Dictionary of Literary Biography

Dictionary of Literary Biography Documentary Series

1 *Sherwood Anderson, Willa Cather, John Dos Passos, Theodore Dreiser, F. Scott Fitzgerald, Ernest Hemingway, Sinclair Lewis,* edited by Margaret A. Van Antwerp (1982)

2 *James Gould Cozzens, James T. Farrell, William Faulkner, John O'Hara, John Steinbeck, Thomas Wolfe, Richard Wright,* edited by Margaret A. Van Antwerp (1982)

3 *Saul Bellow, Jack Kerouac, Norman Mailer, Vladimir Nabokov, John Updike, Kurt Vonnegut,* edited by Mary Bruccoli (1983)

4 *Tennessee Williams,* edited by Margaret A. Van Antwerp and Sally Johns (1984)

5 *American Transcendentalists,* edited by Joel Myerson (1988)

6 *Hardboiled Mystery Writers: Raymond Chandler, Dashiell Hammett, Ross Macdonald,* edited by Matthew J. Bruccoli and Richard Layman (1989)

7 *Modern American Poets: James Dickey, Robert Frost, Marianne Moore,* edited by Karen L. Rood (1989)

8 *The Black Aesthetic Movement,* edited by Jeffrey Louis Decker (1991)

9 *American Writers of the Vietnam War: W. D. Ehrhart, Larry Heinemann, Tim O'Brien, Walter McDonald, John M. Del Vecchio,* edited by Ronald Baughman (1991)

10 *The Bloomsbury Group,* edited by Edward L. Bishop (1992)

11 *American Proletarian Culture: The Twenties and The Thirties,* edited by Jon Christian Suggs (1993)

12 *Southern Women Writers: Flannery O'Connor, Katherine Anne Porter, Eudora Welty,* edited by Mary Ann Wimsatt and Karen L. Rood (1994)

13 *The House of Scribner, 1846–1904,* edited by John Delaney (1996)

14 *Four Women Writers for Children, 1868–1918,* edited by Caroline C. Hunt (1996)

15 *American Expatriate Writers: Paris in the Twenties,* edited by Matthew J. Bruccoli and Robert W. Trogdon (1997)

16 *The House of Scribner, 1905–1930,* edited by John Delaney (1997)

17 *The House of Scribner, 1931–1984,* edited by John Delaney (1998)

18 *British Poets of The Great War: Sassoon, Graves, Owen,* edited by Patrick Quinn (1999)

19 *James Dickey,* edited by Judith S. Baughman (1999)

See also DLB 210, 216, 219, 222, 224, 229, 237, 247, 253, 254, 263, 269, 273, 274, 280, 284, 288, 291, 294, 298, 301, 304

Dictionary of Literary Biography Yearbooks

1980 edited by Karen L. Rood, Jean W. Ross, and Richard Ziegfeld (1981)

1981 edited by Karen L. Rood, Jean W. Ross, and Richard Ziegfeld (1982)

1982 edited by Richard Ziegfeld; associate editors: Jean W. Ross and Lynne C. Zeigler (1983)

1983 edited by Mary Bruccoli and Jean W. Ross; associate editor Richard Ziegfeld (1984)

1984 edited by Jean W. Ross (1985)

1985 edited by Jean W. Ross (1986)

1986 edited by J. M. Brook (1987)

1987 edited by J. M. Brook (1988)

1988 edited by J. M. Brook (1989)

1989 edited by J. M. Brook (1990)

1990 edited by James W. Hipp (1991)

1991 edited by James W. Hipp (1992)

1992 edited by James W. Hipp (1993)

1993 edited by James W. Hipp, contributing editor George Garrett (1994)

1994 edited by James W. Hipp, contributing editor George Garrett (1995)

1995 edited by James W. Hipp, contributing editor George Garrett (1996)

1996 edited by Samuel W. Bruce and L. Kay Webster, contributing editor George Garrett (1997)

1997 edited by Matthew J. Bruccoli and George Garrett, with the assistance of L. Kay Webster (1998)

1998 edited by Matthew J. Bruccoli, contributing editor George Garrett, with the assistance of D. W. Thomas (1999)

1999 edited by Matthew J. Bruccoli, contributing editor George Garrett, with the assistance of D. W. Thomas (2000)

2000 edited by Matthew J. Bruccoli, contributing editor George Garrett, with the assistance of George Parker Anderson (2001)

2001 edited by Matthew J. Bruccoli, contributing editor George Garrett, with the assistance of George Parker Anderson (2002)

2002 edited by Matthew J. Bruccoli and George Garrett; George Parker Anderson, Assistant Editor (2003)

Concise Series

Concise Dictionary of American Literary Biography, 7 volumes (1988–1999): *The New Consciousness, 1941–1968; Colonization to the American Renaissance, 1640–1865; Realism, Naturalism, and Local Color, 1865–1917; The Twenties, 1917–1929; The Age of Maturity, 1929–1941; Broadening Views, 1968–1988; Supplement: Modern Writers, 1900–1998.*

Concise Dictionary of British Literary Biography, 8 volumes (1991–1992): *Writers of the Middle Ages and Renaissance Before 1660; Writers of the Restoration and Eighteenth Century, 1660–1789; Writers of the Romantic Period, 1789–1832; Victorian Writers, 1832–1890; Late-Victorian and Edwardian Writers, 1890–1914; Modern Writers, 1914–1945; Writers After World War II, 1945–1960; Contemporary Writers, 1960 to Present.*

Concise Dictionary of World Literary Biography, 4 volumes (1999–2000): *Ancient Greek and Roman Writers; German Writers; African, Caribbean, and Latin American Writers; South Slavic and Eastern European Writers.*

American Mystery and Detective Writers

Dictionary of Literary Biography® • Volume Three Hundred Six

American Mystery and Detective Writers

Edited by
George Parker Anderson
University of South Carolina

A Bruccoli Clark Layman Book

THOMSON
GALE

Detroit • New York • San Francisco • San Diego • New Haven, Conn. • Waterville, Maine • London • Munich

THOMSON
GALE

Dictionary of Literary Biography
Volume 306: American Mystery and Detective Writers
George Parker Anderson

Advisory Board
John Baker
William Cagle
Patrick O'Connor
George Garrett
Trudier Harris
Alvin Kernan

Editorial Directors
Matthew J. Bruccoli and Richard Layman

© 2005 Thomson Gale, a part of The Thomson Corporation.

Thomson and Star Logo are trademarks and Gale is a registered trademark used herein under license.

For more information, contact
Thomson Gale
27500 Drake Rd.
Farmington Hills, MI 48331-3535
Or you can visit our Internet site at
http://www.gale.com

LIBRARY OF CONGRESS CATALOGING-IN-PUBLICATION DATA

American mystery and detective writers / edited by George Parker Anderson.
     p. cm. — (Dictionary of literary biography ; v. 306)
"A Bruccoli Clark Layman book."
Includes bibliographical references and index.
          ISBN 0-7876-6843-5 (alk. paper)
          1. Detective and mystery stories, American—Bio-bibliography—
Dictionaries. 2. American fiction—20th century—Bio-bibliography—
Dictionaries. 3. Authors, American—20th century—Biography—
Dictionaries. 4. Detective and mystery stories, American— Dictionaries.
5. American fiction—20th century—Dictionaries. I. Anderson,
George Parker, 1957–. II. Series.

PS374.D4A456 2005
813'.08720905—dc22   2004018770

Printed in the United States of America
10 9 8 7 6 5 4 3 2 1

For Rosalind and Mary

Contents

Plan of the Series

. . . Almost the most prodigious asset of a country, and perhaps its most precious possession, is its native literary product—when that product is fine and noble and enduring.

Mark Twain*

The advisory board, the editors, and the publisher of the *Dictionary of Literary Biography* are joined in endorsing Mark Twain's declaration. The literature of a nation provides an inexhaustible resource of permanent worth. Our purpose is to make literature and its creators better understood and more accessible to students and the reading public, while satisfying the needs of teachers and researchers.

To meet these requirements, *literary biography* has been construed in terms of the author's achievement. The most important thing about a writer is his writing. Accordingly, the entries in *DLB* are career biographies, tracing the development of the author's canon and the evolution of his reputation.

The purpose of *DLB* is not only to provide reliable information in a usable format but also to place the figures in the larger perspective of literary history and to offer appraisals of their accomplishments by qualified scholars.

The publication plan for *DLB* resulted from two years of preparation. The project was proposed to Bruccoli Clark by Frederick G. Ruffner, president of the Gale Research Company, in November 1975. After specimen entries were prepared and typeset, an advisory board was formed to refine the entry format and develop the series rationale. In meetings held during 1976, the publisher, series editors, and advisory board approved the scheme for a comprehensive biographical dictionary of persons who contributed to literature. Editorial work on the first volume began in January 1977, and it was published in 1978. In order to make *DLB* more than a dictionary and to compile volumes that individually have claim to status as literary history, it was decided to organize volumes by topic, period, or

*From an unpublished section of Mark Twain's autobiography, copyright by the Mark Twain Company

genre. Each of these freestanding volumes provides a biographical-bibliographical guide and overview for a particular area of literature. We are convinced that this organization—as opposed to a single alphabet method—constitutes a valuable innovation in the presentation of reference material. The volume plan necessarily requires many decisions for the placement and treatment of authors. Certain figures will be included in separate volumes, but with different entries emphasizing the aspect of his career appropriate to each volume. Ernest Hemingway, for example, is represented in *American Writers in Paris, 1920–1939* by an entry focusing on his expatriate apprenticeship; he is also in *American Novelists, 1910–1945* with an entry surveying his entire career, as well as in *American Short-Story Writers, 1910–1945, Second Series* with an entry concentrating on his short fiction. Each volume includes a cumulative index of the subject authors and articles.

Between 1981 and 2002 the series was augmented and updated by the *DLB Yearbooks*. There have also been nineteen *DLB Documentary Series* volumes, which provide illustrations, facsimiles, and biographical and critical source materials for figures, works, or groups judged to have particular interest for students. In 1999 the *Documentary Series* was incorporated into the *DLB* volume numbering system beginning with *DLB 210: Ernest Hemingway.*

We define literature as the *intellectual commerce of a nation:* not merely as belles lettres but as that ample and complex process by which ideas are generated, shaped, and transmitted. *DLB* entries are not limited to "creative writers" but extend to other figures who in their time and in their way influenced the mind of a people. Thus the series encompasses historians, journalists, publishers, book collectors, and screenwriters. By this means readers of *DLB* may be aided to perceive literature not as cult scripture in the keeping of intellectual high priests but firmly positioned at the center of a nation's life.

DLB includes the major writers appropriate to each volume and those standing in the ranks behind them. Scholarly and critical counsel has been sought in deciding which minor figures to include and how full their entries should be. Wherever possible, useful references are made to figures who do not warrant separate entries.

Each *DLB* volume has an expert volume editor responsible for planning the volume, selecting the figures for inclusion, and assigning the entries. Volume editors are also responsible for preparing, where appropriate, appendices surveying the major periodicals and literary and intellectual movements for their volumes, as well as lists of further readings. Work on the series as a whole is coordinated at the Bruccoli Clark Layman editorial center in Columbia, South Carolina, where the editorial staff is responsible for accuracy and utility of the published volumes.

One feature that distinguishes *DLB* is the illustration policy–its concern with the iconography of literature. Just as an author is influenced by his surroundings, so is the reader's understanding of the author enhanced by a knowledge of his environment. Therefore *DLB*

volumes include not only drawings, paintings, and photographs of authors, often depicting them at various stages in their careers, but also illustrations of their families and places where they lived. Title pages are regularly reproduced in facsimile along with dust jackets for modern authors. The dust jackets are a special feature of *DLB* because they often document better than anything else the way in which an author's work was perceived in its own time. Specimens of the writers' manuscripts and letters are included when feasible.

Samuel Johnson rightly decreed that "The chief glory of every people arises from its authors." The purpose of the *Dictionary of Literary Biography* is to compile literary history in the surest way available to us–by accurate and comprehensive treatment of the lives and work of those who contributed to it.

The *DLB* Advisory Board

Introduction

The literature of crime—what historian Howard Haycraft in his essay "Murder for Pleasure" in *The Art of the Mystery Story* (1946) describes as "puzzle stories, mystery stories, crime stories, and stories of deduction and analysis"—has existed since mankind began to record experiences in writing. One might begin with Genesis and the story of Cain and Abel, for example. As a literary genre, however, modern crime writing has evolved through two great movements: the literary mystery story featuring remarkable feats of deduction that developed in the nineteenth century and was refined in the 1920s and 1930s, the period known as the Golden Age of detective fiction; and the hard-boiled crime story that originated in the 1920s, in part as a reaction against the perceived artificiality of the literary mystery. American writers who were key to the development of these movements include Edgar Allan Poe and Anna Katharine Green for the literary mystery and Dashiell Hammett, Raymond Chandler, and Ross Macdonald for the hard-boiled detective story.*

The differences between the two traditions are often matters of class, as the literary mystery usually concerns middle- and upper-class suspects and criminals whereas the hard-boiled detective or character is routinely involved with the criminal underworld. Style and language are also distinguishing characteristics, as hard-boiled writing, particularly in its origins, relies far more on slang and colloquial speech than does the literary mystery. The most important distinction between the writers of the literary mystery and the hard-boiled crime story, however, is that they begin with contrast-

ing understandings of the realities about which they write. In the literary mystery, the world before the murder occurs is stable; the violent act is an aberration; and the identification of the murderer restores order and justice. In the hard-boiled crime story, the world is one in which crime and the threat of violence are endemic; the quest for the truth or justice is quixotic; and any just or harmonious resolution is necessarily temporary.

In *Dictionary of Literary Biography 306: American Mystery and Detective Writers* the influence of these two traditions is evident in the careers of thirty-five authors (thirty-three entries), whose lives span the twentieth century. The authors included in *DLB 306* serve as examples in the complex evolution of an immensely popular genre that has been greatly affected by market forces. Their careers and works reveal changing perspectives on crime and punishment in American society and culture.

The origins of the literary story of detection are traced by critics and historians to Poe and the five tales he wrote in the early 1840s: "The Murders in the Rue Morgue," "The Mystery of Marie Rogêt," "The Purloined Letter," "The Gold Bug," and "Thou Art the Man." Haycraft praised Poe for laying down

> the two great concepts upon which all fictional detection worth the name has been based: (1) That the solvability of a case varies in proportion to its outré character. (2) The famous dictum-by-inference (as best phrased by Dorothy Sayers) that "when you have eliminated all the impossibilities, then, whatever remains, however improbable, must be the truth," which has been relied on and often re-stated by all the better sleuths in the decades that have followed.

Haycraft goes on to list "only a suggestive catalogue" of the motifs that characterize Poe's legacy to the detective story:

> The transcendent and eccentric detective; the admiring and slightly stupid foil; the well-intentioned blundering and unimaginativeness of the official guardians of the law; the locked-room convention; the pointing finger of unjust suspicion; the solution by surprise; deduction by putting one's self in another's position; concealment by means of the ultra-obvious; the staged ruse to force the

*See the Poe entries in *DLB 3: Antebellum Writers in New York and the South; DLB 59: American Literary Critics and Scholars, 1800–1850; DLB 73: American Magazine Journalists, 1741–1850; DLB 74: American Short-Story Writers Before 1880;* and *DLB 248: Antebellum Writers in the South, Second Series.* See the Green entries in *DLB 202: Nineteenth-Century American Fiction Writers* and *DLB 221: American Women Prose Writers, 1870–1920.*

Entries on Hammett, Chandler, and Macdonald (as Kenneth Millar) are in *DLB 226: American Hard-Boiled Crime Writers.* See also *DLB Documentary Series 6: Hardboiled Mystery Writers: Raymond Chandler, Dashiell Hammett, Ross Macdonald; DLB 253: Raymond Chandler: A Documentary Volume;* and *DLB 280: Dashiell Hammett's* The Maltese Falcon: *A Documentary Volume.*

culprit's hand; even the expansive and condescending explanation when the chase is done. . . .

He concludes, "In fact, it is not too much to say—except, possibly, for the influence of latter-day science—that nothing really primary has been added either to the framework of the detective story or to its internals since Poe. . . . Manners, styles, specific devices may change—but the great principles remain where Poe laid them down and left them."

The most esteemed practitioners of the literature of detection in the nineteenth century after Poe were British; they include Charles Dickens, Wilkie Collins, and, most important, Sir Arthur Conan Doyle, whose creation Sherlock Holmes, a detective much in the tradition established by Poe, achieved enormous popularity in the 1890s. One of the most significant American crime writers after Poe was Green, whose *The Leavenworth Case* (1878) featured a professional detective, Ebenezer Gryce, who is aided by the sharp-eyed amateur Amelia Butterworth. In addition to creating the first series detective in American literature and to limiting the suspects to a "closed society"–a household in which all members are equally suspect–Green is credited by critic Alma Murch in *The Development of the Detective Novel* (1958) with plot devices and innovations that became staples of the genre, including "the rich old man, killed when on the point of signing a new will; the body in the library; the dignified butler with his well-trained staff; detailed medical evidence as to the cause and estimated time of death; the coroner's inquest and the testimony of expert witnesses; [and] the authority on ballistics who can identify the gun that fired the shot."

In the early twentieth century, and especially between World Wars I and II, the Golden Age of the literary detective story, the form that came to be called the "cozy" dominated the mystery field in Britain and influenced American writers. The prototypical cozy detective was Agatha Christie's Miss Marple, an elderly spinster who encountered and solved murders in her visits to idyllic villages. Readers of cozies enjoy the challenge of the puzzle, the opportunity to match wits with the detective in the story, sift through the clues, and name the murderer before the author reveals his or her identity. In 1928 writers of mysteries emphasizing the puzzle formed the London Detection Club, the first president or "Ruler" of which was G. K. Chesterton. In the Detection Club Oath, prospective members answered a series of questions affirmatively, including:

Do you promise that your detectives shall well and truly detect the crimes presented to them, using those wits which it may please you to bestow upon them and not placing reliance on nor making use of Divine Revelation, Feminine Intuition, Mumbo-Jumbo, Jiggery-Porkery, Coincidence or the Act of God?

Do you solemnly swear never to conceal a vital clue from the reader?

Do you promise to observe a seemly moderation in the use of Gangs, Conspiracies, Death-Rays, Ghosts, Hypnotism, Trap Doors, Chinamen, Super-Criminals and Lunatics; and utterly and forever to forswear Mysterious Poisons unknown to Science?

The oath-taker also had to vow not to purloin or disclose plots or secrets revealed by other members, "whether under the influence of drink or otherwise."

DLB 306 includes several writers who wrote the literary mystery story in the United States during the Golden Age. Willard Huntington Wright became a best-selling author when, as S. S. Van Dine, he began writing about Philo Vance. Van Dine's article "Twenty Rules for Writing Detective Stories" (*American Magazine*, September 1928) is both more serious in tone and more restrictive than the tongue-in-cheek oath of the Detection Club:

The detective story is a kind of intellectual game. It is more—it is a sporting event. And for the writing of detective stories there are very definite laws—unwritten, perhaps, but none the less binding; and every respectable and self-respecting concocter of literary mysteries lives up to them. Herewith, then, is a sort of Credo, based partly on the practice of all the great writers of detective stories, and partly on the promptings of the honest author's inner conscience.

The rules Van Dine goes on to itemize include three in particular that indicate the chasm he saw between genre and mainstream fiction:

3. There must be no love interest. The business at hand is to bring a criminal to the bar of justice, not to bring a lovelorn couple to the hymeneal altar.

16. A detective novel should contain no long descriptive passages, no literary dallying with side-issues, no subtly worked-out character analyses, no "atmospheric" preoccupations. Such matters have no vital place in a record of crime and deduction. They hold up the action, and introduce issues irrelevant to the main purpose, which is to state a problem, analyze it, and bring it to a successful conclusion. To be sure, there must be a sufficient descriptiveness and character delineation to give the novel verisimilitude.

17. A professional criminal must never be shouldered with the guilt of a crime in a detective story. Crimes by house-breakers and bandits are the province

of the police departments—not of authors and brilliant amateur detectives. A really fascinating crime is one committed by a pillar of a church, or a spinster noted for her charities.

John Dickson Carr, the only American ever to become a member of the London Detection Club, was as uninterested in realism in detective fiction as was Van Dine and often wrote the so-called locked-room mystery. In *The Three Coffins* (1935), his detective, Dr. Gideon Fell, lectures on the intrigue of murder committed in "a hermetically sealed chamber," which he finds "more interesting than anything else in detective fiction." Fell argues that the word "improbable" is "the very last that should ever be used to curse detective fiction" because a "great part of our liking for detective fiction is *based* on a liking for improbability."

Heedful only of the rule of success in the literary marketplace, other Americans writing in the tradition of the literary mystery created distinctive detectives to find their niches in the crowded mystery field. In his series of novels on the Chinese-born detective Charlie Chan, Earl Derr Biggers capitalized not only on the novelty of the first major American ethnic detective but also on the exotic setting of Hawaii. In their long-running series of books, Frances and Richard Lockridge detail the often amusing adventures of Mr. and Mrs. North, in which Pamela North's hunches frequently lead to the murderer. In her series of novels featuring the urbane psychologist Dr. Basil Willing, Helen McCloy contrived to entertain and "play fair" with her readers while always providing surprise endings.

In the 1920s, the same decade in which the London Detection Club was organized, an altogether different approach to crime writing was beginning to develop in the United States. The hard-boiled crime story did not develop through the agency of a club that codified rules for how to write in the genre. Called the only purely American literary style, hard-boiled writing grew out of naturalism and evolved as a collection of individual responses to a rapidly changing and often violent country. By the 1920s, the lawless frontier had disappeared from America, replaced in the popular imagination by an urban society that was just as menacing. The writers of the 1920s had only to open their newspapers to find immediate inspiration for writing about crime. With the passage of the Eighteenth Amendment to the Constitution, which forbade the manufacture and sale of intoxicating beverages, the country overnight had become a nation of scofflaws. As alcohol consumption increased during the decade, gangs organized to create and maintain an underground network for the distribution of illegal drink. The apparent sway of criminals, who were often able to corrupt the police and public officials, created an atmosphere of perceived anarchy. The public fascination with crime created the environment for hard-boiled fiction to emerge and flourish.

As the hard-boiled detective hero was conceived by Carroll John Daly (see entry in *DLB 226*)—the writer credited with the creation of the type—he was clearly a wish-fulfillment figure, a slang-talking tough guy who could cope with an anarchic world with his fists and his guns. Daly's best-known protagonist, Private Investigator Race Williams, initially appeared in a story in the 1 June 1923 issue of *Black Mask*. Although Daly's work—with its crudely drawn characters, unrealistic action, and overwrought prose—was not held in high esteem by *Black Mask* editors, it was commercially successful. During the next dozen years, Daly had some fifty more Race Williams stories published in the magazine, and in 1930 he was voted the favorite author by its readers. The P. I. as a type clearly had strong appeal.

Black Mask and former army captain Joseph T. "Cap" Shaw, its editor from 1926 to 1936, were crucial to the development of hard-boiled fiction. *Black Mask* was one of many pulps—cheap magazines that were printed on rough wood-pulp paper—that thrived in the first half of the century. In 1920, H. L. Mencken and George Jean Nathan, neither of whom cared for detective fiction, founded *The Black Mask* and sold it after six months as a means of subsidizing their literary magazine, *The Smart Set*. When Shaw took over as editor, he "meditated on the possibility of creating a new type of detective story," as he recalled in his introduction to *The Hard-Boiled Omnibus* (1946). Shaw disliked the British type of detective story, which he termed "the deductive type, the cross-word puzzle sort, lacking—deliberately—all other human emotional values." Believing that "the creation of a new pattern was a writer's rather than an editor's job," he searched the magazine "for a writer with the requisite spark and originality." He found Dashiell Hammett.

Hammett, who published his first Continental Op story in *Black Mask* four months after the first Race Williams story had appeared, was as interested as Shaw in remaking the detective story, as Shaw relates:

> It was apparent that Mr. Hammett shared our hope for a medium in which he could achieve his aim while developing his talent into a highly skillful instrument. We pointed out that this particular medium—the magazine mystery story—was both constrained and restrained. We felt obliged to stipulate our boundaries. We wanted simplicity for the sake of clarity, plausibility, and belief. We wanted action, but we held that action is meaningless unless it involves recognizable human character in three-dimensional form.
>
> Dashiell Hammett had his own way of phrasing this: *If you kill a symbol, no crime is committed and no effect is*

produced. To constitute a murder, the victim must be a real human being of flesh and blood.

Simple, logical, almost inevitable. Yet, amazingly, this principle had been completely ignored by crime writers—and still is, in the deductive type of mystery story.

Shaw maintained that "character conflict is the main theme; the ensuing crime, or its threat, is incidental." The style that emerged in *Black Mask,* Shaw writes, "was rather extravagantly tagged as the 'hard-boiled' school." Paul Cain and Lester Dent, included in *DLB 306,* contributed to the hard-boiled style of the magazine. The medium provided by *Black Mask,* as guided by Shaw, focused and sharpened the efforts of writers who were seeking to write realistically and entertainingly about their violent culture.

The success of *Black Mask* inspired many imitations and contributed to a healthy pulp market for mystery fiction, including such periodicals as *Sure-Fire Detective Magazine, Spicy Mystery Stories, Thrilling Detective, True Gang Life, The Shadow, Detective Fiction Weekly, New Mystery Adventures, Underground Detective, Phantom Detective, Ace Detective, Detective Tales, Headquarters Detective, Hardboiled, Federal Agent, Popular Detective, Pocket Detective, Crime Busters, Detective Romances,* and *Detective Story Magazine.* Yet, while the pulp market provided the venue for writers to develop, much of what was regarded as hard-boiled fiction was of poor quality. As Chandler writes in "The Simple Art of Murder" (1950):

> The realistic style is easy to abuse: from haste, from lack of awareness, from inability to bridge the chasm that lies between what a writer would like to be able to say and what he actually knows how to say. It is easy to fake; brutality is not strength, flipness is not wit, edge-of-the-chair-writing can be as boring as flat writing. . . . There has been so much of this sort of thing that if a character in a detective story says 'Yeah,' the author is automatically a Hammett imitator.

Chandler and Macdonald built on Hammett's legacy, establishing a tradition in American letters that began to command serious attention and respect.

The readership for the crime story, in its established literary tradition and its emerging hard-boiled tradition, was probably never more divided than during the pulp era. In "The Simple Art of Murder," Chandler scoffingly imagines "old ladies" jostling each other "at the mystery shelf" for a copy of "*The Triple Petunia Murder Case.*" Just as easy—and probably no less accurate—to imagine are young male readers knocking each other aside for the last copy of *Black Mask.* The one writer in *DLB 306* who in the 1930s tried to bridge this readership gap was Rex Stout, who in the partnership of Nero Wolfe, a Great Detective in the manner of the Golden

Age, and his assistant Archie Goodwin, who acts as a hard-boiled detective, attracted readers of both sexes and all ages.

In the 1950s, with the decline of the pulps and the rise of the paperback original, the market for hard-boiled fiction profoundly changed. As Bill Pronzini and Jack Adrian explain in the introduction to *Hard-Boiled: An Anthology of American Crime Stories* (1995), Fawcett Gold Medal led a group of publishers—including Avon, Dell, Popular Library, and Lion—into the practice of "paying royalty advances on the number of copies printed, rather than on the number of copies sold; thus, writers received handsome initial payments, up to four times as much as hardcover publishers were paying":

> Instead of a bulky magazine full of short stories, Fawcett published brand-new, easy-to-read novels in a convenient pocket-size format. . . . Instead of printing hundreds of thousands of copies of a small number of titles, Fawcett printed hundreds of thousands of copies of many titles in order to reach every possible outlet and buyer. As a result, many Gold Medal novels, particularly in the early 1950s, sold more than a million copies each.

DLB 306 includes four writers who were able to sustain careers in the changing marketplace of the 1950s and beyond: Michael Avallone, the self-proclaimed "King of the Paperbacks"; Gil Brewer, who began his career with Shaw acting as his literary agent; John D. MacDonald, who later found hardback success with his Travis McGee series; and Edward D. Hoch, who has continued the Golden Age "fair play" tradition into the twenty-first century.

Stanley Ellin, Patricia Highsmith, and Evan Hunter—three writers who began their careers in the decade after World War II—brought new dimensions to the literature of crime. Ellin and Highsmith added macabre twists and a new vitality to the mystery story. Ellin explored the nature of crimes and the criminal by creating menacing, suspenseful situations in which seemingly ordinary middle-class people reveal obsessions or flaws. Highsmith, too, had the ability to take her readers into an unsettling world. Through her five novels featuring the "criminal-hero" Tom Ripley, she was able to present an "abnormal" view of twentieth-century life that engages the reader's sympathies while questioning traditional notions of crime and its consequences. In his long-running series of police-procedural novels featuring the 87th Precinct novels that began with *Cop Hater* (1956), Hunter, writing as Ed McBain, has provided a developing portrait of criminals and their pursuers spanning six decades.

DLB 306 features seventeen writers who began their careers in or since the 1960s, five of whom write in the literary mystery tradition. Mary Jane Latsis and Martha Henissart, writing as Emma Lathen, took the mystery into the business world with their detective-hero, banker John Putnam Thatcher, whose first adventure is recorded in *Banking on Death* (1961). Feminist scholar Carolyn Heilburn, writing as Amanda Cross, published her first mystery featuring the young professor Kate Fansler, *In the Last Analysis,* in 1964. Mary Higgins Clark, whose suspenseful novels are typically best-sellers, began her career with *Where Are the Children?* (1975). Ralph McInerny, a Roman Catholic who uses the mystery story to explore moral choices and spiritual consequences, began the series featuring his best-known detective, Father Dowling, in 1977 with *Her Death of Cold.*

Other writers have combined elements of the literary mystery and the hard-boiled tradition in their writings. Robert Campbell, who had a career as a television writer and mainstream novelist before he began writing mysteries, is the author of a hard-boiled series about a private investigator named Whistler and a series about amateur detective Jimmy Flannery, a sewer inspector. The Whistler series, set in Los Angeles, begins with *In La-La Land We Trust* (1986), and the Flannery series, set in Chicago, starts with *The Junkyard Dog* (1986). Judith Van Gieson is another writer who has written two series, the first featuring tough attorney Neil Hamel, and the second, Claire Renier, a librarian who is far more hard-boiled than cozy. The Hamel series began with *North of the Border* in 1988, and the Renier series was initiated in 2000 with *The Stolen Blue.* Elizabeth George, who sets her novels in England and traces the careers of Inspector Thomas Lynley and Sergeant Barbara Havers of New Scotland Yard, has been credited with modernizing and complicating the moral certainties of the cozy. The first novel in George's series, *A Great Deliverance,* was published in 1988.

Dennis Lynds, Robert B. Parker, and Sara Paretsky continue the hard-boiled P. I. tradition established by Dashiell Hammett and Raymond Chandler. Lynds, who writes as Michael Collins, began his Dan Fortune series with *Act of Fear* (1967). His stated purpose in writing detective fiction is to make the reader "see the violence and the darkness as his own." Since *The Godwulf Manuscript* (1973), Robert B. Parker has shown that the P. I. need not face the mean streets alone and has humanized his hero through Spenser's long-term romantic relationship with psychologist Susan Silverman. While Paretsky, like Parker, has surrounded her hero with a network of relationships, V. I. Warshawski remains as capable of dealing with the mean streets of Chicago as any man. V. I. began her investigations into mainly white-collar crime in *Indemnity Only* (1982).

Several writers have used the mystery or crime novel in part as a vehicle for other interests. Tony Hillerman's novels, beginning with *The Blessing Way* (1970), explore Native American culture through Navajo policemen Joe Leaphorn and Jim Chee. Sharyn McCrumb, the author of three series, is best known for her novels that explore Appalachian folklore, beginning with *If Ever I Return, Pretty Peggy-O* (1990). Dominick Dunne has written about crime and issues of justice since the murder of his daughter, beginning with the novel *The Two Mrs. Grenvilles* in 1985. Michael Nava has completed a seven-novel cycle, beginning with *The Little Death* (1986), in which he uses the adventures of Chicano lawyer and sleuth Henry Rios to comment on gay life in America. With *Postmortem* (1990) and her other novels featuring medical examiner Kay Scarpetta, Patricia Cornwell has brought a focus on forensic science to investigative work. Walter Mosley has provided a social history of black Los Angeles in his novels featuring Easy Rawlins, beginning with *Devil in a Blue Dress* (1990). Finally, in thirteen novels, dating from *A Firing Offense* (1992), George P. Pelecanos has reinvigorated the hard-boiled crime novel to explore music, class, and race in blue-collar Washington, D.C.

In the first decade of the twenty-first century, mystery and detective fiction continues to be popular with readers. Genre fiction is now taught in college classrooms, where it is no longer thought of as being necessarily inferior to literary fiction. Beyond genre conventions, good writing is good writing, and some of the best work currently being published is by Americans writing mystery and detective fiction.

—George Parker Anderson

Acknowledgments

This book was produced by Bruccoli Clark Layman, Inc. Penelope M. Hope and Charles Brower were the in-house editors.

Production manager is Philip B. Dematteis.

Administrative support was provided by Carol A. Cheschi.

Accountant is Ann-Marie Holland.

Copyediting supervisor is Sally R. Evans copyediting staff includes Phyllis A. Avant Brown, Melissa D. Hinton, Philip I. Jones Mayo, Nadirah Rahimah Shabazz, Joshu Nancy E. Smith.

Pipeline manager is James F. T

Editorial associate is Jessica

In-house vetter is Catheri

Permissions editor is A

Layout and graphics supervisor is Janet E. Hill. The graphics staff includes Zoe R. Cook and Sydney E. Hammock.

Office manager is Kathy Lawler Merlette.

Photography editors are Mark J. McEwan and Walter W. Ross.

Digital photographic copy work was performed by Joseph M. Bruccoli.

Systems manager is Donald Kevin Starling.

Typesetting supervisor is Kathleen M. Flanagan. The typesetting staff includes Patricia Marie Flanagan and Pamela D. Norton.

Walter W. Ross is library researcher. He was assisted by the following librarians at the Thomas Cooper Library of the University of South Carolina: Elizabeth Suddeth and the rare-book department; Jo Cottingham, interlibrary loan department; circulation department head Tucker Taylor; reference department head Virginia W. Weathers; reference department staff Laurel Baker, Marilee Birchfield, Kate Boyd, Paul Cammarata, Joshua Garris, Gary Geer, Tom Marcil, Rose Marshall, and Sharon Verba; interlibrary loan department head Marna Hostetler; and interlibrary loan staff Bill Fetty, Nelson Rivera, and Cedric Rose.

American Mystery and Detective Writers

Dictionary of Literary Biography

Michael Avallone

(27 October 1924 – 26 March 1999)

Martin Kich
Wright State University–Lake Campus

BOOKS: *Cavalry for Combat* (Munich, 1945);

The Tall Dolores, Ed Noon series (New York: Holt, 1953; London: Barker, 1956);

The Spitting Image, Ed Noon series (New York: Holt, 1953; London: Barker, 1957);

Dead Game, Ed Noon series (New York: Holt, 1954; London: W. H. Allen, 1959);

Violence in Velvet, Ed Noon series (New York: New American Library, 1956; London: W. H. Allen, 1958);

The Case of The Bouncing Betty, Ed Noon series (New York: Ace, 1957; London: W. H. Allen, 1959);

The Case of The Violent Virgin, Ed Noon series (New York: Ace, 1957; London: W. H. Allen, 1960);

The Crazy Mixed-Up Corpse, as Mike Avalone, Ed Noon series (New York: Fawcett, 1957; London: Fawcett, 1959);

The Voodoo Murders, Ed Noon series (New York: Fawcett, 1957; London: Fawcett, 1959);

All the Way (New York: Midwood, 1960; London: Brown, Watson, 1967);

Meanwhile Back at the Morgue, Ed Noon series (Greenwich, Conn.: Fawcett, 1960; London: Muller, 1961);

The Alarming Clock, Ed Noon series (London: W. H. Allen, 1961; New York: Curtis, 1961);

The Little Black Book (New York: Midwood, 1961);

Stag Stripper (New York: Midwood, 1961);

Women in Prison (New York: Tower, 1961);

Flight Hostess Rogers (New York: Midwood, 1962);

Never Love a Call Girl (New York: Tower, 1962);

The Platinum Trap (New York: Tower, 1962);

Sinners in White (New York: Tower, 1962);

Sex Kitten (New York: Tower, 1962);

And Sex Walked In (Beacon, N.Y.: Beacon Signal, 1963);

Michael Avallone (Bruccoli Clark Layman Archives)

The Bedroom Bolero, Ed Noon series (New York: Belmont, 1963; London: Brown, Watson, 1964); republished as *The Bolero Murders* (London: Hale, 1972);

Boris Karloff Presents Tales of the Frightened (New York: Belmont, 1963);

The Doctor's Wife (Beacon, N.Y.: Beacon Signal, 1963);

The Living Bomb, Ed Noon series (London: W. H. Allen, 1963; New York, Curtis, 1972);

Lust at Leisure (Beacon, N.Y.: Beacon Signal, 1963);

The Main Attraction, as Steve Michaels (New York: Belmont, 1963);

Shock Corridor (New York: Belmont, 1963);

There Is Something About a Dame, Ed Noon series (New York: Belmont, 1963);

The China Doll, as Nick Carter (New York: Award, 1964);

Lust Is No Lady, Ed Noon series (New York: Belmont, 1964); republished as *The Brutal Kook* (London: W. H. Allen, 1965);

Felicia, as Mark Dane (New York: Belmont, 1964);

The Night Walker, as Sidney Stuart (New York: Award, 1964);

Run, Spy, Run, as Carter (New York: Award, 1964);

Saigon, as Carter (New York: Award, 1964);

The Spitting Image, Ed Noon series (New York: 1964);

Station Six–Sahara (New York: Popular Library, 1964);

The Copenhagen Affair (New York: Ace, 1965);

Corridor of Whispers, as Edwina Noone (New York: Ace, 1965);

The Dagger Affair (New York: Ace, 1965);

Dark Cypress, as Noone (New York: Ace, 1965);

The Darkening Willows, as Priscilla Dalton (New York: Paperback Library, 1965);

The Doomsday Affair (New York: Ace, 1965);

Heirloom of Tragedy, as Noone (New York: Lancer, 1965);

90 Gramercy Park, as Dalton (New York: Paperback Library, 1965);

The Silent, Silken Shadows, as Dalton (New York: Paperback Library, 1965);

The Thousand Coffins Affair (New York: Ace, 1965; London: New English Library, 1965);

The Victorian Crown, as Noone (New York: Paperback Library, 1965);

Young Dillinger, as Stuart (New York: Belmont, 1965);

The Birds of a Feather Affair (New York: New American Library, 1966; London: New English Library, 1967);

The Blazing Affair (New York: New American Library, 1966);

Daughter of Darkness, as Noone (New York: New American Library, 1966);

Edwina Noone's Gothic Sampler (New York: Universal, 1966);

The Evil Men Do, as Dorothea Nile (New York: Tower, 1966);

The Fat Death, Ed Noon series (London: W. H. Allen, 1966; New York: Curtis, 1966);

The February Doll Murders, Ed Noon series (London: W. H. Allen, 1966; New York: New American Library, 1967);

Kaleidoscope (New York: Popular Library, 1966);

Madame X (New York: Popular Library, 1966);

The Mad Scientist Affair (New York: Ace, 1966);

Mistress of Farrondale, as Nile (New York: Tower, 1966);

The Radioactive Camel Affair (New York: Ace, 1966);

The Second Secret, as Dalton (New York, 1966);

The Second Secret, as Noone (New York: Belmont, 1966);

Terror at Deepcliff, as Nile (New York: Tower, 1966);

The Vampire Affair (New York: Ace, 1966);

The Assassination Affair Affair (New York: Ace, 1967);

The Berlin Wall Affair, as Troy Conway (New York: Paperback Library, 1967);

The Diving Dames Affair (New York: Ace, 1967);

Don't Bite Off More Than You Can Chew, as Conway (New York: Paperback Library, 1967);

The Felony Squad (New York: Popular Library, 1967);

The Invisibility Affair (New York: Ace, 1967);

Is There a Teenage Driver in Your House? by Avallone and Lawrence E. Schlesinger (New York: New American Library, 1967);

The Man From A.V.O.N. (New York: Avon, 1967);

The Monster Wheel Affair (New York: Ace, 1967);

Superkill, as John Tiger (New York: Popular Library, 1967);

Wipeout, as Tiger (New York: Popular Library, 1967);

Assassins Don't Die in Bed, Ed Noon series (New York: New American Library, 1968);

The Big Freak-Out, as Conway (New York: Paperback Library, 1968);

The Billion-Dollar Snatch, as Conway (New York: Paperback Library, 1968);

The Black Angel (New York: Ace, 1968);

The Coffin Things (New York: Lancer, 1968);

Come One, Come All, as Conway (New York: Paperback Library, 1968);

Hawaii Five-O (New York: New American Library, 1968);

The Horrible Man, Ed Noon series (London: Hale, 1968; New York: Curtis, 1972);

The Incident (New York: New American Library, 1968);

It's Getting Harder All the Time, as Conway (New York: Paperback Library, 1968);

Keep It Up Rod, as Conway (New York: Paperback Library, 1968);

Last Licks, as Conway (New York: Paperback Library, 1968);

The Man-Eater, as Conway (New York: Paperback Library, 1968);

Mannix (New York: Popular Library, 1968);

My Secret Life with Older Women, as James Blaine (New York: Lancer, 1968);

Seacliffe, as Noone (New York: New American Library, 1968);

The Vampire Cameo, as Nile (New York: Lancer, 1968);

The Wham! Bam! Thank You, Ma'am Affair, as Conway (New York: Paperback Library Library, 1968);

It's What's Up Front That Counts, as Conway (New York: Paperback Library, 1969);

The Best Laid Plans, as Conway (New York: New American Library, 1969);

The Big Broad Jump, as Conway (New York: Paperback Library, 1969);

The Doomsday Bag, Ed Noon series (New York: New American Library, 1969); republished as *Killer's Highway* (London: Hale, 1970);

Ed Noon, Private Eye, Ed Noon series (New York: New American Library, 1969);

The Flower-Covered Corpse, Ed Noon series (London: Hale, 1969; New York: Curtis, 1969);

A Good Peace, as Conway (New York: Paperback Library, 1969);

Had Any Lately? as Conway (New York: Paperback Library, 1969);

I'd Rather Fight than Swish, as Conway (New York: Paperback Library, 1969);

Just a Silly Millimeter Longer, as Conway (New York: Paperback Library, 1969);

The Killing Star (London: Hale, 1969);

Krakatoa, East of Java (New York: New American Library, 1969);

Missing! (New York: New American Library, 1969);

Terror in the Sun (New York: New American Library, 1969);

Whatever Goes Up, as Conway (New York: Paperback Library, 1969);

All Screwed Up, as Conway (New York: Paperback Library, 1970);

Beneath the Planet of the Apes (New York: New American Library, 1970; Toronto & London: Bantam, 1970);

The Blow-Your-Mind Job, as Conway (New York: Paperback Library, 1970);

A Bullet for Pretty Boy (New York: Curtis, 1970);

The Cloisonne Vase, as Noone (New York: Curtis, 1970);

The Cunning Linguist, as Conway (New York: Paperback Library, 1970);

The Doctors (New York: Popular Library, 1970);

The Haunted Hall, as Vance Stanton (New York: Curtis, 1970);

Hornet's Nest (New York: Popular Library, 1970);

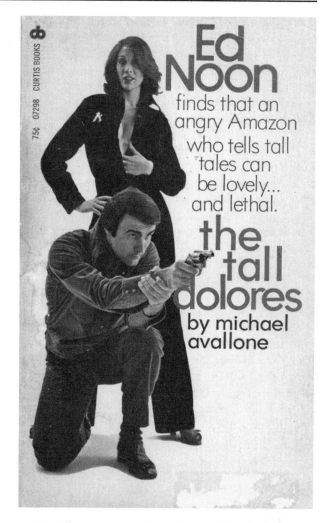

Cover for a 1973 paperback reprint of the first novel to feature Ed Noon, the hard-boiled detective hero who loves movies and baseball. Avallone called it his "swiftest, most economical, most entertaining book" (Bruccoli Clark Layman Archives).

It's Not How Long You Make It, as Conway (New York: Paperback Library, 1970);

The Last Escape, as Max Walker (New York: Popular Library, 1970);

One More Time (New York: Popular Library, 1970);

The Partridge Family, as Stanton (New York: Curtis, 1970);

The Sex Machine, as Conway (New York: Paperback Library, 1970);

Turn the Other Sheik, as Conway (New York: Paperback Library, 1970);

Will the Real Rod Please Stand Up? as Conway (New York: Paperback Library, 1970);

The X-Rated Corpse, Ed Noon series (New York: Curtis, 1970);

The Craghold Legacy, as Noone (New York: Beagle, 1971);

Death Dives Deep, Ed Noon series (New York: New American Library, 1971; London: Hale, 1971);

The Ghost of Graveyard Hill, as Stanton (New York: Curtis, 1971);

The Harder You Try, the Harder It Gets, as Conway (New York: Paperback Library, 1971);

Keith Partridge, Master Spy, as Stanton (New York: Curtis, 1971);

Keith, The Hero, as Stanton (New York: Curtis, 1971);

Little Miss Murder, Ed Noon series (New York: New American Library, 1971); republished as *The Ultimate Client* (London: Hale, 1971);

The Night before Chaos (Paris: Gallimard, 1971);

The Penetrator, as Conway (New York: Paperback Library, 1971);

Son of a Witch, as Conway (New York: Paperback Library, 1971);

A Sound of Dying Roses, as Jean-Anne de Pré (New York: Popular Library, 1971);

A Stiff Proposition, as Conway (New York: Paperback Library, 1971);

The Third Woman, as de Pré (New York: Popular Library, 1971; London: Sphere, 1973);

When Were You Born? (Paris: Gallimard, 1971);

Aquarius, My Evil, as de Pré (New York: Paperback Library, 1972);

The Cockeyed Cuties (New York: Paperback Library, 1972);

The Craghold Creatures, as Noone (New York: Beagle, 1972);

The Craghold Curse, as Noone (New York: Beagle, 1972);

Die, Jessica, Die, as de Pré (New York: Paperback Library, 1972);

The Fat and Skinny Murder Mystery, as Stanton (New York: Curtis, 1972);

The Girl in the Cockpit, Ed Noon series (New York: Curtis, 1972; London: Hale, 1974);

London, Bloody London, Ed Noon series (New York: Curtis, 1972); republished as *Ed Noon in London* (London: Hale, 1974);

Shoot It Again, Sam, Ed Noon series (New York: Curtis, 1972); republished as *The Moving Graveyard* (London: Hale, 1973);

Up and Coming, as Conway (New York: Paperback Library, 1972);

The Walking Fingers, as Stanton (New York: Curtis, 1972);

Who's Laughing in the Grave? as Stanton (New York: Curtis, 1972);

Warlock's Woman, as de Pré (New York: Popular Library, 1973);

And Then There Was Noon, Ed Noon series (New York: 1973);

The Beast with Red Hands, as Sidney Stuart (New York: Popular Library, 1973);

The Craghold Crypt, as Noone (New York: Beagle, 1973);

The Eager Beaver, as Conway (New York: Paperback Library, 1973);

The Gun Next Door (New York: Doubleday, 1973);

The Hot Body, Ed Noon series (New York: Curtis, 1973);

A Hard Man Is Good to Find, as Conway (New York: Paperback Library, 1973);

Killer on the Keys, Ed Noon series (New York: Curtis, 1973);

Kill Her—You'll Like It, Ed Noon series (New York: Curtis, 1973; London: Hale, 1974);

153 Oakland Street, as Dora Highland (New York: Popular Library, 1973);

The Partridge Family: Love Comes to Keith Partridge, as Stanton (New York: Curtis, 1973);

The Third Shadow, as Nile (New York: Avon, 1973);

The Walking Wounded, Ed Noon series (New York: 1973);

Death Is a Dark Man, as Highland (New York: Popular Library, 1974);

Fallen Angel (New York: Warner, 1974; London: Mews, 1976);

The Girls in Television (New York: Ace, 1974);

The Moon Maiden, Ed Noon series (New York, 1974);

The Rubbed-Out Star, Ed Noon series (New York, 1974);

The Werewolf Walks Tonight (New York: Warner, 1974; London: Mews, 1976);

The Craghold Cross, as Noone (New York: Beagle, 1975);

Devil, Devil (New York: Warner, 1975; London: New English Library, 1976);

Only One More Miracle (New York: Scholastic, 1975);

The Big Stiffs, Ed Noon series (London: Hale, 1977); republished as *Blues for Sophia Loren;*

Carquake (London: W. H. Allen, 1977);

CB Logbook of the White Knight: The Open Road Adventures of Dave Dunn, Code Name: White Knight (New York: Scholastic, 1977);

Dark on Monday, Ed Noon series (London: Hale, 1978);

Finest Films of the Fifties (New York: Scholastic, 1978);

Five Minute Mysteries: Cases from the Files of Ed Noon, Ed Noon, no. 37 (New York: Scholastic, 1978);

Name That Movie: A Test Yourself Humor Book (New York: Scholastic, 1978);

Son of Name That Movie: A Test Yourself Humor Book (New York: Scholastic, 1978);

Where Monsters Walk (New York: Scholastic, 1978);

Where Monsters Walk Again (New York: Scholastic, 1978);

The Judas Judge, as Stuart Jason (New York: Pinnacle, 1979);

Slaughter in September, as Jason (New York: Pinnacle, 1980);

Kill Them Silently, as Jason (New York: Pinnacle, 1980);

The Cannonball Run (New York: Nordon, 1981);

Charlie Chan and the Curse of the Dragon Queen (New York: Pinnacle, 1981);

Coffin Corner, U.S.A., as Jason (New York: Pinnacle, 1981);

Death in Yellow, as Jason (New York: Pinnacle, 1981);

The Gunfighters, as Lee Davis Willoughby (New York: Dell, 1981);

The Hoodoo Horror, as Jason (New York: Pinnacle, 1981);

Friday the Thirteenth. Part 3 (New York: Star, 1982);

Go Die in Afghanistan, as Jason (New York: Pinnacle, 1982);

Gotham Gore, as Jason (New York: Pinnacle, 1982);

The Man from White Hat, as Jason (New York: Pinnacle, 1982);

A Woman Called Golda (New York: Leisure, 1982; London: W. H. Allen, 1982);

Red Roses Forever, as Amanda Jean Jarrett (New York: Dell, 1983);

The Rough Riders, as Willoughby (New York: Dell, 1984);

Tender Loving Fear (New York: Blue Heron, 1984);

High Noon at Midnight, Ed Noon series (New York: Paperjacks, 1988);

Since Noon Yesterday, Ed Noon series (New York: 1989);

The Arabella Nude/Open Season on Cops, Ed Noon series (Brooklyn, N.Y.: Gryphon, 1993).

OTHER: "A Great Day Coming," in *Masters of Mayhem,* edited by Edward D. Radin (New York: Morrow, 1965);

"Every Litter Bit Hurts," in *With Malice Toward All,* edited by Robert L. Fish (New York: Putnam, 1968); republished in *The Young Oxford Book of Nasty Endings,* edited by Dennis Pepper (London: Oxford University Press, 1997);

"The Gun Next Door," in *Mirror, Mirror, Fatal Mirror,* edited by Hans Stefan Santesson (New York: Doubleday, 1973);

"The Narrative Hook," in *Mystery Writer's Handbook* (New York: Writer's Digest, 1976);

"Take Me Out to the Ballgame," in *Ellery Queen's Mystery Stories #2* (New York: Bonomo, 1979);

"The Man Who Walked on Air," in *Top Fantasy* (New York: Dent, 1986);

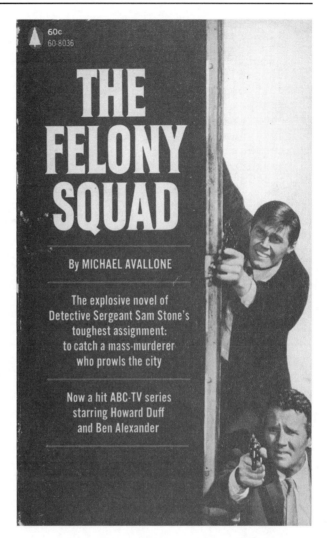

Cover for the paperback original of Avallone's novel based on a television series that premiered in 1966 and ran for three years (Bruccoli Clark Layman Archives)

"Walter Ego," in *A Matter of Crime, Vol. 2,* edited by Matthew J. Bruccoli and Richard Layman (New York: Harcourt, 1987), pp. 229–233;

"The Gun Next Door," in *The Second Black Lizard Anthology of Crime Fiction,* edited by Edward Gorman (New York: Black Lizard, 1988), pp. 15–20.

Michael Avallone viewed himself as the consummate professional writer who was able to produce good work in any genre within even the most rigorous time frames. Such was his commitment to his profession that he claimed never to have taken a "regular" vacation. Described as the "King of the Paperbacks" and self-described as "the fastest typewriter in the East," he once wrote a 1,500-word short

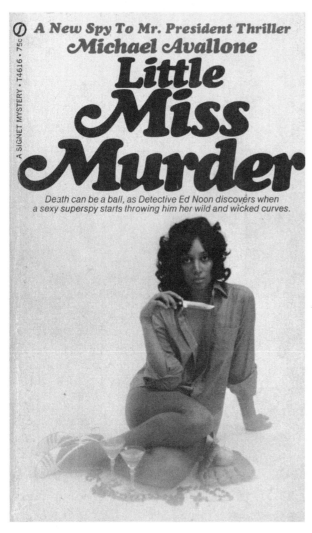

A New Spy To Mr. President Thriller
Michael Avallone
Little Miss Murder

Death can be a ball, as Detective Ed Noon discovers when a sexy superspy starts throwing him her wild and wicked curves.

Cover for one of two paperback originals Avallone published in the Ed Noon series in 1971 (Matthew J. and Arlyn Bruccoli Collection, Thomas Cooper Library, University of South Carolina)

story in twenty minutes–during lunch–and he wrote one full-length novel in a day and a half.

As a novelist and short-story writer for periodicals, Avallone wrote under many personal and "house" pseudonyms, including Michele Alden, James Blaine, Nick Carter, Troy Conway, Priscilla Dalton, Mark Dane, Jean-Anne de Pré, Fred Frazer, Dora Highland, Amanda Jean Jarrett, Stuart Jason, Steve Michaels, Memo Morgan, Dorothea Nile, Ed Noon, Edwina Noone, John Patrick, Stuart Sidney, Vance Stanton, Sidney Stuart, John Tiger, Max Walker, and Lee Davis Willoughby. Some of his books were even published under such variant spellings of his given name as Avalone and Avalione.

Almost all of his books were paperback originals. Estimates of his total output have ranged from two hundred to four hundred books. In his most prolific year,

Avallone claims to have produced twenty-seven books that were eventually published. Given Avallone's production and the nature of paperback market and publishing during his heyday, compiling a complete bibliographic listing of his books is impossible. His known publishers included Ace, Allen, Avon, Award, Beacon, Beacon Popular, Beagle, Belmont, Curtis, Dell, Fawcett, Fawcett Gold Medal, Gallimard, Gryphon, Holt, Lancer, Leisure, Mews, Midwood, New American Library, Paperback Library, Paperjacks, Pinnacle, Popular Library, Scholastic, Signet, Star Books, Tower, and Warner. Some of his books have been translated into French, German, Italian, and several other European languages.

Avallone wrote nonseries mystery-suspense novels, espionage novels, war novels, Westerns, science fiction, Gothic and horror novels, romance novels, gay and lesbian novels, television and movie novelizations, television scripts, radio plays, children's books, scripts of audio recordings for children, short stories, essays, book and movie reviews, and countless letters to editors of periodicals and newspapers. He is best remembered, though, for the more than three dozen mystery novels he wrote featuring Ed Noon.

Michael Angelo Avallone was born 27 October 1924 in New York City, one of seventeen children raised by Michael Angelo and Marie Antoinette (Antonelli) Avallone. During the Great Depression, his father, a stonemason, was out of work for long periods, and at one point the family was evicted from their home. As a child in this crowded and financially strapped household, Avallone found his escape in motion pictures. Francis M. Nevins, mystery novelist and Edgar-winning biographer of Cornell Woolrich, knew Avallone personally and has concluded that Avallone not only had seen every movie released during the 1920s and 1930s but also had seen each one enough times to commit details and dialogue to memory.

Avallone attended Theodore Roosevelt High School in the Bronx. From 1943 to 1946, he served with the mechanized infantry in the European theater, earning two battle stars. At the time of his discharge, he had risen to the rank of sergeant. For the next decade, Avallone worked as a stationery or candy salesman during the day while trying to write the great American novel at night. In 1949 he married Lucille Asero, with whom he had one son, Stephen Michael Avallone.

Avallone was determined to become the Thomas Wolfe of his generation and turned out several hefty "serious" novels for which he could not find a publisher. These early novels included a war story, "All Except Six"; other rejected typescripts had such titles as "Above a Whisper," "Only One More Melody," and "Take Me by the Hand." As the rejection slips accumulated, Avallone began to alter his ambition and gradually found a more receptive market for his work among the publishers of pulp magazines and mass-market paperbacks. During this frustrating period of apprenticeship, his marriage began to unravel.

In 1951 Avallone had his first short story accepted for publication, placing "Aw, Let the Kid Hit" with *Baseball Stories*. In the 1950s, he wrote for a great variety of magazines. To provide an illustrative survey of some of the titles, "The Man Who Walked on Air" appeared in the September 1953 issue of *Weird Tales;* "Headache Hurler" appeared in the October 1955 issue of *Ten Story Sports;* "The Curse of Cleopatra" in the Spring 1956 issue of *Tales of the Frightened;* and "Aces Always Win" in the May 1956 issue of *Western Action*. He also contributed to *The Saint Detective Magazine, The Saint Magazine, Ellery Queen Mystery Magazine, Mystery Monthly, Dolly Doolittle's Crime Club, Weirdbook, Pulp Vault, Hardboiled, Detective Story Magazine,* and *New Mystery*. Writing as "Brett Halliday," for several years Avallone was part of a group of authors who on a rotating basis produced the Shayne novellas featured in each issue of *Mike Shayne's Mystery Magazine* (MSMM). In the early 1960s, Avallone also began a long association with *MSMM* as a contributor of stories under his own name. As an illustrative sampling of his contributions to *MSMM*, "Open Season on Cops" appeared in the September 1962 issue, "A Bullet for Big Nick" in December 1971, "Violin for a Corpse" in May 1974, "Sweet Violets" in October 1980, and "Ed Noon's Minute Mysteries" in the April through December 1980 issues.

Avallone soon went from writing for magazines to also editing them. From 1954 to 1959, he served as editor of some twenty-seven men's magazines. What is more remarkable is that he was also often the chief contributor to these magazines, providing work under various pseudonyms to fill issues. Most notably, from 1956 to 1958, he was employed by Lyle Kenyon Engel of Republic Features, which in 1956 began publishing three short-lived, digest-sized monthlies that were intended to fill niches in newsstand offerings—*American Agent, Space Science Fiction,* and *Tales of the Frightened*. Although Avallone edited all three publications, his name never appeared on the mastheads because the magazines included so much of his work. After his stint with Republic, he worked as an editor for Cape Magazines from 1958 to 1960. But as the heyday of the pulp magazines passed, Avallone, like pulp "masters" such as John D. MacDonald, increasingly devoted his energies to producing paperback "originals."

Two years after the publication of his first story, Avallone had initiated his career as a novelist and the Ed Noon series with *The Tall Dolores* in 1953. Although the series evolved into approximately forty titles pub-

lished over almost four decades, Avallone devoted himself to the series in fits and starts. He wrote and published the first eight novels of the series in a four-year period: *The Tall Dolores, The Spitting Image* (1953), *Dead Game* (1954), *Violence in Velvet* (1956), *The Case of The Bouncing Betty* (1957), *The Case of The Violent Virgin* (1957), *The Crazy Mixed-Up Corpse* (1957), and *The Voodoo Murders* (1957).

Inspired by Mickey Spillane's success with the Mike Hammer novels and stories, Avallone initially attempted to treat hard-boiled subjects with the direct style that became commonplace in the crime genre in the 1940s and 1950s after it had been popularized in *Black Mask Magazine* and with writers such as Dashiell Hammett, James M. Cain, and Raymond Chandler. From the beginning, however, the idiosyncrasies of Avallone's style made Noon much more of an original than were somewhat formulaic hard-boiled heroes such as Mike Shayne.

Noon himself is an eccentric and a throwback. In the entry on Noon in Chris Steinbrunner and Otto Penzler's *An Encyclopedia of Mystery and Detection* (1976), the authors provide this concise portrait of Noon: "Throughout his adventures, Noon remains the ultimate movie and baseball 'nut,' the quintessential 'cock-eyed optimist,' the last true believer in the Hollywood myths of the 1930s and 1940s." The authors also quote a detailed self-appraisal that Noon provides, in the third person, in *Shoot It Again, Sam* (1972):

> Strong, tough, Manhattan-cynical but underneath still a small boy. A movie lover. Cried when dogs got run over, helped little old ladies across the street, works for principle and integrity. Not an anti-hero. He believes the home team will win the old ball game in the ninth, that nice guys will not finish last, and when the climax comes, the Good Guys will always beat the Bad Guys. He grew up that way, through the Depression years, a second World War, and all the time he dreamed in a million darkened movie houses. He embraced the word Hero; he believed there was no other way for a man to be.

The plots of the Noon novels largely defy summary, and their convolutions, bizarre turns, and loose ends became increasingly more pronounced as the series progressed. Whereas Chandler sometimes lost track of the intricacies of his plots, Avallone seems never to have worried much at all about the thoroughness or logic of his story lines or of Noon's detection. From the beginning, the Noon novels were marked by a postmodern exuberance for obsessive-compulsive detailing and linguistic confusion. The novels are full of allusions to the popular culture, especially to movies, and they are full of non sequiturs, mixed metaphors,

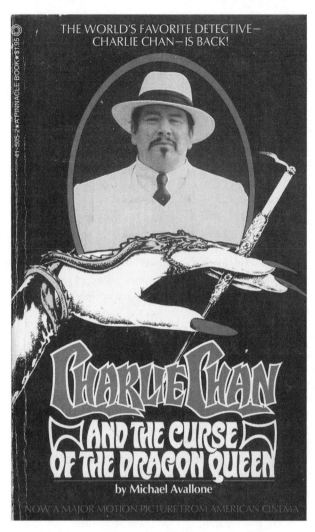

THE WORLD'S FAVORITE DETECTIVE—
CHARLIE CHAN—IS BACK!

CHARLIE CHAN
AND THE CURSE
OF THE DRAGON QUEEN
by Michael Avallone

NOW A MAJOR MOTION PICTURE FROM AMERICAN CINEMA

*Cover for one of six paperback originals Avallone published
in 1981 (Bruccoli Clark Layman Archives)*

rapid-fire coinages, and clichés tormented to the edge of originality. Neither readers nor reviewers—nor, perhaps, Avallone himself—ever clearly understood how much of his freewheeling style was purposeful and how much was the result of self-indulgence or inattention.

In *The Tall Dolores,* Noon is first hired and then stalked by a 6' 3" "Glamazon" and circus performer named Dolores, whose fiancé has gone missing and then turns up murdered. For all of its hard-boiled surface elements, the novel never finds its focus in the sort of sadomasochistic intensity that is thematically at the center of Spillane's Mike Hammer novels. When Noon is involved in violence, whether as its source or as its victim, an odd element of frivolity always exists in the tone. The following passage—in which Noon causes a police car to crash as it is carrying him to jail as a murder suspect—serves as an example: "First, the air whistled out of Monk's throat as the cuffs caught him

heavily in the neck just below his ear. Then Kinney screamed in fright, the tires screeched like four old maids finding a man in the closet, and there was a sickening jolt as the body of the car tried to run right across the locked wheels." Much later, Noon describes the violent death of a criminal in idiosyncratic terms that actually reflect the character's attitude toward this kind of death: "He stared at me. His expression was silly. His tiny mouth was trying to say something. His little eyes looked like marbles behind the big windows of his glasses. His tongue poked out on a long cough of sound. Blood ran out of the corner of his mouth. A giggle ripped out of him suddenly. A high, hysterical bubble of something that was all mixed up with dying and amusement." *The Tall Dolores* remained Avallone's own favorite among his books. In an interview with Gary Lovisi that appeared in *Mean Streets* (December 1999), he described it as "the swiftest, most economical, most entertaining book I've ever written."

Despite Dolores's exoticism in the first novel, the starting points for the plots in the early Noon novels are typically rather run-of-the-mill situations within the detective genre. For instance, in *The Spitting Image,* society girl June Wexler's chauffeur is shot dead. She suspects that she was the intended target and that her twin sister April is behind the attempt to kill her. June hires Noon to find out if her suspicions are true. But early indications also indicate that Avallone was tinkering with the possibility of taking the character in directions away from the milieu of the hard-boiled private investigator. For instance, each of the two issues of *American Agent* included a novella featuring Ed Noon.

Much of Avallone's work during his hectic last half of the 1950s cannot be traced with comprehensiveness or accuracy. Even his work for publications with a shelf life of more than a few issues remains somewhat ambiguous. For instance, although Avallone became part of the rotation of authors who wrote the Shayne novellas featured in each monthly issue of *MSMM,* no ready record exists of who wrote what.

Between 1958 and 1961, as Avallone tried to establish relationships with a variety of paperback publishers, he produced only one novel in the Ed Noon series, *Meanwhile Back at the Morgue* (1960). This novel concerns a series of "accidents" that threaten the staging of a new Broadway musical. The cover copy provides a fairly clear idea of the style of the work: "A blonde on a slab— / A brunette on a bearskin rug— / Ed Noon on a killer's trail!"

On 27 May 1960, Avallone married his second wife, Frances Weinstein. They had two children— Susan, who became a screenwriter, and David Prill, who became a writer and movie director. As Avallone made the transition from working as an editor to making his living as a freelancer, the family relocated from New York City to East Brunswick, New Jersey. In the 1960s, Avallone was active in the MWA (Mystery Writers of America). He served as the director of the New York chapter from 1962 to 1966. In the national organization, he served as the chairman of the television committee from 1963 to 1965, as the chairman of the motion-picture awards committee from 1965 to 1967, and as the chairman of the movie committee from 1965 to 1970. From 1962 to 1965, Avallone edited the MWA newsletter.

In the first years of the 1960s, Avalone wrote softcore pornographic novels, with such titles as *Stag Stripper* (1961), *Sinners in White* (1962), *Never Love a Call Girl* (1962), and *Lust at Leisure* (1963), as well as two books with lesbian themes, *Women in Prison* (1961) and *The Platinum Trap* (1962). He also began writing novelized versions of movies. In 1963, Avallone wrote a novelization of the movie *Shock Corridor*. At the time of his death in 1999, it was one of the few of his hundreds of books still in print. In fact, it has remained continuously in print since its initial publication.

Between 1961 and 1964, Avallone wrote another six titles in the Ed Noon series: *The Alarming Clock* (1961), *The Bedroom Bolero* (1963), *The Living Bomb* (1963), *There Is Something About a Dame* (1963), *Lust Is No Lady* (1964), and *The Spitting Image* (1964). After a one-year pause, he produced the next two Noon novels in 1966, *The Fat Death* and *The February Doll Murders*. During this period, Noon was transformed from a hard-boiled private investigator into a suave espionage agent who works for the president of the United States as a sort of freelance troubleshooter or secret-service agent. Avallone also wrote espionage novels as Nick Carter, Gothic novels as Priscilla Dalton and Edwina Noone, horror novels as Dorothea Nile, and novelizations from the television show *The Man from U.N.C.L.E.* (United Network Command for Law and Enforcement), which ran from 1964 through 1968.

Between 1968 and 1974, Avallone produced almost half of the novels in the Ed Noon series, eighteen: *Assassins Don't Die in Bed* (1968), *The Horrible Man* (1968), *The Flower-Covered Corpse* (1969), *Ed Noon, Private Eye* (1969), *The Doomsday Bag* (1969), *The X-Rated Corpse* (1970), *Death Dives Deep* (1971), *Little Miss Murder* (1971), *Shoot It Again, Sam* (1972), *The Girl in the Cockpit* (1972), *London, Bloody London* (1972), *Kill Her—You'll Like It* (1973), *The Hot Body* (1973), *Killer on the Keys* (1973), *The Walking Wounded* (1973), *And Then There Was Noon* (1973), *The Moon Maiden* (1974), and *The Rubbed-Out Star* (1974). In 1973 alone, six Noon novels were published. Avallone's productivity is all the more amazing when one considers that he published more than sixty other books during this seven-year period, including fifteen

novels in the gay mystery-suspense science-fiction series—The Coxeman—with titles such as *I'd Rather Fight than Swish* (1969) and *Turn the Other Sheik* (1970), as well as novelizations of the television series *The Partridge Family*.

In the entry on Avallone in Steinbrunner and Penzler's *Encyclopedia of Mystery and Detection,* the ways in which Avallone's own experiences made their way into the increasingly bizarre plots of these Noon novels are delineated: "The early chapters of *The February Doll Murders* (1966) are based on Avallone's memories of combat in World War II; *Little Miss Murder* (1971) reflects his love affair with the New York Mets; the spy's shipboard diary in *London, Bloody London* (1972) recreates some of the incidents that occurred during a cruise Avallone took aboard the *Queen Elizabeth II.*"

One of the best novels of this period is *Shoot It Again, Sam.* In his online web page, *A Guide to Classic Mystery and Detection,* Michael E. Grost provides an appreciative analysis of the novel, which focuses on the writer's use of a movie directed by Joseph von Sternberg, which starred Gary Cooper and Marlene Dietrich:

> *Shoot It Again, Sam* . . . shows much of Avallone's gift for verbal expression. It also shows Avallone's vast knowledge of movie history, with a discussion of *Morocco* (1930) being worked into the plot. Avallone, like Sternberg, has his own gift for creating *mise-en-scène.* Sternberg's plots are often as delirious as Avallone's, and Avallone's evocation of Sternberg's dream-like atmosphere blends into Avallone's own surreal chain of events. This section is a cornerstone of the story. It is one structural element, out of which the whole flow of Noon's feelings is contrasted.

While insightful, Grost's analysis hardly hints at the absolute lunacy of the plot of *Shoot It Again, Sam.* At the request of the president of the United States, Noon accompanies the body of an all-American movie star on a cross-country train ride to its final resting place in Hollywood. All of the characters are based on easily identifiable movie stars, but their relationships are surreally contrived. For instance, the dead movie star is clearly based on John Wayne, but one of his former wives is just as clearly based on Lauren Bacall and his son on Peter Fonda. The book is written as if *People* magazine were a family album in which all of the celebrities were actually related by blood or connected by intimacy. Then, just short of the destination of the train, the story abruptly shifts gears from the surreal to the wildly fantastic. The corpse rises from his coffin, and Chinese agents disguised as Jimmy Cagney, Clark Gable, and other Hollywood heavyweights brainwash

A drawing of Avallone with his homage to the writer who used the pseudonym Ross Macdonald (Matthew J. and Arlyn Bruccoli Collection, Thomas Cooper Library, University of South Carolina)

Noon into believing that he is Humphrey Bogart playing Sam Spade. In this persona, he is sent off in a pair of weaponized shoes to assassinate the president. In the entry on Avallone in *Encyclopedia Mysteriosa* (1994), William L. DeAndrea observes, "Reading an Avallone book, especially that work dearest to his heart, the adventures of private eye Ed Noon, is like bodysurfing. By the time you come up gasping for air, you've traveled quite a distance."

In 1977 Avallone was honored by the New Jersey Institute of Technology, which named him a Literary Luminary of the state. This honor was one of the few formal ones that came his way during his long and extraordinarily productive career. The productivity of which he was so proud was the major cause of his critical neglect. In his resentment at this seeming injustice, Avallone often blurred the best and worst aspects of his personality. He possessed a great natural charm—was, in fact, the sort of person who could "take over" a room—and he was capable of great loyalty to longtime

friends. His positive traits, however, were often largely canceled out by transparent jealousies that made him contentious and, at his worst, simply boorish.

For instance, on all sorts of occasions, Avallone repeatedly asserted that Stephen King did not deserve his tremendous success, since almost every noteworthy aspect of King's novels could be traced back to those of Avallone's friend Robert Bloch. A library collection of some four hundred letters between Bloch and Avallone attests to the closeness and durability of their friendship, and Bloch may indeed have felt that King owed him some acknowledgment as a literary forerunner. But it was clear to anyone who heard Avallone's diatribes against King that the underlying issue was Avallone's own need for recognition and not the relative merits of Bloch's and King's works.

In 1978, Francis M. Nevins wrote the only article on Avallone to appear in a mainstream periodical, a profile in *New Republic* titled "The Issue Is Murder: Murder at Noon." The influence of this profile on Avallone's subsequent reputation has been considerable. In a slightly shorter form, the article was republished as the entry on Avallone in the highly regarded *St. James Guide to Crime and Mystery Writers* (1996), edited by Kathleen Gregory Klein, Jay P. Pederson, and Taryn Benbow-Pfalzgraf. In addition, its influence can be seen in every subsequent reference entry on Avallone, in the echoes of Nevins's observations and in the attention to certain works and details of those works.

Although Nevins is direct about Avallone's gaffes as a novelist, the tone of his profile is generally positive. One proof of Nevins's esteem is that Avallone himself, who was quite sensitive to criticism of his work, subsequently referred to Nevins as a "buff" of the Noon series, and the two remained friendly up to Avallone's death. At the heart of Nevins's approach to Avallone's work is this observation:

> Unlike most purveyors of drugstore fiction, Mike Avallone is a true *auteur,* with a unique personality discernible throughout most of his books and especially throughout the Nooniverse. For despite his original intention, Ed Noon is no more than a distant literary cousin of Mike Hammer. Rather, this Manhattan gumshoe is a cockeyed optimist, a motormouthed clown, a movie and baseball nut, a lover of luscious ladies and lousy jokes, . . . an emotional pushover, and in many respects a child in an adult body.

In his profile, Nevins catalogues some of his favorite Noonisms—linguistic idiosyncracies similar in type to Goldwynisms and Yogiisms. (In fact, Nevins has pored through most of Avallone's books of all types and has catalogued pages of what might more accurately be called Avallonisms from each book.) For instance, from just *The Horrible Man,* Nevins has culled the following Noonisms: "She had tremendous hips and breasts encased in a silly short black fur jacket and calf-high boots"; "The cube flashbulbs which could shoot a set of four pictures without bothering to make adjustments was all set"; "Madly Lopez was stark naked, on her knees, still wearing the calf-high boots"; "She . . . unearthed one of her fantastic breasts from the folds of her sheath skirt"; and "My stunned intellect, the one that found death in his own backyard with him standing only feet away, hard to swallow in a hurry, found the answer." At the end of the much more extensive list in his article, Nevins concludes: "'I was all tangled and brangled in mystery and fantasy that made absolutely no sense,' Noon remarks in *Death Dives Deep,* and so is the reader every time he dives into an Avallone novel. But somehow the whole impossible slumgullion lingers on the palate. Those who keep coming back for more servings are known as Noonatics."

The influence of Nevins's profile is also seen in the only other detailed critique of the Noon novels, Bill

Pronzini's *Gun in Cheek,* published four years later in 1982. Like Nevins's profile, Pronzini's book catalogues the lunacies (or Noonacies) of Avallone's work. But in Pronzini's book, that work is not being considered in isolation as a unique, if idiosyncratic, contribution to the genre. Instead, Pronzini has the broader aim of cataloguing the whole spectrum of dismal writing within the crime and mystery genre. The effect is still comical, but the tone is pointedly the equivalent of a sneer rather than a snicker. In his opening chapter, Pronzini delineates his intention:

> The purpose of this book is threefold: first to rectify the neglect of these writers and their works, to give them the critical attention they deserve; second, to provide a different historical perspective on crime fiction—its detectives, its sub-genres, its publishers—and on the social attitudes it reflects (which are more often more pronounced in the bad mystery than in the good one); and third, to add a few chuckles—perhaps even a guffaw or two—to the heretofore sobersided field of mystery criticism.

One can immediately assume that "the critical attention they deserve" will be tantamount to ridicule—rather than the current "neglect"—since they are described pointedly as the authors of "bad" mysteries that inadvertently offer "good" illustrations of trends in the genre. So, when Pronzini asserts, "It is Avallone's lurid, ungrammatical, and often hilarious prose style that distinguishes him and Ed Noon," *distinguishes* clearly does not mean "confers distinction upon." The similarities in Nevins's and Pronzini's methods have, unexpectedly, enhanced the credibility of Pronzini's much less flattering conclusions about the value of Avallone's work. After *Gun in Cheek* (and its sequel *Son of Gun in Cheek* [1988], in which Avallone's work is exposed to further ridicule), to make the case, as Nevins did, became difficult—that Avallone's work is so exuberantly eccentric that its energy transcends or transforms its conspicuous limitations.

In the early 1980s, Avallone contributed many stories to *MSMM,* including "The Shadow," which appeared in the March 1981 issue; "Ms. Found in a Crypt," in July 1981; "Operator 5," in August 1981; "Children of the Night," in April 1982; "The Murder of Mr. Excitement," in November 1982; and "Conversation While Praying," in July 1984. With Frank Hamilton, Avallone also wrote many stories featuring "Doc Savage," which appeared in the magazine throughout 1981—"Doc Savage," in May; "The Spider," in June; "G-8 and His Battle Aces," in July; "The Phantom Detective," in September; "You Can't Kiss a Corpse," in November; and "Fu Manchu," in December.

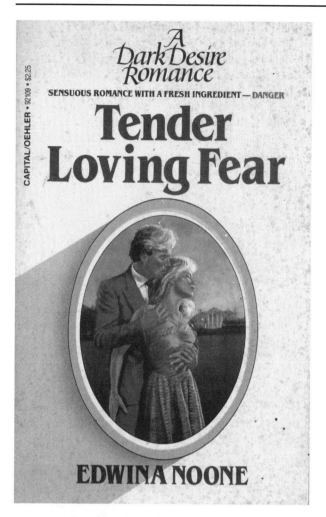

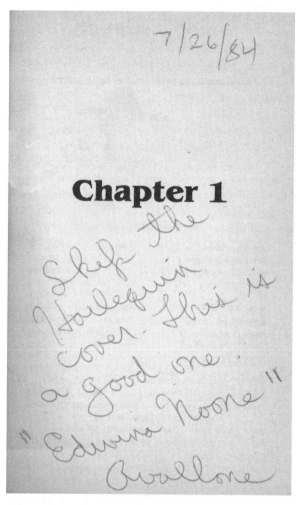

Cover for and inscription in a 1984 paperback original, one of the dozen or more Gothic novels Avallone wrote as "Edwina Noone" (Matthew J. and Arlyn Bruccoli Collection, Thomas Cooper Library, University of South Carolina)

Between 1975 and 1987, Avallone published just one more Noon novel, *The Big Stiffs* (1977), published first in England and then in the United States as *Blues for Sophia Loren*. During this period, Avallone concentrated on the titles he wrote for The Butcher series—a series of grimly brutal action-adventure novels designed to exploit the interest in such prototypical series as The Executioner and The Destroyer.

In 1988, *High Noon at Midnight,* the thirty-ninth Ed Noon book, received much more attention than most of the other novels in the series. Most notably, in 1989, the novel was named a finalist for an Anthony Award in the paperback category. In this novel, as well as in *Since Noon Yesterday* (1989) and the unpublished "The Ninth of Never," Noon confronts an alien menace that threatens all of humanity. The hard-boiled private eye of the Cold War era, who had evolved into an espionage agent providing special services to the president of the United States, had now become an almost folk-heroic

figure in a science fantasy in which Armageddon is not, after all, an exclusively human option.

With this novel, Avallone had come full circle with Noon, reconnecting him to the movie heroes, particularly Gary Cooper, who had inspired his creation some three decades earlier. In the 1999 interview with Lovisi, Avallone described his admiration for the star of *High Noon* and the genesis of much of Ed Noon's personality (and Avallone's own professional persona) in Cooper's on-screen persona:

Everybody needs a hero. To me, a Depression kid with sixteen brothers and sisters . . . , Gary Cooper was the most beautiful man in the world, and still is—nobody on screen today comes close, not even Kevin Costner. . . . The vital thing was, all of Cooper's great heroic movies stress the same central figure and leitmotif: a man of high moral character and purpose taking on impossible odds all by his valiant lonesome—remember *The Virginian, Lives of a Bengal Lancer, Mr. Deeds Goes* to Town, The General Died at Dawn, The Plainsman, Meet John Doe, Sergeant York, Pride of the Yankees, For Whom the Bell Tolls, and, of course, the perfect example, High Noon. The whole world remembers that one. Incidentally, I named Noon for this movie. . . .

Lovisi provided new venues for Avallone's work, publishing several of his stories in the digest-sized periodicals Hardboiled and Hardboiled Detective. "Better Safe Than Sorry," by Avallone and Josh Pachter, appeared in Hardboiled #8 (1987), "The Ten Percent Kill" in Hardboiled Detective, #10 (December 1990), and "Paul Will Know" in Hardboiled #14 (1992). Avallone's review "Chandlerizing and Parker's Big Sleep" also appeared in Hardboiled Detective #12 (1991).

At the end of the entry on Avallone in Encyclopedia Mysteriosa, DeAndrea refers to Avallone's often-quoted remark that "a professional writer ought to be able to write anything from a seed catalog to the Bible." DeAndrea muses: "Those who know his work eagerly await his version of the Good Book." But by the time those words were published in the mid 1990s, Avallone had begun to experience chronic health problems, and his only "new" publications were repackaged works from the early years of his career. He and his wife decided to relocate to Los Angeles to be nearer their children. On 26 March 1999, Avallone died in his sleep at his Los Angeles home. The causes of death were given as heart disease and complications from chronic anemia. In that same year, Avallone's son David wrote and directed a video serial for the website Bijou Café. Based on the Noon novel Since Noon Yesterday, the serial featured David Avallone as the detective's son.

Kevin Burton Smith, editor in chief of the Thrilling Detective website, has succinctly and vividly catalogued the most salient features of Avallone's work:

His wacko characters, his hilariously fragmented sentences, his penchant for improvised, nonsensical plots, his love for movie and baseball trivia, and truly pain-inducing puns, his complete allegiance to a sort of virtual unreality in whatever field he chose to write in was steamrollered by his enthusiasm and his own energetic albeit somewhat skewered version of the world, and the sheer quantity of his work.

The Noon novels deserve to be remembered because they are perhaps the closest thing in existence to postmodern detective stories—though Michael Avallone probably never intended to take the genre in such a direction. To borrow a word from Anne Tyler, he was more an "accidental" postmodernist.

Interview:

Gary Lovisi, "Mike Avallone, Ed Noon, and Tough Guys," Mean Streets, 12 (December 1999): 25–31.

References:

Michael E. Grost, "Michael Avallone," A Guide to Classic Mystery and Detection <http://members.aol.com/MG42731police.htm#Avallone> [accessed 14 September 2004];

Francis M. Nevins, "The Issue Is Murder: Murder at Noon," New Republic (22 July 1978): 26–28;

Bill Pronzini, Gun in Cheek: A Study of "Alternative" Crime Fiction (New York: Coward, McCann & Geoghagan, 1982), pp. 61–64.

Papers:

Michael Avallone's manuscripts and other papers are in the Mugar Memorial Library, Boston University.

Earl Derr Biggers

(26 August 1884 – 5 April 1933)

Marvin S. Lachman

BOOKS: *Seven Keys to Baldpate* (Indianapolis: Bobbs-Merrill, 1913; London: Mills & Boon, 1914);

"Seven Keys to Baldpate": A Mysterious Melodramatic Farce, by Biggers and George M. Cohan (New York & London: S. French, 1914);

Love Insurance (Indianapolis: Bobbs-Merrill, 1914);

Inside the Lines (Indianapolis: Bobbs-Merrill, 1915; New York & London: S. French, 1924); novelization of the play by Biggers and Robert Welles Ritchie (Indianapolis: Bobbs-Merrill, 1915; London & New York: Hodder & Stoughton, 1915);

The Agony Column (Indianapolis: Bobbs-Merrill, 1916); republished as *Second Floor Mystery* (New York: Grosset & Dunlap, 1930);

The House Without a Key (Indianapolis: Bobbs-Merrill, 1925; London: Harrap, 1926);

The Chinese Parrot (Indianapolis: Bobbs-Merrill, 1926; London: Harrap, 1927);

Fifty Candles (Indianapolis: Bobbs-Merrill, 1926);

Behind That Curtain (Indianapolis: Bobbs-Merrill, 1928; London: Harrap, 1928);

The Black Camel (Indianapolis: Bobbs-Merrill, 1929; London: Cassell, 1930);

Charlie Chan Carries On (Indianapolis: Bobbs-Merrill, 1930; London: Cassell, 1931);

Keeper of the Keys (Indianapolis: Bobbs-Merrill, 1932; London: Cassell, 1932);

Earl Derr Biggers Tells Ten Stories (Indianapolis: Bobbs-Merrill, 1933).

PLAY PRODUCTIONS: *If You're Only Human,* 1912;

Inside the Lines, New York, Longacre Theatre, 9 February 1915;

A Cure for Curables, New York, 39th Street Theatre, 25 February 1918;

See-Saw, New York, George M. Cohan's Theatre, 23 September 1919;

Three's a Crowd, by Biggers and Christopher Morley, New York, Cort Theatre, 4 December 1919.

Earl Derr Biggers (Chris Steinbrunner and Otto Penzler, eds., Encyclopedia of Mystery and Detection *[New York: McGraw-Hill, 1976]; Bruccoli Clark Layman Archives)*

SELECTED PERIODICAL PUBLICATIONS–UNCOLLECTED: "The Ebony Stick," *Ellery Queen's Mystery Magazine,* 20 (November 1952): 82–101;

"The Apron of Genius," *Ellery Queen's Mystery Magazine,* 22 (August 1953): 65–76.

Though he already had a successful writing career, Earl Derr Biggers's greatest fame came with the creation in 1925 of Charlie Chan, a Hawaiian police detective of Chinese origin. Adaptations of Chan in various media made him one of the most popular of all fictional detectives, one whose fame endures to the present. Biggers was philosophical regarding the success of his creation, who eclipsed his own fame, telling his Harvard classmates on their twenty-fifth reunion,

"Yet here I am, and with me Charlie Chan. . . . For I know that he and I must travel the rest of the journey together."

Biggers was born in Warren, Ohio, on 26 August 1884, the son of Robert J. Biggers and Emma E. Derr Biggers. He was founder and first editor of the Warren High School newspaper, *The Cauldron,* and then attended Harvard, where some people remembered that he preferred writers of adventure such as Rudyard Kipling and Richard Harding Davis to such authors as John Keats and Henry Fielding. Biggers wrote for the *Harvard Lampoon* and *Harvard Advocate.* After graduating with a B.A. in 1907, he worked briefly on the staff of the *Cleveland Plain Dealer,* then for four years at the *Boston Traveler,* first writing a humor column. In *Murder for Pleasure* (1941), Howard Haycraft quoted Biggers as having said that "writing a humorous column in Boston was a good deal like making faces in church: it offended a lot of nice people, and it wasn't much fun."

Biggers's eventual promotion to writing dramatic criticism led to his being fired because his reviews of productions he considered mediocre or poor were so negative. In 1912, he married Eleanor Ladd, who also had worked for the *Traveler.* They had one son, Bob.

Biggers and his wife moved to New York City, and he began writing plays himself. His first play, *If You're Only Human* (1912), a comedy, was only produced in summer stock, and though it was not a success, one of the people who saw it was George M. Cohan, then the most popular man in American theater.

Biggers also wrote magazine fiction and then his first novel, *Seven Keys to Baldpate,* which was published in 1913 and well received. Neither a murder mystery nor a detective story, it nonetheless has considerable crime and suspense. William H. Magee, writer of popular fiction, goes to Baldpate Inn, an upstate New York hotel closed for the winter, anticipating the solitude he wants in order to write a "serious" novel. He thinks he has the only key, but as the title indicates, seven keys are in circulation, and Magee finds himself dealing with a group of odd characters who are seeking $200,000 locked in the hotel safe. Three contemporary, unsigned reviews summarized Biggers's accomplishment. The reviewer for the *Boston Transcript* (21 February 1913) thought his characters "well described," though the reviewer also said, "The plot is, of course, impossible, but it is no less amusing." Calling the situations "absurd," the *New York Sun* (8 February 1913) still accurately predicted that "All the requirements for a 'best seller' are fulfilled." *The New York Times* (23 February 1913) said, "The brilliant way in which Mr. Biggers has written this, his first novel, gives promise of excellent things to come in his career as a novelist."

Cohan adapted the novel for the Broadway stage, and it became a hit, running 320 performances—a considerable number at the time—beginning 22 September 1913. Cohan changed the plot slightly, making Magee's motivation for his self-exile to Baldpate the winning of a bet.

Love Insurance (1914), Biggers's next novel, is a comedy-mystery about a young English nobleman who takes out insurance with Lloyd's of London against the possibility that his wealthy bride-to-be might change her mind before their wedding. Complications are provided by the presences of another possible heir to the nobleman's title, a blackmailer, a diamond thief, and an actress with compromising love letters. In unsigned reviews, *The New York Times* (27 September 1914) and *Publisher's Weekly* (22 August 1914) praised *Love Insurance* for its humor and cleverness.

In 1915 Biggers wrote his own successful play, *Inside the Lines,* about a love affair between two German spies—one of whom is a British double agent. It ran on Broadway for 103 performances; it also had a long run in London in 1915 and 1916. It was also made into a novel by Biggers and Robert Welles Ritchie, and was made into a silent movie in 1918 and then a movie with a sound track in 1930.

The Agony Column (1916) is a short novel about a young man and woman corresponding through the "agony column," the personal notices of a London newspaper. The man's efforts to impress the woman lead to romance but also to his becoming a suspect in a murder in the rooming house at which he is living. The book was made into a movie four times; the best-known version was titled *The Second Floor Mystery* (1930), starring Loretta Young.

Biggers's next play, *A Cure for Curables,* a comedy, played 112 Broadway performances, beginning 25 February 1918. Biggers's experience with the production was not a happy one. The star, William Hodge, then a popular actor, insisted on changing most of the lines Biggers had written.

In 1919, Biggers demonstrated versatility by adapting *Love Insurance* as the musical *See-Saw* (first performed 23 September 1919) and writing the lyrics for the musical score by Louis Hirsch. It played eighty-nine performances at Cohan's theater. Later that year, with Christopher Morley, Biggers wrote the play *Three's a Crowd,* a comedy that opened 4 December 1919, about former army officers helping a girl in trouble. Despite being the work of two well-known writers, it failed, surviving only twelve performances. Thereafter, Biggers devoted himself to magazine fiction, neither having another play produced nor publishing another novel until 1925.

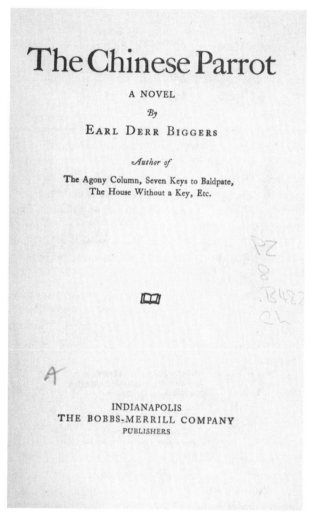

Title page for Biggers's novel in which he provides the history of his Chinese-born detective, Charlie Chan (Thomas Cooper Library, University of South Carolina)

To recover from the stress of being involved in two Broadway productions during the fall of 1919, Biggers went on vacation to Hawaii, where he became enamored of its climate and lifestyle. He also read a newspaper account of the work of two Honolulu plainclothes detectives, Chang Apana and Lee Fook, and stored in the back of his mind the idea of writing a series of mysteries set in Hawaii. Apana later claimed he was the sole basis for Charlie Chan, though Biggers said Chan was not drawn from real life.

In the early 1920s, Biggers, then in poor health, moved from New York to the milder climate of Pasadena, California. The idea of a detective of Chinese origin remained in his mind. He thought of such villains as Sax Rohmer's Dr. Fu Manchu and, as he told an interviewer for *The New York Times* (22 March 1931), decided, "Sinister and wicked Chinese are old stuff, but

an amiable Chinese on the side of law and order had never been used." He continued to write romantic fiction for magazines, but in spring 1925, he also published *The House Without a Key*. Prior to book publication, it, like all future Charlie Chan novels, was serialized in *The Saturday Evening Post,* in seven parts between 24 January and 7 March 1925.

The first Chan mystery is a tale of three cities. Early chapters in the book are set in San Francisco prior to an ocean liner sailing from there to Hawaii. In Honolulu, so many of the characters are drawn from the proper Winterslip family of Boston that one character calls it "a Boston suburb." Miss Minerva Winterslip, portrayed initially as a stereotypical spinster, comes to drink cocktails, attend a luau, and watch the hula, a dance she says she would not dare describe on Beacon Street in Boston, and enjoys them. Her brothers, Amos and Dan, who have not spoken in thirty-one years, carry their feud from Boston to Honolulu, and Dan is murdered, making Amos one of several suspects. Charlie Chan, described as "very fat," does not appear until one-fourth of the book is complete. Though he has a strong reputation as a detective, his role in solving the murder is limited. However, he allows the killer to steal his empty gun for a self-incriminating suicide attempt.

Most reviews of *The House Without a Key* were positive, with the exception of the unsigned review in the *Boston Transcript* (2 May 1925), which called Biggers's attempt at humor "sad" and faulted him for exaggerated characterization. More typical was another unsigned review in the *Saturday Review of Literature* (2 May 1925) that praised it as "an entertaining story well told with a dash of humor to give spice to its mystery, and a skillfully sketched-in background to lend glamour to its incidents." Few reviews mentioned Charlie Chan, who was not yet a series character.

In a retrospective review, in the Spring 1997 publication of *Deadly Pleasures,* Carol Byrd found "Biggers's evocation of territorial Hawaii is nearly hypnotic." Describing the harbor in Honolulu, Biggers wrote that "The carpet of the waters, apple-green by day, crimson and gold at sunset, was a deep purple now. On top of that extinct volcano called Diamond Head a yellow eye was winking, as though to hint there might still be fire beneath." She thought the book was not dated, pointing to Biggers's concern in the 1920s for the effect of overdevelopment on idyllic Hawaii.

Biggers followed his first Chan mystery with his last nonseries crime novel, *Fifty Candles* (1926), in which the host at a birthday party is murdered. Suspects in this short work include the host's wife, her lover, a Chinese servant, and the business partner the host allegedly defrauded. About half the size of the Chan books at 159 pages, its brevity was praised by several reviewers. Will Cuppy in *The New York Herald Tribune's Books* (7 March 1926) and Donald Douglas in *The New York World* (14 March 1926) objected to Biggers's introduction of romance, an apparent carryover from his magazine-fiction writing.

In *The Chinese Parrot* (1926), serialized in *The Saturday Evening Post* in six parts from 26 June through 31 July 1926, the reader learns much of Chan's history, including that after he came to Hawaii from China, he was a houseboy in the home of the wealthy Phillimore family, where he was well treated and learned to read and write English. Understandably, he is most willing to come to California to deliver rare pearls sold by financially strapped Sally Jordan, née Phillimore, through jeweler Alexander Eden. P. J. Madden, the purchaser, is supposed to take delivery in New York, but the location for delivery is changed to Madden's ranch in the California desert.

Chan grows suspicious and sends the jeweler's son ahead without the jewels, arriving later and posing as Ah Kim, a Chinese cook, a job that forces him to avoid using the "fine English words" that he has studied. He even reverses pronunciation of *r* and *l*, saying things such as "Tomallah nice day, you bet," and puts up with racial slurs. Not free from prejudice himself, Chan claims that judo is the only thing he was ever able to learn from the Japanese. Another Chinese cook is murdered, and the only "witness" is a bilingual parrot, who repeats the death cries of the victim but then is poisoned. At the end, Chan uses judo to wrest a pistol from the killer.

The *Boston Transcript* (25 September 1926) praised Biggers's combining humor with mystery. Seasick from his shipboard crossing, Chan says, "All time big Pacific Ocean suffer sharp pain down below, and toss about to prove it. Maybe from sympathy, I am in same fix." *The New York Times* (2 January 1927) praised the intricate plotting in *The Chinese Parrot*.

The Charlie Chan character quickly became enormously popular. In the same year that the second Chan book was published, *The House Without a Key* was made into a silent serial, the first of forty-nine Chan movies. With Charlie Chan in the bookstores, in the pages of the foremost mass-market magazine, and on the screen, readers eagerly anticipated the next novel, *Behind That Curtain* (1928), which was first serialized in *The Saturday Evening Post* in six parts from 31 March through 5 May 1928. Charlie is in San Francisco, where he meets Inspector Duff of Scotland Yard, who tells him of two murders that occurred sixteen years apart. The only fact that connects the victims is that each wore embroidered Chinese slippers. The first murder occurred in London. The second occurred in San Francisco, and the victim is Sir Frederic Bruce,

Dust jacket for the English edition of Biggers's fifth Charlie Chan novel, which begins with a murder in London (John Cooper and B. A. Pike, Artists in Crime: An Illustrated Survey of Crime Fiction First Edition Dustwrappers, 1920–1970 *[Brookfield, Vt.: Ashgate, 1995]; Bruccoli Clark Layman Archives)*

former head of the Criminal Investigation Department at Scotland Yard. Bruce had been frustrated because the London murder was the first case to come to his attention when he became head, and he never was able to solve it. After his retirement, he had followed a lead to California in hopes of finding the murderer.

Chan would like to return to Honolulu, where his wife has just delivered their eleventh child, but he feels honor bound when Duff asks his help in solving the murders and agrees to help because he feels not helping would cause him to "lose face." Chan's joining Duff and Captain Flannery of the San Francisco police, also on the case, causes a surfeit of detectives. As Chan himself says, "The ship with too many steersmen never reaches port." Chan solves the case in San Francisco but allows Flannery to take the credit.

In *The Black Camel* (1929), first serialized in *The Saturday Evening Post* in six parts, from 18 May through

22 June 1929, Chan is home and has been promoted from sergeant to inspector. He is characteristically modest about this advancement, claiming, "I am rewarded far beyond my humble merits." Called in to investigate the murder of Sheilah Fane, a Hollywood movie star, in her Waikiki Beach home, he again faces prejudice; when Charlie arrives on the scene to investigate, an Englishman, who refers to the Chinese as heathens, asks why they could not have sent a white man. Biggers again shows that Chan is not perfect himself, as he belittles Kashimo, his Japanese police assistant.

Early in the case, Chan discovers a letter that might identify the killer. Before he can read it, however, the lights go out, and Charlie is hit on the head and the letter stolen. The murderer is cleverer than most, planting false clues to lead Chan astray. Charlie thinks he has identified the killer, only to discover that his suspect has a perfect alibi, a revelation that forces Chan to reexamine his case. Chan gathers all the suspects together at the house where the murder occurred, the only time such a meeting takes place in one of Biggers's books, though such scenes are a staple of the Chan movies.

This book includes more about Chan's family than any other, and the reader meets some of Chan's children. Chan's older children are relatively informal and Americanized, but they call him "Dad," not "Pop," as the actors who played his sons in movies did. The book opens with the magnificence of Diamond Head as seen from a ship sailing into the harbor, looking "like a great lion . . . crouched to spring." It also includes a description of the view from Chan's home on Punchbowl Hill in Honolulu. In an essay on this book in *1001 Midnights* (1984), Marcia Muller praises Biggers's sense of place in showing Honolulu as it was in the 1920s, citing his description of Waikiki Beach as "a place where flowers bloom unmolested, and the trip into the city itself is a long journey by streetcar."

Again, the reviews of a Biggers book were largely favorable. An unsigned review in *The New York Times* (1 September 1929) said, "Not only is this an excellent detective story, but there is, as in Mr. Biggers's other stories, some very skillful character drawing in it." A review signed by "W.H.C." in the *Boston Transcript* (17 July 1929) called the book "Something very near perfection in the modern mystery tale." Cuppy in the *New York Herald Tribune's Books* section (30 June 1929) called Biggers "generous with hints and clews, at the same time guarding his secret perfectly until the end."

Inspector Duff of Scotland Yard returns in *Charlie Chan Carries On* (1930), first serialized in *The Saturday Evening Post,* in six parts, from 9 August through 13 September 1930, a book that covers more territory and has more action than others in the series. It begins in London with the murder of a Detroit automobile tycoon.

Duff trails his killer, whom he suspects is a passenger on a round-the-world cruise. The suspects are a lumber baron, a society grande dame, a wealthy lawyer, and a stereotypically portrayed Chicago gangster and his "moll."

Charlie Chan does not appear until more than halfway through the book. When Duff is wounded by the killer in Honolulu, Charlie takes his place on the ship for the final lap, the voyage to San Francisco, and the discovery of the killer. Kashimo, who acts as his foil, much in the same way as a Chan son does in most movies, joins him as a stowaway aboard the ship.

Keeper of the Keys (1932), first serialized in *The Saturday Evening Post,* in seven parts, from 11 June through 23 July 1932, is not only the final Chan novel, but it is also the third book in a relatively small oeuvre in which Biggers used the word "key" in the title. Set three weeks after the conclusion to *Charlie Chan Carries On, Keeper of the Keys* finds Charlie still in California, having attended a Chan family dinner in San Francisco. Before returning home, Chan avails himself of the opportunity to see snow for the first time by going to the home of opera singer Ellen Landini near Lake Tahoe. Chan's trip to the Sierras is partly business. Short of money for his return trip, he accepts $1,000 from wealthy Dudley Ward to find Ward's son.

Landini is murdered, and the mystery becomes a classic Golden Age puzzle with a small group of people isolated in a mountain cottage by snow. Landini's former husband seems a prime suspect because he angrily claims she bore him a son and concealed the fact. The solution is one of the best in the series. Isaac Anderson in *The New York Times Book Review* (31 July 1932) called it a "baffling mystery with an intricate but reasonable plot, good characterizations, a touch of comedy. . . ." This novel places more emphasis on clues than do other Chan novels, possibly because of the influence of S. S. Van Dine and Ellery Queen, who had both gained great popularity by then.

Biggers died of heart disease in Pasadena on 5 April 1933. Shortly after his death, his longtime publisher, Bobbs-Merrill, published *Earl Derr Biggers Tells Ten Stories* (1933), a collection of magazine stories originally published in *The Saturday Evening Post* between 1921 and 1928. (To the regret of anthologists, Biggers never wrote a short story—or even a novelette—about Charlie Chan.) Romance is the common feature of these stories, even the two that are about crime. "Moonlight at the Crossroads" is set in Hawaii. "The Dollar Chasers" combines romance and detection as reporter Bill Hammond, while on assignment, tries to discover who stole a lucky piece belonging to the wealthy father of the young woman he loves. "Idle Hands," Biggers's best-known short story, is about Jim

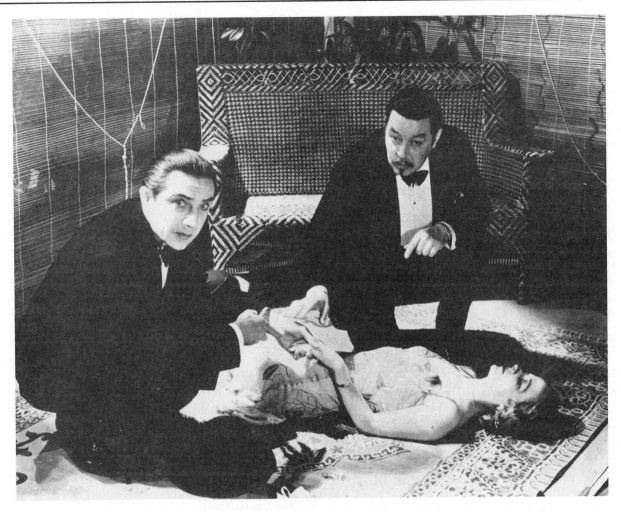

Bela Lugosi as Tarneverro, Warner Oland as Charlie Chan, and Dorothy Revier as the victim in the 1931 movie
The Black Camel *(© 1931 Twentieth Century Fox. All rights reserved.)*

Alden, bored because, on his doctor's advice, he has retired from automobile manufacturing. He secretly goes into a small garage and auto-repair business, which not only makes him happy but also restores his health. "Idle Hands" was made into the 1931 movie *The Millionaire,* with George Arliss.

Biggers's noncriminous stories include autobiographical elements. Three are set in "Mayfield," Indiana, a fictional town apparently drawn from Warren, Ohio, where he grew up. "Broadway Broke" suggests something of Biggers's nostalgia for the old Broadway theater; his protagonist, a onetime stage star, finds the theater of the 1920s increasingly commercial and hard-hearted. Leaving the stage for California—as did Biggers when he abandoned writing plays—she thinks, "It saddens me, but it makes it easier to go—to go and never come back. There's nothing to come back for." Reviews of the collection emphasized the simplicity of the stories. An unsigned review in *Christian Century* (20

September 1933) refers to the contents as "excellent magazine stories but not imperishable literature—the republication of which is justified chiefly as a memorial."

Karl Schriftgiesser, in reviewing *Keeper of the Keys* in the *Boston Transcript* (20 July 1932), said of Chan, "Because of his charm, his quoted Chinese philosophy, and his ability to use his head when those about him are not quite so smart, he has endeared himself to thousands of readers who have long ago forgotten that he is not a real person after all." Schriftgiesser's assessment came as Chan was becoming a popular character in movies.

In the first two movies, *The House Without a Key* (1926), a serial, and *The Chinese Parrot* (1927), Chan has a relatively minor role and is played by Japanese actors. An English actor played him in a third movie, *Behind That Curtain* (1929), again one in which Chan's role was not a major one. With the casting of Warner Oland, a

Cover for a 1948 paperback reprint of Biggers's first novel, originally published in 1913 (Chris Steinbrunner and Otto Penzler, eds., Encyclopedia of Mystery and Detection [New York: McGraw-Hill, 1976]; Bruccoli Clark Layman Archives)

Swedish actor, as the title character in *Charlie Chan Carries On* (1931), Chan's movie reputation was established, though Biggers did not live long enough to benefit financially from it. Eventually, the first five Chan books were made into movies. The only one not to make it to the screen was the last, *Keeper of the Keys,* which in October 1933 was adapted for the Broadway stage by Valentine Davies. William Harrigan, son of famous Irish comedian Ned Harrigan, played Chan. The play was a failure, lasting only twenty-five performances.

The Chan movies were formulaic B pictures, but the formula proved popular with moviegoers. They even reacted well to what became a cliché, the resolution in which Chan gathers all the suspects in a room, details each one's role in the case, and finally turns on the killer saying, "You are murderer!" A son, played first by Keye Luke, was given a prominent role in the movies, thus contrasting a young, slang-spouting mem-

ber of the family with the tranquil father. He was called "Number One Son," a term never appearing in the books, and he frequently calls out, "Hey, Pop, I've got a swell clue."

These low-budget Charlie Chan movies were profitable. Chan, who in books had never traveled anywhere except to California, became more mobile, traveling to Egypt, Paris, London, New York, and Shanghai, among other places. He also solved crimes at a racetrack, an opera house, and the 1936 Olympics.

Although Oland was almost universally considered the best of the screen Chans, his death in 1937 and his replacement by Sidney Toler did not destroy the popularity of the series. When 20th Century-Fox decided to drop it in 1942, it was picked up by Monogram Pictures, and though production values declined, their movies with Toler and then, after Toler died in 1947, with Roland Winters, continued to earn money.

Throughout much of the 1930s and 1940s, Charlie Chan was also a character on radio, with Walter Connolly, Ed Begley, and Santos Ortega playing him at various times. Early in the history of television, *The New Adventures of Charlie Chan,* with J. Carroll Naish in the title role, was a television series in England that was syndicated in the United States beginning in 1957.

From 1938 to 1942, a Charlie Chan comic strip, drawn by Alfred Andriola, appeared in many newspapers. In his analysis of these strips, Ron Schwartz, in *Mystery Readers Journal* (Fall 1987), said that Andriola's Chan "owes more to the movies than the books, with his Chan visually rendered in the likeness of actor Warner Oland."

Though Charlie Chan was born as an antidote to the stereotypical picture of Oriental villains as evil incarnate, by the 1960s he was the subject of protests by militant Asian and African Americans. The former group thought Chan was still a stereotype, albeit a different one. African Americans had a reason to object to the movie series because, beginning with *Charlie Chan in Egypt* (1935), perennially frightened black characters were often added to the cast. Stepin Fetchit was first, playing a character named Snowshoes. Later, for Monogram, Mantan Moreland played chauffeur Birmingham Brown, whose typical reaction to danger was chattering teeth and dialogue such as, "Feets get me out of here." When Chan movies were shown on commercial television networks, protests forced sponsors to remove them from programming in some cities. However, with the ready availability of noncommercial cable television and videotapes by the 1980s, the movie version of Chan remained available for new generations.

A brief resurgence of interest in Chan occurred in the 1970s. Ross Martin played him in a television movie, *Happiness Is a Warm Clue* (1971), and from 1972 to 1974 a television cartoon series, *The Amazing Chan and the Chan Clan* featured younger members of the family trying to solve mysteries. In 1973, a digest-sized magazine, *Charlie Chan Mystery Magazine,* was introduced. Each issue included a new Charlie Chan story written by various authors under the "house name" Robert Hart Davis. The stories are updated to the 1970s and feature a Charlie Chan more apt to use martial arts than in Biggers's original work. The magazine only survived for four issues. Bantam Books commissioned Dennis Lynds to write *Charlie Chan Returns* (1974), a book that updates the series to the 1970s, with Chan vacationing in New York, where his son is a police detective. One of the worst adaptations of the Chan character, in the opinion of most critics, was a 1980 movie, *Charlie Chan and the Curse of the Dragon,* in which Peter Ustinov was badly miscast as Chan. It was picketed by Asian Americans in San Francisco.

Because Chan was considered an object of embarrassment to many militant Chinese Americans, *Charlie Chan Is Dead* became the title of a 1993 anthology of contemporary Asian American fiction, edited by Jessica Hagedorn, whose stated aim was to destroy stereotypes. Most of those who contributed to it gave no indication that they had read the Biggers books, which show Charlie Chan as wise, courageous, modest, patient, devoted to his family, and loyal to his friends.

The best single article about Biggers and Chan, "Murder Number One: Earl Derr Biggers" by Jon L. Breen in *New Republic* (July 1977), describes Chan as "a complex and multifaceted character" compared to the genial, single-dimensional detective portrayed in other media. A victim of discrimination himself, he early shows bias against the Japanese, though he comes to like his clumsy but well-meaning detective assistant Kashimo. Chan is torn between two cultures, East and West. Though he tries to be Americanized, he is subject to pressures, as when he visits older members of the Chan family in San Francisco, and they are critical because his job requires him to work for "foreign devil police."

Charlie prides himself on his ability to speak perfect English, though the words he speaks on his first appearance in *The House Without a Key* are decidedly ungrammatical: "No knife are present in neighborhood of crime." Later, his speech in that book tends toward the picturesque. At a dramatic moment, he tells the killer, "Relinquish the fire arms . . . or I am forced to make fatal insertion in vital organ belonging to you." Even when grammatical errors decrease, his speech remains quaint. For example, in *Behind That Curtain,* he says, "The facts must be upearthed." In *The Black Camel,* a suspect is told, "I could place you beneath arrest."

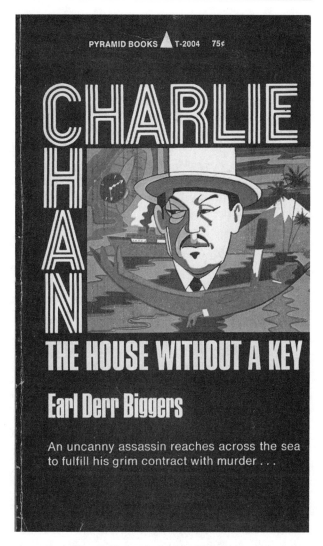

Cover for a 1969 paperback reprint of the first novel that featured Charlie Chan, originally published in 1925 (Collection of Mark McEwan)

Movies with sound are called "talkative films" in *Charlie Chan Carries On.*

By the second book in the series, Chan uses many aphorisms, though never in the quantity that he spouts them in movies. In *The Chinese Parrot,* he quotes a famous Chinese saying: "He who rides a tiger cannot dismount." Along similar lines, in *The Black Camel,* he says, "The man who is about to cross a stream should not revile the crocodile's mother." He warns in *Charlie Chan Carries On,* "The deer should not play with the tiger." One of his best-known aphorisms occurs in his final book: "The fool in a hurry drinks his tea with a fork."

That last saying exemplifies one of the characteristics of Chan's detective methods, his patience. In the first Chan book, he claims, albeit ungrammatically, "Patience are a virtue." As he says in *The Chinese Parrot,* "Detective business consists of one unsignificant detail placed besides others of same. Then with sudden dazzle, light begins to dawn." Biggers himself thought that Chan's strength was in assessing character. In *Twentieth Century Authors* (1942), Biggers is quoted as saying, "If I understand Charlie Chan correctly, he has an idea that if you understand a man's character you can nearly predict what he is apt to do in any set of circumstances." Though Biggers made Chan a smart detective, Judith Weaver was probably correct when, in her article about him in *Mystery Readers' Journal* (Winter 1991–1992) she said of Chan, "His quaint humor, kind philosophy, benevolence and amiability endeared him to fans far more than his detective ability."

The fame and reputation of Biggers has been eclipsed, certainly for the general public, by that of his creation. No full-scale biography of Biggers has appeared. In her article about him in *St. James Guide to Crime and Mystery Writers* (1996), Margaret J. King devotes a single sentence to Biggers, the rest to Chan. Most of Breen's *New Republic* article is devoted to Chan, though Biggers's strengths are noted, including a "gently humorous style and his ability to bring his characters to life within the limits of commercial fiction." Breen echoed most critics when he said that Biggers's greatest achievement was "the creation of one of the immortal fictional detectives."

In *Murder for Pleasure*, Haycraft called Biggers "a skilled and genial craftsman . . . his detective stories are remembered less for themselves than for the wise, smiling, pudgy little Chinese they introduced." As Neil Ellman says in his article "Charlie Chan Carries On," in *The Armchair Detective* (April 1977), "His popularity has outlived the memory of his creator; his name is more a household word than are the names of many of the great detectives admired by whodunit aficionados."

Earl Derr Biggers wrote popular plays and magazine fiction and one nonseries mystery novel that was successful both by itself and in its adaptation for the theater. He was not a prolific writer of detective fiction, but he created the enduring Charlie Chan. In the present era, when the ethnicity of many fictional detectives—for example, Native Americans, Asian Americans, and Hispanics—is stressed, readers should remember that Earl Derr Biggers created the first major ethnic sleuth.

Interview:

New York Times, 22 March 1931, p. 12.

References:

Douglas M. Armato, "Charlie Chan in Books and in Motion Pictures," *Armchair Detective,* 7 (February 1974): 97–99;

Jon L. Breen, "Charlie Chan: The Man Behind the Curtain," *Views and Reviews,* 6 (Fall 1974): 29–35;

Breen, "Murder Number One: Earl Derr Biggers," *New Republic,* 177 (30 July 1977): 38–39;

Breen, "Who Killed Charlie Chan?" *Armchair Detective,* 7 (February 1974): 100, 127;

Harvey Chertok and Martha Torge, *Quotations from Charlie Chan* (New York: Golden Press, 1968);

Fred Dueren, "Charlie Chan: A Biography," *Armchair Detective,* 7 (August 1974): 263;

Neil Ellman, "Charlie Chan Carries On," *Armchair Detective,* 10 (April 1977): 183–184;

Ron Goulart, "What's Your Plan, Charlie Chan?" *Nostalgia Illustrated,* 2 (July 1975): 46–50, 71;

Ken Hanke, *Charlie Chan at the Movies: History, Filmography, and Criticism* (Jefferson, N.C.: McFarland, 1989);

Howard Haycraft, *Murder for Pleasure* (New York & London: Appleton-Century, 1941);

Carole Lovett Koontz, "The Writing Career of Earl Derr Biggers: Struggle for Survival and Success," *Ohiana,* 26 (Winter 1983): 120–123;

Marvin Lachman, "The Enduring Detective," *CADS (Crime and Detective Stories),* no. 16 (May 1991): 43–44;

Anthony Lejeune, "Charlie Chan," in *100 Great Detectives,* edited by Maxim Jakubowski (New York: Carroll & Graf, 1991): 64–66;

Dick O'Donnell, "The Original Charlie Chan," *Pulpsmith,* 7 (Winter–Spring 1988): 46–51;

Otto Penzler, "Charlie Chan," in *The Private Lives of Private Eyes, Spies, Crime Fighters, and Other Good Guys* (New York: Grosset & Dunlap, 1977), pp. 42–51;

Penzler, "Collecting Earl Derr Biggers," *Armchair Detective,* 15 (Spring 1982): 119–125; 15 (Fall 1982): 356;

Michael R. Pitts, "Charlie Chan," in *Famous Movie Detectives* (Metuchen, N.J. & London: Scarecrow Press, 1979), pp. 39–84;

Ron Schwartz, "The Two Dimensional Detective," *Mystery Readers' Journal,* 3 (Fall 1987): 47;

Judith Weaver, "Ah, So, Mr. Chan . . . ," *Mystery Readers' Journal,* 7 (Winter 1991–1992): 12–15.

Gil Brewer

(20 November 1922 – 9 January 1983)

Tim Dayton
Kansas State University

BOOKS: *Satan Is a Woman* (New York: Fawcett, 1951; London: New Fiction Press, 1952);

So Rich, So Dead (New York: Fawcett, 1951; London: Priory, 1951);

13 French Street (New York: Fawcett, 1951; London: New Fiction Press, 1952);

Love Me and Die, as Day Keene (New York: Phantom, 1951);

Flight to Darkness (New York: Fawcett, 1952);

Hell's Our Destination (New York: Fawcett, 1953; London: Fawcett, 1955);

A Killer Is Loose (New York: Fawcett, 1954; London: Moring, 1954);

Some Must Die (New York: Fawcett, 1954; London: Moring, 1956);

The Squeeze (New York: Ace, 1955; London: Priory, 1960);

77 Rue Paradis (New York: Fawcett, 1955; London: Miller, 1959);

—And the Girl Screamed (Greenwich, Conn.: Fawcett, 1956; London: Priory, 1956);

The Angry Dream (New York: Mystery House, 1957); republished as *The Girl from Hateville* (Rockville Centre, N.Y.: Zenith, 1958);

The Brat (Greenwich, Conn.: Fawcett, 1957; Manchester: PBS, 1957);

Little Tramp (Greenwich, Conn.: Fawcett, 1957; London: Red Seal, 1959);

The Red Scarf (New York: Mystery House, 1958; London: Digit, 1958);

The Bitch (New York: Avon, 1958);

Wild (Greenwich, Conn.: Fawcett, 1958; London: Fawcett, 1959);

The Vengeful Virgin (Greenwich, Conn.: Fawcett, 1958; London: Muller, 1960);

Sugar (New York: Avon, 1959);

Wild to Possess (Derby, Conn.: Monarch, 1959);

Appointment in Hell (London: Priory, 1960; Derby, Conn.: Monarch, 1961);

Angel (New York: Avon, 1960);

Backwoods Teaser (Greenwich, Conn.: Fawcett, 1960);

The Three-Way Split (Greenwich, Conn.: Fawcett, 1960; Bridlington, U.K.: Bridbooks, 1960);

Nude on Thin Ice (New York: Avon, 1960);

Play It Hard (Derby, Conn.: Monarch, 1960; London: Priory, 1960);

Taste for Sin (New York: Berkley, 1961);

Memory of Passion (New York: Lancer, 1962);

The Hungry One (Greenwich, Conn.: Fawcett, 1966);

Sin for Me (New York: Banner, 1967);

The Tease (New York: Banner, 1967);

The Campus Murders, as Ellery Queen (New York: Lancer, 1969);

The Devil in Davos (New York: Ace, 1969);

Mediterranean Caper (New York: Ace, 1969);

Appointment in Cairo (New York: Ace, 1970);

Blood on the Ivy, as Hal Ellson (New York: Pyramid, 1970);

Shadowland, as Elaine Evans (New York: Lancer, 1970);

A Dark and Deadly Love, as Evans (New York: Lancer, 1972);

Mouth Magic, as Mark Bailey (Chatsworth, Cal.: Barclay House, 1972);

More Than a Handful, as Luke Morgann (New York: Bee-Line, 1972);

Ladies in Heat, as Morgann (New York: Bee-Line, 1972);

Gamecock, as Morgann (New York: Bee-Line, 1972);

Tongue Tricks, as Morgann (New York: Bee-Line, 1972);

Black Autumn, as Evans (New York: Lancer, 1973);

Murder Mission! as Al Conroy (New York: Lancer, 1973);

Strangle Hold! as Conroy (New York: Lancer, 1973);

Wintershade, as Evans (New York: Popular Library, 1974);

Eleven Bullets for Mohammed, as Harry Arvay (New York: Bantam, 1975);

Operation Kuwait, as Arvay (New York: Bantam, 1975);

Togo Commando, as Arvay (New York: Bantam, 1975; London: Corgi, 1976);

The Piraeus Plot, as Arvay (New York: Bantam, 1975).

SELECTED PERIODICAL PUBLICATIONS–
UNCOLLECTED: "With This Gun," *Detective Tales,*
47, no. 4 (1951): 46–55;

"It's Always Too Late," *Detective Fiction,* 156, no. 1
(1951): 27–35;

"Final Appearance," *Detective Tales,* 48, no. 3 (1951):
54–62;

"Moonshine," *Manhunt,* 3, no. 3 (1955): 42–50;

"My Lady Is a Tramp," as Bailey Morgan, *Pursuit Detective Story Magazine,* 9 (1955): 1–15;

"Gigolo," as Morgan, *Pursuit Detective Story Magazine,* 10
(1955): 57–68;

"The Screamer," as Eric Fitzgerald, *Pursuit Detective Story
Magazine,* 11 (1955): 1–44;

"I Saw Her Die," *Manhunt,* 3, no. 10 (1955): 37–43;

"Die, Darling, Die," *Justice,* 2, no. 1 (1956): 57–77;

"Sauce for the Goose," as Fitzgerald, *Pursuit Detective
Story Magazine,* 13 (1956): 94–107;

"Mow the Green Grass," as Jack Holland, *Pursuit Detective Story Magazine,* 14 (1956): 101–108;

"Short Go," as Holland, *Hunted Detective Story Magazine,*
10 (1956): 111–120;

"The Gesture," *Saint Detective Magazine,* 5, no. 3 (1956):
104–109;

"Return to Yesterday," as Fitzgerald, *Pursuit Detective
Story Magazine,* 16 (1956): 62–72;

"Wife Sitter," as Morgan, *Pursuit Detective Story Magazine,*
16 (1956): 73–82;

"Whiskey," as Morgan, *Pursuit Detective Story Magazine,*
18 (1956): 45–62;

"The Axe Is Ready," *Trapped Detective Story Magazine,* 1,
no. 4 (1956): 39–50;

"On a Sunday Afternoon," *Manhunt,* 5, no. 1 (1957):
128–141;

"Sympathy," *Mike Shayne Mystery Magazine,* 25, no. 1
(1969): 125–128;

"The Getaway," *Mystery Monthly,* 1, no. 1 (1976): 58–66;

"Family," *Alfred Hitchcock's Mystery Magazine,* 23, no. 3
(1978): 54–61.

One of the writers associated with Gold Medal
publishers in the 1950s, Gil Brewer was a prolific
author of paperback originals until personal difficulties
began to curb his output in the early 1960s. While he
also wrote Gothic and pornographic novels, it is as a
writer of crime novels that Brewer will likely prove of
some continuing interest to readers. Brewer's crime
novels fall roughly into two groups: novels about
femmes fatales, such as *13 French Street* (1951), which
revolve around the figure of an alluring, powerful
woman; and novels about hunted, innocent men, such
as *The Red Scarf* (1958), in which the main character

finds himself the object of the attention of the police, the
criminal underworld, or both. Frequently, Brewer's
novels combine elements of both of these narrative
types, as in, for example, *The Brat* (1957).

Gilbert John Brewer grew up in Canandaigua, in
the Finger Lakes region of upstate New York, where he
was born on 20 November 1922, the son of Gilbert
Thomas and Ruth Wilhelmina (Olschewske) Brewer.
In a brief, unpublished account of Brewer's life, his
wife, Verlaine (Morris) Brewer, notes that Brewer's
family life was not happy. Brewer "worshiped" his
father–also, according to Verlaine, a writer–but he had
a difficult relationship with his mother, who "had no
understanding of writers." This difficulty was worsened
by the fact that both father and son were alcoholics.

Brewer claimed to have written his first short
story when he was nine years old, emulating his father,
and in high school he imposed upon himself the discipline of writing a story every day. This practice was
good preparation for a writer who produced hundreds
of short stories and dozens of novels between 1950 and
the late 1970s. Brewer was drafted into the United
States Army during World War II, serving in Europe.
While he was serving in the army his family moved to
St. Petersburg, Florida, where, following his discharge,
he rejoined them in 1947. Brewer's career as a writer
began in 1948, when after a brief attempt at "serious"
fiction Brewer began "writing to sell."

Brewer had met Verlaine Morris the previous
year, in 1947. At the time she was married, with two
teenage children. Her husband agreed to a divorce and
to take custody of the children. Brewer and Verlaine
were married in 1950. Soon after the marriage, Brewer
learned that his first short story had been accepted for
publication. Literary agent Joseph T. "Cap" Shaw, the
legendary former editor of *Black Mask,* saw Brewer's
work and took him on as a client, placing Brewer's first
three novels, *Satan Is a Woman* (based on his short story
"With This Gun"), *So Rich, So Dead,* and *13 French Street*
with Gold Medal in 1951.

Satan Is a Woman–the title came from Gold
Medal; Brewer's title for the novel was "Satan's Rib"–
features what became typical Brewer characters and
themes. Larry Cole owns and tends bar at the Pink
Goat, a small and not lucrative bar in Tampa. Cole has
been raised by his older brother, Tad, who, like many a
Cole before him, is a hardened criminal. Tad has
attempted to keep his younger brother away from a life
of crime, however, warning Larry, "Don't get to thinking about champagne and caviar. Stick to beer and pretzels. It's safer. And to be honest, it's more fun."

As a grown man, Larry abides by Tad's advice,
though Tad himself has been convicted of murder.
Larry's law-abiding ways become threatened, however,

once Joan Turner walks into the Pink Goat. Turner is a typical Brewer femme fatale, honey-blonde, tall, "warm and cool at the same time, with eyes like pale blue diamonds, and soft, moist lips." Cole is overwhelmed by Turner and becomes slowly but surely drawn by her into dishonesty and to the brink of criminality. The story reaches a turning point when Cole helps Turner to dispose of the corpse of a man she claims had broken into her bedroom and attempted to rape her. Turner talks Cole into concealing the man's death because it would draw attention to her and Cole, attention that would ruin their chance to stage a robbery that Turner has planned and to which Cole reluctantly consents to be an accomplice.

Finally, Cole cannot bear living with guilt and resolves to confess his role in disposing of the body and to convince Turner not to commit the robbery. Cole, however, is slugged on his way to the scene of the robbery, and when he comes to and makes his way there finds that Turner has apparently gone ahead without him. Cole discovers that Tad has escaped from prison and confronts Turner, who, it turns out, is a jilted former lover of Tad's and has set up the robbery as a chance to frame Tad's younger brother for the murder of a night watchman. The man whose body Larry had dumped into the ocean had been sent by his brother to warn him. In the final scene, Tad and Joan shoot and kill one another, and Larry learns, finally, what Tad has tried to teach him. Turner has kept Larry in tow and made him a vehicle for her revenge by manipulating his sexual desire, making him want "champagne and caviar." Perhaps more than the figure of the femme fatale, the vulnerability of the male protagonist to the manipulation of a sexually powerful woman is the point of emphasis in *Satan Is a Woman;* it reverberates through much of Brewer's fiction.

Brewer already had *So Rich, So Dead*—written before *Satan Is a Woman*—ready to send to Fawcett when they asked to see more from him. *So Rich, So Dead* begins as a hard-boiled detective novel, but when the main character, Bill Maddern, finds his partner (who is also his brother) and their secretary shot dead in their office, a suspense plot is introduced. Maddern becomes a suspect and must elude both the police and a slew of criminals in order to find the guilty party and absolve himself. While the novel is satisfying as the story of a man trying to clear his name while simultaneously avoiding being murdered, the background elements are perhaps even more compelling than the main narrative. For example, when Maddern, his face and hands covered with cuts and scrapes incurred as he fled the police, stops in a butcher's shop to make a phone call, the exchange between him and the butcher exemplifies the darkness that pervades the novel:

Cover for Brewer's 1954 novel in which an unemployed man is forced to accompany a young psychopath on a killing spree (<www.biblio.com/books/11354949.html>)

I . . . glimpsed the phone on a dirty, fly-littered windowsill behind an open crate of dried figs. As I reached for it, the fat man said, "Sho now. Was she a mite too much for you, son? I always say you got to show 'em who's boss once in a blue moon. Heh-heh. Don't bloody up that ere brand-new telyphone, son. I always wash my hands first, myself. Buyin' folks air peculiar about bloody telyphones."

Brewer's third novel, *13 French Street,* was enormously successful. A femme fatale novel in the extreme, *13 French Street* concerns Alex Bland, a World War II veteran, who visits his wartime buddy Verne Lawrence at his home on 13 French Street in the fictional town of Allayne, apparently modeled on Brewer's hometown. While Bland thinks of the trip as a visit to see his old comrade, he has, in fact, mostly been in contact with his friend's wife, Petra. Bland and Petra have exchanged letters over the course of several years.

Verne has in five years turned into a wealthy but physically drained man. Petra is, predictably enough, beautiful, but Brewer makes her physical attractiveness convincingly threatening as well. This combination of allure and danger is central to the considerable sexual tension that Brewer achieves, which in turn motivates the action of the novel. Of these two elements, tension and action, the former predominates, as Brewer exploits the reader's uncertainty as to whether or not Bland will succumb to Petra's powers of attraction. When Bland eventually does succumb, the action pivots on how far he will follow his seductress—a question posed when, just as the tension built up over the course of the first ten chapters is about to be relieved, Verne's aged mother catches Bland and Petra half-undressed and Petra hurls the old woman out of a second-floor window. Bland keeps to himself his knowledge of Petra's role in the death, because she threatens to claim that Bland killed Verne's mother after she witnessed Bland assaulting Petra.

Petra's deviousness comes to dominate the novel, with Bland torn between his self-destructive, and nearly murderous, obsession with the woman and his sorely tested loyalties both to his friend and to Madge, the woman he plans someday to marry. By the time Petra proposes murdering Verne, Bland's loyalties are frayed nearly to the breaking point, as he has had sex with Petra while Verne selected a headstone for his mother's grave.

Bland, however, recovers his senses when he goes to meet Cecil Emmetts, the hired man on a nearby farm. Emmetts witnessed the murder of Verne's mother and tries to blackmail Bland and Petra. Rather than paying Emmetts off, Bland, disregarding the consequences, beats him severely and in doing so apparently purges himself of his obsession with Petra. The violence of the beating Bland inflicts seems to work as a purgative precisely because of the undercurrent of violence in Bland's relationship with Petra.

The violence of the novel reaches its climax in the conclusion, which Brewer manages to bring about swiftly but without forcing the rapid pace. Returning from his encounter with Emmetts, Bland, after a last run-in with Petra, attempts to tell Verne the truth; Verne has already been told by Emmetts. At this point Petra appears and informs Verne and Bland that she had planned the whole course of events: to seduce Bland, kill Verne's mother, and, finally, kill both Verne and Bland, leaving Petra unencumbered to enjoy Verne's money. Petra's seemingly passionate character is thus revealed to be an act, concealing her cold-hearted manipulations.

As Petra aims a pistol at Bland and begins to squeeze the trigger, however, Verne shoots her with "an Army Colt .45" in a momentary return to his old, wartime self, as Verne himself notes: "'I still hit what I aim at,' he said. 'I always did. Even with a lousy pistol. You remember, Alex?'" The graphic description of Petra's wounds—which emphasizes the contrast between her former beauty and her disfigurement—and the affirmation of male wartime companionship suggest that Brewer taps into the same fund of misogynistic energy as did Mickey Spillane in *I, the Jury* (1947), while the lurid exoticism of Brewer's descriptions of Petra, her clothes, and her accoutrements suggests James M. Cain's *Double Indemnity* (1936).

Brewer published his next novel, *Love Me and Die* (1951), under the name of Day Keene. This pseudonymous effort is his purest hard-boiled detective novel and, like some of his short stories, suggests that he could have been a successful commercial writer in the straight hard-boiled manner. The main character of *Love Me and Die,* Johnny Slagle, a former cop turned private detective, works on retainer for Consolidated Studios, bailing out misbehaving Hollywood stars. The novel features characteristic elements of the hard-boiled novel: Slagle is knocked unconscious twice, framed for murder, and offered a lucrative deal if he minds his own business. Brewer, however, also changes the formula by making Slagle married. Indeed, he begins the novel with Slagle torn from his domestic life by a middle-of-the-night phone call. Unlike the typical hard-boiled detective hero, Slagle must think of his wife and the consequences for her of his actions.

The last of Brewer's Gold Medal crime novels handled by Shaw, *Flight to Darkness* (1952), concerns a Korean War veteran, Eric Garth, haunted by a recurring dream in which he bludgeons to death his much-hated adopted brother, Frank. When the novel begins, Garth is a patient in a psychiatric hospital, where he meets and begins an affair with Leda, a nurse. Upon Garth's release, he and Leda drive cross-country to Garth's childhood home in Florida, where he plans to resume life as the son of a prosperous family and return to his calling as a sculptor. Garth worries about the reaction of his former girlfriend, Norma Dean, who is not likely to be pleased by the presence of Leda. His return, however, is complicated well before the couple makes it to Florida, when Garth is taken into custody as a suspect in a hit-and-run accident. Shortly after he is incarcerated, Leda phones Frank, who flies up, ostensibly to see his brother through his troubles. Garth is shipped to a psychiatric hospital, and after a short while Leda mysteriously disappears.

In the psychiatric hospital Garth loses contact with the outside world, but manages to place a phone call to the police, who inform him that all charges against him have been dropped; Garth flees from the hospital and returns to Florida, where he discovers that while Norma has faithfully awaited his return, Leda has married Frank. In addition to his girlfriend, Frank has taken Garth's money and property, convincing their dying mother that he, Frank, should rightly inherit the family's wealth. So when Frank is found bludgeoned to death, suspicion falls heavily on Garth. In the protracted climax of the novel, Garth and Leda flee into the wild Florida countryside, until Leda reveals that she has masterminded his series of disasters, from the hit-and-run to Frank's murder, in order to get his family's money. When they come to blows, Leda is revealed as possibly Brewer's most feral and appetitive female character, and Garth's desire for her is presented as ultimately pathological.

The pathology of sexual desire was seen by Shaw as a device that Brewer needed to move beyond. As Brewer's literary agent Shaw was both supportive and demanding of his client. He clearly saw him as a talent with considerable potential but also as a writer who needed careful handling. In his letters Shaw urged Brewer to work at a reasonable pace so as to avoid burning himself out and also to consider writing stories that did not rely on sex to drive their plots. On 27 July 1951 Shaw wrote to Brewer that "backed by that quality of writing, distinctive of restraint, makes me want to talk with you of better things, of better stories, without sex, for I feel confident that you can achieve the same emotional effects without it."

Shaw's opinion was shared by Dick Carroll, executive editor of Gold Medal. Writing to Max Wilkinson, one of the agents employed by Brewer after Shaw's death, Carroll wrote in a letter of 5 February 1953, "I wish you could persuade Gil to use his tense, exciting writing in a novel whose basic theme is not sexual obsession. . . . I think Brewer has a better writing talent than he has yet shown, even in his successful books for us." Shaw and Carroll each believed that Brewer relied too much and too often on sexual obsession to drive his plots, with his treatment of sex becoming a kind of default mechanism used to enliven his stories and novels. Furthermore, Carroll wrote in the same letter, while Brewer often began his novels strikingly, his characters were "already boiling on the front page with nothing left thereafter but for the pot to overflow hissingly."

Brewer took Shaw's and Carroll's advice seriously, to judge from his next three crime novels: *Hell's Our Destination* (1953), *A Killer Is Loose* (1954), and *The Red Scarf*. These three novels all concern hunted, innocent men, although each in its own distinctive manner. In *Hell's Our Destination* the main character, Simon Lewt, has helped a criminal stash nearly $300,000 in a Florida

Cover for Brewer's 1955 novel that was published in an Ace Double paperback edition along with Frank Diamond's Love Me to Death (<www.people.uncw.edu/smithms>)

swamp, the ways of which he knows intimately. Lewt becomes obsessed with finding the money–the exact location of which he does not know–and using it to escape from the swamp with his girlfriend, Verna Lee. His obsession with the money, however, has begun to change him and to sour his relationship with Verna. Meanwhile, the criminal, James Lister, has escaped from prison with another prisoner, Henry Bliss, who in turn murders Lister, apparently with the object of finding his stashed money. To further complicate matters, the missing money is being pursued by an insurance investigator, Lew Steggins, and–seemingly unrelated–a photographer, Cora Payne, hires Lewt to guide her in the swamp as part of a magazine feature on which she is working.

The novel centers on Lewt's internal conflict as he finds himself compulsively pursuing money that he realizes is ruining any chance of a happy life with Verna–his original motivation for seeking it. This internal conflict is paralleled by tensions between the various characters, with Cora providing a foil to Verna and Steggins to Bliss. Brewer plays out these tensions and conflicts skillfully and presents Lewt's deterioration powerfully.

A Killer Is Loose is an unusual Brewer novel in that it relies on neither money nor sex to fuel the plot. While the first-person narrator is Steve Logan, the focal character is Ralph Angers, the killer of the title. When the novel opens, Logan is in the middle of a hard-luck streak, unemployed and without the prospect of changing this status soon; his wife, Ruby, is pregnant. Logan decides to try to collect on a debt from Harvey Aldercock, a rich yachtsman for whom he has worked, bringing with him the last piece in his sold-off gun collection, a Luger, with the intention of either using it to prompt Aldercock to pay up or selling it to a friend. When Logan fails to collect from Aldercock, he heads off to sell the Luger, but on the way sees a man about to step in front of a speeding bus. Logan saves the young man, who then insists that they go for a drink. On the way to the bar, Logan learns that Ruby has been taken to the hospital and is in labor. At this point the main action of the novel begins to unfold, against the background of Logan attempting to join his wife at the hospital.

When Logan tries to sell his Luger to the owner of the bar, Jake Halloran, the young man, for no apparent reason, shoots Halloran in the head and then introduces himself to Logan as Ralph Angers. Thus begins a nightmarish journey on which Angers forces Logan, whom he regards as his "pal," to accompany him. Logan watches as Angers kills several people who threaten to hinder him, repeatedly eludes the police, and simultaneously makes fitful progress on his fanciful project of building a hospital specializing in eye surgery. Angers tells Logan that he is an eye surgeon whose desire to open a hospital has been thwarted; this medical specialty connects him to Logan, since Logan suffered an eye injury that began his bad luck. Perhaps because of this connection, or because Logan's own failure makes Angers's frustration more understandable to him, Logan finds himself feeling sympathetic toward Angers, even though he also fears him. Brewer's handling of the ambivalent relationship between Logan and Angers makes *A Killer Is Loose* one of his more satisfying novels. In his article on Brewer in *The Big Book of Noir* (1998) Bill Pronzini asserts it is "probably the best of his Fawcett originals."

The Red Scarf, while not as flamboyantly powerful as *13 French Street*, may be Brewer's best novel, though it was rejected by Fawcett, an action Pronzini calls inexplicable. The first-person narrator is a Florida motel owner, Ray Nichols, who, unlike Simon Lewt in *Hell's Our Destination*, finds himself caught up in the criminal world more as a result of sheer misfortune than of bad judgment. The novel opens as Nichols—hitchhiking back from Chicago, where he has failed in an attempt to enlist his brother's support in bailing out his failing motel—catches a ride with Noel Teece and Vivian Rise. Teece drinks heavily, drives too fast, and crashes, spilling Nichols and Rise from the car, while Teece is apparently killed. As Nichols gathers himself and Rise to walk away from the crash, he sees her close and pick up a satchel full of money. Nichols helps Rise secure a car before once again hitching a ride back home to his wife.

Nichols returns home to the unpromising prospect of telling his faithful but long-suffering wife that he has failed to raise the money necessary to save their business. His business woes fall into the background, however, when Rise reappears and checks into the motel. Nichols quickly finds himself embroiled in her attempt to flee with the money, which, it turns out, Teece had stolen from the mob, for whom he was a courier. The narrative takes Nichols through several plot turns as he finds himself caught between the police and the mob, driven by a desperate desire to preserve his and his wife's modest existence. Brewer avoids steering the plot toward an ending not in keeping with the sober tone of the novel as a whole, and his prose is tightly controlled and well-suited to the portrayal of a man who finds himself suddenly in tight and dangerous circumstances.

Originally published in the *Mercury Mystery Book-Magazine* in 1955, *The Red Scarf* was published in book form in 1958—Brewer's second and last appearance in hardback (his first being *The Angry Dream* in 1957)—by Thomas Bourgey's Mystery House and then picked up as a Crest reprint by Fawcett five years after their initial rejection. In *The New York Times Book Review* (21 September 1958) Anthony Boucher—no great fan of Brewer—praised *The Red Scarf* as "the best Gil Brewer novel I've seen: a short but full-packed story, pointed and restrained." Pronzini finds that "the characterization is flawless, and the prose is Brewer's sharpest and most controlled."

After this run of three exceptional novels, Brewer largely returned to his former devices in *The Squeeze* (1955), a novel flawed both by the rather strained premise by which the plot is initiated and Brewer's overworked theme of the destructive power for men of sexual obsession. Yet, he managed to produce several more novels that moved his work into new territory, sometimes literally. *77 Rue Paradis* (1955) is set in Marseille, a city in which Brewer had been stationed during the war, and tells the story of Frank Baron, a successful aircraft manufacturer whose business, reputation, and personal life were destroyed when some of his planes failed, with fatal consequences, during use in the Korean War. Baron knows, but is unable to prove, that the failures were the result of sabotage. His attempt to track down the person responsible for his ruin has led him to Marseille, where he appears uncertain whether he is still pursuing his unknown nemesis or merely dissipating himself.

In this enervated condition Baron is put severely to the test when he is abducted by a vile underworld figure, Hugo Gorsmann, who informs Baron that he has kidnapped Baron's daughter, Bette. Gorsmann threatens to kill Bette unless Baron betrays his friendship with a French aircraft manufacturer, Paul Chevard, and delivers to Gorsmann the secret plans to a new and revolutionary aircraft engine design. To make matters worse, Gorsmann works for the unknown party who has already done Baron so much harm and who plans to use the new aircraft technology to advance the cause of a neo-Nazi group. Baron finds himself torn between his love for his daughter, his hatred for his unknown enemy and the henchman Gorsmann, and his affection for Chevard. Baron emerges against the nicely delineated background of postwar Europe as one of Brewer's best "innocent man" characters. In a familiar complaint, Boucher objected to Brewer's "resolute inserts of gratuitous sexuality" (*The New York Times Book Review,* 9 January 1955).

Several times in his career, Brewer used a short story as the basis for a novel, as he did when he published an expanded version of "The Screamer," originally published in 1955 in *Pursuit Detective Story Magazine* under the name Eric Fitzgerald, as *—And the Girl Screamed* (1956). This novel features as the main character a former cop, Cliff Reddick, barred from a return to active duty because of an injury. Reddick takes on the policeman's role once again when he is mistakenly considered the prime suspect in the murder of a young woman. The novel intertwines the story of Reddick's attempt to find the woman's murderer with an exposé of teenagers run amok; perhaps with a wink, Brewer has Reddick mention the movie *Blackboard Jungle* (1955) early in the novel.

Brewer makes a seemingly ideal high-school football player both a murderer and the leader of the Hounds, the youth gang that menaces Reddick. The basic plot features of the novel are similar to those of the typical Brewer "innocent man" tale, with the main character trapped between the forces of law and order and the criminal underworld, although in this case criminality is represented by a gang of teenage delinquents rather than by adults. As is usual with Brewer, he works the main character convincingly into a box and presents his dilemma in a dramatic and compelling manner; but as is often also the case, Brewer relies too much on coincidence to extricate his protagonist.

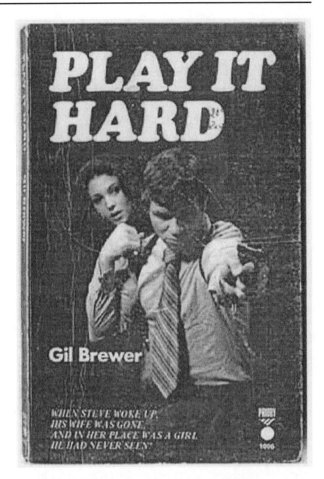

Cover for the British edition of Brewer's 1960 novel in which a newly married man awakens to find a strange woman pretending to be his wife (<auctionstockroom.com>)

In *The Angry Dream* Brewer returns to a setting like that of *13 French Street,* a place that suggests the upstate New York in which Brewer lived until the time of his military service. Main character and narrator Al Harper returns to his boyhood home of Pine Springs after an absence of eight years, during which time Harper's father, president and owner of the local bank, has killed himself, leaving the vaults of the bank empty. Harper's father never participated in the Federal Deposit Insurance Corporation (FDIC), so the bank has failed, ruining many of the townspeople. Furthermore, while he was alive Harper's father was a predatory businessman, driving family after family into ruin, while coming to own most of the businesses and land in the town.

As a result, Harper's return to Pine Springs is not warmly received by anyone, including his former fiancée, Lois Gerhard, daughter of a slightly shadowy local farmer, Sam Gerhard, and sister to the withdrawn but menacing Weyman Gerhard. Harper is advised to leave town by everyone, including the local sheriff. He refuses to do so, however, because he is determined to find out what happened to the more than $200,000 that should have been in the bank when his father was found dead. Harper's experiences—his house is vandalized, his dog is killed, and he is beaten and framed for murder—lead him to believe that someone in Pine Springs is threatened by his attempt to arrive at the truth about his father and the bank. While he draws and uses the northern winter background effectively, Brewer undercuts the compelling main story line by inserting yet another good girl/bad girl dichotomy into the plot. Harper is finally forced to choose between Lois and Norraine, a former girlfriend whom he suspects of having been involved in a theft ring.

Similar to *The Squeeze* in that it combines the "innocent man" formula with that of the femme fatale, *The Brat* is somewhat more successful because its premise—that the wife of the main character, Lee Sullivan, has framed him for theft and murder—is superior. Brewer, however, also sets up a familiar and melodramatic contrast between Sullivan's evil wife, Evis, and her younger sister, Rona, with Rona functioning as both Sullivan's devoted admirer and his ally in his attempt to escape the frame Evis has concocted. Brewer panders to readers almost embarrassingly by having Rona rip off her shirt so that Sullivan may see her breasts. Together Sullivan and Rona defeat Evis, and Rona takes her rightful place as the object of Sullivan's affection.

Little Tramp (1957), like *—And the Girl Screamed,* is a tale of youth gone bad. The protagonist, Gary Dunn, is a carpenter, targeted to be the stooge in a false kidnapping scheme concocted by a rich girl, Arlene Harper, putting the squeeze on her own father. Dunn finds himself drawn into a trap from which there is apparently no escape, and which turns decidedly worse when a private detective hired by Arlene's father to keep an eye on her decides to turn her plot to his advantage. *Little Tramp*—its first chapter in particular—is curiously similar in its working-class setting and emphasis on class differences to a proletarian novel, and, like many novels of Jim Thompson, helps one to see the close connection between that form and hard-boiled and "tough-guy" writing in general.

Wild (1958) is a fairly straightforward hard-boiled detective novel, with Chandleresque qualities, particularly in the concern the main character, Lee Baron, shows for his client, Ivor Hendrix. Ivor is Baron's high-school sweetheart, and his first job as a private detective after returning to Florida after many years is a largely pro bono affair, protecting her, he thinks, from her estranged husband. Baron runs afoul of the police in the course of his investigation, even as he is beaten and shot at by a professional killer trying to keep him from unraveling a criminal scheme he only half understands. Brewer combines the plot elements—lost love, the return home, a "defective detective"—effectively but fails to produce a wholly satisfying novel because of a weak conclusion. Boucher called the novel "sometimes crude, but undeniably effective" in the 3 August 1958 *New York Times Book Review*.

Wild to Possess (1959)—the title was imposed by the publisher, replacing Brewer's choice, "The Screaming Lullaby"—is one of the writer's better efforts. It concerns a sign painter, Lew Brookbank, who, while putting up some of his work, overhears a man and a woman discussing a scheme to kidnap and ransom the man's wife. Brookbank identifies the two kidnappers and intervenes in the plot, intending to get the ransom money and to save the kidnap victim from being murdered. Brookbank's situation is complicated because he is in hiding himself, having found his wife and her lover murdered before the novel opens. Fearing that he will be accused of the double murder—a fear that materializes when Herbert Clarkson, brother of his dead wife's lover, appears—Burbank believes that the ransom money will enable him to remain successfully and permanently hidden.

Brookbank has begun to dissolve in the wake of his wife's death, feeling "a sick, aching hunger that was gradually twisting into an obsession of loss." Drinking too much and failing to eat or sleep properly, he views his plan to disrupt the kidnapping as a needed distraction: "This was what he needed. Something to think about, to help him get to sleep. A sort of lullaby." While the plot depends upon coincidence perhaps more than it should, Brewer presents skillfully a man battling both a variety of antagonists and his own self-destructive tendencies.

In addition to novels, throughout the 1950s Brewer also published short fiction, ranging in length from short stories to novellas. He published these works under a variety of pseudonyms—Bailey Morgan, Eric Fitzgerald, Jack Holland, Frank Sebastian, Roy Carroll, and Barry Miles, as well as under his own name. The major outlets for Brewer's work in short fiction were *Manhunt* and *Pursuit Detective Story Magazine* (in which he published an astonishing amount, considering that it lasted only eighteen issues), though he also published a great deal elsewhere, including such short-lived magazines as *Accused Detective Story Magazine* and *Justice*. Brewer's short fiction, whether published under his own name or another, is generally competent, if often uninspired. Occasionally, it rises above this level, as in the haunting, disturbing "Moonshine" (*Manhunt*, 1955), in which a jealous husband's murderous rage expands beyond his wife and her lovers and envelops his children and himself. Brewer crafted this story carefully, weaving lunar imagery throughout. Also noteworthy is "The Gesture" (*The Saint Detective Magazine,* 1956), a psychological study. A man consumed by jealousy decides to murder a photographer who is visiting the secluded island on which the man and his wife live. When the man comes across a letter written by the photographer, the reader learns that the man and his wife are quite elderly and that the jealousy of the man is truly pathological. Faced with the reality that he has kept his wife a virtual prisoner, he kills himself in an act of atonement.

The technical mastery of which Brewer was capable was well represented in the July 1956 issue of *Pursuit Detective Story Magazine,* which carried two Brewer stories, "Return to Yesterday" (as Eric Fitzgerald) and "Wife Sitter" (as Bailey Morgan). "Return to Yesterday" follows an innocent man who has escaped from prison in order to murder his wife as revenge for setting him up in the murder of a woman whose husband, he suspects, was having an affair with his wife. Upon seeing his wife, however, he has a change of heart and refuses to believe that she betrayed him. As he begins to reconcile with her, her lover emerges and kills him, confirming that his initial suspicions were correct.

While "Return to Yesterday" was told as a restrained third-person narration, Brewer wrote "Wife Sitter" in a broad first-person, making it more of a "voice" story than is common for him. In it the protagonist has embezzled funds from the bank for which he works. Staying in a hotel on his way to New Orleans, whence he plans to fly to South America, he sees a handsome man saddled with a drunken, shrewish wife. The nondescript protagonist identifies with the husband and offers to "wife-sit" for him so that he may attend a party. After he becomes enraged and murders the woman, he makes his escape to South America—but only after marrying a woman who becomes a shrew, just like the one he killed.

While Brewer wrote prolifically in the 1950s, by the last years of the decade his alcoholism was beginning to take a toll on him: his productivity and his ability to construct a novel carefully from the opening paragraph to the conclusion—never a strong point in the best of times—were declining. For example, *The Three-Way Split* (1960), a novel he began in 1953 and resumed and completed in 1959, presents a compelling conflict between the main character, Jack Holland (named with one of Brewer's pseudonyms), and his father, Sam, a high-rolling con man. When Jack discovers a sunken Spanish treasure ship, Sam finds out and sees it as an opportunity to appease the Mob, which is trying to collect a debt he owes them. Brewer sets up and plays out the conflict well but appears to run out of

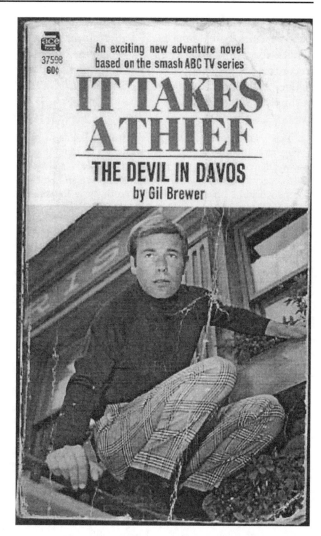

Cover for the first of three novels that Brewer wrote based on the television series It Takes a Thief, *published in 1969 (<www.people.uncw.edu/smithms>)*

narrative energy by the end of the novel, steering it to a happy ending that seems dishonest in that it diminishes the emotional toughness of the work as a whole.

Still, despite its shortcomings, Brewer's work continued to have merit. *Play It Hard* (1960) qualifies as a minor classic of paranoia. As the novel opens, narrator Steve Nolan, a newlywed, comes briefly to consciousness only to find that he is in the company of a woman dressed in his wife's clothes, wearing his wife's perfume, but most definitely not his wife. Because none of Nolan's friends or family had met his wife, no one can affirm that the woman is not she; quite the opposite, they accept that she is his wife and think his conviction otherwise is simply an effect of the nervous breakdown from which he is recovering. In reality Nolan has been drugged and his wife murdered, as he discovers in the course of his self-consciously amateurish investigation.

By the early 1960s, however, Brewer realized that his capacities had diminished. Under an entry in his ledger for *Flight to Darkness,* in which he originally recorded his payment for publication rights in the United Kingdom ($180.00), Brewer added in July 1962 a somber reflection:

> This book was the last thing Capt. Joseph T. Shaw, my agent at the time, read before he died. . . . J. T. Shaw was the very best. . . . To my knowledge, he was one of the very last men of heart in the publishing and editorial world. . . . He believed in my work; what I wanted to do, that is. In 10 yrs. I have not done it. Yet.

These lines were written early in a bleak period in which Brewer did not write anything for publication and eventually–drunk–wrecked his Porsche, nearly killing himself. Brewer refers to the accident in his private writing but never provides a date. The sense of unfulfilled potential remained with Brewer throughout his life.

By the late 1960s even the lesser work of the earlier part of the decade was beyond Brewer's capacity, and he settled increasingly into the role of a journeyman, turning out fiction for any market he could work his way into. He wrote three novels, published in 1969 and 1970, based on the television series *It Takes a Thief.* He also published four Gothic novels under the name Elaine Evans between 1970 and 1974. For a fee of $2,500, Brewer served as the ghostwriter of four or five books for Israeli soldier Harry Arvay. (An otherwise accurate list of books written by Brewer and compiled by Verlaine Brewer lists five Arvay publications, one of which, *The Twelfth Bullet,* was likely published under a different title.) Perhaps most tellingly, Brewer published five pornographic novels in 1972. Obviously attempting to write them as efficiently as possible, Brewer typically took the characters and plot of one of his crime novels, added a sexual subplot, and interlarded sex scenes, with bizarre results as a 1950s noir aesthetic meets that of 1970s pornography.

In the 1970s Brewer continued to write for the mystery magazines, but the market for his type of crime fiction had declined, and his personal problems had become overwhelming. By the late years of the decade he was extolling the virtues of MD 20/20 (a "fortified wine" with a 20 percent alcohol content) as a writer's aid in letters to friends. He joined, quit, and rejoined Alcoholics Anonymous but was unable ultimately to give up drinking. By the end of the decade his longtime agent, Scott Meredith, parted company with him. The early 1980s brought no interruption of this downward spiral, and on 9 January 1983, Verlaine Brewer–from whom he had separated, though she continued to live nearby–found him dead in his apartment.

An uneven writer who never quite delivered on his potential, Gil Brewer remains of interest for at least two reasons. First, his career illustrates the difficulties and dangers that beset the authors of paperback originals in the 1950s and 1960s. Brewer's alcoholism, sense of personal isolation, and frustrated artistic ambitions, while not caused by his working in the paperback industry, certainly were abetted by it. At the same time, he was capable of turning out compelling work that illustrates the high level of craft that many paperback novelists brought to their writing. In Brewer's case, few of even his least accomplished crime novels are without memorable scenes, while some entire works, such as *The Red Scarf,* are excellent. If Brewer does not compel readers' interest because he achieves the heights–or depths–attained by Raymond Chandler or Thompson, he remains of interest precisely because his work, while retaining a personal quality, is in many ways typical of his time and genre.

References:

Richard Hill, "Gil Brewer Writes to Live and Lives to Write," *Tallahassee Floridian,* 20 July 1969, pp. 24–27;

Marianne Kelsey, "Gil Brewer–Profile of an Author: Writing Is His Work and His Hobby," *St. Petersburg Independent,* 14 April 1967, p. B6;

Bill Pronzini, "Forgotten Writers: Gil Brewer," in *The Big Book of Noir,* edited by Lee Server, Edward Gorman, and Martin H. Greenberg (New York: Carroll & Graf, 1998), pp. 191–200.

Papers

Gil Brewer's papers, which include Verlaine Brewer's unpublished manuscript "Gil Brewer: His Writing Life," are in the American Heritage Center, University of Wyoming, Laramie.

Paul Cain
(Peter Ruric, George Sims)
(30 May 1902 – 23 June 1966)

Peter Gunn
University of Texas at Austin

BOOKS: *Fast One* (Garden City, N.Y.: Doubleday, 1933; London: Constable, 1936);

Seven Slayers (Hollywood: Saint Enterprises, 1946).

Editions and Collections: *Fast One* (N.p.: Shaw Press, 1944);

Fast One, afterword by Irvin Faust (Carbondale: Southern Illinois University Press, 1978);

Fast One, introduction by David A. Bowman (Berkeley: Black Lizard, 1987);

Fast One: The Graphic Novel, illustrated by Geoff Grandfield (Harpenden: No Exit, 1991).

PRODUCED SCRIPTS: *Gambling Ship,* motion picture, story by Cain, script by Max Marcin and Seton I. Miller, Paramount, 1933;

The Black Cat, motion picture, Universal, 1934;

Affairs of a Gentleman, motion picture, adapted for the screen by Cain as Ruric, Cyril Hume, and Milton Krims, Universal, 1934;

Jericho, motion picture, script by Cain as Ruric, Frances Marion, George Barraud, and Robert N. Lee, Buckingham Productions, 1937;

Twelve Crowded Hours, motion picture, story by Cain as Ruric and Garrett Fort, RKO, 1939;

The Night of January 16th, motion picture, script by Delmer Daves, Robert Pirosh, and Eve Greene, contribution to script by Cain as Ruric, Paramount, 1941;

Grand Central Murder, motion picture, M-G-M, 1942;

Mademoiselle Fifi, motion picture, script and story by Cain as Ruric and Josef Mischel, RKO, 1944;

Alias a Gentleman, motion picture, story by Cain as Ruric, script by William R. Lipman, M-G-M, 1948;

The Lady in Yellow, television, Screen Gems, 1960.

SELECTED PERIODICAL PUBLICATIONS–
UNCOLLECTED: "Hunch," *Black Mask,* 17 (March 1934): 10–33;

"Trouble-Chaser," *Black Mask,* 17 (April 1934): 60–71;

"Chinaman's Chance," *Black Mask,* 18 (September 1935): 98–107;

"555," *Detective Fiction Weekly,* 98 (14 December 1935): 128–131;

"Death Song," *Black Mask,* 18 (January 1936): 63–74;

"Sockdolager," *Star Detective Magazine,* 4 (April 1936): 6–26;

"Dutch Treat," *Black Mask,* 19 (December 1936): 117–125;

"The Tasting Machine, Part I," as Peter Ruric, *Gourmet,* 9 (November 1949): 10–11, 28, 30–32;

"The Tasting Machine, Part II," as Ruric, *Gourmet,* 9 (December 1949): 12–13, 42–47;

"Viva las Castañetas: a Spanish [Mostly Mallorquin] Letter," as Ruric, *Gourmet,* 11 (June 1951): 14–15, 40–47.

Paul Cain's reputation in American crime fiction rests exclusively on stories published in *Black Mask* magazine during the 1930s. Five of these stories went on to form Cain's only novel–*Fast One* (1933)–repeatedly championed as one of the most brutal and unrelentingly hard-boiled tales ever to appear in print. Cain's stories were published by *Black Mask* during a period of prominence and innovation for the magazine, when it was flourishing under the editorship of Joseph T. Shaw, who assembled an impressive group of writers including, most notably, Dashiell Hammett, Raymond Chandler, and Horace McCoy. In later years, these writers came to be known collectively as "The *Black Mask* Boys," responsible for establishing the hard-boiled school of detective fiction.

While Cain's best work fits squarely into this same hard-boiled tradition, it also departs from recognized early conventions of the genre in significant ways. For instance, whereas most writers from the *Black Mask* era preferred a heroic and world-weary private investigator for their protagonists, Cain wrote *Fast One* from the vantage point of Gerry Kells–a gangster, murderer,

You've read

● THE MALTESE FALCON
 ● GREEN ICE
  ● LITTLE CAESAR
   ● IRON MAN

hard, fast stories all, but now comes the hardest, toughest, swiftest novel of them all

FAST ONE

Two hours of sheer terror, written with a clipped violence, hypnotic in its power. The author is

PAUL CAIN

See Back Cover

Cover for the advance copy of Paul Cain's 1933 novel, which depicts gangster Gerry Kells's attempt to dominate the criminal underworld in Los Angeles. It was republished in 1978 by Southern Illinois University Press in its Lost American Fiction series (left: Christie's New York, item number 25, 24 September 2002; right: Matthew J. and Arlyn Bruccoli Collection, Thomas Cooper Library, University of South Carolina).

extortionist, and thief. As Jack Adrian and Bill Pronzini point out in the introduction to *Hard-Boiled: An Anthology of American Crime Stories* (1995): "Paul Cain's Gerry Kells was neither a hero nor a detective; Kells, in fact, was in many ways the first true antihero in noir fiction." In his ability to create narrative drive and reader sympathy for a criminal protagonist, Cain anticipates the work of a more famous writer with the same surname, James M. Cain, as well as such later crime novelists as Jim Thompson, Peter Rabe, and David Goodis. In fact, Wilbur Needham, in a *Saturday Night* review (17 February 1934) of *The Postman Always Rings Twice* (1934), speculated that James M. Cain was the "mysterious bearded gentleman who wrote 'A Fast One' [*sic*] under the name of Paul Cain last season." The mistaken identity was perhaps inevitable.

Paul Cain was born George Carrol Sims on 30 May 1902 in Des Moines, Iowa. His father, William

Sims, was a police detective, and his mother, Eva Freberg, according to David Bowman in his introduction to the 1987 Black Lizard edition of *Fast One*, was "a frail, well-read woman who wrote poetry." Cain's parents were separated when he was six years old. Beyond this information, however, little is known about Cain's formative years. In a discarded introduction to *The Hard-Boiled Omnibus* (1946), which E. R. Hageman quotes in his article "Introducing Paul Cain and His Fast One," Joseph Shaw suggests that Cain spent some of his youth in Illinois, professing to have overheard "recollections of his boyhood experiences in Chicago where [Cain] saw something of life in its toughest phases." Shaw further speculates that Cain "drew from these first-hand glimpses" when writing *Fast One* (the protagonist, Kells, grew up in Chicago), but Cain's Chicago connection has yet to be substantiated outside of Shaw's testimony. The uncertainty about biographical details is a recurrent pattern with Cain, whom Bowman calls "the J. D. Salinger of pulp writers" because of his desire to remain anonymous.

Cain's father moved to Los Angeles in 1918, and his mother followed a few years later. Presumably, Cain accompanied one or the other of his parents in the journey west, although the exact date of his arrival in Los Angeles is not known. While in California, Cain decided to change his name from George Sims to Peter Ruric, and the transition is marked by a screen credit given to "George Ruric" as production assistant on Joseph Von Sternberg's first movie–*Salvation Hunters*–released in 1925.

As reported in *Myrna Loy: Being and Becoming* (1987), Cain was a member of an "artistic avant-garde" in Hollywood at this time. Among the members of this group was Myrna Williams, then a struggling actress trying to break into the movie industry. She describes the group as being made up of "writers and would-be writers, painters, sculptors–young people in the arts who would have lived in Greenwich Village if we'd been in New York." The group decided that Williams should change her name to something more appropriate for the screen, and a series of "awful combinations" were mentioned before "Peter Rurick [*sic*], a wild Russian writer of free verse, suddenly came up with 'Myrna Loy.'" Peter Ruric was the name Cain used for his movie work and also the one he preferred in his personal life. How he hit upon the name is not known, although possibly he derived it from reading about Peter the Great–a direct descendant of the Russian "House of Rurick"–who shares the same birth date as Cain (30 May).

Reserved for his work in crime fiction, the Paul Cain pseudonym initially appeared in March 1932 with the publication of the first installment of *Fast One* in *Black Mask*. Originally published as five separate but interconnected stories–"Fast One" (March 1932), "Lead Party" (April 1932), "Velvet" (June 1932), "The Heat" (August 1932), and "The Dark" (September 1932)–*Fast One* is by far Cain's most important and critically discussed work. The dense and convoluted plot deals with Gerard A. Kells and his attempts to take over the organized crime rackets in 1930s Los Angeles. With a reform party currently in control of the political situation, but a new election due to take place in weeks, prohibition Los Angeles is a city ripe for a power grab. Four principal gangsters compete for control of offshore gambling, political power, and cocaine trafficking in the city. Kells is a wild card with a New York reputation for toughness, and the competing gangsters try to recruit him for their organizations. Kells, however, prefers to stand alone. He knows that organization is the key to city control, but he also

maintains that "the fun in an organization is being head man." Kells ultimately finds himself "in a swell spot to play both ends against the middle," and he proceeds from there to carry out a systematic elimination of his gangland competition.

Before Kells can succeed in his takeover bid, however, the position of a rival gangster–Jack Rose–becomes solidified to the point that further efforts seem ill-advised. Kells is about to leave the city with his girlfriend, Grandquist, before learning that his friend Shep Berry has been gunned down in a drive-by shooting ordered by Rose. Out of loyalty to his friend and a desire for revenge, Kells heads back into town to hunt down Rose in a final confrontation. Kells succeeds in his elimination of Rose: "Kells went to him swiftly and put the muzzle of the automatic against the back of his head and fired three times," but only after suffering multiple gunshot wounds and an ice pick between the shoulder blades. Kells survives long enough to reunite with Grandquist for a final run at escape along the twisting roads leading out of Los Angeles. In a letter to James M. Sandoe on 4 February 1953, Chandler calls *Fast One* "some kind of high point in the ultra hard-boiled manner. And the last episode in it is about as murderous and at the same time poignant as anything in that manner that has ever been written."

Published as a book by Doubleday on 25 October 1933, *Fast One* received generally positive contemporary reviews. *The Saturday Review of Literature* for 28 October 1933 called it "The hardest-boiled yarn of a decade. So h.-b. it gets funny. But it moves like a machine-gun. Zowie!" In the 28 October 1933 edition of the *New York Evening Post*, Norman Klein described the novel as "all so *tough,* and so very taut." The reviewer for *The New York Times* on 29 October 1933 had this to say: "Publishers' blurbs are prone to overestimate the virtues of their respective products, but with the accompanying statement that 'Fast One' is 'the toughest, swiftest, hardest novel of them all,' we almost concur. It is in truth a ceaseless welter of bloodshed and frenzy, a sustained bedlam of killing and fiendishness, told in terse staccato style . . . there is no minute's let-up in the saturnalia of 'black-and-blue passion, bloodlust, death.'"

Constable published a British edition of *Fast One* in March of 1936, and the reviewer from *The Times Literary Supplement* (*TLS*, 18 April 1936) showed similar respect for the novel:

> . . . for those who can keep pace with the changing motives the book will not be easy to put aside. None of the familiar tricks of suspense or the clichés of characterization seem in evidence, and it is only when the book is finished that the reader will realize how com-

Cary Grant and Benita Hume in a scene from the 1933 Paramount motion picture Gambling Ship, *for which Cain provided the original story (© John Springer Collection/CORBIS)*

pletely the mannered style has bemused him into thinking the story real for a moment. American writers are becoming increasingly adept at this method of hypnotism and this author has obviously learned the various passes thoroughly.

Later reviewers of *Fast One* generally follow this same pattern of commenting on the driving pace of Cain's narrative and the leanness of his prose style.

The swift pacing of *Fast One* is attributable in large part to the narrative technique Cain employs. Cain's technique is distinctive among hard-boiled writers, although it does share certain affinities with the third-person-objective narration used by Dashiell Hammett in *The Maltese Falcon* (1930). Most of *Fast One* is told from a detached vantage point that stays focused on Kells while also denying the reader access to his internal motivations. Like Hammett, Cain shuns the use of internal monologue and instead utilizes external details to divulge his protagonist's state of mind. For instance, in the midst of a critical situation, Cain simply shows Kells consuming two aspirin tablets—a detail that keeps

the pace moving and allows readers to formulate their own opinions about Kells's internal conflicts and attitudes. Cain, however, is not so exacting in his approach as Hammett, and he does allow the reader to enter into Kells's thoughts at times. For example, upon waking from a state of unconsciousness (induced by a severe physical beating and bolstered by a large amount of morphine), Kells catches the fleeting image of a small zebra—"striped red, white, blue"—galloping up and down at the foot of his bed. Cain momentarily situates readers on the level of Kells's immediate sense perception, allowing them to view the vision in its mediated form—a point of view that is not possible in a strictly objective narration, such as the one used in *The Maltese Falcon*.

The prose style Cain utilizes in *Fast One* is notable for its economy of expression. Cain prefers simple and direct sentences focused on action, and uses adjectives and adverbs only sparingly. In *Danger Is My Business: An Illustrated History of the Fabulous Pulp Magazines, 1896–1953* (1993), Lee Server calls Cain's style "so lean and mean it makes Hammett's sentences read like the work of Rafael Sabatini." Perhaps James Ellroy took the hard-boiled style to even further extremes of minimalism with the telegraphic prose of *L. A. Confidential* (1990) and *White Jazz* (1992), but in fiction coming from the *Black Mask* school, no greater example of sheer pacing and swift action exists than *Fast One*. Still, as Irvin Faust points out in his afterword to the 1978 Southern Illinois University Press edition, the emphasis on pace comes at a cost: "The price is that the pace takes over, is itself a major character, perhaps *the* major character, and it controls the book." But though Cain took the hard-boiled style about as far as anyone would ever want to, he did not wholly sacrifice character development.

In March 1932, as the first installment of *Fast One* was being published in *Black Mask,* Cain was living in New York, where he became romantically involved with actress Gertrude Michael. Originally from Talladega, Alabama, Michael arrived in New York in 1930. After two years of struggling to find roles, she was finally cast on Broadway in March 1932–opposite Tex Ritter–in *Roundup.* The play had a short run, but Michael's performance caught the eye of an M-G-M talent scout who offered her travel expenses to come to Hollywood for a screen test in spring 1932. By this time she and Cain were deeply involved, and Cain accompanied her on the trip west. Both Cain and Michael were heavy drinkers, and several critics have speculated that Michael served as the real-life model for Grandquist–Kells's dipsomaniac lover–in *Fast One.* Cain dedicated the first edition of *Fast One* to Michael in 1933, although by then their relationship was starting to dissolve, and by 1934 she was reportedly engaged to Rouben Mamoulian, a prestigious Hollywood director of the early sound period.

Nearly a year after returning to Hollywood from his sojourn in New York, Cain received screen credit for the Paramount release of *Gambling Ship.* The movie stars Gary Cooper and was released in July 1933–just months before *Fast One* was published by Doubleday. Cain's exact contribution to *Gambling Ship,* and the movie's connection to *Fast One,* is a matter for speculation. An "original stories" credit is given to "Paul Cain" on the movie, but the British press book gives a solo credit to "Peter Ruric" as "Author." In any case, as David Wilt notes in *Hardboiled in Hollywood* (1991), "*Gambling Ship* is certainly far from a faithful adaptation of Ruric's stories in plot and tone," and aside from a few minor scenes, the movie has little to do with Cain's novel. The closest *Fast One* has ever gotten to a visual representation is Geoff Grandfield's 1991 graphic version, which reads like a set of preproduction storyboards.

In addition to the five serialized installments of *Fast One,* Cain published twelve other stories in *Black Mask* between 1932 and 1936. From March to September 1932, by far his most productive period, Cain placed stories in seven straight issues of the magazine, including two in the lead position. From there, however, his work in *Black Mask* markedly dropped off. Only three Cain stories were published in the magazine in 1933, two in 1934, one in 1935, and a final three stories in 1936. After Shaw left as editor of the magazine late in 1936, Cain never published in *Black Mask* again. Cain did publish at least two stories in other pulp magazines during this period, "555" in *Detective Fiction Weekly* and "Sockdolager" in *Star Detective Magazine,* but as 1936 came to a close, so did Paul Cain's (known) prose work in crime fiction.

Three general points are evident when Cain's short stories are considered as a whole: Cain employs a variety of narrative techniques to produce varying effects upon his readers; he prefers criminal protagonists, although they represent a range of wealth and status; and his recurrent themes mirror the concerns of his own life–alcoholism, gambling, divorce, Hollywood, and hidden identity. Critics have generally neglected Cain's short works, preferring instead to focus on *Fast One,* although two stories have received a small amount of recognition as examples of his best work done outside the novel–"Red 71" and "Murder Done in Blue."

"Red 71" was originally published in the December 1932 issue of *Black Mask.* Hagemann considers it Cain's "best (although marred) story," and it was also selected by Shaw for inclusion in *The Hard-Boiled Omnibus.* Shaw explained his selection in a 29 November 1945 letter to Cain, who was then living in Los Angeles, saying "I agree that it is one of the best [stories] you did at that time." "Red 71" is the story of two converging love triangles that ends with the murder of nearly everyone involved. Dick Shane, the protagonist, is an investor whose wealth is of unknown origin. Shane sinks $15,000 into Red 71–a gambling house, run by Charley Rigas, which is in financial trouble because of a 50 percent rate increase from the protection rackets. Shane is fond of Loraine Rigas–Charley's wife–and as the story unfolds, small details begin to suggest that Shane himself could be behind the rate increase (among other things) in an effort to rid himself of his competition for Loraine's affection. The story is told from a detached third-person point of view similar to the one employed in *Fast One.* Cain's use of this technique leaves readers unsure about Shane's motives, and the story ends on a purposefully ambiguous note about who is truly responsible for the murders.

"Murder Done in Blue" appeared in *Black Mask* in June 1933, a time when Cain was residing at the Montecito Hotel Apartments in Hollywood. The story was later anthologized under the title "Gundown" in *The Black Mask Boys* (1985), in which editor William F. Nolan says it "ranks on an equally high level with *Fast One*" in narrative toughness and intensity. The story opens with three seemingly random episodes, each describing an execution from the third-person perspective of the character being killed. Johnny Doolin, a former Hollywood stuntman, reads the morning paper and draws a connection between those who died and those who had witnessed a gangland shooting months before. Doolin uses his information to hire on as the bodyguard for a fourth possible witness–Nelson Halloran–who turns out to be the drug lord responsible for all the killings. A confrontation, which comes near the end of the story, culminates in the same type of hypnotic violence that runs throughout *Fast One*. The multiple-perspective narration alone sets "Murder Done in Blue" off from the rest of Cain's work, but this story also has a rich sense of characterization that does not appear in his other tales. For example, readers are allowed to view Doolin's interactions with his wife, even though they have no direct bearing on the plot, and his character becomes more three-dimensional as a result.

Diminishing appearances of Cain's stories in the pulps were accompanied by a corresponding increase in his movie work. He went to work for Universal Pictures in the early months of 1934, receiving screen credit for *The Black Cat* and *Affairs of a Gentleman*. *The Black Cat* is Cain's most remembered motion picture today, but more because it was the first to costar cult icons Bela Lugosi and Boris Karloff than for any work Cain did on the script. Cain also labored on several unproduced scripts, including "A Very Naughty Girl" and "One for the Money," before leaving Hollywood for Europe in the summer of 1934. He spent the next four years overseas, where he did some screenwriting for various London motion-picture companies. He apparently also did movie work in Spain and France, although no specific credits have been unearthed. In 1937, *Jericho* (released in the United States as *Dark Sands*) was produced by Buckingham Productions out of London, but little is known about the rest of Cain's work done during this time.

Cain was back in the United States by 1938, working on an unproduced script titled "Graustark" for Samuel Goldwyn. Cain's next realized screen credit came after a collaboration with Garrett Fort, according to *The New York Times* (20 October 1938), yielded "What's Your Number?"–a "'Thin Man' type story" that RKO Radio Pictures purchased in October 1938 and released the following year as *Twelve Crowded Hours*. Cain met a "cigarette girl" named Virginia late in 1939 and then persuaded her to change her name to

Mushel Ruric when they were married. She was apparently much younger than Cain, and their marriage was stormy and marred by alcohol abuse. Bowman, who once interviewed Mushel Ruric, reports, "Finally, she couldn't take his drinking anymore, and they divorced in 1943, the same year [Peter] Ruric's father died."

Cain worked briefly for Globe pictures in 1940, then moved over to Paramount, where he received contribution credit for the screen adaptation of Ayn Rand's *The Night of January 16th*. Cain's tenure at Paramount was also brief, and from there he relocated to M-G-M. According to an article in *The New York Times* (18 March 1947), Cain sold "Sir Smith"–a screen story about a confidence man–to M-G-M in 1941. The story was adapted several times before finally being released in 1948 as *Alias a Gentleman*. News of "a projected episodic film, 'Now We Are Twenty-one,' which Peter Ruric is writing from a radio program by Jerry Schwartz" appears in the 29 April 1942 edition of *The New York Times*. The movie was planned to showcase "seven young Metro directors" using a cast of stock players, but like at least six other Hollywood projects Cain worked on between 1940 and 1942, the project was never produced. Cain's most notable work for M-G-M was *Grand Central Murder* (1942), which Wilt suggests "may very well be the best example of his [Ruric's] motion picture work" as a whole. The most striking and successful feature of *Grand Central Murder* is its use of narrative flashbacks to unfold the plot incrementally from the point of view of each murder suspect. Cain signed a six-month contract extension with M-G-M early in 1943, but his only other screen credit came on the RKO Radio release of *Mademoiselle Fifi* in 1944. Primarily assigned to B-movie projects as a genre specialist, Cain had a movie career that was certainly of a lower caliber than his prose work.

Cain moved back to New York in October 1944, renting an apartment on East 73rd Street just as his earlier crime fiction was starting to experience a modest renewal of interest from the mass-market paperback field. The Shaw Press republished *Fast One* as a digest-sized paperback in 1944, marketing it with a dynamic blurb on the back cover: "This is not a detective story, not a mystery, not a saga of gangland, but a new kind of novel, written with clipped and brutal violence, hypnotic in its ruthless power." Avon reprinted *Fast One* in 1948 and 1952 in mass-market paperback editions. The blurbs on covers of the Avon reprints call the novel "a package of literary T.N.T." in 1948, and "a fast-moving, hard-boiled yarn that rates with the best of its kind!" in 1952. After the Avon reprints, *Fast One* remained out of print for a full quarter of a century before Southern Illinois Univer-

Sam Levene (left), Tom Conway, Van Heflin, and Virginia Grey in the 1942 M-G-M motion picture Grand Central Murder, *for which Cain (as Peter Ruric) wrote the screenplay. The story is told through flashbacks from the point of view of each murder suspect (MGM/The Kobal Collection).*

sity Press republished it in hardcover in 1978 as part of their "Lost American Fiction" series.

Soon after the Shaw Press edition of *Fast One* came out, Cain began to compile a short-story collection, *Seven Slayers* (1946), comprising seven of his best stories originally published in *Black Mask:* "Black" (May 1932), "Red 71" (December 1932), "Parlor Trick" (July 1932), "One, Two, Three" (May 1933), "Murder in Blue" (June 1933), "Pigeon Blood" (November 1933), and "Pineapple" (March 1936). Tear sheets of the stories, now housed in the Joseph Shaw file at UCLA, show the 'Paul Cain' byline crossed out and substituted with 'Peter Ruric' on each title page. The name change was not observed when the collection came out, but the back cover does include a rare and revealing statement about the author:

> Paul Cain isn't his real name. He is slender, blond, bearded, 30-odd years old. He spent the bulk of these years in South and North America, Africa, the Near East, Europe. He was, intermittently, a bosun's-mate, a Dada painter, a gambler, and a 'no' man in Hollywood. He likes: Mercedes motor cars, peanut butter, phonograph records of Leslie Hutchingson, Scotch whiskey, some of the paintings of Chirico, Garbo, Richebourg 1904, and Little Pam. He dislikes: parsnips, the color pink, sopranos, men who wear white nylon sox, backgammon, cigars, and a great many men, women, and children.

Aside from the fact that Cain would have been in his forties when the statement was made, one can think of no other reason to doubt the veracity of what he says. Likewise, verifying it is impossible. Nevertheless, this short autobiographical statement provides one of the most intriguing glimpses into Cain's enigmatic personal life.

Early in 1946, when Shaw was preparing *The Hard-Boiled Omnibus,* he sent a letter to Cain requesting biographical information to be included in the volume. Cain's bizarre response, which Shaw chose not to use, begins with a list of titles that have never been located under any name:

He is the author of 'Hypersensualism, A Practical Philosophy for Acrobats'; 'Syncopaen'; 'The Naked Man'; 'Advertisement for Death'; 'Broad'; 'The Cock-Eyed Angel'; 'Seven Men Named Caesar' and 'The Ecstasy Department,' a play to be produced in the Fall of '46–a couple of dozen films, here and abroad, and, under the Paul Cain *nom de shocker,* twenty odd short stories and novelettes.

Cain then repeated the same list of travel locations and previous employments given on the back cover of *Seven Slayers,* but he also augmented it by claiming that he was formerly an "editor, consulting gynocologist [*sic*], and balloonist. He is, at this writing, dividing his time between three plays, a definitive work on the sexual implications of Oncidium Fuchsias, and Warner Brothers."

Once again, all of the new information remains largely unsubstantiated: no record exists of Cain's ever having worked for Warner Brothers; no trace of the production of the play has been found; and only nineteen Paul Cain stories have been located. Cain's authorial claims obviously smack of exaggeration, and one is immediately tempted to discard them as mere comic hyperbole; yet, Cain does mention his continued work on "The Ecstasy Department" in personal correspondence as late as 1959, perhaps an indication that the play was not simply a figment of his imagination. The same cannot be said for the other titles, however, and until some are located, Cain's assertions, if not altogether dismissible, must be treated with skepticism.

In 1949, *Fast One* appeared in France as *A Tombeau Ouvert,* the thirty-sixth volume in the prestigious Série Noire crime series, translated by the series founder, Marcel Duhamel, and Jacques-Laurent Bost. Cain wrote to Duhamel from Hollywood, and the two met in France sometime in the late 1940s or early 1950s. Duhamel describes the encounter vividly in his memoir *Raconte Pas Ta Vie* (1972):

> . . . one morning, I saw a derelict of undetermined age land at the office, his mien more crumpled than his neglected attire. However, his face would have to be called handsome, the personage seductive. Small and thin in stature, gray hair, washed-out blue eyes, a lost look, he suddenly clung to me the next moment like a blood-sucker and told me the story of his life. Hollywood had done him in. A reputed scriptwriter, a favorite at parties, disgusted with work beneath him, he ended up seeking his inspiration in alcohol. This led to emotional let-downs, two divorces, three detoxification cures, and psychoanalysis. He came to Europe looking for some return to wholeness after having tried everything else. (Translated by Judithe Jacob)

Cain had apparently suffered the most recent in what appears to have been a series of traumatic events, and his life was spiraling downward in a mire of alcoholism, insomnia, and a "fear of being alone." Duhamel found Cain to be an insufferable guest: "This limp being, inoffensive and child-like, was a vampire of the worst sort, such as Polanski would not dare to make up." Wanting to be rid of him, Duhamel finally convinced Cain that he needed a vacation in Spain to restore his energies. To finance the trip, Duhamel got the Gallimard publishing house to publish Cain's collection of noir stories, and *Seven Slayers* was eventually translated in 1955 by Henri Robillot as *Sept Tueurs,* the 243rd title in the Série Noire.

Duhamel's story of Cain is in sharp contrast to the comic tone of Cain's autobiographical statements; which representation gives the more accurate depiction of Cain's life as a whole is difficult to know. A year after Cain left him, Duhamel reports that he received another letter from the author: "from Alicante, written in firm handwriting, and in a normal style, in which the octopus informed me that he had married a drop-dead gorgeous Spanish woman, that he was the happy father of a charming baby boy, that he was as sturdy as the Pont-Neuf, and that he was going back to his job in Hollywood with his family." The stability afforded by family life was brief, for the family was soon separated, with Cain remaining in California while his wife and children eventually settled in Richmond, Virginia. Letter evidence suggests that "Peggy" was the name of Cain's third wife, although given her Spanish origins and Cain's fondness for such procedures, the name was most likely assumed. Together they had two sons: Peter Craig and Michael Sean Ruric.

Late in 1949, Cain published "The Tasting Machine" under the name Peter Ruric in *Gourmet* magazine. More science fiction than hard-boiled in conception, "The Tasting Machine" is unlike anything else Cain is known to have written. The story concerns an eccentric master chef who keeps a beautiful young woman cloistered away in the upper rooms of his apartment building. A young inventor falls in love with the woman and attempts to win her freedom by giving the chef a "tasting machine" as a gift. The tasting machine is armed with utensils and an orifice for one mission–to go around tasting and critiquing things in its environment. The story reaches its climax when the machine begins "tasting" the young woman, while the chef, hearing her screams, is left to hack away at the locked door with an ax.

Cain's final appearance in *Gourmet* came in June 1951. "Viva las Castañetas: a Spanish [Mostly Mallorquin] Letter" is a typical *Gourmet* article describing Cain's eating (and drinking) habits during his stay in Spain. Cain's whereabouts for much of the 1950s remains difficult to verify, although he is known to have lived in Cuba for a period late in the decade. A New Year's letter to his wife and children, written through the night of 31 December 1958 and on into the morning of 1 January 1959, places Cain in harbor aboard a German ship, waiting anxiously to leave the country just hours before Castro's historic march into Havana to remove the last remnants of the Batista government. The same letter also mentions a lost manuscript titled "Truce," which was apparently a novel Cain wrote and submitted to Doubleday, only to have it rejected as being too "uncompromisingly sexual" for publication.

One last creative effort surfaced in 1960, when Cain received screen credit on the television show *The Lady in Yellow*. A lone postcard from San Francisco in 1962 shows Cain still estranged from his family, yet resolutely clinging to the hope that they will someday be reconciled. The day apparently did not arrive before Cain died of ureter cancer on 23 June 1966 at his home in Los Angeles. According to Bowman, Cain's "body was cremated, and the box of ashes sat in a Glendale cemetery's storage room until 1968 when it was shipped to Hawaii" to the care of a woman who remains unidentified. Cain's death certificate states that he lived in Los Angeles for forty-eight years and that he was a writer for forty-three of them.

In the late 1970s, Cain's work experienced a modest revival with the republication of *Fast One* by Southern Illinois University Press. The edition was followed immediately by Hagemann's ground-breaking article in *The Armchair Detective*, which has served as the main biographical source on Cain for decades: "Introducing Paul Cain and His *Fast One*: A Forgotten Hard-Boiled Writer, a Forgotten Gangster Novel." *Fast One* and *Seven Slayers* have been reprinted multiple times since then, and both are still being read today.

Paul Cain is and will be remembered for his association with *Black Mask*—the pulp magazine seen as instigating and developing the hard-boiled school of detective fiction—as well as for his authorship of *Fast One*. As an individual work, *Fast One* compares favorably to any written by Hammett or Chandler, particularly when judged on narrative pace and style. But where Hammett and Chandler have benefited from modern critical inquiries into their works, no such efforts have been made for Cain. If *Fast One* is ever to rise above its current position as a novel that hard-boiled aficionados "should read," a fully developed critical analysis must be made to see if it can stand up under the scrutiny of modern critical methods. Until that time, Cain will continue to be remembered as one of the most enigmatic members of the "*Black Mask* Boys," who wrote one of the darkest novels of his generation, during one of the darker periods in American history.

Bibliography:

E. R. Hagemann, *A Comprehensive Index to* Black Mask, *1920–1951* (Bowling Green, Ohio: Bowling Green State University Popular Press, 1982).

References:

Marcel Duhamel, *Raconte Pas Ta Vie* (Paris: Mercure de France, 1972);

E. R. Hagemann, "Introducing Paul Cain and His *Fast One*: A Forgotten Hard-Boiled Writer, a Forgotten Gangster Novel," *Armchair Detective,* 12 (1979): 72–76;

James Kotsilibas-Davis and Myrna Loy, *Myrna Loy: Being and Becoming* (New York: Knopf, 1987);

Lee Server, *Danger Is My Business: An Illustrated History of the Fabulous Pulp Magazines, 1896–1953* (San Francisco: Chronicle Books, 1993);

David Wilt, *Hardboiled in Hollywood* (Bowling Green, Ohio: Bowling Green State University Popular Press, 1991).

Papers:

The bulk of Paul Cain's manuscripts and papers have never been located. Tear sheets for eight Paul Cain stories (which eventually made up *Seven Slayers*) are housed in the Shaw Correspondence file at UCLA. The best collection of biographical information on Cain, together with some scattered personal correspondence from his later years, can be found in box 33 of the E. R. Hagemann Papers and Collection of Detective Fiction (collection 1672) in the Department of Special Collections, University Research Library, University of California, Los Angeles.

Robert Campbell

(9 June 1927 – 21 September 2000)

Martin Kich
Wright State University–Lake Campus

BOOKS: *The Spy Who Sat and Waited,* as R. Wright Campbell (New York: Putnam, 1975; London: Weidenfeld & Nicolson, 1976);

Circus Couronne, as R. Wright Campbell (New York: Putnam, 1977);

Where Pigeons Go to Die, as R. Wright Campbell (New York: Rawson, 1978; London: Sidgwick & Jackson, 1978);

Killer of Kings, as R. Wright Campbell (Indianapolis: Bobbs-Merrill, 1979);

Malloy's Subway, as R. Wright Campbell (New York: Atheneum, 1981; London: Hale, 1981);

Fat Tuesday, as R. Wright Campbell (New Haven, Conn.: Ticknor & Fields, 1983);

The Tin Cop, as F. G. Clinton (New York: Pinnacle, 1983);

In La-La Land We Trust (New York: Mysterious Press, 1986; London: Mysterious Press, 1987);

The Junkyard Dog (New York: NAL/Signet, 1986; London: Mysterious Press, 1987);

Honor, as R. Wright Campbell (New York: St. Martin's Press, 1987);

The 600-Pound Gorilla (New York: NAL/Signet, 1987; London: Mysterious Press, 1989);

Hip-Deep in Alligators (New York: NAL/Signet, 1987; London: Hodder & Stoughton, 1991);

Alice in La-La Land (New York: Poseidon, 1987; London: Century, 1988);

Thinning the Turkey Herd (New York: NAL/Signet, 1988);

The Cat's Meow (New York: NAL/Signet, 1988; London: Coronet, 1990);

Juice (New York: Poseidon, 1988; London: Alison & Busby, 1990);

Plugged Nickel (New York: Pocket Books, 1988);

Nibbled to Death by Ducks (New York: Pocket Books, 1989; London: Coronet, 1991);

Red Cent (New York: Pocket Books, 1989);

Sweet La-La Land (New York: Poseidon, 1990; London: Century, 1990);

Robert Campbell (photograph by Dennis Wyszynski; from the back cover for Juice, *1990 paperback; Collection of Mark McEwan)*

The Gift Horse's Mouth (New York: Pocket Books, 1990; London: Hodder & Stoughton, 1993);

In a Pig's Eye (New York: Pocket Books, 1991; London: Hodder & Stoughton, 1993);

Boneyards (New York: Pocket Books, 1992; London: Hodder & Stoughton, 1993);

Sauce for the Goose (New York: Mysterious Press, 1994; London: Hodder & Stoughton, 1994);

The Wizard of La-La Land (New York: Pocket Books, 1995);

The Lion's Share (New York: Mysterious Press, 1996);

Pigeon Pie (New York: Mysterious Press/Warner, 1998).

PLAY PRODUCTIONS: *Wondersmith,* 1977;
The Glendorian Reality, 1992;
Mr. Pipple-Popple's Pet Shop, 1992;
An Evening with Frost and Sandburg, 1996.

PRODUCED SCRIPTS: *The Loretta Young Show,* tele-
    vision, various episodes by Campbell, NBC,
    1953–1961;
Medic, television, various episodes by Campbell, NBC,
    1954–1956;
Cheyenne, television, various episodes by Campbell,
    ABC, 1955–1963;
Five Guns West, motion picture, American Releasing,
    1955;
Gun for a Coward, motion picture, Universal Interna-
    tional, 1957;
Quantez, motion picture, Universal International, 1957;
Man of a Thousand Faces, motion picture, by Campbell,
    Ivan Goff, and Ben Roberts, Universal Interna-
    tional, 1957;
Maverick, television, episode by Campbell, ABC, 1958;
Machine Gun Kelly, motion picture, American Interna-
    tional, 1958;
A New World, motion picture, Azteca, 1958;
Teenage Caveman, motion picture, American Interna-
    tional, 1958;
Mr. Garlund, television, CBS, 1960;
The Night Fighters, motion picture, United Artists, 1960;
The Young Racers, motion picture, American Interna-
    tional, 1963;
Twelve O'Clock High, television, ABC, 1964–1967;
The Masque of the Red Death, motion picture, by Camp-
    bell and Charles Beaumont, American Interna-
    tional, 1964;
The Secret Invasion, motion picture, United Artists, 1964;
Hells Angels on Wheels, motion picture, U.S. Films, 1967;
Marcus Welby, M.D., television, various episodes by
    Campbell, ABC, 1969–1976;
Captain Nemo and the Underwater City, motion picture, by
    Campbell, Pip Baker, and Jane Baker, M-G-M,
    1969;
Born Free, television, various episodes by Campbell,
    NBC, 1974;
Harry O, television, various episodes by Campbell,
    ABC, 1974–1976.

Robert Campbell had a long and varied career as
a writer. For about two decades, from the early 1950s
to the end of the 1960s, he was employed primarily as a
screenwriter. Then, in the mid 1970s, he turned to writing novels, and during the next decade he wrote a half
dozen novels that, for lack of a more exact classifica-

tion, might be described as mainstream fiction.
Although these novels were fairly well received critically, their sales were disappointing to Campbell. At a
friend's instigation, he turned to writing mystery novels, and since the late 1980s his original and prolific
work in the genre has gained him not only a place in
the front rank of contemporary mystery writers but
also a substantial and loyal readership.

Born on 9 June 1927 in Newark, New Jersey,
Robert Wright Campbell was the son of William James
and Florence Gladys (Clinton) Campbell. His father
was an employee of the city water department, and his
mother, a homemaker. Probably not coincidentally,
Jimmy Flannery, the central character of Campbell's
most extended series of mystery novels, works as an
inspector of sewers, and scenes of quietly fulfilling
domestic life provide a comfortable and credible locus
from which Flannery can consider the exotic circumstances surrounding some brutal crimes. Moreover, in
an interview with Paul Engleman published in the 27
November 1992 issue of the *Chicago Tribune,* Campbell
acknowledged that he decided to locate the Flannery
novels in Chicago because "it was to me the last city
that seemed to be actively involved in machine politics
as I knew them back in Newark, N.J."

In 1947 Campbell received a certificate in illustration from Pratt Institute in Brooklyn. For the next three
years, he worked as an illustrator. Then, from 1950 to
1952, he served in the U.S. Army during the Korean
War. After he was discharged from the military, he
agreed to help his brother drive a Chevrolet across the
country to southern California. His brother, William,
embarked on a career as a movie and television actor.
Initially seeking work as an illustrator, Campbell soon
found his niche as a screenwriter. In effect, he turned
his skills and training as an illustrator into some of his
most remarkable characteristics as a writer: his ability
to convey in a few bold strokes the most telling qualities
of a scene, his attention to the significance of fine
details, and his intuitive grasp of the nuances in seemingly casual remarks, gestures, and postures.

Campbell's first credit as a motion-picture screenwriter was for *Five Guns West* (1955), a low-budget
Western set during the American Civil War that
focuses on a Confederate plan to use Yankee prisoners
to rob a stagecoach of a shipment of Yankee gold.
Campbell also appears as an actor in the movie, playing
a younger version of the character played by his
brother, William. *Five Guns West* was Roger Corman's
directorial debut, and Campbell subsequently wrote
scripts for six movies directed and produced by Corman. Two years later, in 1957, three movies were produced from Campbell's screenplays. Two of these—*Gun
for a Coward* and *Quantez,* both westerns starring Fred

Dust jacket for Campbell's 1986 novel that introduces Whistler,
a former children's show host turned private investigator
(Richland County Public Library)

Charles Beaumont the screenplay for the successful *The Masque of the Red Death* (1964), a Gothic vehicle for Vincent Price. Campbell's last three feature credits were for *The Secret Invasion* (1964), a movie with the same premise as *The Dirty Dozen,* which was made three years later; *Hells Angels on Wheels* (1967), which is remembered primarily for providing one of Jack Nicholson's first starring roles; and *Captain Nemo and the Underwater City* (1969).

Campbell's long experience as a screenwriter is evident in the narrative structures, the pacing, and the development of his novels. One is struck again and again by how easily his novels might be adapted to movies or to television. Campbell knew well how to frame an incident, how to juxtapose incidents in order to achieve ironic effects, how to move a story efficiently along, and how to characterize people with a single remark or image. Likewise, when it suited his purposes, he knew how to play out a conversation or a series of actions in order to wring out of them all of their potential comedy and pathos. Campbell's novels are not free of cynicism, but his cynicism comes across as something earned through experience, rather than as an expedient attitude.

During his two decades in Hollywood, Campbell became disillusioned with the secondary role of the screenwriter in the process of making a movie and with the mercenary attitudes of many of those involved in the business. His disenchantment echoes that of the many novelists who have derided Hollywood as the great betrayer and wrecker of literary talent, but his disgust drove him to transform himself from a tired screenwriter into a new novelist. Still, as he made this transition, Campbell supported himself by writing teleplays for such series as *Born Free, Cheyenne, Harry O, The Loretta Young Show, Marcus Welby, M.D., Maverick, Medic, Mr. Garlund,* and *Twelve O'Clock High.* In 1975 he moved to a new home in Carmel and found the discipline required of a full-time novelist.

Campbell wrote seven novels as "R. Wright Campbell": *The Spy Who Sat and Waited* (1975), *Circus Couronne* (1977), *Where Pigeons Go to Die* (1978), *Killer of Kings* (1979), *Malloy's Subway* (1981), *Fat Tuesday* (1983), and *Honor* (1987). These novels range widely in their subjects and settings, but they all use elements of characterization, plot, and tone that became staples of Campbell's three later mystery series featuring the Chicago sewer inspector Jimmy Flannery, the Los Angeles private investigator Whistler, and the railroad detective Jake Hatch.

The premise of *The Spy Who Sat and Waited* is that, following the 1918 Armistice, the Germans place a spy in the Orkney Islands, near the Royal Navy base at Scapa Flow. For twenty years the spy lives a truly ordi-

MacMurray—are largely forgettable, but the fourth was *Man of a Thousand Faces,* the highly acclaimed biography of Lon Chaney, with Jimmy Cagney in the lead role. It earned Campbell an Academy Award nomination for best screenplay.

In 1958 three more movies were produced from Campbell's screenplays: again, two of the three—*A New World* and *Teenage Caveman*—were inconsequential, but the third, *Machine Gun Kelly,* was a successful vehicle for Charles Bronson, who made the gangster with the deceptively deadly moniker a fiercer presence on the big screen than he had been in life. Campbell not only wrote the screenplay for *The Night Fighters* (1960) but also acted in it—in this instance, as the brother of the character played by William Campbell. During this period, Campbell had become afflicted with Bell's palsy, a partial paralysis of the face, and he later deflected criticism of his poor acting by dryly pointing out that it had been difficult to be expressive with only about half of his facial muscles functioning. Following work on *The Young Racers* (1963), Campbell wrote with

nary life, until, during World War II, he directs an air and submarine attack against the British fleet. A moving study of conflicted loyalties, the novel was nominated for a National Book Award. *Circus Couronne* has a similarly clever historical premise, but is as much a detective story as a suspense story. After Archduke Francis Ferdinand has been assassinated, igniting World War I, Swiss police inspector Yves Faucon trails an unidentified eighth assassin. The case takes on exotic dimensions when its resolution requires him to join a small circus.

The most atypical of Campbell's novels, *Where Pigeons Go to Die,* is a coming-of-age parable. A boy learns much from his grandfather's recovery from a stroke and from the outcome of a pigeon race in which they compete together. In a striking contrast, *Killer of Kings* concerns a group of eccentrics—really freaks—who join together in a tawdry Manson-like family and plot to massacre the participants in the Academy Awards ceremony. Several FBI agents make a late appearance, and a handsome actor does good work as an amateur sleuth.

Malloy's Subway is a taut suspense story in which a serial killer named Julius Bean stalks the New York subway system, while policeman Martin Malloy tries to stop him. In its memorable characterizations of the human detritus who inhabit the subway tunnels, this novel anticipates the more crowded galleries of lowlifes in the Whistler novels, as well as in *Juice* (1988).

In *Fat Tuesday,* a New York newspaperman goes to New Orleans in 1916, ostensibly to find his runaway daughter, but as he moves through Storyville, the red-light district of the city, he becomes an initiate in one depraved sexual activity after another. The novel becomes a series of loosely connected set pieces reminiscent of such Victorian pornography as the anonymous *My Secret Life* (circa 1890). Still, the novel does anticipate the emphasis on sexual perversion, sexual violence, and suspect respectability in the whole series of Whistler novels and the use of Louisiana settings in *In La-La Land We Trust* (1986).

During the early 1980s, Campbell overcame a drinking problem and a four-pack-a-day cigarette habit, allowing him to increase his productivity as a novelist, most apparent in his decision to develop several mystery-detective series simultaneously. All of his novels as R. Wright Campbell, except for *Honor* in 1987, were published before he began writing his three detective series as "Robert Campbell." Two circumstances somewhat complicate this seemingly convenient division of his work as a novelist, however. First, in 1983 he wrote a novel, *The Tin Cop* (1983), under the pseudonym "F. G. Clinton." That he then chose to write his mystery series as "Robert Campbell" suggests that he was not com-

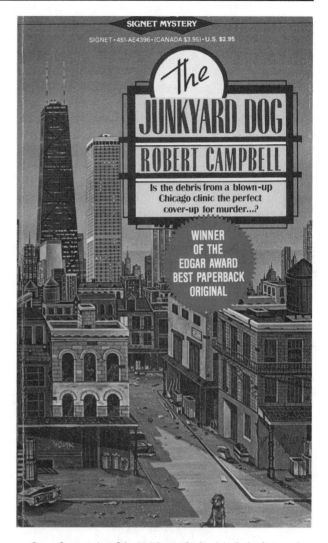

Cover for a reprint of the 1986 paperback original, the first novel in a series that follows the career of Jimmy Flannery, an honorable Chicago city official who becomes involved in the problems of his constituents (Collection of Mark McEwan)

pletely comfortable with dividing his work so definitively as, for example, Evan Hunter has done by writing his mainstream novels under that name (which initially was itself a pseudonym) and his mystery novels as Ed McBain. Second, Campbell has published as Robert Campbell two novels, *Juice* and *Boneyards* (1992), that do not belong to any of his mystery series. Clearly, in their content and styles, these two novels have gained much from Campbell's experience as a mystery novelist. Because of their subjects and their tones, however, they could also be classified easily with the seven novels he has written as R. Wright Campbell.

In 1986, with *The Junkyard Dog,* Campbell introduced his most successful and extensive series of mystery novels, featuring Jimmy Flannery, a sewer inspector and the precinct captain in the Twenty-seventh Ward in Chi-

Dust jacket for Campbell's second Whistler novel, published in 1987,
in which the detective acts as a bodyguard for a woman seeking
a divorce from her famous and vindictive husband
(Richland County Public Library)

cago. Flannery is a born politician—a smooth talker, a close listener, and a clear thinker who can recognize a scam as quickly as he can run one. What most pointedly separates him from the corruption that has touched almost everyone he comes in contact with—from politicians to civil servants to lawyers and police—is that he is incorruptible. As good-hearted as he is prone to getting into bizarre situations, Flannery knows how to manipulate the system for the benefit of his constituents, who include not only the residents of his ward but also just about anyone who needs his help. He is careful, though, not to manipulate the system or circumstances for his own advancement or profit. For all of his political wits, he is willing to let his political future depend on his actual accomplishments. A man of steady principles, he is as tolerant of other individuals, regardless of their backgrounds or sexual preferences, as he is skeptical of most political agendas and popular "causes."

As the series progresses, readers see Flannery's life evolve both publicly and privately: he rises from a precinct captain to a committeeman and, by the tenth and last novels in the series, *The Lion's Share* (1996) and *Pigeon Pie* (1998), he is considered a credible candidate for alderman of the Fifth Ward, Mayor Richard Daley's old ward; likewise, he goes from being a confirmed bachelor to a husband and then a father. The series features a regular, though gradually evolving, cast of characters: most importantly, Flannery's father, Mike, a retired fireman; his wife, Mary, a registered nurse; James "Chips" Devlin, head of the Sewer Department and Flannery's "Chinaman," or political mentor; Wally Dunleavy, head of Streets and Sanitation; and Janet Canarias, a "lipstick lesbian" who bucked the Chicago political machine and still managed to get elected alderman of Flannery's ward. In addition, there are recurring characters from Flannery's apartment building and immediate neighborhood, from the police and the coroner's office, and from the local political hierarchy. When Campbell mixes in a new group of high-stakes players and lowlifes with each new case, there is plenty for Flannery to comment on in his wry way. For example, in *The Junkyard Dog* he observes about a lawyer he is talking to: "He lets his eyes go soft, like he's suffering a secret pain, and I know this Streeter as good as I'll ever know anybody. He's an actor and a liar. He'd tell a lie to an elephant in Africa on the long shot that the elephant is shipped to a zoo in Chicago and tells the story to a talking giraffe which tells it to somebody who might come to Streeter with a deal."

Beyond the characterizations, the first-person narration, and the dialogue, the series provides a strong sense of the setting itself, as Campbell deftly integrates information about the history, the architecture, and the ethnic culture of each neighborhood that Flannery has occasion to visit. The detail Campbell provides is not just window dressing, for he typically uses it to enhance his characterizations or to add some further layer of complexity to the mystery. While the resolutions of these mysteries have often been judged weaker than their premises, the novels have been so rich in other respects that the complaints have been muted. In *The Junkyard Dog,* Flannery investigates the death of a young woman in a bomb explosion at an abortion clinic, and the novel approaches the volatile subject in a level-headed rather than incendiary manner. Reviewing the novel for the 23 May 1986 issue of *Publishers Weekly,* John Mutter concluded: "Written in appealing argot, the mystery has full characters, a satisfying ending, and a nice balance of hardboiled action and romantic tenderness." The Mystery Writers of America awarded *The Junkyard Dog* an Edgar for best first novel.

In La-La Land We Trust introduced Campbell's other major series detective, a private eye named Whistler. In this first novel Whistler focuses on the sordid business of making snuff movies. *In La-La Land We Trust* sets the tone for the series in its contrast between the old-fashioned, hard-boiled nobility of the detective and the contemporary sordidness and lunatic-fringe depravity of the cases he investigates.

Readers learn relatively little about Whistler's past: he came to Los Angeles in 1974, became a clown who hosted a children's cartoon show, and then, as the Sandman, became the host of a late-night, call-in show. Several tragedies, which he believed might have been preventable, led him to get a private investigator's license. He now works out of Gentry's Diner, operated by a one-armed, well-read, and philosophic Vietnam veteran named Bosco Silverlake. His closest friend on the police force is Isaac Canaan, an aging vice investigator who specializes in crimes against children and who is haunted by the horrible murder of his own niece. The only other significant piece of personal information that readers learn about Whistler is that he is a recovering alcoholic.

Campbell purposely made Whistler a nearly anonymous, ordinary person. Even his investigative techniques are pointedly unextraordinary: he carefully sifts through the debris of human lives, looking for clues to what has made them turn out as they have, and when necessary he relies on his intuition about what might be relevant and connected. Because the novels draw on the milieu made familiar in Raymond Chandler's novels, Campbell had to distinguish Whistler from Philip Marlowe, who is also rather anonymous in terms of his personal life but has a personality that is anything but ordinary. In addition, the contrast between Whistler's ordinariness and the extraordinarily seedy and vicious world in which he works makes both seem more credible and compelling. Reviewing the novel for the Fall 1987 issue of *The Armchair Detective,* George Harvey observed: "Campbell cuts an icy picture of cold-blooded realism and explores a bizarre world of passion and madness. He has created a savage mystery thick with snappy dialogue and haunting imagery. Whistler is a tough new face, a knight of incorruptible strength."

Honor, the last of the novels Campbell wrote as R. Wright Campbell, mixes the detective novel and the espionage thriller. It opens with the murder of an officer in the Yugoslavian military counterintelligence service, known by the acronym KOS. When municipal police detective-sergeant Michael Karel is assigned to solve the case, he must work around the antipathy of KOS and others in the government. Campbell skillfully integrates a great deal of background on the turmoil in Yugoslavia during World War II. The central issues explored are the nature of honor as both a private and a public concern and the tension between maintaining such an absolute principle and making those necessary and judicious compromises that allow one to survive politically and emotionally. In somewhat different forms, this dilemma runs throughout Campbell's detective fiction, in which the pervasive corruption of urban life serves to emphasize it by providing a broad and constant ironic counterpoint.

In 1987 Campbell also published the second and third entries in the Jimmy Flannery series and the second entry in the Whistler series. In *The 600-Pound Gorilla,* two men are found dead in a gay bathhouse where Flannery has arranged to house a gorilla temporarily displaced from the city zoo. *Hip-Deep in Alligators* begins with Flannery's discovery of a body that has been bitten cleanly in half and involves his exposure of an ingenious narcotics-smuggling operation. The titles of the novels in the Flannery series all feature some sort of animal, and they are usually somewhat comically inaccurate. For instance, the gorilla in the second novel actually weighs less than three hundred pounds, and the reptiles in the third novel are actually caimans, not alligators. In *Alice in La-La Land* Whistler serves as the bodyguard for a woman seeking a divorce from her famous husband, who is both kinky and vindictive; as it turns out, the case involves a mess of dark sexual secrets. The reviewer for the 1 October 1987 issue of *Kirkus Reviews* observed: "The neo–Ross MacDonald plotting here is downright baroque, complete with wild coincidences and the most unlikely sex-secret since Josephine Tey's *To Love and Be Wise.* But, unlike most chronicles of down-decadent-and-dirty L.A., Campbell dishes up the ugliness in spare, crisply deadpan narration, long on repartee and short on purple prose. So, for those who like it nasty, grim, and garish: a classy, vivid nightmare."

In 1988 Campbell introduced what became an abbreviated series comprising only two novels, featuring Jake Hatch, a railroad detective for the Burlington Northern Railroad. *Plugged Nickel,* the first of the two, is set in Nebraska. Hatch literally stumbles onto what seems to be a severed corpse dumped onto the tracks, but the pieces turn out to be the top and bottom halves of two corpses. In each of Hatch's cases, an almost cosmopolitan cast of suspects emerges despite the rural, remote settings. Campbell pointedly characterizes Hatch as an anachronism, but the whole premise seems to have been too dated to inspire a great deal of interest. The reviewer for *Booklist* (1 April 1988) made some interesting observations on what distinguishes this series from Campbell's others: "*Plugged Nickel* is a kind of stripped-down version of Campbell's earlier works.

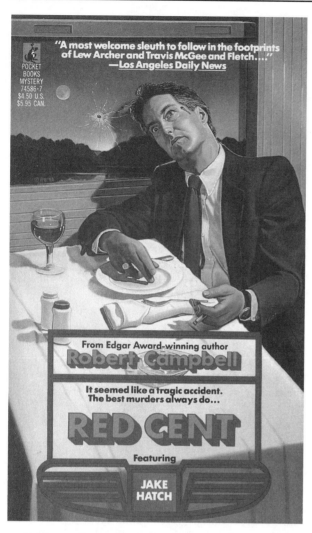

Cover for the paperback original, published in 1989, of Campbell's second novel about Jake Hatch, a railroad detective for the Burlington Northern Railroad (Collection of Mark McEwan)

Nearly absent from this novel are two of the author's calling cards—detailed and idiosyncratic characterization and a setting firmly grounded in a particular time. The focus here is almost solely on plot, as Campbell capably mixes a host of beguiling clues, demonstrating both lightness of touch and narrative cunning."

Campbell also added two novels to the Flannery series in 1988. In *Thinning the Turkey Herd* Flannery tries to identify the serial killer of young models. In *The Cat's Meow* an old priest dies in the midst of what seem to be satanic rituals, shortly before his church is scheduled to be demolished and replaced by a gas station. Reviewing *The Cat's Meow* for the 1 October 1988 issue of *Library Journal*, Rex E. Klett remarked that the novel is "a tidy little set piece, featuring a grammatically fractured but warm-hearted narrator, lively characterization, and just a smidgen of humor."

In this same year—one of the most productive in Campbell's career—he also produced *Juice,* one of his highly regarded nonseries crime novels. In this novel Campbell presents a carefully paced, consistently engaging, wholly ugly story that several reviewers rightly compared to Elmore Leonard's novels. The narrative is both disarmingly terse and startlingly comic, perfectly matched to the characters' narrowly angled views of life. Everyone here, from the police and prosecutors to the lawyers and businessmen, is trying to run some sort of deal. From loan shark Alphonso "Puffy" Pachoulo to the bookie Benny Cheeks to the "gamoosh" Billy Ray, the petty criminals are colorful and cheap. There is nothing glamorous about them, but there is little at all that is glamorous in this take on Los Angeles. Published two years later, Leonard's *Get Shorty* features characters out of much the same milieu, but compared to *Juice,* his novel is all "Hollywood," seemingly written with adaptation for the screen in mind.

In 1989 *Red Cent,* the second Jake Hatch novel, was published, along with the sixth novel in the Flannery series, *Nibbled to Death by Ducks. Red Cent* is set in Iowa. After a group of drunken Indians shoot at the "iron horse," a millionaire passenger is found shot to death. Despite the announcement that Campbell was working on a third novel in the series, tentatively titled "Thin Dime," the series stalled out without its being published. In *Nibbled to Death by Ducks,* Flannery investigates nursing-home fraud. In her review for the 10 December 1989 issue of *The New York Times Book Review,* Marilyn Stasio commented: "Mr. Campbell hangs a lot on his modest plot: dialogue so breezy it stings your eyeballs; spirited characterization of Jimmy's proud ethnic neighbors; and the ward heeler's cocky defense of the old ways, the old values, and the old politics."

Campbell extended both the Flannery and Whistler series in 1990. In *The Gift Horse's Mouth,* Flannery investigates the strange death of Goldie Hanrahan, the longtime receptionist and confidante of political boss Ray Carrigan. *Sweet La-La Land* concerns the murderous predations of a hillbilly satanist, and one of the victims is the killer's former wife, a past girlfriend of Whistler's with whom he had become reconnected. Although not entirely positive, the review in the 15 February 1990 issue of *Kirkus Reviews* conveyed the peculiar energy of the novel—and the series: "Campbell's dense, juicy narration pin-wheels from Whistler's search to Bitsy's hustler-world to Younger's psycho-rampage to the movie-mogul's slimy machinations. So there's little suspense, as well as little credibility, as the mayhem translates into a grisly, multihomicidal reunion for Bitsy, mom, and dad. Still, for fanciers of Sunset Boulevard raunch and neon pathos: harshly vivid, depress-

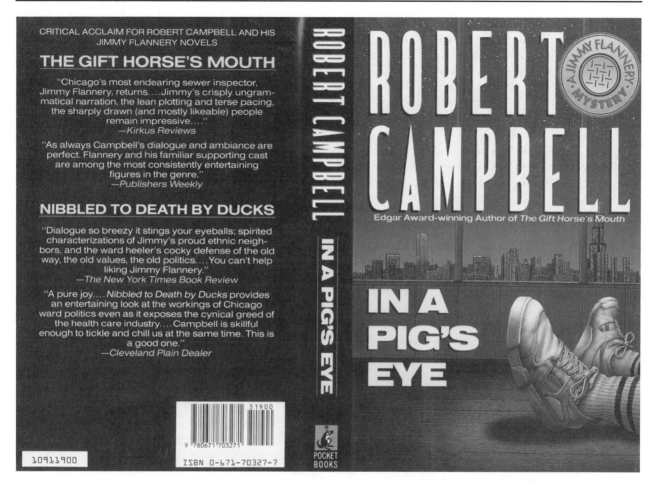

Dust jacket for Campbell's eighth Jimmy Flannery novel, published in 1991, which begins with the death of a man who signs in as "Mr. P. Pig" at the Paradise Health Club (Collection of Julie and George Anderson)

ingly sharp vignettes from an assured stylist." Published in 1991, the eighth Flannery novel, *In a Pig's Eye,* presents a riddle involving an unidentified corpse.

In 1992 Campbell produced the second of his highly regarded nonseries crime novels. *Boneyards* convincingly, if grimly, details the circumstances that come together to ruin Chicago cop Ray Sharkey. Known as the "City Hall Pimp" because of his knack for providing lewd entertainment for after-hours political functions, Sharkey has become routinely corrupt in his twenty-six years as a policeman. Knowing that he is being set up by a mayoral candidate running on an anti-corruption platform, Sharkey cannot help trying to beat the setup. He is too mixed up about his personal problems to think straight. His wife is finally dying after a long and expensive battle with cancer. The expenses to keep their retarded daughter in a private sanatorium keep going up. His sister, Wilda, for whom he has always felt, to his great shame, barely repressed desires, returns to the city and is seeing a black musician—which in itself is enough to send Sharkey, an unapologetic rac-

ist, over the brink. His racism is not enough to keep him from getting involved with a black prostitute named Roma Chounard, however—an involvement that inevitably puts him up against her pimp, Jaspar Tourette. In their willingness to play out what seem in retrospect to be their fated roles, these characters are somewhat reminiscent of those in John Gregory Dunne's *True Confessions* (1977).

For the first year in a decade, no Campbell novel appeared in 1993. From 1994 to 1996, though, one Flannery or Whistler novel appeared each year. In *Sauce for the Goose* (1994), Flannery goes to night school and gets involved in a case involving his teacher, a lawyer with expensive tastes, and one of his classmates, an enforcer for the mob. Reviewing the novel for the Winter 1996 issue of *The Armchair Detective,* Edward Lodi closed: "The Jimmy Flannery mysteries are notable for their breezy dialogue and likeable characters. . . . This is sauce to make a meal of." *The Wizard of La-La Land* (1995) brings the previous Whistler story lines together dramatically as well as thematically: the unusual murder of an AIDS patient dying in a hospice leads Whistler to expose satanists who have sexually abused children before sacrificing them; in the process, he gets involved again with the man he ruined for financing snuff movies, and he also falls in love again, this time with a nurse named Mary Bucket, who happens also to be a practicing white witch. Although it was not presented as the final novel in the Whistler series, *The Wizard of La-La Land* provides a good deal of closure to the ongoing concerns of the series and its characters' situations. *The Lion's Share* mixes Devlin's death, some hardball politics with Flannery's future at stake, and his awkward discovery of a naked woman's corpse in a bathtub.

Campbell's final novel, *Pigeon Pie,* was published in 1998. The eleventh Flannery novel, it seems a coda for the series. The mystery involves the drive-by shooting of Flannery's office manager, a transsexual former cop who has been a recurring and gradually more significant character in the series. The solution to this mystery is clearly secondary to the exploration of the themes that the murder highlights–the ethical cost of political ambition, the transitions between generations within families and public institutions, and the ways in which the mundane events of everyday life are sifted to provide the "facts" of personal and public histories. In her review in the 19 April 1998 issue of *The New York Times,* Stasio commented: "Mabel's passing is a sad

occasion for fans of this series, but other familiar characters survive, talking a blue streak and reaffirming Jimmy's faith in the values that sustain his grand old neighborhood."

After a period of time in hospice, Robert Campbell died on 21 September 2000 in Monterey, California. Although his series featuring Flannery and Whistler are different in tone, both manage to be both nostalgic and current. The series will be remembered as a significant contribution to the already considerable library of mystery and detective novels set in Chicago and Los Angeles. Still, the Flannery novels will continue to be notable for their vivid treatment of precinct-level politics and Chicago, whereas the Whistler novels may remain noteworthy primarily because of their catchy, ironically trite titles. Campbell's *Juice* may provide a more definitive treatment of the underside of life in late-twentieth-century Los Angeles than the Whistler novels.

Interviews:

W. C. Stroby, "Inside Books: Finding a Novel's Sense of Place with Robert Campbell," *Writer's Digest,* 69 (February 1989): 50–51;

Paul Engleman, "Crime Pays: Chicago's the City That Works for Novelist Robert Campbell," *Chicago Tribune,* 27 November 1992, V, pp. 1–2.

John Dickson Carr

(30 November 1906 – 27 February 1977)

Douglas G. Greene
Old Dominion University

BOOKS: *It Walks by Night* (New York & London: Harper, 1930);

The Lost Gallows (New York: Harper, 1931; London: Hamilton, 1931);

Castle Skull (New York: Harper, 1931; London: Severn House, 1976);

The Corpse in the Waxworks (New York: Harper, 1932); republished as *The Waxworks Murder* (London: Hamilton, 1932);

Poison in Jest (New York: Harper, 1932; London: Hamilton, 1932);

Hag's Nook (New York: Harper, 1933; London: Hamilton, 1933);

The Mad Hatter Mystery (New York: Harper, 1933; London: Hamilton, 1933);

The Bowstring Murders, as Carter Dickson (New York: Morrow, 1933; London: Heinemann, 1934);

The Blind Barber (New York & London: Harper, 1934);

The Eight of Swords (New York: Harper, 1934; London: Hamilton, 1934);

Devil Kinsmere, as Roger Fairbairn (New York: Harper, 1934; London: Hamilton, 1934);

The Plague Court Murders, as Dickson (New York: Morrow, 1934; London: Heinemann, 1935);

The White Priory Murders, as Dickson (New York: Morrow, 1934; London: Heinemann, 1935);

Death-Watch (New York: Harper, 1935; London: Hamilton, 1935);

The Three Coffins (New York & London: Harper, 1935); republished as *The Hollow Man* (London: Hamilton, 1935);

The Red Widow Murders, as Dickson (New York: Morrow, 1935; London & Toronto: Heinemann, 1935);

The Unicorn Murders, as Dickson (New York: Morrow, 1935; London & Toronto: Heinemann, 1936);

The Arabian Nights Murder (New York: Harper, 1936; London: Hamilton, 1936);

The Murder of Sir Edmund Godfrey (New York: Harper, 1936; London: Hamilton, 1936);

John Dickson Carr (from Papa Là-Bas, *1968; Richland County Public Library)*

The Magic-Lantern Murders, as Dickson (London: Heinemann, 1936); republished as *The Punch and Judy Murders* (New York: Morrow, 1937);

The Burning Court (New York: Harper, 1937; London: Hamilton, 1937);

The Four False Weapons (New York: Harper, 1937; London: Hamilton, 1938);

The Peacock Feather Murders, as Dickson (New York: Morrow, 1937); republished as *The Ten Teacups* (London: Heinemann, 1937);

The Third Bullet, as Dickson (London: Hodder & Stoughton, 1937);

The Crooked Hinge (New York: Harper, 1938; London: Hamilton, 1938);

Death in Five Boxes, as Dickson (New York: Morrow, 1938; London & Toronto: Heinemann, 1938);

The Judas Window, as Dickson (New York: Morrow, 1938; London & Toronto: Heinemann, 1938); republished as *The Crossbow Murder* (New York: Berkley, 1964);

To Wake the Dead (New York: Harper, 1938; London: Hamilton, 1938);

Fatal Descent, by Dickson and John Rhode (New York: Dodd, Mead, 1939); republished as *Drop to His Death* (London: Heinemann, 1939);

The Problem of the Green Capsule: Being the Psychologists' Murder Case (New York & London: Harper, 1939); republished as *The Black Spectacles* (London: Hamilton, 1939);

The Problem of the Wire Cage (New York: Harper, 1939; London: Hamilton, 1940);

The Reader Is Warned, as Dickson (New York: Morrow, 1939; London & Toronto: Heinemann, 1939);

The Man Who Could Not Shudder (New York: Harper, 1940; London: Hamilton, 1940);

And So to Murder, as Dickson (New York: Morrow, 1940; London & Toronto: Heinemann, 1941);

Nine—And Death Makes Ten, as Dickson (New York: Morrow, 1940); republished as *Murder in the Submarine Zone* (London & Toronto: Heinemann, 1940); republished as *Murder in the Atlantic* (London: World, 1959);

The Department of Queer Complaints, as Dickson (New York: Morrow, 1940; London: Heinemann, 1940);

The Case of the Constant Suicides (New York: Harper, 1941; London: Hamilton, 1941);

Death Turns the Tables (New York & London: Harper, 1941); republished as *The Seat of the Scornful* (London: Hamilton, 1941);

Seeing Is Believing, as Dickson (New York: Morrow, 1941; London: Heinemann, 1942); republished as *Cross of Murder* (London: World, 1959);

The Emperor's Snuff-Box (New York: Harper, 1942; London: Hamilton, 1943);

The Gilded Man, as Dickson (New York: Morrow, 1942; London & Toronto: Heinemann, 1942); republished as *Death and the Gilded Man* (New York: Pocket Books, 1947);

She Died a Lady, as Dickson (New York: Morrow, 1943; London & Toronto: Heinemann, 1943);

He Wouldn't Kill Patience, as Dickson (New York: Hampton, 1944; London & Toronto: Heinemann, 1944);

Till Death Do Us Part (New York: Harper, 1944; London: Hamilton, 1944);

The Curse of the Bronze Lamp, as Dickson (New York: Morrow, 1945); republished as *Lord of the Sorcerers* (London & Toronto: Heinemann, 1946);

He Who Whispers: A Dr. Fell Mystery (New York: Harper, 1946; London: Hamilton, 1946);

My Late Wives, as Dickson (New York: Morrow, 1946; London & Toronto: Heinemann, 1947);

Dr. Fell, Detective, and Other Stories (New York: American Mercury, 1947);

The Sleeping Sphinx: A Doctor Fell Detective Story (New York: Harper, 1947; London: Hamilton, 1947);

The Skeleton in the Clock, as Dickson (New York: Morrow, 1948; London: Heinemann, 1949);

Below Suspicion (New York: Harper, 1949; London: Hamilton, 1950);

The Life of Sir Arthur Donan Doyle (New York: Harper, 1949; London: Murray, 1949);

A Graveyard to Let, as Dickson (New York: Morrow, 1949; London: Heinemann, 1950);

The Bride of Newgate (New York: Harper, 1950; London: Hamilton, 1950);

Night at the Mocking Widow, as Dickson (New York: Morrow, 1950; London: Heinemann, 1951 [i.e., 1952]);

The Devil in Velvet (New York: Harper, 1951; London: Hamilton, 1951);

The 9 Wrong Answers (New York: Harper, 1952; London: Hamilton, 1952);

Behind the Crimson Blind, as Dickson (New York: Morrow, 1952; London: Heinemann, 1952);

The Cavalier's Cup, as Dickson (New York: Morrow, 1953; London: Heinemann, 1954);

The Third Bullet and Other Stories (New York: Harper, 1954; London: Hamilton, 1954)—comprises "The Third Bullet," "The Clue of the Red Wig," "The House in Goblin Wood," "The Wrong Problem," "The Proverbial Murder," "The Locked Room," and "The Gentleman from Paris";

The Exploits of Sherlock Holmes, by Carr and Adrian Conan Doyle (New York: Random House, 1954; London: Murray, 1954); republished as *The New Exploits of Sherlock Holmes* (New York: Ace, 1956);

Captain Cut-Throat (New York: Harper, 1955; London: Hamilton, 1955);

Patrick Butler for the Defence (New York: Harper, 1956; London: Hamilton, 1956);

Fear Is the Same, as Dickson (New York: Morrow, 1956; London: Heinemann, 1956);

Fire, Burn! (New York: Harper, 1957; London: Hamilton, 1957);

The Dead Man's Knock (New York: Harper, 1958; London: Hamilton, 1958);

Scandal at High Chimneys: A Victorian Melodrama (New York: Harper, 1959; London: Hamilton, 1959);

In Spite of Thunder (New York: Harper, 1960; London: Hamilton, 1960);

The Witch of the Low-Tide: An Edwardian Melodrama (New York: Harper, 1961; London: Hamilton, 1961);

The Demoniacs (New York: Harper, 1962; London: Hamilton, 1962);

The Men Who Explained Miracles (New York: Harper, 1963; London: Hamilton, 1964);

The Grandest Game in the World (New York: Davis, 1963);

Most Secret, as Roger Fairbairn (New York: Harper, 1964; London: Hamilton, 1964);

The House at Satan's Elbow (New York: Harper, 1965; London: Hamilton, 1965);

Panic in Box C (New York: Harper, 1966; London: Hamilton, 1966);

Dark of the Moon (New York: Harper, 1967; London: Hamilton, 1967 [i.e., 1968]);

Papa Là-Bas (New York: Harper, 1968; London: Hamilton, 1968 [i.e., 1969]);

The Ghosts' High Noon (New York: Harper, 1969; London: Hamilton, 1970);

Deadly Hall (New York: Harper, 1971; London: Hamilton, 1971);

The Hungry Goblin: A Victorian Detective Novel (New York: Harper, 1972; London: Hamilton, 1972);

The Door to Doom and Other Detections (New York: Harper, 1980; London: Hamilton, 1981 [i.e., 1980]);

The Dead Sleep Lightly (Garden City, N.Y.: Doubleday, 1983);

Crime on the Coast [by Carr and others] and *No Flowers by Request* [by Dorothy L. Sayers and others] (London: Gollancz, 1984; New York: Berkley, 1987)— Carr wrote the first two chapters of the first story; the other chapters were by Valerie White, Laurence Meynell, Michael Cronin, Joan Fleming, and Elizabeth Ferrars;

Fell and Foul Play (New York: International Polygonics, 1991);

Merrivale, March and Murder (New York: International Polygonics, 1991);

Speak of the Devil (Norfolk, Va.: Crippen & Landru, 1994).

Edition: *The Crooked Hinge,* introduction by Robert E. Briney (San Diego: University of California, 1976).

John Dickson Carr, one of the dominant figures in the Golden Age of fictional detection between World Wars I and II, was a master of the locked-room mystery novel, of fair-play puzzlement in historical settings, and of eerie atmosphere combined with rational detection. His detective stories have a special flavor. They not only ask "Whodunit?" but also "How could it have been done?" Carr's fictional crimes seem to have been committed without human agents. Murders take place in rooms with entrances locked and sealed; bodies are found alone in buildings surrounded by unmarked snow or sand; people enter a house or dive into a swimming pool and utterly disappear. And for fully three-quarters of the story, Carr suggests that only a vampire, a witch, or a ghost could have committed the crimes. Striding through these adventures and bringing order and reason to what seems a world dominated by the dark powers are Carr's four towering figures of detective fiction–Henri Bencolin of the Sûreté, Dr. Gideon Fell, Sir Henry Merrivale, and Colonel March of Scotland Yard's Department of Queer Complaints.

John Dickson Carr was born on 30 November 1906 in Uniontown, Pennsylvania, the only child of Julia and Wooda Nicholas Carr, and grew up in comfortable circumstances. His father, a lawyer and later a congressman, encouraged him to read at the age of four, and though Carr later insisted that he had been no prodigy, he was soon reading the Oz books of L. Frank Baum and the historical romances of Alexandre Dumas *père* and Robert Louis Stevenson. The strain of swashbuckling adventure of the great historical novelists is evident throughout Carr's stories, but the influence of Baum's imaginative fantasies has less often been recognized. Carr's interest in improbabilities and in witchcraft and magic, whether genuine or humbug, can be traced back to his love of the Oz books.

Carr's interest in crime and detection seems to have begun when he read some of the law books and accounts of true crime in his father's library. But Carr was not entranced by the sordid realism of crime. He believed that, like history, crime can be romantic, and he devoured the stories of Sir Arthur Conan Doyle, Jacques Futrelle, L. T. Mead and Robert Eustace, and Thomas W. Hanshew. "In those days," Carr wrote in a 21 October 1941 letter to Frederic Dannay, "it was the custom to begin with an arrestingly grotesque or impossible situation, and supply a twist ending which was sometimes naive but always ingenious." G. K. Chesterton's Father Brown tales, with their emphasis on atmosphere, paradox, the past, and tricks and impossibilities, were an important influence on Carr's taste in detective fiction.

Carr entered the Hill and Preparatory School in Pottstown, Pennsylvania, in 1921, where he wrote stories for the English club and engaged in such activities as fencing in the moonlight. Four years later he went on to Haverford College. In March 1926, his "As Drink the Dead . . ." appeared in Haverford's monthly literary

*Dust jacket for Carr's 1933 novel, the second featuring Dr. Gideon Fell, whom the author
modeled after his friend and fellow mystery writer, G. K. Chesterton (<jdcarr.com>)*

magazine; in its combination of historical romance and death by seemingly impossible means the story foreshadows Carr's later work. Both his writing ability and his enthusiasm must have impressed his colleagues, for he became associate editor of *The Haverfordian* in April 1926 and editor two months later. He was such a prolific writer that often several of his stories or poems appeared in a single issue—under his own name, under several pseudonyms, or anonymously. His detective stories written at Haverford—published in *The Door to Doom and Other Detections* (1980)—feature Sir John Landervorne of Whitehall and Henri Bencolin, Prefect de Police of Paris. Each story has an impossible crime—a man is murdered in a locked train compartment or disappears from a guarded chamber—and each reveals the strong influence of Chesterton. In a book review for *The Haverfordian,* of November 1926, Carr described one of Chesterton's Father Brown collections as "the best detective stories of the year, and not even Conan Doyle has ever come within pistol-shot or knife-throw of them. We have haunted castles, winged daggers,

vanishing men—and over it all the genial, lovable priest who plays detective."

Carr's Bencolin short stories, like most of his later tales, are Chestertonian in their atmosphere, their impossibilities, and their plot structure. As in the Father Brown stories, the detective does not solve the crime by interviewing witnesses or by examining fingerprints, cigarette ashes, and other physical clues; instead, Bencolin discovers the pattern the events form. Bencolin's evidence includes voice inflections, glances, and half-completed sentences. Carr's detectives more commonly use their imagination rather than their reason to reconstruct the crime. Bencolin says in "The Murder in Number Four" (*The Haverfordian,* June 1928) that

the great chess player is the one who can visualize the board as it will be after his move. The great detective is the one who can visualize the board as it has been when he finds the pieces jumbled. He must have the imagination to see the opportunities that the criminal saw, and act as the criminal would act. . . . Nobody is more apt than a detective to say a lot of windy, fancy things about reasoning, and deduction, and logic. He too frequently says "reason" when he means "imagination." I object to having a cheap, strait-laced pedantry like reason confused with a far greater thing.

Carr's stories written at Haverford are astonishingly mature, but at times both the historical romances and the Bencolin tales are too intricately textured and too claustrophobic in atmosphere. As Carr remarked in a 26 May 1946 letter to Dannay about another writer's first short stories, problems frequently arise "from the novice's frantic wish to cram as many surprises as possible into the narrowest limits."

In 1928, Carr went to Paris to study (or so his parents thought) at the Sorbonne. He never showed up at his class; he was determined to use the time to become a writer. He wrote two long manuscripts in the main genres that interested him, historical romance and detective fiction. He completed an historical novel, but it did not please him, and he destroyed it. All that is known of it is Carr's comment, quoted in Howard Haycraft's *Murder for Pleasure* (1941), that it had "lots of Gadzookses and sword-play." But his detective story, a short novel about Bencolin, called *Grand Guignol*, was published in *The Haverfordian* in 1929, and, with considerable lengthening, it appeared as *It Walks by Night*, published the next year by Harper. It was a moderate success, going through at least four printings in its first year, and Carr turned toward writing detection rather than historical novels as his career.

Carr's next three novels—*The Lost Gallows* (1931), *Castle Skull* (1931), and *The Corpse in the Waxworks* (1932)—appeared at approximately six-month intervals, and they all feature Bencolin. Each is highly ingenious with bizarre murders; each is a pure puzzle novel, playing fair with the reader and featuring a carefully concealed least-likely villain; and each is heavily atmospheric with hints of the supernatural before Bencolin produces a natural, human solution. Although the Bencolin novels have frequently been reprinted, Carr looked back on them as crude and immature. About *It Walks by Night*, Carr told Haycraft, "I think it's pretty terrible, but I hope it's entertaining—to me the one unforgivable sin is being dull. . . . And, thank heaven, it is not 'significant.' But if it gives the nervous reader a bad night or the puzzle-connoisseur a headache, I shall be satisfied." He was less kind about *The Lost Gallows* in a 1939 letter to fellow writer Clayton Rawson: "I twice tore up twenty or thirty thousand words, and, when I had finished it, it was poor stuff." As for *Castle Skull*, Carr was even harsher in a 1 December 1975 letter to Francis M. Nevins Jr.: "I have come to dislike the book as much as I regret it, and hope it's never again issued by anybody." Carr, like many authors, was too hard on

his first books, but he became uncomfortable with some of the formulas of the Bencolin novels. An air of unreality, of madness and decay, hangs over them, and by 1932 Carr no longer liked the sardonic and sometimes sadistic Bencolin.

Carr's decision to write detective novels set in England and featuring English sleuths was connected with his meeting Clarice Cleaves of Bristol, England, on a transatlantic trip in 1930. He gave her a copy of *It Walks by Night*, arranged to meet her on shore, and married her on 3 June 1932. Early in 1933 they went to England for what they planned as a brief trip of a few weeks, but Carr found the country so congenial that they made England their home for the next sixteen years. Carr's love of England had several levels, all of them reflected in his books. The British Isles seemed to him the perfect place to write detective novels. In one of his radio scripts, "A Razor in Fleet Street" (broadcast in 1948 on the CBS show *Cabin B-13*), an American who like Carr married an Englishwoman explains that "London is home to me, too, in a way. It's put a spell on my imagination ever since I was a boy so-high. Sherlock Holmes! Dr. Fu-Manchu! Hansom-cabs rattling through the fog. . . ." In contrast to the sometimes brash, moneymaking life in America, England seemed to Carr the place where the past continually influenced the present, where the values he treasured still existed, where honor, chivalry, and fair play still had meaning in the world.

Three of Carr's first four books written in England are told from the viewpoint of an American visitor to the British Isles. In *The Bowstring Murders*, (1933), published under the pseudonym of Carr (later, Carter) Dickson, Professor Michael Tairlaine finds England an escape from a dull and predictable existence. "What sort of adventures did I ever have?" Carr has Tairlaine ask a friend, who replies, "What do you mean by 'adventure' anyway? Do you mean in the grand manner? A slant-eyed adventuress, sables and all, who suddenly slips into this compartment, whispers 'Six of diamonds—north tower at midnight—beware of Orloff'?" "Yes," Tairlaine admits in the book, "I suppose I did mean something like that." Tairlaine's adventures in the remainder of the book demonstrate Carr's love of England and the past. Even the name of the detective, John Gaunt (who appears only in *The Bowstring Murders*), brings up an historical parallel (John of Gaunt, son of King Edward III), and the events take place in a fifteenth-century castle filled with a collection of medieval arms and armor assembled by the "more than half-cracked holder of the Barony of Rayle."

Hag's Nook (1933), written about the same time as *The Bowstring Murders*, is dominated by "a feeling which can haunt the traveller only in the British Isles. A feeling that the earth is old and enchanted; a sense of reality in all the flashing images which are conjured up by that one word 'merrie'. . . . The English earth seems (incredibly) even older than its ivy-bearded towers. The bells at twilight seem to be bells across centuries. . . ." The American Tad Rampole's enchantment with England is matched by the feelings of the detective, Dr. Gideon Fell, who, making his first appearance in this work, solves crimes in Carr's books for almost thirty-five years. Dr. Fell, described both as a lexicographer and an historian, has a fund of miscellaneous information about all aspects of the English past, especially those things that make history live–games and sports, royal mistresses, and drinking customs, about which he eventually writes an immense tome. ("To write good history," Carr remarks in *The Murder of Sir Edmund Godfrey* [1936], "is the noblest work of man.")

Fell was modeled after Carr's literary idol, G. K. Chesterton. With his huge girth, his bandit's mustache, his unruly hair, Fell resembles photographs of Chesterton. The plot of *Hag's Nook* is also Chestertonian in its feeling for the past, as modern crimes seem to repeat ancient murders. Dorothy L. Sayers first recognized the influence of Chesterton on Carr's early style. In a 24 September 1933 review of the second Dr. Fell novel, *The Mad Hatter Mystery* (1933), in *The Sunday Times*, she pointed out that "Chestertonian are the touches of extravagance in character and plot, the sensitiveness to symbolism, to historical association, to the shapes and colours of material things, to the crazy terror of the incongruous."

These characteristics are also evident in the first Sir Henry Merrivale novel, *The Plague Court Murders* (1934), published under Carr's Carter Dickson pseudonym. This book, too, emits the feeling that the past is living in the present, as the ghost of a seventeenth-century hangman's assistant seems responsible for the murders. For this novel Carr again uses a vividly depicted English detective. H.M. (as his friends call him) superficially resembles Dr. Fell: he is corpulent and fond of speaking in non sequiturs. But unlike Dr. Fell, whose speech is full of Johnsonian formality, Sir Henry is disrespectful and often insulting: the Prime Minister is "Horseface"; a jury is made up of "fatheads"; and women are addressed as "my wench" or "my dolly." Carr later said that H.M. was not based on any individual, but as the 1930s progressed and war became imminent, H.M. took on some of the pugnacious public personality of Winston Churchill.

Another aspect of the Carr style appeared in 1934 with the publication of a detective farce, *The Blind Barber*, probably his most controversial book. Some critics, notably Kingsley Amis, disliked the story because the humor focuses on drunkenness. Others, including Anthony Boucher, have found it one of Carr's most successful novels. "Laughter and death," Boucher wrote in his introduction to the 1962 Collier edition of *The Blind Barber*, "are old friends."

During the 1930s Carr experimented with the detective novel. He never dropped its fundamental characteristics; his stories always play fair with the reader since the detective solves the crime by clues that the reader also possesses; the criminal is usually the least-likely suspect; and the solution is kept hidden until the end of the book. Carr realized that such elements can be combined with high (and low) comedy in *The Blind Barber* and in many of the later Sir Henry Merrivale novels; with ghost stories in "The Man Who Was Dead" and "The Door to Doom" (written in 1935 but not collected until 1980 when they appeared in *The Door to Doom and Other Detections*); with true-crime reconstruction in *The Murder of Sir Edmund Godfrey*, which presents a fair-play solution to an unsolved murder of 1678; and with witchcraft in *The Burning Court* (1937). Once again Carr combined detection and historical romance. Several of his novels set in the present, such as *The Red Widow Murders* (1935), have sections in which a tale from the past sets the scene for present crimes; these brief tales can be read almost independently. Even when Carr wrote an historical novel, *Devil Kinsmere*, published in 1934 under the pseudonym Roger Fairbairn, he included two mysteries and enough clues for the reader to foresee the conclusion.

In the Dr. Gideon Fell and Sir Henry Merrivale stories of the middle and later 1930s, Carr brought together the elements that set his work apart from that of other writers. His consciousness of the past is connected with punctilious attention to physical detail. He researched each book carefully, often spending more time in investigating the background than in the actual writing. He often built the plot around an artifact of the past, such as the watch in the shape of a skull in *Death-Watch* (1935), or the seventeenth-century card game in *The Four False Weapons* (1937), or the tarot fortune-telling cards in *The Eight of Swords* (1934), or the life-size automation in *The Crooked Hinge* (1938). Dr. Fell and H.M. were ready to lecture on almost any obscure subject at the drop of a clue. Most of the time, these discursive sections turn out to be relevant to the plot, but they contribute to the complaint that a few Carr books are so rich in extraneous detail that they lack focus. But whether relevant to the plot or not, such passages play a part in the total effect of Carr's work; they help to sustain the mood of the continuing and pervasive influence of ancient crime.

Carr often began a book with a bizarre scene–a clergyman in false whiskers in *The Arabian Nights Murder* (1936); the clockworks, watches, and phosphorus in the

Dust jacket for Carr's first novel (published in 1934) in his series of Sir Henry Merrivale mysteries, which he published under the pseudonym Carter Dickson (<jdcarr.com>)

pockets of drugged suspects in *Death in Five Boxes* (1938); the four weapons found at the murder scene in *The Four False Weapons;* and the extraordinary Wode-houseian coincidences that have detective chasing detective in *The Magic-Lantern Murders* (1936). Carr loved finding romance in the humdrum, as Robert Louis Stevenson had done in *The New Arabian Nights* (1882). The Baghdad-on-the-Thames atmosphere appears in several of Carr's works during the 1930s, especially the epidemic of hats in *The Mad Hatter Mystery,* and, in conscious imitation of Stevenson, the drawing of cards to enter the death room in *The Red Widow Murders.*

The greatest bizarrerie in Carr's books is the locked rooms and other impossible crimes. The motif of the victim found murdered where no one could have approached him had appeared in Carr's early Bencolin short stories and in his first novel, *It Walks by Night,* but then it played a minor role in Carr's books until 1934 and 1935. The first Sir Henry Merrivale novels are

based on seeming impossibilities—a victim poisoned in a sealed room in *The Red Widow Murders,* or murdered in a house surrounded by unmarked snow in *The White Priory Murders* (1934), or impaled in front of witnesses by what seems an invisible unicorn in *The Unicorn Murders* (1935). Dr. Fell's first locked-room case, *The Three Coffins* (1935), is considered by many experts the finest "miracle problem" ever written, despite that the explanation was far more complex than those Carr himself usually admired. The book also includes the problem of how a man can be shot at point-blank range when no one is near him. But *The Three Coffins* is probably most praised for Dr. Fell's famous "Locked-Room Lecture." Carr simply stops the action to allow Dr. Fell to discourse for a full chapter on the ways and means of creating the effect of murder in a hermetically sealed chamber. And, should the reader object, Dr. Fell announces that "we're in a detective story, and we don't fool the reader by pretending we're not. Let's not invent elaborate excuses to drag in a discussion of detective stories. Let's candidly glory in the noblest pursuit possible to characters in a book."

Although "The Locked-Room Lecture" has taken on a life of its own and been printed independently of *The Three Coffins,* it plays an important part in that book. Carr was often careful to contrast the comfortable security of English club and tavern life with the terror of seemingly supernatural crime. Dr. Fell's lecture takes place "under the dark gleam of armour and armorial bearings" when "the coffee was on the table, and wine-bottles were empty, cigars lighted." Many of Carr's other stories from this period have similar contrasts. *The Mad Hatter Mystery* begins in "a lounge like a club, brown panels and easy-chairs, in red leather, with brass-bound kegs behind the bar." The opening scene of *The Crooked Hinge* takes place in a room where "the late July sunlight turned the floor . . . to gold. The somnolent heat brought out an odour of old wood and old books." Such scenes make the crimes seem, in contrast, more removed from everyday life, more inexplicable. Sometimes the terror is introduced immediately, as in "The Man Who Was Dead" (collected in *The Door to Doom and Other Detections*), when a man in the Naughts-and-Crosses Club remarks that he has just read his own obituary in a newspaper. More often, Carr allows this "crazy terror of the incongruous" (to quote Sayers) to grow until the reader is certain that a vampire, a witch, or someone lighter than air must have committed the crime.

A majority of Carr's books written during the late 1930s include impossible crimes. In *The Crooked Hinge,* the victim is killed behind a low hedge that no one could have approached without being seen. *To Wake the Dead* (1938) includes a murder in a guarded room. In *The Problem of the Wire Cage* (1939), a man is strangled on a soft-clay tennis court with no footprints but his own. Sir Henry Merrivale solves even more impossibilities than does Dr. Fell. In *The Peacock Feather Murders* (1937), Carr includes page references in footnotes to show the reader that all the clues to the solution of the locked-room murder had been fairly given in the story. The murder in *The Reader Is Warned* (1939) is seemingly committed by "thought-waves." *Fatal Descent* (1939), written by Carr in collaboration with John Rhode, demonstrates various means of murder in a closed elevator. (The book was actually written almost entirely by Carr but using a method for the crime devised by Rhode.) Most ingenious of all is *The Judas Window* (1938), in which H.M. proves that even the most securely locked room has one "window" through which death can come. Carr's power of narration and his sleight of hand in misleading the reader reached such a level that several readings of *The Judas Window* are required to realize that the trick could not have worked. But Carr, like

a magician, makes his audience so fascinated with the trappings of the trick that they must make an effort to realize that the ace was never there.

The effect of these miracle crimes is to make the reader doubt rational cause and effect, and this response in turn makes Dr. Fell's and H.M.'s explanations of the trick more spectacular. Most readers are relieved that the world is operating normally again and that they can retreat happily to the safety of their clubs or homes. To increase this effect, Carr uses supernatural legends as background to many of his stories. He plays not only on readers' fears of a world turned upside down, but also on their dread of powers beyond human explanation. Seances, witch lore, and night monsters play major roles in Carr's stories. In short, many Carr books read as though they are occult novels, ghost stories written by Algernon Blackwood or Montague Rhodes James, until Dr. Fell and Sir Henry Merrivale restore an ordered universe.

By the late 1930s, Carr was recognized as one of the most proficient practitioners of the detective novel. Sponsored by Anthony Berkeley and Sayers, he became the only American member of the exclusive Detection Club, which in its oath of membership enforced the rule of fair play. Most of Carr's novels were serialized in popular magazines, and *The Sketch, The Illustrated London News,* and *The Strand* commissioned short stories from him. Nine of these tales (out of about twenty short stories Carr wrote between 1935 and 1941) feature Colonel March of Scotland Yard's Department of Queer Complaints, which handles problems that "do not seem to bear the light of day or reason." Colonel March refers in passing to such cases as the thief who steals only green candlesticks, but the adventures that Carr records are far more spectacular. "The New Invisible Man" involves a gun fired by disembodied hands. "The Footprint in the Sky" includes a new explanation of murder in a house surrounded by unmarked snow. Best of all may be "The Crime in Nobody's Room," in which an entire flat disappears from a building. Colonel March, teetering on his heels and resembling "a stout colonel in a comic paper," solves these cases primarily because he is never surprised by anything.

As the decade came to an end, Carr decided to try his hand as a scriptwriter. For a brief time, he worked with J. B. Priestley on a script for the Korda movie studios, but he never finished his part of the project. His work depended so much on the intricate relationship of every plot detail that he had difficulty sharing responsibilities with a co-author. Moreover, Carr disliked contending with the changing ideas of movie barons about what they wanted in a script. In a letter to Rawson, Carr moaned that "they are madder

Dust jacket for Carr's 1935 Gideon Fell mystery, in which the detective lectures for an entire chapter on how someone who is alone in a hermetically sealed room might be murdered (<jdcarr.com>)

than a crate-load of coots; and why I still preserve some vestige of my reason remains a mystery."

In 1939 Carr sent a three-part Dr. Fell radio play—"Who Killed Matthew Corbin?"—to the British Broadcasting Corporation (BBC). The presentation of this play, in December 1939 and January 1940, began a long period of association between Carr and the radio network. During 1940 and 1941 he wrote several more mysteries for the BBC, including an eight-part serial, "Speak of the Devil," which combines his interests in historical romance and impossible crime. The setting is Regency England, and the story involves the apparently ghostly manifestations of a young woman who was hanged for a murder a year earlier. ("On my last public appearance, I was hanged by the neck until dead.") For the most part, however, Carr's time was occupied in writing and narrating propaganda scripts. "Black Gallery: Heinrich Himmler" retells the life of a Nazi leader. ("I am Heinrich Himmler. Let me shake your hand. Wouldn't you like to be ruled by me?") Other plays told the British to obey the blackout

("Britain Shall Not Burn"), to refuse to purchase black-market chocolate ("Black Market, the Exposure of a Criminal Organization"), or to accept women's military role in the war ("Women on the Guns").

Propaganda work is seldom creative, for normally the author's sole duty is to present a predetermined message; nevertheless, some of Carr's anti-Nazi plays deserve to be remembered. "Denmark in Chains" makes the Nazis seem ridiculous as well as sinister. *The Silent Battle,* a series of six plays, emphasizes the emotions and cleverness of the underground resistance in occupied countries. Carr makes his points in this series with unexpected plot twists, including two miraculous problems. In one episode, the Polish underground hides a large radio transmitter where even the most thorough search by the Gestapo fails to find it. In another, Hitler disappears from a hermetically sealed chamber.

But Carr did his most successful radio work for several mystery programs. In 1942 and 1943, while in the United States waiting for the government to assign him duties for the war effort, he wrote more than twenty half-hour episodes for the program *Suspense* on Columbia Broadcasting System (CBS). Of these, the most popular was "Cabin B-13," about a terrified bride and the impossible disappearance of her young husband and even her cabin on an ocean liner. This show was rebroadcast several times on American and British radio; it was adapted as a television drama; and it became the basis for a feature-length movie by 20th Century-Fox, *Dangerous Crossing* (1953). Almost as popular was his adaptation of Edgar Allan Poe's "The Pit and the Pendulum," written after CBS claimed that the story could never be done on the radio. Carr also wrote mysteries set in the past ("The Body Snatchers," "Lord of the Witch Doctors"); impossible crimes ("The Moment of Darkness," "The Dead Sleep Lightly"); anti-Nazi pieces ("Menace in Wax," "Death Flies Blind"); and adaptations of his own stories and gimmicks ("Fire Burn and Cauldron Bubble," "Nothing up My Sleeve").

Back in England by the end of 1943, Carr persuaded Val Gielgud of the BBC to run his *Suspense* scripts as *Appointment with Fear*. Gielgud wanted to try United States radio techniques, including knife chords and timing controlled to the split second, and the series opened with "Cabin B-13." British audiences reacted favorably to what Gielgud in his book *Years of the Locust* (1947) called "the unabashed histrionicism" of *Appointment with Fear*. The title of the series became familiar enough that at least three British newspapers used it in political cartoons. Carr's *Suspense* scripts were soon exhausted, and he wrote a second and then a third series of new plays for British audiences, including an adaptation of a Father Brown story and retellings of tales by Stevenson, Melville Davisson Post, and Ambrose Bierce.

Carr later wrote other radio plays—for *Cabin B-13* on CBS in 1948 and for a revival of *Appointment with Fear* in 1955—but the characteristics of his radio work had already been set in the early 1940s. His plays make effective use of the limitations of the medium. Carr knew that the listener fills in physical details with his own imagination, and in several of his plays he counted on fooling his audience by allowing them, in a sense, to imagine too much. Carr also used sound masterfully. In "The Black Minute," for example, the effect of sound in darkness is a major clue—that to locate the origin of a sound in a pitch-black room is difficult. In many plays, Carr introduced a single background sound to set the mood and to lead, or mislead, the audience. Especially noteworthy examples are the musical glasses in "The Devil's Saint," the whirl of the roulette wheel in "Death Has Four Faces," and the thud of the darts in "The Man Who Couldn't Be Photographed." Carr, who seldom had trouble devising plots, looked on radio work as a welcome relaxation from writing novels.

During the years that he was concentrating on radio work, Carr's production declined to about two novels a year rather than the four or five he had written in the previous decade. But among these books are some of the finest of his career; they are more tightly constructed and humanly compelling than many of his books before or after this period. Rather than using entertaining but occasionally irrelevant discourses by Dr. Fell and Sir Henry Merrivale, Carr organized his books so that almost every word and gesture contributes to the final solution. In addition, Carr's books during the early 1940s pull the reader more directly into the story. His earliest works usually have the American visitor to Britain or the Continent be an outside, through sensitive, observer; but Carr's later novels are told from the viewpoint of a young man who is directly concerned with the solution to the mystery—often because he is attracted to a woman who is the chief suspect or who is withholding information. Moreover, some misunderstanding between the male and female leads commonly provides the impetus for much of the action, and Carr uses it to build tensions and to mask the essential clues.

Writing under his own name, Carr gave Dr. Fell two locked rooms and a Scottish setting in *The Case of the Constant Suicides* (1941), which with its combination of atmosphere, ingenuity, and sexual tensions between the male and female main characters is one of his best books. *The Emperor's Snuff-Box* (1942) is atypical in its French setting and its lack of an impossible crime, but it has beautifully contrived suspense and clever misdirection. *Till Death Do Us Part* (1944) has a compelling situation: can you trust your wife or fiancée if a police officer says that she is a compulsive killer? *He Who Whispers: A Dr. Fell Mystery* (1946) has a perfectly developed neo-Gothic atmosphere, several impossibilities (which Carr implies are caused by vampires), and a rational solution.

As Carter Dickson, Carr made the H.M. novels of the same period emphasize comedy rather than the seemingly supernatural terror of most of the Dr. Fell stories. *Nine—And Death Makes Ten* (1940) includes a new type of miracle problem for Carr. The body is not discovered in a locked room, but the fresh fingerprints at the scene do not match those of anyone who could have committed the crime. In *She Died a Lady* (1943) Sir Henry explains how someone can be shot at close range on a cliff when only the victim's footprints appear. *He Wouldn't Kill Patience* (1944) involves a murder that occurs in one of the most completely inaccessible rooms in all fiction, with all the doors and windows sealed on the inside with gummed tape. In *The Curse of* the Bronze Lamp (1945), a young lady vanishes almost before the eyes of the witnesses. Carr had been experimenting with seemingly impossible disappearances since his first Bencolin short story, "The Shadow of the Goat," published almost twenty years earlier, and he worked several more variations on the same "miracle problem" but never executed it more successfully than in *The Curse of the Bronze Lamp*. Indeed, Carr wrote only one weak novel during these years, *Seeing Is Believing* (1941), which begins with an unfair gimmick. (The second sentence in the book, which reads "That was the admitted fact," turns out not to be a fact at all.) The plot is clever enough that Carr had no need to resort to complete misstatements to fool the reader.

With the end of the war and the election of a socialist government in 1945, Carr became dissatisfied with living in England. He disliked postwar austerity and the tendency to solve problems through nationalization and regulation–herd existence, Carr called it. He stayed in England until 1948 to work on his biography of Sir Arthur Conan Doyle, based on papers preserved by the Doyle family. Carr had met Doyle's son, Adrian, at the BBC while assisting in the production of radio shows based on Doyle's stories. So much primary material survived that Carr was able to write *The Life of Sir Arthur Donan Doyle* (1949) by using Doyle's own words in many scenes. Carr returned to the United States in 1948 and the next year became president of the Mystery Writers of America.

Carr's fictional works reflected his growing dissatisfaction with the post–World War II world. Dr. Fell often crossed the line separating Chestertonian warmth from meaningless declamations, and in general the Fell novels lacked the enthusiasm of Carr's earlier books. Above all, *Below Suspicion* (1949), with its unfair descriptions of characters and its unbelievable witchcraft, showed that Carr could no longer consistently count on his old formulas. Sir Henry Merrivale continued to appear in novels until 1953, but the later books lack the spontaneity of the earlier ones. Carr seems to have compensated for the grimness of life in the late 1940s by making H.M. almost a buffoon and minimizing the mystery. Even the impossible crimes and their solutions were not always convincing. Many attentive readers discover before H.M. how the wife murderer in *My Late Wives* (1946) makes corpses disappear. The explanation of the locked room in *Night at the Mocking Widow* (1950) seems forced. The impossible crime in the final Merrivale novel, *The Cavalier's Cup* (1953), is ingenious, but it is lost in some markedly unfunny horseplay about an American congressman chasing a British lady in her underwear. Carr produced one stunning miracle problem, the disappearance of a man from a swimming pool in *A Graveyard to Let* (1949), but the mystery is not

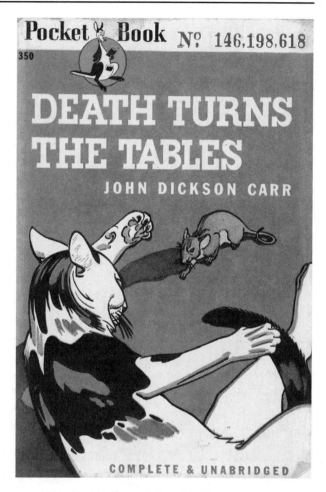

Cover for a 1946 paperback reprint of Carr's 1941 novel
(Bruccoli Clark Layman Archives)

developed, a flaw that leads the reader to wonder if the idea might better have been handled in a short story.

H.M., however, did have a splendid final case in "Ministry of Miracles," a novelette that appeared in a British magazine, *The Housewife,* in three parts, January through March 1956, but not as a book until 1963, when it was published under the title "All in a Maze" in *The Men Who Explained Miracles.* The problem–that, although the victim is alone in a locked room, someone turns on the gas jets–is excellent in its simplicity, and the story has much of the warmth and enthusiasm of Carr's earlier tales.

Although the H.M stories continued until the mid 1950s, and the Dr. Fell novels appeared off and on until 1967, Carr's major focus for the rest of his writing career was historical detective novels. *The Bride of Newgate* (1950), his first historical novel in sixteen years, includes a fine mystery and a minor-miracle problem, but it is primarily an adventure story of swordplay and romance in Regency England. Carr's unhappiness with the mid twentieth century is clearly revealed in his his-

Dust jacket for Carr's 1969 historical mystery, set in the United States in 1911 (Richland County Public Library)

and detection. It takes place against a background of Napoleon's camp in 1805 as the Grande Armée prepares to invade England. Carr carefully increases suspense as a British agent tries to discover French plans in the face of a series of mysterious killings committed by what seems to be an invisible man.

Carr's books through the early 1960s maintain high standards of ingenuity and storytelling. Noteworthy among his historical novels are *Fire, Burn!* (1957) and the final Carter Dickson book, *Fear Is the Same* (1956), both of which have modern heroes transported to the past. Another good example of Carr's later style is *The Witch of the Low-Tide* (1961), subtitled "An Edwardian Melodrama." It features David Garth, a detective-story writer who, as a specialist in impossible crimes, represents Carr's view of his craft. A true detective story, says Garth, is "the exercise of one's ingenuity, the setting of the trap and the double-trap, the game you play chapter after chapter against a quick-witted reader." The miracle crime in *The Witch of the Low-Tide,* murder in a building surrounded by unmarked sand, is one of the best in Carr's later books, and the re-creation of England in 1907 is accurate and colorful. The hero knows the identity of the killer early on but must fend off the official police in order to protect the woman he loves. Only two novels from these years, *The Dead Man's Knock* (1958) and *In Spite of Thunder* (1960), both about Dr. Fell, are disappointments. The crimes are clever enough, but Fell is wooden, and the stories are dominated by cryptic remarks that are frustrating rather than intriguing.

From about 1962 until his death on 27 February 1977, Carr fought increasing illness. Occasionally, his final books substitute speeches for conversation, and some of his stories have so much mystification that following the main thread of the plot is difficult; but almost all of his books continue to be carefully detailed in setting and ingeniously constructed in detection. *The House at Satan's Elbow* (1965), praised by Boucher in a *New York Times* review as "a happy return to the Golden Age of detection," has Carr's simplest and most convincing explanation of the locked-room puzzle. *Panic in Box C* (1966) has a well-developed theatrical background and a chilling conclusion in the crazy world of "the Old Haunted Mill" at an amusement park.

In 1965, after another socialist government took power in Britain, Carr moved to the American South. His final Dr. Fell novel, *Dark of the Moon* (1967), takes place near his new home in South Carolina. His next three novels are set in old New Orleans. The best of them, *Papa Là-Bas* (1968), has an intriguing combination of voodoo, riverboats, and a cleverly constructed alibi by the murderer. But after the 1972 publication of *The Hungry Goblin: A Victorian Detective Novel,* in which

torical novel *The Devil in Velvet* (1951), in which the hero so longs to leave his own age that he bargains with Satan to be transported to the England of Charles II. *The Devil in Velvet* was always Carr's favorite among his mysteries in a period setting.

With the defeat of the socialist government in 1951, Carr returned to England, but his books again showed some of the heaviness they had suffered from a few years earlier. He was seriously ill for almost three years, but he did not take time off, as he admitted in an 8 October 1954 letter to Boucher: "like I fool I *would* write during this time against all advice." *Behind the Crimson Blind* (1952) indicates how difficult writing had become for Carr. The story has an excellent Tangiers setting, based on the Carrs' five-month stay there, but the problem—the identification of a Robin Hood character—is not compelling. After an emergency operation in the summer of 1953 and a long period of recuperation, however, Carr again produced stories of uniformly high quality.

Captain Cut-Throat (1955), Carr's first book after his recovery, is a fine combination of historical romance

Wilkie Collins is the detective, Carr wrote no more fiction. He planned to write a detective novel set in the 1890s with Sir Arthur Conan Doyle as the main detective, and twice he began new novels, but he did not complete more than a few pages. His proposed volume of reminiscences, "Culprit Confesses," suffered the same fate. He did, however, contribute a lively and refreshingly idiosyncratic book-review column to *Ellery Queen's Mystery Magazine*, and he began a nonfiction series about criminals of the past, but only the first installment was published.

At his death, tributes to John Dickson Carr poured in. Perhaps the one that sums up his achievement most fully came from fellow mystery novelist Edmund Crispin: "for subtlety, ingenuity and atmosphere, he was one of the three or four best detective-story writers since Poe that the English language has known."

References:

Robert C. S. Adey, *Locked Room Murders and Other Impossible Crimes* (London: Ferret, 1979), pp. 13–16, 43–48, 59–62;

Lillian de la Torre, "John Dickson Carr's Solution to *The Mystery of Edwin Drood*," *Armchair Detective*, 14 (Autumn 1981): 291–294;

Larry L. French, *Notes for the Curious, a John Dickson Carr Memorial Journal* (St. Louis: Privately printed, 1978);

Douglas G. Greene, "Adolf Hitler and John Dickson Carr's Least-Known Locked Room," *Armchair Detective*, 14 (Autumn 1981): 295–296;

Greene, "John Dickson Carr: The Man Who Created Miracles" and "A Bibliography of the Works of John Dickson Carr," in *The Door to Doom and Other Detections* (New York: Harper, 1980; London: Hamilton, 1981), pp. 9–26, 327–351;

Greene, *John Dickson Carr: The Man Who Explained Miracles* (New York: Otto Penzler/Simon & Schuster, 1995)–includes a complete list of Carr's radio scripts, pp. 486–490;

Greene, "John Dickson Carr, Alias Roger Fairbairn, and the Historical Novel," *Armchair Detective*, 11 (October 1978): 339–342;

Howard Haycraft, *Murder for Pleasure* (New York: Appleton-Century, 1941), pp. 199–203;

Roger Herzel, "John Dickson Carr," in *Minor American Novelists*, edited by Charles Alva Hoyt (Carbondale: Southern Illinois University Press, 1970), pp. 67–80;

S. T. Joshi, *John Dickson Carr: A Critical Study* (Bowling Green, Ohio: Bowling Green University Popular Press, 1990);

Roland Lacourbe, *John Dickson Carr, Scribe au Miracle* (Amiens: Ecrage, 1998);

Tony Medawar, "Duels, Devilment, and Infidelity," in *Speak of the Devil* (Norfolk, Va.: Crippen & Landru, 1994), pp. 9–25;

Francis M. Nevins Jr., "The Sound of Suspense, John Dickson Carr as a Radio Writer," *Armchair Detective*, 11 (October 1978): 334–338;

LeRoy Panek, "John Dickson Carr," in *Watteau's Shepherds* (Bowling Green, Ohio: Bowling Green University Popular Press, 1979), pp. 145–184;

Julian Symons, *Bloody Murder, from the Detective Story to the Crime Novel* (London: Faber & Faber, 1972), pp. 119–121;

Robert Lewis Taylor, "Profiles: Two Authors in an Attic," *New Yorker*, 27 (8 September 1951): 39–48; (15 September 1951): 36–49.

Papers:

The correspondence of John Dickson Carr with his British agent, David Higham, and his correspondence with Frederic Dannay are held at the Harry Ransom Humanities Research Center, University of Texas at Austin.

Mary Higgins Clark
(24 December 1929 –   )

Wendi Arant
Texas A&M University

BOOKS: *Aspire to the Heavens: A Portrait of George Washington* (New York: Meredith Press, 1969); republished as *Mount Vernon Love Story: A Novel of George and Martha Washington* (New York: Simon & Schuster, 2002);

Where Are the Children? (New York: Simon & Schuster, 1975; London: Talmy Franklin, 1975);

A Stranger Is Watching (New York: Simon & Schuster, 1978; London: Collins, 1978);

The Cradle Will Fall (New York: Simon & Schuster, 1980; London: Collins, 1980);

A Cry in the Night (New York: Simon & Schuster, 1982; London: Collins, 1983);

Stillwatch (New York: Simon & Schuster, 1984; London: Collins, 1984);

Weep No More, My Lady (New York: Simon & Schuster, 1987; London: Collins, 1987);

The Anastasia Syndrome and Other Stories (New York: Simon & Schuster, 1989; London: Century, 1990);

While My Pretty One Sleeps (New York: Simon & Schuster, 1989; London: Century, 1989);

Loves Music, Loves to Dance (New York: Simon & Schuster, 1991; London: Century, 1991);

All Around the Town (New York: Simon & Schuster, 1992; London: Century, 1992);

I'll Be Seeing You (New York: Simon & Schuster, 1993; London: Century, 1993);

Mary Higgins Clark: Three Novels in One Volume (London: Cresset, 1993)—comprises *While My Pretty One Sleeps, Loves Music, Loves to Dance,* and *Anastasia Syndrome;*

Death on the Cape and Other Short Stories (Bath, U.K.: Century, 1993);

Remember Me (New York: Simon & Schuster, 1994; London: Simon & Schuster, 1994);

The Lottery Winner: Alvirah and Willy Stories (New York: Simon & Schuster, 1994);

Mary Higgins Clark: Three Complete Novels (New York: Wings, 1995)—comprises *The Cradle Will Fall, A Stranger Is Watching,* and *Where Are the Children?;*

Mary Higgins Clark (from Kitchen Privileges: A Memoir, *2002; Thomas Cooper Library, University of South Carolina)*

Let Me Call You Sweetheart (New York & London: Simon & Schuster, 1995);

Silent Night (New York & London: Simon & Schuster, 1995);

Mary Higgins Clark: Three New York Times Bestselling Novels (New York: Wings, 1996)—comprises *While My Pretty One Sleeps, Loves Music, Loves to Dance,* and *All Around the Town;*

Moonlight Becomes You (New York: Simon & Schuster, 1996; London: Simon & Schuster, 1996);

My Gal Sunday (New York: Simon & Schuster, 1996; London: Simon & Schuster, 1997);

Pretend You Don't See Her (New York: Simon & Schuster, 1997; London: Simon & Schuster, 1997);

All Through the Night (New York: Simon & Schuster, 1998; London: Simon & Schuster, 1998);

You Belong to Me (New York: Simon & Schuster, 1998; London: Simon & Schuster, 1998);

We'll Meet Again (New York: Simon & Schuster, 1999; London: Simon & Schuster, 1999);

Before I Say Goodbye (New York: Simon & Schuster, 2000; London: Simon & Schuster, 2000);

Deck the Halls, by Clark and Carol Higgins Clark (New York: Simon & Schuster, 2000; London: Simon & Schuster, 2000);

He Sees You When You're Sleeping, by Clark and Carol Higgins Clark (New York: Scribner/Simon & Schuster, 2000; London: Simon & Schuster, 2001);

On the Street Where You Live (New York: Simon & Schuster, 2001; London: Simon & Schuster, 2001);

Daddy's Little Girl (New York: Simon & Schuster, 2002; London: Simon & Schuster, 2002);

Kitchen Privileges: A Memoir (New York: Simon & Schuster, 2002);

The Second Time Around (New York: Simon & Schuster, 2003; London: Simon & Schuster, 2003);

Nighttime Is My Time (New York and London: Simon & Schuster, 2004).

OTHER: *Murder on the Aisle: The 1987 Mystery Writers of America Anthology,* edited by Clark (New York: Simon & Schuster, 1987);

"That's the Ticket," in *Mistletoe Mysteries,* edited by Charlotte MacLeod (New York: Mysterious Press, 1989), pp. 101–118;

"As It Was in the Beginning," in *Malice Domestic 2,* edited by Martin H. Greenberg (New York: Pocket Books, 1993), p. ix;

The International Association of Crime Writers Presents: Bad Behavior, edited by Clark (San Diego: Harcourt Brace, 1995);

"Definitely, a Crime of Passion," in *Murder for Love,* edited by Otto Penzler (New York: Delacorte, 1996), pp. 43–76;

The Plot Thickens, edited by Clark (New York: Pocket Books, 1997);

"Power Play," in *Murder for Revenge,* edited by Penzler (New York: Delacorte, 1998), pp. 35–70;

"Lady Sleuth, Lady Sleuth, Run Away Home," in *Murder on the Run* (Berkeley, Cal.: Adams Round Table, 1998), pp. 27–58;

The Night Awakens, edited by Clark (New York: Pocket Books, 2000);

"The Funniest Thing Has Been Happening Lately," in *Murder in the Family,* edited by the Adams Round Table (New York: Berkley Prime Crime, 2002), pp. 19–41.

SELECTED PERIODICAL PUBLICATIONS–UNCOLLECTED: "Beauty Contest at Buckingham Palace," *Saturday Evening Post,* 234, no. 29 (22 July 1961): 16–19;

"Suspense Writing," *Writer,* 93 (September 1980): 9–12;

"Always a Storyteller," *Writer,* 100 (August 1987): 9–11;

"A Husband Beyond Compare," *Reader's Digest,* 135 (December 1989): 92–94;

"My Wild Irish Mother," *Reader's Digest,* 139 (July 1991): 83–86;

"Taking the Plunge: Writing the Category Romance Novel," *Writer,* 105 (July 1992): 5–6;

"By the End of August," *Mary Higgins Clark Mystery Magazine,* 26 (Summer 1993): 53;

"Suppose? And What If?" *Writer,* 109 (March 1996): 13;

"Haven't We Met Before?" *Mary Higgins Clark Mystery Magazine,* 25 (Summer 1999): 57;

"Edgar Smith: The Human Copperhead," *Mystery Scene,* 63 (1999): 32–42.

Novelist Mary Higgins Clark has written more than twenty best-sellers in her thirty years as a mystery novelist. In addition, she has received many awards, including the Horatio Alger Award and the Grand Prix de Literature of France. She was the president of the Mystery Writers of America (MWA) in 1987, chairman of the International Crime Congress in 1988, and the Grand Master of the Edgar Awards of the MWA in 2000. She has received thirteen honorary doctorates, from such universities as Villanova, Fordham, and Seton Hall. Critics have likened her novels to the works of Alfred Hitchcock in her talent for weaving stories around ordinary people in highly intense and terrifying situations, while her short stories are said to have a somewhat acerbic, O. Henry–like quality.

In the tradition of Agatha Christie, Clark's books have been referred to as "cozy mysteries" or "suspense tales in the English style"–referring to their lack of violence and sordid details. While she is considered a master of mystery/suspense, Clark's novels include no sex and violence in spite of the often serious nature of her subjects. "I've always just preferred the idea of implied violence. The Hitchcock way. How many ways can you shoot people up. I think footsteps . . . can be scarier. And I think the sexiest line written this century is,

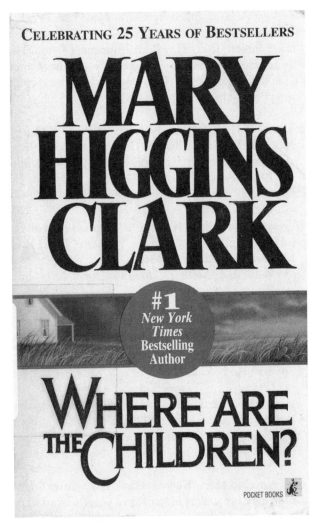

Cover for a 1975 paperback reprint of Clark's first best-selling novel, which was initially turned down by publishers who feared that the theme of children in danger was too upsetting for women readers (Richland County Public Library)

'You'll not shut me out of your bedroom tonight.' I swear that's sexier than all this rolling in the hay," Clark opined to Dave Weich in an interview for Powells.com dated 13 May 1999.

Clark attributes her success as a writer to her Irish heritage, explaining that "the Irish are, by nature, storytellers" as she is quoted as saying on the Simon and Schuster website. Her father, Luke Joseph Higgins, was a first-generation Irish immigrant who owned and managed the Higgins Bar and Grille in New York City. He married Nora C. Durkin, a buyer for B. Altman Department Stores, who then resigned to raise their family. On 24 December 1929, Mary was born, the middle child and the Higginses' only daughter. She was so close with her brothers that according to her memoir, when she and her siblings were all in the St. Francis

Xavier School and instructed to write J.M.J. (Jesus, Mary, and Joseph) on the top of their papers, she thought the initials were a tribute to her and her brothers— Joseph, Mary, and John.

Clark wrote her first poem at seven. To Weich, she recounted,

> I still have it. It's pretty bad, but my mother thought it was beautiful and made me recite it for everyone who came in. I am sure the captive audience was ready to shoot me, but that kind of encouragement nurtures a budding talent. From the time I was seven, I also kept diaries. I can read them now and look back at what I was like at different ages. I still keep diaries; they are a great help to my novels. No one has seen them—they are locked in a trunk.

She also wrote skits, which she bullied her brothers into performing with her, although she was writer, director, producer, and star, to her brothers' dismay. She recounts in her memoir that she told them, "When you write it, you can be the star."

The Higgins family struggled during the Depression era; Luke Higgins worked as many as twenty hours a day, struggling to support his family. Perhaps as an escape from hardship, Mary loved to read, at first taking great delight in fairy tales and later graduating to mystery stories and Nancy Drew novels. The first story she sent out for publication was to *True Confessions* when she was sixteen—it was not published because the editor found her characters too "upscale," a defining attribute of her later novels that has not hindered their popularity.

In 1939 Mary experienced a grave loss when her father died unexpectedly of a heart attack, the first of many tragedies that she overcame, gaining from them traits that she celebrates in her novels, strength of character and determination. With little money and a mortgage to pay, her mother was forced to return to work at a series of menial jobs in order to support her daughter and two sons. The family took in boarders, and Mary took a job while she was still a student to help make ends meet. Eventually, the family had to move to a three-room apartment.

Just prior to her graduation from Villa Maria Academy, a Roman Catholic high school, Mary experienced a second loss when her older brother, Joe, a new naval recruit, died unexpectedly of spinal meningitis. The death of her brother had a profound impact on Clark in two ways. As she recounts in her memoir, "We three siblings had been so close, Joseph, Mary, and John. J.M.J. Joe's death multiplied a thousand times the sense of loss that I'd felt since that May morning five years earlier when I came home to the news that 'Daddy's dead.'" Her brother's death also spurred her to choose secretarial school rather than college; she wanted to "grow up . . . earn money . . . marry young and have children."

Forgoing a college scholarship, Mary Higgins went to Ward Secretarial School and on to a job as an advertising assistant at Remington Rand, working to help support her family. This employment lasted until the chance remark of a stewardess friend, "God, it was beastly hot in Calcutta," captured Mary Higgins's imagination, and she immediately changed careers, putting off marriage to her sweetheart, Warren F. Clark, and going to work for Pan American Airlines. "My run was Europe, Africa and Asia," Clark recalled in an interview with Lisl Cade at Simonsays.com. "I was in a revolution in Syria and on the last flight into Czechoslovakia before the Iron Curtain went down. I flew for a year and then got married." On 26 December 1949, Mary Higgins married Clark, an airline executive and longtime friend of the family, whom she had known since she was sixteen.

Clark gave birth to five children in the first eight years of her marriage—Marilyn, Warren, David, Carol, and Patricia. But even the concerns of marriage and motherhood did not dissuade her from pursuing her interest in writing: she started taking creative-writing courses at New York University, writing romance fiction about flight attendants for the next few years. Clark told Cade,

There, I got advice from a professor which has always served me well. He said: "Write about what you know. Take a dramatic incident you are familiar with and go with it." I thought of my experience on the last flight to Czechoslovakia and gave my imagination free rein. "Suppose," I reflected, "the stewardess finds an 18-year old member of the Czech underground hiding on the plane as it is about to leave." The story was called "Stowaway." It took six years and 40 rejection slips before I sold it to *Extension* magazine in 1956 for $100. I framed that first letter of acceptance.

Many of Clark's stories include a distinctly personal element—from settings in Cape Cod, where she has a summer home, or New York, where she has an apartment (Clark describes herself as a "nice, Catholic girl from the Bronx"), to characters modeled on people she observed, even those close to her. Clark says she wrote *A Cry in the Night* (1982), a Cinderella story gone wrong, with her daughter Carol in mind, and in the movie adaptation, Carol played the lead role.

Another valuable feature that Clark took from the class was a peer writing group: it met once a week, starting in 1950, and continued for more than forty years. Clark attributes its longevity to the structure, saying to Betta Ferendelli, "We had strong rules and

that's why it survived. Two people read each time and they could read for 20 minutes each—that way nobody would hog the time. We had one person who was the chairman with a stopwatch, and we each had three minutes to criticize. You know, that way nobody could be long-winded." This writing workshop, founded by Clark and Thomas Chastain, has evolved into the Adams Round Table—a name that pays homage to the Algonquin Round Table—and has led to the publication of five collections of short fiction.

Clark kept a disciplined schedule for her writing, rising at 5:00 A.M. and writing until 7:00 A.M., when her children woke up. She published a few short stories and continued to write stories resolutely until two events occurred: the short-story market faltered, and, when she was thirty, Warren Clark learned that he was suffering from severe arteriosclerosis and was not expected to live much longer.

In 1964, after five children and fifteen years of marriage, Clark's husband died of a heart attack, leaving her to care for her children alone—the same situation her mother had faced. Clark turned to her natural talent for writing to support her family and went to work for Robert G. Jennings as a radio scriptwriter. She learned to write concisely for radio, building the action quickly and catching and holding the audience's attention. She expressed to Ferendelli that "Each one was four minutes long and in that time you had to tell a story and leave room for two messages from the sponsor. It taught me to write tightly." She wrote a serialized radio production about the life of George Washington titled *Portrait of a Patriot,* what Clark called a "three-year tutorial in history," a detailed account that required in-depth research into the first United States president's life and work, research that was the basis of her first book.

Her first attempt at writing a book-length work was hardly a best-seller, but it was critically acclaimed, earning Clark the New Jersey Author Award in 1969. The biographical novel about George Washington, *Aspire to the Heavens* (1969), had a run of just 1,700 copies and was "remaindered as it came off the press," notes Fakih. Nevertheless, Clark had taken a significant step in her transition from writing radio scripts into the mainstream publishing market. Clark recounts in her memoir, "I did know that I considered the book a triumph. And I also knew that I had what it took to actually write a book. Now I wanted to try to write a book that would sell." Taking the monetary failure of the Washington biography in stride, she decided to write what she liked to read—mystery and suspense. Her particular favorites were the works of Agatha Christie, Mary Roberts Rinehart, and Charlotte Armstrong. A couple of years later, in 1970, Clark left Robert G. Jennings to take a position as vice president and creative director with Aerial Communications.

Although Clark's suspense novels have not brought her the critical acclaim she received for the biography of George Washington, they have garnered her best-seller profits and a following of millions of readers. The lack of praise from critics has not bothered Clark. She told Jean Westmoore of the *Buffalo News* (14 November 2000): "I want the books to be like a roller-coaster ride, I want you to feel when you get on you're going to be entertained and a little scared but you can't get off until the end of the ride. I love when someone says 'I was up until 4 in the morning reading your darned book.' I say, 'then you got your money's worth.'" Clark, who said in the interview with Cade that she taught herself to write suspense stories by studying Daphne du Maurier's *Rebecca* (1938), took a year and a half to write her first suspense novel and another year and a half to rewrite it. Originally titled "Die a Little Death," it was inspired by a news story about the trial of Alice Crimmins, a woman in New York accused of murdering her children. Cade quotes Clark as saying that she wove a plot around the premise "suppose your children disappear and you are accused of killing them—and then it happens again." Clark used Cape Cod as the setting, imbuing the tale with a shadowy and vaguely sinister quality: she said of the locale that its "mists and fogs, churning surf, nor'easter storms, weather-beaten captains' houses perched high on embankments above the sea . . . enhance the atmosphere of terror and gloom." Such a description is indicative of the stimulating way in which Clark paints a scene—providing subtle details and setting the mood so that readers feel as if they are there.

Clark turned in the manuscript to agent Patricia Myer, who tried to sell it to Doubleday and to Harper and Row, both of which turned it down because, as Lucy Freeman reports in "Mary Higgins Clark," *Armchair Detective: A Quarterly Journal Devoted to the Appreciation of Mystery, Detective, & Suspense Fiction* (Summer 1985), they "felt that children in jeopardy would upset women readers." Her agent then sent the manuscript to Simon and Schuster, where upon finishing a first reading of the book, editor Phyllis Grann called back with "Don't show Mary Higgins Clark's book to anyone else. I want it." The deal was sealed in May 1974, and Simon and Schuster has published every Clark novel since. Ultimately, the title was changed to *Where Are the Children?* (1975). In the same year as the successful sale of the manuscript, though, Clark's brother Johnny died at the age of forty-two because of complications from a fall.

Linda Claycomb Pelzer says of *Where Are the Children?* that "Clark tapped into the deepest fears of her readers. She forced them to confront the underside of their ordinary lives and to acknowledge the evil lurking in the shadows of their quiet existence." It earned her a $3,000 advance. The immediate success of the work, which became a best-seller, led to $100,000 in paperback royalties for Clark, providing financial security for the family and for her children's education. That is also when Clark sat down and made a wish list of things that she had always wanted to do; "It was headed by college," recounts Freeman. Clark continued her studies in philosophy at Fordham University, which she had entered in 1974. While pursuing a bachelor's degree in philosophy, she continued to work as a radio scriptwriter, and she started on her second suspense novel.

Clark's second novel, *A Stranger Is Watching* (1978), was also inspired by news reports, this time the 1976 Supreme Court ruling on *Gregg* v. *Georgia* reinstating the death penalty and specifically addressing the case of a man who had committed armed robbery and deliberately shot two men in the process. Initially titled "Crossroads," Clark's book does not mirror the events of the real crime; instead, Clark writes of a young child who was witness to the brutal murder of his mother and uses the story as a vehicle to question the morality of capital punishment. The character development languishes despite all the vivid description of settings and actions, and in spite of the climactic ending. Clark received a $500,000 advance for *A Stranger Is Watching,* a sum that allowed her to devote more of her time to her writing. In 1979, she graduated summa cum laude from Fordham, and in 1980, the paperback rights for this third novel sold for $1,000,000, permitting her the security to quit working with Aerial Communications and to write full-time.

A signature element of Clark's novels is the fast-paced action. Susan Toepfev of *People* magazine (15 June 1992) remarked, "There are mystery writers who concoct more sophisticated plots, more realistic settings, more profound characters. But for sheer storytelling power—and breathtaking pace—Clark is without peer." Although the works start quickly, the length of time covered may vary. *The Cradle Will Fall* (1980) takes place over the space of a week; the action of *A Stranger Is Watching* covers three days; and *Where Are the Children?* spans a single day. Clark is a master at relating relevant facts or historical information needed for the story through dialogue or through such conventions as a story within a story and conveying simultaneous episodes, all without breaking the pace.

The Cradle Will Fall is reminiscent of Robin Cook's medical thrillers, the story inspired by the pictures of Baby Louise, the first test-tube baby. As Pelzer says, Clark borrowed the title of a well-known lullaby for the book, and as she points out through the "allusion to the lullaby . . . the cradle, or mother's womb . . . is threatened by the very person who seems to support it." Clark has become fond of borrowing song titles for the titles of her books. Kristin Tillotson of the *Minneapolis Star Tribune* (19 October 1998) says that "they often have a dark side; they can be either promising or chilling, depending on how you interpret them."

With *A Cry in the Night,* Clark was looking for "a cross between *Rebecca* and *Psycho,*" and indeed there are Gothic undertones in the story of a "poor, deceived young woman who is swept off her feet by a 'Prince Charming' and transported to a remote Minnesota farm where her days are filled with loneliness and her nights with terror," as Thomas Whissen reports. The plot is not only evocative of du Maurier's classic, but also clearly echoes Clark's own experience with her second husband, an attorney who owned a farm in Minnesota. On 8 August 1978, Clark married Raymond Charles Ploetz and moved with him to Minnesota. The marriage was later annulled in 1986, and of her ill-fated eight-year liaison with Ploetz, Clark said to Hubbard of *People,* "Everyone is entitled to one colossal mistake. That was mine." Jenny MacPartland's mistake is in allowing herself to be rescued by a charismatic but mysterious man, a decision that ultimately puts the lives of her daughters in jeopardy. The heroine of *A Cry in the Night* is Clark's most helpless, and what would normally be admirable qualities—innocence and a willingness to please—are detrimental and even dangerous.

In appraisals of Clark's first four novels, reviewers often draw comparisons between her work and that of other established mystery novelists, as if recognizing that Clark was trying out possibilities before she found her own style. If this is the case, *Stillwatch* (1984) can be viewed as a transitional work between her early novels and the books written in what became her signature style. It was also the first of her novels to exhibit the opulence and high society that characterize her later works, as if some of her own success has permeated her novels. Clark's own experience with a break-in was the impetus for *Stillwatch,* a political thriller with two strong female protagonists, each successful and each haunted by her past. By seeing the main characters' points of view and knowing what they are thinking, the reader gets to know them quickly and becomes deeply involved in the story. Pelzer says that "The emphasis on the heroine's struggles indicates the importance of character to the suspense novel. Unlike the classical mystery or detective novel . . . , the sus-

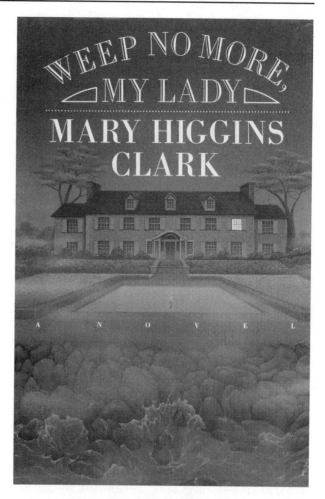

Dust jacket for Clark's sixth novel, published in 1987, a murder mystery set at an exclusive California health spa (Richland County Public Library)

pense novel depends upon fully realized characters for the effect." In addition to constructing a believable and sympathetic heroine, Clark creates a realistic and menacing, oftentimes deranged, killer. In most of her stories, the 'whodunit' is revealed as the story unfolds, and the perpetrator's motivation and possible future misdeeds provide the suspense, a technique that has been criticized as a weakness by reviewers looking for a serious mystery. Again, as with so many of Clark's novels, the premise for *Stillwatch* was inspired by reality—specifically, the potential for a female vice president of the United States in Geraldine Ferraro.

The next novels are all so unmistakably Clark as to be almost formulaic. They are all set in New York City with a more affluent cast of characters and a more sophisticated, but still sensitive and strong, heroine than had been the case in her first four novels. Richard Dyer of the *Boston Globe* (11 June 1996) in "Murder Most Polite" reports that Clark "writes about, and for, the kind of fantasy-person she herself appears to be on her jacket photographs–couture-clad, elegantly bejeweled, elaborately and immaculately coiffed, nails incarnadined and face subtly maquille, wealthy beyond imagination but far too tasteful to make an ostentatious show of it." The similarity in the pattern of her works may occur because she always follows what has proven to be a rewarding method for her writing: "At my first writing class, I was told to think of a true situation and then ask myself, 'Suppose' and 'What if?' To that I have added a third question, 'Why?'–there must be motivation. Those rules have made it easy for me," Clark relates in *The Writer* (March 1996).

Weep No More, My Lady (1987) is rather more of a mystery than a suspense novel: the identity of the killer is unknown and there is no lack of suspects in the cast of characters. Clark provides only fleeting glimpses of the killer's mind, enough details to ascertain that the heroine is in danger but not enough to determine the identity or motivation of the killer. The book is essentially a fictionalized celebrity mystery "in the tradition of Thomas Tryon," Pelzer asserts. It is set at an exclusive spa. In addition, *Weep No More, My Lady* introduces the only recurrent characters in any of Clark's novels–Alvirah and Willy Meehan, a working-class couple who won the lottery. The Meehans provide an element of comic satire as well as an earthy foil for the lavish celebrity characters in the story. Originally, Clark intended to kill off Alvirah, but her daughter Carol prevailed upon her mother to change her mind, and the Meehans resurfaced in some adventures of their own in *Death on the Cape and Other Short Stories* (1993) and *The Lottery Winner: Alvirah and Willy Stories* (1994). The majority of Clark's novellas and shorter stories have a Dickensian bittersweet or satiric quality. *The Anastasia Syndrome and Other Stories* (1989) includes three stories originally published in *Woman's Day*, fast-paced suspense stories comparable to her longer works, but with a supernatural edge.

Clark chose another extravagant venue for her next novel, focusing on the world of high fashion with *While My Pretty One Sleeps* (1989). It includes all the suspenseful elements of her earlier novels with a more romantic air. The story centers on a family–Neeve Kearney, owner of an exclusive boutique; her father, a retired police commissioner; and the ghost of her murdered mother. Remembrances of Neeve's parents' tender early life together are interspersed with Neeve's falling in love with a reporter and her father's involvement with a murder witness. The devoted but strained relationship between father and daughter underscores such themes as filial independence, defining one's own life, and feelings of guilt.

Starting with *Loves Music, Loves to Dance* in 1991, Clark has completed and published one book a year

and sometimes two. Some critics took her industry as reflecting poorly on the quality of the works and charged her with selling out, placing more importance on the payoff than the product. If there is any deficiency in these novels, it is that they are too much in her style–the gripping suspense and quick pace, the genuine and strong female protagonist, the vivid settings all combined in a scenario springing from a contemporary social issue. Many reviewers accuse her of being predictable, which may be the case, but the public has made all but her first book best-sellers, with more than twenty made into movies. The popular attraction may be that she is not disappointing or depressing. Her heroines are strong, and while the books usually include a touch of romance and the almost inevitable 'Prince Charming,' the heroines rescue themselves.

In spite of writing specifically for a popular audience and keeping to her winning formula, Clark includes profound psychological and philosophical elements in her novels. Many, especially the earlier ones, are concerned with the heroine confronting an often-ominous past. Most of the works address parent-child relationships, whether thriving or corrupt, and the heroine's realization of her individual strength and courage in a kind of trial-by-fire approach. Clark's later novels, while more glamorous in setting than the earlier ones, deal with such penetrating issues as the nature of beauty, artificial insemination, the death penalty, and child abuse, while practically all of them at some level raise the issue of justice and portray the struggle between good and evil. Clark suffers no ambiguity in her characters; the readers are supposed to identify with the heroines just as they are meant to vilify the murderers. For example, as Pelzer states, Carl Harmon, the killer in *Where Are the Children?* "embodies every dark intent, every wicked impulse of which humans are capable . . . Carl's crime, pedophilia, and his pleasure in it prevent readers from developing any sympathy."

Loves Music, Loves to Dance looks at the dangers of using personal ads to find romance. Clark was inspired when she attended a lecture by an FBI agent when she was chairman of the International Crime Congress in 1987. He was talking about a serial killer who had enticed his victims through personal ads. *All Around the Town* (1992), an intricate story involving kidnapping and child sexual abuse, emanated from the request for an autograph. A friend of Clark's daughter Carol came to visit. An art therapist from the National Center for Treatment of Dissociative Disorders in Denver specializing in the treatment of multiple personality disorder, she wanted Clark to sign a book for one of her patients. When asked for the name, the therapist hesitated and wondered, "Now which one of her personalities reads your books?" *I'll Be Seeing You* (1993) revisits Clark's fascination with genetic manipulation and in-vitro fertilization. *Moonlight Becomes You* (1996) is set in a nursing home where a questionable death occurs. This passage highlights Clark's talent for evoking the details of a scene, the growing fear and futility:

> She remembered him bending over her, whispering, "Maggie, think of the bell ringers." After that, she remembered nothing.
>
> Still disoriented and terrified, she struggled to understand. Then suddenly it came flooding back. The bell ringers! Victorians had been so afraid of being buried alive that it became a tradition to tie a string to their fingers before interment. A string threaded through a hole in the casket, stretching to the surface of the burial plot. A string with a bell attached to it.
>
> For seven days a guard would patrol the grave and listen for the sound of the bell ringing, the signal that the interred wasn't dead after all. . . .
>
> But Maggie knew that no guard was listening for her. . . .
>
> Oh, God! She was buried alive!

Pretend You Don't See Her (1997) treats a woman in the federal witness protection program. *You Belong to Me* (1998) deals with a radio psychologist investigating women who have disappeared. Clark has also written several Yule-inspired mysteries: *Silent Night* (1995), a holiday mystery about a kidnapped boy; *All Through the Night* (1998), a parable-like story wherein Alvirah and Willy investigate the story of an abandoned baby; and *Deck the Halls* (2000), a collaborative effort between Clark and daughter Carol featuring Regan Reilly, Carol Higgins Clark's established sleuth, and the Meehans in a investigation of a kidnapping.

With *Let Me Call You Sweetheart* (1995), Clark again provides a novel that is more mystery than suspense, the action concerning the quest for the truth in the Sweetheart Murder case. Pelzer points out the use of an innovative device: "Clark limits her reader's exposure to the criminal's mind and thereby keeps his identity shrouded in mystery." Plastic surgery figures in the plot, as it does in *We'll Meet Again* (1999), a thriller speaking to HMOs and the medical industry. The idea of using plastic surgery as a theme emanated from a conversation with Clark's editor, Michael Korda. He raised the question "What if a plastic surgeon keeps giving the exact same face to a number of women?"

Dust jacket for Clark's 1989 collection of stories that mix suspense elements and the supernatural (Richland County Public Library)

Considered one of her best novels, *Remember Me* (1994) recalls *A Cry in the Night* in its Gothic setting, sinister ambience, and story growing out of a contemporary social issue—in this case, post-traumatic stress disorder and child death. Like some of her other earlier works, it is set in Cape Cod, but unlike those first novels, *Remember Me* has a supernatural element, set as it is in a haunted house and having an eighteenth-century story line that parallels the modern one. Clark tackles another fantastic topic in *Before I Say Good-Bye* (2000), threading psychic phenomena throughout the political suspense story.

In July 1996, Clark launched *Mary Higgins Clark Mystery Magazine*. It includes mystery and suspense stories by both well-known and first-time authors, for which Clark does the introduction, "In defense of suspense."

My Gal Sunday (1996) is a small departure from Clark's usual suspense story. Henry Britland Parker IV, a former U.S. president, and his young wife, Sun-

Dust jacket for Clark's 2003 novel, in which a company that produces cancer drugs is involved in financial improprieties (Richland County Public Library)

day, a congresswoman, combine to sleuth their way through several puzzles in this mystery reminiscent of the exploits of Nick and Nora Charles, with a dash of politics thrown in for good measure.

Clark told *Contemporary Authors* that "a good suspense novel can and should hold a mirror up to society and make a social comment." When asked by Claire White of writerswrite.com if she kept an 'idea book,' Clark responded, "Not really. But I do cut out clippings and just throw them into one drawer. . . . I never use the entire true story—it's just a springboard for my ideas." In addressing contemporary social issues, Clark explores the truth of the old adage "bad things happen to good people," but for all that, her books are optimistic: the reader knows the heroine and can count on a happy ending wherein the protagonist survives, the stronger for her turmoils, ready to face the future, often with a love interest in tow. Clark's heroine "is an ordinary woman driven by terrifying circumstances to do extraordinary things," notes Whissen.

Prior to her third marriage, to John Conheeney, retired CEO of Merrill-Lynch Futures, Inc., on 30 November 1996, Clark spent most of her time writing in Manhattan, even sharing an apartment with her daughter Carol Higgins Clark. Clark and her husband renovated a house in Spring Lake, New Jersey—the setting of *On the Street Where You Live* (2001), a modern-day murder mystery with historical imagery of Victorian life.

Throughout her life, Clark has kept a diary and based her memoir *Kitchen Privileges: A Memoir* (2002) on it. The title evokes the time when Clark's mother took in boarders and had a sign that read "Furnished rooms—Kitchen privileges." The memoir includes many of the anecdotes that have previously been published in various interviews, but it offers new insight into her early family and work life prior to her success as a novelist.

He Sees You When You're Sleeping (2000) is another collaboration by Clark and Carol Higgins Clark. Set around the holidays, this story is more of a parable with bittersweet undertones than the suspense fiction that Clark usually writes. This book was followed by *Daddy's Little Girl* (2002), which stands apart from her more recent fiction in the use of the first-person point of view, a new device for Clark, which she also employs in *The Second Time Around* (2003), a plot dealing with the world of Wall Street and involving a financial conspiracy within a company that makes cancer drugs. Again, Clark is holding a mirror up to society, for the plot of the former bears some similarities to the Martha Moxley murder while the latter is perhaps inspired by ImClone Systems. *Nighttime Is My Time* (2004) has a stalker who calls himself the Owl.

At seventy-five, Clark shows no signs of quitting. In the early 1980s, she joked to Roy Hoopes of *Modern Maturity* (August/September 1989) of a commentator calling her the next Christie, saying that "Agatha Christie wrote about 100 novels, so I only have ninety-five to go." She has passed on her passion for storytelling to her children as well. In addition to her daughter Carol, two of her other children, Marilyn, a criminal judge in New Jersey, and Warren, a lawyer, are considering taking up writing.

While many reviewers have criticized Clark's work for a lack of character development, calling her personalities flat and wooden, as well as accusing her of being too formulaic, the formula works. Perhaps the lack of character development is what allows the reader to become so absorbed in the plot, to insert herself or himself into the story. Clark focuses her eye for detail on setting the scene and describing the action. Her penchant for drawing controversial stories or widespread issues into her plots also speaks to the universal appeal of her works.

As Cassandra Jardine observed in the *Daily Telegraph* (London) of 19 June 2000, "Death stalked Mary Higgins Clark for the first 45 years of her life. One after another, those dearest to her died suddenly, sometimes in horrible circumstances. And then she turned the tables. For the past 25 years, she has stalked death." The tragic experiences of her life–the untimely deaths of her father, brothers, and husband–developed her fortitude and courage, attributes reflected in the strong, sympathetic women in her novels.

Interviews:
H. Edward Hunsburger, "Interview: Mary Higgins Clark," *Crime Digest* (September/October 1982): 17–20;

Marlys Millhiser, "Interview with Mary Higgins Clark," *Mystery Scene,* 40 (1993): 46, 71;

Betta Ferrendelli, *Mystery Scene* (January–February 1996): 51.

References:
Linda Claycomb Pelzer, *Mary Higgins Clark: A Critical Companion* (Westport, Conn.: Greenwood Press, 1995);

Jean Swanson and Dean James, "Clark, Mary Higgins," in *By a Woman's Hand: A Guide to Mystery Fiction by Women* (New York: Berkley, 1994), pp. 45–46;

Thomas Whissen, "Mary Higgins Clark," in *Great Women Mystery Writers: Classic to Contemporary,* edited by Kathleen Gregory Klein (Westport, Conn.: Greenwood Press, 1994), pp. 66–69.

Patricia Cornwell
(9 June 1956 –   )

Charles L. Etheridge Jr.
McMurry University

BOOKS: *A Time for Remembering: The Story of Ruth Bell Graham* (San Francisco: Harper & Row, 1983; London: Triangle, 1984); revised as *Ruth, a Portrait: The Story of Ruth Bell Graham* (New York: Doubleday, 1997; London: Hodder & Stoughton, 1998);

Postmortem (New York: Scribners, 1990; London: Macdonald, 1990);

Body of Evidence (New York: Scribners, 1991; London: Macdonald, 1991);

All That Remains (New York: Scribners, 1992; London: Little, Brown, 1992);

Cruel and Unusual (New York: Scribners, 1993; London: Little, Brown, 1993);

The Body Farm (New York: Scribners, 1994; London: Little, Brown, 1994);

From Potter's Field (New York: Scribners, 1995; London: Little, Brown, 1995);

Cause of Death (New York: Putnam, 1996; London: Little, Brown, 1996);

Hornet's Nest (New York: Putnam, 1996; London: Little, Brown, 1997);

Unnatural Exposure (New York: Putnam, 1997; London: Little, Brown, 1997);

Point of Origin (New York: Putnam, 1998; London: Little, Brown, 1998);

Southern Cross (New York: Putnam, 1998; London: Little, Brown, 1999);

Scarpetta's Winter Table (Charleston, S.C.: Wyrick, 1998);

Black Notice (New York: Putnam, 1999; London: Little, Brown, 1999);

Life's Little Fable, illustrated by Barbara Leonard Gibson (New York: Putnam, 1999);

The Last Precinct (New York: Putnam, 2000; London: Little, Brown, 2000);

Food to Die For: Secrets from Kay Scarpetta's Kitchen, by Cornwell and Marlene Brown (New York: Putnam, 2001; London: Little, Brown, 2001);

Isle of Dogs (New York: Putnam, 2001; London: Little, Brown, 2001);

Patricia D. Cornwell (from the dust jacket for Cruel and Unusual, *1993; Collection of George and Julie Anderson)*

Portrait of a Killer: Jack the Ripper–Case Closed (New York: Putnam, 2002; London: Little, Brown, 2002);

Blow Fly (New York: Putnam, 2003; London: Little, Brown, 2003);

Trace (New York: Putnam, 2004; London: Little, Brown, 2004).

Patricia Cornwell was one of the first authors to make laboratory work, collecting trace evidence at murder sites, and autopsies essential elements in solving mysteries. Long before popular movies and television series were weaving scientific evidence into compelling narratives, Cornwell's Kay Scarpetta novels drew on her professional and personal experience with forensic science and police work to create some of the most authentically detailed crime fiction ever written.

An intensely private person, Cornwell is reticent concerning her personal history. She was born as Patricia Daniels on 9 June 1956 in Miami, Florida. Her father, Sam Daniels, an attorney, and mother, Marilyn Zenner Daniels, divorced when Patricia was five. Two years later Marilyn moved with Patricia and her two brothers to Montreat, North Carolina. Patricia, then called Patsy, befriended an elderly woman named Virginia Bell because, as she writes in *Ruth, a Portrait: The Story of Ruth Bell Graham* (1997), she was homesick for her own grandmother. Virginia Bell was the mother of Ruth Bell Graham, wife of evangelist Billy Graham and a formidable evangelist in her own right. Initially, Daniels "wasn't aware of who [Billy Graham] was" and was more interested in Ruth's "beauty, her gentleness, and her spontaneous laughter."

Her friendship with Graham became one of the most important relationships in Daniels's life. When Daniels's mother began to suffer from clinical depression and grew unable to care for her family, Graham arranged for the children to be cared for by Manfred and Lenore Saunders, missionaries the Grahams knew.

After graduating from high school, Daniels enrolled briefly at King College, a Presbyterian institution in Bristol, Tennessee. Soon she transferred to Davidson College in Davidson, North Carolina, where she was awarded a tennis scholarship. An English major, Daniels worked on the school newspaper and yearbook, distinguishing herself both as a writer and a cartoonist. During her time at Davidson her acquaintance with Graham began to blossom into friendship. The older woman encouraged Daniels to develop as a writer.

After graduating in 1979, Daniels went to work at the *Charlotte Observer,* initially reporting on unglamorous stories such as local holiday events (her first *Observer* piece, published on 29 June 1979, was "Take Your Pick of 4th of July Celebrations in Charlotte"). Eventually, she began to work as an investigative reporter. Many of her experiences mirror those of Andy Brazil, the young reporter who is one of the protagonists of her novel *Hornet's Nest* (1996). Daniels distinguished herself with a series of articles on prostitution, which garnered her a 1980 investigative reporting award given by the North Carolina Press Association.

Later in 1980, Daniels married Charles Cornwell, one of her former college professors. Charles soon decided to go to divinity school, and in 1981 they moved to Richmond, Virginia, where Charles attended Union Theological Seminary.

Finding her career as a reporter interrupted by the move, Patricia Cornwell decided to try writing a biography of her friend Graham–an idea that Graham resisted strongly at first. Cornwell finally convinced Graham that she was being selfish by not allowing a biography to be written because, as she wrote in *Ruth, a Portrait* (addressing Graham) it would be "denying those who have never met you and never will" the chance to know her. Graham finally relented. Cornwell's first book, *A Time for Remembering,* was published to generally good reviews. The process of writing and publishing the book strained the friendship between author and subject, however, and the two did not speak for nearly eight years. (The story of how the biography came to be written is told in *Ruth, a Portrait: The Story of Ruth Bell Graham,* a 1997 revised edition of *A Time for Remembering,* which also includes personal reflections by Cornwell about her relationship with Graham.)

Drawing on her background as an award-winning crime reporter, Cornwell turned to detective fiction in 1984. In her first attempts, her protagonist was a traditional male police detective named Joe Constable, described by Mary Cantwell in a profile of Cornwell for *The New York Times* (14 July 1996) as "walking-wounded, poetic, . . . handsome." Cornwell wrote three books before writing *Postmortem* (1990), her first published book-length fiction. Recognizing the limitations of the Constable character and frustrated by her inability to get published, Cornwell took the advice of Sara Ann Fried, an editor at Mysterious Press, who suggested that the "male detective just wasn't believable" and that Cornwell should make Kay Scarpetta, a minor character in the Constable novels, the protagonist.

Through a friend, Cornwell met Marcella Fierro, a deputy chief medical examiner in Richmond. The meeting was a revelation; as Cornwell later told Joanne Tangorra in *Publishers Weekly,* "I was shocked by . . . how absolutely little I knew" about the duties of a medical examiner. The meeting between Cornwell and Fierro eventually led to Cornwell's employment in the office of the chief medical examiner, where the aspiring writer worked as a computer analyst and helped in the morgue. In *Portrait of a Killer: Jack the Ripper–Case Closed* (2002) Cornwell describes the experience:

I scribed for the forensic pathologists, weighed organs, wrote down trajectories and the size of wounds, inventoried the prescription drugs of suicide victims who would not take their antidepressants, helped undress fully rigorous people who rigidly resisted our removing their clothes, labeled test tubes, wiped up blood, and saw, touched, smelled, and even tasted death because the stench of it clings to the back of one's throat.

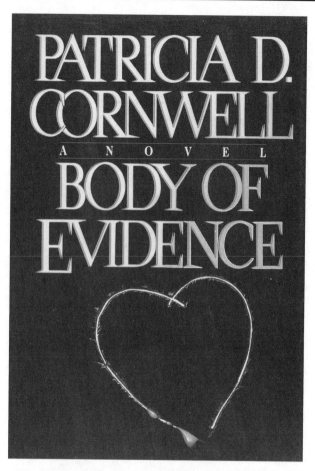

*Dust jacket for Cornwell's 1991 novel, the second to feature
Kay Scarpetta, the chief medical examiner for the
Commonwealth of Virginia (Collection of
George and Julie Anderson)*

The experience gave her a sense of purpose: "Murder is not a mystery, and it is my mission to fight it with my pen." Fierro, who was later named chief medical examiner for the Commonwealth of Virginia, provided the inspiration for Scarpetta, the protagonist of Cornwell's most successful novels. (Cornwell also used Fierro's middle name, Farinelli, as the last name of Scarpetta's niece, Lucy, a recurring character in the novels.)

In 1987, a series of stranglings of Richmond-area women, one of whom was a physician, caused Cornwell to muse about how Scarpetta would react: "I wanted to approach it from a psychological perspective–Scarpetta projecting the life of this murdered female physician and identifying with her. That's how *Postmortem* evolved." A chance meeting in Miami in 1988 with Edna Buchanan, a Pulitzer Prize–winning *Miami Herald* reporter, gave Cornwell a connection to literary agent Michael Congdon, who later agreed to represent her.

That same year, Charles Cornwell was offered the pastorate at a Texas church. Patricia Cornwell decided not to move, and the two separated amicably, divorcing in 1990.

Postmortem was rejected several times before it was accepted by Scribners in 1990. The publication of the novel not only significantly changed Cornwell's life, but also American detective fiction. It is the only novel to earn the Edgar award (presented by the Mystery Writers of America), the Creasey Award (given by the British Crime Writers Association), the Anthony Award (presented each year at the Bouchercon World Mystery Convention), the Macavity Award (presented by Mystery Readers International), and the French Prix du Roman d'Aventure in the same year.

Loosely based on the Richmond strangling murders, *Postmortem* introduces Kay Scarpetta, the forty-three-year-old chief medical examiner of the Commonwealth of Virginia. Set in Richmond, a city known at the time for its high homicide rate, the novel follows the investigation of the rapes and brutal murders of several women. The first three victims have little in common except their gender. In the opening sections of the book, Scarpetta is called to a murder scene and discovers a fourth victim, a doctor, Lori Peters. Processing the crime scene is especially difficult because the medical examiner identifies with the victim both as a woman and a doctor.

Perhaps the biggest battle Scarpetta must fight is with sexism. Pete Marino, the detective sergeant assigned to investigate the killings, is chauvinistic. Her supervisor, Health Commissioner Alvin Amburgey, blames Scarpetta for information leaks and faults her for difficulties involved in the investigation of the crimes. (In later novels, she becomes embroiled in disputes with congressmen, attorneys, and the governor of Virginia.) In each of these conflicts Scarpetta must endure doubts about her competence that seem to be based primarily on misogynistic assumptions that women cannot be effective members of the law enforcement community.

Several recurring characters are introduced. Marino initially distrusts Scarpetta but grows to respect her. Benton Wesley, a Federal Bureau of Investigation (FBI) profiler, assists Scarpetta in her investigations. Scarpetta's ten-year-old niece, Lucy Farinelli, is more of a daughter to her. Nels Vander, a minor but important character, is a fingerprint expert nonpareil. (Scarpetta's relationships with each of these characters evolve into helpful, beneficial ones later in the series.)

The morgue is where Scarpetta's expertise is fully apparent, however, and the realistic autopsy scenes make Cornwell's novels distinctive. As she examines wounds, weighs organs, and determines cause of death, the medical examiner creates a narrative that tells the story and offers clues as to how the victim died. As she prepares to autopsy Peters, Scarpetta muses: "The dead are defenseless, and the violation of this woman . . . had just begun. . . . A violent death is a public event, and it was this facet of my profession that so rudely grated against my sensibilities. But there was little I could do after the person became a case number, a piece of evidence passed from hand to hand. Privacy is destroyed as completely as life." A medical doctor, Scarpetta views murder victims as patients and her quest to find killers' identities as healing. She becomes the victims' advocate, their champion in death. As Cornwell told Paul Duncan in *Mystery Scene,* Scarpetta "is the healer. She heals these people."

By the late 1990s, strong female detectives had emerged in American crime fiction; most—for example, Marcia Muller's Sharon McCone, Kate Wilhelm's Barbara Holloway, Sara Paretsky's V. I. Warshawski, and Sue Grafton's Kinsey Millhone—are tough-woman private eyes in the hard-boiled tradition of Carroll John Daly, Dashiell Hammett, and Robert B. Parker. Scarpetta differs dramatically from these traditional women sleuths in several ways. The first and most obvious is that she is neither police nor private eye. Logic, reasoning, proof, evidence, and the scientific method are all central to her methods, which largely stem from her medical and legal backgrounds (she also attended law school).

Second, she is flawed. Traditional protagonists of detective fiction, or at least many created by men, tend to be static, code-driven heroes who rarely make mistakes and who do not change over the course of time. Parker's Spenser is a prime example; he has a Hemingwayesque code of behavior (often referred to as "the rules") that he follows in every situation. Scarpetta, in contrast, is consumed with doubt. She worries about relationships with her coworkers and with Lucy. She has a series of disastrous relationships; lasting love remains out of reach. Friends betray her. She is often wrong, and even occasionally makes a choice of questionable morality. She is equal to challenges but constantly in danger of being overcome by them. Most different is that she empathizes with her victims. Her powerful command of reason, mixed with her personal flaws, makes her a new kind of hero in criminal fiction.

In addition to the awards it garnered, *Postmortem* was a critical success. The reviewer for the *Washington Post Book World* (21 January 1990) wrote, "Cornwell makes looking through a microscope as exciting as a hot-pursuit chase." In the *Winston-Salem Journal* it was called "well-plotted, well-written" and "gripping." The reviewer for the *Times* (London) called it a "terrific first novel, full of suspense, in which even the scientific bits

grip." The novel was a best-seller, and Cornwell was soon a successful author with a multibook contract.

Body of Evidence, the second Scarpetta novel, was published in 1991. It revolves around the murder of novelist Beryl Madison. Readers are allowed to get to know Madison before her death, which makes the scene describing her autopsy difficult to read. As with the murder of Lori Peters in the previous novel, much of Scarpetta's ruminations revolve around identifying with the victim—in this case, wondering why Madison allowed the killer to enter her home. Meanwhile, Mark James, an old flame from Scarpetta's days at Georgetown Law School, comes back into her life. Scarpetta and Marino become convinced that the key to Madison's murder lies in the manuscript she was working on at the time of her death, now missing. Scarpetta finds herself being stalked by Madison's killer. The need to solve the case to save her own life becomes a recurring motif in the Scarpetta novels. Most reviews were positive, focusing on Cornwell's concerns about violence against women. The reviewer for the *San Francisco Chronicle* called it "one of the few slasher/stalker novels that is neither exploitive nor salacious." In the *Washington Post Book World* (17 February 1991) the novel was deemed "excellent" and "compelling"—a "complex, multi-layered novel with enough twists and turns for two books."

Negative criticism of the novel centered around Scarpetta's character. The reviewer for *The New York Times* complained that the "red-herring subplots" force Scarpetta "into situations that compromise both her professionalism and her common sense" (24 February 1999). Complaints about Scarpetta's character become a recurring theme in reviews. Some find her unsympathetic—"self-aggrandizing" is a term used more than once. Ann Sanders Cargill, writing in *Clues: A Journal of Detection* in 2001, is quite positive in her analysis of Scarpetta but notes that many women readers find her "too distant." Others question her plausibility—the fact that she has completed law school, medical school, and residencies, has worked for many years as a forensic pathologist, and has been in the job of chief medical examiner of Virginia for years and is still in her early forties strains credibility for some readers. In later novels, Scarpetta displays previously unmentioned skills such as scuba diving (she can even dive in icy water, something only expert divers do) and shooting like an expert marksman. The most common criticism, however, concerning the believability of Scarpetta's character relates to whether a medical examiner would be so intimately involved in murder investigations. Ellen Bleiler, writing in *Mystery and Suspense Writers: The Literature of Crime, Detection, and Espionage* (1998), asserts that Scarpetta's "adventures are so far-fetched as to bring

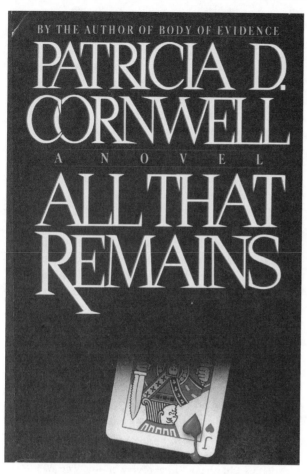

Dust jacket for Cornwell's 1992 novel, in which Scarpetta hunts a serial killer who preys on young couples (Collection of George and Julie Anderson)

the author dangerously close to self-parody." Others, such as Cargill, look at the same circumstances and suggest that it is Scarpetta's "willingness and ability to get close to death that is most memorable" and that she goes to extraordinary measures because of her "intense sense of responsibility" to the dead.

Negative comments neither hurt sales of Cornwell's books nor affected her production. Throughout the 1990s, she produced a novel a year. In *All That Remains* (1992) the murder victims are young couples. The cases are especially difficult for Scarpetta to solve because they are found months after their deaths, the bodies in varying states of decomposition, which makes the cause of death difficult to determine. Curiously, a playing card, the jack of hearts, is found with the bodies of the victims.

Cruel and Unusual (1993) may be the best novel in the Scarpetta series. Scarpetta is at her most sympathetic—Mark James has died in a terrorist attack at Victoria Station in London. The plot is complex yet plausible, and Scarpetta's duties are primarily in the

morgue. A man they assume to be Ronnie Joe Waddell, convicted of the capital murder of a Richmond-area television reporter long before Scarpetta was made chief medical examiner, is executed by electric chair. When his body comes into the morgue, an envelope is found in his back pants pocket; written on the outside is a request, apparently from Waddell, that the envelope be buried, unopened, with the remains. When the body is processed, Scarpetta finds blood and bruises that are unusual for an execution. Soon Nicholas Grueman, Waddell's attorney and a former law professor of Scarpetta's, is protesting that the execution of the man they suppose is Waddell was cruel and unusual.

Meanwhile, a series of apparently sexually motivated murders is occurring in Richmond. What appears to be Waddell's fingerprints are found at one of the crime scenes. When Scarpetta tries to match the crime-scene prints with the fingerprint card taken of Waddell at his autopsy, she finds that the card is gone, along with many important records concerning other cases. Computer records have been tampered with (something Lucy, now a teenager and a computer whiz, discovers). A lab assistant, who has been acting strangely, suddenly quits and is later found murdered. Scarpetta comes under suspicion for the murder and must turn to former adversary Grueman for legal help. Her competence and character is increasingly questioned, and the governor pressures her to resign.

Scarpetta convinces a grand jury of her innocence, and her legal troubles are resolved. Eventually, the former husband of one of the murder victims gives her a briefcase that had been in Waddell's possession, presumably taken from the victim's house on the night of her murder. The briefcase belongs to the governor, who had been having an affair with the deceased newswoman. Investigation, evidence, and speculation lead Scarpetta and Marino to conclude that the man executed actually was Waddell, and that the governor used his influence with the warden of the state penitentiary to release a criminal to secure the briefcase and to protect the governor from scandal. The released man's fingerprints were substituted for those of Waddell, and his actual identity is "erased" from law-enforcement databases. Unknown to the governor or the warden who participated in the scheme, the convict in question is a nascent serial killer. He is Temple Brooks Gault, who becomes a recurrent villain, Moriarty to Scarpetta's Sherlock Holmes. Gault escapes capture; his escape would not have been discovered had Grueman not protested about Waddell's death.

Reviews were overwhelmingly positive. *Newsweek* (5 July 1993) called the novel "taut, high tech and eerily credible," and said of the author "with each book, her scalpel is getting sharper." *Kirkus Reviews* called it Cornwell's "best book yet" and "a new high point in her meteoric rise." *The New York Times Book Review* proclaimed, "The elaborate plot shows expert engineering, and the lucid descriptions of forensic procedures that make her story so grimly fascinating are delivered in an authoritative voice." Some reviewers, however, were concerned that the plots of the Scarpetta novels had become repetitive.

The novel resonated with readers for several reasons. Scarpetta is equal to her task professionally but is also personally vulnerable. In addition to grieving for the loss of Mark, she experiences strains in her other relationships—with Lucy, Marino, her mother, and her sister—and Scarpetta seems, for the first time in the series, to deal with daily stresses that most of Cornwell's readers experience. In the early 1990s, the possibilities and pitfalls of the Internet and of computerized record keeping by law enforcement were novel subjects for a thriller; with his fingerprints altered and his electronic record wiped clean, the evil Gault is invisible to police and is free to cause mayhem.

Most importantly, in her testimony before the grand jury, Scarpetta provides a passionate explanation for why she has chosen her particular profession: "It is my intense concern for the living that makes me study the dead . . . What we learn from the dead is for the benefit of the living, and justice is for those left behind." This simple, elegant statement explains Scarpetta's lifework and is a concise justification for all of the novels. It sets the stage for the next two novels, both of which prominently feature Gault. In the closing pages of *Cruel and Unusual*, FBI profiler Benton Wesley invites Scarpetta to join a federal violent-crime task force, a development that allows Cornwell to create plots that take Scarpetta out of her lab in Richmond.

The Body Farm (1994) is the first novel in the series to show Scarpetta taking part in federal investigations. Lucy, now in college, is also interning at the FBI, helping to create CAIN, the Crime Artificial Intelligence Network. Lucy is also becoming romantically involved with a coworker, Carrie Grethen, who becomes a recurring character in the series.

Eleven-year-old Emily Steiner has been found murdered in the small North Carolina town of Black Mountain. Scarpetta, Marino, and Wesley are called in to investigate. Injuries to the body make Scarpetta suspect that the killing is the work of Gault. After another killing, she requests tests from the Decay Research Facility at the University of Tennessee (a research facility popularly known as "The Body Farm"). Soon, the local FBI agent in charge is found dead from an apparent suicide. Scarpetta and Wesley begin an affair, as do Marino and the first victim's mother. Cornwell learned to fly a helicopter while writing this novel, and helicop-

ters play an important role in many of her subsequent novels.

Reviewers were pleased with the greater character development in *The Body Farm*. *Kirkus Reviews* called the novel "as insidious a study of evil as Cornwell has turned in." *Publishers Weekly* noted that Cornwell casts "a wider, surer narrative net" in the novel than in her previous works and applauds her portrayal of Scarpetta as "increasingly complex." *Booklist* suggested that "This deserves a place in every mystery collection." *The New York Times Book Review* was more tepid, suggesting that the "novel nearly redeems itself" and noting that it "may not be the best novel in the Scarpetta series."

From Potter's Field (1995) completes the Temple Gault trilogy, taking Scarpetta to New York, where the murder of a homeless woman convinces Kay she is once again on the trail of Gault. Picking up on themes established first in *Cruel and Unusual*, the security of CAIN, the FBI criminal database, has been breached—probably with the help of Grethen, who has teamed up with Gault. Scarpetta follows Gault into the New York subway system, where a gun battle ensues. *Cause of Death* (1996) begins with a scuba-diving Scarpetta investigating the death of a reporter and winding up on the trail of cult-related killers, subsequently resulting in her being taken hostage by the cult, only to be rescued by Lucy, now an FBI agent.

Response to the Scarpetta novels during the mid 1990s was sometimes tepid or hostile, though often still positive. In a review of *The Body Farm* in the *Christian Science Monitor*, Gault was described as "irrational": "It is difficult to imagine someone so evil, so intelligent, and yet so reckless." The review goes on to call Scarpetta's qualms about her affair with Benton "not credible." The reviewer for *Publishers Weekly* likewise commented "there's something faintly unconvincing about Gault." The reviewer for *The New York Times Book Review* praised Cornwell's technical descriptions in *Cause of Death* but asserted: "I wouldn't give you two cents for the silly villains in this piece." *Publishers Weekly* lamented that "the hurried, almost slapdash pace of the climactic scenes is disappointing from so accomplished a writer."

In the same year that *Cause of Death* was published, Cornwell launched a second series with the novel *Hornet's Nest*. Written in the third person and set in Charlotte, North Carolina (where Cornwell began her career as a crime reporter), the novel follows the interconnected stories of Chief of Police Judy Hammer, Deputy Chief Virginia West, and Andy Brazil, a young reporter who serves as a volunteer police officer (a profession and an avocation also followed by Cornwell early in her career). The novel is an attempt at humor, something that was not clear to the readers expecting gritty realism in the style of the Scarpetta novels.

*Dust jacket for Cornwell's 1993 Scarpetta novel, which introduces the medical examiner's nemesis, serial killer Temple Gault
(Collection of George and Julie Anderson)*

A serial killer is prowling the streets of Charlotte, slaying men, whose bodies are found in their cars. West is asked to allow Brazil to ride along with her during her duties; the assumption is that the stories Brazil will write will provide good public relations for the police department. A great deal of time is spent on character analysis—Hammer had a bad marriage; West has a stormy relationship with a male friend; Brazil's dead father was a cop; and his dysfunctional mother has taken to drink. Like Cornwell herself, Brazil attended Davidson College on a tennis scholarship, and, like Scarpetta, he is athletic and attractive. Initially, West and Brazil do not get along, but they earn each other's mutual respect, and, when Brazil shoots the two men responsible for the killings, West promises to help the reporter. Along the way, West's cat discovers a money-laundering scheme.

The reviewer for *Publishers Weekly* wrote that the characters in this new series "are preternaturally competent automatons, obsessive and utterly devoid of self-

awareness" and that "there is nothing to believe in on these pages beyond Charlotte itself." The reviewer for *The New York Times Book Review* called the character development "exhaustive" and suggested that Brazil is "just plain creepy."

Unnatural Exposure (1997) introduces to the Scarpetta series the threat of an epidemic, as in the medical thrillers of Robin Cook. *Kirkus Reviews* suggested that the "best-selling formula—in-your-face forensics, computer terrorism, agency infighting, soap-opera romance, penny-dreadful villain" is "wearing a little thin." Interestingly, however, *Unnatural Exposure* has been written about in academic circles more than any other of the Scarpetta novels. In "Authority, Social Anxiety and the Body in Crime Fiction: Patricia Cornwell's *Unnatural Exposure*" (2000), Peter Messent notes that Cornwell's fiction "addresses the problems confronting a woman writer working with what is recognized as a 'masculine genre.'" He notes that "bodily violations and exposure" are key elements to the Scarpetta novels and argues that the connection between urban anxieties and female victimization" is one on which "the crime novel commonly relies."

Grethen, by now a full-fledged serial murderer in her own right, appears prominently in *Point of Origin* (1998), waging a letter-writing campaign to East Coast newspapers accusing Scarpetta, Lucy, and Benton of framing her. Lucy, now with the Bureau of Alcohol, Tobacco, and Firearms (ATF), left the FBI because of sexism and prejudice against her sexual orientation. Scarpetta investigates a series of murders that are being masked by arson. At the end of the novel Wesley is killed, a development that significantly affects Scarpetta in the subsequent novels.

By this point in the Scarpetta series, reviewers increasingly suggested that the books were losing quality but that loyal readers would continue to make them best-sellers. *Kirkus Reviews,* which had been positive early in Cornwell's career, sniped that "Cornwell's most compelling characters tend to be dead." The reviewer in *Library Journal* wrote that "the series seems to be losing momentum" and that "Scarpetta herself seems to be growing increasingly weary of it all." Perhaps the most damning condemnation of all came from the reviewer in *Entertainment Weekly,* who argued: "The meat-and-potatoes plot, unpolished language, and are-we-there-yet pacing of this new volume are what happens when an author's work suddenly has to keep time with the exigencies of book contracts and a publisher's burning need for a big summer title rather than with the less predictable dictates of her own imagination."

Southern Cross (1998), the second novel in the series about Hammer, West, and Brazil, transplants the trio to Richmond. A National Institute of Justice grant has brought Chief Hammer in to combat corruption in the Richmond Police Department and gang violence on the streets. Brazil is now a police officer. Again, there are multiple plotlines. One involves West overhearing a cell-phone conversation between Bubba Fluck and a friend. West mistakenly assumes Bubba is planning a murder when he is actually planning a hunting trip (ever the researcher, Cornwell even went on an all-night coon hunt). More-serious plotlines include the sabotage of police computers (a now-familiar Cornwell motif) and, most compellingly, a talented young artist trapped in a street gang. Brazil interacts briefly with Scarpetta.

Reviews were mixed but were much more positive than those for *Hornet's Nest.* The reviewer for *Library Journal* recommends the book, "especially for those who've appreciated Cornwell in the past but have grown weary of her Scarpetta books," and calls *Southern Cross* a "looser, funnier, more satirical novel where Cornwell allows the minor characters to upstage the

plot." The reviewer in *Publishers Weekly* objected that the "tone is all over the place, veering from faux-Wambaugh low-jinks to hard-edged suspense" and judged that Cornwell "lacks control over the third-person narration."

With both Gault and Grethen dispatched, *Black Notice* (1999) introduces a new recurring villain to the Scarpetta series. Jean-Baptiste Chandonne suffers from hypertrichosis, an extremely rare medical condition that gives its victims facial irregularities and a covering of fine hair, so that they resemble werewolves. Nicknamed "Loup-garou" (French for *werewolf*), Chandonne is the child of one of the scions of the Chandonne family, a powerful international crime syndicate. The novel is set immediately after the events of *Point of Origin; Black Notice* and *The Last Precinct* (2000) immediately follow chronologically, so that each of the three books seems like a volume of one continuous novel.

Scarpetta, still reeling from Wesley's death, has not yet begun the grieving process when badly decomposed remains are found in a cargo container on a ship just arrived from Belgium. The autopsy reveals an odd mark on the body, which turns out to be part of a tattoo identifying the victim as a member of the Chandonne crime syndicate. Meanwhile, the new chief of police in Richmond, Diane Bray, is masquerading as Scarpetta on the Internet and otherwise trying to sabotage the chief medical examiner. Women are being brutally beaten, raped, and then murdered, their faces beaten in by an unidentifiable blunt instrument. Trying to uncover the threads that link the various crimes she is investigating, Scarpetta travels to France, giving the series what George Beahm, in *The Unofficial Patricia Cornwell Companion* (2002), calls "a much needed change of locale." She meets and has a brief fling with Jay Talley, an ATF agent supposedly investigating the Chandonne family in France. Bray is murdered, and Chandonne comes for Scarpetta with a chipping hammer. She manages to disable him at the last moment with a bucket of chemicals, holding him off until Lucy comes and apprehends him. Talley offers to escort Scarpetta to the hospital.

Scarpetta's character is more fully developed in this novel; she spends much of her time alone, contemplating her grief and the loss of Wesley. *Publishers Weekly,* in its most positive review of a Cornwell novel since *The Body Farm,* suggested that the most compelling elements in the novel are "the deep-hearted responses of Kay, as real a hero as any thriller in fiction, to the evil . . . that threatens." *Kirkus Reviews* interpreted the events of the novel differently but also judged the characterization positively: "It's fascinating to watch Scarpetta and her supporting cast . . . become more and more themselves." The novel is "brilliantly paced,"

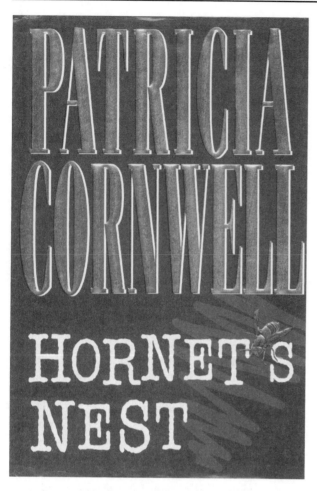

*Dust jacket for Cornwell's 1996 novel, the first in a series
featuring investigative reporter (later policeman) Andy
Brazil and Charlotte, N.C., police chief Judy Hammer
(Richland County Public Library)*

according to the *Kirkus* reviewer, although the plot "isn't believable for a minute."

The Last Precinct again emphasizes character as much as plot. It begins minutes after the events of *Black Notice* conclude. Although Chandonne was caught red-handed and police appeared on the scene minutes after his attempted murder, the case against him is disintegrating, primarily because the hammer he used to attack Scarpetta has disappeared. As in *Cruel and Unusual,* Scarpetta is again suspected of murder (this time for the death of Bray), and she finds that someone has been sabotaging her professionally. Lucy is on leave from the ATF, having been traumatized during a drug bust gone bad, and has joined a private detective agency called the Last Precinct.

Sexual assaults and murders similar to those in *Black Notice* continue after Chandonne has been apprehended, and an examination of the suspect reveals that his congenital disease has left him sexually impotent. It is thus literally impossible for him to have committed

the rapes of which he is suspected. DNA evidence from the crimes, however, is a near-perfect match to Chandonne's. Further investigation reveals he has a twin brother, nearly identical but lacking the genetic defect that gave Chandonne his physical abnormality. The mysterious twin turns out to be Talley, the ATF officer who was present at Chandonne's capture and who, presumably, stole the crucial chipping hammer. Talley has been working in tandem with his brother during the killings. He escapes; Chandonne remains in custody; and Scarpetta is again exonerated by a grand jury. She has become disillusioned, however, with the bureaucracy and the politics of law enforcement. It is strongly suggested that she will soon make changes in her life.

Reviews for *The Last Precinct* were mixed. The reviewer in *Publishers Weekly* condemned the "excessive emoting" in the novel, dismissing the plot as a "law-and-order soap opera" and the book itself as "overlong" and "sluggish." The reviewer for *Library Journal* suggested that "This may be Cornwell's least action-oriented" book.

Isle of Dogs (2001), another entry in the series about Hammer, West, and Brazil, continues to try to balance realistic crime drama with broad comedy. The governor of Virginia orders a statewide system of speed traps and begins a pilot program on Tangiers Island, noted for its hard-living, independent people. Brazil, now a helicopter pilot and state trooper, is charged with ferrying the governor's daughter about as well as flying out to the island to enforce the governor's speed trap—even though few of the residents on Tangiers have cars. In his spare time, Brazil is running a website under the name "Trooper Truth," answering citizens' questions concerning law enforcement. In the Trooper Truth vignettes Cornwell manages to include some fascinating snippets of Southern history. Tangiers secedes from Virginia, declares war, and takes the town dentist hostage. Cornwell's brush strokes are more broadly humorous, and several commentators have compared the novel to Carl Hiaasen's darkly comedic works. The governor's spoiled-brat daughter emerges as an unlikely hero.

Reviewers were more polarized in their responses to *Isle of Dogs* than to the first two books in the series. Many overseas reviewers were positive; the *New Zealand Herald* called it "a jolly, silly romp," and the *Advertiser,* an Australian periodical, called the novel "an irreverent portrait of politically driven law enforcement run amok, with a wry tale of life and turmoil behind the thin blue line." Many responses were extremely negative; Beahm writes that the "novel misses the mark by a country mile," and the reviewer for the *Scotsman* declared "Patricia Cornwell has become so famous that no editor would ever dream of rejecting her work" and suggested that the book would have never been published if it had been written by an unknown.

Criticism of this second series has centered on its labyrinthine plots and unsympathetic, unbelievable characters. A third objection is that the crime-solving and comedic elements together create a disjointed reading experience. At the same time, Cornwell seems to be growing more confident mixing comedy and mystery, focusing on Brazil, who is a departure for the author.

Cornwell took a three-year hiatus between *The Last Precinct* and the next Scarpetta novel, *Blow Fly,* which was published at the end of 2003. Whether motivated by the desire to take Scarpetta in a new direction or by a desire to try new things as a writer, she devised *Blow Fly* as a much different tome from the previous eleven works in the series. Unlike the others, the novel is not narrated by Scarpetta but is told in the third person. Rather than closely following Scarpetta, the action continually changes characters and locales, and many more characters' perspectives are presented; Scarpetta disappears from the book for long stretches.

The novel introduces a new investigator, Nic Robillard, a young crime-scene technician and single mother from the small town of Zachary, Louisiana. There has been a series of unsolved murders of women in the formerly peaceful town. Nic studies under Scarpetta, who is teaching a seminar at the National Forensic Institute. The older woman encourages the younger. Scarpetta has made significant changes in her life, having resigned her post in Virginia and moved to Miami, her hometown, where she is now working as a consultant.

Several story lines are interwoven. Still at large, Talley has retreated to the bayous and backwaters of rural Louisiana, where he continues to kill women for pleasure. Meanwhile, Lucy travels to Eastern Europe to assassinate Rocco Caggiono, Pete Marino's son, who has become a lawyer for the Chandonne crime family, because Rocco is planning on killing Marino.

Marino travels to meet with a member of the Witness Protection Program—who turns out to be Benton Wesley. Supposedly, Wesley was not actually killed by Carrie Grethen in *Point of Origin*. Instead, his efforts against the Chandonne crime syndicate had created such personal danger for him that it was necessary for him to fake his own death to protect himself and Scarpetta. Chandonne, now convicted and on death row, wants Scarpetta to agree to administer the lethal injection to him. In exchange, he will give her enough information to significantly damage the Chandonne syndicate. Ultimately, he escapes.

The novel is unsuccessful for several reasons. Although one can understand Cornwell's desire to try new things, what made the series most distinct and captivating is Scarpetta's proficiency in forensic medicine. The methodological and scientific intricacies of her novels captured the imagination and engrossed the reader. These qualities are absent from *Blow Fly*. Several important characters act implausibly—Lucy, now partnered with a man who once tried to rape her (they are friends now), has become a vigilante. Marino not only forgives Lucy for the murder of his son, but tells her he is glad that she did it. The plot resolution happens almost entirely offstage, and the independent, strong, admirable Scarpetta must rely upon a man to save her—perhaps the most unsettling character violation of them all.

The reviewer for the *Houston Chronicle* declared that *Blow Fly* "feels as if it were imploding, a book that fans will want to read for the sheer voyeuristic quality of watching the characters they know so well go beyond their limits." Joan Smith in the *Times* (London, 19 October 2003) not only panned *Blow Fly* but used it to criticize Cornwell's success:

> What makes this phenomenon so puzzling is that she is an amateurish writer, who has to rely on ever more baroque plots to keep the Scarpetta series going. The plot of Blow Fly is nearly incomprehensible and displays the worst features of the earlier novels in spades; Scarpetta inhabits a paranoid universe, where decent people are menaced by sickos, psychos and sadists, to the point where it is permissible for the good guys to take the law into their own hands.

In the Scarpetta novel *Trace* (2004), Cornwell returns to Richmond, the scene of her most successful stories. She also reincorporates some of the more successful techniques that she abandoned in *Blow Fly,* specifically Scarpetta's first-person narration of some sections of the novel and realistic, detailed scenes of her in the morgue lab, investigating causes of death. Scarpetta is called back to Virginia by her successor as chief medical examiner, Joel Marcus, to consult on the unexplained, sudden death of Gilly Paulson, an apparently healthy fourteen-year-old girl. After a five-year absence, she returns to Richmond, Marino in tow.

Scarpetta arrives to find her old building undergoing demolition and the new facility, which she had painstakingly designed while she was still chief, poorly run. The few staff who remain from her tenure are furtive and defensive, and Marcus proves hostile to Scarpetta and uninvolved in the day-to-day management of the Office of the Medical Examiner.

Two other plotlines unfold. Benton Wesley cares for an unstable former actress named Henri, who has been assaulted. Were it not for information provided by Lucy, Benton might have dismissed the erratic Henri's story of being attacked as a bid for attention. His biggest obstacle to investigating is Henri herself, whose personality has become more volatile since the assault. She repeatedly uses her long red hair and athletic body to tempt Wesley into sexual liaisons, but he is aware of her manipulations and does not respond. The other plotline follows Edgar Allan Pogue, named after Gothic writer and former Richmond resident Edgar Allan Poe. Pogue travels with the cremated remains of elderly women he has killed and is obsessed with his mother, whose image he draws on the walls of his apartment.

Political machinations abound–Marcus did not want Scarpetta involved but only called upon her at the insistence of a superior, and Marino discovers a mysterious FBI connection to the case. The three seemingly unrelated story lines are connected, with the deranged Pogue proving to be both the perpetrator of the assault on Henri and the murderer of Gilly.

Trace is neither the best nor the worst novel in the Scarpetta series. Cornwell still seems unsure what to do with Scarpetta–her role as a consultant does not necessarily lend itself to gripping crime fiction. Long-time devotees of the series have found the return to Richmond rewarding, however. The presence of multiple story lines is sometimes distracting: although it is interesting to see secondary characters developed, the most effective sections of the book are those from Scarpetta's point of view. *Trace* is a much stronger work than *Blow Fly,* however, and in it, Cornwell may have found a way to re-create some of the dramatic tension that was lost when Scarpetta resigned from her duties as a public official.

In addition to her series novels, Cornwell has written a children's book, *Life's Little Fable* (1999); a cookbook, *Food to Die For: Secrets from Kay Scarpetta's Kitchen* (2001), with Marlene Brown; and *Portrait of a Killer: Jack the Ripper–Case Closed. Portrait of a Killer* is the most personally revealing of Cornwell's work. In it she writes: "I fight crime with my pen . . . And if I benefit from writing crime novels, it's important to invest some time and resources to helping catch evil people. It's a way of giving back." She also describes, in vivid detail, her personal experiences working with the Medical Examiner's Office in Virginia.

Using several million dollars of her own money, Cornwell has compiled DNA and other forensic evidence as well as psychological analysis to argue that Jack the Ripper was, in fact, Walter Sickert, a British painter and actor. Like the fictional Chandonne, Sickert suffered from a sexual dysfunction that fueled his rage against women. The work is also noteworthy in its carefully researched, thorough examination of the plight of poor women during the Victorian era. Cornwell argues

that her case against Sickert is so compelling that a deputy assistant commissioner from Scotland Yard told her that, were Sickert alive, "We'd be happy to put the case before the crown prosecutor."

Although reviewers express skepticism that a writer could have solved murders that occurred more than a century earlier, many found the book fascinating. The reviewer for *Booklist* wrote that Cornwell "adeptly sets the whole horrifying story within the tenor of life in Victorian England, and the result is a well-constructed, endlessly fascinating account that is sure not only to arouse debate but also to generate considerable demand." *Publishers Weekly* proclaimed that the book "turns potentially dry material into an enthralling exploration." Cornwell's case failed to convince many, though. A reviewer for the *Buffalo News* stated that, if he were on the jury, "Sickert would walk," and the *Portland Oregonian* contended that "Cornwell hasn't closed the case and caught Jack the Ripper" but conceded that "she has written an interesting true-crime book."

Patricia Cornwell's Scarpetta series brought science into the mainstream of crime fiction. She continues to write fast-paced, compelling fiction; while some reviewers complain, her books are still best-sellers. She is growing in stature as a comedy writer, and she has taken the Scarpetta series in a new direction. Her fiction will likely continue to be commercially successful; whether she will be artistically successful in her new ventures remains to be seen.

References:

George Beahm, *The Unofficial Patricia Cornwell Companion* (New York: St. Martin's Minotaur, 2002);

Ellen Bleiler, "Patricia Cornwell," in *Mystery and Suspense Writers: The Literature of Crime, Detection, and Espionage,* volume 1, edited by Robin W. Winks and Maureen Corrigan (New York: Scribner, 1998), pp. 243–250;

Mary Cantwell, "How to Make a Corpse Talk," *New York Times,* 14 July 1996;

Ann Sanders Cargill, "Chief Medical Examiner Kay Scarpetta," *Clues: A Journal of Detection,* 22 (2001): 35–48;

Paul Duncan, "Patricia Cornwell: Verbal Evidence," *Mystery Scene,* 57: 45–49;

Peter Messent, "Authority, Social Anxiety and the Body in Crime Fiction: Patricia Cornwell's *Unnatural Exposure,*" in *The Art of Detective Fiction,* edited by Warren Cherniak, Martin Swales, and Robert Vilain (Basingstoke, U.K.: Macmillan / New York: St. Martin's Press, 2000), pp. 124–137.

Amanda Cross
(Carolyn G. Heilbrun)
(13 January 1926 – 9 October 2003)

Charles L. Etheridge Jr.
McMurry University

BOOKS: *The Garnett Family,* as Carolyn G. Heilbrun (New York: Macmillan, 1961; London: Allen & Unwin, 1961);

In the Last Analysis (New York: Macmillan, 1964; London: Gollancz, 1964);

The James Joyce Murder (New York: Macmillan, 1967; London: Gollancz, 1967);

Christopher Isherwood, as Heilbrun (New York & London: Columbia University Press, 1970);

Poetic Justice (New York: Knopf, 1970; London: Gollancz, 1970);

The Theban Mysteries (New York: Knopf, 1971; London: Gollancz, 1972);

Toward a Recognition of Androgyny: Aspects of Male and Female in Literature, as Heilbrun (New York: Knopf, 1973); republished as *Towards Androgyny* (London: Gollancz, 1973); republished as *Toward a Recognition of Androgyny: A Search into Myth and Literature to Trace Manifestations of Androgyny and to Assess Their Implications for Today* (New York & London: Norton, 1993);

The Question of Max (New York: Knopf, 1976; London: Gollancz, 1976);

Reinventing Womanhood, as Heilbrun (New York & London: Norton, 1979);

Death in a Tenured Position (New York: Dutton, 1981); republished as *A Death in the Faculty* (London: Gollancz, 1981);

Sweet Death, Kind Death (New York: Dutton, 1984; London: Gollancz, 1984);

No Word from Winifred (New York: Dutton, 1986; London: Virago, 1987);

Writing a Woman's Life, as Heilbrun (New York: Norton, 1988);

A Trap for Fools (New York: Dutton, 1989; London: Virago, 1990);

Hamlet's Mother and Other Women, as Heilbrun (New York: Columbia University Press, 1990; London: Women's Press, 1991);

Amanda Cross (photograph © Katy Raddatz; from the dust jacket for The Education of a Woman: The Life of Gloria Steinem, *1995; Richland County Public Library)*

The Players Come Again (New York: Random House, 1990; London: Virago, 1990);

The Education of a Woman: The Life of Gloria Steinem, as Heilbrun (New York: Dial, 1995; London: Virago, 1996);

An Imperfect Spy (New York: Ballantine, 1995; London: Virago, 1995);

Amanda Cross: The Collected Stories (New York: Ballantine, 1997);

The Last Gift of Time: Life beyond Sixty (New York: Dial, 1997);

The Puzzled Heart (New York: Ballantine, 1998);

Women's Lives: The View from the Threshold, as Heilbrun (Buffalo: University of Toronto Press, 1999; London & Toronto: University of Toronto Press, 1999);

Honest Doubt (New York: Ballantine, 2000);

The Edge of Doom (New York: Ballantine, 2002);

When Men Were the Only Models We Had: My Teachers Barzun, Fadiman, and Trilling, as Heilbrun (Philadelphia: University of Pennsylvania, 2002).

OTHER: Lady Ottoline Violet Anne Cavendish-Bentinck Morrell, *Lady Ottoline's Album: Snapshots and Portraits of Her Famous Contemporaries (and of Herself),* edited by Heilbrun (New York: Knopf, 1976; London: Joseph, 1976);

The Representation of Women in Fiction, edited by Heilbrun and Margaret R. Higgonet (Baltimore & London: Johns Hopkins University Press, 1983);

But Enough about Me: Why We Read Other People's Lives, edited by Heilbrun and Nancy K. Miller (New York: Columbia University Press, 2002).

Probably America's most popular writer of academic mysteries, Amanda Cross was herself a mystery for many years. Only after she achieved tenure in 1972 in the Department of English and Comparative Literature at Columbia University did the noted feminist critic Carolyn G. Heilbrun reveal that she and Amanda Cross were one and the same.

Carolyn Gold was born on 13 January 1926 in East Orange, New Jersey. Her father, Archibald Gold, had emigrated from Russia as a boy and later achieved success as an accountant; her mother, Estelle Roemer, was born in Manhattan to Austrian immigrants. Although both her parents were of Jewish heritage, both rejected their Jewish backgrounds, as did their only daughter, although, as Julia B. Boken says, Heilbrun later came to realize that the veiled anti-Semitism she experienced in her younger years contributed to the development of her feminist thinking.

The family moved to Manhattan in 1932, where Carolyn attended various private schools. In an interview with a Wellesley College on-line publication, she said her favorite childhood activities included going "roller skating for hours and devouring biographies." Stories of people's lives became a lifelong interest of hers. During her childhood, most of the biographies written were about men; she commented on the dearth of women's biographies in *Writing a Woman's Life* (1988).

Gold enrolled at Wellesley College in 1944 and graduated Phi Beta Kappa in 1947, having married James Heilbrun in 1945 (on the evening before he was shipped overseas during World War II). According to

Boken, Heilbrun kept the fact of her early marriage secret for years, "Not wanting to be seen as a role model for young women considering the same." Heilbrun was, J. M. Purcell says, "married at 19 (1945) and earned all her degrees from B.A. to doctorate while raising three kids." After briefly working in the communications industry, Heilbrun enrolled at Columbia University for graduate study in English literature, receiving her M.A. in 1951 and her Ph.D. in 1959. She taught a year at Brooklyn College, then moved to Columbia, where she spent more than thirty years, retiring in 1993.

Her career at Columbia was long and distinguished. She was a Guggenheim fellow (1965–1966), served as president of the Modern Language Association (1984), and was invited to teach at several universities, including Yale (1974), the University of California at Santa Cruz (1979), Princeton (1981), and Yale Law School (1989). She served on many advisory boards, including those of the Columbia University Press and *Twentieth Century Literature,* was a senior fellow for the National Endowment for the Humanities, and ended her career as Avalon Professor in the Humanities at Columbia. During this full professional career, she wrote more than twenty books and edited two more.

These brief biographical facts reflect the difficulty in conveying the major events experienced by anyone living the academic life. Were one to look merely at the outer events of Heilbrun's life, one might say, "She was well educated and taught a long time. Now she's retired." However, the period during which she began her career and the cultural events of her time were critical to her development both as a mystery writer and as an original thinker in the field of literary studies.

When Heilbrun began teaching at Columbia, the undergraduate school was still all male (and remained so until 1983), and Heilbrun was among the first women professors hired. The move to "integrate" the faculty was not uniformly well received; according to Anne Matthews, Heilbrun's major graduate professor, Lionel Trilling, supposedly said, "This [hiring women] is not at all a good idea. . . . Older men should teach younger men and younger men should then go out and encounter women as the Other." Heilbrun continued to be a trailblazer throughout her career, becoming the first woman to achieve tenure at Columbia. Much of her earlier professional work was "traditional scholarship"; her first book, *The Garnett Family* (1961), was a study of a family who deeply influenced nineteenth-century British literature, and her second, *Christopher Isherwood* (1970), was a standard bio-critical study of that author's work. Still, a challenge to traditional ways of looking at literature emerged early, as evidenced by her 1957 piece "The Character of Hamlet's Mother," published in the *Shakespeare Quarterly* and collected in *Hamlet's Mother and Other Women* (1990).

Heilbrun's biggest "rebellion," however, may have been her other, secret career as a mystery writer. At the time Heilbrun began that career, assistant professors at Columbia, especially assistant professors who aspired to earn tenure, did not engage in such frivolities as novel writing. Not only did she choose to write novels, she found doing so personally necessary, although in order to protect her identity (and her position at Columbia), she had to create a new identity to write under—Amanda Cross.

The invention of "Amanda Cross" is as significant to an understanding of these novels as is the invention of their protagonist, Kate Fansler. According to Carmen Birkle, Heilbrun creates "a new space for herself by moving between the fictional self in the text and the real self in academia." The act of creating both a pseudonymous identity to write under (Amanda Cross) and a fictional alter ago (Kate Fansler) is a form of autobiographical writing called "autogynography," which grows out of women's "need to inscribe themselves in the text, to give voice to their own experiences and to the tensions within a male-dominated world on the one hand, and the danger of too much public exposure on the other hand."

Heilbrun came to academe at a time when few women were tenure-track professors. Initially, her writing and scholarship were in the traditional mode of New Criticism that, according to Birkle, dominated academe at the time; she did not become an active feminist critic until later. The act of writing detective fiction became a way for her to explore, if not resolve, the tensions she felt as a woman professor and a woman scholar in a male-dominated institution (the university) whose prevailing attitude toward literature held that great works are "universal" and that issues of gender were irrelevant. In *Writing a Woman's Life,* Heilbrun wrote, "I must have wanted . . . to create a space for myself."

The idea of "creating a space" is a strong echo of Virginia Woolf's familiar feminist concept developed in *A Room of One's Own* (1929), an idea central to nearly all of the Kate Fansler mysteries. Woolf contrasts "the safety and prosperity of one sex"—that is, men—with "the poverty and tradition and insecurity of the other and of the effect of tradition and of the lack of tradition upon the mind of a writer" to show how women need "spaces" to reenvision the world around them. Heilbrun and others adapted this concept of "a room of one's own" to include the idea of a "psychic space"; in the case of Heilbrun herself, the action of writing as Amanda Cross provided the necessary room.

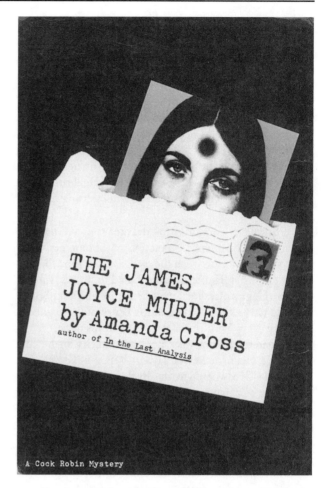

Dust jacket for Cross's 1967 novel, the second to feature her amateur detective, literature professor Kate Fansler (Richland County Public Library)

The traditional elements of detective fiction, which apparently limit a writer's choices, gave her a freedom not available in other kinds of writing, as she points out in *Hamlet's Mother:* ". . . with the momentum of a mystery and the trajectory of a good story with a solution, the author is left free to dabble in a little profound revolutionary thought. In [her] opinion, detective fiction, often called formula fiction, has almost alone and with astonishing success challenged the oldest formulas of all." Birkle draws an analogy between Heilbrun's writing of detective fiction and the manner in which she chose to negotiate the labyrinth of academe, saying that the author "accepted the given conventions in the same way in which she had to accept the traditional rules of the society she lived in, but decided to act freely within these boundaries."

Readers should not, however, read each novel as a roman à clef, assuming that Kate Fansler is Carolyn Heilbrun and that the New York City university that employs Kate is Columbia. Purcell cautions that "it would be preferable terminology to say that Heilbrun invented Cross as Cross invented Kate Fansler." According to Birkle, the pseudonym "Amanda Cross is allowed to present a Kate Fansler who possesses all the possibilities Carolyn Heilbrun does not have." In *Writing a Woman's Life,* Heilbrun says of Kate: "I created a fantasy. Without children, unmarried, unconstrained by the opinions of others, rich and beautiful, the newly created Kate Fansler now appears to be a figure out of never-never land. . . . I wanted to give her everything and see what she could do with it." The single, independently wealthy Kate was a contrast to Heilbrun's own experience of earning her degrees while raising her children.

Scholars continue to debate the relationship between Heilbrun and Amanda Cross. Some deny any deep significance between the two, as does Purcell, who says that "what 'Heilbrun' contributed to 'Cross' was . . . the working professional experience to make authoritative the Cross continuation of the genre of the academic mystery story" and little else. Others disagree, saying she hoped to show women new possibilities for life and for living. Heilbrun herself says in *Writing a Woman's Life,* "Amanda Cross could write, in the popular, unimportant form of detective fiction, the destiny she hoped for women, if not exactly, any longer, for herself: the alternate life she wished to inscribe upon the female imagination." Birkle concludes that "Based on the new psychic and social spaces created by Heilbrun for her fictional character Kate Fansler, Heilbrun and the female reader can create their own new spaces."

The Kate who emerges throughout the series is likable, an odd mix of the traditional and the revolutionary. She is from an old, wealthy family, and her wealth allows her freedom that other professors do not have as her investigations "usually end up costing her money." Despite her work to advance women's causes, she is not completely politically correct—she drinks and smokes, and she is not exactly egalitarian (she often decries the decline of manners, and is distressed when people overuse first names). She does not claim to like children, although she has close relationships with a few nieces and nephews. She refuses to cook. According to Trisha Yarbrough, readers also admire "her unfailing ability to provide an appropriate quote for any occasion."

Heilbrun's first Amanda Cross mystery, *In the Last Analysis* (1964), introduces the character Kate Fansler, a young, single professor of literature at an unnamed university that resembles Columbia. Chapter 1 begins with an allusion to T. S. Eliot's *Waste Land* (1922), followed by Kate's wry musings on American academic life. The opening establishes elements that recur in the Amanda Cross series—the use of relevant literary allusion (for, after all, Kate is an English profes-

sor) and the satiric look inside academe. By the end of the first page, Kate has already engaged in a witty banter with a fellow professor (use of witty dialogue is another oft-commented-upon feature of the novels) and, after the exchange has ended, is "startled" that the male colleague, who has "a strong distaste for all female writers since Jane Austen," would or could quote from a poem by Edna St. Vincent Millay. Amanda Cross is moving in advance of Carolyn Heilbrun, stating in the early 1960s a feminist concern about the lack of regard for women writers that did not become an open part of the debate in literary studies for another decade.

In the Last Analysis, which was nominated for an Edgar by the Mystery Writers of America, illustrates the enduring appeal of the Amanda Cross series. The comments on the tenor of the times, as well as the literary allusions, grow organically out of the story and the situations in which characters find themselves. The early novels are interesting as period pieces showing early moments in the feminist movement; however, they are also mystery tales of enduring merit. Critics often compare these novels to the works of Dorothy L. Sayers, another mystery novelist who was also a noted scholar, whose influence Heilbrun openly acknowledges. In *Writing a Woman's Life,* Heilbrun says of Sayers, "It is impossible to overestimate the importance of her detective novels in my life . . . and through her wit, her intelligence, her portrayal of a female community and a moral universe, I caught sight of a possible life."

Kate in *In the Last Analysis* comes to the aid of psychiatrist friend Emanuel Bauer, whose young patient Janet Harrison (a student of Kate's) has been found murdered in Bauer's office. Kate enlists the help of assistant district attorney friend Reed Amhearst, who appears in all the novels. At one point, Kate is accused of being the murderer, although the plot later reveals that Janet was killed by a man who has assumed the identity of Dr. Michael Barrister. The pretender has an office across the hall from Emanuel, and Janet, who had known and once been in love with the real Michael Barrister, recognizes the killer as an imposter.

Psychoanalysis and the work of Sigmund Freud both figure prominently in the novel. Kate refers to "freudful errors—all those nonsensical conclusions leaped to by people with no reticence and less mind," and then goes on to explain that "It isn't Freud himself one quarrels with. . . . It's the dissemination of his ideas in the modern world." As she later tells police, "A youngster today, moving in intellectual circles, will, in trouble, turn to psychiatry." An uneasy respect—both for Freud and for psychiatry—appears in several novels.

As evidenced by its nomination for an Edgar, the novel was well reviewed. *Library Journal* wrote that it was "pure entertainment, a delightful exploration of the tribal customs of the couch and of the academy." Some reviewers were far less positive; *Book Week* found the narrative style of the novel "lecture-talky, at times pompous and patronizing." Kate's character and Cross's wit are both highly praised. Later critical responses are more evenhanded. Many, like Steven R. Carter, suggest that "the major source of interest is unquestionably the puzzle" rather than character development or other issues, and the consensus seems to be that it "is minor; it succeeds in its aims, but its aims are limited." Some object that the ending of the novel is contrived; Purcell calls the plot "simplistic," objecting to the plot device of a nightmare to cast suspicion on the faux Barrister. Feminist critics, such as Mary Rose Sullivan, object that Reed is the one who provides the critical clue and in effect solves the case, resulting in an "odd displacement" of Kate "as the protagonist."

The next novel, *The James Joyce Murder* (1967), according to Yarbrough, is another "routine whodunit," which deals with a homicidal academic who kills because he does not want others to know he also writes popular fiction; the only connection to James Joyce is that Kate is editing an edition of Joyce's letters at the time of the killing. The next two mysteries, *Poetic Justice* (1970) and *The Theban Mysteries* (1971), do not actually involve murders, although they include deaths. *Poetic Justice* is of interest because the attitudes that Frederick Clemance expresses are remarkably similar to Lionel Trilling's. As the 1960s go on, Kate becomes more outspoken about relevant issues of the time, from student uprisings on campus to the hiring of women faculty. For example, although Miss Tyringham, headmistress of the Theban School, "took no political stands," she showed "that change was possible" by hiring "young married women" and recruiting African American students "before Martin Luther King."

The Theban Mysteries is notable because a major change has taken place in Kate's life: she has married Reed, despite repeated vows during the first three Amanda Cross novels to remain single—in *Poetic Justice,* Kate says "marriage for a woman spoils the two things that make life glorious: learning and friendship." Some feminists found Kate's marriage a betrayal of her ideals. But others, such as Yarbrough, suggest that the Kate Fansler–Reed Amhearst union proves that "marriage" can be an "egalitarian partnership" and "not a refuge and a trap," concluding that "marriage has not been detrimental to Kate's feminism." When Miss Tyringham refers to Kate as Mrs. Amhearst, Kate replies, "I hope you don't mind, but professionally, and you do want a professional I take it, I use the name Kate Fansler." Rather than express offense or outrage, Miss Tyringham says only, "Good for you." This exchange appeared in 1971, a year before *Ms.* magazine

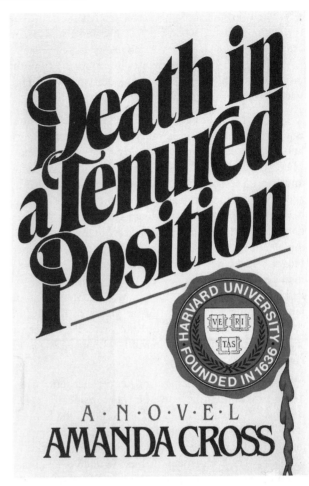

Dust jacket for Cross's 1981 novel, in which Fansler investigates the death of the first tenured woman English professor at Harvard (Richland County Public Library)

first appeared and helped introduce the idea of a marriage-neutral term for women (combining "Mrs." and "Miss") to a national audience. And in keeping with her interest in both feminism and biography, Heilbrun in 1995 published *The Education of a Woman: The Life of Gloria Steinem,* about the founder of *Ms.* Interestingly, an important element in *The Theban Mysteries* is Sophocles' *Antigone* (circa fifth century B.C.), a work of classic literature in which a strong woman opposes the existing social order.

Many consider Cross's 1981 work, *Death in a Tenured Position,* to be the best of the Kate Fansler novels; it is certainly her best known, and it won the 1981 Nero Wolfe Award for mystery fiction. The most overtly political of the Cross novels, Boken has called it "a clear frontal attack, a veritable laser beam of satire and anger, directed at Harvard University's idea of itself as the best university in the United States." The victim, Janet Mandelbaum, is the first woman to be granted tenure in the English department at Harvard University. She is an unsympathetic character who, according to Jeanne Addison Roberts, "has rejected feminine sisterhood because she believes she has risen to her status . . . entirely through her own efforts." At the time the novel was published, the English department at Harvard had never given a woman professor tenure.

What first brings Kate onto the Harvard campus is a cruel prank played on Janet, who has been drugged and left in a bathroom on the Harvard campus. Luellen May, a Cambridge woman, asks Kate to investigate, and she agrees, arranging to spend time at Harvard by accepting a research fellowship. Janet and Kate had been contemporaries in graduate school, although they have not kept in touch. Kate solves the mystery of the initial attack, tracing it to a graduate student named Howard Falkland. When Janet is later found dead in a men's room, poisoned by cyanide, suspicion falls on Falkland and later on Milton "Moon" Mandelbaum, Janet's former husband, a former flame of Kate's (the romance between Moon and Kate is fondly and comically remembered by Kate in the 1998 novel *The Puzzled Heart*).

Time and Kate's inquiries reveal that Janet Mandelbaum was hired because she was considered "safe"; she was not a feminist, nor did she support the feminist agenda. Cross uses the novel to examine the biases and minefields facing a woman in academe, from Howard Falkland's cross statement "I think women are happier when they're looking up to some man and having kids, which is what nature intended them for" to the more hypocritical Clarkville, who says that prejudice against women is "just in the nature of things" and sees no irony in his own discriminatory stance even though he is homosexual, a member of another group often the target of the reactionary opinions he himself espouses.

Kate reconstructs Janet's death as a biographer and a literary scholar would, and the novel is probably the most vivid demonstration in the Cross canon that the skills of the detective and the skills of the scholar are complementary. The study of sonnets and soliloquies has prepared Kate to sleuth. The dead professor had been reading George Herbert's poetry as well as a biography of Eleanor Marx, Karl Marx's daughter. The literary clues move the detective toward a solution of the mystery. One of the Herbert poems Janet had been reading was "Hope"; Kate concludes that Janet began to realize that her hope of acceptance from the male faculty in her department would go unfulfilled. The biography of Eleanor Marx is more instructive; she was well known as a translator of Gustave Flaubert's *Madame Bovary* (1857), a woman driven to suicide, and Marx herself was also a suicide, poisoning herself with cyanide.

In her quest to reconstruct the life of Janet Mandelbaum, Kate discovers that Janet's death had been preceded by a faculty meeting that had been devastating to her. The department had been asked to offer women's studies courses, which Janet was expected to teach. She refused, arguing that "she was a scholar in the seventeenth century and did not know what the woman's point of view was in Milton, Marvell, or Donne." A department member informed Janet that she had been hired because she was a woman, not because of her qualifications (which are considerable):

> Since it is only the efforts of those women's studies devotees who have brought you here, Professor Mandelbaum, I can't imagine why you want to take so high and mighty a tone. Of course, women's studies are nonsense, pure nonsense. So is affirmative action. . . . But since we've got saddled with you, it does seem the least you could do would be to take care of this problem for us.

Kate examines what she knows of Janet personally–her reading and the devastating blow given to her self-esteem by the crass comments of her colleagues–and realizes that Janet committed suicide. Clarkville later confirms this theory, revealing that Janet had killed herself in the office of the department chairman, perhaps as a kind of protest, and that he had moved the body to the men's room of the building, where it was later discovered.

Although Janet's death was a suicide, Kate concludes that both the English department and Harvard University as a whole are guilty parties, nonetheless. One woman notes, "Janet was murdered all the same. . . . We all conspired in it. We isolated her, we gave her no community. Only death welcomed her." Kate, too, wishes she had recognized Janet's distress and had been more supportive. The theme of the necessity for women to support and nurture one another is prominent in this novel and becomes more so in later Kate Fansler fiction. Janet has, to some extent, contributed to her own victimization by turning her back on the female community and is typical of Cross's female victims who, Roberts says, are "destroyed women who represent for her antiquated modes of female behavior, particularly those characterized by the submerged anger and neurotic need for revenge engendered by enforced dependency in a patriarchal society."

The novel ends with a promise of change: Harvard is going to endow two professorships for women, and women will be on the search committee. The traditional order is not restored, as it often is in detective fiction, but rather Cross holds out the hope that a new, more egalitarian order can be established.

Not surprisingly, the novel was controversial. Many reviewers felt, as Boken, that as a mystery novel, *Death in a Tenured Position* has a "weak plot/puzzle," but applauded Cross for confronting the male-dominated power structure that made life difficult for the real-life Janet Mandelbaums of the world. Jean White, writing for the *Washington Post,* argued that this novel proves that a murder mystery "can be told in a civilized, witty, and learned fashion with an observant eye on society's pretensions and pomposities." John Leonard, writing for *The New York Times,* was less favorable, saying that the author "not only makes her point; she also hammers on it, leaving a nail in our skulls."

The mixed reaction to *Death in a Tenured Position* illustrates some of the tensions that arise from Cross's detective fiction. Originally, Heilbrun began writing pseudonymously in the genre because it provided a kind of freedom she did not have either in her life as Carolyn Heilbrun or in her writing as a rising professor at the then-traditional Columbia University. However, the genre makes specific demands of the writer, and the reader approaches it with set expectations. The author is supposed to provide a series of clues that hint at the identity of the criminal, and, if she is skillful, another set of clues—the "red herrings"—that conceal the identity of the guilty party by pointing to another suspect. The process of reading becomes something of a game; the author is expected to "play fair" by providing the necessary clues, and the reader tries to "play along" and solve the puzzle. Even if the reader does not solve the mystery before the author reveals the solution, the reader should at least be able to look back at the series of clues given and see how the detective came to her conclusion.

Cross has always been caught in a kind of double bind. If she provides a satisfying mystery, one that fulfills the expectations of the average mystery reader, the novel is "merely" a mystery, as evidenced by Carter's comments about *In the Last Analysis:* the puzzle "is an end in itself"; although the novel is "engrossing and entertaining," it is "limited." These comments reflect the traditional academic bias against genre fiction and against much fiction with a strong narrative drive—that if it is "a good read," it cannot be "a good book." On the other hand, if Cross does take on more serious issues, either by criticizing the academic establishment, as she does in *Death in a Tenured Position,* or by experimenting with narrative technique, as she does in *The Players Come Again* (1990), she fails to satisfy the demands of the mystery critics. Purcell is scathing on this point, writing that Cross "enjoys herself by putting her view of the U.S. into print, writing off the top of her head to some extent, faking at times on matters of theme and structure, and never seriously attempting the

more disturbing world of illusion and betrayal that we find in the structurally skilled mystery novel." If Cross writes a good mystery, she's being "simplistic," and if she takes on "real issues," she is not a good mystery writer.

Other critics have suggested a third approach—that Cross is trying to redefine the genre of the mystery, that she tries to honor the tradition of mystery writing while finding new expressions of it. Roberts writes, "It is a sign of her extraordinary skill that she has introduced change without losing the large popular audience which the genre attracts and has established herself as an important practitioner of the art"; the novels "read well the first time and richly repay rereading." Yarbrough writes that "Cross's mysteries offer no safe, formulaic plot with a fixed, static detective. Instead, in her shifting approach to the mystery genre, in the fluid nature of her protagonist, and in the complexly evolving portraits of women, especially professional women, Cross stands alone among contemporary American writers of detective fiction."

Many of Cross's mysteries written during the 1980s and 1990s are not conventional mystery novels. *No Word from Winifred* (1986), for example, involves the disappearance of Winifred Ashby rather than a murder. Cross experiments with different ways of storytelling—through diaries, letters, and reports. The central "clue" is Winifred's diary, which Kate reads, coming to "know" the vanished woman, who is witty, independent, well read, and who at one point writes: "What marks a writer is this: until she—or he, of course—writes down whatever happened, turns it into a story, it hasn't really happened. . . . I think so many women keep diaries and journals in the hope of giving some shape to their inchoate lives." In her Amanda Cross fiction, Heilbrun is writing women's lives, and *No Word from Winifred* immediately preceded the publication of the Heilbrun book *Writing a Woman's Life,* which explores the necessity of autobiography for many women's self-exploration.

Kate, however, fails to piece together Winifred's narrative properly and creates (with Reed's help) a spectacularly wrong solution to Winifred's disappearance—that she was murdered by a former lover, Martin Heffenreffer. Kate and Reed confront the so-called killer, only to learn that Winifred is alive and well but has left the United States to escape Martin. Winifred, although she never appears in the novel except as a diarist, is considered by Boken as "a role model for feminism, completely independent." Winifred has found Woolf's mythical room of her own—in this case, the whole world, which she has set out to explore.

The novel is experimental in its use of various modes of writing to tell a story, a technique used by

*Dust jacket for Cross's 1986 novel, in which Fansler investigates
a woman's disappearance by reading her diary for clues
(Richland County Public Library)*

literary one (although Kate does unearth a concealed murder of a famous author, a secret she promises to keep).

Kate is at a personal and professional crossroads, having finished a well-received book on Thomas Hardy, and is wondering "if another project would ever occur to her." She is approached by Simon Pearlstine, an editor who wants Kate to write a biography of Gabrielle Foxx, the wife of Emmanuel Foxx, an English novelist from the modern (early-twentieth-century) period, who had "devoted an entire book, linguistically revolutionary, exquisitely crafted, to the life and thoughts and passions of a woman." In fact, the portrayal of womanhood in *Ariadne* was so convincing that scholars have always wondered how Foxx did it; some speculated that the novel was written by Gabrielle and not by Emmanuel. In order to tempt Kate into taking the project, Simon gives her an unpublished memoir written by Anne Gringold, an American woman who grew up a close friend of Nellie Foxx, granddaughter of Emmanuel and Gabrielle, and of Dorinda Goddard, whose family took in Nellie when World War II threatened.

The Kate Fansler narrative stops at this point, and the next sixty pages of the novel are Anne's memoir, written in her own voice. As she did in *No Word from Winifred,* Cross is experimenting with different women's voices and different lives. Anne's narrative reveals that, long after Emmanuel's death, Anne met with Gabrielle and was given a massive collection of papers, some of which were letters by Foxx, and others of which were written by Gabrielle. The papers were put in a bank vault for safekeeping and remain in Anne's possession. Their existence has been secret up until this point, and any biographer with access would score a major coup by being able to present previously unknown information. The existence of the papers excites Kate enough that she takes a "fatal leap into biography."

Kate eventually meets with Anne, Dorinda, and Nellie. After careful perusal of the papers, Kate discovers something of greater literary interest than letters and drafts of Emmanuel Foxx's work–that Gabrielle wrote "a kind of counter novel to *Ariadne* that "stands in contradiction to Emmanuel's version." Kate assures Simon, the editor, that it's "rather wonderful"–high praise from the usually reserved professor. After some negotiations–in which, comically acting against type, the book publisher insists Kate *not* return her advance for the biography she's decided not to write–the two agree that Kate will edit the novel and will provide a biographical sketch of Gabrielle, which will "do wonderfully well" for the publishing house.

several women writers in the 1980s, particularly in Alice Walker's *The Color Purple* (1982), which revives the epistolary form. *The Players Come Again,* also, as Boken points out, uses "no epigraphs and almost no literary quotes," a real departure for the series. However, in this novel, Kate fumbles badly in her role as detective. Reviews were lukewarm. Writing for *The Los Angeles Times,* Charles Champlin called the novel "clever enough," but complained about the "pedantic dialogue . . . in this and the earlier Fansler mysteries."

Although she returned to a more traditional "academic whodunit" with the 1989 *A Trap for Fools,* the later novels have been more experimental, either in the storytelling modes created or in the ways the detection is handled. *The Players Come Again* is probably the most "experimental" Kate Fansler novel. Its title comes from Woolf's *The Waves,* another nod to that revolutionary feminist thinker. *The Players Come Again* is not a detective novel in any recognizable sense; the mystery solved is a

The Players Come Again received mixed reviews. In *Newsday,* Vicki Weisman wrote, Kate "who was lively has now become precious. Despite endless information on . . . mythology . . . this mystery fails to grip. It is too academic, its principle players are too long gone, to engage." Doris Batliner of the *Louisville Courier-Journal* suggested that it was all right for Cross to make the requirements of the mystery genre secondary and applauds the novel for its "strong character studies of . . . women and their interwoven lives." The same question raised with *Death in a Tenured Position* surfaces again: it may be a good novel, but is it a good mystery novel?

Kate's tale of literary sleuthing introduces a theme that becomes a centerpiece of the Amanda Cross tales of the 1990s—that society ignores older women, rendering them invisible, but that a woman can take advantage of being ignored and can accomplish amazing things. Rather than lamenting her lost youth, Kate seems grateful for the wisdom—and joie de vivre—that comes with aging. She describes her delight in getting to know Anne, Dorinda, and Nellie, who are described as "a coven of good witches," who are "all in their sixties" yet who seem "young women" in terms of "attitude, manner, vigor." Kate continues, "It's as though they only found the point of youth when it stopped oppressing them." The joy a woman can feel in aging has been a constant theme in the later Cross/Heilbrun works—it recurs in all the Kate Fansler novels after *The Players Come Again* and even in a book Heilbrun published under her own name, *The Last Gift of Time: Life beyond Sixty* (1997).

The idea that women can disappear—and take advantage—is established in the opening pages of *An Imperfect Spy* (1995). The title pays homage to John le Carré, whose work Kate (and Cross) often admire, and his detective George Smiley, memorialized in such spy novels as *A Perfect Spy* (1986). *An Imperfect Spy* begins with the last known appearance of a woman professor, who is predictably dismissed by her male airline seatmate as "Old and heavy. Out of shape," who must have come from "Central Casting." Her marginal status is affirmed: "who knew better than a woman professor that disappearing into thin air was what most professional men, given their druthers, would have required of her?" The woman then hides in plain sight for most of the novel, her identity not revealed until its climax, although Cross provides the reader with ample clues to her identity.

Kate and Reed, both on leave, are invited to teach at Schuyler Law School, which has had a hidebound, stifling curriculum and a hidebound, stifled faculty, all male since the death of its lone female professor. Kate has been invited to team-teach a seminar on women

and the law, and Reed has been asked to set up a legal aid clinic. Neither is made welcome by the majority of the faculty, although they are welcomed by the students and by the le Carré-quoting secretary, Harriet Furst. Kate investigates two deaths. The first is the mysterious death of the woman professor, whose demise proves to have been accidental. Through his legal aid work, Reed encounters Betty Osborne, imprisoned for the murder of her husband—one of the Schuyler faculty. Kate and Reed are able to persuade the courts to reexamine Betty's case, and along the way they discover that Harriet is Betty's mother, who says, in order to save her child, she "had to" take the job at Schuyler, "the place that had condemned her." Harriet's final words to Kate are on the subject of aging: "Think of me, and remember that it's fun."

Harriet Furst figures prominently in *The Puzzled Heart,* having taken a job as a private investigator after the events of *An Imperfect Spy.* She and Kate have become friends, and Harriet turns to Kate after Reed is kidnapped. Kate is given an ultimatum: she must "publicly recant" her "insane feminist position" or Reed "may come to harm"; she is also warned not to contact the police. Harriet and her partner Toni pursue leads as Kate reviews her past, trying to determine who would be angry enough at her to want to kidnap her husband in retaliation. The two detectives persuade Kate to take temporary ownership of a St. Bernard named Banny (after Anne Bancroft), which will provide apartment-dwelling Kate frequent reason to go out, thus creating opportunities for Harriet and Toni to pass messages on the street without arousing the suspicions of Reed's kidnappers. Harriet takes full advantage of her "invisible" status as an aging woman to go unsuspected into various locations where Reed might have been held and eventually locates and frees him. Reed is restored a third of the way through the novel, having been held hostage by a group of right-wing students angered by Kate's feminist views. But a deeper mystery remains: who was behind the kidnapping? All concerned think that the students were put up to the plot and that some older, more experienced, malevolent person is at work.

Suspicion falls upon Kenneth, a right-wing student, and his mother, an organizer of right-wing causes. The family, however, appears to have a black sheep, Dorothy Hedge, a dog-kennel owner who tells Kate at one point that feminism "saved my life." While Harriet and Toni work to establish the connection between Kenneth and the kidnapping, Kate, working on the basis that the right wing might not be responsible, remembers a woman who might have held a grudge for many years. In her college years, Kate's brother William had been questioning whether Muriel, the woman he had chosen to marry, was right for him. In consulta-

Dust jacket for Cross's tenth Fansler novel, published in 1990, in which her research into the life of a famous author's wife involves her in the lives and secrets of "three good witches" (Collection of George and Julie Anderson)

tion with her then-boyfriend, Moon Mandelbaum (of *Death in a Tenured Position*), Kate helps William devise a scheme that reveals that Muriel loves him for his money and family position, not for himself. Convinced that William has renounced worldly possessions and is going to start a commune with Moon, Muriel breaks off the engagement. Where, Kate wonders, is Muriel now?

Toni is attacked in her office and is critically wounded, eventually dying. Kate begins to doubt Dorothy's sincerity, wondering if she is really colluding with the family she claims to be estranged from. Eventually, Muriel is revealed to be Marjorie, the breeder who provided Banny to Kate, and Dorothy is revealed to be a woman who was denied tenure at the university where Kate teaches. Kate, acting on behalf of the Association of Tenured Women, had examined Dorothy's case and determined that she was, quite simply, unworthy of tenure. Dorothy had nursed a grudge for many years and had masterminded the kidnapping, including hiring Toni, who was in on the plot and was probably

killed because she was about to reveal her secret (although Dorothy's guilt in Toni's death is never explicitly proven).

Cross's most direct attack on conservative values since *Death in a Tenured Position, The Puzzled Heart* drew far less vitriol from reviewers who disagreed with its politics than did the earlier work. In a 26 January 1998 review for *The New York Times*, Marilyn Stasio suggested that "Kate is right on the ball." Associated Press reviewer Mary Campbell praised *The Puzzled Heart* as "an engrossing, different kind of novel." This novel is one the critics felt struck a balance between the mystery/puzzle demands of the detective genre and Kate's resistance toward the status quo.

The penultimate Kate Fansler novel, *Honest Doubt* (2000), is not actually a Kate Fansler novel. Its first-person narrator, Estelle Aiden Woodhaven, called Woody, is in some ways the anti-Kate—corpulent where Kate is slender, a motorcycle rider, a martial artist, a hockey coach, and a thoroughgoing outsider to academe. Kate is present, but in a consulting role; Woody has been hired to solve the murder of Charles Haycock, a universally loathed professor at a college in New Jersey, and she needs Kate to explain the ins and outs of academe.

The novel is almost a rewrite of Cross's 1989 *A Trap for Fools*, in which Kate is engaged to solve the murder of Canfield Adams, a universally loathed professor at her own university. The motives in this and the earlier work for engaging a detective are similar; in both *Honest Doubt* and *A Trap for Fools* the woman detective is brought in because she is expected to fail. The murder in *Honest Doubt* is overtly patterned after the killing in Agatha Christie's *Murder on the Orient Express*, in which nearly all the principal characters participate in the killing. In *Honest Doubt*, most members of Haycock's department participated in poisoning his drink. All of them are killers—and thus get away with murder, because Woody cannot pin the blame on a particular killer.

The novel is interesting for the presence of Woody and because for the first time (except in a few short stories), Kate is viewed from the outside and from the point of view of a woman who initially does not like her. The two women do become friends, aided in part by their mutual admiration of the dog Banny, whom Kate still has. The interplay between the two detectives, one amateur and one professional, has been praised. Stasio of *The New York Times* noted that Kate is "gracious but unwittingly condescending" while Woody is "quick to admit that she's out of her depth," an admission giving her an "endearing honesty." Stasio concluded that she hoped to see what Woody could do with another assignment.

The Edge of Doom (2002), Cross's final novel, finds Kate confronted with the mystery of her own birth. She is approached by a man claiming to be her biological father. Largely through conversations with Reed, she alternates between arguing that her biological paternity does not matter—she is a Fansler—and toying with the idea that having a different father from her brothers might explain why she always felt as if she did not fit in with the Fanslers.

DNA tests prove that "Jason Smith" is, in fact, her biological father. The Fansler family must deal with the fact of their deceased mother's infidelity to their father. The brothers are appalled, while Kate is happy to think that her mother might not have been as "conventional" as she had thought. "Jason Smith," it turns out, is in the Witness Protection Program because he was involved in art theft many years ago. Those who have been imprisoned because of his testimony have been released from prison, and he is trying to avoid his former accomplices in crime while establishing a relationship with Kate.

The ending is melodramatic. "Jason," whose real name is Jay, is kidnapped by a member of his former cohorts, and Kate must try to rescue him. A showdown with Jay's armed captor ensues, and Kate is able to secure her father's release. Cross/Heilbrun's last book, *The Edge of Doom* was probably the least effectively plotted of the entire series.

On 9 October 2003, Carolyn Heilbrun took her own life. Much controversy about her suicide and its meaning played out in the local New York media. Heilbrun herself maintained her right to end her life when she wanted (a discussion of her ideas concerning suicide can be found in the preface to *The Last Gift of Time: Life beyond Sixty*). Both of Carolyn G. Heilbrun's careers were remarkable. She achieved a high reputation as a scholar and gained a large, loyal following as a mystery writer. She was a pioneer both at her university and in the field of women's studies. Few academics have managed to share their ideas with such a wide audience, and few mystery writers have been taken so seriously in academic circles.

References:

Carmen Birkle, "'To Create a Space for Myself': Carolyn Heilbrun a.k.a. Amanda Cross and the Detective Novel," *Amerikastudien/American Studies,* 39 (1994): 525–535;

Julia B. Boken, *Carolyn G. Heilbrun* (New York: Twayne, 1996);

Steven R. Carter, "Amanda Cross," in *Ten Women of Mystery,* edited by Earl F. Bargainnier (Bowling Green, Ohio: Bowling Green University Press, 1981), pp. 270–296;

Anne Matthews, "Rage in a Tenured Position," *New York Times,* 8 November 1992, pp. 47, 72–73, 75, 83;

J. M. Purcell, "The 'Amanda Cross' Case: Sociologizing the U.S. Academic Mystery," *Armchair Detective* (Winter 1980): 36–40;

Jeanne Addison Roberts, "Feminist Murder: Amanda Cross Reinvents Womanhood," *Clues: A Journal of Detection,* 6 (Spring–Summer 1985): 2–13;

Eugene Schleh, "Character Development of Kate Fansler in the Amanda Cross Novels," *Clues: A Journal of Detection,* 13 (Spring–Summer 1992): 73–79;

Mary Rose Sullivan, "Amanda Cross," in *Mystery and Suspense Writers: The Literature of Crime, Detection, and Espionage, I–II,* edited by Robin W. Winks (New York: Scribners, 1998), pp. 271–280;

Trisha Yarbrough, "The Achievement of Amanda Cross," *Clues: A Journal of Detection,* 15 (Spring–Summer 1994): 93–104.

Papers:

Smith College has a collection of papers called the Carolyn G. Heilbrun papers, 1946–1979. The remaining papers of Amanda Cross (Carolyn G. Heilbrun) are held in the Sophia Smith Collection; they are sealed until 2015.

Lester Dent

(12 October 1904 – 11 March 1959)

Katherine M. Restaino
Fairleigh Dickinson University

BOOKS: *The Man of Bronze,* as Kenneth Robeson (New York: Street & Smith, 1933; London: Corgi, 1975);

The Land of Terror, as Robeson (New York: Street & Smith, 1933; London: Tandem, 1965);

Quest of the Spider, as Robeson (New York: Street & Smith, 1933);

Dead at the Take-Off (Garden City, N.Y.: Doubleday, 1946; London: Cassell, 1948); republished as *High Stakes,* with John N. Makris's *Nightshade* (New York: Ace, 1953);

Lady to Kill (Garden City, N.Y.: Doubleday, 1946; London: Cassell, 1949);

Lady Afraid (Garden City, N.Y.: Doubleday, 1948; London: Cassell, 1950);

Lady So Silent (London: Cassell, 1951);

Cry at Dusk (New York: Fawcett, 1952; London: Fawcett, 1959);

Lady in Peril (New York: Ace, 1959);

The Thousand-Headed Man, as Robeson (New York: Bantam, 1964; London: Corgi, 1975);

Meteor Menace, as Robeson (New York: Bantam, 1964; London: Corgi, 1975);

The Polar Treasure, as Robeson (New York: Bantam, 1965);

Brand of the Werewolf, as Robeson (New York: Bantam, 1965);

The Lost Oasis, as Robeson (New York: Bantam, 1965);

The Monsters, as Robeson (New York: Bantam, 1965);

Quest of Qui, as Robeson (London: Bantam, 1965; New York: Bantam, 1966);

The Mystic Mullah, as Robeson (New York: Bantam, 1965; London: Bantam, 1966);

The Phantom City, as Robeson (New York: Bantam, 1966);

Fear Cay, as Robeson (New York: Bantam, 1966);

Land of Always-Night, by Dent and Ryerson Johnson as Robeson (New York: Bantam, 1966);

The Fantastic Island, by Dent and Johnson as Robeson (New York & London: Bantam, 1966);

The Spook Legion, as Robeson (New York: Bantam, 1967);

The Red Skull, as Robeson (New York: Bantam, 1967);

Lester Dent (from Lee Server, Danger Is My Business: An Illustrated History of the Fabulous Pulp Magazines *[San Francisco: Chronicle, 1993]; Bruccoli Clark Layman Archives)*

The Sargasso Ogre, as Robeson (New York: Bantam, 1967);

Pirate of the Pacific, as Robeson (New York: Bantam, 1967);

The Secret in the Sky, as Robeson (New York & London: Bantam, 1967);

The Czar of Fear, as Robeson (New York: Bantam, 1968);

Fortress of Solitude, as Robeson (New York: Bantam, 1968);

The Green Eagle, as Robeson (New York: Bantam, 1968);

Death in Silver, as Robeson (New York: Bantam, 1968);

Mystery under the Sea, as Robeson (New York: Bantam, 1968; London: Bantam, 1969);

The Deadly Dwarf, as Robeson (New York: Bantam, 1968);

The Other World, as Robeson (New York & London: Bantam, 1968);

The Flaming Falcons, as Robeson (New York & London: Bantam, 1968);

The Annihilist, as Robeson (New York & London: Bantam, 1968);

Hex, by Dent and William G. Bogart as Robeson (New York: Bantam, 1969; London: Bantam, 1969);

The Squeaking Goblin, as Robeson (New York: Bantam, 1969);

The Terror in the Navy, as Robeson (New York: Bantam, 1969);

Dust of Death, by Dent and Harold A. Davis as Robeson (New York: Bantam, 1969; London: Bantam, 1969);

Resurrection Day, as Robeson (New York: Bantam, 1969; London: Bantam, 1969);

Red Snow, as Robeson (New York: Bantam, 1969);

World's Fair Goblin, by Dent and Bogart as Robeson (New York: Bantam, 1969);

The Dagger in the Sky, as Robeson (New York: Bantam, 1969);

Merchants of Disaster, by Dent and Davis as Robeson (New York: Bantam, 1969);

The Gold Ogre, as Robeson (New York: Bantam, 1969);

The Man Who Shook the Earth, as Robeson (New York: Bantam, 1969);

The Sea Magician, as Robeson (New York: Bantam, 1970);

The Midas Man, as Robeson (New York: Bantam, 1970);

The Feathered Octopus, as Robeson (New York: Bantam, 1970);

The Sea Angel, as Robeson (New York: Bantam, 1970);

Devil on the Moon, as Robeson (New York: Bantam, 1970);

The Vanisher, as Robeson (New York: Bantam, 1970);

The Mental Wizard, as Robeson (New York: Bantam, 1970);

The Golden Peril, by Dent and Davis as Robeson (New York: Bantam, 1970);

The Giggling Ghosts, as Robeson (New York: Bantam, 1971);

Poison Island, as Robeson (New York: Bantam, 1971);

The Yellow Cloud, as Robeson (New York: Bantam, 1971);

The Majii, as Robeson (New York: Bantam, 1971);

The Living Fire Menace, as Robeson (New York: Bantam, 1971);

The Pirate's Ghost, as Robeson (New York: Bantam, 1971);

The Submarine Mystery, as Robeson (New York: Bantam, 1971);

The Motion Menace, by Dent and Johnson as Robeson (New York: Bantam, 1971);

Mad Mesa, as Robeson (New York: Bantam, 1972);

The Freckled Shark, as Robeson (New York: Bantam, 1972);

The Mystery on the Snow, as Robeson (New York: Bantam, 1972);

Spook Hole, as Robeson (New York: Bantam, 1972);

The Metal Master, as Robeson (New York: Bantam, 1973);

The Seven Agate Devils, as Robeson (New York: Bantam, 1973);

The Derrick Devil, as Robeson (New York: Bantam, 1973);

The Land of Fear, by Dent and Davis as Robeson (New York: Bantam, 1973);

The South Pole Terror, as Robeson (New York: Bantam, 1974);

The Devil Genghis, as Robeson (New York: Bantam, 1974);

The Crimson Serpent, by Dent and Davis as Robeson (New York: Bantam, 1974);

The King Maker, by Dent and Davis as Robeson (New York: Bantam, 1975);

The Stone Man, as Robeson (New York: Bantam, 1976);

The Evil Gnome, as Robeson (New York: Bantam, 1976);

The Red Terrors, as Robeson (New York: Bantam, 1976);

The Mountain Monster, as Robeson (New York: Bantam, 1976);

The Boss of Terror, as Robeson (New York: Bantam, 1976);

The Angry Ghost, by Dent and Bogart as Robeson (New York: Bantam, 1977);

The Spotted Men, as Robeson (New York: Bantam, 1977);

The Roar Devil, as Robeson (New York: Bantam, 1977);

The Magic Island, as Robeson (New York: Bantam, 1977; London: Bantam, 1977);

The Purple Dragon, by Dent and Davis as Robeson (New York: Bantam, 1978);

The Awful Egg, as Robeson (New York: Bantam, 1978);

Hades and Hocus Pocus, introduction by Will Murray, edited by Robert Weinberg (Chicago: Pulp Press, 1979);

The Hate Genius, as Robeson (New York: Bantam, 1979);

The Red Spider (New York: Bantam, 1979);

Mystery on Happy Bones, as Robeson (New York: Bantam, 1979);

Doc Savage: Satan Black; and, Cargo Unknown, as Robeson (New York: Bantam, 1980);

Doc Savage: Hell Below; and, The Lost Giant, as Robeson (New York: Bantam, 1980);

Doc Savage: The Pharaoh's Ghost; and, The Time Terror, as Robeson (New York: Bantam, 1981);

Doc Savage: The Whisker of Hercules; and, The Man Who Was Scared, as Robeson (New York: Bantam, 1981);

Doc Savage: They Died Twice; and, The Screaming Man, as Robeson (New York: Bantam, 1981);

Doc Savage: Jiu San; and, The Black, Black Witch, as Robeson (New York: Bantam, 1981);

Doc Savage: The Shape of Terror; and, Death Had Yellow Eyes, as Robeson (New York: Bantam, 1982);

Doc Savage: One-Eyed Mystic; and, The Man Who Fell Up, as Robeson (New York: Bantam, 1982);

Doc Savage: The Talking Devil; and, The Ten Ton Snakes, as Robeson (New York: Bantam, 1982);

Doc Savage: Pirate Isle; and, The Speaking Stone, as Robeson (New York: Bantam, 1983);

The Incredible Radio Exploits of Doc Savage, edited by Will Murray (Melrose, Mass.: Odyssey, 1984);

Doc Savage: The Golden Man; and, Peril in the North, as Robeson (New York: Bantam, 1984);

Doc Savage: The Laugh of Death; and, The King of Terror, as Robeson (New York: Bantam, 1984);

Doc Savage: The Three Wild Men; and, The Fiery Menace, as Robeson (New York: Bantam, 1984);

Doc Savage: The Goblins; and, The Secret of the Su, as Robeson (New York: Bantam, 1985);

Doc Savage: Four Complete Novels in One Volume: The All-White Elf, The Running Skeletons, The Angry Canary, The Swooning Lady, as Robeson (New York: Bantam, 1986);

Doc Savage: Four Complete Novels in One Volume: King Joe Cay, The Thing That Pursued, The Mindless Monsters, The Headless Men, by Dent and Alan Hathway as Robeson (New York: Bantam, 1987);

Doc Savage: Four Complete Novels in One Volume: The Spook of Grandpa Eben, Measures for a Coffin, The Three Devils, Strange Fish, as Robeson (New York: Bantam, 1987);

Doc Savage: Four Complete Novels in One Volume: Mystery Island, Men of Fear, Rock Sinister, The Pure Evil, as Robeson (New York: Bantam, 1987);

The Sinister Ray, introduction by Will Murray (New York: Gryphon Books, 1987);

Doc Savage: Five Complete Novels in One Volume: No Light to Die By, The Monkey Suit, Let's Kill Ames, Once Over Lightly, I Died Yesterday, as Robeson (New York: Bantam, 1987);

Doc Savage: Four Complete Novels in One Volume: The Awful Dynasty, The Magic Forest, Fire and Ice, The Disappearing Lady, by Dent and Bogart as Robeson (New York: Bantam, 1988);

Doc Savage: Four Complete Novels in One Volume: The Men Vanished, Five Fathoms Dead, The Terrible Stork, Danger Lies East, as Robeson (New York: Bantam, 1988);

Doc Savage: Four Complete Novels in One Volume: The Mental Monster, The Pink Lady, Weird Valley, Trouble on Parade, as Robeson (New York: Bantam, 1989);

Doc Savage: Four Complete Novels in One Volume: The Invisible-Box Murders, Birds of Death, The Wee Ones, Terror Takes Seven, as Robeson (New York: Bantam, 1989);

Doc Savage: Four Complete Novels in One Volume: The Devil's Black Rock, Waves of Death, Terror and the Lonely Widow, The Too-Wise Owl, as Robeson (New York: Bantam, 1989);

Doc Savage: Five Complete Novels in One Volume: Se-Pah-Poo, Colors for Murder, Three Times a Corpse, Death Is a Round Black Spot, The Devil Is Jones, as Robeson (New York: Bantam, 1990);

Doc Savage: Five Complete Novels in One Volume: Death in Little Houses, Bequest of Evil, Target for Death, The Death Lady, The Exploding Lake, by Dent and Bogart as Robeson (New York: Bantam, 1990);

Doc Savage: Five Complete Novels in One Volume: The Derelict of Skull Shoal, Terror Wears No Shoes, The Green Master, Return from Cormoral, Up from Earth's Center, as Robeson (New York: Bantam, 1990);

The Compleat Adventures of the Gadget Man, with commentaries by Murray and Robert Weinberg (Shelburne, Ontario: Battered Silicon Dispatch Box, 2004).

PRODUCED SCRIPTS: *Scotland Yard,* radio, 1931;
Doc Savage, radio, September 1934–March 1935—26 episodes by Dent.

OTHER: "The Pulp Paper Master Fiction Plot," in *Writer's Digest Yearbook, 1936* (Cincinnati: Writer's Digest, 1936), pp. 25–26;

"Wave Those Tags," in *Writer's Digest Yearbook, 1940* (Cincinnati: Writer's Digest, 1940);

"Sail," in *The Hard-Boiled Omnibus: Early Stories from Black Mask Magazine,* edited by Joseph T. Shaw (New York: Simon & Schuster, 1946), pp. 300–337;

"Angelfish," in *The Hardboiled Dicks,* edited by Ron Goulart (Los Angeles: Sherbourne Press, 1965; London: Boardman, 1967); republished in *The Hard-Boiled Detective: Stories from Black Mask Magazine (1920–1951),* edited by Herbert Ruhm (New York: Random House, Vintage, 1977), pp. 165–200.

SELECTED PERIODICAL PUBLICATIONS–
UNCOLLECTED: "River Crossing," *Collier's,* 122 (25 August 1948): 8;

"The White Posts," *Nation's Business,* 40 (November 1952): 42–44;

"Savage Challenge," *Saturday Evening Post,* 230 (2 February 1958): 28–29.

With works in progress simultaneously at three or four typewriters and stories under his own name as well as the house name Kenneth Robeson and pseudonyms H. O. Cash, Harmon Cash, Cliff Howe, Tim Ryan, C. K. M. Scanlon, and Robert Wallace, Lester

Dent produced hundreds of stories, mostly for the pulp magazines, from the early 1930s through the early 1950s. Later, he complained that his pulp-writing habits ruined his opportunities to publish more stories in the high-paying "slicks" such as *Collier's* and *The Saturday Evening Post*. A many-faceted man—dairy farmer, aerial photographer, gadgeteer, master sailor, pilot, and hunter of lost treasure—Dent found in his life much of the material for his fiction and is best known for his Doc Savage novellas, written under the house name of Kenneth Robeson. He had wanted the series to appear under his own name, but the publisher, concerned that Dent might defect to another house, insisted on his using the name of Robeson. Only once, through an editor's error, was Dent's byline used for a Doc Savage story, *The Derelict of Skull Shoal* (March 1944).

Lester Dent, the creator of the intellectual and physical giant who became the hero of so many male adolescents, was the only child of Bernard and Alice Norfolk Dent. He was born on 12 October 1904 in La Plata, Missouri, on the farm owned by his maternal grandparents, John and Eliza Norfolk. Shortly after his birth, he and his mother went to live on the farm his father had bought in Broken Arrow, Oklahoma. A few years later, the Dents relocated to a sheep and cattle farm in Pumpkin Buttes, Wyoming, and, when Lester was eight, to another ranch on the other side of the state. In 1918 the Dents returned to La Plata, which became the writer's permanent home when he was not living in New York City or traveling the world in search of adventure.

An only child who had no neighboring children as playmates and who in his early years was taught at home by his mother, a former schoolteacher, Dent lacked the social skills to develop friendships when he finally did go to school. His status as an outcast was further exacerbated by his uncommon size: at fourteen years of age he was more than six feet tall and weighed slightly more than two hundred pounds. His wardrobe consisted of farmer's coveralls, and his village schoolmates complained of his "farm" odor. Dent was not considered a good student, even in English, but his teacher passed him because of his imaginative essays. Marilyn Cannaday's critical study of Dent, *Bigger than Life: The Creator of Doc Savage* (1990), shows the influence of his early years on remote farms and ranches on such stories as "River Crossing" (*Collier's,* 25 August 1948) and the Doc Savage adventures *The Running Skeletons* (*Doc Savage,* June 1943), *Mystery on Happy Bones* (*Doc Savage,* July 1943), *King Joe Cay* (*Doc Savage,* July 1945), and *The Angry Canary* (*Doc Savage Scientific Magazine,* July–August 1948).

After Dent graduated from high school in 1923, he enrolled in Chillicothe Business College in Missouri,

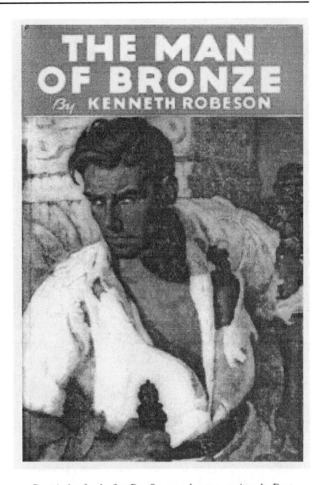

Dust jacket for the first Doc Savage adventure, written by Dent and published by Street and Smith in 1933 under the house pseudonym Kenneth Robeson (<members.aol.com/ the86floor/the86floor.html>)

where he planned to study banking but switched to telegraphy when he learned that good-paying jobs were available in that field. He taught telegraphy at the college for one year after he completed the course and then accepted a position as manager of the Western Union Telegraph office in Carrollton, Missouri. He needed an assistant, and when he advertised for a student to learn telegraphy, Norma Gerling applied. Dent and Gerling became coworkers and sweethearts. Dent changed jobs twice in Oklahoma before their marriage in 1925. Shortly after, the Dents moved to Tulsa, where he worked as a telegrapher for the Associated Press (AP).

One of Dent's AP colleagues spent his unoccupied hours in the office writing stories, and Dent decided to do the same. He wrote fourteen stories before *Top-Notch Magazine* accepted "Pirate Cay" (September 1929), followed the next year by "Death Zone" (*Top-Notch Magazine*, April 1930), "The Thirteen Million Dollar Robbery" (*Popular Magazine*, May 1930), "Buccaneers of the Midnight Sun" (*Top-Notch Magazine*, May

Cover for the January 1937 issue of the magazine featuring Dent's best-known creation (from Lee Server, Danger Is My Business: An Illustrated History of the Fabulous Pulp Magazines *[San Francisco: Chronicle, 1993]; Bruccoli Clark Layman Archives)*

1930), "Vulture Coast" (*Air Stories,* September 1930), and "The Devil's Derelict" (*Action Stories,* December 1930). From the beginning, Dent's stories covered a wide range of types popular with readers of the pulps: action, adventure, detective, and air stories. His 1931 publications included six aviation stories for *Sky Riders* and *Air Stories* and six detective stories for *Scotland Yard.*

Dell Publishing Company, a major publisher of pulp material, recognized Dent's talent and offered him a job in New York to write for its publications for a salary of $500 a month. The Dents arrived in New York City, where they stayed on and off for ten years, on New Year's Day, 1931. During a short period when Dell had to cut back on its publications because of the Depression, Dent and a La Plata friend, Jasper Madison, spent six weeks touring California and other areas of the Southwest, where they prospected for gold nuggets. From these experiences Dent developed many story ideas that he used when he returned to New York.

Dent quickly realized that he could make more money by selling stories as a freelancer, so by 1932 he increased his output to twenty-six stories, with a major focus on Western stories appearing in *Western Trails, Western Romances,* and *All-Western Magazine.* He published aviation tales and war stories in *Flying Aces, Skybirds,* and *War Aces.* Detective stories bought by *Detective-Dragnet Magazine* included "The Invisible Horde," which Dent published under his own name, and "Black Loot," under the pseudonym of Cliff Howe, both of which were in the September issue.

As a freelancer, Dent created arresting scientific detectives in the mold of Arthur B. Reeve's Craig Kennedy, who relied on the scientific analysis of evidence and clues to solve cases. Dent created Lynn Lash for *Detective-Dragnet* (1932), Lee Nace for *Ten Detective Aces* (1933), and Foster Fade, the "Crime Spectacularist," for *All-Detective Magazine* (1934). All three detectives used the Sherlock Holmes scientific approach to detection and are described by Ron Goulart in *The Dime Detectives* (1988) as "off-beat private eyes . . . wild and wacky" who use powers of deduction and principles of scientific investigation to solve cases. Three Lash stories—"The Sinister Ray," "The Mummy Murders," and "The Flame Horror"—were republished in 1987 as *The Sinister Ray,* with an introduction by Will Murray, a Dent biographer and bibliographer as well as the literary agent for the Lester Dent estate. The simple, direct, and frightening beginning of the first chapter of "The Sinister Ray" demonstrates how Dent created situations that compelled his audience to read on: "A woman screamed—piercing shrieks between hoarse gasps of indrawn breath. 'My eyes! My eyes!'" Lash's successful resolution of the case results from his ability to decode symbols he finds scratched on the bottom of a chair. The symbols are a formula for creating a ray that can cause human blindness and will be used to cause a diplomatic break in relations between the United States and certain countries in the Far East. Lash works backward, constructing the ray from the formula and then devising another formula to defuse it.

With the twenty-seven stories Dent published in 1933, he resorted to a favorite pulp-writer stratagem: the pseudonym, which enabled authors to publish more than one story in the same issue of a magazine. He published a story under his own name and one as Cliff Howe in each of the March, April, August, and December issues of *Ten Detective Aces.* He wrote stories for *Crime Busters* as Dent and Kenneth Robeson.

Smith and Street selected Dent to write the Doc Savage series, published in *Doc Savage Magazine.* Henry Rabson and John Nanovic, two Smith and Street executives, wrote an outline for the plot and characters. Although the first story, *The Man of Bronze* (15 February 1933), carried the byline of Kenneth Roberts, by the next issue the name was changed to Kenneth Robeson once the publisher discovered that there was a real Kenneth Roberts who wrote historical novels. Dent wrote a sixty-thousand-word story each month for *Doc Savage;* according to the terms of his contract, he was allowed to contract story assignments to other writers, including Norman Daniels, Alan Hathaway, William C. Bogart, Laurence Donovan, and Harold A. Davis. Even with the contracted writers, Dent still spent much time developing extensive plot outlines for the stories and editing his surrogates' work.

Clark Savage Jr., better known as "Doc," is literally a physical and intellectual giant, especially striking because of the bronze color of his skin; because of Clark Savage Sr.'s premature death from the mysterious "Red Death" three weeks before *The Man of Bronze* begins, Doc has had to assume his father's heroic work earlier than expected. As they explained in their outline for the series (a document reproduced in its entirety in Cannaday's *Bigger than Life*), Ralston and Nanovic expected Doc Savage "to go here and there, from one end of the world to the other, looking for excitement and adventure; striving to help those who need help; to punish those who deserved it." Doc's headquarters, known as "The Wizard's Den," is in the Empire State Building, never cited by name but recognizable to readers by its description. The members of his entourage include Renny, an engineer with a gigantic physique; Long Tom, an electronics expert who is extremely thin; Johnny, a geologist and physicist; Monk, a chemist, who resembles an ape; and Ham, a lawyer and Harvard graduate.

Doc grew up a lonely child because his mother died when he was young and his father traveled the world in fulfillment of his mission to do good. Educated by scientists, he is a linguist fluent in fifty languages as well as sign language and hobo markings, a violinist, an athlete, and an inventor. Fifteen-year-old Savage enlisted in the air force during World War I, and he was shot down and placed in a German prisoner-of-war camp. After the war he attended Johns Hopkins University, became a doctor, and studied brain surgery and neurology in Vienna, where he also attended lectures by Sigmund Freud. In 1928 Doc built a secret college in upstate New York, designed to cure individuals of their antisocial, criminal behavior.

Street and Smith thought Dent was the ideal writer for the series because of his own sense of adventure and his love of gadgets, which he invented for his own use, such as an electric garage-door opener, a burglar alarm, and an electric light timer that turned lights on and off at set times. The publisher was impressed also by Dent's earlier scientific detectives, Lynn Lash and Lee Nace. Later, in 1937, Dent used his interest in gadgets to create another scientific detective for the

Street and Smith *Crime Busters:* Clickell Rush, "the Gadget Man," created inventions to get him out of whatever situation he was in: a shoe heel that could explode, wiretapping devices, portable x-ray machines, a bulletproof vest, and possibly, according to Goulart in *The Dime Detectives,* more than a thousand such criminal-stopping devices.

The Doc Savage adventures were the lead stories in *Doc Savage Magazine,* published monthly from March 1933 to March 1947, bimonthly in March 1947, and quarterly from fall 1948 through summer 1949. For a brief period in 1947–1948 the title of the magazine was changed to *Doc Savage, Scientific Detective* in a bid to attract new readers in a declining pulp market, but the original title was resumed in 1949. The final adventure was *Up from Earth's Center* (Summer 1949). Dent earned $500 per story when he began the series; $750 during the height of the series' popularity; and $650 when the readership started to decline in the early 1940s.

Dent wrote 165 of Doc Savage's 181 adventures. Doc traveled to five continents, as well as lost civilizations such as the Mayan kingdom (*The Golden Peril,* December 1937). He faced such monsters as Maximus, an eight-foot-tall hairy man (*World's Fair Goblin,* December 1939). During World War II he also faced Axis villains, as in *The Hate Genius* (January 1945), a story about Adolf Hitler's double. Although *Doc Savage Magazine* and all the other pulps fell out of favor, the character has been remembered with affection. Science-fiction writer Philip José Farmer's fictional biography, *Doc Savage: His Apocalyptic Life* (1973), pays homage to Dent's creation by linking Doc in an imagined genealogy to his literary forebears Tarzan, Sherlock Holmes, and Arsène Lupin. Bantam paperbacks republished the Doc Savage adventures separately or in omnibus editions in the 1960s, 1970s, and 1980s, and fans maintain Internet sites and chat rooms about Doc Savage.

Dent's Doc Savage stories as well as many others he wrote for the pulps emphasized action and adventure over character and setting. The characters were often stereotypes, such as the Oriental villain, the daredevil pilot, the treasure hunter, and the superhuman monster. Thumbnail characterizations were achieved through tag names that pinpoint a character's major trait. Most of the women in Dent's stories, *Doc Savage* and others, were stereotypes as well, such as the seductress, the blonde bombshell, or the tempestuous redhead.

The Dent formula consists of several key elements: a fast-moving plot with much physical action; a hero who is unusually tall and thin; superficial characterization; and exotic locales. He used SCT–his acronym for "Some Clever Tricks"–to extricate the hero or detective from a dangerous situation, though he limited

Cover for the 27 November 1937 issue of Argosy *magazine, which featured an installment of Dent's serial novel inspired by Edgar Rice Burroughs's Tarzan adventures (from John Gunnison,* Belarski: Pulp Art Masters *[Silver Spring, Md.: Adventure House, 2003]; Bruccoli Clark Layman Archives)*

himself to three such tricks per story. Dent kept copious files of newspaper and magazine articles, as well as notes on true crimes, scientific and medical discoveries, and story ideas that occurred to him when he was doing other things.

The prolific Dent produced an average of sixty-five thousand words a week; he spent more time creating and outlining a story than he did in actually writing it. He disliked revision and almost preferred to write a new story in place of a revised one. An exception occurred with the two stories he wrote for *Black Mask:* "Sail" (October 1936) and "Angelfish" (December 1936). Joseph "Cap" Shaw, the influential editor of *Black Mask* from 1926 to 1936, insisted that Dent make changes to assure a better flow of the action of the story, more direct language, and greater consistency in the point of view. In a letter dated 19 July 1936, Shaw reminded Dent that "Mr. Average Reader would have to go through the dictionary a score of times through the page. In the first place, he hasn't the dictionary, and

in the second, if he had, it would be extremely doubtful if he would bestir himself to do so even once." As Cannaday quotes him in *Bigger than Life,* Dent later said that if Shaw had not been fired from *Black Mask* in 1936, Dent probably would have continued to pay more attention to style: "I wrote reams of salable crap which became my pattern, and gradually there slipped away the bit or power with words Shaw had started awakening in me."

In "Sail" and "Angelfish," which are frequently mentioned in hard-boiled reference works, Dent makes use of his own experiences. In 1934 he and his wife purchased a boat they christened the *Albatross,* which they used for frequent ocean voyages on the Atlantic from New York to Florida and the Caribbean. Their ocean trips included treasure hunts, which, although unsuccessful for them, did provide many future story ideas and served as a basis for a motion-picture documentary they made, *The Voyage of the Albatross.* Like the *Albatross,* Oscar Sail's boat in "Sail" there is a bugeye, a small boat with a flat bottom, a centerboard, and two raked masts.

"Sail" and "Angelfish" are adventure stories featuring much physical action and a hero modeled after Dent and other figures he created. Oscar Sail is a tall, muscular, deeply suntanned man with weathered skin who resorts to inventive tricks and devices to escape discovery or dangerous situations. "Sail" deals with a search to find a sunken boat, *Lady Luck,* that supposedly has a hidden cache of jewelry. In "Angelfish" Nan Moberly, an oil company executive, arranges to be the victim of a fake assault and robbery in order to outwit representatives from a rival company who want to obtain an important geological map of an undeveloped oil site. Hard-boiled writers were known for their colorful figures of speech; while such writing was not characteristic of Dent's style at the time, in "Sail" there is a picturesque description of Oscar Sail by another character: "They sure left the faucet on too long when they poured you."

Dent must have considered 1936 an auspicious year. He heard that *Argosy,* his favorite pulp magazine, was looking for new material. His serialized novel *Hades* appeared in the 5, 12, and 19 December issues. The following year, *Hocus Pocus* was published in the May 22 and 29 and June 5 issues. His final *Argosy* story, *Genius Jones,* a clone of Edgar Rice Burroughs's Tarzan stories, was serialized in the fall of that year. Murray has two of Dent's *Argosy* tales, *Hades and Hocus Pocus* (1979), in which he describes their respective protagonists, Alexander Titus and Cal Merton, as men who mirror both Dent and Doc Savage.

Not one to deny his reliance on formula writing, Dent published an often-quoted article, "The Pulp

Paper Master Fiction Plot," in the 1936 *Writer's Digest Yearbook*. Dent's blueprint for a six-thousand-word story deals with content, structure, atmosphere, and narrative devices. He advises writers to devise

1. A DIFFERENT murder method for villain to use
2. A DIFFERENT thing for villain to be seeking
3. A DIFFERENT locale
4. A menace which is to hang over the victim like a cloud.

As examples of different approaches, Dent suggests murder by the poison from scorpions or from germs carried by flies or other insects rather than by stabbing or shooting. A writer's story does not have to be different in every way; the method can be ordinary but the motive different or unusual.

Dent divided the story into four parts of 1,500 words each. The hero should be introduced in the first line; in the first section the writer should "swat him with a fistful of trouble" and "create menace and suspense." More grief and conflict should be placed on the hero in the second part, along with a surprising twist or trick in the story line. The third section should cause added grief for the hero, who has had some slight success in battling the menace but now experiences serious difficulties because of another twist in the plot. By the final 1,500 words, the hero should be devastated and close to losing his life, but clever tricks then enable him to overcome the forces of evil.

Whether on land or sea, Dent wrote steadily and stockpiled Doc Savage adventures and other stories for future use. He drew much inspiration for Doc Savage adventures from some frightening experiences he and Norma had while on a six-month tour of Europe in 1938, when Nazism was emerging as a threat. Tired of New York, Miami, and travel in general, the Dents moved back to La Plata permanently in 1941, where they built a home, called the House of Gadgets by the locals, combining traditional and avant-garde features. Although there was nothing remarkable about its exterior, it included a kitchen in front of the house, an electric garage-door opener created by Dent, an intercom system, and a burglar alarm. The rooms were decorated to reflect Dent's interests, hobbies, and work, including replicas of the cattle brands used on the ranches he had lived on as a boy and nautical motifs reminiscent of the *Albatross*. Dent was an involved member of the community and an active supporter of youth groups though he and his wife had no children. In addition to his writing, he earned income from dairy farming and from Airviews, an aerial photography business that he established. He continued to write for *The*

Avenger, Clues, 10-Story Detective Magazine, and *Doc Savage.*

In a second *Writer's Digest Yearbook* essay, "Wave Those Tags" (1940), Dent describes a formula for characterization, with specific emphasis on identifying an individual's most significant trait and most prominent physical characteristic. He observed that Dashiell Hammett's Sam Spade was aptly named because of Spade's habit of digging into an investigation. Manly names should be used for heroes, names of flowers for pretty young women, geographical names for foreign characters. Doc Savage's retinue is defined in terms of such tags, as are most of Dent's other detectives.

The pulp market started to dry up in the 1940s and died out completely in the early 1950s. Dent began to experiment with a different type of story, a straight mystery with an action hero, amateur detective Chance Malloy, who made his debut in *Dead at the Take-Off* (1946), written for the Doubleday Crime Club. Malloy, a wealthy, thirty-nine-year-old bachelor, runs his own aviation business in South America. His attempt to buy surplus military planes is thwarted for political reasons by Senator Lord. Hoping to persuade the senator to change his mind, Malloy develops a friendship with Lord's daughter, Janet, when they are on the same plane to New Mexico. Janet recognizes a supposed invalid (really a corpse) as her nephew; he had been killed because he tried to blackmail the senator. Janet and Malloy are in extreme danger and expect to be killed once Janet realizes that her nephew has been murdered. When they arrive in New Mexico, there is a confrontation with the senator, who is killed in a gun battle with some gangsters he hired to frighten his nephew. The senator never asked the men to kill his nephew, an action they took on their own. The novel ends with the promise of some romantic interest between Malloy and Janet. In his essay "After the Bronze Man," Robert Sampson in *Lester Dent: The Man Behind Doc Savage* (1974) describes Malloy as a man like Doc Savage, striving for perfection and deliberately seeking the right thing to do, a man "who made no allowances willingly, ever, for any compromise, in what he considered his moral goals." *The New Yorker* reviewer (13 April 1946) found the novel "exciting in a curious way," while Isaac Anderson, in his review for *The New York Times* (14 April 1946), considered the novel "spotty in the beginning, but it gains in coherence as it proceeds towards a startling climax." The reviewer for *Kirkus Reviews* (1 March 1946) commented favorably on "its sustained interest and superior suspense."

Anthony Boucher's review of Dent's *Lady to Kill* (1946) in the *San Francisco Chronicle* (3 November 1946) credits the work as "fast, medium hard, and highly readable." The adventures of Malloy and his two assis-

Cover for Dent's 1952 novel, in which a young man's search for lost treasure leads him to confront the men who murdered his father ten years earlier (<www.people.uncw.edu/smithms>)

tants—George, a private investigator who likes girlie magazines, and Miss Kiggins, Malloy's executive secretary—begin with Malloy's planned purchase of airplane parts for his business. Again, a woman's life is endangered. Julie Edwards leaves Chicago for New York City, where she plans to visit her friend Martha Baxter, secretary to Paul Copeland, owner of the plant that has the surplus parts. If Julie should reach New York, she will realize that Copeland's secretary is impersonating the murdered Martha (the real Martha was never Copeland's secretary). Most of the action takes place on the railroad train, and the sense of confined space contributes to the mood of suspense.

Lady Afraid (1948) switches the action from planes to boats and features a woman instead of a man as the main character. Sarah Lineyack, a boat designer, is preparing for the launch of the *Vameric,* a racing sloop commissioned by a crooked financier named Arbogast, a partner with her father-in-law in a shady deal. Captain Most, the captain of the *Vameric,* helps Sarah in her quest to reclaim her son, Jonnie. Because Dent was fond of using names as tags to signify important actions or qualities, it is possible to regard the captain as one who is doing his most to help Sarah at a time of great stress and danger. The reader learns that when Sarah had been seriously injured two years earlier in an automobile accident that killed her husband, she lost custody of her son to her in-laws through a legal maneuver. Frustrated in her attempts to regain Jonnie legally, Sarah and Most kidnap him. The boy is then kidnapped again in a plot engineered by Arbogast and Sarah's father-in-law to prevent Alice Mildred, Jonnie's grandmother, from divulging their scheme. The two men hope to gain control of Alice's assets in order to obtain more capital for their fraudulent schemes. Their plan is to have the old woman committed to an institution. Because Alice has been living in her own shadowy world, it takes her a while to understand the danger that she and her grandson face. The motive for the second kidnapping is somewhat strained, but all ends happily with the grandmother safe and sane. The novel reveals Dent's familiarity with piloting boats in the waters around Miami. The suspense is increased by the rapidity of the action, which takes place within a twenty-four-hour time frame.

Although *Lady Afraid* is not a Chance Malloy story, Dent chose to continue the "Lady" motif in other titles. *Lady So Silent* (1951) is a mystery in more ways than one for Dent aficionados. The book was published in England, but not in the United States, and no manuscript is included in Dent's papers.

Cry at Dusk (1952) is an original paperback written for Fawcett's Gold Medal Books, an imprint that published, as Lee Server describes the formula in *Over My Dead Body: The Sensational Age of the American Paperback, 1945–1955* (1994), "the small-scale, contemporary suspense story with sex. . . . The ingredients: an ordinary Joe, a slightly out-of-the-ordinary Jane, a dead body, a bitter ending." Johnny Marks seems to have a shady past; when the novel opens, he is attending a Midwestern college, where he plays on the football team, under the name of Oliver Stringer. Johnny and his Uncle Walter doctored someone else's transcripts so that Johnny could get into the college. Both men are on the run, but Johnny does not know why Walter keeps moving until after his uncle is murdered. Ten years earlier, Johnny's father, a sailor, was killed while he was skipper on a boat that had been hired by a treasure hunter. Before he was murdered, he sent a package to himself, and two men, Hermie Bouncett and Pedro Tamus, have been searching for it ever since. Bouncett and Tamus believe that Uncle Walter can lead them to the lost treasure.

Bouncett, a gangster, brothel owner, and sexual pervert, tried to engage Johnny in homosexual behavior when the two were childhood classmates and made him doubt his own masculinity, a fact that has prevented him from having a sexual relationship with Jennifer Wills, whom he has loved since his youth. Jennifer is kept as Bouncett's companion; she stays with him even though he ran her over with a car and caused one leg to become crippled. Johnny and Jennifer are able to consummate their love only when they think they are going to die. The story ends with a treasure hunt, death to the wicked, and the promise of a new life for Johnny and Jennifer.

Vivid metaphors add to the style of the novel. Johnny comments about Pedro Tamus: "If the bastard is half as dangerous as I think he is, he could make an oak tree shed its leaves just by walking past." Elsewhere he declares that Bouncett "is like the measles–he turns up everywhere." In "The Pulp Paper Master Fiction Plot" Dent stresses the importance of realistic language and the need to appeal to the reader's senses of touch, sight, taste, smell, and hearing.

Lady in Peril (1959), published a few months after Dent's death on 11 March 1959, reflects another area of the author's expertise–farming. Grocer Jones, who is about to appear as a key witness in a price-fixing scandal involving the Ploughman Food Cooperative, has been found dead. The coroner states suicide as the cause of death; however, Gabriella Loneman, Grocer's sister, whose husband works for the cooperative, tries to prove that her brother was murdered. She is kidnapped, but when she is first reported as missing it is suspected that she might have committed suicide because of psychological problems. After several red herrings, Gabriella and her kidnapper, Grocer's killer, are found. The suspense is well-maintained, according to Boucher in his *New York Times* "Criminals at Large" column (3 May 1959). He asserts that *Lady in Peril* "is especially weak in the sketchy handling of important medical and psychological material, but it's fast, skillful and happily unhackneyed."

Perhaps Lester Dent's career can best be described as energetic, adventuresome, and imaginative. Dent was successful in capturing the reader's attention immediately with his introduction of either his main character or the situation in his stories and novels. Goulart in *The Dime Detectives* maintains that "nobody can open a story any better than Lester Dent." His full bibliography will never be known, because he wrote under so many names. A driven writer who could not stop inventing stories, gadgets, and memorable charac-

ters, Dent wrote according to formula, but he studied writing carefully. By analyzing the stories a magazine published and using the types as models, he could create the desired product. Although writing for the pulps made Dent a wealthy man, there remains a sense of unrealized promise about his career. The novels written in the 1940s and 1950s showed more depth in characterization and careful plot development than his previous work, but they are far from classic genre novels. Dent is and will be remembered best as the creator of Doc Savage.

Bibliography:

Will Murray, "The Secret Kenneth Robesons," *Duende,* 2 (Winter 1975–1976): 3–9.

Biographies:

Marilyn Cannaday, *Bigger than Life: The Creator of Doc Savage* (Bowling Green, Ohio: Bowling Green State University Popular Press, 1990);

M. Martin McCarey-Laird, *Lester Dent: The Man, His Craft and His Market* (West Des Moines, Iowa: Hidalgo, 1994).

References:

Philip José Farmer, *Doc Savage: His Apocalyptic Life* (Garden City, N.Y.: Doubleday, 1973; revised edition, St. Albans, U.K.: Panther, 1975);

Ron Goulart, *The Dime Detectives* (New York: Mysterious Press, 1988), pp. 82, 193–195, 197–199;

Will Murray, *Doc Savage: Reflections in Bronze* (Melrose, Mass.: Privately printed, 1974);

Murray, *The Doc Savage Files* (Melrose, Mass.: Privately printed, 1985);

Murray, "Lester Dent: The Last of Joe Shaw's *Black Mask* Boys," *Clues: A Journal of Detection,* 2 (Fall–Winter 1981): 128–134;

Murray, "A Lester Dent Biography" (10 May 1996) <http://www.vintagelibrary.com/pulp/dent>;

Murray, *Secrets of Doc Savage* (Melrose, Mass.: Privately printed, 1981);

Murray, "Six Decades of Doc Savage," in *Doc Savage Omnibus #13* (New York: Bantam, 1990), pp. 419–430;

Robert Weinberg, ed., *Lester Dent: The Man behind Doc Savage* (Oak Lawn, Ill.: Privately printed, 1974).

Papers:

Lester Dent's papers are held in the Lester Dent Collection, 1924–1984, Joint Collection of University of Missouri Western Historical Manuscripts Collection and the State Historical Society of Missouri Manuscripts, located in Columbia, Missouri.

Dominick Dunne

(29 October 1925 –   )

Katherine M. Restaino
Fairleigh Dickinson University

BOOKS: *The Winners: Part II of Joyce Haber's The Users* (New York: Simon & Schuster, 1982; Sevenoaks, U.K.: New English Library, 1983);

The Two Mrs. Grenvilles (New York: Crown, 1985; London: Sidgwick & Jackson, 1986);

Fatal Charms and Other Tales of Today (New York: Crown, 1987; London: Sidgwick & Jackson, 1987); revised in *Fatal Charms and Other Tales of Today; and, The Mansions of Limbo* (New York: Ballantine, 1999);

People like Us: A Novel (New York: Crown, 1988; London: Sidgwick & Jackson, 1988);

An Inconvenient Woman (New York: Crown, 1990; London: Sidgwick & Jackson, 1990);

The Mansions of Limbo (New York: Crown, 1991; New York & London: Bantam, 1993); revised in *Fatal Charms and Other Tales of Today; and, The Mansions of Limbo* (New York: Ballantine, 1999);

A Season in Purgatory (New York: Crown, 1993; London: Bantam, 1993);

Three Complete Novels (New York: Wings, 1994)—comprises *The Two Mrs. Grenvilles, People like Us,* and *An Inconvenient Woman;*

Another City, Not My Own: A Novel in the Form of a Memoir (New York: Crown, 1997);

Fatal Charms and Other Tales of Today; and, The Mansions of Limbo (New York: Ballantine, 1999);

The Way We Lived Then: Recollections of a Well-Known Name Dropper (New York: Crown, 1999);

Justice: Crimes, Trials, and Punishments (New York: Crown, 2001; London: Warner, 2002).

SELECTED PERIODICAL PUBLICATIONS–UNCOLLECTED:

FICTION

"Somebody Knows," *Vanity Fair,* 56 (April 1993): 176–179;

"Guess Who's Coming to Dinner," *Vanity Fair,* no. 447 (November 1997): 278–283.

NONFICTION

"*Architectural Digest* Visits: Dyan Cannon," *Architectural Digest,* 14 (February 1984): 78–83;

Dominick Dunne *(photograph by Barry Marcus, from the dust jacket for* Justice: Crimes, Trials, and Punishments, *2001; Richland County Public Library)*

"An Author's Maison de Plume: Dominick Dunne in his New York Penthouse," *Architectural Digest,* 44 (September 1987): 146–149, 151;

"*Architectural Digest* Visits: Dominick Dunne," *Architectural Digest,* 49 (May 1992): 108–115;

"A Death in the Family," *Vanity Fair,* no. 523 (March 2004): 212–218;

Monthly diary for *Vanity Fair.*

Dominick Dunne's fiction and nonfiction writing about monied society reflect his dual roles as observer and participant. Dunne understands the worlds of wealthy Irish Catholics, the nouveau riche, and the Hollywood-Beverly Hills set, all of which were disdained by the WASPs and those with "old money." His work combines the genres of the roman à clef, a novel in which actual people are portrayed in a fictional guise, and the novel of manners, with its focus on the customs, mores, and behavioral conventions of a particular social class. But beyond his fascination with the celebrity class, Dunne's deeper concern is crime and punishment, and in his fiction he often explores the issues raised by his reporting on trials for *Vanity Fair*.

Dominick Dunne was born in Hartford, Connecticut, on 29 October 1925 to Richard Edwin Dunne, a cardiac surgeon and president of St. Francis Hospital, and Dorothy B. Dunne. One of six children, Dunne attended the Kingswood School in West Hartford and later enrolled at the Canterbury School, a well-known Catholic boarding school for boys, where he stayed until he was drafted by the United States Army in January 1944. Dunne served in the infantry, and on 20 December 1944 during the Battle of the Bulge, he and another infantryman, Hank Bresky, rescued two wounded men stranded behind enemy lines. Dunne and Bresky were each awarded the Bronze Star, and for the first time in his life, Dunne's father acknowledged his son in a positive way. (According to the entry on Dunne in the 1999 *Current Biography Yearbook*, Dunne's father ridiculed him and beat him with wooden hangers because he believed his son was not competitive enough, especially in sports. Jan Hoffman in her *New York Times* profile of Dunne [27 January 2000] wrote that the beatings caused Dunne to lose some of his hearing.)

After the war, Dunne matriculated at Williams College in Massachusetts, where he acted in plays, spent much time going to the theater in New York, and made friends with Stephen Sondheim. In summer 1947, between his sophomore and junior years, Dunne convinced his mother to let him study Spanish in Guatemala. While he admits to learning little Spanish, he met and became friends with Gore Vidal, who was just making his reputation as a novelist, as well as Anaïs Nin. In *The Way We Lived Then: Recollections of a Well-Known Name Dropper* (1999), Dunne describes an impromptu sexual interlude he and Nin enjoyed in a neighbor's pool. Years later, when a much older Nin met Dunne and his son Griffin, she exclaimed, "You're the same age your father was when I first met him." Dunne completed his bachelor's degree in 1949 and moved to New York City, where he studied acting with Sanford Meisner at the Neighborhood Playhouse. In 1951 he began his show business career as the stage manager for *The Howdy Doody Show*, a popular children's television show that aired five times a week. He

Dominique Dunne, the Dunnes' only daughter, who was murdered by a former boyfriend in 1982. Dunne's decision to write about the murder and its ramifications transformed his literary career, making him feel "in step with my destiny" (from Fatal Charms and Other Tales of Today, *1987; Richland County Public Library,).*

then became stage manager for *Robert Montgomery Presents,* a highly regarded weekly drama anthology show. Dunne earned a reputation as an efficient and pleasant stage manager; several major movie actors—including Ginger Rogers, Frank Sinatra, and Humphrey Bogart—asked that he stage-manage their television debuts.

Dunne married Ellen Beatriz Griffin (also known as "Lenny" and "Peach") in April 1954 at her family's cattle ranch in Nogales, Arizona. Dunne's mother was impressed by Griffin's background: a Catholic who possessed inherited wealth, excellent social status, and good political connections. When Dunne proposed to Griffin, she promised she would respond in a week. Dunne later duplicated the formality of her written reply in his second novel, *The Two Mrs. Grenvilles* (1985), in which "Miss Ellen Beatriz Griffin accepts with pleasure the kind invitation of Mr. Dominick

Dunne to be his lawful wedded wife" becomes "Miss Ann Arden accepts with pleasure the kind invitation of Ensign William Grenville Junior. U.S.N.R. to become his lawful wedded wife."

When Martin Manulis hired Dunne in 1957 to be his assistant on *Playhouse 90,* a landmark live television drama series, the family moved to Los Angeles, where they rented Harold Lloyd's beach cottage in Santa Monica before buying their own home on Walden Drive in Beverly Hills in 1960. Eventually, Dunne became vice president for production at Four Star Television, a company founded by Dick Powell, David Niven, and Charles Boyer. Dunne also produced some motion pictures, including *The Boys in the Band* (1970); *The Panic in Needle Park* (1971), with a screenplay by Dunne's brother John Gregory Dunne and his wife, Joan Didion; *Play It As It Lays* (1972), which was based on Didion's novel of the same title; and *Ash Wednesday* (1973), starring Henry Fonda and Elizabeth Taylor.

The Dunnes were social people who entertained and were entertained constantly. During their first two years in California, they became close friends with Peter and Patricia Kennedy Lawford, their immediate neighbors. Always starstruck and proud of his celebrity friends, Dunne took many photographs of guests at his parties; after a while, he was asked to take pictures at other people's parties. He kept all the photos, invitations, and announcements of these years in scrapbooks, later using the material as the basis of his memoir, *The Way We Lived Then: Recollections of a Well-Known Name Dropper*. During their years at Walden Drive, the Dunnes' many parties included their famous black-and-white ball in celebration of their tenth wedding anniversary, as described in both the memoir and the April 1997 *Vanity Fair* article "The Best of Times: The Author's Black and White Anniversary Ball in Beverly Hills, 1964." The Dunnes had five children, including two infant girls who died shortly after birth from respiratory complications and two boys—Griffin, the older son, who became an actor and movie director, and Alexander, a teacher and writer. Their youngest child and their only daughter to live into adulthood was Dominique Dunne, an actress who appeared in the movie *Poltergeist* and some television shows before she was murdered at age twenty-two, an event that changed her father's life and career.

The Dunnes' Beverly Hills-Hollywood life unraveled for several reasons—the excessively hectic social life, a tendency to live beyond their means, the critical and financial failure of *Ash Wednesday,* and finally, Dunne's abuse of drugs and alcohol. In 1966, Lenny and Dominick Dunne divorced. Dunne moved to an expensive duplex on Spalding Drive in Beverly Hills; later this apartment became his only source of income, because he was able to sublease it for a higher rent than he was paying, a detail he makes use of in his first novel, *The Winners: Part II of Joyce Haber's The Users* (1982).

Dunne reached a time when he lost most of his friends and was unable to get work in television or the movies. He believes he was blackballed because he told a scurrilous joke about a major Hollywood agent, and the story was mentioned in a *Hollywood Reporter* gossip column. Dunne realized he was finished in the entertainment business, so in 1979 he sold many of his belongings—except for his clothes, typewriter, and precious scrapbooks—and started driving north toward Oregon and Washington State with no particular destination in mind. His plan was to take a vacation for about a week in order to think about his future.

Dunne was driving through the Cascade Mountain Range when he had a flat tire and stopped by Camp Sherman, a colony of one-room cabins. He stayed there for six months during the late fall and the early part of winter. While there, he achieved two major accomplishments: withdrawal from substance abuse and near-completion of his first novel, a sequel to Joyce Haber's novel, *The Users* (1976). In his introduction to *Justice: Crimes, Trials, and Punishments* (2001), Dunne recalls how he began his writing career:

> I didn't start writing until I was fifty years old although an observer's eye had been observing for forty of those fifty years, while trying out different areas of occupation. My career in television and movies in Hollywood had come to a permanent halt, and I had nowhere else to turn. The thought of writing had been lurking within me for some time, but I didn't actually begin until I finally removed myself from the glamorous world in which I no longer belonged to a one-room cabin in the Cascade Mountains of Oregon. There I began my second career as a writer and a recorder of the social history of the time. The plot of that first book had been played out in front of me the year before I left Hollywood.

While Dunne was staying at Camp Sherman, he received a letter from Truman Capote, whose work he admired. Capote, who also dealt with alcohol and drug problems, urged Dunne to return to civilization, "to return to your own life." Dunne's re-emergence into civilization was precipitated by the suicide of his younger brother, Stephen. His Aunt Harriet sent Dunne the money to fly east for the funeral, where he was reunited with his children. Dunne decided to move east, took an apartment on Perry Street in Greenwich Village, attended Alcoholics Anonymous (AA) meetings on a regular basis, and completed *The Winners*.

Dunne with Ann Margaret (left) and Claudette Colbert, who played the title characters in the 1987 television movie made from his first bestseller, The Two Mrs. Grenvilles *(from* The Way We Lived Then: Recollections of a Well-Known Name Dropper, *1999; Thomas Cooper Library, University of South Carolina)*

Although *The Winners* was not well received critically, as an apprentice novel, it gave Dunne confidence as well as a little money. Apparently, Haber had been given an advance to write the sequel to *The Users* but did not do it because of other commitments as a gossip columnist; she did not want to return the advance, and her agent paid Dunne to write the book. Dunne was able to write about what he knew—Hollywood society, the rise and fall of movie people, and the differences between the old movie moguls and the young upstart deal-makers without conscience.

The Winners describes the rise of Mona Berg—a powerful, unattractive woman—who starts in the entertainment business as an agent's secretary, becomes an agent herself, and, eventually, a studio head. Her star discovery is sexy beefcake actor Frankie Bozzaci, renamed Franklyn Bassett, a former pool man and bartender, who becomes a popular star in a tropical adventure series. Marina Vaughan, a movie star whose career has declined because of substance abuse, bad breaks, and deliberate lies told by Mona Berg, has experiences

similar to Dunne's, particularly when she repeats an obscene joke. Abe Grossman, head of Grossman-Dragonet television productions, is modeled after producer David Begelman. Dunne had given a newspaper reporter the unlisted telephone numbers of entertainment executives to contact for details about the Begelman-Robertson scandal, in which actor Cliff Robertson was one of the accusers in an embezzlement scandal about Columbia Pictures executive David Begelman; in Dunne's novel, Marina Vaughan performs a similar role, helping to break the story of the Grossman-Bassett scandal.

In *The Winners,* Dunne created characters he has used in subsequent books: Dolores (renamed Dolly) DeLongpre, who writes the column "People Like Us"; Faye Converse, a popular movie star who supports charitable causes and is modeled after Elizabeth Taylor; and Dom Belcanto, a fictional version of Sinatra. Capote was the model for writer Basil Plant.

The critical reception of *The Winners* noted the difficulties of writing a Hollywood genre novel. Critic

Leslie Raddatz stated in her *Los Angeles Times* review (16 May 1982) that she preferred Dunne's work to Haber's. Nora Johnson commented in her *New York Times* (30 May 1982) review that to write a Hollywood novel is a challenge because Hollywood caricatures itself.

Dunne writes about the experience that gave his writing career its focus in his introduction to *Justice:*

> A tragic event in my personal life changed me forever. In 1982, my only daughter, Dominique, was murdered by a former boyfriend, John Sweeney, who stalked her and strangled her. I had never attended a trial until that of the man who murdered my daughter. In fact, I had been a feather in the breeze until that cataclysmic event–here, there, everywhere, never sure of who I was or what I was supposed to be. What I witnessed in that courtroom enraged me and redirected me. The lies that are tolerated shocked me, as did the show-business aspect that has taken over the justice system.

Dunne was outraged "that the rights of the victim do not equate with the rights of the defendant. Anything can be said about the dead, and much was, but the killer's grave past offences as a beater of women were kept from the jury." His daughter's killer served only two and a half years of a six-year sentence. In seeking a release for his rage, Dunne decided to write about the murder:

> . . . not just about the fact of the story but about the emotional upheaval and permanent scars my wife, my sons, and I suffered during that terrible period. The first magazine article I ever wrote is the story of that trial. It appeared in *Vanity Fair* in March 1984. The affirmative reaction to the article, titled "Justice," made me realize the power of the written word. It was read in some law schools to show just how badly a trial could go. I was proud of that. For the first time in my life, I felt I was in step with my destiny.

His writing since has assumed a purposeful theme–the search for justice. Tina Brown, the editor of *Vanity Fair* who had encouraged Dunne to keep a journal of Sweeney's trial, gave Dunne an opportunity to write about people he knew as well as the causes that were important to him.

The Two Mrs. Grenvilles, Dunne's first best-seller, was based on the fatal shooting of banking-fortune heir William Woodward II by his wife, Ann, who claimed that she thought he was a prowler. Dunne had kept the issue of *Life* magazine (14 November 1955) that featured the Woodward case, because the details and the people involved intrigued him. His novel depicts the rise of a woman from a pedestrian Midwestern background to social prominence. Like the real Woodwards, Dunne's Ann and Billy Grenville constantly attend parties, mingle with an international set that includes the duke and duchess of Windsor, and raise prizewinning race horses. Ann, like her real-life counterpart, learns to dress well, buy furniture, and entertain, but she never really fits into the world of old money. Given to temper tantrums, assaulting people in public, and drunken displays, Ann alienates her husband and her friends. Early in the novel, Billy's best friend, Bratsie Bleeker, advises Ann not to emulate her mother-in-law or her four sisters-in-law, but to be herself. Later, Ann says to another friend, "I want to talk like them, dress like them, handwrite like them, think like them. *Then* I'll add my own special thing on top of that."

Billy's mother, Alice, gives Ann financial security in exchange for silence about the circumstances of Billy's death. For the sake of family honor and the protection of her grandchildren, Alice Grenville stands behind Ann. Ann endures further heartbreak when her son, William Grenville III, always called "Third," committed suicide by jumping out a fifth-floor window of his grandmother's townhouse. The other Woodward son committed suicide in a similar manner.

Basil Plant, modeled on Capote, narrates the story in flashback. He and Ann meet on a cruise, and he convinces her to tell him the story she has been paid to keep a secret. When Basil betrays Ann by writing an article titled "Annie Get Your Gun" for *Monsieur* magazine, she takes a fatal combination of Seconal and vodka. The real Ann Woodward had been sent an advance copy of *Esquire* magazine in which appeared Capote's short story "La Cote Basque," later included as a chapter in his unfinished novel, *Answered Prayers* (1987); after reading the fictional account of her husband's death, Woodward ingested cyanide on 9 October 1975. Dunne believed that the story led to Woodward's suicide, though Capote denied the connection.

Campbell Geeslin claimed in *People Weekly* (29 July 1985) that "books like this . . . give *roman à clef* a bad name," and Joyce Cohen in *The New York Times Book Review* (8 September 1985) said that the Woodward story "must have made a more compelling news account than it does a novel." Charles Champlin, however, in his review for *The Los Angeles Times* (19 July 1985) described the novel as "a popular entertainment, a fast and enjoyable piece of reading." The best-seller was made into a successful miniseries starring Claudette Colbert and Ann-Margaret.

Fourteen of Dunne's *Vanity Fair* essays were collected in *Fatal Charms and Other Tales of Today* (1987). In addition to "Justice," other trial narratives include "The

Woman Who Knew Too Much," about the Vicki Morgan murder case, and "Fatal Charm: The Social Web of Claus Von Bulow," a man who was tried and acquitted twice of the attempted murder of his heiress wife. Dunne's celebrity profiles focus on Aaron Spelling's wife, Candy ("Candy's Dynasty"); Imelda Marcos ("Imelda in Exile"); Diane Keaton ("Hide-And-Seek with Diane Keaton"); Ava Gardner ("Ava Now"); Gloria Vanderbilt Cooper ("Gloria's Euphoria"); and Elizabeth Taylor ("The Red Queen"). "The Mortimer's Bunch," about the socially exclusive New York City restaurant run by Glenn Bernbaum, and "The Women of Palm Beach" capture the mores of an exclusive social stratum. "Beverly Hills Coup" deals with the battle of the Silberstein sisters (Muriel Slatkin and Seema Boesky) and their spouses for control of the Beverly Hills Hotel. The pieces, written with verve, are marked by an insider's knowledge. In his green leather-bound notebooks sent to him each year by Graydon Carter, who succeeded Tina Brown as editor, Dunne records anecdotes, facts, and trivia for future reference. Through *Vanity Fair,* Dunne reaffirmed his métier, as he describes in the preface to the 1999 edition of *Fatal Charms*—to write about "the rich and the powerful in a criminal situation." In a *Washington Post* review (27 December 1986), Charles Canzoni described Dunne as "an extremely competent reporter."

Many of the *Vanity Fair* essays provide themes and background for *People like Us: A Novel* (1988), in which Dunne develops three important plot points: the murder of Gus Bailey's daughter, Becky; the rise and fall of Ruby and Elias Renthal; and the death of Lil Altemus's son from AIDS. *People like Us* reflects the demise of an old society, represented by the Altemuses, and the establishment of a new one by the Renthals. The prologue of the novel is set in Clarence's restaurant, Dunne's fictional counterpart of the old Mortimer's. All the patrons fall silent as Gus and Ruby walk in. The story is told in flashback, and at the end of the novel, Gus and Ruby leave without eating; they are ready to move on to new lives.

In the flashback, the reader learns that Gus Bailey, a news reporter and Dunne's alter ego, is following an insider-trading story. Like Dunne, Bailey leaves Los Angeles after his divorce from "Peach," who suffers from multiple sclerosis. Also, like Dunne, Bailey believes that justice is not served in Lefty Flint's trial for the murder of Becky Bailey. Unlike Dunne, Bailey intends to kill the murderer. Ruby Renthal, who had been beaten by Lefty Flint but had not pressed charges, feels that she is partially responsible for Becky's death—a connection that brings the two story lines together.

People like Us contrasts old money and social stature (Lil Altemus and her family) with the nouveau

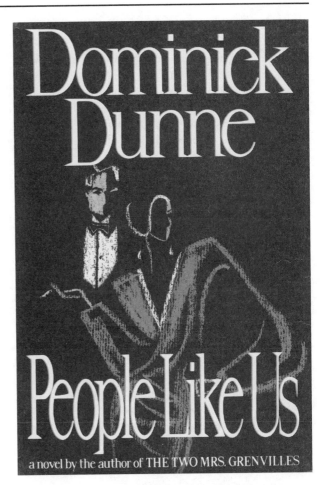

Dust jacket for Dunne's third novel, published in 1987, in which a reporter following a developing insider-trading scandal begins to come to terms with his daughter's murder (Richland County Public Library)

riche (Elias and Ruby Renthal) on New York's upper East Side. The action, set in the 1980s, culminates with the debacle of Black Monday in October 1987, caused by insider trading, mergers and acquisitions, junk bonds, and arbitrage. These activities led to the downfall of Ivan Boesky, Michael Milken, Dennis B. Levine, Saul Steinberg, and the firm of Drexel Burnham Lambert. Although the *Wall Street Journal* printed some excerpts from *People like Us* and attempted to match each fictional character with a real-life counterpart, Dunne claimed in a *Los Angeles Magazine* interview (May 1990): "The people in my novels are always composites despite what people think."

The Renthals are people who use money to buy power, prestige, and culture. Like Ann Grenville, Ruby learns taste and impeccable manners through observation. She is the one character in the novel who undergoes an amazing transformation; she removes herself from society, becomes reclusive, and atones for the excesses of her life and the damage Elias inflicted on people through insider trading. Dunne likes to show society undergoing an evolution. In *People like Us,* the Grenvilles are simply another generation whose name has little meaning for the people of the 1980s. The Renthals own Merry Hill, the country estate that was formerly the Grenvilles' Playhouse. When the Renthal triplex and all its furnishings are sold, the latest vulgar upstarts, Yvonne Lupescu and Reza Bulbenkian, attempt to buy the apartment and are turned down by the co-op board; however, they do purchase all the furnishings, antiques, and artwork.

Appearances are important in *People like Us;* Lil Altemus denies her son Hubert's homosexuality and his AIDS. His partner, who also will die of AIDS, accomplishes a good deed by leaving his entire estate to fund an AIDS hospice, to be named the Hubert Altemus Jr. AIDS Hospice, and also embarrasses Lil with this public affirmation of her son's lifestyle. Kit Reed, in *The New York Times Book Review* (10 July 1988), acknowledged *People like Us* as "an anthropologically fascinating picture of Manhattan's high society in the 1980s" and praised the humor of the ballroom scene. Reed also commented on Dunne's technique: "Engaging us in his characters' concerns and then pulling multiple story strands into a tight knot, Dominick Dunne demonstrates with wit and accuracy the delicate, merciless distinction between 'people like that' and 'people like us.'"

The story of Alfred Bloomingdale, founder of the Diners Club, and Vicki Morgan, his mistress, is told with some alteration in *An Inconvenient Woman* (1990). In this novel, Dunne connects two disparate, wholly unrelated events that occurred four years apart–the 1983 murder of Vicki Morgan and the 1987 murder of Alfred de la Vega, a popular "walker," or escort for socially prominent women. De la Vega, who led a second life as a gay man and picked up hustlers for rough sex, was shot three times in the heart. The cause of death, however, was listed as suicide, and little of the story was mentioned in the news.

Bloomingdale and his wife, Betsy, close friends of Ronald and Nancy Reagan, were the models for Jules and Pauline Mendelson, who live at Clouds, a magnificent estate in the hills of Bel Air, inspired by Misty Mountain, the former home of Dr. Jules Stein, cofounder of Music Corporation of America (MCA), and his wife, Doris. Flo March is an older and nicer version of Vicki Morgan. Lonny Edge, Flo's roommate, is the only character who Dunne says is not a composite. Although he is a fictional version of Marvin Pancoast, Vicky Morgan's murderer, Dunne based the characterization on Johnny Holmes, a hustler and porn film

actor who died of AIDS. The counterpart to Alfred de la Vega is Hector Hubert Luis Paradiso Gonsalvo. Dunne's alter ego, Phillip Quennell, a writer from New York who does not believe that Hector Paradiso committed suicide or that Lonny Edge killed Flo March, helps to connect the two cases.

The Bloomingdale-Morgan affair lasted twelve years. Betsy learned of the arrangement, and after her husband was diagnosed with cancer, she cut off Morgan's allowance, reputed to be $12,000 a month. Morgan filed an unsuccessful palimony suit and tried to support herself by selling her story and a set of videotapes of herself having sex with Bloomingdale and various government officials. No tapes were ever found. In July 1983, three weeks after Morgan took in Pancoast, a psychotic homosexual, as a roommate, she was bludgeoned to death with a baseball bat. Pancoast was convicted of her murder. In the novel, Flo March has recorded forty hours of audiotapes for her autobiography, which she hopes to sell as a book, a movie, or a television special. After Flo's death, only six hours of tape are found. Each chapter of *An Inconvenient Woman* is interspersed with an excerpt from Flo's tapes.

The manners of monied Beverly Hills society are exquisitely depicted: glamorous parties, floral arrangements of rare orchids raised by Pauline, and priceless artworks. The need to maintain appearances is especially important for Pauline, who does not tell her guests when she excuses herself from the dinner table that Jules, victim of a serious stroke, is upstairs in his suite, on the verge of death. Jules, who suffered his stroke while having intercourse with Flo, never believed that his second life would be discovered, nor did he attempt to provide security for Flo until it was too late. For him, Flo was an employee entitled to privileges but not to permanent fringe benefits.

In her review of *An Inconvenient Woman* for the *New York Times Book Review* (10 June 1990), Jill Robinson described the book as

> a smart novel because Dominick Dunne understands the distance between Los Angeles society and the spicy bazaars of Hollywood. And what makes Mr. Dunne not only first-rate but also different from other writers about the very rich in late 20th-century America, is his knowledge that there is more to it than getting the labels and the street names right. He shows he knows by the way he tells you how his people feel, the way they listen, the things they cover up and the things they don't. He's lived in L.A. and gets it right, but he has the perspective you only get when you leave. He knows every story there is to tell, precisely how it happened and why it happened. He also knows there's nothing up there in society to envy.

In his May 1990 *Los Angeles Magazine* article, "Dominick Does It to L.A.," Mark MacNamara described the novel as a "little morality play about power."

Dunne first used the title of his next collection of *Vanity Fair* articles, *The Mansions of Limbo* (1991), as the title of a movie that Philip Quennell admires in *An Inconvenient Woman*. Although Dunne cannot recall in the introduction to this collection where he first heard the expression "the mansions of limbo," he describes Limbo as "a blissful repository for the souls of infants who died before they were baptized, a community whose perfection was marred only by the fact that they were denied the sight of God." Later in the introduction, Dunne broadens the concept to mean "a state of privileged oblivion with a missing ingredient."

The essays collected in the volume include "Nightmare on Elm," the story of Lyle and Erik Menendez, who killed their parents; "Teardown," in which millionaires raze houses in the Platinum Triangle of Beverly Hills, Holmby Hills, and Bel Air to build larger, more monstrous, more expensive houses that show a lack of taste and grace; and "The Windsor Epilogue," which describes the auction of Wallis Simpson's jewelry. The celebrity profiles include "Queens of the Road" (Joan and Jackie Collins), "High Roller" (singer Phyllis McGuire), "Jane's Turn" (Jane Wyman), and "Robert Maplethorpe's Proud Finale."

A Season in Purgatory (1993) was inspired by a case that has had a renaissance of interest because of the 2002 indictment and conviction of Michael Skakel, nephew of Ethel Kennedy, for the 1975 murder of fifteen-year-old Martha Moxley, a neighbor of the Skakels in Greenwich, Connecticut. The case, which went unsolved for years—possibly because of a cover-up, lack of sufficient evidence to convict, or careless police investigation—is one Dunne feels strongly about. Dunne had been in touch with Martha Moxley's mother regarding his interest in the case, did considerable research on it, but wrote a fictional rather than a nonfictional account because some facts were still to be revealed. Dunne, however, shared his notes with Mark Fuhrman, a detective in the O. J. Simpson case, and when Fuhrman published *Murder in Greenwich* (1998), Dunne wrote the introduction in which he declares, "In both fiction and crime reportage, I make no secret of the fact that I hate killers who get away with murders, and I am utterly without respect for the kind of lawyers who cheat and lie to win an acquittal for a guilty man."

In *A Season in Purgatory,* Dunne writes of the murder of Winifred Utley by Constant Bradley, the youngest of five boys, who does not seem as gifted or as intelligent as his brothers. The resemblance between the fictional Bradley family and the Kennedys is suggestive, but neat one-to-one correspondences cannot be

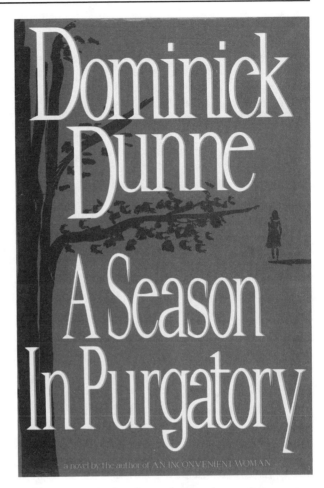

Dust jacket for Dunne's 1993 novel, inspired by the 1975 murder of Martha Moxley, for which Ethel Kennedy's nephew Michael Skakel was convicted in 2002 (Richland County Public Library)

drawn. The Bradleys are a large family, with the boys educated in Catholic prep schools and the girls in a convent school run by the Madams of the Sacred Heart; two sons are in politics; the father keeps mistresses while his wife overlooks her husband's infidelities and devotes her time to her children and her religion; one daughter is institutionalized; and the family has a history of scandals in which the Bradley boys have caused serious injury or death to others. Dunne, who came from a wealthy Irish Catholic family, uses some of his own background in the novel. Like the fictional patriarch Gerald Bradley, Dunne's grandfather started as a grocer and a butcher, developed a successful chain of food stores, and then went into banking. Desmond Bradley, one of Constant's brothers, like Dunne's father, is a hospital president and once held the heart of a young boy in his hand while he removed a bullet. Desmond disappoints his father by becoming a doctor and marrying an Irish maid; the marriage is annulled.

The structure of the novel consists of three parts. The first part, which begins in 1972, is narrated by Harrison Burns, Constant's friend and classmate. The first part of *A Season in Purgatory* establishes the relationship between the Bradleys and Burns, who is attracted to them and appreciative of their paying for his tuition and of their connections. For his part, Burns performs a variety of services for Constant, which range from writing an essay that enables Constant to be readmitted to school after his expulsion at the end of junior year to providing Constant with an alibi and helping him clean up after Winifred's murder.

The second part opens in 1989 and is a third-person account of Burns's involvement with the Bradleys, whom he has not seen in years. Burns is now a successful, well-known crime writer living in New York City, married but separated from his wife and father of two-year-old twins. A chance encounter in a Manhattan restaurant with Winifred's mother rekindles Burns's troubled conscience. Coincidentally, as he is leaving the restaurant, Harrison sees an old prep-school classmate, who tells of his cousin's attack and molestation by Constant in a Chicago hotel room. Burns is later brought back into the Bradley orbit when he encounters Kitt Bradley Chadwick, Constant's younger sister, who had a teenage crush on Burns. When Gerald Bradley asks Burns to write a family history to be used as part of Constant's campaign for governor, Burns finally begins to face his conscience. Although he believes that he can withstand the pressure put on him by Gerald Bradley and his sons, he does not wish to jeopardize a developing romantic relationship with Kitt.

In the third part of *A Season in Purgatory*, set in 1993, Burns realizes that he must tell the truth about the Utley murder, even at the risk of being charged as an accessory after the fact and ending his relationship with Kitt. Part 3 reverts to first-person narration by Burns, who is fulfilling a destiny foretold by Sally Steers, one of Gerald Bradley's mistresses, in Part 1. Sally said that someday Burns would write a book about the Bradleys: "You're a damn fool if you don't. What is writing but putting down what you see, what you know. You are having a bird's-eye view of a dynasty in formation. Remember it all. Keep a journal."

As the novel moves toward its conclusion, the Bradleys show they do not trust Burns, and Johnny Fuselli, a bodyguard and chauffeur for the Bradleys, is asked to stage a drowning accident in which Burns will die. Fuselli dies of a heart attack while he is struggling in the water with Burns, but he does tell Burns where the bag containing the murder weapon and Constant's bloody clothes was dumped. Because the detectives cannot find the evidence, Constant is acquitted. However, the epilogue of the novel hints at justice in the future when two boys who are fishing in Whalebone Cove pull up a bag instead of a fish.

Grace Bradley, the family matriarch, explains the significance of the title of *A Season in Purgatory*: "Purgatory," she says, "is a place for contemplation of what is ahead, for atonement of what is behind, for purification, for expiation. It is preparation for the sight of God." Harrison Burns undergoes that expiation, and so, too, at a later time, will Grace Bradley. Dunne leaves the reader to wonder about the other Bradleys.

Although Maureen Dowd was not impressed by yet another attempt to tell Kennedy stories, in *The New York Times Book Review* (6 June 1993), she did recognize Dunne's ability in "fiction and nonfiction . . . to prick at the pretension of his own class." Gerald Clarke described the novel in his *Harper's Bazaar* (April 1993) review as "a lurid and irresistible story."

Beginning in 1995, Dunne wrote a series of articles in *Vanity Fair* about the O. J. Simpson trial that were later collected in *Justice: Crimes, Trials, and Punishments*: "L.A. in the Age of O. J." (February 1995), "The Two Mrs. Simpsons" (April 1995), "All O. J., All the Time" (May 1995), "The Lady Vanishes" (June 1995), "Follow the Blood" (July 1995), "If the Gloves Fit . . . " (August 1995), "The Two Faces of O. J." (September 1995), "The 'N' Word: Not Guilty" (November 1995), "O. J.'s Life Sentence" (December 1995), and "Closing Arguments" (April 1997). He explores his experience in an alternative fashion in *Another City, Not My Own: A Novel in the Form of a Memoir* (1997), which describes Gus Bailey's coverage of the Simpson trial for his *Vanity Fair* monthly column, "Letter from Los Angeles."

The focus of *Another City, Not My Own* is not on the murders of Nicole Simpson and Ron Goldman but rather on one man's reaction to the trial: the presentation of the evidence, the interaction of witnesses with the prosecution and the defense, the way Judge Lance Ito conducts the trial, the behavior of the spectators, and the feelings of the three families involved–the Simpsons, the Browns, and the Goldmans. Bailey's story is Dunne's story. Both have returned to the city that was the home of their personal and professional failure. Both make the Chateau Marmont the base of their operations. Both are assigned courtroom seats near the Goldman family, presumably because they, too, are fathers of murder victims. The schedule for both the author and his fictional alter ego is the same: appearances on early morning and late evening talk shows, lunches and dinners with celebrities who want insights about the trial, after-dinner lectures, and preparation of the monthly *Vanity Fair* column. Both Dunne and Bailey endure a frightening five-day period when their younger sons–Dunne's Alex and Bailey's Zander–are missing in an Arizona mountain range. Much of *Another*

City, Not My Own is devoted to the nature of the writing process and to the author's favorite themes—the quest for justice, outrage when justice is not served, and "the celebrity type of fame."

Little of *Another City, Not My Own* is recognizably fiction, but Dunne adds a strange twist with the introduction of Andrew Cunanen, the murderer of fashion designer Gianni Versace. Cunanen appears in the novel as a guest at some of the celebrity parties Bailey attends. Some of Dunne's friends objected to being portrayed as sitting next to Cunanen and also to being quoted about their reactions to the Simpson murder trial. Dunne's defense is simply that people should know the type of books he writes and not be surprised when he uses something that he has heard in a social context.

Even though the book opens with a reference to Bailey's fate, that he was killed in the media room of Clouds, his country home in Prud'Homme, Connecticut, the murder is still a shock to the reader. A few months later, when A. Scott Berg, biographer of Samuel Goldwyn and Charles Lindbergh, is sifting through materials in Bailey's desk, he finds an audiotape of Bailey's last moments. Dunne concludes by posing an interesting question: "Had Gus still been with us, he would have easily understood Scott Berg's dilemma. Should he pick up the telephone and call the home of State Trooper Conrad Winalski, whose number was in Gus's book, or should he save it for the final chapter of his biography of Gus Bailey?"

In his *New York Times* (20 November 1997) review, Christopher Lehmann-Haupt raised the question of truth versus fiction and asked if Dunne used fiction "to protect himself from the wrath (and litigation) of countless people he tells tales about out of school. . . ." Irene Lacher commented in *The Los Angeles Times* (18 December 1997): "When Dunne destroys, he does it with far more precision—stiletto-sharp words in an odd-hybrid book."

According to Bob Sudyk's article, "Dunne's Trials," in *Northeast* (24 May 1998), Dunne ended Gus Bailey's life when he decided not to cover murder trials after *Another City, Not My Own*. *Fatal Charms and Other Tales of Today; and, The Mansions of Limbo* was republished in 1999 as a single volume with updates on the essays and two new pieces on fashion shows in Paris ("Paris When It Sizzles") and on personalities associated with the Menendez and Simpson trials ("The Three Faces of Evil").

Dunne's *The Way We Lived Then: Recollections of a Well-Known Name Dropper,* also published in 1999, is a chronicle of social celebrity history and the Hollywood crowd from the late 1950s to the mid 1970s. A pictorial history with accompanying narrative, the book is culled from Dunne's sixteen scrapbooks. While it may be read

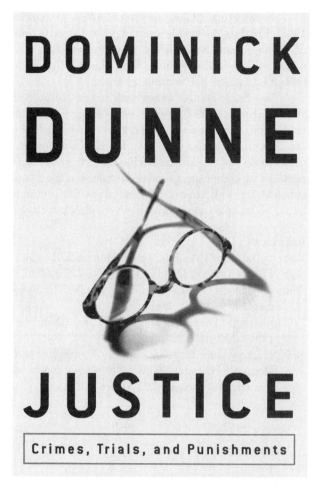

Dust jacket for Dunne's 2001 collection of his writing for Vanity Fair, *which includes his reporting on the O. J. Simpson trial (Richland County Public Library)*

as a popular, sociological account about people of wealth and power, it also serves as an index to people and incidents Dunne later portrayed in his novels. Liz Smith commented on the book in her syndicated column: "The charm and power of the book is in its capsule clarity. Dunne does not waste words; he has no need to. His tales are both fabulous and terrible. . . ."

In 1991 Dunne bought a country home in Hadlyme, Connecticut, which he named Clouds as a homage to the Mendelson estate. The house is a compilation of pieces of old houses on the property, some of Revolutionary War vintage. Clouds faces Whalebone Cove, to which Dunne alludes in the final paragraph of *A Season in Purgatory*. Dunne also maintains an apartment in Manhattan, is active on the lecture circuit, and assists in a support group, Parents of Murdered Children. Even though his wife and Dunne divorced, they remained close, and Dunne delivered the eulogy at her funeral in 1997.

In his article "Close to Home" (*Buzz,* December 1997), Eric Lax quotes Dunne as saying that he is tired of writing about high society and murder. The next novel will be called "A Solo Act," about a man who finds it is better to live without a partner.

Dominick Dunne writes with passion about the abuses of power and justice; with style, verve and satiric humor about a society he knows well; and with compassion for people who have failed. His dialogue is captivating and well paced. His characters, whether portraits or composites, transcend type. His plots and subplots are well connected, not just within a single book, but as crossovers and bridges to other novels.

Interviews:

Robert Dahlin, "PW Interviews Dominick Dunne," *Publishers Weekly* (28 June 1985): 76–77;

Anthony Haden-Guest, "Dominick Dunne," *Interview* (September 1985): 76–77;

"20 Questions: Dominick Dunne," *Playboy* (December 1995): 158–160;

"CNN: Larry King Live," transcript of interview with Dominick Dunne (20 May 2002). <CNN.com/Transcripts> [accessed 23 March 2004].

References:

Christopher Bagley, "Party Tyme," *W* (October 1999): 313–314, 362–363;

J. Collins, "L.A. Confidential," *Time* (17 November 1997): 95–96;

Valerie Grove, "Interview with Dominick Dunne," *Times* (London), 11 June 1993, pp. 12–13;

Eric Lax, "Close to Home," *Buzz* (December 1997): 74–76, 78–82;

Theodora Lurie, "Close-Up: Dominick Dunne, Chronicler of the Rich," *Macleans* (1 December 1986): 6–7;

Mark MacNamara, "Dominick Does It to L.A.," *Los Angeles Magazine* (May 1990): 129–134;

Piper Monroe, "The Walter Winchell of the Elites: The Triumph of Celebrityism in High-Brow America," *Washington Monthly,* 30 (April 1998): 34–35;

Mary Rourke, "Dominick Dunne's Dangerous Game," *Los Angeles Times,* 7 June 1998, pp. 1, 3;

Bob Sudyk, "Dunne's Trials," *Northeast* (24 May 1998): 11–14.

Stanley Ellin

(6 October 1916 – 31 July 1986)

Katherine M. Restaino
Fairleigh Dickinson University

BOOKS: *Dreadful Summit: A Novel of Suspense* (New York: Simon & Schuster, 1948; London: Boardman, 1958); republished as *The Big Night: A Novel of Suspense* (New York: New American Library, 1966);

The Key to Nicholas Street (New York: Simon & Schuster, 1952; London: Boardman, 1953);

Mystery Stories (New York: Simon & Schuster, 1956; London: Boardman, 1957); republished as *Quiet Horror* (New York: Dell, 1959); republished as *The Specialty of the House and Other Stories* (New York: Penguin, 1968)–comprises "The Specialty of the House," "The Cat's Paw," "The Orderly World of Mr. Appleby," "Fool's Mate," "The Best of Everything," "The Betrayers," "House Party," "Moment of Decision," and "Broker's Special";

The Eighth Circle (New York: Random House, 1958; London: Boardman, 1959);

The Winter after This Summer: A Novel about Different Kinds of Love (New York: Random House, 1960; London: Boardman, 1961);

The Panama Portrait (New York: Random House, 1962; London: Macdonald, 1963);

The Blessington Method, and Other Strange Tales (New York: Random House, 1964; London: Macdonald, 1965)–comprises "Robert," "The Seven Deadly Virtues," "The Blessington Method," "You Can't Be a Little Girl All Your Life," "Unreasonable Doubt," "The Nine-to-Five Man," and "The Question My Son Asked";

House of Cards (New York: Random House, 1967; London: Macdonald, 1967);

The Valentine Estate (New York: Random House, 1968; London: Macdonald, 1968);

The Bind (New York: Random House, 1970); republished as *The Man from Nowhere* (London: Cape, 1970);

Mirror, Mirror on the Wall (New York: Random House, 1972; London: Cape, 1973);

Stanley Ellin (from The Luxembourg Run, *1977; Richland County Public Library)*

Stronghold (New York: Random House, 1974; London: Cape, 1975);

Kindly Dig Your Grave and Other Wicked Stories, edited by Ellery Queen (New York: Random House, 1975)–comprises "Death of an Old-Fashioned Girl," "The Other Side of the Wall," "The Crime of Ezechiele Coen," "The Twelfth Statue," "The Day the Thaw Came to 127," "The Corruption of Officer Avakadian," "The Last Bottle in the World," "Coin of the Realm," and "Kindly Dig Your Grave";

The Luxembourg Run (New York: Random House, 1977; London: Cape, 1978);

The Specialty of the House and Other Stories: The Complete Mystery Tales, 1948–1978 (New York: Mysterious Press, 1979; London: Orion, 1979);

Star Light, Star Bright (New York: Random House, 1979; London: Cape, 1979);

The Dark Fantastic (New York: Mysterious Press, 1983; London: Deutsch, 1983);

Very Old Money (New York: Arbor House, 1985; London: Deutsch, 1985).

PRODUCED SCRIPT: *The Big Night,* motion picture, by Ellin, Joseph Losey, Ring Lardner Jr., and Hugo Butler, United Artists, 1951.

OTHER: "The Ungentle Art of Revision," in *Mystery Writer's Handbook by the Mystery Writers of America* (Cincinnati: Writer's Digest, 1976), pp. 165–169;

"The Mystery Writer's Wife: A Special Case," in *Murderess Ink: The Better Half of the Mystery,* edited by Dilys Winn (New York: Workman, 1979), pp. 131–133;

"The Ledbetter Syndrome," in *Ellery Queen's Crime Cruise Round the World,* 35th annual (New York: Davis/ Dial, 1981);

"Graffiti," in *The Best Short Stories of 1983,* anonymous editor (New York: Davis, 1984);

"Mrs. Mouse," in *The Year's Best Mystery and Suspense Stories, 1984,* edited by Edward D. Hoch (New York: Walker, 1984);

"Unacceptable Procedures," in *The Year's Best Mysteries and Suspense Stories 1986,* edited by Hoch (New York: Walker, 1986);

"Just Desserts," in *Crime a la Carte,* edited by Cynthia Manson (New York: Signet, 1994).

SELECTED PERIODICAL PUBLICATIONS–
UNCOLLECTED: "Fat Girl," *Cosmopolitan,* 134 (May 1953): 80–85;

"Fan Letter," *Cosmopolitan,* 136 (March 1954): 48–53;

"Romantic," *Ladies Home Journal,* 74 (January 1957): 36–37;

"The Irony of It," *Writer,* 70 (November 1957): 7–10;

"Writing a Mystery Novel," *Writer,* 73 (November 1960): 7–10;

"Sea Horse," *Redbook,* 118 (December 1961): 36–37;

"Viewpoint and the Mystery Short Story," *Writer,* 76 (May 1963): 7–9;

"Planning a Mystery Back to Front," *Writer,* 79 (December 1966): 11–13, 44;

"Ideas for Mystery Fiction," *Writer,* 80 (December 1967): 11–13;

"Stanley Ellin Talks about Himself and His Writing," *Mystery Readers Newsletter,* 2 (February 1969): 13–14;

"From Our New President," in *Mystery Writers' Annual* (New York: Mystery Writers of America, 1969);

"From Our Former President," in *Mystery Writers' Annual* (New York: Mystery Writers of America, 1970);

"Options, Anyone?" in *Mystery Writers' Annual* (New York: Mystery Writers of America, 1971);

"Mystery Novel or Crime Novel," *Writer,* 86 (January 1973): 22–24;

"Specialty of the House: Edwardian Style," in *Mystery Writers' Annual* (New York: Mystery Writers of America, 1976);

"Inside the Mystery Novel," *Writer,* 92 (December 1979): 9–11, 43;

"The Destiny of the House," *Armchair Detective,* 12 (Winter 1979): 195;

"What Makes Good Suspense Fiction?" *Writer,* 95 (August 1982): 9–11;

"Under Financial Duress," in H. R. F. Keating's "How I Write My Books," *Writer's Digest,* 63 (October 1983): 22–30;

"The Specialty of the Shipyard," in *Mystery Writers' Annual* (New York: Mystery Writers of America, 1983);

"Description in the Mystery Novel," *Writer,* 98 (February 1985): 5–7.

Many people familiar with Stanley Ellin's work often fail to remember his name. But when people old enough to have seen *Alfred Hitchcock Presents* are asked if they recall a famous episode about a gourmet who becomes the specialty of the house in a Manhattan restaurant, they recognize the story. Although Ellin may be a forgotten man in name, his stories remain popular. Since 1948, with the exception of 1997, at least one Ellin story a year has been included in a mystery-story anthology.

In his article "Inside the Mystery Novel," published in *The Writer* (December 1979), Ellin wrote that the elements of a good story must be seamless and fit together: "Plot is the skeleton, characterization, the flesh, and everything else the clothing." Although his characters appear to be ordinary people, they harbor bad intentions and are often caught in maelstroms of terror, mental aberrations, or unanticipated twists of fate. From his first published short story, "The Specialty of the House" in 1948, to his last novel, *Very Old Money* (1985), Ellin created situations with an undercurrent of quiet menace and escalating suspense in locations he knew well–the familiar New York City neighborhoods of Brooklyn and Manhattan; the environs of Miami Beach, Florida, where he maintained a second home; and his favorite places abroad (London, Paris, Italy, Switzerland, Belgium). He believed that one mistake in a road map could mar the effectiveness of a story, as he explained in an interview with Matthew J. Bruccoli published in *Conversations with Writers II* (1978). Patience, exactitude, creativity, meticulous craftsmanship, ironic vision, as well as Ellin's abilities to use memorable brush strokes of characterization, to find the mot juste, and to create excitement and surprise are just a few descriptors of a writer whose short stories continue to be anthologized more than fifteen years after his death.

Stanley Bernard Ellin was born 6 October 1916 in Brooklyn, New York, to Louis and Rose (Mandel) Ellin. Louis Ellin, a Russian immigrant, loved to read both pulp and slick magazines and instilled in his son a love for the short story as a genre. After Ellin graduated from New Utrecht High School in Brooklyn, he enrolled, one month shy of his sixteenth birthday, at Brooklyn College, where he majored in English, edited the college literary magazine, and was awarded his bachelor of arts degree in 1936, one month before his twentieth birthday. In 1937 he married Jeanne Michael, a college classmate who became a freelance copyeditor. They later had one child, Susan.

After graduation, Ellin held a variety of jobs—including dairy farmer, ironworker, instructor in a junior college, and "pusher" for a newspaper distributor—all the while writing short stories that were not accepted for publication. For most of this period, he was an ironworker, until he was drafted into the United States Army in 1944 to serve in World War II. His experiences as a farmer and ironworker provided important background for *The Winter after This Summer: A Novel about Different Kinds of Love* (1960), the settings for which varied from the Brooklyn waterfront to upstate New York to the Florida coast. Following his discharge from the army in 1945, Ellin spent one full year trying to become a writer. Jeanne Ellin supported the family by working on other people's books. Ellin wrote constantly, but with no commercial success.

One evening, when food rationing was still in effect, the Ellins, hungry for steak instead of Spam, treated themselves to a dinner at the famous Gage & Tollner restaurant in Brooklyn. A waiter took their order, but far beyond the time that the steaks could have been served well-done, the Ellins still did not have their meal. Their waiter seemed to have disappeared. Another waiter was summoned, took the order, and delivered the food quickly. The Ellins were intrigued. What happened to the first waiter? Did he disappear into the kitchen, never to be seen again? The incident was the genesis of Ellin's first published short story, "The Specialty of the House."

When *Collier's* and *The Saturday Evening Post* rejected the story, Jeanne Ellin suggested that her husband submit it to *Ellery Queen's Mystery Magazine (EQMM)*. Frederic Dannay, one of the two cousins who wrote and edited as

Ellery Queen, first saw the story in 1946, and Queen awarded it a special prize for the Second Annual Short Story Contest, 1947, for best first short story. Queen said later that the award should have been for best short story of the year. The story was finally published in *EQMM* in May 1948.

"The Specialty of the House," set in a gourmet restaurant in a nondescript brownstone over a two-week period, brings Costain, the diner, from the delight of discovering a restaurant with a special treat, Lamb Amirstan, to an invitation to enjoy a distinctive meal, only to become part of the menu itself in a strongly suggested offstage cannibalistic experience. Costain ignores the waiter's advice: "Do not go into the kitchen sair." Anthologized many times since, the story establishes the pattern for Ellin's fiction: ordinary people placed in unremarkable situations that are transformed into the macabre by a twist of fate. The story gained further renown when it was adapted as an unforgettable episode for *Alfred Hitchcock Presents* (CBS-TV, 13 December 1959).

In his 1966 article for *The Writer*, "Planning a Mystery Back to Front," Ellin indicates how difficult developing a satisfactory story line for "The Specialty of the House" was. Finally, he realized that he should work on the ending first; he "had to make it plain that this customer was a lamb for slaughter. The lines I decided on read: 'The restaurateur held his kitchen door invitingly wide with one hand, while the other rested, almost tenderly, on his customer's meaty shoulder.'" Ellin's wry sense of humor was revealed in the final paragraph of his article "Description in the Mystery Novel" (*The Writer*, February 1985), in which he alludes to a letter a reader had sent forty years earlier: "Human flesh does not taste like lamb, it tastes like veal." Ellin never responded but was still "wondering how to answer it."

The year of apprenticeship was a good investment for the Ellins because Simon & Schuster accepted Ellin's first novel, *Dreadful Summit: A Novel of Suspense* (1948), thus making him a "Selling Writer," as he described himself in the 1966 article for *The Writer*. The novel was in bookstores one month before "The Specialty of the House" appeared in print. The planned direction of Ellin's career veered from straight fiction to stories of crime and suspense. Ellin conceived *Dreadful Summit* as "a story exploring the nature of a crime and the criminal," as he explained in his conversation with Bruccoli. "It was intended to be a novel—and not a mystery novel. In a sense I was hijacked into the mystery field."

Dreadful Summit is more than a crime story. It is a bildungsroman in which George Le Main learns about life on the night of his fourteenth birthday when his father, Andy, owner of Handy Andy's bar in the Chelsea section of Manhattan, publicly receives a brutal physical beating at the hands of Al Judge, an irascible sports col-

"–so in THE EIGHTH CIRCLE are the liars, flatterers, and sellers of office, the fortune tellers, hypocrites, and thieves, the pimps and grafters, and all such scum."

A RANDOM HOUSE MYSTERY BY STANLEY ELLIN

Dust jacket for Ellin's 1958 novel about police corruption, winner of the 1959 Mystery Writers of America Edgar award (Richland County Public Library)

umnist for a daily newspaper. George, who does not know the reason for his father's humiliation, steals his father's gun and sets out on a search for Judge. His quest takes him to parts of Manhattan he has never seen. In one night he has his first drink, is introduced to sex, commits his first crime, and returns home to discover that his father has been killed by a rookie cop, who mistakenly thought that Andy was pointing a loaded gun at him.

In *The New York Times Book Review* (2 May 1948), Isaac Anderson commended Ellin's ability to depict "an adolescent mind driven by a compulsion which it does not understand and which it is unable to resist," but the reviewer for *The New Yorker* (24 April 1948) found some of the same material "repetitious." In *The Saturday Review of Literature* (24 April 1948), *Dreadful Summit* was described as "distinguished but not pretty." The novel is included in "The Haycraft-Queen Definitive Library of Detective-Crime-Mystery Fiction" in the second edition of *The Armchair Detective Book of Lists* (1995).

Ellin and Joseph Losey—who, mailing drafts between the coasts, worked long distance and never met each other—were credited with the screenplay of *Dreadful Summit*, released in 1951 by United Artists as *The Big Night*, starring John Barrymore Jr. In August 2000, the Writers Guild of America acknowledged additional screen credits for two blacklisted writers, Ring Lardner Jr. and Hugo Butler. In "Stanley Ellin Talks about Himself and His Writing" in *The Mystery Reader's Newsletter* (February 1969), Ellin described the screenwriting experience as "traumatic." He later told Bruccoli, however, that he had enjoyed the process of screenwriting but feared that his story might no longer be his because so many people had had a hand in the process.

From 1949 through 1952 Ellin won Ellery Queen Awards for his short stories, usually written at the rate of one a year. "The Cat's Paw" (*EQMM*, June 1949), inspired by Sherlock Holmes's "The Red-Headed League," describes the evolution of Mr. Crabtree from an unemployed, punctilious clerk to a murderer who satisfies his boss by throwing a man out of the office window. *Alfred Hitchcock Presents* re-created the story under the title "Help Wanted" (CBS-TV, 1 April 1956). In "Death on Christmas Eve" (*EQMM*, January 1950), a brother holds his sister responsible for his wife's fatal fall down the hallway stairs twenty years before. The story was the basis for the *Alfred Hitchcock Presents* episode "The Festive Season" (CBS-TV, 4 May 1958). "The Orderly World of Mr. Appleby" (*EQMM*, May 1950), also a Hitchcock episode (CBS-TV, 15 April 1956), reveals the frustration of a seemingly meek antiques dealer who asserts himself when his overbearing wife wants to get rid of all the junk that is his raison d'être. In "Fool's Mate" (*EQMM*, November 1951), George Huneker receives a chess set from his employer, who is retiring. Because his hypochondriac wife, Louise, does not like to entertain, George plays himself in chess, answering the moves of the opponent, who always plays white. As he assumes a double personality, his actions are governed by Mr. White, his alter ego, who triumphs over Louise. A quote from the story often appears in chess websites: "You know that the way a man plays chess demonstrates that man's whole nature."

In "How to Start a Short Story," written for *The Mystery Writer's Handbook* (1956), Ellin explained how he began a story: "I usually start with what might be called a sociological concept: tragedy of the civil service mentality which sells everything for economic security, effects of a murder on an apparently rock-ribbed secure middle class family. . . . I choose characters who answer the demands of the concept, and put them into action." The success of his approach is evident in "The Best of Everything" (*EQMM*, September 1952) and in his second novel, *The Key to Nicholas Street*, also published in 1952.

"The Best of Everything" traces Arthur's struggle to achieve professional success, financial reward, and social status by aping Charlie Prince, his roommate, a black sheep paid by his father to stay away from his socially prominent family. Arthur borrows Charlie's clothes, imitates his manners, assumes his interests, kills him, and then forges Charlie's name on the monthly allowance checks. "The Best of Everything" was made into a successful British movie, *Nothing But the Best* (Royal, 1964), starring Alan Bates.

The sociological significance of *The Key to Nicholas Street* derives from its setting–the small, fictional upstate community of Sutton, New York. Harry and Lucille Ayres and their children, Bettina and Dick, a highly conventional family, contrast sharply with Katherine Ballou, their weekend neighbor, an advertising executive who lives and works in New York City during the week. When Bettina falls in love with Matt Chaves, Katherine's beatnik employee, and Harry commits adultery with Katherine, the conflicts emerging from a rejection of conventional morals, coupled with Lucille's insistence that the family maintain the appearance of respectability, lead to Katherine's murder and the destruction of Dick's life. Even though the reader wants to know "who did it," the more important issue is the disintegration of the family unit. The novel was adapted as a French movie, *Leda* (Times Films, 1961), directed by Claude Chabrol and starring Jean Paul Belmondo. Anthony Boucher, in his review in *The New York Times* (20 April 1952), described *The Key to Nicholas Street* as a "study of small-town mentality, of ingrown respectability, of cannibalistic relationships." James Sandoe wrote in the *New York Herald Tribune Book Review* (27 April 1952) that the novel was " the sort of mystery that proves the vitality of the form."

From 1953 through the publication of *The Eighth Circle* (1958), Ellin wrote several highly praised stories, beginning with "The Betrayers" (*EQMM,* June 1953), in which a young man overhears but does not see a fatal altercation in an adjoining apartment. Determined to seek justice for the victim, he follows clues, discovers a motive, and reports his findings to the New York City Police Department, only to discover that the so-called victim is the other occupant of the room. Pauline Bloom selected "The Betrayers" as the perfect illustration in "How to Achieve Story Structure," written for the 1976 edition of *The Mystery Writer's Handbook.*

"The House Party" (*EQMM,* May 1954) won the Mystery Writers of America Edgar in 1955 for best short story. Miles Owen, a Broadway actor, spends every weekend in his country home in Nyack, but because of his fear of routine, actually a fear of responsibility, he plans to leave both his wife and his profession. As Miles leaves the house party, he simply moves from one hell to another. He imagines himself in hell when Hannah, his discarded wife, shoots and wounds him. The story ends with the same dialogue with which it opens: " *'He's coming around,' said the voice.*"

"Moment of Decision" (*EQMM,* March 1955) has been a popular anthology selection because of its thematic adaptability. It was included in *Alfred Hitchcock Presents Stories They Wouldn't Let Me Do on TV* (1957) as well as two volumes of stories about magicians: *Ellery Queen's Magicians of Mystery* (1976) and Otto Penzler's *Whodunit? Houdini: Thirteen Tales of Magic, Murder and Mystery* (1976). Janet Hutchings chose the story for *The Deadliest Games: Tales of Psychological Suspense from Ellery Queen's Mystery Magazine* (1993), and most recently, Tony Hillerman included it in *The Best American Mystery Stories of the Century* (2000).

In "Moment of Decision," Ellin adapted a situation from an Edgar Allan Poe story. In Ellin's story, an obsessed man challenges his neighbor, a retired magician, to allow himself to be walled in a cellar room and then use his powers to escape. He makes the challenge during a dinner party, and the guests, along with the host, watch the magician's attempt to free himself. When the magician claims to be having a heart attack, the reader and the guests wonder whether the man will release the magician, or will they discover "what a man can learn of himself when he is forced to look into his own depths. . . ." The story was the basis for an Alcoa Premiere segment aired on ABC-TV (7 March 1962).

"Broker's Special" tells the story of a broker who daily takes the same train from his home in a Connecticut suburb to his Wall Street office and back again. One day he has to leave the office early in order to be home in time for a dinner party he and his wife must attend. The change in routine, disturbing to him, coupled with coincidence, leads him to an uncharacteristic act. After he leaves the train and gets into his car for the final part of his trip home, he passes his wife's car, going in the opposite direction, as he drives over the railroad track crossing. In less than a moment, he deliberately causes his wife to die in a fatal wreck. Ellin resorted to some of his favorite motifs: an unprepossessing man who commits an act that seems alien to his personality and temperament, and a contrast between the supposed dangers of the city and the hidden violence found in a rural or suburban setting.

Critics and peers have long recognized Ellin's skill in conceiving and writing short fiction. *Mystery Stories* (1956), his first volume of collected short stories (nine), appears on many lists of works considered outstanding in the mystery-suspense-crime field. It is the only collection of short stories included in H. R. F. Keating's *Crime and Mystery: The 100 Best Books* (1987). Ellery Queen added it to *Queen's Quorum: The 125 Most Important Books of*

PS
3555
.L56
H6
c.2

Title page for Ellin's 1967 novel, in which an American
expatriate attempts to rescue the kidnapped son of a
right-wing European politician (Thomas Cooper
Library, University of South Carolina)

Detective-Crime-Mystery Short Stories (1951; 1969). Julian Symons notes in *Bloody Murder* (1972; third edition, 1992), his history of mystery fiction, that Ellin's stories can be read many times for the "pleasure" they provide. Boucher, in his review for *The New York Times* (20 May 1956), referred to Ellin as "one of the modern masters" of the short story. Sergeant Cuff, in *Saturday Review* (26 June 1956), described the stories as "crown jewels."

"The Blessington Method" (*EQMM,* June 1956), winner of the 1957 Mystery Writers of America Edgar for the best short story, describes a discreet approach to disposing of elderly people unable to care for themselves. Mr. Treadwell, an upright middle-management executive, cannot resist the logic of the proposal from the Blessington Foundation and signs a contract for his father-in-law's death by means of a planned accident. Treadwell's mind, however, becomes unsettled as he begins to wonder what will happen to him as he gets

older. The popularity of the story is apparent by its inclusion in nine anthologies and as the source of an *Alfred Hitchcock Presents* episode (CBS-TV, 15 November 1959).

"The Faith of Aaron Menafee" (*EQMM,* September 1957), adapted by Ray Bradbury for *Alfred Hitchcock Presents* (NBC-TV, 30 January 1962), reveals Ellin's playfulness as the title character, Aaron Menafee, an interesting amalgamation of faith, fate, humor, and rambunctiousness, avenges a wrong. In "Robert" (*Sleuth Mystery Magazine,* October 1958), a pathological sixth-grader terrorizes his teacher, who runs to her death in front of a moving car. When Robert asks his mother for "some milk and cookies, please," the reader recognizes him as truly evil. "You Can't Be a Little Girl All Your Life" (EQMM, May 1958), re-created as an *Alfred Hitchcock Presents* episode (NBC-TV, 21 November 1961), describes the psychological terror a young wife experiences when, after she and her husband move out of the city, she finally realizes the identity of the man who raped her. In a favorite Ellin theme, the hidden evil of the country, which on the surface seems idyllic and wholesome, is contrasted with the obvious dangers of urban life.

The Eighth Circle, sometimes considered the forerunner of Roderick Thorpe's *The Detective* (1966), has as its basic metaphor the eighth circle of Dante's *Inferno.* Ellin reminds the reader that the "liars, flatterers, and sellers of office, the fortune tellers, the hypocrites and the thieves, the pimps and the grafters, and all such scum" are in this circle. They signify the low types Murray Kirk, a private detective, encounters as he tries to prove the innocence of a policeman convicted of graft. Ellin's eighth circle, set symbolically on Manhattan's West Side between Eighth and Ninth Avenues, is not as ordered as Dante's, but the sins and transgressions against humanity are the same. In Dante's hell, the eighth circle is penultimate, coming just before the final circle of treachery, the most egregious sin of all. If Ellin's characters cross Ninth Avenue, they are moving into territory from which they may not return. If Kirk betrays his client's trust, he, too, will be guilty of betrayal.

The Eighth Circle, voted best American crime novel of 1958 by *Books and Bookman,* and winner of the Mystery Writers of America Edgar for best novel in 1959, was inspired by a real bribery trial for which Ellin was on the jury that convicted the defendant. After the trial was over, he could not forget the sad expression on the face of the officer's wife as she sat in the courtroom cradling her infant son in her arms. In "Ideas for Mystery Fiction," published in *The Writer* (December 1967), Ellin recalled the doubts that haunted him after the trial. Would the outcome of the trial have been different if the wife had hired a private investigator to find evidence that would exonerate her husband? What would happen if the detective fell in love with the wife? What if the convicted officer was really innocent? From these suppositions, Ellin created the story of Ruth Vincent, who hires Kirk to prove the innocence of her fiancé, Arnold Lundeen.

Ellin carefully researched *The Eighth Circle,* interviewing private detectives, officers in local Brooklyn precincts, and a judge to learn about crime investigation, arrest, booking suspects, and arraignment, indictment, and courtroom procedures. Kirk visits every borough of the city, except the Bronx, which is given only a fleeting mention, and Ellin traveled to every site mentioned in the novel so that he could verify the accuracy of the settings.

Kirk, like Ellin's two other private eyes, Jake Dekker of *The Bind* (1970) and John Milano of *Star Light, Star Bright* (1979) and *The Dark Fantastic* (1983), is a tough guy in a tough city, but as Robert A. Baker and Michael T. Nietzel argue in *Private Eyes: 101 Knights* (1985), these men do not fit the classic mold of the down-at-the-heels, hard-boiled investigator. Posh Manhattan apartments decorated with expensive paintings, luxury cars, custom-made suits and monogrammed shirts, dinners at Gallagher's Steakhouse and the Russian Tearoom describe a world at odds with that investigated by most fictional private eyes, unlike Ellin's detectives who specialize in insurance investigation.

Sandoe referred to *The Eighth Circle* in his *New York Herald Tribune* review (28 September 1958) as demonstrating "a good writer's perfect sense of proportion." Boucher of *The New York Times* (12 October 1958) regarded Ellin's novel as "a book that defies categories" and wondered if it was "a suspense story . . . or a serious novel about a private detective?" Nevertheless, he declared it "one of the most absorbingly readable books of the season."

One of Ellin's most popular and moving stories, "The Day of the Bullet" (*EQMM,* October 1959), was nominated for an Edgar for best short story in 1960. Martha Foley and David Burnett included it in *The Best American Short Stories, 1960.* It was also an *Alfred Hitchcock Presents* episode (CBS-TV, 14 February 1960). When the narrator, a Manhattan resident, reads about the murder of Ignace Kovac in the morning paper, he recalls a summer day thirty-five years earlier, his last day in Brooklyn before his parents moved to Manhattan. He remembers Kovac, his boyhood playmate, their fascination with Mr. Rose, a local gangster who lived on the block, and the night they were "fishing" for golf balls in the swamp at the Dyker Heights public golf course in Brooklyn. The two boys grew up that night because they saw a man being beaten by Rose's hoods. But when they reported the incident to the police, they learned in a child-like way that Mr. Rose could do no wrong. That night their lives

changed. Because the narrator moved "to the city" the next day, he did not learn of his friend Izzy's later connection with the rackets until he read the newspaper story of Izzy's death.

A child's perspective is a significant motif in Ellin's fiction. The children in his stories either represent evil, as in "Robert," or, as in "The Day of the Bullet," they learn something that affects the rest of their lives. Fractured father-child relationships are explored more fully in *The Winter after This Summer.* In *The Mystery Reader's Newsletter* (February 1969), Ellin described the novel as his favorite because it is "where I have gone deepest into myself." The title of the book was inspired by the closing line of Thucydides's *History of the Peloponnesian War* (circa 411 B.C.): "When the winter after this summer is over, the twenty-first year of this war will be completed."

A problem in communication, a failure and an unwillingness to negotiate a treaty, caused the prolonged war between Sparta and Athens. Ellin uses this analogy to study Daniel Egan's relationships with others and to analyze his self-perception. Egan becomes estranged from his wealthy Manhattan family and friends when Ben Gennaro, his college roommate, dies in a fire in their room at the fraternity house. Ben was an outstanding athlete whose family owns a farm in upstate New York where Egan spent many summers. When Ben dies, people suspect that Egan might have caused the fire. If he did not set the fire, did he really attempt to save Ben? If not, why not? To answer the questions, Egan must find his own identity, his place in his family, and his role in life as a worker or a patrician.

Egan has withdrawn into himself and cannot or will not communicate with others; thus, he leaves himself open to suspicion. Near the end of the novel, Samuel Fisher, one of Egan's coworkers, connects Thucydides's closing line with Egan's situation: "Do you see how it applies to your own hotheaded case? Here's Athens and Sparta, two peoples speaking the same language, full of the need to understand each other, but lunging at each other's throats in a blind fury of ignorance, not only yesterday and today, but tomorrow as well. Was there ever a better description of the disaster brought about by the failure of communication among men?"

Many hallmarks of Ellin's work are evident in *The Winter after This Summer.* The action occurs in upstate New York, New York City's Upper East Side, the Brooklyn waterfront, and the Miami shore. Egan exemplifies Ellin's own belief in a strong work ethic; he takes the lowest-level job in a Brooklyn shipyard, where he heats rivets. He lives in a boardinghouse, where he meets Michael Avery, another shipyard employee, and Avery's wife, Barbara. Michael, also employed in the shipyard, is a religious fanatic who abuses his wife and later exhibits psychotic behavior. Egan does reconcile with his family

Dust jacket for the British edition of Ellin's 1970 novel, originally published in the United States as The Bind
(Richland County Public Library)

at one point and works with his uncle in the family business, but he returns to the shipyard. Egan learns that a man "can live with himself in peace, and can eat and drink and rejoice in his labor unafraid."

Primitivism, sexual aberrations, insanity, and the search for a long-lost painting by Gauguin are some of the challenges Ben Smith faces in *The Panama Portrait* (1962). When he is sent to the island of Santo Stefano to purchase land from the wealthy Bambas-Quincy family for Seaways, Inc., to establish a rock-lobster processing plant, Smith does not suspect that the deal depends on his marrying Elissa Bambas-Quincy, a nymphomaniac and sexual exhibitionist. Fortunately, Smith learns of the family secret before it is too late. Ellin links two story lines, the family's history of sexual promiscuity and the search for the Panama portrait, with the annual festival of Ajaxa, a weeklong event in which members of the local Indian tribe attempt to emulate the feat of Ajaxa, their ancient forebear, who was saved from death on the gallows when a knife was thrust miraculously in his hands and he cut himself free. The modern festival is a metaphor for the thesis of the novel: "Life is a series of cruel dilemmas which are the ropes which would hang us. Courage is the knife in our hands." Ben Smith real-

izes that he has survived the gallows of life and is a better man for it.

Critical reception of *The Panama Portrait* was mixed. The reviewer for the *New York Herald Tribune* (2 September 1962) considered the story a "first-rate tale of suspense and intrigue" but thought that the novel lacked depth. The reviewer for *Time* (31 August 1962) also recognized the suspenseful nature of *The Panama Portrait* but was bothered by Ellin's "pretentious symbolism." With *The Panama Portrait,* Ellin introduced new motifs into his fiction, previously confined to settings in New York and Florida. The action takes place outside the United States on an imaginary island; the theme and symbol of survival are preeminent; adventure and suspense are significant plot elements.

Between 1963 and 1967, when *House of Cards* was published, Ellin wrote several short stories that continue to be anthologized. Ellin's second anthology, *The Blessington Method, and Other Strange Tales* (1964), includes seven stories. Ellin's playfulness emerges in "The Nine-to-Five Man," in which a man with an extraordinary occupation, a torcher of buildings so that their owners can collect insurance, follows the life of any ordinary breadwinner.

In "The Question My Son Asked," poignancy is evident when a son asks his father, who moonlights as an executioner, "What do you do for a living, Dad?"

"The Crime of Ezechiele Coen" (*EQMM,* November 1963) is the first of several short stories set outside the United States. When Noah Freeman, a New York City police officer, goes to Rome on vacation, he clears the name of the title character, a neighborhood doctor who was stomped to death during World War II because people thought he had betrayed members of the Resistance to the Nazis. Freeman identifies the real murderer and finds the money the doctor was supposed to have stolen. Because Freeman had been accused of bribery, was found innocent, but was still treated as if he were guilty, he could empathize with Coen's situation. The story was nominated for an Edgar in 1964.

Other stories from this period include "The Great Persuader" (*EQMM,* March 1964), in which an elderly, penniless, Miami Beach socialite outcons a con man, and "The Day the Thaw Came to 127" (*EQMM,* March 1965), in which a landlord who refuses to heat the building is disposed of by his tribe of tenants. In "Death of an Old-Fashioned Girl" (*EQMM,* June 1966), the story of two artists, the unnamed narrator and Paul Zachary, who met when they were living in Paris twelve years before, is told through flashbacks about the men's friendship and subsequent falling-out. "Death of an Old-Fashioned Girl" opens with a police officer investigating the death scene, Elizabeth Ann's body on the floor of the studio. After the narrator describes, through a flashback, his relationship with Paul, the story ends with a description of the suicide itself.

"The Twelfth Statue" (*EQMM,* February 1967) deals with out-of-work Hollywood moviemakers who accept an assignment outside of Rome to work on a soft-porn movie, *Emperor of Lust.* Alexander File, the producer, hated by everyone on the set, disappears, and the discovery of his body months after his disappearance provides the subject for this masterpiece of wit and humor. Ellin's familiarity with Rome and with the movie business, as well as his interest in the classics, provide a realistic basis for a story set in a make-believe world. The complicated plan for revenge in "The Twelfth Statue" is a forerunner of the motivation that drives Ellin's characters in *The Luxembourg Run* (1977), *The Dark Fantastic,* and *Very Old Money.*

The structure of the novel *House of Cards* is based on the symbolism of certain tarot cards used to predict one's destiny. The adventures of Reno Davis, an American expatriate, former professional boxer, and aspiring writer, parallel five cards: the Fool (Flesh and Folly), the Tower (Disaster), the World (Journeying), the Hanged Man (Duty), and the Wheel (Rewards). Reno accepts a position as bodyguard and tutor for Paul de Villemont,

son of Anne and Henri de Villemont. Paul's father was supposedly killed in Algeria, but thanks to plastic surgery he has assumed a new identity, Dr. Hubert Morillon, in order to continue his campaign to eliminate any government espousing liberalism. Anne and Reno fall in love, plan to run away to Italy, but are sidetracked when Paul is kidnapped. Suspense intensifies, and espionage becomes an important element as the reader learns of the de Villemont family's right-wing activities and its attempts to overthrow governments espousing philosophies opposed to theirs. Anne and Reno's search for Paul brings them through France, Belgium, Switzerland, and Italy. Much of the final section of the novel depends on the element of the chase, brutal physical encounters, and life-threatening situations. The excitement and fast pace of *House of Cards* made it a natural candidate for movie adaptation. The movie of the same title, starring Orson Welles, George Peppard, and Inger Stevens, was directed by William Guillerman (Universal, 1969).

Reviewers of *House of Cards* noted the veracity of its European setting but found problems with the story itself. *The Christian Science Monitor* (23 February 1967) critic thought readers would not think real people were being "threatened" or their lives at risk. In his article for *The New York Times Book Review* (26 February 1967), Boucher borrowed a metaphor from Ellin's world of art to explain the failure of the novel as the work of "a miniaturist who attempts a gigantic canvas in the manner of Louis David." Boucher also believed the book was too long.

In *Conversations with Writers II,* Ellin described his appreciation of European cultures, evident in much of his later fiction. When the Ellins traveled in Europe, they spent a long period of time in a particular city, visited all the tourist sites, went to local bars, walked around different neighborhoods, and followed the local media. They recorded their impressions in a daybook, which Jeanne edited and typed. Ellin reread these typescripts, usually three hundred pages, until he had the feel of a place and could write about it without consulting his notes. *House of Cards* gave Ellin an international reputation as a writer; the French and Italians considered him a major author, and his work has been translated into twenty-two languages.

The Valentine Estate (1968) was Ellin's first novel to establish a pattern, according to Carlton Smith's essay on Ellin in *American National Biography Online* (2000), in which "a young hero in Europe or Miami Beach . . . finds himself embroiled in a deadly contest over an estate or legacy." Chris Monte, a tennis pro and amateur tournament winner based in Miami Beach, is paid $50,000 to marry Elizabeth "Beth" Jones so that she can claim the late Clive Valentine's estate. Valentine ran a book club that served as a cover for a phony passport

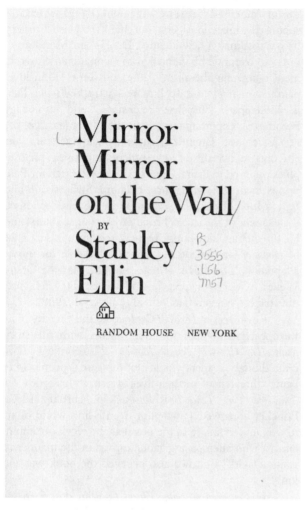

Title page for Ellin's 1972 novel, in which a prostitute's murder leads the protagonist to recall his painful family history (Thomas Cooper Library, University of South Carolina)

ring. Although the reader understands that Beth and Chris will divorce once she gains the estate, plans change when they fall in love. A trail of terror develops as Chris and Beth go from Florida to Boston and then to London.

In "Stanley Ellin Talks about Himself and His Writing" he uses *The Valentine Estate* to demonstrate the connection that should exist between location and character. The hero's background as a tennis pro "made his Miami background plausible; the nature of my heroine, the Boston background I endowed her with. As a climactic locale, I chose London. Each locale then provided characters to complicate the narrative, and out of all this came the book." *The New Yorker* review (8 November 1968) considered the "action . . . very tricky, utterly preposterous, and highly diverting." The reviewer for *The Times Literary Supplement* (26 September 1968), described the story as "sufficiently exciting but somewhat contrived."

Settling an estate is central to the action of *The Bind,* in which Jake Dekker, a freelance private eye for a Manhattan insurance company, is sent to Miami Beach to prove that the holder of a double indemnity policy was not murdered but committed suicide. Dekker establishes an elaborate cover by moving into the house adjacent to the dead man's and hiring a young actress from New York to pose as his wife. The fraudulent scheme Dekker is investigating is linked to an important art collection that belongs to the estate. Allen J. Hubin's review for *The New York Times* (12 July 1970) described *The Bind* as "underpaced"; the reviewer for *The New Yorker* (17 October 1970) thought the book was too long, an opinion that was sometimes echoed by critics of Ellin's later novels. *The Bind* was the basis for the movie *Sunburn* (Bird/Hemdale/Tuesday Films, 1979), starring Farrah Fawcett and Charles Grodin, but the screenplay that Ellin had written was not used.

Much of Ellin's fiction from 1963 on was set in Europe, a period when he and his wife went abroad frequently. "The Last Bottle in the World" (*EQMM,* February 1968) is a story featuring oenophiles and adultery. When Drummond, a wine merchant, finally agrees to sell the only existing bottle of Nuits Saint-Oen 1929 to Kyros Kassoulas, the two men who brokered the deal, Drummond and Max de Marechale, could not have imagined Kassoulas's revenge for his wife's liaison with de Marechale. Ellin's penchant for detail is obvious as he correlates the stages of the sedimentation process with the increasing tension and suspense in the story. In 1969 the story was nominated for an Edgar; Ellin received a second nomination that year for *The Valentine Estate* as best novel.

From 1968 through 1974 Ellin produced a novel every two years and a short story annually. *Mirror, Mirror on the Wall* (1972) is a tale of psychological torment, family guilt, transvestitism, and a complicated father-son relationship. The action begins within a compressed time frame on Good Friday, when Peter Hibben finds the body of a murdered whore on the bathroom floor of his Sheridan Square apartment. Through a series of flashbacks, Hibben recalls his unhappy childhood, his parents' miserable marriage, his father's mistress (whom the dead prostitute mirrors), his own failed marriage, and his relationship with his son. The mirror reflects Hibben's distorted image of himself and his family. Hibben dreams that he is on trial for the prostitute's murder; the jury consists of family members such as his parents, sister, father's mistress, as well as his former wife and her second husband, who serves as Hibben's lawyer.

The anguish is resolved with a murder-suicide on Good Friday, a symbolic day in Christian belief for expiation of sin. The protagonist, Peter Hibben, is one of

Ellin's most tortured characters. In "What Makes Suspense Fiction Good?" (*The Writer*, August 1982), Ellin compares the unmasking of Hibben's character as "the peeling away of the layers of the man's being . . . and the geography of the book becomes the geography of his mind." The action—set in New York City, Miami Beach, and Copenhagen—reveals the broader worldview Ellin developed in his later career. Keating regards *Mirror, Mirror on the Wall*, which won the 1975 Le Grand Prix de Littérateur Policiere, as one of the one hundred best crime novels. H. C. Veit, in *Library Journal* (1 October 1972), characterized *Mirror, Mirror on the Wall* as a "brilliant, kinky" novel. O. L. Bailey in *The Saturday Review* (26 August 1972) focused on the psychological pathology of crime and the unexpected ending. Newgate Callendar (*New York Times Book Review*, 26 August 1972) commented that Ellin "suddenly socks the reader in the teeth" with the ending. Ellin captured some of the same psychological sexual fantasy in "The Other Side of the Wall" (*EQMM*, August 1972), a story about a psychiatrist who imagines elaborate trysts with his receptionist.

Memories of an unhappy childhood provide the motive in *Stronghold* (1974), a novel that reflects the Quaker beliefs Ellin espoused in his adult life. The plot focuses on a kidnapping as retaliation for a youth's humiliating sexual experience. *Stronghold* has two narrators: James Flood, who heads a band of four kidnappers, all former inmates of a Florida prison; and Marcus Hayworth, a successful bank president and leader of the Quaker community in upstate New York. The narrators tell their stories in alternating chapters, beginning with Flood and ending with Hayworth. When Flood was orphaned, he was raised by the Hayworth family. His first sexual encounter as a teenager was with Janet Hayworth, now a successful officer in her father's bank. The kidnappers plan to hold all the women in the Hayworth household hostage, demand a $4,000,000 ransom, and charter a plane to fly with the hostages to the West Indies, where they plan to negotiate for political asylum in either South America or Africa. But Flood does not anticipate Hayworth's reliance on the Quaker principle of peaceful resistance to bring the story to its harrowing but successful conclusion.

Many secrets are found in *Stronghold*—those of the four convicts as well as Janet's hidden addiction to barbiturates and amphetamines. The title is symbolic of the perspectives of both narrators: Hayworth's home functions as a stronghold of Quaker beliefs as well as a fortress for the kidnappers. The combination of suspense, kidnapping, and the use of drugs within a Quaker setting apparently had potential as entertainment value and was adapted as a television movie, *The July Group*, by the Canadian Broadcasting Corporation (1982). In 1997 the novel was the basis for a teleplay, *A Prayer in the Dark*,

winner of the Julian Marks Award for best feature film at the Santa Clarita International Film Festival.

Ellery Queen edited Ellin's third volume of nine collected short stories, *Kindly Dig Your Grave and Other Wicked Stories* (1975), none of which had appeared in previous collections. The title story (*EQMM*, November 1970) is a humorous account of revenge and blackmail wreaked on a greedy art dealer who pays her artists subsistence wages. Edward Hoch notes in his commentary on Ellin in *The St. James Guide to Crime and Mystery Writers* (1996) that the stories in *Kindly Dig Your Grave and Other Wicked Stories* "seem a little less remarkable . . . because of the high standards he [Ellin] has set with the previous books." Two stories in the collection are outstanding, but for different reasons. "The Corruption of Officer Avakadian" (*EQMM*, December 1973) presents a humorous view of an ethical New York City police officer, father of four, who participates in a scheme in which doctors do not wish to report that they have been kidnapped to make house calls. The dilemma Avakadian confronts is not as serious as that found in "The Payoff" (*EQMM*, November 1971), in which a man proves, on a bet, that he can walk into a Florida swim club, kill the first man he sees, and escape.

The Luxembourg Run tells the story of the three lives of David Hanna Shaw. Son of a wealthy diplomat and a manic-depressive mother, young David keeps a journal about his father's love affairs. When Oscar Wiley, David's roommate, sells the journal to a tabloid, David leaves college, has plastic surgery, and starts a new life in Paris. David emerges first as Jean Lespere and then as Jan van Zee, a mentor for hippies who frequent Vondel Park in Amsterdam. David earns his living by making courier trips throughout Europe to deliver drugs in hollowed-out Bibles. His work becomes more dangerous and more lucrative when he begins to deliver money that has to be laundered. During a run to Luxembourg with Annekee, his pregnant mistress, the money is stolen, and Annekee is killed. Van Zee, thanks again to plastic surgery, assumes his former identity as Shaw and devises an elaborate scheme to avenge all the wrongs he has endured. John Leonard's critique for *The New York Times* (15 November 1977) characterized Ellin as "a Walter Payton of the crime gridiron," who uses "weakness of character" to gain vengeance. Callendar of *The New York Times Book Review* (16 October 1977) thought the book was too long and overplotted.

Johnny Milano, private detective and art aficionado, makes his first appearance in *Star Light, Star Bright*. The title was inspired by Vincent van Gogh's *The Starry Night* and by the nursery rhyme "Star light, star bright. . . ." Milano works for Watrous Associates, a New York City agency that specializes in recovering stolen property for which people have submitted insurance claims. He has been called to the Andrew Quist estate in Miami Beach to

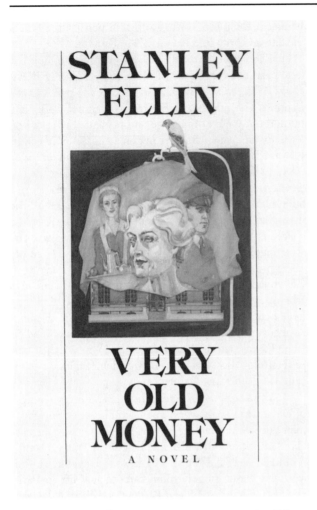

Dust jacket for Ellin's last novel, published in 1985, in which a socialite takes revenge on the woman who caused her blindness fifty-five years earlier (Richland County Public Library)

act as a bodyguard for Kalos Daskalos (alias Walter Kondracki, astrologer to movie stars), whose life has been threatened. Despite Milano's efforts, Daskalos is killed. Although Milano's mission is not successful, he uncovers a major art fraud as well as a planned revolt against Fidel Castro. Ellin wrote *Star Light, Star Bright* with such conviction because he knew art well, learned the intricacies of investigation when he first started writing novels, and understood the strong political feelings of the many Cuban expatriates living in Florida. Callendar's review in *The New York Times Book Review* (8 August 1979) recognized certain Agatha Christie features, such as a group of people isolated on a remote estate; he thought that Ellin wrote a readable, entertaining novel. The reviewer in *The New Yorker* (9 August 1979) considered the novel one of Ellin's best, but Callendar thought Milano was a stereotype of the private eye.

Otto Penzler, head of The Mysterious Press, convinced Ellin that a collection of all his short stories was

needed, and in 1979 *The Specialty of the House and Other Stories: The Complete Mystery Tales, 1948–1978* was published, a fitting acknowledgment of Ellin's work over a thirty-year period. The collection includes most of the stories Ellin wrote after *Kindly Dig Your Grave and Other Stories*. Penzler insisted that Ellin write his own introduction, in which he explained the common thread in his work: "All the stories in this collection except one deal with that streak of wickedness in human nature which makes human nature so deplorably fascinating." The exception, "Beidenbauer's Flea," makes the imaginary flea, rather than its owner, the focus of the story. The Mystery Writers of America named Ellin a Grand Master in 1981 in recognition of his outstanding work in the field.

The Dark Fantastic, a novel that Ellin spent a long time writing, was a major setback in his career, at least from the viewpoint of Random House, his publisher since 1958. Ten other publishing houses rejected the novel before it was finally accepted by Otto Penzler's fledgling Mysterious Press. Publishers feared the backlash that might result from a story about a white racist landlord, Charles Walter Kirwan, who wants to eliminate the black tenants in an apartment house he owns by blowing up the building. Of further concern was the interracial relationship between Milano and Christine Bailey, an attractive black receptionist who works at Rammeart's, a West 57th Street art gallery. The two meet when Milano asks for her help in finding a stolen painting, which he believes is in the Rammeart Gallery. They have a further connection because Christine's family lives in Kirwan's building.

Kirwan and Milano are the narrators in alternating chapters, the same technique Ellin used successfully in *Stronghold* to present differing perspectives. Kirwan, now terminally ill, is a retired history professor from Borough College, a thinly disguised version of Ellin's alma mater. Kirwan, a closet racist, lives in a decaying family mansion at 407 Witter Street in the East Flatbush section of Brooklyn and owns the adjacent apartment building at 409. Kirwan plans to destroy the building so that it will implode and not damage his mansion. *The Dark Fantastic*, the most ambitious of Ellin's sociological novels, explores the impact of a change in the population of a neighborhood. Ellin weaves much Brooklyn history into *The Dark Fantastic*, starting with its settlement by the Dutch in the Flatbush and Fulton Street areas, as well as his knowledge of architecture.

When Philippe Van Rjndt reviewed *The Dark Fantastic* in *The New York Times Book Review* (17 March 1985), he declared it would become one of the most debated books of the year because of its racial content, but he also wrote that it was "a novel that transcends its own genre." The book did not cause protests or create negative reactions toward Ellin. The Private Eye Writers of America nominated *The Dark Fantastic* for the Shamus Award for Best PI Novel of 1984.

Ellin's final novel, *Very Old Money,* is a story of revenge enacted fifty-five years after Margaret Durie was blinded from a fall down a winding staircase. Margaret, a member of a wealthy family that traces its heritage back to colonial America, was an artist before the accident. Adela Taliaferro, the wife of Margaret's art instructor, pushed Margaret down the stairs after discovering that Adela's husband and Margaret were having an affair. Margaret's insanity and the reason for her accident have been kept secret by three of the family's servants, but when Mrs. McEye, the housekeeper, decides to retire, Michael and Amy Lloyd, unemployed former private-school teachers, join the household as a servant couple—Michael as chauffeur and Amy as secretary and administrative assistant. Amy does not realize that she is being used to exact Margaret's revenge until Margaret kills Kim Lowry, who is the Taliaferros' granddaughter.

Very Old Money, a Book-of-the-Month Club selection, is an interesting study in social classes and the mores of an elite family who reside in the Upper East Side Historic District, located between Madison and Fifth Avenues. The Lloyds come from a decidedly middle-class background and have to adjust to a quieter, more restrained manner of behavior. Melik Kaylin, who reviewed the novel for *The New York Times Book Review* (17 March 1985), was disappointed in the work as a suspense or crime novel and found that Ellin strayed "too far from the exigencies of the genre in pursuit of a moral . . . that very old money is corrupt and alluring."

With *The Dark Fantastic* and *Very Old Money,* Stanley Ellin stopped his worldwide wanderings and returned to Manhattan and Brooklyn, the two New York City boroughs he loved most. On 31 July 1986, he died of a heart attack in Brooklyn's Kings County Hospital. His obituary in *The New York Times* (1 August 1986) alluded to the regard his peers had for Ellin and recalled Boucher's comparison of Ellin to Raymond Chandler. In his tribute in *The Armchair Detective* (Winter 1987), Willis Colby wrote that Ellin had "an exquisite curiosity, superb intelligence, and an alarming, awesome, infinite imagination" and characterized him as a "fastidious revisionist." Ellin had told Bruccoli that he did not move to the second page until the first page was exactly right.

Praise for Ellin's short stories has been consistently high; critical reception to the novels has been mixed. The short stories are acclaimed for their logical presentation of detail, accuracy in presenting the criminal mind, and the surprise twist in the resolution. The novels have sometimes been criticized for being too long, resorting to unnecessary plot maneuvers, and moving toward solutions that are not always credible. But even with those faults, the novels, like the short stories, entertain readers while making them reflect on the vagaries of human nature.

Through Ellin's fiction, readers are introduced to more than murder and psychological motivation. His writing reflects the mind of a man who saw an alliance between fiction and sociology, as reflected in his later novels, particularly *The Dark Fantastic.* He captured the ethos of a civilization or society in a given period. Ellin's penchant for detail, developed largely through his many walks in Brooklyn and Manhattan, created an aura in his work that is both romantic and realistic.

Interview:

Conversations with Writers II, volume 3 (Detroit: Gale, 1978), pp. 3–20.

References:

Robert A. Baker and Michael T. Nietzel, *Private Eyes: 101 Knights: A Survey of American Detective Fiction 1922–1984* (Bowling Green, Ohio: Bowling Green State University Popular Press, 1985), pp. 192–197, 325;

Herbert Brean, ed., *The Mystery Writers Handbook: A Handbook on the Writing of Detective, Suspense, Mystery, and Crime Stories by the Mystery Writers of America* (New York: Harper, 1956); revised as *Mystery Writer's Handbook by the Mystery Writers of America* (Cincinnati, Ohio: Writer's Digest, 1976), pp. 41–47, 165–169;

Edward D. Hoch, "Stanley Ellin," in *The St. James Guide to Crime and Mystery Writers,* edited by Jay P. Pederson (London & New York: St. James Press, 1996), pp. 337–338;

Marvin S. Lachman, "Stanley Ellin," in *Mystery and Suspense Writers: The Literature of Crime, Detention, and Espionage,* edited by Robin Winks and Maureen Corrigan, volume 1 (New York: Scribners, 1998), pp. 357–366;

Carlton Smith, "Stanley Ellin," *American National Biography Online* <http://www.anb.org/article/16/16/0356.html>;

Julian Symons, *Bloody Murder: From the Detective Story to the Crime Novel: A History,* third edition (London: Pan Books, 1992), pp. 87, 196–197;

Dilys Winn, *Murder Ink: The Mystery Reader's Companion* (New York: Workman, 1977), p. 5.

Papers:

Stanley Ellin's papers are at the Mugar Memorial Library of Boston University. The papers include manuscripts and drafts of stories and novels written between 1960 and 1985, corrected proofs, some reviews of his books, and some correspondence.

Elizabeth George

(26 February 1949 –   )

Karl L. Stenger
University of South Carolina Aiken

BOOKS: *A Great Deliverance* (New York: Bantam, 1988; London: Bantam, 1989);

Payment in Blood (New York: Bantam, 1989; London: Bantam, 1989);

Well-Schooled in Murder (New York: Bantam, 1990; London: Bantam, 1990);

A Suitable Vengeance (New York: Bantam, 1991; London: Bantam, 1991);

For the Sake of Elena (New York: Bantam, 1992; London: Bantam, 1992);

Missing Joseph (New York: Bantam, 1993; London: Bantam, 1993);

Playing for the Ashes (New York: Bantam, 1994; London: Bantam, 1994);

In the Presence of the Enemy (New York: Bantam, 1996; London: Bantam, 1996);

Deception on His Mind (New York: Bantam, 1997; London: Hodder & Stoughton, 1997);

In Pursuit of the Proper Sinner (New York: Bantam, 1999; London: Hodder & Stoughton, 1999);

The Evidence Exposed (London: Hodder & Stoughton, 1999); revised and enlarged as *I, Richard: Stories of Suspense* (London: Hodder & Stoughton, 2001; New York: Bantam, 2002)—comprises "Exposure," "The Surprise of His Life," "Good Fences Aren't Enough," "Remember, I'll Always Love You," and "I, Richard";

Remember, I'll Always Love You (Clarkston, Mich.: ASAP Publishing, 2001);

A Traitor to Memory (New York: Bantam, 2001; London: Hodder & Stoughton, 2001);

A Place of Hiding (New York: Bantam, 2003; London: Hodder & Stoughton, 2003);

Write Away: One Novelist's Approach to Fiction and the Writing Life (London: Hodder & Stoughton, 2004; New York: HarperCollins, 2004).

OTHER: *Crime from the Mind of a Woman: A Collection of Women Crime Writers of the Century,* edited and introduced by George (London: Hodder & Stoughton, 2002); republished as *A Moment on the Edge: 100*

Elizabeth George (photograph © Bruce Stromber/Images.com/Picture Quest; from the dust jacket for Write Away: One Novelist's Approach to Fiction and the Writing Life, *2004; Thomas Cooper Library, University of South Carolina)*

Years of Crime Stories by Women (New York: Harper-Collins, 2004).

When Elizabeth George's first novel, *A Great Deliverance,* was published in 1988, reviewers showered it with accolades and marveled at the accurate depiction of British life and mores by a Californian. The novel garnered George nominations for a Macavity Award and an Edgar and won the Anthony and Agatha Awards as well as Le Grande Prix de Littèrature

Policière in France. George's subsequent eleven literary mysteries, each of which has outdone the previous one in terms of plotting, character development, and length, have met with considerable commercial and critical success. Her novels have been translated into thirteen languages and are especially popular in Germany, where they have consistently been best-sellers.

In George's books, the Golden Age tradition of the English mystery meets contemporary reality. But though George evokes conventions of the English mystery, she chooses to write crime fiction because, as she told Tom Nolan of *Mystery Scene* (2001), "one can use this particular form as a skeleton on which you hang all kinds of stuff." From the beginning of her career, her primary interests have been the psychology of her characters and the dynamics of dysfunctional family relationships, not the solution of the mystery. She has continued to focus on these interests to an ever-deepening degree. In an interview with Crow Dillon-Park for *Deadly Women: The Woman Mystery Reader's Indispensable Companion* (1998), she characterized her books as "why-dunits" rather than "whodunits."

Susan Elizabeth George was born on 26 February 1949 in Warren, Ohio, the younger of two children of Robert Edwin George, who estimated large-job costs for a conveyor company, and Anne Rivelle George, a registered nurse. When George was one and a half years old, the family relocated to the San Francisco Bay area because her father hated the Midwestern weather and wanted to get his wife away from her large Italian family. Growing up in the small town of Mountain View—now part of Silicon Valley—George missed being surrounded by her relatives. "I grew up without any extended family, and I really, my entire life, missed and mourned that," she told Nolan. Her parents awakened in George at an early age the love for the written word. In a profile in the 23 August 1993 issue of *People*, "No True Brit," she told Marjorie Rosen, "We weren't a family that had a lot of money. We turned to the world of imagination." She recalls her six-year-old brother being struck in the eye by an arrow and, while he had his eyes bandaged, their parents spending hours reading to him as she listened. In *Write Away: One Novelist's Approach to Fiction and the Writing Life* (2004), George states, "I was more or less conditioned to the writing life through exposure, straitened financial circumstances, and the encouragement of my parents." While George was in elementary school, she started writing short stories on an ancient typewriter her mother gave her. "I knew from the age of seven that I was meant to be a writer," she told David A. Fryxell of *Writers Digest* in a February 2002 interview. When she was twelve, she wrote her first "Nancy Drew-like" novel, "The Mystery of Horseshoe Lake."

George attended St. Joseph Grammar School and Holy Cross High School and escaped boredom by immersing herself in literature. Midway through high school, she wrote her second novel, "The Glass Pillar." When the British invasion reached American shores in the 1960s, George became interested in British literature and pop culture. She began studying the works of William Shakespeare and traveled to London in the summer of 1966 in order to participate in a Shakespeare seminar. She was able to explore the city and immediately fell in love with it, as she explained in an undated essay for amazon.com: "Somehow, I found myself at home. And recognizing that home, I never left it. Physically, of course, I had to. I wasn't even 20 years old. I hadn't even graduated from high school. I had to return to California. But my heart and my creative soul remained behind. And there they have resided ever since." Eventually, George purchased a three-bedroom flat in South Kensington, which came with its own ghost, and she visits England on a regular basis, especially while doing extensive research for her novels.

When George entered college, she chose classes oriented toward English rather than American literature. Having attended Foothill Community College, George received a B.A. in English and her secondary teaching credentials from the University of California, Riverside, in 1970. There she met Ira Jay Toibin, an economics major, and they married on 28 May 1971; their marriage lasted twenty-four years, ending in divorce in November 1995. Along with ten other teachers, George was fired from her first job, at Catholic Mater Dei High School in Santa Ana, for union activity. Her website states, "When the courts ordered the school to rehire all of the teachers, she was unavailable as she had quickly moved on to El Toro High School in El Toro (now called Lake Forest), California, where she remained for the rest of her career as a high school English teacher." George spent almost fourteen years teaching English (1974–1987). During that time she also took courses, earning an M.S. degree in counseling and psychology from California State University, Fullerton, in 1979. In 1981 she was honored as the Orange County Teacher of the Year.

While teaching a high-school course on mystery novels in 1983, she started playing with the idea of writing one herself. Looking back, she admitted to Lisa See of *Publishers Weekly* (11 March 1996): "I knew I wanted to write, but I didn't have a lot of confidence." The turning point came in 1983 when her husband bought one of the earliest IBM computers: "Once the computer came into my home it was a simple jump from thinking about writing a novel to actually doing it," she told Galina Espinoza in "English Lessons," for *People* magazine (26 August 2002). More bluntly, she explained

Dust jacket for George's first novel, in which the relationship between Detective Inspector Thomas Lynley and Detective Sergeant Barbara Havers is complicated by class differences (Richland County Public Library)

tral theme of the novel was "the redemption of St. James and how he came back to science in an attempt to save Lynley, the man who put him in the position of being handicapped in the first place," as George told Barbara Hopfinger in *San Diego Writers Monthly* (March 1992). In the See interview, George conceded that her first effort was not a good book: "It was a clunky, old fashioned, Agatha Christie-style mystery where St. James took everyone into the library and explained the crime." Even though her manuscript was rejected by several publishers, the writing of the novel was a seminal experience for George, for it not only gave her the confidence that she could be a writer but also introduced the four main characters in her published series. "Something to Hide" is the only George manuscript not held by Muger Memorial Library at Boston University.

During her next summer vacation, in 1984, George traveled to Cornwall to do research for the novel later published as *A Suitable Vengeance* (1991), again focused on Allcourt-St. James. Although this novel, too, was rejected by several publishers, George was undaunted. In summer 1985, she traveled to Yorkshire to work on the novel that became *A Great Deliverance*. Having completed the novel in just forty-two days, George was certain that she had created a success. As she told See, "I knew that everything was right—the story, the approach, the characters, a nice twist." Kate Miciak at Bantam Books accepted the novel, and George left her teaching position at El Toro High School in 1987 to become a full-time writer. Despite her success as a novelist, George has not completely abandoned teaching. In addition to directing a weekly seminar for aspiring writers at her home in Huntington Beach, she has taught creative writing at various colleges and at the Maui Writers' Retreat.

Whereas the spotlight in her two unpublished novels was on forensic scientist Allcourt-St. James, in *A Great Deliverance,* George shifted the focus to New Scotland Yard detective Thomas Lynley. The novel also introduced his working-class sergeant, Barbara Havers. George explains this shift on her website:

to See: "I thought, this is put up or shut up time." George began writing her first novel, "Something to Hide," on 28 June 1983, finishing it in a little more than two months, on 5 September.

The central character of "Something to Hide" was forensic scientist Simon Allcourt-St. James, who became a recluse after a serious car accident left him partially disabled. George conceived him, as she states on her website, as an "eccentric detective" in the tradition of Edgar Allan Poe's Auguste Dupin and Sir Arthur Conan Doyle's Sherlock Holmes. She partnered Allcourt-St. James with Thomas Lynley, Lord Asherton, a detective from New Scotland Yard, "who was designed to come to St. James with his pressing problems." Two female characters, Deborah Cotter and Helen Clyde, conceived to be assistants in solving crimes in future novels as well as the men's romantic interests, rounded out the cast of characters. The cen-

I decided to see if Lynley could solve a case on his own. Giving him a case meant giving him a partner, so I designed Barbara Havers to work with him. She would be his polar opposite and she would serve the function of introducing the reader to Lynley through her eyes and in her mind before the reader ever saw the man himself. I hoped in this way to prepare the reader to like—rather than to dislike—Lynley. Since Barbara hated him so much in that first novel and since she herself was fairly unlikable, it seemed to me reasonable to conclude that however she felt about someone, the reader was likely to feel the opposite.

George did not realize at the time that the ever-developing relationship between these two diametrically opposed characters would become the center of most of her novels. Many of her readers are more absorbed by the complicated lives of Lynley and Havers and their friends and families than they are in the crimes depicted in the novels.

At the beginning of *A Great Deliverance,* Detective Sergeant Havers, "a decidedly unattractive woman, but a woman who appeared to be doing everything possible to make herself so," is summoned to her supervisor's office. After eight miserable months of street patrol as a punishment for having been incapable of getting along with anyone in the Criminal Investigation Division, she is given another chance to prove herself and is ordered to work with Detective Inspector Thomas Lynley, the eighth earl of Asherton and New Scotland Yard's "golden boy," on the investigation of a murder in Yorkshire. Havers balks at having to work with "that sodding little fop," especially since he has the reputation of being a ruthless womanizer and she appears to be the only female who is safe from his amorous advances. In searching out Lynley, Havers crashes the wedding reception of Allcourt-St. James and Deborah Cotter, a woman Lynley is still deeply in love with. Havers's inferiority complex and resentment surface as she watches the elegant and self-assured aristocrat: "His movements were graceful, fluid, like a cat's. He was the handsomest man she had ever seen. She loathed him."

The mismatched detectives set off for Keldale, Yorkshire, where they investigate the brutal decapitation of William Teys, a respected member of the community. His mutilated body was found by Father Hart, the village's Catholic priest, along with the corpse of the family dog and the murder weapon. Roberta, the murdered man's nineteen-year-old daughter, was discovered sitting next to the remains, dressed in her Sunday best and muttering, "I did it. I'm not sorry," before lapsing into a catatonic state and being taken to a mental hospital. During their investigation Lynley and Havers uncover many secrets hidden by the Teys family, the villagers, and even the Catholic priest, including child abuse, incest, the death of a newborn, bigamy, and suicide. Despite that George offers several suspects who all have believable motives for Tey's murder, the reader can easily anticipate the final revelation.

In *A Great Deliverance,* the closed world of the village, a locus classicus of the so-called cozy mystery popularized by Agatha Christie, is invaded by the cruelty and injustice of the modern world. In his essay "Truth, Justice, the American Way: Martha Grimes and Elizabeth George," Carl D. Malmgren argues that George has modernized mystery fiction by modifying its two basic predicates: "In the modern world, simply put,

Truth prevails but Justice fails. In the modern mystery, crimes occur, are detected, and are usually solved, but justice becomes much more problematic, sometimes hard to define, other times harder to uphold." In the case of *A Great Deliverance,* the victim is revealed as the victimizer and the murderer as the ultimate victim.

Although George's first novel won favorable reviews—the *Booklist* reviewer called it a "tricky, multi-layered, ambitious, and ultimately breathtaking debut" and compared Lynley to P. D. James's Adam Dagleish—it also created controversy. Martha Grimes, another American author who sets her mystery novels in England, accused George of literary imitation and, according to Sarah Lyall in a 25 July 1993 article in the *New Orleans Times-Picayune,* "Writing Well Is the Best Revenge: The Dueling Pens of Martha Grimes and Elizabeth George," hired someone to uncover similarities between her novel *Help the Poor Struggler* (1985) and *A Great Deliverance.* Grimes's subsequent novel, *The Horse You Came In On* (1993), employed the theme of literary pilfering and featured a female author who plagiarizes a rival's work. George refused to be drawn into a turf war and responded in Rosen's profile with puzzlement: "I've always been nonplused by Martha's allegations. She writes the 'tea cozy,' or light-hearted romp through murder. And I write the literary mystery. There's really nothing that can be compared beyond the superficial."

In George's second novel, *Payment in Blood* (1989), the setting, a Scottish manor house that has been converted into a hotel, and the group of suspects, who are members of a close-knit group (in this case a theatrical company) hark back to the Golden Age tradition. The company has gathered to prepare the production of a new play by Joy Sinclair, an abrasive writer who also specializes in books about real crimes and murders. When Sinclair is found viciously stabbed to death in her bed, Lynley, Havers, and Allcourt-St. James are sent to Scotland to solve the heinous crime. At the beginning of their investigation, Sinclair's play, a murder mystery that reveals secrets about some of the company members, appears to be the trigger for the murder. The more Lynley and Havers delve into the mystery, however, the more Sinclair's intention emerges—to reveal a past murder, which had been camouflaged as a suicide, in her upcoming nonfiction book, "Hanging's Too Good," and this impending exposure appears to be the motive for the murder.

The investigation is complicated by Lynley's and Havers's personal antipathies and prejudices. When Lynley discovers that Lady Helen Clyde, the woman he is in love with, had an amorous encounter in the room adjacent to the murder victim's bedroom with Rhys Davies-Jones, the Welsh director of the play, Lyn-

*Dust jacket for George's third novel, published in 1990, about pedophilia, sadism, blackmail, and murder
at a prestigious English school for boys (Collection of Julie and George Anderson)*

ley's personal resentment and wounded pride take over, and he declares Davies-Jones the prime suspect. Havers realizes "that, for Lynley, the situation had the potential of developing into a personal crisis of some considerable proportions." Her ever-present class resentment also leads her to suspect that Lynley has been asked to investigate the case because one of the suspects is stage producer Stuart Rintoul, Lord Stinhurst. She is afraid that Lynley's class allegiance clouds his judgment and keeps him from considering Lord Stinhurst a strong suspect in the murder. Havers is proven right when Lord Stinhurst's older brother Geoffrey is revealed to have been a Russian spy who had been murdered and whose murder had been covered up by the government.

When Lynley realizes that he has lost his objectivity and that he has been used by his superiors for a cover-up, he is devastated and decides to resign his position at New Scotland Yard. Superintendent Webberly, Lynley's superior, acknowledges that Lynley's idealism has suffered a serious blow, and he exhorts

him to be more realistic: "Welcome to the club, Inspector. You're not perfect any longer. . . . Learning to forgive yourself is part of the job, lad. It's the only part you've never quite mastered." Not only is Lynley disillusioned by the machinations of the political and justice systems but he also realizes his personal relationship with Helen Clyde is in a shambles. He has treated her shabbily during the murder investigation, and in an attempt to atone, he declares his love and asks her to marry him. Helen's predictable response is, "I don't want to see you, Tommy. Not for a while," and she leaves for foreign parts. At the end of the novel, a chastened and disillusioned Lynley sits in a London bar drowning his sorrows in single-malt scotch with Havers, who, for the first time, is able to empathize with her partner: "Barbara sighed, felt the weighty, sore blanket of his unhappiness, and found to her surprise that she wore it as her own."

In spite of Lynley's realization that he lost his objectivity because of class allegiance, he agrees to take on his next case in *Well-Schooled in Murder* (1990) because of old school loyalties. John Corntel, Lynley's former schoolmate at Eton, who is now housemaster at Bredgar Chambers, a prestigious public school for boys in West Sussex, turns to the Inspector because Matthew Whateley, one of his students, has disappeared. Lynley, Havers, and Allcourt-St. James travel to the claustrophobic school to find the missing boy. All three are also trying to escape their personal woes. Lynley is still smarting from his rejection by Helen Clyde, who has fled to Greece; Havers is unable to cope with the responsibility of caring for a sick father and an increasingly demented mother; and Allcourt-St. James is dumbfounded by the rapid disintegration of his marriage. The reason for the growing alienation between Allcourt-St. James and his wife, Deborah, is revealed when she visits the area during one of her photographic assignments and finds the naked and tortured body of the missing boy in the same graveyard where Thomas Gray composed his famous "Elegy Written in a Country Churchyard." She has suffered four miscarriages during the past eighteen months and blames herself for her condition, having undergone an abortion six years ago while in America and without Allcourt-St. James's knowledge. Finding the child's corpse exacerbates her feelings of guilt.

During the murder investigation, the seemingly respectable school is revealed to be marked by homosexuality, pedophilia, sadism, and blackmail. When a cache of pornographic photos of a masochistic and pedophilic nature is discovered in Corntel's possession, and he becomes one of the murder suspects, Lynley's judgment is compromised by their past history. He suppresses the incriminating material because "There was—and always would be—the old school tie." As in George's previous novels, much of the mystery in *Well-Schooled in Murder* is found in buried family secrets. The author has stated in several interviews that the central theme of her novels is the dysfunctional family.

The gloom that suffuses what is certainly one of George's darkest books is only slightly alleviated by developments in the lives of the four central characters. For Havers's long-suffering father, death comes as a blessing. Allcourt-St. James magnanimously suggests to his wife to use Lynley as a sperm donor in case he is genetically unable to produce children, and his unselfishness prompts Deborah to admit that she had an abortion when she was eighteen and pregnant with Lynley's baby. Not only does the Allcourt-St. James marriage seem saved at the end of the novel, but also Lynley and Helen find a measure of reconciliation: "Lynley took what pleasure he could from Helen's hand on his arm. He drew a measure of contentment from the pressure of her shoulder against his, from her presence at his side, from the sound of her voice. It was

not all what he wanted from her. It never would be. But he knew it would have to suffice for now." *Well-Schooled in Murder* was praised in *People* (October 1990) as "a compelling psychological study probing skittish personalities as sharply as it examines the case at hand," and its creator was favorably compared to James, a master of the genre. The novel was awarded the coveted German prize for international mystery fiction, the MIMI.

A Suitable Vengeance, set before the action of the first three novels, offers the reader a glimpse into the tangled lives of the major characters before Barbara Havers entered the mix. When George's original manuscript was rejected in 1984, she put it aside, returning to revise it radically six years later, as she explained in her interview with Hopfinger: "I rewrote the whole book. I threw out the first version . . . and started all over again from ground zero, did character analysis, did a setting design, did a running plot outline, and then just rewrote the book without reference to the original. So it was basically a new book. It was a much better book." The novel has the hallmarks of most of George's novels—a seemingly idyllic and remote setting, a close-knit group of characters bound by secrets and animosities, the intrusion of the evils of contemporary life, and the focus on the dysfunctional family.

A Suitable Vengeance focuses on Thomas Lynley and his family. When he takes his fiancée, Deborah Cotter, to Howenstow, the family's home in Cornwall, to celebrate their engagement, tensions immediately surface. Lynley has been estranged from his mother since his father's death because he has accused her of infidelity. He also does not get along with his brother, Peter, a drug addict who has made a shambles of his life. George adds other characters to this volatile situation—Peter's drug-addicted girlfriend, Sasha Nifford; Simon Allcourt-St. James, who is still in love with Deborah; as well as Simon's younger sister, Sidney, and her unsavory boyfriend, Justin Brooke, a bon vivant who is also addicted to drugs. Not only is Mick Cambrey, the village newspaper publisher, murdered and castrated, but also Justin Brooke and Sasha Nifford are killed. Once the case is closed, Lynley's departure from Howenstow is bittersweet. On the one hand, he has resolved his differences with his brother and mother. On the other hand, he has lost Deborah to Allcourt-St. James, whose wedding takes place at the beginning of *A Great Deliverance*. Upon his return to London, Lynley buries himself in work and refuses to see anyone until Helen Clyde pierces his isolation and offers him a shoulder to cry on. While *Publishers Weekly* (12 April 1991) praised the deftly handled plot of George's "darkly vibrant modern English mystery," it found "the paths etched by her anguished, memorable characters" even more intricate.

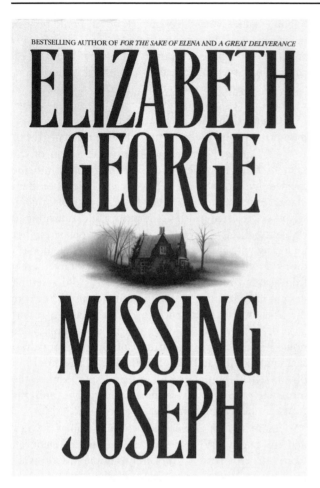

*Dust jacket for George's sixth novel, in which Lynley investigates
a vicar's "death by misadventure" in a rural northern village
(Collection of Julie and George Anderson)*

Like *Well-Schooled in Murder,* George's next novel,
For the Sake of Elena (1992), is set in an academic milieu.
Elena Weaver, an English student at fictitious St.
Stephen's College in Cambridge, is bludgeoned and
strangled during her daily jog, and the administration at
the university asks for the help of New Scotland Yard.
Lynley volunteers for the job in order to be close to
Helen Clyde, who is in Cambridge helping her sister
Pen recuperate from a difficult pregnancy and birth.
When Lynley and Havers investigate the murder victim's background, they encounter a chameleon. While
Elena projects the image of innocence and helplessness
to some, she appears to others as unbalanced, sexually
predatory, and manipulative. The investigation reveals
she had an affair with a married history professor and
tried to entrap him, rebuffed one of her fellow students
after using him to get pregnant, and accused an English
professor of sexual harassment. These men quickly
become suspects because, with the savage nature of the
murder, Lynley "felt that the nature of the crime itself

suggested a personal involvement, perhaps, more than
that, a settling of scores." While Lynley knows from
experience "that murder was often an obviously
cut-and-dried affair in which the likeliest suspect was
indeed the perpetrator of the crime," he is also aware
that "some deaths grew from darker places in the soul
and from motives far more convoluted than were suggested by the initial evidence." The latter holds true for
Elena's murder, as the investigators turn from the likeliest suspects to Elena's dysfunctional family to solve the
crime.

Having witnessed a family in disarray, Havers re-
evaluates her own domestic situation. She has been
reluctant to move her mother, who suffers from severe
senile dementia, to Hawthorn Lodge, an assisted-living
facility, because Havers fears "being judged as a callous
and indifferent child—by what she knew was largely a
callous and indifferent world." She finally realizes that
putting her mother in the care of experienced professionals represents the ultimate act of love and unselfishness.

In *Missing Joseph* (1993), Havers's decision proves
to have been the right one. Not only does it benefit her
mother, but it also offers the sergeant the chance of a
new beginning. While Havers's life has taken a positive
turn, the Allcourt-St. James marriage is again on the
brink of dissolution as Deborah's emotions clash with
Simon's scientific and analytical outlook. Simon's
"worldview—indeed, his world itself—was different from
hers. He could say, Listen to me, Deborah, there are
other bonds besides those of blood. . . . Life was
defined in different terms for her." While Simon wants
to adopt a child, Deborah insists on "a family that's
real, one that we create, not the one that we apply for."

The Allcourt-St. Jameses are soon caught up in a
case that raises questions about the nature of family and
parenthood. Stranded in London's National Gallery
because of a fierce storm, Deborah encounters a vicar
in front of Leonardo da Vinci's exquisite and famous
drawing of the Virgin and Child and is startled by his
observation, "Haven't you noticed? Isn't it always
Madonna and Child? . . . Or Virgin and Child. Or
Mother and Child. Or Adoration of the Magi with a
cow and an ass and an angel or two. But you rarely see
Joseph. Have you never wondered why?" Deborah
instantly senses a kinship with the clergyman and persuades her husband to take her on a holiday to remote
and idyllic Winslough, Lancashire, where she hopes to
mend their marital rift and to visit the vicar. When the
Allcourt-St. Jameses arrive in the village, they discover
that the vicar has died. While the coroner returns a ver-
dict of "death by misadventure," or, more specifically,
"a case of accidental poisoning," many villagers suspect
that the vicar was murdered.

When the Allcourt-St. Jameses ask Lynley for help, he gladly interrupts his holiday after a disagreement with his new lover, Helen, over the nature of their relationship. He joins his friends in Lancashire only to discover a closed community where "there were secrets layered upon secrets." Ultimately, the vicar's past provides the key to unlock the mystery of his death. At the end of the book, Lynley is forced to question his own concept of justice and morality, and he realizes, "There's no black or white for me in what happened. Grey stretches forever, despite the law and my professional obligations to it." *Missing Joseph* was named one of the ten best crime novels of the year by *The Los Angeles Times,* and the *Richmond Times-Dispatch* (11 July 1993) called it "as much a meditation on parenthood as . . . a fine whodunit."

In *Playing for the Ashes* (1994), George, who has said that she tries to create a challenge for herself in each book, experiments with structure by weaving two novels into one. One of the narratives consists of the journal of Olivia Whitelaw, a young woman who is estranged from her family, has a history of prostitution and drug addiction, and is slowly wasting away from amyotrophic lateral sclerosis, or Lou Gehrig's disease. Like a stray dog, Olivia has been rescued from the street by idealistic Chris Faraday, an animal-rights activist with whom she now shares a barge on the river Thames. Initially, Olivia does everything she can to shock and alienate the reader of her manuscript. Abrasive, hateful, profane, even obscene, she revels in her rebelliousness. She retells with glee, for example, how she was able to sexually arouse her own father: "He'd gone hard as a fire iron. And I loved the joke of it, the beautiful power of it. . . . To have got a reaction from taciturn, passionless Gordon Whitelaw. If I could do that, here in public, in front of God only knows how many witnesses, I could do anything. I was omnipotence personified." In Carroll Lachnit's article "Perfectly Murderous" (1995), George conceded that she was apprehensive about the level of sexuality in *Playing for the Ashes:* "I was especially worried about Olivia's narration. But I wanted to write a first-person narrative that was not my voice, that was totally different from me, that my mother would read and say 'Where did that come from?'" Through George's skill, Olivia's initially repulsive persona gradually and believably gives way to that of a fragile, sensitive girl who desperately yearns for her mother's love.

Miriam Whitelaw, however, has cut all ties with her outlaw daughter and has found a substitute in Ken Fleming, a former student of hers who comes from a poor blue-collar family. As the second narrative opens, Ken is a star player and member of the national cricket team who is torn between his dedication to his wife,

Jeannie, and their troubled sixteen-year-old son, Jimmy, and his passion for beautiful Gabriella Patten, whose husband is a major sponsor of the national cricket team. When Fleming is found asphyxiated, Lynley and Havers are asked to assist in the investigation because of the high-profile victim. Lynley is convinced Jimmy, who confesses to the killing, is innocent, and he suspects that the perfect crime has been committed, "one in which none of the evidence collected at the scene could be attached—beyond the law's required shadow of a doubt—to the killer." Ultimately, Olivia's journal names the murderer and reveals the motive.

George uses the lives of her recurrent characters as a positive counterpoint to her heartbreaking depiction of thwarted filial and parental love and disastrous relationships. Lady Helen Clyde finally agrees to marry Lynley, and the reclusive and prickly Havers is slowly but inexorably drawn in by her new neighbors, the gentle and shy Taymullah Azhar, a Pakistani professor of microbiology, and his vivacious eight-year-old daughter, Khalidah Hadiyyah.

George's concern with the psychology of her characters, increasingly clear as her career has progressed and evident in *Playing for the Ashes,* is even more pronounced in her 1996 novel, *In the Presence of the Enemy.* As in her previous novel, only one murder takes place, and the focus of the 517-page book is on the psychological development of each character and the tangled relationships among the protagonists. Detective Inspector Lynley does not even enter the scene until page 204.

As is the case for most of George's novels, the seed of *In the Presence of the Enemy* was suggested to her by an actual incident. In her interview with See, George said that the 1993 kidnapping and murder of twelve-year-old Polly Klaas in California provided her with the inspiration for creating a similar kidnapping in London society: "I wondered, why does Scotland Yard become involved? . . . The kidnaped girl had to be the daughter of someone prominent—a member of Parliament and a single mother. Wouldn't Lynley look to the father? What if the father is someone that the mother wouldn't want anyone to know about? What if he was one of those scumbag tabloid guys?" Such questions led George to fashion a multilayered novel that again has dysfunctional family relationships at its core.

In his 15 March 1996 review of *In the Presence of the Enemy* in *Entertainment Weekly,* Mark Harris asserted that George's "books are comedies of manners, social studies, psychological case histories, and always, finally, tragedies. . . . The novel's theme—what parents do to their children in the name of love, greed, hate, or self-interest—ricochets through half a dozen relationships, almost always unpredictably, and by the end, nobody remains unaffected." In the 12 May 1996 issue of *The Los Angeles Times Book Review,* Margo Kaufmann praised George as "arguably the finest writer working in the mystery genre today."

Deception on His Mind (1997), George's ninth novel, features Barbara Havers, the favorite character of many readers in the United States. In a 1992 interview with Nancy-Stephanie Stone in *Armchair Detective,* George noted this preference: "Americans are absolutely fascinated with Sergeant Havers. Most of my mail concerns her, and readers recommend what should happen to this poor woman. British readers are not as connected to her. I think Americans have a tendency to really attach themselves to the underdog." As the novel opens, Lynley and Helen, newly married, are enjoying their honeymoon, while Havers is still suffering physically and psychologically from her involvement with the kidnapping-murder case from *In the Presence of the Enemy.* She is ordered to take time off, and the thought of enforced leisure fills her "with the horror of a woman who kept her private life, her wounded psyche, and her raw emotions in order by not having time to attend to them." When her neighbor Taymullah Azhar and his daughter Khalidah Hadiyyah leave for the decaying seaside town Balford-le-Nez on the coast of Essex, where the murder of a Pakistani businessman has sparked a potentially dangerous racial conflict, she follows them partly out of curiosity, partly out of concern for her new friends.

Haytham Querashi, the murder victim, had recently arrived from Pakistan in order to enter into an arranged marriage with Sahlah Malik, the daughter of the most prominent Pakistani businessman of the town. Sahlah, however, is in love with Theodore Shaw, the grandson of Malik's fiercest opponent, and she is apparently pregnant with his child. Muhannad Malik, Sahlah's older brother, uses Querashi's murder to fan the flames of racial unrest by claiming that the police investigators are focusing on Pakistani suspects while ignoring the English community of the town. Azhar, who is related to the Malik family, is called in as an "expert in the politics of immigration" and as an arbitrator between the two communities. The chief inspector for the town, Emily Barlow, an ambitious policewoman, knows Havers from a course they took together, and Havers assigns Barlow the unofficial role of liaison to the Pakistani community.

When Barlow digs into the murder victim's background, she discovers that he was known in the gay subculture of the town and that he had had a homosexual affair. While George had touched on the theme of homosexuality in *Well-Schooled in Murder, For The Sake of Elena, In the Presence of the Enemy,* and *Playing for the Ashes,* it gains in significance in *Deception on His Mind* because it

symbolizes the conflict between the rules and traditions of the Pakistani community and those of the English citizenry. The investigation eventually uncovers the organized smuggling of illegal Pakistani immigrants into the country and their exploitation by Muhannad Malik, who has used the murder investigation to distract the police from his illegal activities.

The novel closes with an exciting chase sequence in which Havers and Barlow pursue Muhannad Malik, who flees for the Continent with little Hadiyyah as hostage. When the police boat catches up with Muhannad, he tries to buy himself time by throwing the girl overboard. When Havers's superior refuses to turn the boat around to save Hadiyyah because she is just "some goddamn Paki brat," Havers forces the action at gunpoint. Even though her insubordination saves the girl's life, it puts her own career in jeopardy. In addition, the revelation of Barlow's prejudice further disillusions Havers: "She realized that every time she felt she'd got a leg up on understanding her fellowman, something happened to whip the rug out from under her." Such experiences explain her reluctance to accept Taymullah Azhar's offer of friendship:

> She wondered if she really wanted to face the unknown and take the risk of engaging her heart–there it was again, that flaming, unreliable organ–where it might well be broken. But then she realised that, insidious arbiter of behaviour that it was, her heart was already entirely engaged and had been so from the moment she'd encountered the man's elfin daughter. What, after all, was so terrifying about adding one more person to the crew of the largely untidy ship upon which she appeared to be sailing in her life?

George's ambitious and multilayered 1999 novel, *In Pursuit of the Proper Sinner,* which Margo Kaufman of *The Times* (London) called "labyrinthine," was inspired by an incident that occurred near her South Kensington apartment, as she recalled in an essay for amazon.com:

> The novel took its genesis from a postcard that I found on Cromwell Road in London, when I was walking home to my flat with my grocery shopping. My cousin Georgia Ann was with me, and we both stopped when we saw this card and when we noticed that there appeared to be a proliferation of them on the pavement. I picked one up. She picked up two more. We read them. We looked at each other, eyebrows raised. We thought at the same moment, no doubt, what I said: "There's a novel here, and I'm going to write it."

Similar postcards, advertising various kinds of sexual services, link the two murder victims who are found on Calder Moor, Derbyshire, near an ancient circle of stones known as Nine Sisters Henge. One of the bodies is that of Nicola Maiden, the daughter of retired under-cover operations officer Andy Maiden, who has opened a bed-and-breakfast after leaving the force. Nicola, a troubled and rebellious young woman, has dropped out of law school and has, at her father's insistence, moved home for the summer to work for a firm of solicitors. The other murder victim found on the moor is Terry Cole, a struggling London artist who had no scruples when it came to supplementing his meager income.

At first no connection between the victims can be established, and by special request of Maiden, his former mentor, Detective Inspector Thomas Lynley, is brought in to investigate the vicious attack. Havers has been demoted to Detective Constable after a three-month suspension and an investigation for assault and attempted murder, and Lynley has distanced himself from his former partner. In an obvious affront to Havers, he picks Detective Constable Winston Nkata, an ambitious black policeman and former gang member, who has played a subordinate role in previous novels, to accompany him to Derbyshire. Nkata, however, surprises Havers by asking her to investigate the case on the London end, a wise decision that ultimately leads to the solution of the double murder.

The investigation reveals that Nicola Maiden had turned to prostitution, specializing in S–M, with Terry Cole acting as her "card boy" by distributing ads for her services. As the story comes to a close, Andy Maiden, in an attempt to keep Nicola's life as a prostitute hidden from his wife, commits suicide by slashing his throat and leaves an "apocryphal confession to the murder of a daughter he had deeply loved." Maiden's wife, however, is aware of their daughter's secret, and his self-sacrifice turns out to have been in vain. Lynley feels partially responsible for the needless death of his mentor because he let personal affection and admiration cloud his judgment, and he did not follow procedure: "I let my feelings for the man get in the way. I made the wrong decision, and as a result he died. His blood is on my hands as indelibly as if I'd wielded the knife." This realization causes Lynley to reevaluate Havers's rescue of Hadiyyah, and, acknowledging that one cannot "separate the decision from the outcome," he is finally able to concede: "You made the right decision, Barbara." Whereas Francine Fialkoff of the *Library Journal* thought that "George may have gone overboard here with her penchant for complex plotting" and found her particular brand of psychological mystery/ morality tale tedious, a reviewer for *Publishers Weekly* praised the "intricate, swiftly paced tale" and, above all, the "multifaceted surprise ending to the taut, suspenseful plot." The German translation of the novel, *Undank ist der Vaeter Lohn,* was extremely successful when it was

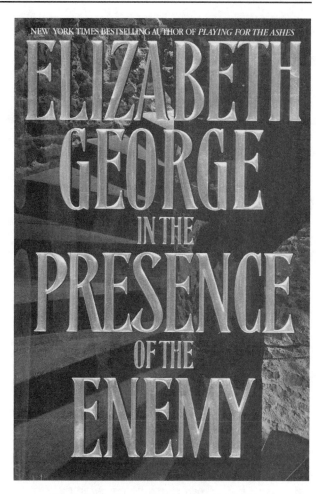

Dust jacket for George's eighth novel, which involves a kidnapping-murder case (Richland County Public Library)

published in an astonishingly large first printing of 250,000 copies.

After the short-story collection *The Evidence Exposed* (1999) and the revision and enlargement, *I, Richard: Stories of Suspense* (2001), in which Lynley appears only briefly, George published her eleventh novel, *A Traitor to Memory,* in 2001. The seed for this book, called a "sprawling epic" by *Publishers Weekly* (4 June 2001), was the trial and conviction of the English nanny Louise Woodward for the death of the baby under her care. As she told amazon.com, George developed her "nanny book" into a complex study of a family in crisis, an exploration of "the nature of denial and how denial of the past operates not only to distort memories but also to influence an individual's ability to function in the present." When she began the novel, George says, "I decided that the real story was about more than the terrible death of a child. Indeed, I decided that the heart of the novel was about the death of that child's mother, which would happen twenty years later. I saw the novel as two stories intertwined, with the principal characters the same of both." The author challenged herself "to write one of the stories as a first person stream-of-consciousness narrative, something I had never attempted before. I decided to up the stakes for myself and make it a first person narrative in a male point of view." This narrative takes the form of a journal kept by violin virtuoso Gideon Davies, who has suddenly and inexplicably lost the ability to play and suffers from psychogenic amnesia.

He gradually and painfully unearths buried childhood memories about the death of his younger sister, Sonia, a Down's syndrome baby. The child had drowned in her bath, and the nanny, a young German woman named Katja Wolff, had been convicted of Sonia's murder and sent to prison. As the third-person narrative reveals, Katja's recent release from prison coincides with the hit-and-run murder of Eugenie Davies, the drowned child's mother. Other hit-and-run attacks follow. While the official police investigation focuses on the hit-and-run murders, Davies's exploration of his past reveals that Wolff did not kill his sister but that she agreed to take the fall in exchange for a considerable monetary reward. *Publishers Weekly* found *A Traitor to Memory* George's most ambitious work and stated that "though some plot developments are initially confusing due to the book's occasionally non-linear style, the author's handling of narrative is consistently inventive." P. G. Koch in a 2001 review in the *Houston Chronicle* called the book a "masterly performance," saying: "Even more so than P. D. James and Minette Walters, with whom she inspires comparison, George seems to embrace the narrative depth and reflective pace of the 19th century novel."

While *A Place of Hiding* (2003) maintains the depth and pace of her previous novels, George chose the isolated Channel island of Guernsey as its setting and, more importantly, shifted the focus from Lynley and Havers to forensic scientist Simon Allcourt-St. James and his wife, Deborah. Deborah, who had spent three years in California with the River family when she was a troubled teenager, is asked by Cherokee River to help his sister, China, who has been arrested and accused of murdering Guy Brouard, a wealthy Guernsey landowner. China and Cherokee had been hired by Brouard to deliver architectural plans for a museum designed to document the resistance of the island against the Nazi occupation. Brouard and his sister Ruth had been the only members of their Jewish family to escape persecution by the Nazis. When Simon and Deborah travel to Guernsey in order to assist China, they find a closed community intent on protecting its secrets. According to the review in *Publishers Weekly* (2

June 2003), the "theme of hiding—of hopes, of the past, of secret places—underpins this intricate story about friendship, anger, loyalty and betrayal."

As in Elizabeth George's previous books, the whodunit is less important than the whydunit and "her nuanced characterizations drive the novel," according to *Booklist* (15 May 2003). George took a considerable risk when she decided to assign the murder investigation to the Allcourt-St. Jameses and to keep Lynley and Havers offstage. Even though Allcourt-St. James is "actually the character that's nearest and dearest to my heart," as she told Stone, George is aware "that Lynley will always emerge as an important character, no matter what I'm doing." The reviewer for *Entertainment Weekly* (8 August 2003) found the Allcourt-St. Jameses "not as vivid as some of George's other regulars" and the 2003 one for *Booklist* "perhaps the least vigorous of George's customary cast." Many of George's fans were disappointed by the unconvincing pair, as many reviews on amazon.com show, and many readers missed Lynley and Havers and especially objected to the character of Deborah, whom they found immature and annoying. Another indication for the deep affection George's readers have for Lynley, Helen, and Havers is the negative reaction of many to the choice of actors for the title roles in *The Inspector Lynley Mysteries* on PBS—*A Great Deliverance, Well-Schooled in Murder, Payment in Blood, For the Sake of Elena, Missing Joseph, Playing for the Ashes, In the Presence of the Enemy, A Suitable Vengeance,* and *Deception on His Mind.* George's fans are undoubtedly looking forward to another intricately plotted mystery, a psychologically astute rendering of a family in disarray, and, above all, fascinating glimpses into the complicated lives of Lynley and Havers.

Interviews:

Barbara Hopfinger, "Q & A with George," *San Diego Writers' Monthly,* 2 (March 1992): 18–24;

Nancy-Stephanie Stone, "An Interview with Elizabeth George," *Armchair Detective,* 25 (Summer 1992): 260–269;

Lisa See, "Elizabeth George: An American in Scotland Yard," *Publishers Weekly,* 243 (11 March 1996): 38–39;

Crow Dillon-Park, "Interview with Elizabeth George," in *Deadly Women: The Woman Mystery Reader's Indispensable Companion,* edited by Jan Grape, Dean James, and Ellen Nehr (New York: Carroll & Graf, 1998), pp. 199–203;

Tom Nolan, "Elizabeth George," *Mystery Scene,* 73 (2001): 56–59;

David A. Fryxell, "The Core Need of Elizabeth George," *Writers Digest* (February 2002): 32–33, 60;

Elizabeth George, "Frequently Asked Questions," Elizabeth George On-Line Web Site <http://elizabethgeorgeonline.com/faq.htm>;

Elizabeth George, "Batty for Britain: Elizabeth George's Anglomania" <http://www.amazon.com/exec/obidos/tg/feature/-/4955/103-7369367-8975022>;

Elizabeth George, "In Pursuit of Elizabeth George: Elizabeth George talks about *A Traitor to Memory*" <http://www.amazon.co.uk/exec/obidos/tg/feature/-/ 175749/026-5131897-7125246>;

"Interview: Elizabeth George, author of *A Great Deliverance*" <http://www.pbs.org/wgbh/mystery/programs/lynley/interview.html>.

References:

Raimund Borgmeier, "Alte Muster - neue Funktionen: Elizabeth George und die Tradition des Detektivromans," in *Unterhaltungsliteratur der achtziger und neunziger Jahre,* edited by Dieter Petzold and Eberhard Spaeth (Erlangen: Universitaetsbund Erlangen-Nuernberg, 1998), pp. 29–41;

Carroll Lachnit, "Perfectly Murderous," *Orange Coast* (August 1995): 82–88;

Sarah Lyall, "Writing Well Is the Best Revenge: The Dueling Pens of Martha Grimes and Elizabeth George," *New Orleans Times-Picayune,* 25 July 1993, pp. E7–E8; reprinted in *New York Times,* 14 July 1993, pp. B2, C13;

Carl D. Malmgren, "Truth, Justice, the American Way: Martha Grimes and Elizabeth George," *Clues,* 21 (Fall/Winter 2000): 47–56; reprinted in Malmgren, *Anatomy of Murder: Mystery, Detective, and Crime Fiction* (Bowling Green, Ohio: Bowling Green State University Popular Press, 2001).

Papers:

Elizabeth George's manuscripts are in the Mugar Memorial Library, Boston University.

Patricia Highsmith

(19 January 1921 – 4 February 1995)

Karl L. Stenger
University of South Carolina, Aiken

BOOKS: *Strangers on a Train* (New York: Harper, 1950; London: Cresset, 1950);

The Price of Salt, as Claire Morgan (New York: Coward-McCann, 1952); republished as *Carol* (London: Bloomsbury, 1990); republished as *The Price of Salt,* as Highsmith (New York: Norton, 1990; revised edition, Tallahassee: Naiad, 1993);

The Blunderer (New York: Coward-McCann, 1954; London: Cresset, 1956); republished as *Lament for a Lover* (New York: Popular Library, 1956);

The Talented Mr. Ripley (New York: Coward-McCann, 1955; London: Cresset, 1957);

Deep Water (New York: Harper, 1957; London: Heinemann, 1958);

Miranda the Panda Is on the Veranda, by Highsmith and Doris Sanders (New York: Coward-McCann, 1958);

A Game for the Living (New York: Harper, 1958; London: Heinemann, 1959);

This Sweet Sickness (New York: Harper, 1960; London: Heinemann, 1961);

The Cry of the Owl (New York: Harper & Row, 1962; London: Heinemann, 1963);

The Two Faces of January (Garden City, N.Y.: Doubleday, 1964; London: Heinemann, 1964);

The Glass Cell (Garden City, N.Y.: Doubleday, 1964; London: Heinemann, 1965);

A Suspension of Mercy (London: Heinemann, 1965); republished as *The Story-Teller* (Garden City, N.Y.: Doubleday, 1965);

Plotting and Writing Suspense Fiction (Boston: Writer, 1966; London: Poplar Press, 1983; revised and enlarged edition, New York: St. Martin's Press, 1990);

Those Who Walk Away (London: Heinemann, 1967; Garden City, N.Y.: Doubleday, 1967);

The Tremor of Forgery (London: Heinemann, 1969; Garden City, N.Y.: Doubleday, 1969);

Eleven (London: Heinemann, 1970); republished as *The Snail-Watcher and Other Stories* (Garden City, N.Y.: Doubleday, 1970);

Ripley under Ground (Garden City, N.Y.: Doubleday, 1970; London: Heinemann, 1970);

A Dog's Ransom (London: Heinemann, 1972; New York: Knopf, 1972);

Ripley's Game (London: Heinemann, 1974; New York: Knopf, 1974);

The Animal-Lover's Book of Beastly Murder (London: Heinemann, 1975; New York: Penzler, 1986);

Kleine Geschichten für Weiberfeinde, translated by W. E. Richartz (Zurich: Diogenes, 1975); republished as *Little Tales of Misogyny* (London: Heinemann, 1977; New York: Penzler, 1986);

Edith's Diary (London: Heinemann, 1977; New York: Simon & Schuster, 1977);

Slowly, Slowly in the Wind (London: Heinemann, 1979; New York: Mysterious Press, 1979);

The Boy Who Followed Ripley (London: Heinemann, 1980; New York: Lippincott & Crowell, 1980);

The Black House (London: Heinemann, 1981; New York: Mysterious Press, 1988);

People Who Knock on the Door (London: Heinemann, 1983; New York: Penzler, 1985);

Mermaids on the Golf Course (London: Heinemann, 1985; New York: Penzler, 1988);

Found in the Street (London: Heinemann, 1986; New York: Atlantic Monthly, 1986);

Tales of Natural and Unnatural Catastrophes (London: Bloomsbury, 1987; New York: Atlantic Monthly, 1989);

Ripley under Water (London: Bloomsbury, 1991; New York: Knopf, 1992);

Small g: A Summer Idyll (London: Bloomsbury, 1995; New York: Norton, 2004);

Nothing That Meets the Eye: The Uncollected Stories of Patricia Highsmith (New York: Norton, 2002).

Edition and Collections: *Eleven,* foreword by Graham Greene (Harmondsworth, U.K.: Penguin, 1972);

The Talented Mr. Ripley, Ripley under Ground, Ripley's Game, Everyman's Library (New York: Random House, 1999);

Patricia Highsmith in 1991 (photograph by Horst Tappe; Hulton Archive/Getty Images)

The Selected Stories of Patricia Highsmith (New York: Norton, 2001).

In his foreword to the 1972 edition of *Eleven* (1970), Patricia Highsmith's first collection of short stories, English novelist Graham Greene dubs her "the poet of apprehension rather than fear" and characterizes her achievement:

> She is a writer who has created a world of her own—a world claustrophobic and irrational which we enter each time with a sense of personal danger, with the head half turned over the shoulder, even with a certain reluctance, for these are cruel pleasures we are going to experience, until . . . the frontier is closed behind us, we cannot retreat, we are doomed to live till the story's end with another of her long series of wanted men.

Highsmith has been acclaimed as a great writer by authors such as Brigid Brophy, Julian Symons, and Peter Handke and has long been widely read in England, France, Spain, Germany, Switzerland, and Austria. European movie directors, including René Clé-

ment, Claude Miller, Claude Chabrol, Wim Wenders, and Hans W. Geissendorfer, have adapted Highsmith's books to the screen.

Having enjoyed a brief burst of fame in the United States when Alfred Hitchcock made a movie of her first novel, *Strangers on a Train* (1950), in 1951, Highsmith during her life was largely ignored by the American reading public. Many of her books quickly fell out of print in the United States, and her popularity and reputation declined. Several reasons have been cited for the lengthy neglect Highsmith and her work suffered. One of them is the relentlessly negative depiction of the American middle class and of American politics in her works. Another reason mentioned is the fact that Highsmith was labeled a "suspense writer" at the outset of her career and that this label prevented serious consideration of her books. An additional reason given for the reluctance of the American public to embrace the writer is Highsmith's reclusive and prickly personality.

After Highsmith settled in Europe permanently in 1963, she only grudgingly promoted her books and avoided book signing tours and readings as much as possible. Even though she granted interviews, she ferociously protected her privacy and deliberately shocked her interviewers with such outrageous statements as her 1976 assertion to Peter Ruedi (collected in *Patricia Highsmith: Leben und Werk* [1996], edited by Franz Cavigelli, Fritz Senn, and Anna von Planta): "If I saw a kitten and a little human baby starving in the street, I would feed the kitten provided no one saw me." Otto Penzler, one of Highsmith's American publishers, attested to her abrasive personality in *Entertainment Weekly* on 14 January 2000: "She was a mean, cruel, hard, unlovable, unloving human being. I could never penetrate how any human being could be that relentlessly ugly. . . . But her books? Brilliant." Gary Fisketjon, who published her late novels, added: "She was very rough, very difficult. But she was also plainspoken, dryly funny, and great fun to be around." It is difficult to assess to what extent Highsmith's misanthropy was genuine and to what extent it was a pose to safeguard her privacy. Since Highsmith's death in 1995 her reputation has risen in the United States. Her five novels featuring Tom Ripley have been republished, gaining the author an increasing readership. Anthony Minghella's 1999 movie version of *The Talented Mr. Ripley* (1955) helped to solidify her growing popularity in the United States. In 2003 Liliana Cavani chose *Ripley's Game* (1974) as the starring vehicle for John Malkovich, whose assumption of the title role was described as "quintessential" by *The New Yorker* and "definitive" by London's *New Statesman*. Additional movies based on her novels are in development, and her out-of-print books are being republished. Interest in the author is further attested to by the 2003 publications of Marijane Meaker's memoir *Highsmith: A Romance of the 1950's* and Andrew Wilson's *Beautiful Shadow: A Life of Patricia Highsmith*. As Mark Harris stated in *Entertainment Weekly* (24–31 August 2001), "Highsmith is in the final lap of a posthumous victory mile that should cement her standing as a no-longer-neglected master of character-driven suspense fiction."

Highsmith was born Mary Patricia Plangman in Fort Worth, Texas, on 19 January 1921, the only child of Jay Bernard Plangman, a graphic artist of German extraction, and Mary Coates Plangman, an illustrator and fashion designer. Patricia's parents were divorced five months before her birth, and she was raised together with her cousin Dan Coates, who was like a brother to her, by her maternal grandparents in Fort Worth until she was six years old. She did not meet her father until she was twelve years old, and even though she found him likable, they had nothing to say to each other. In 1925 Patricia's mother married Stanley Highsmith, an advertising illustrator, and the family moved to New York City two years later. Patricia Highsmith recalled in a 1979 interview with Noelle Loriot (published in *Patricia Highsmith: Leben und Werk*) the trauma she suffered because of the move: "Something went to pieces in me when I left my grandmother. I completely withdrew into myself." Stanley Highsmith did not officially adopt his stepdaughter, but her mother registered her as Patricia Highsmith when she enrolled her in elementary school. Patricia later decided to keep the name as a tribute to this extremely patient and upright man.

While she liked her stepfather, Highsmith did not love her mother and, as she revealed to Loriot, blamed the failure of her second marriage on her quarrelsomeness and selfishness: "Why don't I love my mother? First, because she turned my childhood into a little hell. Second, because she herself never loved anyone, neither my father, my stepfather, nor me." Her feeling that she was unloved and unwanted was confirmed when her mother confessed that, while she was pregnant with Highsmith, she had unsuccessfully tried to induce abortion by drinking turpentine.

In an attempt to escape the frequent quarrels that she was forced to witness in the cramped two-room apartment in Greenwich Village, Highsmith immersed herself in the works of Fyodor Dostoevsky, Charles Dickens, Henry James, Edgar Allan Poe, Robert Louis Stevenson, Hugh Walpole, and T. S. Eliot. She was also fascinated by Karl Menninger's *The Human Mind* (1930), a book including case studies of kleptomaniacs, pyromaniacs, and serial killers, because she realized that the man, woman, or child next door could be strange even while appearing normal and that anybody one meets in the street could be a kleptomaniac, a sadist, or even a murderer.

Highsmith discovered the power of language when her composition about her trip to the Endless Caverns in Virginia, which had been discovered by two boys chasing a rabbit through a crevice, left her classmates spellbound. Her first short stories and poems appeared in *The Bluebird,* the Julia Richmond High School magazine, and the story "Mighty Nice Man" won first prize, which consisted of copies of Marcel Proust's *Du côté de chez Swann* (1913) and Virginia Woolf's *Mrs. Dalloway* (1925). Having graduated from high school in 1938, Highsmith enrolled in Barnard College at Columbia University and studied English, Latin, and Greek. She published short stories in the *Barnard Quarterly* on a regular basis, eventually serving as editor of the periodical. "The Heroine," a story she wrote in 1941 about a governess who sets the house of her employers on fire so that she can save the children, was rejected by *Barnard Quarterly* but eventually published in 1944 by *Harper's Bazaar* and included in *O. Henry's Best Short Stories of 1946*.

Upon graduating from college in 1942, Highsmith moved into a room of her own on Sixtieth Street in Manhattan and eked out a living by composing text for comic strips such as *Superman* and *Batman*. She continued writing short stories and immersed herself in the bohemian life of Greenwich Village, meeting Truman Capote, Paul and Jane Bowles, and Carson McCullers. In 1943 she spent five months in Taxco, Mexico, where she worked on the unfinished novel titled "The Click of the Shutting" and considered becoming a professional painter. The novel revolves around the relationship between two New York boys, prefiguring the pattern Highsmith later followed in many of her works, namely "the meeting, the close friendship of two people who are unlike one another," as she stated in a 1987 speech quoted by Wilson.

Having moved to a cold-water flat on East Fifty-sixth Street in 1944, Highsmith began work on *Strangers on a Train*. After the first chapters of the novel had been rejected by six publishers, she was admitted to Yaddo, the artists' colony in Saratoga Springs, New York, based on recommendations by Capote, the composer David Diamond, and Mary Louise Aswell, the chief editor of *Harper's Bazaar*. Freed from external pressures and provided with an ideal working environment, Highsmith was able to rewrite the novel from scratch. While at Yaddo she also got engaged to Marc Brandel, a fellow writer, only to break off the engagement shortly before the wedding ostensibly because of her fear of being a mother: "I would not have had the patience to raise children," Highsmith admitted to Loriot.

Soon after its completion *Strangers on a Train* was acquired by Harper and Sons and published in 1950. Hitchcock purchased the movie and stage rights for $6,800 and put Raymond Chandler in charge of writing the screenplay. The collaboration between the opinionated men, however, was strained, and Chandler was eventually replaced by Czenzi Ormonde, an associate of Ben Hecht's. When the movie was released in 1951, it was a great success, and Highsmith became famous overnight.

Strangers on a Train established a pattern that recurs, with variations, in many of Highsmith's works. In her book *Plotting and Writing Suspense Fiction* (1966), which offers a fascinating glimpse into the writer's work, Highsmith describes this motif: "The theme I have used over and over again in my novels is the relationship between two men, usually quite different in make-up, sometimes an obvious contrast in good and evil, sometimes merely ill-matched friends." In *Strangers on a Train* the two men are Guy Daniel Haines, a twenty-nine-year-old aspiring architect, who is traveling by rail to Texas in order to pressure his estranged wife

Highsmith in May 1949, leaving New York for a tour of England, France, and Italy (photograph ©Swiss Literary Archives, Berne; from Andrew Wilson, Beautiful Shadow: A Life of Patricia Highsmith, *2003; Thomas Cooper Library, University of South Carolina)*

into agreeing to a divorce so that he can marry his new girlfriend, and Charles Anthony Bruno, a young ne'er-do-well who lives off his rich parents. The aimless Bruno immediately latches on to the initially reserved and aloof Guy, being attracted by his apparent seriousness of purpose. Guy is repelled by Bruno's appearance, effete mannerisms, and "the desperate boredom of the wealthy"; yet, he is also fascinated by Bruno's bold suggestion to commit perfect murders by exchanging victims: "We murder for each other, see? I kill your wife and you kill my father! We meet on the train, see, and nobody knows we know each other! Perfect alibis!"

Even though Guy himself had once thought of murdering his wife's lover, he rejects Bruno's assertion that any person is capable of murder: "I'm not that kind of person." In spite of Guy's clear rejection of the murderous plan, Bruno travels to Texas several weeks later and strangles Guy's wife in an amusement park. He then pressures and eventually blackmails an initially resisting Guy into killing Bruno's hated father. The plan to commit perfect murders, however, gradually unravels when Guy is racked by guilt and pestered by

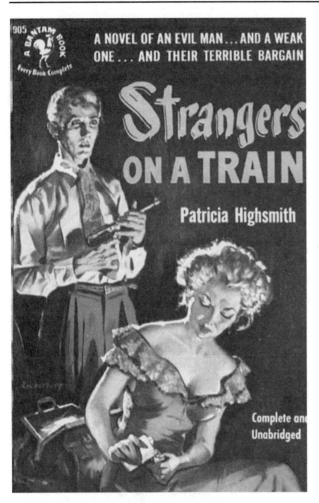

Cover for the paperback edition of Highsmith's first novel, originally
published in 1950, in which a man is pressured by a passing
acquaintance into participating in a murder scheme (from
Richard A. Lupoff, The Great American Paperback
[Portland, Ore.: Collectors Press, 2001]; Bruccoli
Clark Layman Archives)

Bruno, who has developed a homoerotic attachment to
his involuntary fellow conspirator. Bruno subsequently
invites himself to Guy's wedding as well as to a house-
warming party and showers Guy with gifts, which
causes Guy to reflect: "He might have been Bruno's
lover . . . to whom Bruno had brought a present, a
peace offering." Because of Bruno's obsessive behavior
a detective is able to establish a connection between the
two murderers, and they eventually receive their just
deserts. At the end of the novel Guy accepts the inevitable punishment. His last words to the detective are
"Take me."

When one compares Highsmith's novel and
Hitchcock's movie, the differences in focus and plot are
readily apparent, as MaryKay Mahoney has shown in
her essay "A Train Running on Two Sets of Tracks:
Highsmith's and Hitchcock's *Strangers on a Train*"

(1994). Whereas Hitchcock clearly contrasts Bruno, the
psychopath, with Guy, the innocent hero who "will
eventually emerge uncorrupted from the world of darkness into which Bruno has temporarily plunged him,"
Highsmith focuses on the two men as "inextricably
linked doubles." Guy becomes the author's mouthpiece
when he declares, having murdered Bruno's father, that
"love and hate, . . . good and evil, lived side by side in
the human heart, and not merely in differing proportions in one man and the next, but all good and all evil.
One had merely to look for a little of either to find it all,
one had merely to scratch the surface."

Highsmith's second published novel, *The Price of
Salt* (1952), was a considerable departure from her first.
In the afterword to the 1993 edition of the novel, which
she originally published pseudonymously as Claire
Morgan, Highsmith writes of how, to her surprise, she
became a "suspense writer" overnight when *Strangers on
a Train* was published as "A Harper Novel of Suspense," even though the novel was not categorized in
her mind as such. For her it was "simply a novel with
an interesting story." Highsmith's publisher and agent
urged her to write another book of the same type in
order to strengthen her reputation as a suspense writer.
Highsmith, having just completed a novel about a lesbian relationship, decided to publish her new work
under a pseudonym partly to escape the label of
"lesbian-book writer": "I like to avoid labels. It is
American publishers who love them."

Highsmith goes on in her afterword to detail the
genesis of *The Price of Salt*. Before *Strangers on a Train*
was published, Highsmith had taken a temporary job in
the toy department of Bloomingdale's in Manhattan
during the 1948 Christmas rush. There she was fascinated one day by a blonde woman in a mink coat who
"seemed to give off light." The woman bought a doll
from Highsmith, providing her name and address
because the doll was to be delivered out of state. While
the encounter was a routine transaction, Highsmith
"felt odd and swimmy in the head, near to fainting, yet
at the same time uplifted, as if I had seen a vision."
Even though the odd feeling revealed itself the next day
as the beginning of a chicken pox infection, the germ
for the novel was born. Highsmith immediately wrote
down the entire story line of the novel in less than two
hours: "It flowed from my pen as if from nowhere–
beginning, middle and end." Because of Highsmith's
predilection for letting ideas simmer for a while, the
novel was not completed until 1951.

The Price of Salt tells the story of Therese Belivet, a
nineteen-year-old stage designer who has taken temporary work as a salesgirl at Frankenberg's department
store. Her inability to find a permanent position in her
chosen field is aggravated by the confusion she is expe-

riencing in her personal life. Her boyfriend of ten months, a painter with whom she has been intimate on several occasions, has proposed marriage to her, but she has rejected his proposal because her feeling toward him bears no resemblance to what she had read about love: "Love was supposed to be a kind of blissful insanity." Therese suddenly and unexpectedly experiences such a passion when she meets customer Carol Aird, a married woman and a mother. Carol eventually relinquishes all rights to her daughter in order to be with Therese, and Therese in turn realizes after an unsuccessful attempt to be with a lesbian actress that "it was Carol she loved and would always love."

As Highsmith acknowledges in her afterword, *The Price of Salt* was most likely the first novel about homosexuals that ended on a happy note. When the book was published in hardcover in 1952 and as a paperback in nearly a million copies a year later, Highsmith received many fan letters addressed to Claire Morgan from women as well as men thanking her for her positive portrayal of a loving relationship among well-adjusted lesbians. After Highsmith had acknowledged her authorship of the novel in 1991, she admitted in an interview with Janet Watts, collected in *Patricia Highsmith: Leben und Werk,* that she had fallen in love with the woman–identified by Wilson as Kathleen Senn–who had served as the prototype for Therese, though she stopped short of declaring her lesbianism.

The financial success of her first two novels enabled Highsmith–who had visited England, France, and Italy briefly in 1949–to begin a European sojourn in 1952 that lasted more than two years. She traveled in the footsteps of her literary idol, James, from London to Paris, Munich, Salzburg, Trieste, and Florence. In the southern Italian town of Positano she rented a house and, watching a young, possibly American man walk along the deserted beach one morning lost in thought, she was inspired to invent a story about a young American vagabond who is sent to Europe with the mission to convince another American to return to the States. Having returned to the United States at the beginning of 1954, Highsmith moved into a cottage near Lenox, Massachusetts, where she began writing the first in a series of five adventures featuring her best-known creation, Tom Ripley.

Before Ripley made his appearance, however, Highsmith published another novel, *The Blunderer* (1954), that involves another perfect murder as well as a pair of murderers, one an ice-cold psychopath, the other a bumbling blunderer. Melchior Kimmel, a pornographic book dealer, has murdered his wife by assaulting her at a rest stop on a bus trip, having arranged a secure alibi. Although police assume that Kimmel's wife was killed by a stranger, Walter Stackhouse, a lawyer who is locked in a miserable marriage with "a pint-size Medusa," is able to piece together the true circumstances of the murder based on newspaper reports and his empathy with the murderer. When Stackhouse's wife commits suicide before Stackhouse can emulate Kimmel's crime, the lawyer's feeling of guilt at having planned her murder causes him to act suspiciously. Because of his obsessive urge to seek out Kimmel, he unwittingly directs suspicion toward the source of his inspiration. Stackhouse eventually does turn into a murderer, and Kimmel is arrested after a policeman witnesses him stab Stackhouse, his "enemy number one," to death, calling him "murderer, idiot, blunderer, until the meaning of the words became a solid fact like a mountain sitting on top of him, and he no longer had the will to fight against it."

James Sandoe, reviewer for the *New York Herald Tribune Book Review,* accorded Highsmith underhanded praise when he stated that she "manages so well with the understandable if mussy Stackhouse that she can trample plausibility and drag us along in spite of it. Her fancy is at once extravagant and acute." He preferred *The Blunderer* to Highsmith's first novel: "She has written a remarkable tale and a far more telling one (for me, at least) than its celebrated predecessor, *Strangers on a Train.*" Symons, in *The New York Times Book Review,* proclaimed *The Blunderer* one of the one hundred best detective novels of all time.

In Highsmith's best-known and arguably most accomplished novel, *The Talented Mr. Ripley,* the "criminal-hero," as she calls him in *Plotting and Writing Suspense Fiction,* receives no punishment for his misdeeds and escapes scot-free. Tom Phelps Ripley, a twenty-five-year-old unsettled and unemployed aspiring actor who has an amazing gift for mimicry, is asked by Herbert Greenleaf, the well-to-do owner of a small shipbuilding company, to convince his son, Dickie, who has been living in Southern Italy for two years dabbling in painting, to return to the States and to take over the family firm. Tom, whose life is based on the philosophy that "something always turned up," accepts the mission because it provides him with a clean slate: "He was starting a new life. Good-bye to all the second-rate people he had hung around and had let hang around him in the past three years in New York. He felt as he imagined immigrants felt when they left everything behind them in some foreign country, left their friends and relations and their past mistakes, and sailed for America."

When Tom meets Dickie and his girlfriend, writer Marge Sherwood, in Mongibello, he is immediately fascinated by their carefree and luxurious way of life, their independence, and their air of sophistication. Tom insinuates himself into Dickie's life: he confesses

Robert Walker (right) as the psychopathic Bruno and Farley Granger as his unwitting conspirator in murder in Alfred Hitchcock's
1951 motion-picture adaptation of Highsmith's Strangers on a Train *(Warner Bros. / The Kobal Collection; from Andrew*
Wilson, Beautiful Shadow: A Life of Patricia Highsmith, *2003;*
Thomas Cooper Library, University of South Carolina)

the true reason for his trip and switches sides by supporting Dickie's plan to remain in Italy. Their friendship, which includes an ever-increasing element of homoeroticism, grows until Dickie witnesses Tom impersonating him in front of a mirror and pretending that he is strangling Marge. Tom eventually kills Dickie and assumes his identity. He later kills Dickie's friend Freddie Miles to protect his secret. Whereas Tom regrets having murdered Dickie, he feels no qualms about Freddie's murder: "He hadn't wanted to murder, it had been a necessity." When he seems about to be caught, Tom slips back into his old identity and eventually manages to convince Dickie's father that his son committed suicide. Dickie's will, which has been forged by Tom to his advantage, is accepted as authentic, and Tom is assured the life of luxury he had yearned for.

The positive ending of the novel has drawn comparisons with André Gide's *Les Caves du Vatican* (1914;

translated as *The Vatican Swindle,* 1925) in which, according to Anthony Channell Hilfer in *The Crime Novel: A Deviant Genre* (1990), "by a chain of extraordinary coincidence Lafcadio escapes the consequences of the gratuitous murder he has committed." Consequently, Highsmith, like Gide, was accused by some of promoting an amoral and even immoral worldview. *The New Yorker* (7 January 1956), for example, called the novel "remarkably immoral" and its protagonist "one of the most repellent and fascinating characters," and Craig Brown stated in *The Times Literary Supplement (TLS):* "it is a rare villain or psychopath whom the reader does not find himself willing toward freedom, a rare investigator or victim (sometimes the one becomes the other) whom the reader is unhappy to see dead." The following 1942 entry from Highsmith's notebook, quoted by Wilson, shows that her accusers were not far off the mark:

The abnormal point of view is always the best for depicting twentieth-century life, not only because so many of us are abnormal, realizing it or not, but because twentieth-century life is established and maintained through abnormality. I should love to do a novel with all the literary virtues of *Red Badge of Courage* about one abnormal character seeing present day life, very ordinary life, yet arresting through it, abnormality, until at the end, the reader sees, and with little reluctance, that he is not abnormal at all, and that the main character might well be himself.

German critic Michael Dunker has shown that Highsmith masterfully employs the literary device of the third-person narrator who provides the reader with an insight into the criminal-hero's state of mind and his motivations, subtly manipulating the reader's sympathies toward the protagonists in all her novels.

Highsmith publicly responded to the accusations of promoting amorality in *Plotting and Writing Suspense Fiction* with characteristic bluntness. She stressed that "art essentially has nothing to do with morality, convention or moralizing" and threw back a charge of hypocrisy: "I find the public passion for justice quite boring and artificial, for neither life nor nature care if justice is ever done or not. The public wants to see the law triumph, or at least the general public does, though at the same time the public likes brutality." Tellingly, in Clément's movie adaptation of *The Talented Mr. Ripley*, *Plein Soleil* (1959), the ending of the novel is changed and Ripley is caught. Even in Anthony Minghella's 1999 version, Tom does not entirely escape punishment. Although he is not caught by the police, he suffers a retribution of his own making: he is forced to kill the man he really loves in order to safeguard his future. Highsmith's first Ripley novel was given a special award by the Mystery Writers of America in 1956 and the Grand Prix de Litterature Policiere and the Edgar Allan Poe Scroll of the Mystery Writers of America the following year.

Highsmith followed up her masterful Ripley novel with another masterpiece. *Deep Water* (1957), the exploration of a hellish marriage and its deadly consequences, is considered by Russell Harrison, author of *Patricia Highsmith* (1997), as one of the writer's most accomplished novels and characterized by Anthony Boucher in the 6 October 1957 issue of *The New York Times Book Review* as a "full-fleshed novel of pity and irony." Victor Van Allen, the independently rich publisher of limited luxury books, is chained to a "wild horse" of a wife who, as a sign of her "constitutional rebelliousness," has many extramarital affairs while refusing to agree to a divorce. Victor does not object to Melinda's affairs per se but rather to the fact that she picks "idiotic, spineless characters" and that she is not

discreet, flaunting her affairs in their small, conservative Berkshire town. During a pool party Victor manages to drown one of his wife's lovers without being observed and without experiencing any guilt. Melinda suspects that her husband is guilty of the murder but is unable to prove it. When Melinda later threatens to leave Victor to marry a building contractor, Victor throws the new lover down a cliff and submerges the body in a deserted quarry. When he is drawn back to the scene of the crime to check on the status of the corpse, he is discovered by Don Wilson, a hack writer who has suspected him of murder for some time. In an explosion of violence Victor strangles the woman who has made his life a living hell: "Medea. Mangler of children and castrator of husbands. Fate had overtaken her at last." He accepts his punishment defiantly:

> . . . it was not bad at all to be leaving them. The ugly birds without wings. The mediocre who perpetuated mediocrity, who really fought and died for it. He smiled at Wilson's grim, resentful, the-world-owes-me-a-living face, which was the reflection of the small, dull mind behind it, and Vic cursed it and all it stood for. Silently, and with a smile, and with all that was left of him, he cursed it.

Boucher called the novel Highsmith's "coming of age as a novelist; less startling than *Strangers,* it is incomparably stronger in subtlety and depth of characterization."

After collaborating with Doris Sanders on a children's book, *Miranda the Panda Is on the Veranda* (1958), Highsmith published *A Game for the Living* (1958), a novel that even after four rewrites she considered her "one really dull book." In *Plotting and Writing Suspense Fiction* she blames its failure on her own weakness in constructing a whodunit: "I had tried to do something different from what I had been doing, but this caused me to leave out certain elements that are vital for me: surprise, speed of action, the stretching of the reader's credulity, and above all that intimacy with the murderer himself. I am not an inventor of puzzles, nor do I like secrets."

Despite its shortcomings, the novel is of interest because of its exotic location and the portrayal of the relationship of two mismatched friends. Theodore Schiebelhut, a rich German painter who has adopted Mexican citizenship, and his friend Ramon Otero, a professor and devout Catholic, are suspected of brutally raping, murdering, and mutilating Lelia, a woman who had an intimate relationship with both. While the two men initially suspect each other, they gradually learn to appreciate each other's similarities and differences. As Noel Dorman Mawer shows in her 1991 essay "From Villain to Vigilante," Highsmith is no longer confining herself "to the mutually destructive

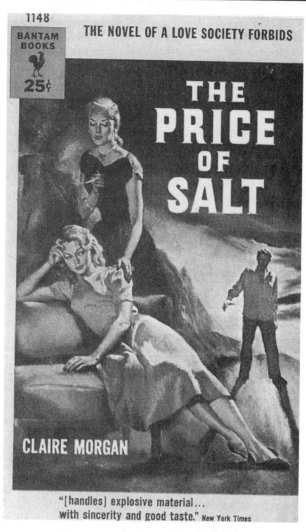

1148
BANTAM
BOOKS
25¢

THE NOVEL OF A LOVE SOCIETY FORBIDS

THE
PRICE
OF
SALT

CLAIRE MORGAN

"[handles] explosive material...
with sincerity and good taste." New York Times

*Cover for the paperback edition of Highsmith's pseudonymously
published 1952 novel about a young woman's dawning
realization that she is a lesbian (from Andrew Wilson,
Beautiful Shadow: A Life of Patricia Highsmith,
2003; Thomas Cooper Library, University
of South Carolina)*

effects of complementary pathologies, but rather is portraying the mutual misunderstandings of two essentially rational, humane people who have contrasting cultural backgrounds." Because the novel focuses on the relationship between the friends, the solution of the murder mystery—a marginal figure is revealed as the perpetrator—seems tacked on and unsatisfactory.

Highsmith moved to a house in the Catskills near Palisades, New York, in 1958, and two years later she shared an old farmhouse outside New Hope, Pennsylvania, with the lesbian author Meaker. Highsmith's next two novels, *This Sweet Sickness* (1960) and *The Cry of the Owl* (1962), complete what Harrison calls her "exurban trilogy," which she had begun with *Deep Water*. Both books are set in claustrophobic and narrow-minded small-town America, and both describe a character's obsessive fixation on an inappropriate object of desire and the clash between fantasy and reality.

In *This Sweet Sickness,* David Kelsey, the chief engineer of a fabrics manufacturing plant, is not able to adjust to the fact that Annabelle, a former girlfriend of his, has married another man. He creates a fantasy world in which Annabelle and his alter ego, "William Neumeister," can live happily together. While residing in a dingy boardinghouse during the week, he spends the weekends in a house that he has furnished in preparation for his reunion with Annabelle. Even though she keeps rejecting his persistent overtures, David blames "the Situation" on the fact that Annabelle is not herself and that she is not able to see anything in perspective: "she was immersed, drowned now in what she considered reality."

David himself is being romantically pursued by Effie Brennan, a secretary who lives in the same boardinghouse. When Annabelle's husband, Gerald, pays a surprise visit to David in his dream house one Sunday in order to warn him off, David kills him accidentally during a scuffle. He takes the body to the police and, in the guise of William Neumeister, reports the accident. Since David's fantasy world has been breached, he sells the house, gives up his job, and moves to another city. The tables are turned on him when an obsessed Effie pursues him to his new residence and sullies the bed that was meant solely for Annabelle: "He was through with the house. Effie had ruined it. There was nothing in it that he wanted any longer. . . . he would never come back. Never." Having killed Effie accidentally while dragging her from the bed and throwing her to the floor, David flees to New York City and, being pursued by the police, throws himself off an apartment building. In his last moments he desperately clings to his fantasy: "Thinking no more about it, he stepped off into that cool space, the fast descent to her, with nothing in his mind but a memory of a curve of her shoulder, naked, as he had never seen it."

Highsmith explored the theme of obsession with an unresponsive love object again two years later in *The Cry of the Owl.* Robert Forester, a lonely and depressed aeronautics engineer whose marriage has collapsed, starts spying on Jenny Thierolf, a young woman who lives alone in a secluded house. Robert's peeping serves as a palliative to the fiasco of his marriage and allows him to create, in Harrison's phrase, a "fantasy of perfect domesticity."

When Robert is discovered by Jenny and invited into the house, reality does not match up with the fantasy he has created. Although he enters into a nonsexual relationship with Jenny, he does so without much enthusiasm. Greg Wyncoop, Jenny's former fiancé, eventually provokes a fight with Robert, who saves Greg from drowning when he falls into a river. Greg and Robert's vindictive former wife, Nickie, hatch an involved plot to frame Robert for Greg's faked death, which in the end results in Jenny committing suicide and Greg being arrested for attempted murder. While out on bail Greg stabs Nickie to death when she tries to break up a fight he is having with Robert. The wary Robert makes sure that he is not implicated in the stabbing: "The knife was at his feet, not a bloodstain on it that he could see. He bent to pick it up, then stopped. Don't touch it, he thought, don't touch it." Hitchcock purchased the rights to the novel in 1961 and used it as the basis for an hour-long segment of his television series, *Alfred Hitchcock Presents,* titling it "Annabelle."

In both novels Highsmith portrays the protagonists' community as a vengeful and unreasonable mob. A suicidal David Kelsey is urged on by a heckling crowd to jump off the building, and Robert Forester is immediately suspected by his community of a murder that may or may not have taken place. Harrison makes a convincing case that by portraying the community "as a collection of prejudiced, irrational, witch-hunting individuals . . . Highsmith has constructed something like an allegorical tale of the witch-hunt, of the blacklist, in short, of McCarthyism." The writer, whose political sympathies rested with the Left, alluded to political developments in the United States increasingly in subsequent novels. The political and cultural changes the country experienced in the early 1960s may have been one of the reasons why Highsmith moved to Europe permanently. After a third extended trip to Rome and Positano in 1961–1962 she settled in the south of England in 1963 to be with her lover, Barbara, the wife of a London businessman.

The first novel to be published after Highsmith's permanent move to Europe was *The Two Faces of January* (1964). Like several of her works the novel features an exotic locale–in this case Greece–and two men chained to each other in a love-hate relationship. Rydal Keener, a young American with an air of melancholy, has a chance encounter in an Athens hotel with Chester MacFarland, a crook who has fled the United States, where he has committed stock fraud, and his wife, Colette. Rydal is attracted to Chester, because he strongly resembles his recently deceased father, and to Colette, who reminds him of his first love, Agnes. Rydal is soon caught up in Chester's criminal activities and becomes a suspect when Chester kills a police official. When Rydal's attraction to Colette intensifies, Chester attempts to murder his rival but kills his own wife by mistake. Faced with exposure, the two men close ranks against the police and protect each other.

Chester's false deathbed confession absolves Rydal from any guilt. Whereas Rydal had deliberately missed his own father's funeral, his decision to attend Chester's signals his reconciliation with the past. Highsmith was highly gratified when the novel, which had been rejected twice by Harper and Row, was awarded the Silver Dagger for best foreign novel by the Crime Writers Association of Great Britain.

Highsmith also had difficulty finding a publisher for *The Glass Cell* (1964). In *Plotting and Writing Suspense Fiction* she describes the genesis of the novel in great detail, including its rejections and revisions. The book is based on the theory of "the deleterious effect of exposure to brutality in prison, and how this can lead to anti-social behavior after release." Philip Carter, an engineer, is made the fall guy for his employer's illegal scheme to overcharge customers for inferior building materials. In prison he is exposed to constant brutality, injustice, and degradation. When Max, a forger who has befriended Philip, is brutally killed during a prison riot, Philip avenges the murder by killing the likely perpetrator. Eventually his ten-year sentence is reduced by three years for good conduct, and Philip is released into a hostile world. Unable to find suitable employment because of his prison record, he gradually discovers that his wife, Hazel, is having an affair with his lawyer, David Sullivan. Philip kills David, "the lily-livered swine," in a fit of uncontrollable rage and subsequently a blackmailer who has knowledge of the murder. Having been punished for a crime he did not commit, a hardened Philip escapes punishment for the murders he has committed. Highsmith explains, "because Carter has been through so much in prison, I wanted to have him cleared of his post-prison murder. A double miscarriage of justice, if you like. I wanted him by some quirk to go free."

Highsmith followed up the grim depiction of prison life and its effects with *A Suspension of Mercy* (1965), a novel of black humor in which she examines the theme of fantasy versus reality through another portrayal of an unhappy marriage. Sydney Smith Bartleby, the American protagonist, is the creator of a British television adventure show titled *The Whip,* about a charming criminal who is never caught. Bartleby loathes his wife, Alicia, and frequently thinks of killing her. Instead of realizing his fantasies, however, he writes them down in his notebook with the plan to use them in his fiction. When she disappears, the notebook leads the police to suspect Sydney of murder. His elderly neighbor is convinced of his guilt because "Americans are violent. Everyone knows that." After Sydney discovers that Alicia has assumed a new identity to protect her affair with Edward Tilbury, a London lawyer, she commits suicide, and Sydney exacts revenge on Ali-

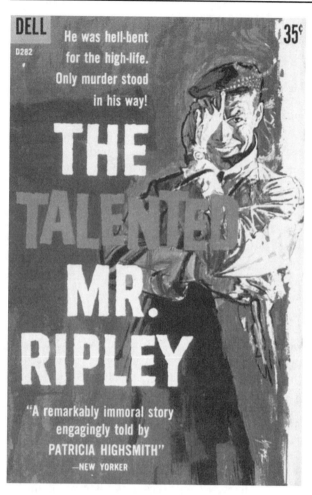

DELL D282

He was hell-bent for the high-life. Only murder stood in his way!

35¢

THE TALENTED MR. RIPLEY

"A remarkably immoral story engagingly told by PATRICIA HIGHSMITH"
—NEW YORKER

Cover for the 1957 paperback edition of Highsmith's 1955 novel, the first of five she wrote about the sociopathic title character (from Richard A. Lupoff, The Great American Paperback *[Portland, Ore.: Collectors Press, 2001]; Bruccoli Clark Layman Archives)*

cia's lover by forcing him to swallow an overdose of sleeping pills. When the police accept the lawyer's death as a suicide, Sydney feels invincible: "As he touched the notebook, Sydney thought that he would write a description of the Tilbury murder in it, while his recollection was still very clear, because the notebook was now, after all, the safest place in which to write it."

Bored with England and mourning the demise of her four-year relationship with Barbara, Highsmith moved to France in 1967 and purchased a house in Samois-sur-Seine, where she lived with her close friend Elizabeth Lyne. In her next two novels she featured some of the exotic and picturesque locales she had visited during her frequent trips. *Those Who Walk Away* (1967) is set in Venice and describes yet another cat-and-mouse game between two men. The American painter Ed Coleman blames his son-in-law, Ray, for the

death of his daughter, who has committed suicide during her honeymoon. He pursues Ray through the canals and piazzas of Venice and makes several attempts on his life. Ray, like Greg in *The Cry of the Owl*, hides after one attack, and Coleman is suspected of his murder. Coleman eventually ceases the assaults, and Ray begins to understand his father-in-law's grief: "he wasn't on the defensive or angry with Coleman any longer, and he could afford to feel sorry for him, even sympathize."

The Tremor of Forgery (1969), set in Tunisia, was Highsmith's (as well as Greene's) favorite of her novels and, in Harrison's view, marks a watershed in her career because it and subsequent works are less concerned with crime and more focused on political and social issues. Howard Ingham, an American writer, is sent to Tunis, where he is supposed to write the script for a movie to be directed by his friend John Castlewood. While waiting for the director to arrive, Ingham is bewildered by the strange country and its customs and befriends Anders Jensen, a homosexual Danish painter who feels comfortable in the alien land. When Ina Pallant, Ingham's fiancée and script supervisor for the movie, arrives, Ingham learns that Castlewood has committed suicide because Ina, with whom he has had an affair, was unwilling to leave Ingham. One night Ingham surprises a burglar trying to break into his bungalow, and he throws his heavy typewriter at the intruder, wounding him. Hotel employees remove the burglar's body as well as any signs of the attack; thus, the only act of violence in the novel is one of self-defense, and Highsmith leaves open the question of whether it has serious consequences.

Initially Ingham feels guilty about the incident and considers informing the police, but eventually he adopts the fatalistic attitude of the natives. He decides to stay on in Tunisia in spite of the fact that the movie has been canceled, and he immerses himself in the local customs, with Jensen as his expert guide. One sign of Ingham's learning process is his changing attitude toward homosexuality. Early in the novel he is propositioned by Jensen and refuses the offer. Throughout the novel the two men get closer and Ingham's reluctance to have sex with a man is less pronounced:

> . . . Ingham recalled one night when he'd gone along to the coffee-house called Les Arcades, and had come near to taking home a young Arab. The Arab had sat at the table with him, and Ingham had stood him a couple of beers. Ingham had been both sexually excited and lonely that evening, and the only thing that had deterred him, he thought, was that he hadn't been sure what to do in bed with a boy, and he hadn't wanted to feel silly. Hardly a moral reason for chastity.

Harrison points out in *Patricia Highsmith* that the gradual loosening of sexual barriers and the break with Western conventions is reminiscent of Gide's novel *L'Immoraliste* (1902; translated as *The Immoralist,* 1930). The novel also shows the influence of Albert Camus's *L'Etranger* (1942; translated as *The Stranger,* 1946). Harrison argues that "the treatment of the political issues . . . reflects Highsmith's position as a representative of a formally noncolonialist power suffering internal divisions over its neoimperialist project in Vietnam."

From 1970 to 1991 Highsmith published not only eight novels, including four featuring Tom Ripley, but also seven collections of short stories. These stories attest to the wide range of the author's interests and talent and include a variety of genres, such as horror, science fiction, fantasy, and fairy tale. Only a few of the stories deal primarily with crime. The first collection, *Eleven,* gathers some of her best stories, including "The Heroine," the short story that had been published in *O. Henry's Best Short Stories of 1946,* and Greene's favorite story, "When the Fleet Was in at Mobile," the portrait of a young woman who unwittingly exchanges a life of prostitution for an abusive marriage. "The Cries of Love" details the disturbing relationship between two elderly women who torture each other by destroying each other's favorite possessions. In "The Snail Watcher" and "The Quest for Blank Claveringi," animals take revenge on humans, and in the memorable story "The Terrapin" a young boy avenges the cruel killing and dismemberment of a soup turtle by subjecting his mother to a similar treatment.

At the beginning of *Ripley under Ground* (1970) the criminal-hero has settled down in Villeperce-sur-Seine near Paris, where he and his wife, Heloise, a rich, cultured, and amoral Frenchwoman, enjoy a life of luxury in their villa, called "Belle Ombre." Ripley collects paintings by such artists as Vincent Van Gogh, René Magritte, and Chaim Soutine; enjoys good food and drink, classical music, and traveling; tends his garden; and commits occasional crimes in order to supplement his income. He has devised a scheme with friends in London to sell fake paintings, pretending they are the work of Derwatt, a famous painter who is supposedly leading the life of a recluse in Mexico but who actually committed suicide in Greece three years before.

When Thomas Murchison, a rich and knowledgeable American art collector, suspects the fraud, Ripley impersonates the dead painter in an attempt to allay Murchison's suspicions. Failing to do so, he kills the collector in his wine cellar with a bottle of his best Margaux while feeling no remorse: "Tom didn't feel that it was a crime." Although Ripley is able to deflect the suspicions of the police, the situation becomes precarious when Bernard Tufts, the young painter who produces the fake Derwatt paintings, threatens to expose the scheme. After Tufts attacks Ripley and leaves him for dead, Ripley is able to haunt the painter like a ghost, causing his suicide. The police are suspicious of Ripley but are unable to connect him to either of the deaths. He has gotten away with murder once more.

In 1971 Highsmith moved to Montmachoux and later to Moncourt, both situated near Fontainebleau. In his article "The Woman Who Was Ripley" (*The Independent on Sunday Magazine,* 13 January 2000), Wilson suggests a possible explanation for the writer's restlessness: "her romantic attachments were far from settled—she lived with a handful of women, none for longer than a couple of years at a time, often moving countries in a bid to escape the emotional fall-out that accompanied the breakdown of a relationship." Frequent trips to the United States provided Highsmith with the inspiration for four non-Ripley novels that include unflattering portrayals of her former homeland.

A Dog's Ransom (1972) depicts New York City as a dangerous urban jungle, torn apart by class and ethnic hatred, in which muggings, burglaries, kidnappings, and blackmail are the order of the day. Kenneth Rowajinski, a former construction worker of Polish extraction who is living on disability, kills a dog belonging to Ed and Greta Reynolds and extorts a ransom from the couple, pretending that the dog has been kidnapped. The Reynoldses, who lost their daughter in a drug-related shooting, are devastated by the loss of their beloved pet: "A dog, a daughter—there should be a great difference, yet the feeling was much the same." Clarence Duhamell, a young policeman who has been assigned to the case, quickly becomes obsessed with tracking down the dognapper in order to win the couple's approbation and gratitude. When the policeman discovers the perpetrator, a deadly game of cat and mouse ensues. Rowajinski, "the Pole," taunts Duhamell and harasses his girlfriend, Marilyn. When the policeman finds Rowajinski lurking around Marilyn's apartment, he beats him to death with his revolver. Having taken the law into his own hands, Duhamell is shot by one of his colleagues. The novel was savaged by *TLS* on 12 May 1972: "Patricia Highsmith's new novel belongs in what is becoming a depressingly substantial sector of her total output—it is a mechanical exercise in self-pastiche, employing all her familiar devices and rehearsing most of her familiar obsessions, but with none of the vigor, inventiveness or intensity which in her best work makes those devices and obsessions seem so riveting." In contrast, Harrison has shown that *A Dog's Ransom* "reveals social and economic conflict more clearly than any of the author's other novels. But at the

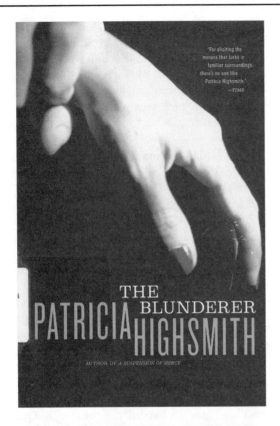
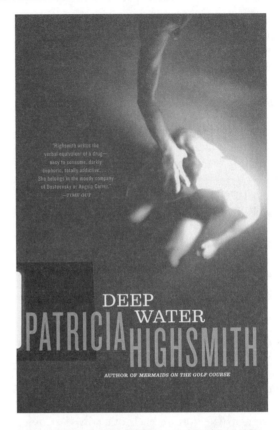
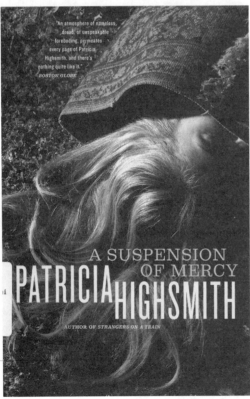
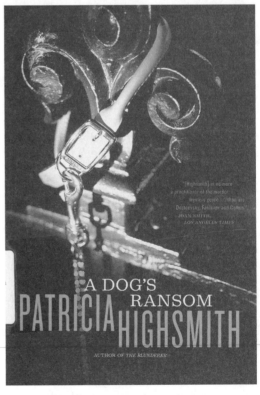

Covers for the paperback reprints, published by W. W. Norton, of four of Highsmith's suspense novels
(Richland County Public Library)

same time, the author's inability to resolve successfully any of these conflicts makes *A Dog's Ransom* both an authentic expression of its times and an unusually moving, if flawed, novel."

Ripley's Game, which takes place six months after *Ripley under Ground,* is the darkest of all the Ripley novels. When Ripley is commissioned to assassinate two mafiosi who threaten illegal gambling activities in Hamburg, Germany, he rejects the offer because the Derwatt episode has not blown over yet and because he "detested murder unless it was absolutely necessary." He hatches, however, a fiendish plan in order to punish Jonathan Trevanny, an Englishman who owns a small picture-framing shop, for "sneering" at him once at a party. Ripley, knowing that Trevanny suffers from leukemia, spreads the false rumor that Trevanny is dying and manages to falsify medical reports to that effect. He hopes to make Trevanny receptive to the murder scheme in order to provide for his family, a challenge made especially attractive by the fact that Trevanny "looks the picture of decency and innocence." Trevanny initially rejects the plan but, believing that he is about to die, eventually agrees to it and travels to Hamburg, where he shoots one of the mafiosi. When Ripley realizes that his experiment to corrupt an innocent has succeeded, he helps Trevanny murder the second mafioso. Several mafiosi track the assassins to France, and Ripley has to join forces with Trevanny in order to eliminate them. Trevanny is killed in a shootout, and his wife, Simone, who hates Ripley for having corrupted her husband, cannot resist the lure of the blood money: "Simone was just a trifle ashamed of herself, Tom thought. In that, she joined much of the rest of the world. Tom felt, in fact, that her conscience would be more at rest than that of her husband, if he were still alive."

Highsmith, a fervent animal lover who was surrounded by cats and snails throughout her life, allows such diverse animals as elephants, camels, dogs, cats, pigs, horses, chickens, hamsters, and ferrets to avenge the cruel treatment they have been subjected to by humans in the appropriately titled collection *The Animal-Lover's Book of Beastly Murder* (1975). In the same year Highsmith, who had frequently been accused of promoting misogyny in her novels, deliberately poured gasoline on the fire when she published *Kleine Geschichten für Weiberfeinde,* translated two years later as *Little Tales of Misogyny.* The stories, with such telling titles as "The Coquette," "The Fully-Licensed Whore, or, The Wife," "The Breeder," "The Mobile Bed-Object," and "The Perfect Little Lady," are clearly written tongue in cheek, and Highsmith was obviously thumbing her nose at the critics while trying to *épater le bourgeois* (to shock the middle classes). She was no doubt highly

gratified when she and Roland Topor, illustrator for the book, received the French Grand Prix de l'Humour Noir in 1977.

Edith's Diary (1977), another novel in Highsmith's American cycle, is one of her most accomplished novels. Since the writer did not acknowledge authorship of her lesbian novel *The Price of Salt* until 1991, *Edith's Diary* was the first Highsmith book to provide the readers with a positive depiction of a strong female protagonist. The fact that Highsmith's novel revolves around an intelligent, educated, and accomplished woman who is destroyed by an oppressive patriarchal society helped to allay somewhat the charge that her novels promoted misogyny. Edith Howland, a freelance writer and housewife, tries "to organize and analyze her life-in-progress" by keeping a diary. Slowly but inextricably her life becomes a living nightmare when her husband, Brett, unexpectedly demands a divorce so that he can marry a younger woman. He leaves Edith caring for his bedridden and sickly Uncle George, who refuses to move to a nursing home even though he requires constant care. Edith is also left in charge of their son, Cliffie, a good-for-nothing who drops out of school, moves from one part-time job to the next, gets hooked on alcohol and drugs, injures a man in a drunken driving accident, and eventually kills Uncle George by administering an overdose of codeine. Edith's diary increasingly serves as her means to escape an unbearable reality. She invents an imaginary son who, having graduated from Princeton University, works as a successful and well-paid engineer in Kuwait. While the real Cliffie is reduced to masturbating into socks at night, Edith's imaginary Cliffie has married a beautiful wife and fathered two adorable children. Edith is aware of the fictional and therapeutic character of her diary entries, but those around her start questioning her sanity. When two doctors, hired by her former husband, insist on having her examined by a psychiatrist, Edith accidentally slips on the stairs and falls to her death. In her final moments the fantasy of a beautiful son is replaced by Edith's "personal sense of injustice."

Highsmith's collection *Slowly, Slowly in the Wind* (1979) includes two of her strongest stories, "The Network" and "Broken Glass." Both stories reflect, according to Harrison, "socioeconomic changes as they affect that free-floating urban middle class . . . with remarkably unsettling results for the reader." In "The Network" middle-class New Yorkers, who feel that they have been disfranchised in favor of minorities, bond together in the attempt to deal with an increasingly threatening environment. In "Broken Glass" Andrew Cooperman, an eighty-one-year-old retired newspaper typesetter who is living on a meager pension, is mugged by a young black man. Cooperman refuses to become a

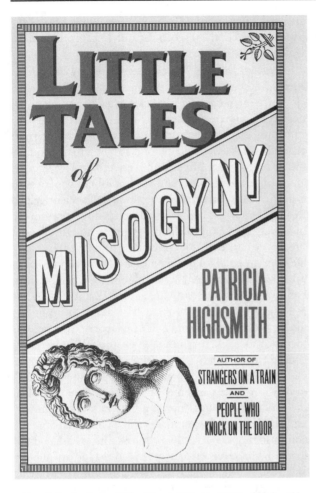

Dust jacket for the first U.S. edition, published in 1986, of Highsmith's
collection of satirical stories named for different feminine
stereotypes, originally published in German in 1975
(Richland County Public Library)

prisoner in his own apartment—as have many of his elderly neighbors—and fights the same mugger the next
time he encounters him, stabbing him in the stomach
with a pane of glass. His action, however, leads to his
death when he is attacked by the injured mugger's
friends.

Ripley the corrupter undergoes a dramatic meta-
morphosis in *The Boy Who Followed Ripley* (1980), as he
turns into the compassionate protector of a young man.
When Frank Pierson, a sixteen-year-old American who
has pushed his wealthy, wheelchair-bound father off a
cliff and who has been on the run since the murder,
shows up on Ripley's doorstep, Ripley offers him shel-
ter. Frank is racked with guilt and hopes to gain absolu-
tion by confessing his deed: "Frank felt guilt, which was
why he had looked up Tom Ripley, and curiously Tom
had never felt such guilt, never let it seriously trouble
him." Ripley and Frank quickly develop an intense
friendship with a strong homoerotic undercurrent.

While spending a weekend in Berlin they find themselves accidentally in a gay bar called "Glad Ass,"
where Ripley enjoys the attention he and his friend
attract: "Tom himself was an object of envy for having
a nice looking boy of sixteen in his company. Tom
could in fact see that now, and it made him smile."
When Frank is kidnapped, Ripley delivers the ransom
money and frees the boy. He eventually convinces
Frank to return to the United States and to face his family. Although he prevents Frank from jumping off a cliff
at one point, he is ultimately unable to prevent the
young man's redemptive suicide.

Highsmith presents a blackly humorous view of
old age in "Old Folks at Home," one of the best stories
in her collection *The Black House* (1981). When Lois and
Herbert McIntyre, a couple of young, successful professionals, decide to "adopt" an elderly couple from an
old-age home, their good deed turns into a nightmare.
The elderly couple turns out to be argumentative,
demanding, and incontinent. An attempt to return the
adoptees to the old-age home fails, and the young couple has to rent offices outside their own home in order
to be able to work. When their house catches on fire,
the McIntyres save their books and papers but leave the
old folks to their fate.

In the last ten years of Highsmith's life her literary output dwindled considerably, and the writer isolated herself more and more. In 1982 she moved from
France to Switzerland, first settling in Aurigeno and
then in Tegna, where she withdrew into a house that
she had built according to her own designs. The home
resembled a bunker: situated at the foot of the Alps, it
kept the world at bay.

In *People Who Knock on the Door* (1983), a "mordant
indictment of contemporary middle America" according to Holly Eley in *TLS* (4 February 1983), Highsmith
savagely attacks fundamentalist religion, moral hypocrisy, and the right-wing government of Ronald Reagan.
Richard Alderman, an insurance salesman in a small
Indiana town, embraces fundamentalist Christianity
when Robbie, his younger son who has become seriously ill, is seemingly saved through the power of
prayer. Richard is transformed into a rigid and uncompromising moralist overnight, and he turns his eldest
son, Arthur, out of the house when he discovers that
Arthur has helped his pregnant girlfriend to obtain an
abortion. Richard, however, does not practice what he
preaches and is caught having an extramarital affair
with Irene, a former prostitute whom he has taken
under his wing. When Robbie, who has become a
reborn Christian as well, discovers that his father is
responsible for Irene's baby, he shoots him in a fit of
righteous indignation, claiming "Dad deserved it!"

Highsmith's last two collections of short stories, *Mermaids on the Golf Course* (1985) and *Tales of Natural and Unnatural Catastrophes* (1987), reveal the writer's growing fascination with an apparently decaying American society and her desire to explore current political and social concerns. Such a desire is also evident in her last novel set in her homeland, *Found in the Street* (1986). Like *People Who Knock on the Door,* it also features an obsessed moralist who believes it is his mission to protect the innocent in what he considers the debauched cesspool of New York City. Ralph Linderman, an eccentric security guard who has named his dog "God," latches on to naive and innocent Elsie Tyler, who has just moved to New York. He tries to protect her from such seemingly predatory men as Jack Sutherland, a book illustrator who has befriended the woman. Linderman harasses and badgers Sutherland and blames him for Elsie's death when she is murdered. In fact, he is so blinded by his moral outrage that he does not realize that Elsie is a lesbian and that she has been murdered by the jealous partner of one of her former girlfriends. While Highsmith in most respects paints a positive picture of the gay world in the novel, Harrison suggests that her use of a highly unrealistic gay-on-gay murder points to some ambivalence on her part: "This misrepresentation of reality would seem to suggest a mild antipathy or unease toward the milieu that Highsmith has–at least ostensibly–been painting in such 'normal,' even flattering colors."

In 1990 Highsmith was honored by the French government when she was named Officier dans l'Ordre des Arts et des Lettres (Officer of the Order of Arts and Letters), and in 1991 she was nominated for the Nobel Prize in literature. The same year she published *Ripley under Water* (1991), the last novel of the cycle, in which Ripley is the victim of a meddlesome American couple, David and Janice Pritchard, who have moved into the French village to torture him with their knowledge of some of his youthful offenses. First they call Ripley, pretending to be Dickie Greenleaf; then they follow him and his wife to Tangier, Morocco. They eventually succeed in recovering the remains of Thomas Murchison, the art collector Ripley killed in *Ripley under Ground,* which they leave on Ripley's doorstep. Ripley's response to the constant harassment is unusually restrained. Even though he considers killing Pritchard on several occasions, he does not give in to this urge. The Pritchards get their just deserts, though, when they drown in their own pond while trying to recover Murchison's remains after Ripley has deposited the "bag of bones" there. Ripley disposes of the last incriminating object, one of Murchison's rings, in the nearby river, ensuring his unencumbered future. Some critics have considered the later Ripley books less successful than the first ones; Symons, for example, in the third edition of *Bloody Murder* (1993), blames the fact that Highsmith "has been self-indulgent" in relation to her favorite character for the preposterousness of Ripley's later exploits. Tellingly, the Ripley omnibus published by Knopf as part of the Everyman's Library in 1999 only includes the first three novels of the series.

Highsmith died in a Locarno hospital on 4 February 1995 of cancer, and her ashes were interred in Tegna on 11 March. She bequeathed her $3,000,000 estate to Yaddo, the Upstate New York artists' colony that had been instrumental in launching her career. Shortly after her death her last novel, *Small g: A Summer Idyll* (1995), was published in London. This book hearkens back to *The Price of Salt* and features a large cast of gay, bisexual, and heterosexual characters whose goal is to live peacefully side by side. They mingle in a Zurich saloon called Jakobs Bierstube, the clientele of which is predominantly straight during the week. On weekends the bar is known as "Small g," a reference to its mixed clientele of gays and straights. The tranquil atmosphere is threatened when Renate Hagenauer, a prudish and homophobic fashion designer, incites violence in an attempt to break up relationships. Renate eventually dies in an accident, and the balance is restored. While the lovers in *The Price of Salt* form a monogamous relationship that mirrors a heterosexual marriage, the protagonists in *Small g* have to be satisfied with nonexclusive relationships: Rickie Markwalder is content sharing his boyfriend, Fredy Schimmelmann, a married policeman, with his wife; and bisexual Luisa Zimmermann forms a ménage à trois with the lesbian Dorrie Wyss and the heterosexual Teddie Stevenson.

Whereas *Small g* rapidly sold almost forty-six thousand copies in French translation, the novel was not published in the United States until almost 10 years later. Its fate is indicative of the reception of most of Patricia Highsmith's books, as is noted by Harrison in his study: "for the American author who expatriated herself to Europe for most of her adult life, whose novels often dealt in evasions of various sorts, this last European success and American failure seem a not altogether unfitting conclusion." A boom in interest in Highsmith's life and art in the United States, however, may be righting this imbalance. Her out-of-print books are being republished by Norton; *The Selected Stories of Patricia Highsmith* (2001), which includes all her previously published short-story collections except for *Eleven,* became a best-seller; and *Nothing That Meets the Eye: The Uncollected Stories of Patricia Highsmith* was published in 2002. Even *The New Yorker,* the magazine in which Highsmith had most fervently hoped to be published during her lifetime, helped renew interest in her work by printing her short story "The Trouble with

Dust jacket for the U.S. edition of Highsmith's 1986 novel, set in New York City, her last work to treat life in her native country (Collection of Julie and George Anderson)

Mrs. Blynn" in 2002. Not only is the American reading public taking note of this seminal writer who had previously been relegated to marginality, but also the academy is following suit. In his essay "Reality Catches Up to Highsmith's Hard-Boiled Fiction" from the *Chronicle of Higher Education* (20 February 2004), Leonard Cassuto expains why the author, who was once belittled as a "dime-store Dostoyevsky," is more popular than ever in the United States, and why she is being canonized as a major American artist:

> Never at home in her own context, she fits perfectly into ours. . . . it's clear that the politics—sexual and otherwise—of her dangerously unstable fictional world are a lot like our own. Homosexuals are out, but still the center of political and cultural (to say nothing of religious) debate. And life in today's age of terrorism creates the kind of anxious foreboding that Highsmith evoked again and again. People never know whether something (or someone) might explode next to them. We also live in an era where surveillance is everywhere, and where people live at risk of being turned in and taken away. These times are the closest we've ever come to the '50s, when anxiety boiled beneath the surface of the prosperous facade of American living.

We've moved to the creepy neighborhood where Patricia Highsmith lived all her life.

Ed Siegel, writing in the *Boston Globe* (27 January 2002), also believes that changes in American society have contributed to the reassessment of Highsmith's importance: "In the wake of September 11, Highsmith's world is not only more like ours, where crime and punishment or cause and effect don't necessarily go hand in hand, she seems a more important writer than ever."

Interviews:

Diana Cooper-Clark, "Patricia Highsmith—Interview," *Armchair Detective,* 14 (Spring 1981): 313–320;

"Profile of a Writer—Patricia Highsmith," London Weekend Television, BBC, 1982;

Joan Dupont, "Criminal Pursuits," *New York Times Magazine,* 12 June 1988, pp. 61–66;

Mavis Guinard, "Patricia Highsmith: Alone with Ripley," *International Herald Tribune* (Paris), 17/18 August 1991, p. 20;

Craig Little, "Patricia Highsmith: The Reclusive Writer Has Another Book about Her Antihero Ripley," *Publishers Weekly,* 239 (2 November 1992): 46–47;

Christa Maerker, "'Ich liebe Klarheit . . .,'" *Horen,* 38 (1993): 146–153.

Bibliography:

Franz Cavigelli, "Bibliographie," in *Patricia Highsmith: Leben und Werk,* edited by Cavigelli, Fritz Senn, and Anna von Planta, revised and enlarged edition (Zurich: Diogenes, 1996), pp. 262–309.

Biographies:

Andrew Wilson, "The Woman Who Was Ripley," *Independent on Sunday Magazine,* 13 January 2000;

Marijane Meaker, *Highsmith: A Romance of the 1950's: A Memoir* (San Francisco: Cleis, 2003);

Wilson, *Beautiful Shadow: A Life of Patricia Highsmith* (New York & London: Bloomsbury, 2003).

References:

Julie Abraham, *Are Girls Necessary? Lesbian Writing and Modern Histories* (New York & London: Routledge, 1996), pp. 10–20;

Michael Bronski, "Patricia Highsmith," in *The Gay and Lesbian Literary Companion,* edited by Sharon Malinowski and Christa Brelin (Detroit: Visible Ink, 1995), pp. 253–258;

Brigid Brophy, "Highsmith," in her *Don't Never Forget: Collected Views and Reviews* (New York: Holt, Rinehart & Winston, 1967), pp. 149–155;

Leonard Cassuto, "Reality Catches Up to Highsmith's Hard-Boiled Fiction," *Chronicle of Higher Education* (20 February 2004);

Franz Cavigelli, Fritz Senn, and Anna von Planta, eds., *Patricia Highsmith: Leben und Werk,* revised and enlarged edition (Zurich: Diogenes, 1996);

Michael Dunker, *Beeinflussung und Steuerung des Lesers in der englischsprachigen Detektiv- und Kriminalliteratur: Eine vergleichende Untersuchung zur Beziehung Autor-Text-Leser in Werken von Doyle, Christie und Highsmith* (Frankfurt am Main & New York: Peter Lang, 1991);

Russell Harrison, *Patricia Highsmith* (New York: Twayne, 1997);

Anthony Channell Hilfer, *The Crime Novel: A Deviant Genre* (Austin: University of Texas Press, 1990);

Hilfer, "'Not Really Such a Monster': Highsmith's Ripley as Thriller Protagonist and Protean Man," *Midwest Quarterly,* 25 (Summer 1984): 361–374;

Andrew Jeffcoat, "Noir Transformations: Gender, Place and Identity in *The Talented Mr Ripley* and *Dirty Weekend,*" *Crimeculture.com* (Winter 2003) <http://www.crimeculture.com/Contents/NewAndrewJeffcoat1.html>;

Kathleen Gregory Klein, "Patricia Highsmith," in *And Then There Were Nine . . . More Women of Mystery,* edited by Jane S. Bakerman (Bowling Green, Ohio: Bowling Green State University Popular Press, 1985), pp. 168–197;

MaryKay Mahoney, "A Train Running on Two Sets of Tracks: Highsmith's and Hitchcock's *Strangers on a Train,*" in *It's a Print! Detective Fiction from Page to Screen,* edited by William Reynolds and Elizabeth A. Trembley (Bowling Green, Ohio: Bowling Green State University Popular Press, 1994), pp. 103–114;

Noel Dorman Mawer, "From Villain to Vigilante," *Armchair Detective,* 24 (Winter 1991): 34–38;

Mawer, "Patricia Highsmith," in *Mystery and Suspense Writers: The Literature of Crime, Detection, and Espionage,* 2 volumes, edited by Robin W. Winks and Maureen Corrigan (New York: Scribner, 1998), I: 503–516;

Margaret Caldwell Thomas, "Patricia Highsmith: Murder with a Twist," in *Women of Mystery: The Lives and Works of Notable Women Crime Novelists,* by Thomas and Martha Hailey DuBose (New York: St. Martin's Minotaur, 2000), pp. 326–339;

Alex Tuss, "Masculine Identity and Success: A Critical Analysis of Patricia Highsmith's *The Talented Mr. Ripley* and Chuck Palahniuk's *Fight Club,*" *Journal of Men's Studies,* 12 (Winter 2004): 93–102;

Julie Walker, "'The World of Fear': Engendering Unease in the Novels of Patricia Highsmith," *Crimeculture.com* (Winter 2003) <http://www.crimeculture.com/Contents/New-JulieWalk.htm>.

Papers:

Patricia Highsmith's papers are at the Swiss Literary Archive in Berne, Switzerland.

Tony Hillerman

(27 May 1925 –)

Marvin S. Lachman

See also the Hillerman entry in *DLB 206: Twentieth-Century American Western Writers.*

BOOKS: *The Blessing Way* (New York: Harper, 1970; London: Macmillan, 1970);

The Fly on the Wall (New York: Harper & Row, 1971);

The Boy Who Made Dragonfly: A Zuni Myth, with illustrations by Laszlo Kubinyi (New York: Harper & Row, 1972);

Dance Hall of the Dead (New York: Harper & Row, 1973; London: Pluto, 1985);

The Great Taos Bank Robbery and Other Indian Country Affairs (Albuquerque: University of New Mexico Press, 1973);

New Mexico, text by Hillerman, photographs by David Muench (Portland, Ore.: Graphic Arts Center, 1975);

Rio Grande, text by Hillerman, photographs by Robert Reynolds (Portland, Ore.: Graphic Arts Center, 1975);

Listening Woman (New York: Harper & Row, 1978; London: Macmillan, 1979);

People of Darkness (New York: Harper & Row, 1980; London: Gollancz, 1982);

The Dark Wind (New York: Harper & Row, 1982; London: Gollancz, 1983);

The Ghostway (San Antonio, Tex.: Dennis McMillan, 1984; London: Gollancz, 1985);

Indian Country: America's Sacred Land, text by Hillerman, photographs by Béla Kalman (Flagstaff, Ariz.: Northland Press, 1987);

Skinwalkers (New York: Harper & Row, 1987; London: Joseph, 1988);

A Thief of Time (New York: Harper & Row, 1988; London: Joseph, 1988);

Tony Hillerman's Indian Country Map & Guide, with Florence Lister and Peter Thorpe (Mancos, Colo.: Time Traveler Maps, 1988);

Talking God (New York: Harper & Row, 1989; London: Joseph, 1990);

Tony Hillerman (from Skinwalkers, *1987; Richland County Public Library)*

The Joe Leaphorn Mysteries (New York: Harper & Row, 1989)–comprises *The Blessing Way, Dance Hall of the Dead,* and *Listening Woman;*

Coyote Waits (New York: Harper & Row, 1990; London: Joseph, 1991);

The Jim Chee Mysteries (New York: HarperCollins, 1990)–comprises *People of Darkness, The Dark Wind,* and *The Ghostway;*

Hillerman Country: A Journey through the Southwest with Tony Hillerman, text by Hillerman, photographs by Barney Hillerman (New York: HarperCollins, 1991);

The Perfect Murder: Five Great Mystery Writers Create the Perfect Crime, by Hillerman, Lawrence Block, Sarah Caudwell, Peter Lovesey, and Donald Westlake, edited by Jack Hitt (New York: HarperCollins, 1991);

New Mexico Rio Grande and Other Essays, text by Hillerman, photographs by David Muench and Robert

Reynolds (Portland, Ore.: Graphic Arts Center, 1992);

Sacred Clowns (New York: HarperCollins, 1993; London: HarperCollins, 2000);

Finding Moon (New York: HarperCollins, 1995; London: Joseph, 1996);

The Fallen Man (New York: HarperCollins, 1996; London: Joseph, 1997);

The First Eagle (New York: HarperCollins, 1998; London: HarperCollins, 1999);

Hunting Badger (New York: HarperCollins, 1999; London: HarperCollins, 2000);

Buster Mesquite's Cowboy Band, with illustrations by Ernest Franklin (Gallup, N.Mex.: Buffalo Medicine, 2001);

Seldom Disappointed: A Memoir (New York: HarperCollins, 2001);

The Wailing Wind (New York: HarperCollins, 2002);

The Sinister Pig (New York: HarperCollins, 2003).

OTHER: *The Spell of New Mexico,* edited by Hillerman (Albuquerque: University of New Mexico Press, 1976);

Philip Varney, *New Mexico's Best Ghost Towns: A Practical Guide,* foreword by Hillerman (Albuquerque: University of New Mexico Press, 1987);

The Best of the West: An Anthology of Classic Writing from the American West, edited by Hillerman (New York: HarperCollins, 1991);

Howard Bryan, *Robbers, Rogues, and Ruffians: True Tales of the Wild West in New Mexico,* foreword by Hillerman (Santa Fe: Clear Light, 1991);

The Best of the West: An Anthology of Classic Writing from the American West, edited by Hillerman (New York: HarperCollins, 1991);

"The Case of the Whimsical Attack Dog (or How I Learned to Stop Outlining Plots)," introduction to new edition of Hillerman's *Listening Woman* (New York: Otto Penzler, 1994);

Introduction to new edition of *People of Darkness* (New York: Otto Penzler, 1994);

The Mysterious West, edited by Hillerman (New York: HarperCollins, 1994);

Robert Allen Rutland, *A Boyhood in the Dustbowl 1926–1934,* introduction by Hillerman (Boulder: University of Colorado Press, 1995);

The Oxford Book of American Detective Stories, edited by Hillerman with Rosemary Herbert (Oxford & New York: Oxford University Press, 1996);

John Martin Campbell, *Few and Far Between: Moments in the North American Desert,* foreword by Hillerman (Santa Fe: Museum of New Mexico Press, 1997);

Best American Mystery Stories of the Century, edited by Hillerman, with Otto Penzler (Boston: Houghton Mifflin, 2000).

SELECTED PERIODICAL PUBLICATION–UNCOLLECTED: "A Canyon, an Egret . . . And a Mystery," *Audubon,* 91 (July 1989): 30–36.

By creating the first Native American detectives to be featured in a series of mystery novels, Tony Hillerman led a trend to increase the diversity of protagonists in that genre. He also helped to popularize the American regional mystery through his authentic depictions of the Southwest.

Anthony Grove Hillerman was born in Sacred Heart, Oklahoma, on 27 May 1925, the youngest child of August Alfred and Lucy Grove Hillerman. His father taught at a one-room school in rural Texas and then was a farmer, cowboy, farrier, and storekeeper. His mother was a homemaker. Between 1930 and 1938, Tony, his brother, Barney, and sister, Mary Margaret, were among a handful of white children attending St. Mary's Academy, a boarding school for Indian girls in Sacred Heart. In *Seldom Disappointed: A Memoir* (2001) Hillerman says of his childhood: "Everybody was poor and when you're a kid you don't know you're deprived unless you see someone who isn't." He grew up with children of the Potawatomi and Seminole tribes as playmates and said the experience permitted him to feel comfortable among Indians.

Beginning in 1939, Hillerman attended Konawa (Oklahoma) High School, graduating in 1942. He spent one semester at Oklahoma Agricultural & Mechanical College in 1942, working as a dishwasher and ditchdigger to pay tuition and expenses. He then returned to work on the family farm when his brother enlisted in the army; his father had died in 1941 of heart disease. In 1943, his mother, whom he credits with teaching him to seek adventure and never to whine or be afraid, consented to his enlisting in the army. He went to France in 1944 as a mortar gunner in the 410th Infantry Regiment, seeing combat in the Ardennes during the Battle of the Bulge and receiving a Silver Star and a Bronze Star with Oak Leaf Cluster. In 1945 he stepped on a landmine and was temporarily blinded and suffered broken legs and severe burns. He received the Purple Heart.

After five months of hospitalization in France, Hillerman was returned to the United States. While still on convalescent leave from the army in 1945, he took a job transporting oil-field equipment. On one trip to the Navajo Reservation, he observed an Enemy Way curing ceremony for Navajos who had

Hillerman covering politics for the Santa Fe New Mexican *in 1954 (Hillerman,* Seldom Disappointed: A Memoir, *2001; Thomas Cooper Library, University of South Carolina)*

served in the marines. The purpose of the ceremony was to cure them of the evil influences they had encountered in seeing death in the war and to restore them to harmony with the Navajo people. It sparked his interest in learning more about the tribe.

In 1946, Hillerman enrolled at the University of Oklahoma under the G.I. Bill, majoring in journalism. While there, he met Marie Unzner, a fellow student, from Shawnee, Oklahoma. The couple married in 1948, the year Hillerman graduated with a B.A. degree, and have raised six children, five of whom were adopted.

Hillerman also embarked on his career in journalism in 1948, accepting a job as a newspaper reporter, first in Borger, Texas, for the *News Herald* and then in Lawton, Oklahoma, as news editor of the *Morning Press* in 1949 and as city editor for the *Constitution* in 1950. He worked for United Press in Oklahoma City in 1952 and later that year became their bureau chief in Santa Fe, New Mexico. He left United Press in 1954 to become managing editor at the *Santa Fe New Mexican,* but in 1963 he left to enroll as a graduate student at the University of New Mexico, obtaining an M.A. in English in 1965. He taught classes in journalism at the school and became chairman of its journalism department. He also worked as an administrative assistant to the president of the university.

Hillerman had long wanted to write fiction, and in the late 1960s, despite the pressures of supporting a large family, he was encouraged to do so by his wife and began working on a novel. (He sold articles while working as a reporter and while attending graduate school and teaching, but no fiction.) Hillerman enjoyed mystery fiction and had been impressed by Arthur W. Upfield, who created a part-Aborigine Australian police detective who often solves cases in his country's "outback," using his knowledge of native culture and his ability to track and interpret physical clues. Hillerman decided to set his mysteries among the Navajos, whose reservation covers more than sixteen million acres in the "four corners" area where New Mexico, Arizona, Utah, and Colorado abut.

Hillerman introduced Joe Leaphorn, a lieutenant in the Navajo Tribal Police, in his first novel, *The Blessing Way* (1970). In the initial draft of this book, a white anthropology professor, Bergen McKee, plays a larger role than Leaphorn. In his memoir, Hillerman recalls that his agent, Ann Elmo, recommended that he "Get rid of the Indian stuff." The editor at Harper and Row, Joan Kahn, to whom Hillerman then submitted the manuscript directly, liked it and advised him to increase the amount of the book devoted to Leaphorn and Navajo culture.

The Blessing Way starts with the meeting between Luis Horseman, a young Navajo hiding from the tribal police, and a mysterious man in a wolf skin, a figure considered a witch in Navajo tradition. Such a belief is the type of superstition that McKee is investigating. Regarding Horseman, Hillerman has Leaphorn wonder, as he often does, about Navajos who cannot cope in the dominant white culture or in their own culture. He calls Horseman, who is even inept at crime, "Just another poor soul who didn't quite know how to be a Navajo and couldn't learn to act like a white."

Later in the book, the focus shifts to McKee, who is held captive by the mysterious "wolfman" in an Anasazi cliff dwelling, with Leaphorn going to rescue him. Critics differed on how suspenseful the book was, with A. L. Rosenzweig writing in the 10 May 1970 issue of *Book World* that Hillerman was ". . . weak on twanging the nerves," while Sergeant Cuff in the *Saturday Review* of 28 March 1970 opined, "Here's suspense enough for anyone." Reviewers generally agreed that Hillerman's writing about Navajo culture had added a dimension to the mystery, causing W. H. Farrington in *Library Journal* (15 May 1970) to conclude, "Here we have that rarity: a mystery with literary value, one you can recommend to people who don't like mysteries."

Despite favorable reviews and a nomination for the Edgar Allan Poe Award of Mystery Writers of America (MWA) as best first novel, *The Blessing Way* did not entirely satisfy Hillerman. Twenty years later, in an interview with Ernie Bulow in *Talking Mysteries* (1991), Hillerman agreed with criticisms of this book for inaccuracies regarding the Navajos, saying, "a lot of it makes me flinch." Hillerman has done considerable research into Navajo culture since his first book.

For his second novel, Hillerman abandoned the Navajos and turned to his newspaper background for *The Fly on the Wall* (1971), a book that earned him another Edgar nomination, this time as best novel of the year. The title refers to what Walter Lippmann once described as the role of the journalist. Set in the capital of an unnamed state (Hillerman later said it was based on Oklahoma City), the book has as protagonist political reporter John Cotton. He is stalked by a killer while investigating the death of a fellow reporter who, after hinting he had a "big story" regarding fraud in state government, fell from the capitol rotunda. Originally intending it as a mainstream novel, Hillerman added the elements of crime fiction to its theme of ethics in journalism and politics. Reviewers praised the authenticity of Cotton's investigation, and generally agreed regarding the strength of the mystery. Newgate Callendar in *The New York Times Book Review* of 7 November 1971 found it "flawlessly plotted." Hillerman also got high marks for suspenseful writing, with

several reviewers praising as "thrilling" the scenes in which Cotton is menaced by the killer in the New Mexico mountains and when he returns to the capitol building. In 1972 Hillerman published *The Boy Who Made Dragonfly,* a children's book retelling a Zuñi myth about a dragonfly bringing wisdom to children.

Hillerman returned to the Navajo Reservation and Joe Leaphorn with *Dance Hall of the Dead* (1973), a novel in which he also explores the culture of the Zuñi tribe. The title refers to Kothluwalawa, the Zuñi heaven. As he searches for two missing teenage friends, one Zuñi and one Navajo, Leaphorn ponders the beliefs of both tribes and their relations with each other. Though the book includes few whites, Hillerman shows the Navajo attitude toward Jason's Fleece, a hippie commune whose "New Age" beliefs appear to have co-opted Indian philosophy. One Navajo "rated the residents of Jason's Fleece as generous, ignorant, friendly, bad mannered but well intentioned." The use of peyote is raised when Leaphorn finds a member of Jason's Fleece "spaced out" and says that if he used peyote he will be all right in a couple of hours; if not, he needs to see a doctor. Hillerman implies that Leaphorn will overlook the use, though illegal, because many Indians feel it is part of their religion. In this book, Hillerman also raises the question of jurisdiction on the Navajo Reservation, a theme that recurs in his books as federal agencies as well as state and county police vie with the Navajo Tribal Police. On the first of many occasions, Leaphorn is critical of a Federal Bureau of Investigation (FBI) agent, who he says is primarily concerned with favorable publicity to build a record for promotion. Hillerman earned his third straight Edgar nomination for this book, and this time won the prize for best novel with what many feel is his best book. H. R. F. Keating, critic and mystery writer, included *Dance Hall of the Dead* in *Crime and Mystery: The 100 Best Books* (1987).

Five years passed before Hillerman's next mystery appeared, but during the interim, he published much nonfiction. *The Great Taos Bank Robbery and Other Indian Country Affairs* (1973) is a collection of essays Hillerman wrote regarding the various cultures of New Mexico. The title essay about Taos and its clumsy criminals is regarded as Hillerman's funniest writing. Travel books that followed were *New Mexico* (1975), *Rio Grande* (1975), *The Spell of New Mexico* (1976), and *Indian Country* (1987).

The third Leaphorn novel, *Listening Woman* (1978), depends more on police procedure than its predecessors, with Joe working on several cases at once. One involves "Goldrims," named for his glasses, a stranger to the reservation. As Leaphorn is transporting a young Navajo prisoner charged with stealing sheep, he is run off the road by Goldrims in his Mercedes. The

Dust jacket for Hillerman's 1982 novel, his second to feature Jim Chee of the Navajo Tribal Police (Richland County Public Library)

prisoner escapes, as does Goldrims, who proves to be a member of a militant Indian group, the Buffalo Society, which has robbed an armored truck.

In this book, Navajo traditions are represented by Margaret Cigaret, a blind Navajo medicine woman who is trying to diagnose and cure Hosteen Tso, a man she believes may be ill because of witchcraft. Hillerman's research into Navajo religion is apparent in his discussion of the Mountain Way and Black Rain Chants, which Cigaret sees as needed to cure Tso, and later in the Kinaalda ceremony she conducts for a young girl. When Tso and Margaret's niece are murdered, Leaphorn has another case to solve. During the course of his investigation, he visits John McGinnis, a white trading-post operator who is a recurring character in Hillerman's books. During their conversation, Hillerman has McGinnis express the opinion that Navajos do not *plan* murders; they only commit them because of alcohol or anger from a fight. Leaphorn agrees.

Listening Woman includes more action than do prior books, and it ends with a seventy-page chase that

includes Leaphorn and a group of Boy Scouts being held prisoner in Canyon de Chelly. Jon L. Breen, writing in *The Tony Hillerman Companion* (1994), considered this book the best of the three involving Leaphorn alone. Callendar summed up the aspect of Hillerman's work that most frequently drew praise by saying in *The New York Times Book Review* of 7 May 1978, ". . . as in the previous books, there are insights into the way Indians today think and function. Hillerman . . . obviously has done a great deal of research into Indian customs and religion." Another favorable review, by K. S. Hurwitz, appeared in the November 1978 *School Library Journal,* a publication designed for school librarians. (Hillerman has frequently said he wanted to attract young readers, especially among the Navajos, and that is why he avoids explicit sex and obscenity in his books.) *Listening Woman* earned Hillerman his fourth Edgar nomination early in 1979, and later that year he was guest of honor at Bouchercon (the World Mystery Convention) in Los Angeles.

In *People of Darkness* (1980), Hillerman turned to a new policeman, Jim Chee, also of the Navajo Tribal Police but about twenty years younger than Leaphorn and more traditional in his religious beliefs. Though a graduate of the University of New Mexico with a degree in anthropology, Chee feels confused as to the ways of whites but is curious enough to want to learn more. However, he is insistent on not giving up his Navajo heritage. Hillerman has called Chee "less culturally assimilated" than Leaphorn. Physically, Chee is tall and lean and is described as good looking. Lieutenant Leaphorn does not appear in this book, but it includes a reference to a call from a "Captain" Leaphorn, apparently intended by Hillerman as an inside joke, because it is a call Chee never returns. Explaining his temporary abandonment of Leaphorn, Hillerman cited as one reason his having signed away the rights to him as a movie character while attempting to negotiate a deal in Hollywood. In his spare time, Chee studies to become a *Yataalii,* a singer qualified to conduct Navajo religious rites such as the Blessing Way and the Enemy Way. These ceremonies, lasting from three to nine days, involve elaborate preparation of food and helpers for the singer and are designed to effect cures and restore harmony.

The novel starts with an explosion in a hospital parking lot in Albuquerque, one that destroys the pickup truck belonging to Emerson Charley, a member of a family that is unusually prone to cancer. The bomber is one of several white hired killers to be found in Hillerman's books. Chee ultimately connects the bomber's crime to an oil-field explosion in the 1940s, and Breen in *The Tony Hillerman Companion* notes that "the plot has a Ross Macdonald feel, as a long-past event casts shadows in the present."

Despite their differences, Chee and Leaphorn both accept *hozho,* the Navajo sense of harmony, and use it in their detective work, seeking to find where a criminal has destroyed a pattern in life. Something that does not belong or is missing is considered as upsetting the balance of *hozho* and can be regarded as a clue. In *People of Darkness* Chee uses his tracking ability and knowledge of his physical surroundings to find a buried skeleton.

The novel initiates a motif that is present in all the novels in which Chee appears—his romantic involvement with a woman develops and defines him as a Navajo. In *People of Darkness,* the woman is Mary Landon, a white schoolteacher on the reservation. He meets Mary while looking for Emerson Charley's son at an Indian rug auction at the school where she teaches, and they are attracted to each other. She accompanies him during his investigation. The reader learns that Chee has been accepted by the FBI Academy and is considering going, though he has doubts because he thinks "you can't be both a Navajo medicine man and an FBI agent."

Chee proved to be as popular as Leaphorn and returned in *The Dark Wind* (1982), in which Hillerman again combined the cultures of two tribes. During a Hopi ceremony to end a drought on Hopi-Navajo joint-use land, a Navajo corpse is discovered. Chee works with Hopi sheriff Cowboy Dashee, a boyhood friend, on this case as well as on one involving the crash of a small plane. The cargo of the plane, presumably illegal drugs, is missing, and in another instance, describing federal misconduct, Hillerman has agents of the Drug Enforcement Agency beat Chee, claiming he stole drugs from the plane. Skin was removed from the corpse, raising the possibility that "corpse powder" was wanted for witchcraft. The white pilot was apparently murdered, and his sister tells Chee that she wants the killer punished. Hillerman portrays Chee as unable to accept the concept of revenge because his Navajo upbringing has taught him that a criminal is out of control: "The dark wind had entered him and destroyed his judgment."

The Dark Wind was not only praised for its descriptions of physical setting—the vast reservation space, the daily summer thundershowers, and the colors of the sky—but also as a detective story. Robin Winks in *The New Republic* for 20–27 September 1982 thought it Hillerman's best book and praised his "turning the mystery and its solution upon the intricate social and religious life of the Indians of the American Southwest." Breen, in *The Tony Hillerman Companion,* finds the plot "beautifully worked out, with a stronger whodunit

element than usual and possibly Hillerman's best fair-play puzzle."

The Ghostway (1984), in which Chee is hunting a Navajo armed fugitive whom the FBI also wants, is less notable for its detective elements than for its continuing development of Chee as a character and its further insights into Navajo culture. Though Chee graduated from the FBI Academy, he chose not to join the bureau, feeling he would lose his identity while away from the *Dineh* ("the People"), as Navajos call themselves. His decision leads to a conflict with Mary Landon, who, he thinks, considers him "another unambitious Navajo." The fugitive is found buried near the abandoned hogan of Hosteen Begay. Chee has trouble entering the hogan where death took place, realizing a conflict exists between his Navajo beliefs in avoiding death and his duties as a police officer. Begay is missing, as is his granddaughter, and they may have gone to Los Angeles, where members of his clan relocated. Chee goes there to find her.

Hillerman's writing about Los Angeles, in which he contrasts it with the reservation and emphasizes the former's constant freeway traffic, smog, and noise, some critics found outstanding. Chee, who considers himself a good driver in New Mexico, is anxious and cautious driving there, lacking the "confidence in their immortality that L.A. drivers brought to their freeway system." However, T. J. Binyon, in his 27 December 1985 review in *TLS: The Times Literary Supplement,* thought the setting rendered *The Ghostway* closer to "more ordinary crime novels."

With *Skinwalkers* (1987), Hillerman first made the best-seller list. In it he brings back Leaphorn while retaining Chee, thus allowing for contrast between the older detective and the younger, more emotional policeman. Chee is uncomfortable around Leaphorn and in awe of him because he is "the famous Leaphorn of tribal police legends."

Though the personal problems of both detectives play a major role in the book, Hillerman places equal emphasis on their working together as detectives. The novel starts with Leaphorn investigating three apparently separate homicides that he suspects are connected because murder is rare on the reservation. Some suggest a skinwalker (a Navajo witch) is responsible, though Leaphorn doubts it. He is also burdened with administrative duties as well as demands placed on him by politicians on the Navajo tribal council. Leaphorn's wife, Emma, is ill, moreover, and he fears that she has Alzheimer's disease. Chee, who is less tactful than Leaphorn, gets into trouble by accusing Yellowhorse, a doctor and tribal council member, of being a fake who uses crystal gazing as well as medicine and exploits the superstitions and fears of his patients.

Dust jacket for the first novel in which Hillerman brings together his two main series detectives, Joe Leaphorn and Jim Chee (Richland County Public Library)

Separated from Mary Landon, who has gone to teach in Wisconsin after having accused him of caring more about being a Navajo than about her, Chee meets the woman who occupies his emotions for many books to come, Janet Pete, a Navajo lawyer whose mother is white. Chee's new romance does not free him from conflict, however. Having decided that he and Mary cannot live in each other's worlds, he comes to fear that getting involved with Pete might also mean that he would "quit being a Navajo" and be a *belagaana* (a white) since, though half-Navajo, she is not at all traditional. Chee continues to pursue his religious training and gets his second job as a *Yataalii*, performing a Blessing Way.

Hillerman won the Western Writers of America's Spur Award and the Bouchercon Anthony Award, both for best novel, for *Skinwalkers*. Maryell Cleary, reviewed it in *The Mystery Fancier* (Summer 1988), saying of Hillerman, "he has so penetrated the Native-American worldview that he can present it to us lovingly, as inevitably right for these people and that place." Breen in *The Tony Hillerman Companion* ranks it among the best in the series

to date. In 1987, Hillerman had received a Special Friend of the Navajo Award and won the Macavity Award of Mystery Readers International. In 1988, he was president of MWA, and in 1991, he received their most prestigious award, the Grand Master.

Hillerman's own favorite among his books, *A Thief of Time* (1988), rose high on the best-seller lists. One of the thieves of Navajo culture is anthropologist Eleanor Friedman-Bernal, who disappears while illegally searching for Anasazi pottery in a cliff dwelling. She justifies her action by saying that finding the pottery might provide clues as to where the Anasazi Indians went when they disappeared from the area in the fourteenth century. Emma Leaphorn dies during surgery for what proves to be a brain tumor, and Joe, having difficulty in coping with his loss, wants to retire. However, he agrees to join in the search for the anthropologist as a favor to a friend. The investigations of Leaphorn and Chee take them to a revival meeting of a Navajo evangelist, whose sermon emphasizes the difficulty Navajos have in practicing their traditional religion, pointing to intrusions on their sacred mountains such as radio towers and roads built to facilitate exploration for oil.

Reviews of Hillerman's work continued to be favorable. An unsigned review in *Time* on 4 July 1988 said, "Hillerman's most striking virtue is his evocation of the Southwest: the barren, craggy land and the complex social interactions between whites and Native Americans and among mutually mistrustful Navajo, Hopi and Apache." Michael Dorris, in *The New York Times Book Review* for 3 July 1988, gave a cogent reason why Hillerman's work had found favor with the people about whom he wrote: "Mr. Hillerman's picture of modern American Indians is never patronizing, never hokey, never precious." In *The Tony Hillerman Companion,* Breen concluded, "Besides including one of Hillerman's best-woven plots . . . , *A Thief of Time* has some of his deepest explorations of religious values and the varieties of religious belief and expression."

Hillerman's use of current issues in his books, apparent in the focus on stolen Native American artifacts in *A Thief of Time*—a subject that had received national attention—is also evident in his next book, *Talking God* (1989), which is based on the protests and lawsuits surrounding the refusal of some museums to return the Indian skeletons in their collections to tribal members. Activist Henry Highhawk, one-fourth Navajo, digs up the bones of the grandparents of the Smithsonian Museum's lawyer from a New England cemetery and mails them to her. Chee arrests him, and Janet Pete, now in Washington, D.C., is selected to defend him. Meanwhile, Leaphorn, not yet retired, investigates the finding of a body in a case that might be connected to Highhawk's. He still misses Emma, who has been dead for a year, and recalls how he discussed his cases with her, often using her advice.

Both Chee and Leaphorn go to Washington for extended stays, and therein lies the fault that some critics had with *Talking God*. Phoebe-Lou Adams in *The Atlantic* for October 1989 said, "If Mr. Hillerman's latest is less exciting than the best, blame the setting. Washington is a dreary place compared to New Mexico." Breen, concluding that Hillerman's series characters "do not transplant well to other locations," was not high in his praise of this Hillerman book but asserted that "the least of his books belongs to the upper echelons of detective fiction." Timothy Foote, in *The New York Times Book Review* of 18 June 1989, however, found the Washington-Smithsonian background effective.

Coyote Waits (1990), Hillerman's third Leaphorn-Chee book in three years, starts with a traumatic event for Chee when he unsuccessfully tries to save a fellow tribal police officer, Delbert Nez, whose car is on fire. A killer had set fire to the car after shooting Nez. Chee, though burned in the attempted rescue, feels guilty because he delayed responding to Nez's call that he was running low on gas while trying to apprehend a suspect he referred to as the "phantom painter."

Conflicts arise for Chee when he arrests a Navajo shaman, Hosteen Ashie Pinto, for Nez's death, and Janet Pete, now a public defender for the Department of Justice, is picked to defend Pinto. Chee also finds that Leaphorn has been asked by Emma's relatives, who think Pinto is innocent, to look into the case. He still feels he must prove himself to Leaphorn. In this book, Leaphorn makes a new friend, Louisa Bourebonette, a professor in American studies at Northern Arizona University. She had been interviewing Pinto in connection with a book she was writing. This relationship proves to be important for Leaphorn and shows his recovery from Emma's death. The relationships of Chee and Leaphorn with women continue to be handled discreetly, with no sexual descriptions, allowing Hillerman's books to be recommended for high-school readers.

In a highly favorable review in *The New York Times Book Review* of 24 June 1990, Robert F. Gish wrote that Hillerman "expands the boundaries of his special form—the detective Western—and shares with readers the power of words in the ratiocination of his detectives and in the Native American culture about which he writes." Later, Gish describes Hillerman "as one of the nation's most convincing and authentic interpreters of Navajo culture, as well as one of our best and most innovative modern mystery writers." That Hillerman has received the highest awards of both MWA

and the Western Writers of America indicates that he crosses genres.

Shortly before *Coyote Waits* was published, Hillerman had another experience with Hollywood when in 1990 he agreed with Robert Redford to make a movie of *The Dark Wind*. Their original discussion has become part of Hillerman lore, as he refused Redford's offer of sending a private airplane to Albuquerque to bring him to Redford's retreat in the Utah mountains because the invitation clashed with Hillerman's weekly poker game. The two men did eventually meet and toured the reservation together. The movie, made in 1991, with Lou Diamond Phillips as Chee, was a disappointment, described by critic Leonard Maltin as "a ponderously slow, muddled account of a young Navajo cop." It was finally released in 1994, but only in video-rental stores.

Hillerman's health problems (resulting in two operations for cancer) led to a three-year hiatus before the publication of his next book, *Sacred Clowns* (1993). It opens with Chee watching a kachina dance ceremony at the Tano Pueblo, with masked dancers representing ancestral spirits, while he looks for a missing schoolboy who may have information about a murder, which had taken place on the previous day, of a teacher on the Navajo Reservation. The sacred clowns of the title, the *Koshares,* perform slapstick comedy as part of the ceremony. One clown is clubbed to death, and Chee, though nearby, is unable to prevent it. Chee's diffidence around Leaphorn, who is now Chee's direct supervisor, leads Chee into frequent errors. He sees the schoolboy at the ceremony but lets him get away. Leaphorn is unhappy that Chee invited Janet Pete to be with him there while he was supposed to be working. Also interfering with his work are his budding romance with Janet Pete and the conflict between his career as a police officer and his desire to be a Navajo shaman. As a nontraditional Navajo, Pete is not even aware of the clan to which she belongs, so Chee is afraid that in a love affair with her he might be violating a Navajo taboo against incest.

Reviewers had more reservations about *Sacred Clowns* than about most Hillerman books. In *The New York Times Book Review* of 17 October 1993, Verlyn Klinkenborg, calling this Hillerman's most "pallid" mystery, questioned his tendency to make whites guilty of murder as well as insensitive to Indians. Though feeling that the identification of the killer did not ring true, Barry Gardner in *Mostly Murder* (Fall 1993) praised the description of Leaphorn and Chee as characters: "Their lives and problems are very much part of the story, and each here is struggling with a personal relationship that troubles and confuses him." Yet, for Jim Bencivenga, in *Christian Science Monitor* of 2 October 1993, their interaction causes the book to "bog down . . .

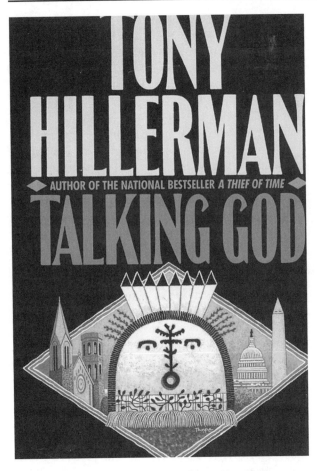

Dust jacket for Hillerman's ninth novel about Navajo policemen, published in 1989, in which Chee and Leaphorn work cases that take them to Washington, D.C. (Collection of George and Julie Anderson)

gives too much effort to analysis of each man's psychological plight, more than is given to solving two murders central to the book."

Hillerman had long wanted to publish a mainstream novel, but he had turned to mystery fiction as a surer means of being published. In the 1960s he had contemplated a novel set in the newly independent Belgian Congo. When he returned to his original idea in the 1990s, he decided to change his setting to Vietnam in April and May 1975, as the United States military was preparing to leave. In *Finding Moon* (1995), Hillerman's protagonist, "Moon" Mathias, is a newspaper editor in a small Colorado city, whose mother asks him to go to Vietnam when she learns that his brother, killed in a plane crash there, left behind a baby daughter. Fueled by guilt because his mother has always been disappointed in him, Mathias goes to Vietnam, despite misgivings.

Although the novel is not a mystery, *Finding Moon* has as much suspense as any book in the Leaphorn-Chee series. Mathias's perilous journey through the Philip-

pines and Vietnam, so different from New Mexico in their greenery and dampness, is well described, especially the "river of roaches" Moon encounters in Manila, and Hillerman does a good job of limning different cultures. Early in the book, Hillerman shows his knowledge of editing a newspaper. Later, he devises an effective way to give the reader a biography of "Moon," having him tell of his life during a confession to a priest. Hillerman, a devout Catholic, seldom refers to his own religion in the Navajo books.

Hillerman returned to his Leaphorn-Chee series with *The Fallen Man* (1996), which opens as a group of climbers spot a skeleton near the peak of Ship Rock on the Navajo Reservation. Since the skeleton is in an area inaccessible to climbers, how did it get there? Leaphorn, finally retired and bored, recalls a missing-person case involving a wealthy rancher's son eleven years before and gets involved now because of his frustration at having left that case unsolved. Meanwhile, Chee, an acting lieutenant, is dealing with several active investigations plus administrative duties and is not anxious to tackle the "Fallen Man" case until he learns of a possible connection between the skeleton and Janet Pete's former boss at a Washington law firm.

Jim and Janet, planning to marry, are increasingly aware of their cultural differences, though both are nominally Navajo. He wants a traditional Navajo wedding, while she tells him, "My culture is Stanford sorority girl, Maryland cocktail circuit, Mozart and tickets to the Met." Chee in turn assesses himself as she might see him, "a just-plain cop and genuine sheep-camp Navajo as opposed to the more romantic and politically correct Indigenous Person."

Chee's relations with Janet—and with Leaphorn—remain engrossing throughout, but reviewers were not satisfied with the resolution of the mystery. Reviewing *The Fallen Man* in *Mostly Murder* (November-December 1996), Terry Collins noted how its interesting subplot of modern-day cattle rustling was abandoned and finds that even the resolution of the main case is "too convenient and some questions remain unanswered. The confrontation with the killer is too pat and predictable."

Bubonic plague, which still occurs in his region, is a subject that has long interested Hillerman. One of his essays in *The Great Taos Bank Robbery,* "All Fall Down," is about an outbreak of plague in New Mexico. A hantavirus, causing plague-like symptoms, struck the Southwest in 1993, resulting in deaths in the four-corners region. Hillerman uses it as background for *The First Eagle* (1998).

In the beginning of the novel, acting lieutenant Chee comes upon the body of Navajo tribal policeman Benny Kinsman on a butte. Kinsman had requested backup, and because no one else was available, Chee had gone there himself. He arrests a Hopi man who has a history of illegally poaching eagle feathers and whom he saw crouching over Kinsman's body. Leaphorn, now retired for a year and working as a freelance detective, becomes involved when a scientist who is collecting fleas from desert animals goes missing in the same vicinity as the murder. Leaphorn reminds Chee, as he often has, to be wary of coincidences.

Chee and Janet Pete, now a public defender in the region, are again on opposite sides. Jim is convinced the Hopi is guilty, while Janet is defending him. Jim and Janet have grown further apart, with Jim satisfied he has found "the good life in a rusty trailer house" and having decided that Janet's life of "Kennedy Center culture" is not compatible with his traditional Navajo beliefs.

A conflict arises regarding the plague, with many local people believing that witchcraft is responsible for the illnesses. Leaphorn, the Navajo agnostic, does not believe in witches, though he does believe that many Navajos do believe in them and act accordingly. Meanwhile, scientists, including the one who is missing, have been seeking a more objective explanation, and one raises an issue that Leaphorn thinks important to the case—the tendency for bacteria to become resistant to antibiotics.

In *The New York Times Book Review,* (16 August 1998), Marilyn Stasio praised Hillerman's narrative voice and storytelling in *The First Eagle.* Other reviewers were less enthusiastic, pointing out that a lack of legitimate suspects existed and that the identity of the killer was increasingly obvious after the first half of the book. In her review in *Library Journal* for July 1998, Wilda Williams thought *The First Eagle* no more than a "routine mystery in which Chee's and Leaphorn's personal lives are more interesting than their professional ones."

In *Hunting Badger* (1999), Hillerman was inspired by a real event, the May 1998 murder of police officer Dale Claxton of Cortez, Colorado, by three men who later wounded three other officers who were trying to catch them. The unsuccessful manhunt for the criminals involved more than five hundred officers from at least twenty federal, state, and tribal agencies, as well as bounty hunters eager for the reward offered by the FBI. Hillerman describes these events in an author's note to *Hunting Badger* and in *Seldom Disappointed* calls it "an FBI-orchestrated, incredibly bungled, Keystone Cops manhunt."

Police officers in *Hunting Badger* refer often to the Claxton case, and the novel includes similarities as three men raid a Ute Tribe casino, kill its security chief, and wound Deputy Sheriff Teddy Bai, moonlighting there as a security guard. Bai is suspected of having been involved in the robbery, so Navajo Tribal Police officer Bernadette Manuelito, who believes Bai innocent, asks Jim Chee to investigate. Leaphorn also agrees to look into the case at the request of an old friend, who is afraid of the three robbers, who are possibly members of a militia group.

The FBI takes over the investigation and manhunt, allowing the tribal police only such minor duties as traffic control, and throughout the book the native police offer negative views of federal agencies, one calling the FBI the "Federal Bureau of Ineptitude." An example of a bureau blunder is the erasing of tracks by agents flying helicopters over the crime scene. The investigations by Chee and Leaphorn, at first separate, combine for a solution, one involving Ironhand, a legendary Ute bandit-hero from the early years of the twentieth century.

Hillerman again explores Chee's personal life as he becomes romantically interested in Bernadette and compares her favorably to Janet Pete, wondering whether the latter's sophistication is not merely shallowness. Chee has interrupted his shaman studies with Hosteen Frank Sam Nakai (who is on his deathbed), but still gets sage advice from the latter that allows him to help Leaphorn to solve the case. Some reviewers showed signs of growing tired of Hillerman's formula. Williams in *Library Journal* (15 November 1999) said, "*Hunting Badger* offers a paint-by-the-numbers plot with cardboard villains." However, other reviewers were more favorable. In *Booklist* (15 October 1999), Bill Ott said, "Hillerman returns to top form in this tale. . . . As with other long-running series, this one has fluctuated in recent years between maintaining comfortable rhythms and slipping into tired sameness. The rhythm is back this time." Stasio in *The New York Times Book Review* (21 November 1999) was also favorable: "The dual investigations converge, restoring the internal harmony of the natural world that Hillerman describes with such heartfelt wonder."

Hillerman took the title for his memoir *Seldom Disappointed* from his mother's favorite aphorism: "Blessed are those who expect little. They are seldom disappointed." Hillerman's three years in the army receive a large amount of space because that period in his life was clearly significant to him. Characteristically, his experiences, in addition to being a vivid narrative of battles and the boredom between them, are told with great modesty. He is equally humble regarding his accomplishments as a writer, and 80 percent of the book is about his life before he began publishing fiction. He minimizes the importance of his awards and believes his ability to attract nonmystery readers is the hallmark of success. Hillerman writes that some feel guilty just "reading for idle amusement . . . they read my books because of the

Adam Beach (left) and Wes Studi as Jim Chee and Joe Leaphorn in the 2002 adaptation of Skinwalkers *for the PBS television series* Mystery! *(<www.jsonline.com>)*

tribal cultural material. They want to learn a bit about American Indians."

In *The Wailing Wind* (2002), Bernadette Manuelito, increasingly a major character in the series, finds a dead man in a truck at the bottom of a dry wash. The discovery poses a conflict for her as both a police officer and a Navajo. Since traditional Navajos fear contamination from the dead, Bernadette thinks she will need a curing ceremony. Chee, as her boss, finds that she mishandled matters: she did not realize the dead man had been murdered; she failed to secure the crime scene; and she removed evidence, seedpods and burr that she took away in a tobacco tin. Chee defends her but also asks Leaphorn's help in secretly returning the evidence. Because Jim is falling in love with her, he realizes there is a problem in his also being her supervisor. A man wants to hire Leaphorn as a private detective to find his wife, missing many years, a case still unsolved when Leaphorn retired. He finds the old case is connected to the body Manuelito found. In proof of Hillerman's continued popularity, the book immediately appeared close to the top of *The New York Times* best-seller list.

Despite two failed attempts to transfer Hillerman's characters to the screen, moviemakers continued to be interested in his works, and *Skinwalkers* was adapted during the 2002–2003 season as the first motion picture on the public television series *American Mystery!* It was followed during the next season by *Coyote Waits,* with PBS airing *A Thief of Time* in 2004. Neither *Skinwalkers* nor *Coyote Waits* received especially good reviews. Of the latter, Virginia Heffernan concluded in *The New York Times:* "Neither the murder nor the western expanse nor the intimations of mortality quicken the imagination."

In addition to regularly producing novels that are best-sellers, Tony Hillerman has become arguably the most interviewed and written-about mystery writer in America since 1970. His books are as popular with critics as they are with the public because they are not only superior escape fiction, with suspenseful narratives and satisfying detection, but they also explore social problems through their depiction of a native culture previously unrepresented in crime fiction.

Interviews:

Patricia Holt, "PW Interviews Tony Hillerman," *Publishers Weekly* (24 October 1980): 6–7;

Bruce Taylor, "Interview with Tony Hillerman," *Armchair Detective,* 14 (Winter 1981): 93–95;

Harriet Stay, "An Interview with Tony Hillerman," *Mystery News,* 7 (July/August 1988): 1–2;

Ernie Bulow, *Talking Mysteries: A Conversation with Tony Hillerman,* illustrations by Ernest Franklin (Albuquerque: University of New Mexico Press, 1991);

Lynn Kaczmarek, "A Stringer of Beads: An Interview with Tony Hillerman," *Mystery News,* 16 (September/October 1998): 1–3.

Bibliographies:

Louis A. Hieb, *Tony Hillerman: From The Blessing Way to Talking: A Bibliography* (Tucson: Press of the Giant Hound, 1990);

Hieb, *Fifty Foreign Firsts: A Tony Hillerman Checklist,* with Hillerman (Santa Fe: Parker Books of the West, 1991);

Hieb, *Collecting Tony Hillerman: A Checklist of the First Editions of Tony Hillerman with Approximate Values and Commentary,* with Hillerman (Santa Fe: Vinegar Tom Press, 1992);

Hieb, *Tony Hillerman Abroad: An Annotated Checklist of Foreign Language Editions* (Santa Fe: Parker Books of the West, 1993);

Tony Hillerman: A Reader's Checklist and Reference Guide (Middletown, Conn.: Checkerbee Checklist, 1999).

References:

Katrine Ames, "In the Heart of Navajo Country," *Newsweek,* 97 (19 June 1981): 60–61;

Jane S. Bakerman, "Cutting Both Ways: Race, Prejudice, and Motive in Tony Hillerman's Detective Fiction," *Melus,* 11 (Fall 1984): 17–26;

Bakerman, "Hunter and Hunted. Comparison and Contrast in Tony Hillerman's *People of Darkness,*" *Mystery Fancier,* 5 (January/February 1981): 3–10;

Bakerman, "Joe Leaphorn and the Navajo Way: Tony Hillerman's Detective Fiction," *Clues,* 2 (Spring/Summer 1981): 9–16;

Bakerman, "Tony Hillerman's Joe Leaphorn and Jim Chee," in *Cops and Constables: American and British Fictional Policemen,* edited by George N. Dove and Earl F. Bargainniner (Bowling Green, Ohio: Bowling Green University Popular Press, 1986), pp. 98–112;

Ernie Bulow, *Words, Weather and Wolfmen: Conversations with Tony Hillerman* (Gallup, N.Mex.: Southwestern, 1989);

Fred Erisman, *Tony Hillerman,* Western Writers Series, no. 37 (Boise, Idaho: Boise State University Press, 1989);

Judith Tabor Gaugenmaier, "The Mysteries of Tony Hillerman," *American West,* 26 (December 1989): 46–47, 56–58;

Martin Greenberg, ed., *The Tony Hillerman Companion: A Comprehensive Guide to His Life and Work* (New York: HarperCollins, 1994);

Laurence D. Linford, *Tony Hillerman's Navajoland: Hideouts, Haunts and Havens in the Joe Leaphorn and Jim Chee Mysteries* (Salt Lake City: University of Utah Press, 2001);

Michael Parfit, "Weaving Mysteries That Tell of Life among the Navajos," *Smithsonian,* 21 (December 1990): 92–96, 98, 100, 102, 104–105;

Betty and Riley Parker, "Hillerman Country," *Armchair Detective,* 20 (Winter 1987): 4–14;

Tom Quirk, "Justice on the Reservation," *Armchair Detective,* 18 (Fall 1985): 364–370;

Jack Schneider, "Crime and Navajo Punishment: Tony Hillerman's Novels of Detection," *Southwest Review,* 67 (Spring 1982): 151–160;

John Sobol, *Tony Hillerman, A Public Life* (Toronto: ECW Press, 1994);

Ellen Strenski and Robley Evans, "Ritual and Murder in Tony Hillerman's Indian Detective Novels," *Western American Literature,* 16 (November 1981): 205–216;

Alex Ward, "Navajo Cops on the Case," *New York Times Magazine* (14 May 1989): 38–39, 50, 56–58.

Papers:

Tony Hillerman's manuscripts are held by the Zimmerman Library of the University of New Mexico.

Edward D. Hoch

(22 February 1930 –   )

Marvin S. Lachman

BOOKS: *The Shattered Raven* (New York: Lancer, 1969; London: Hale, 1970);

City of Brass (North Hollywood: Leisure, 1971);

The Judges of Hades and Other Simon Ark Stories (North Hollywood: Leisure, 1971);

The Spy and the Thief: 14 Stories about Rand and Nick Velvet (New York: Davis, 1971);

The Transvection Machine (New York: Walker, 1971; London: Hale, 1974);

The Blue Movie Murders, as Ellery Queen (New York: Lancer, 1972; London: Gollancz, 1973);

The Fellowship of the Hand (New York: Walker, 1972 [i.e., 1973]; London: Hale, 1976);

The Frankenstein Factory (New York: Warner Paperback Library, 1975; London: Hale, 1976);

The Monkey's Clue and The Stolen Sapphire (New York: Grosset & Dunlap, 1978);

The Theft of the Persian Slipper (New York: Mysterious Press, 1978);

The Thefts of Nick Velvet (New York: Mysterious Press, 1978);

The Quests of Simon Ark (New York: Mysterious Press, 1984);

Leopold's Way, edited by Francis M. Nevins Jr. and Martin H. Greenberg, introduction by Nevins (Carbondale & Edwardsville: Southern Illinois University Press, 1985);

Tales of Espionage, by Hoch, Brian Garfield, and Robert Edward Eckels (Secaucus, N.J.: Castle Books, 1989);

The People of the Peacock (Eugene, Ore.: Mystery Scene Press, 1991);

The Spy Who Read Latin and Other Stories (Helsinki: Eurographica, 1991);

The Night, My Friend: Stories of Crime and Suspense, edited by Nevins (Athens: Ohio University Press, 1992);

The Theft of the Rusty Bookmark (New York: Mysterious Bookshop, 1995);

Edward D. Hoch (photograph by Michael Culligan; from The Velvet Touch, *2000; Richland County Public Library)*

Diagnosis: Impossible–The Problems of Dr. Sam Hawthorne (Norfolk, Va.: Crippen & Landru, 1996; revised, 2000);

Five Rings in Reno (Norfolk, Va.: Crippen & Landru, 1997);

The Ripper of Storyville and Other Ben Snow Stories (Norfolk, Va.: Crippen & Landru, 1997);

The Adventure of the Cipher in the Sand (New York: Mysterious Bookshop, 1999);

The Gold Buddha Caper (Norfolk, Va.: Crippen & Landru, 2000);

The Velvet Touch (Norfolk, Va.: Crippen & Landru, 2000);

Assignment: Enigma (Norfolk, Va.: Crippen & Landru, 2001);

Bouchercon Bound (Norfolk, Va.: Crippen & Landru, 2001);

The Night People and Other Stories (Waterville, Me.: Five Star, 2001);

The Old Spies Club and Other Intrigues of Rand (Norfolk, Va.: Crippen & Landru, 2001);

The Iron Angel and Other Tales of the Gypsy Sleuth (Norfolk, Va.: Crippen & Landru, 2003).

OTHER: *Dear Dead Days: The 1972 Mystery Writers of America Anthology,* edited by Hoch (New York: Walker, 1972; London: Gollancz, 1974);

Best Detective Stories of the Year 1976, edited by Hoch (New York: Dutton, 1976);

Best Detective Stories of the Year 1977, edited by Hoch (New York: Dutton, 1977);

Best Detective Stories of the Year 1978, edited by Hoch (New York: Dutton, 1978);

Best Detective Stories of the Year 1979, edited by Hoch (New York: Dutton, 1979);

Best Detective Stories of the Year 1980, edited by Hoch (New York: Dutton, 1980);

All But Impossible!: An Anthology of Locked Room and Impossible Crime Stories by Members of the MWA, edited by Hoch (New Haven & New York: Ticknor & Fields, 1981; London: Hale, 1983);

Best Detective Stories of the Year 1981, edited by Hoch (New York: Dutton, 1981);

The Year's Best Mystery & Suspense Stories 1982, edited by Hoch (New York: Walker, 1982);

The Year's Best Mystery & Suspense Stories 1983, edited by Hoch (New York: Walker, 1983; London: Severn House, 1983);

The Year's Best Mystery & Suspense Stories 1984, edited by Hoch (New York: Walker, 1984; London: Severn House, 1984);

The Year's Best Mystery & Suspense Stories 1985, edited by Hoch (New York: Walker, 1985; London: Severn House, 1985);

The Year's Best Mystery & Suspense Stories 1986, edited by Hoch (New York: Walker, 1986; London: Severn House, 1986);

Great British Detectives, edited by Hoch and Greenberg (Chicago: Academy Chicago, 1987);

The Year's Best Mystery & Suspense Stories 1987, edited by Hoch (New York: Walker, 1987);

Women Write Murder, edited by Hoch and Greenberg (Chicago: Academy Chicago, 1987);

The Year's Best Mystery and Suspense Stories 1988, edited by Hoch (New York: Walker, 1988); republished as *Great Mystery and Suspense Stories* (London: Severn House, 1988);

Murder Most Sacred: Great Catholic Tales of Mystery and Suspense, edited by Hoch and Greenberg (New York: Dembner, 1989);

The Year's Best Mystery and Suspense Stories 1989, edited by Hoch (New York: Walker, 1989);

The Year's Best Mystery and Suspense Stories 1990, edited by Hoch (New York: Walker, 1990);

The Year's Best Mystery and Suspense Stories 1991, edited by Hoch (New York: Walker, 1991);

The Year's Best Mystery and Suspense Stories 1992, edited by Hoch (New York: Walker, 1992);

The Year's Best Mystery and Suspense Stories 1993, edited by Hoch (New York: Walker, 1993);

The Year's Best Mystery and Suspense Stories 1994, edited by Hoch (New York: Walker, 1994);

The Year's Best Mystery and Suspense Stories 1995, edited by Hoch (New York: Walker, 1995);

Twelve American Detective Stories, edited by Hoch (Oxford & New York: Oxford University Press, 1997);

C. Daly King, *The Complete Curious Mr. Tarrant,* introduction by Hoch (Norfolk, Va.: Crippen & Landru, 2003);

Joseph Commings, *Banner Deadlines,* memoir of author by Hoch (Norfolk, Va.: Crippen & Landru, 2004).

SELECTED PERIODICAL PUBLICATIONS–
UNCOLLECTED:
FICTION
"Jealous Lover," *Crime and Justice,* no. 4 (March 1957): 29–42;

"Dawn for Dawn Stevens," *Fast Action Detective and Mystery Stories,* 6 (February 1958): 6–28;

"Desert of Sin," *Double-Action Detective and Mystery Stories,* no. 10 (May 1958): 6–43;

"The Spy Who Walked Through Walls," *Ellery Queen's Mystery Magazine,* 48 (November 1966): 37–47;

"The Murder Parade," *Mike Shayne Mystery Magazine,* 25 (November 1969): 74–91;

"The Spy and the Intercepted Letters," *Ellery Queen's Mystery Magazine,* 63 (January 1974): 134–148;

"The Murder of Captain Leopold," *Ellery Queen's Mystery Magazine,* 68 (October 1976): 144–159;

"The Theft of the Child's Drawing," *Ellery Queen's Mystery Magazine,* 70 (October 1977): 143–159;

"The Problem of the General Store," *Ellery Queen's Mystery Magazine,* 74 (November 1979): 143–158;

"Vulcan's Widow," *Mike Shayne Mystery Magazine,* 44 (March 1980): 91–104;

"Deduction, 1996," as R. L. Stevens, *Ellery Queen's Mystery Magazine*, 76 (6 October 1980): 29–40;

"Fiction," *Alfred Hitchcock's Mystery Magazine*, 25 (27 October 1980): 109–122;

"Captain Leopold's Gamble," *Alfred Hitchcock's Mystery Magazine*, 25 (19 November 1980): 42–60;

"The Problem of the Gypsy Camp," *Ellery Queen's Mystery Magazine*, 79 (1 January 1982): 141–157;

"The Flying Fiend," *Ellery Queen's Mystery Magazine*, 80 (Mid-July 1982): 6–19;

"The Doom Balloons," *Mike Shayne Mystery Magazine*, 47 (June 1983): 82–97;

"Captain Leopold Beats the Machine," *Ellery Queen's Mystery Magazine*, 81 (June 1983): 137–152;

"Suddenly in September," *Ellery Queen's Mystery Magazine*, 82 (September 1983): 6–25;

"The Problem of the Graveyard Picnic," *Ellery Queen's Mystery Magazine*, 83 (June 1984): 6–18;

"Captain Leopold and the Mystery Woman," *Ellery Queen's Mystery Magazine*, 84 (September 1984): 137–155;

"The Problem of the Crying Room," *Ellery Queen's Mystery Magazine*, 84 (November 1984): 4–18;

"Sleeper Assignment," *Espionage*, 2 (August 1986): 116–129;

"The S.S.S.," *Mystery Scene* (November 1986): 46–49;

"The Spy and the Short-Order Cipher," *Ellery Queen's Mystery Magazine*, 89 (June 1987): 3–18;

"A Game for Spies," *Ellery Queen's Mystery Magazine*, 91 (June 1988): 74–88;

"Sacajawea's Gold," *Ellery Queen's Mystery Magazine*, 93 (January 1989): 4–18;

"The Theft of the Empty Birdcage," *Ellery Queen's Mystery Magazine*, 94 (July 1989): 43–58;

"The Spy Who Went to Camelot," *Ellery Queen's Mystery Magazine*, 95 (March 1990): 4–21;

"The Gypsy Delegate," *Ellery Queen's Mystery Magazine*, 96 (October 1990): 114–129;

"The Problem of the Haunted Tepee," *Ellery Queen's Mystery Magazine*, 96 (December 1990): 4–18;

"The Problem of the Country Church," *Ellery Queen's Mystery Magazine*, 98 (August 1991): 56–70;

"A Winter's Game," *Armchair Detective*, 24 (Fall 1991): 446–456;

"A Parcel of Deerstalkers," *Ellery Queen's Mystery Magazine*, 105 (January 1995): 4–22;

"The Theft of the Bogus Bandit," *Ellery Queen's Mystery Magazine*, 108 (July 1996): 74–89;

"Dagger Money," *Ellery Queen's Mystery Magazine*, 109 (January 1997): 56–71;

"Duel at Dawn," *Ellery Queen's Mystery Magazine*, 111 (March 1998): 53–65;

"The Phantom Lover," *Ellery Queen's Mystery Magazine*, 113 (April 1999): 37–53;

"Master of Miracles," *Ellery Queen's Mystery Magazine*, 113 (May 1999): 64–81;

"The Problem of the Potting Shed," *Ellery Queen's Mystery Magazine*, 116 (July 2000): 67–82;

"The San Agustin Miracle," *Ellery Queen's Mystery Magazine*, 117 (January 2001): 23–35;

"A Visit to Saint Nicholas," *Strand Magazine*, no. 7 (2001): 27–29;

"The Problem of the Traveler's Tale," *Ellery Queen's Mystery Magazine*, 119 (June 2002): 72–85;

"Pandora's Socks," *Ellery Queen's Mystery Magazine*, 122 (November 2003): 52–67.

NONFICTION

"A Simon Ark Bibliography," *Armchair Detective*, 3 (July 1970): 248–249;

"Writing the Mystery Short Story," *Writer* (April 1974);

"Hans Stefan Santesson and the Unicorn Mystery Book Club," *Armchair Detective*, 8 (May 1975): 185–192;

"Growing Up with Ellery Queen," *Armchair Detective*, 12 (Summer 1979): 200;

"A Mirror to Our Crimes," *Armchair Detective*, 12 (Summer 1979): 280–285;

"Stockholm in June: Crime Writers 3rd International Congress," *Armchair Detective*, 14 (1981): 323–326;

"Second City Skulduggery: Chicago's Bouchercon XV," *Armchair Detective*, 18 (Spring 1985): 160–163;

"The Mystery Short Story," *Mystery Writers' Annual* (1986): 10;

"Open and Shut Cases: Writing Beginnings and Endings in Fiction," *Writer's Digest* (September 1986): 39–40;

"Bouchercon XVII: Mysterious Goings-On in Baltimore," *Armchair Detective*, 20 (Spring 1987): 190–191;

"Short Stories Around the World," *Mystery Writers' Annual* (1988): 54–55;

"From Bath to Bouchercon," *Armchair Detective*, 21 (Spring 1988): 194–196;

"The Short Story, Then and Now," *Mystery Writers' Annual* (1995): 30;

"Writing and Editing Short Stories," *Mystery Readers Journal*, 15 (Fall 1999): 22–23.

Not only is Edward D. Hoch the most prolific of modern writers of mystery short stories, with more than nine hundred stories published by 2004, but he virtually singlehandedly maintains the "fair play" tradition of the Golden Age of the mystery between World Wars I and II, by writing whodunits in which the clues that his detectives use to solve crimes are presented to readers in such a way that they, too, can work the case. He specializes in having his sleuths solve such seemingly impossible crimes as disappearances under unusual circumstances and murders in locked rooms. He has published a story in every issue of what is generally considered the leading mystery short-story magazine, *Ellery Queen's Mystery Magazine (EQMM),* since May 1973. Of the many books he has published, only five are novels; the rest are individual short stories or short-story collections. He has published no novels since 1975.

Edward Dentinger Hoch was born in Rochester, New York, on 22 February 1930, the son of Earl G. and Alice Dentinger Hoch. His father was vice president of a bank; his mother was a homemaker. After attending Sacred Heart School and Aquinas Institute High School, he went to the University of Rochester, leaving after two years in 1949. While attending high school and college, he wrote and submitted short stories, though none were accepted for publication. He became interested in detective fiction when he first listened to *The Adventures of Ellery Queen* on radio in 1939. He also credits reading Queen's *The Chinese Orange Mystery,* which was reprinted in paperback that year, as exerting a major influence on his life. In 1949 Hoch joined Mystery Writers of America (MWA) as an unpublished, affiliate member. He attended MWA meetings in New York, especially during the years 1950 to 1952 when he was in the army, serving in the military police at Fort Jay, on Governor's Island. After being discharged, he worked for the publisher Pocket Books in a noneditorial capacity, handling adjustments to dealers. In late 1953, he returned to Rochester, where in January 1954 he took a job writing for an advertising agency. On 5 June 1957, he married Patricia McMahon, with whom he has lived in the Charlotte neighborhood of Rochester ever since.

Hoch continued to write stories in his spare time while working in advertising. "Village of the Dead" was the first of his stories to be accepted for publication, and it appeared in the December 1955 issue of *Famous Detective Stories,* one of the last of the pulp magazines. In it Hoch introduced Simon Ark, an eccentric detective who travels the world seeking to eradicate the devil and other manifestations of evil. In "Sword for a Sinner," which appeared in *The Saint Mystery Magazine* (October 1959), Ark implies that he may have been a Coptic priest two thousand years ago: "In Egypt, long ago, I practiced in the Coptic rite." Ark speaks of himself as having lived in the first century after Christ and having been "doomed to walk the earth forever." In Ark's first adventure, "Village of the Dead," he appears in the western United States town of "Gidaz" after hearing that the entire population (seventy-three people) leaped to their deaths from a cliff. A religious leader who had mesmerized the population may be responsible, though

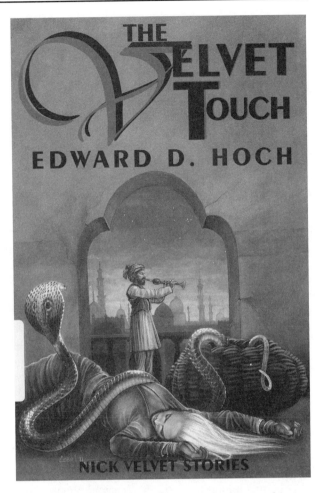

Cover for 2000 paperback original edition of stories, one of three Hoch collections that feature the thief and sometime detective Nick Velvet (Richland County Public Library)

he denies it. Although the plot of "Village of the Dead" and future plots include the possibility of supernatural influence, Hoch's detective solves his mysteries by strictly rational means. "Village of the Dead" was reprinted in two Simon Ark collections, *The Judges of Hades and Other Simon Ark Stories* (1971) and *The Quests of Simon Ark* (1984). A third Ark collection is *City of Brass* (1971).

Hoch's stories soon were published widely in the "pulps" and then the digest-sized magazines that replaced them. Among the long-since defunct magazines in which his works appeared in the 1950s were *Manhunt, Crack Detective and Mystery Stories, Fast Action Detective and Mystery Stories, Keyhole Detective Stories, Off Beat Detective Stories, Tightrope Detective Magazine,* and *Two-Fisted Detective Stories.*

Beginning early in his career, Hoch employed pseudonyms because he found that editors were reluctant to have more than one story by an author in a single issue of a magazine. In March 1956, using his middle name, he published the first of twenty-three stories over the next twenty years as "Stephen Dentinger." He published three stories, in 1956–1957, as "Irwin Booth." Later, as "Pat McMahon" (his wife's maiden name), he wrote four stories, published 1962–1966. Only sixty of his stories have been pseudonymous—and only one since 1989.

From the beginning of his career, Hoch wrote science fiction and Westerns, as well as mysteries. "Zoo," in the June 1958 issue of *Fantastic Universe,* about the annual visit to Earth of Professor Hugo's Interplanetary Zoo, is perhaps Hoch's most popular story. It has been reprinted, according to Hoch's estimate, at least ninety times through 2002, often in literature textbooks for schools.

Though many of Hoch's early stories feature Ark, others are nonseries stories and more hard-boiled than his later work. Ark becomes a private detective in 1959 and 1960 stories for the more hard-boiled *Double-Action Detective and Mystery Stories,* and the titles of his stories there, such as "The Case of the Naked Niece" in the September 1959 issue, reflect the titillation evident in the marketing of the magazine. Hoch's second major series character was a New York City private detective, Al Darlan, who first appeared as Al Diamond in "Jealous Lover" (*Crime and Justice,* March 1957), an uncollected story, but after two stories was renamed in 1958 in order to avoid confusion with radio-television detective Richard Diamond.

Captain Jules Leopold, the detective about whom Hoch has written most often—more than one hundred stories, nineteen of which were collected in *Leopold's Way* (1985), the only Leopold collection—appeared in a minor role in "Jealous Lover." Leopold was not featured until "Circus," published under Hoch's earliest pseudonym, Stephen Dentinger, in the British edition of *The Saint Mystery Magazine* in November 1961. In this story, set, as is most of the Leopold canon, in a medium-sized fictional Connecticut city, Leopold demonstrates (as he investigates the murder of a small boy) two of his most characteristic traits—humanity and patience. He is deeply affected by the child's death but unwilling to blame the crime on an obvious suspect he feels is innocent. Though a captain, he rings doorbells and talks to neighbors to obtain evidence.

"The Oblong Room," a Leopold story first published in *The Saint Magazine* (July 1967), won the coveted MWA Edgar Award as the best short story of the year. It was collected in *Leopold's Way.* A university student, the only suspect, is found standing over the body of a murder victim, and he has been there for twenty-two hours. Though Leopold appears, this story is more a mystery of abnormal psychology than of physical clues, with the key question being why the killer did not attempt to escape. In selecting it for his anthology of the best stories of 1967, Anthony Boucher praised its "deceptively simple plot . . . patient detection, strong creation of mood . . . and a final breath-taking shock of illumination." One of Hoch's most popular stories, it has been reprinted at least thirteen times.

Leopold gradually ages, and by "Finding Joe Finch" (*EQMM,* February 1984), more than twenty years after his divorce, he marries young attorney Molly Calendar, who is twenty-seven years younger than he. After his retirement, he remains available to help Lieutenant Fletcher and Connie Trent, the police detectives with whom he worked for two decades. Leopold's earlier cases include police procedural elements, but later he was just as likely to solve impossible crimes, as in "Leopold and the Broken Bride" (*EQMM,* July 1987), in which a bride disappears before walking down the aisle at her wedding.

In the September 1961 issue of *The Saint Mystery Magazine,* Hoch introduced one of his most popular characters, Ben Snow, in "The Valley of Arrows." Most of Snow's adventures take place during the last two decades of the nineteenth century or the first decade of the twentieth. He is a reluctant gunfighter because there are persistent rumors that he is really the outlaw Billy the Kid, and he is often forced to solve the murders of which he, as a supposed criminal, is suspected. "The Valley of Arrows" is more Western thriller than detective story, with Snow at a fort that is besieged by Navajo Indians near the Arizona–New Mexico border. Snow's adventures take him to most of the western states and Canada, but he also pursues killers in the red-light district of New Orleans in "The Ripper of Storyville" (*The Saint Mystery Magazine,* December 1963), at the Buffalo Pan-American Exposition when President McKinley is assassinated in "The Man in the Alley" (*The Saint [UK],* April 1962; *The Saint,* June 1963), and in North Carolina during the Wright Brothers' first flight in "Brothers on the Beach" (*EQMM,* August 1984). Snow evolves into a detective who can solve impossible crimes, as in "The San Agustin Miracle" (*EQMM,* January 2001), in which he solves the murder of someone who vanishes from a hot-air balloon that is aloft and being watched by a crowd.

By 1962, *EQMM* and *Alfred Hitchcock's Mystery Magazine (AHMM)* were the leading mystery short-story magazines, most of the other "digests" having ceased publication because of competition with increasingly popular paperback original books. In this year, Hoch published his first stories in these magazines. "Twilight Thunder" (January 1962) was the first of more than a hundred stories—mostly nonseries—in *AHMM* through 2004. "Death in the Harbor," a Leopold story published in December 1962, was his first story in *EQMM.*

The height of popularity of spy fiction occurred during the mid 1960s, largely because of successful movies based on Ian Fleming's James Bond and a best-selling novel, *The Spy Who Came in from the Cold* (1965), by John Le Carré. A new series character created by Hoch, appearing first in "The Spy Who Did Nothing" (*EQMM,* May 1965), combines some elements of both, having a four-letter name similar to Bond, Jeffrey Rand, and titles beginning "The Spy Who . . . ." However, the series focuses less on sensational aspects of espionage—Rand is a cryptologist for Britain's Department of Concealed Communications—and little of the cynicism and angst of Le Carré are present. By the time of "The Spy Who Died Twice" (*EQMM,* July 1977), Rand has retired and married Leila Gaad, an Egyptian professor of archaeology, with whom he worked on three Cold War cases. However, he remains busy, often being asked by his former superiors to solve "one more case" or becoming involved with murder investigations when he travels with his wife. Rand appears in eighty-two stories, twenty-six of which appear in the following collections: *The Spy and the Thief: 14 Stories about Rand and Nick Velvet* (1971), *Tales of Espionage* (1989), *The Spy Who Read Latin and Other Stories* (1991), and *The Old Spies Club and Other Intrigues of Rand* (2001). Fifteen other Rand stories have been reprinted in anthologies.

Religion is an important part of Hoch's early work, especially the Simon Ark series. In 1964, Hoch introduced amateur sleuth Father David Noone, a Roman Catholic parish priest at Holy Trinity Church, who shares Hoch's religious affiliation. He has appeared in seven stories, but no collection of Noone stories has been published.

In May 1965 the first of Hoch's stories to be adapted for television, "Winter Run" (*AHMM,* January 1965), retitled *Off Season,* appeared on the last broadcast of *The Alfred Hitchcock Hour.* Three of Hoch's stories were televised on *McMillan and Wife,* a series with Rock Hudson as Police Commissioner McMillan and Susan Saint James as his wife, Sally. Hoch's work has also appeared on *Night Gallery* and *Tales of the Unexpected.* He did not work on any of the scripts.

Nick Velvet is arguably Hoch's most unusual detective, certainly the most unusual thief in crime fiction, since he only steals objects that are on the surface valueless. They include a toy mouse, a used tea bag, and a bag of garbage. Of course, the item has sufficient value to Velvet's client, who is willing to pay $20,000 for the theft. That is Velvet's fee when the series begins with "The Theft of the Clouded Tiger" (*EQMM,* September 1966), in which he is paid to steal, as a diversion, a tiger from a zoo. Velvet raises his rate to $25,000 in a 1983 case and to $30,000 in 1999, and he charges more for unusual risk or expenses. Because

Cover for a 2001 paperback original collection of Hoch's nonseries stories, originally published between 1957 and 1979 (Richland County Public Library)

during the course of his thefts Velvet often happens upon murders, he frequently is forced to become a detective, if only to keep himself from being arrested. Eighty-two Velvet stories were published, thirty-two of which appear in three collections—*The Spy and the Thief* (1971), *The Thefts of Nick Velvet* (1978), and *The Velvet Touch* (2000).

Hoch turned to writing novels and, after signing a contract for his first book, left his job in advertising to become a full-time writer. That book, a paperback original, *The Shattered Raven* (1969), allowed him to use his knowledge of MWA as background. A murder occurs at MWA's annual banquet when a secret device in the microphone explodes as the recipient of the Raven Award is making his acceptance speech. The case is solved by a new Hoch sleuth, mystery writer Barney Hamet, who later appears in two short stories, "Murder at the Bouchercon" (1983) and "The Unpleasantness at the Arts and Letters Club" (1992), solving murders committed at other gatherings of mystery writers.

In 1969, for a science-fiction anthology, Hoch created Carl Crader and Earl Jazine, agents for the fictional federal Computer Investigation Bureau. They later appear in three science-fiction novels, set in the twenty-first century: *The Transvection Machine* (1971), *The Fellowship of the Hand* (1972), and *The Frankenstein Factory* (1975). Reviews of these novels were few and unenthusiastic, confirming Hoch in his natural bent as a short-story writer. In an interview in *Armchair Detective* (Spring 1990), he commented, "It's difficult for me to write novels. There are writers who can turn out a novel in a week, but I'm not one of them. I think the fastest I've ever written a novel has been about two months. I just find that, toward the end of that time, I'm really sort of losing interest in it and I want to get on to the next project. This never happens with short stories. They're just the right length for me–something to work on for two or three weeks."

Writing as "Mr. X," Hoch published "The Will-o'-the-Wisp Mystery," a six-installment serial in *EQMM,* from April through September 1971, featuring David Piper, also known as "The Manhunter," director of a fictional state agency, the Department of Apprehension. The story was later reprinted under Hoch's own name in *Ellery Queen's Anthology* (1982) and *Maze of Mysteries* (1982). In July 1971 Hoch published, in *EQMM,* the first of twenty-five stories written as "R. L. Stevens," the pseudonym he used most often. The last Stevens story was published in 1989. Hoch has not used a pseudonym since then.

In 1972 Hoch had the opportunity to use the name of the writer who so influenced him more than thirty years before when Frederic Dannay and Manfred B. Lee, who wrote as Ellery Queen, allowed Hoch to publish a paperback original novel, *The Blue Movie Murders,* under their pseudonym. Ellery Queen was not the detective in this book, though he was in a short story, "The Reindeer Clue," which Hoch published as Queen in 1975.

Because of his vast mystery reading since childhood, Hoch is acknowledged as one of the leading experts in the field, especially regarding the mystery short story. He was selected to edit the 1972 annual MWA anthology, *Dear Dead Days.* From 1976 through 1995, Hoch edited the annual volume of the best mystery stories of the year. He has also edited five other anthologies, including *All But Impossible!: An Anthology of Locked Room and Impossible Crime Stories by Members of the MWA* (1981), reflecting his interest in impossible crime stories, and *Murder Most Sacred: Great Catholic Tales of Mystery and Suspense* (1989), reflecting his interest in religion.

During the 1970s, Hoch created many new series characters, though, with the exception of Dr. Sam Hawthorne, they were dropped by the 1980s. In addition to Piper, they include con man Ulysses S. Bird in four stories; the Interpol team of Sebastian Blue and Laura Charme in fourteen tales; Paul Tower, known as "The Lollipop Cop" because he does public-relations work for the police department in schools in three stories; Barnabus Rex, a sleuth in two science-fiction stories; Tommy Preston, a zookeeper's son, who appears in two juvenile mysteries collected in *The Monkey's Clue and The Stolen Sapphire* (1978); and Nancy Trentino, a police detective in four stories. The stories of these characters were not collected, though seven of the Interpol stories are included, along with other detectives created by Hoch, Brian Garfield, and Robert Edward Eckels, in *Tales of Espionage.*

Dr. Sam Hawthorne, who first appeared in "The Problem of the Covered Bridge" in *EQMM* (December 1974), has proven to be one of Hoch's most popular and enduring detectives. As this historical series starts, Hawthorne looks back from 1974 to March 1922 when, as a recent medical school graduate, he is getting started as a general practitioner in the fictional small New England town of Northmont. Hawthorne grows older as the series progresses, so that by the sixty-fifth Hawthorne case, "The Problem of the Candidate's Cabin," published in *EQMM* for July 2004, it is October 1942, and the United States is in World War II. The "problems" the doctor solves are impossible crimes–for example, the disappearance of a horse and buggy that was seen to enter a covered bridge but not to emerge from it and the stabbing of a person alone in a voting booth. The only Hawthorne collection is *Diagnosis: Impossible–The Problems of Dr. Sam Hawthorne* (1996), which includes the first twelve stories.

Hoch is a prolific writer of nonfiction, his work appearing in such varied publications as *Exploring the Unknown, Publishers' Weekly, Sybil Leek's Astrology Journal,* and *Writer's Digest.* Using the pseudonym "R. E. Porter," he wrote sixty columns of mystery news under the title "Crime Beat" for *Ellery Queen's Mystery Magazine,* from 18 August 1980 through March 1985. As much a fan as a professional mystery writer, Hoch often attends the World Mystery Convention (Bouchercon) and has written about four of these conventions, as well as about the Crime Writers International Congress, for *The Armchair Detective.* For that journal, he also wrote a column of news and reviews of short stories, "Minor Offenses," from 1982 through 1989.

Hoch often contributes to *The Mystery Writers' Annual,* published by MWA each year for the Edgar awards banquet. He is active in MWA affairs, traveling from Rochester to New York City for its meetings.

From 1982 through 1983 he served as president of MWA, the organization he first joined as a teenager.

More Hoch series characters were introduced in the 1980s, and, again, only one continues to appear. Among those characters who were short-lived are Charles Spacer, who first appeared in "Assignment: Enigma," which Hoch published in the 10 September 1980 *EQMM,* under the pseudonym "Anthony Circus." Four further cases regarding Spacer, an executive for an electronics firm, who is also a United States undercover agent, were published under Hoch's own name. Another 1980s series character is Sir Gideon Parrot, who was featured in five parody-pastiches of "Golden Age" mysteries. Parrot was based on Agatha Christie's Hercule Poirot (he says he pronounces his name the French way), and the impossible crimes he solved were based on Christie's cases, taking place at dinner parties or among people stranded on remote islands. In the best case, "The Flying Fiend" (*EQMM,* Mid-July 1982), several people are found with their throats cut on the beach, but the sand leading up to the bodies is unmarked. Yet another short-lived 1980s detective was Libby Knowles, a private detective who works as a bodyguard. From 1984 through 1985, Hoch outlined the plots for three paperback original mysteries about criminology professor Matthew Prize. They were written by other authors in conjunction with Otto Penzler.

The only detective Hoch created in the 1980s that he continues to write about is Michael Vlado. When the first Vlado story, "The Luck of a Gypsy," appeared in an anthology, *The Ethnic Detectives,* in 1985, the hero, a Romanian Gypsy king, was living under a repressive communist government. Since the fall of the "Iron Curtain" in 1989, Hoch has included evolving Romanian politics in his Vlado stories, along with information regarding Gypsy customs. He has written twenty-eight Vlado stories, with fifteen collected in *The Iron Angel and Other Tales of the Gypsy Sleuth* (2003), the only collection about him.

Remaining as prolific as ever, Hoch introduced two new series characters in the 1990s—Susan Holt, who buys for department stores and encounters crime during her frequent travels, and Alexander Swift, another historical detective, who solves mysteries that crop up as a result of his role as troubleshooter for George Washington during and after the Revolutionary War. In 2002 Hoch created Walt Stanton and Juliet Ives, graduate students. Stanton accepts work, helped by Ives, as a courier, allowing Hoch to give their first adventure the "punny" title "Courier and Ives."

Though much of Hoch's fame is the result of the twenty-seven series detectives he has created, at least a third of his output has consisted of nonseries stories, and in them he has been more likely to deal with impor-

Cover for the 2003 paperback original edition of Mike Vlado stories, set in Romania (Richland County Public Library)

tant ideas and issues in American society than in the series stories. A notable example is "The Detective's Wife," which first was published in the October 1990 issue of the literary journal *Crosscurrents.* In it, Hoch uses the pursuit of a serial killer to explore the effects of crime on a marriage. The frustrations of Roger, a police detective who is unable to catch the killer, threatens his marriage to Jenny.

In addition to fourteen collections of stories about Hoch's series detectives, two collections are of nonseries stories. *The Night, My Friend: Stories of Crime and Suspense* (1992) is a collection of twenty-two stories published in the 1960s, and the variety of these tales is impressive. They include one of Hoch's best impossible-crime stories, "The Long Way Down," originally published in *AHMM* (February 1965), in which a man jumps out of a twenty-first-floor window in Manhattan and does not land until almost four hours later. "To Slay an Eagle" concerns the nature of war and the guilt of an American World War II veteran who returns to the city he bombed while in the Air Force. "A

Girl like Cathy" is a "big caper" yarn with a subtle touch of humor, as the narrator remarks about the coverage of robbery in *The New York Times,* "They always liked museum robberies; there was something cultural about them."

The Night People and Other Stories (2001) is composed of twenty nonseries stories published between 1957 and 1979. Again, variety is the keynote. "The Impossible 'Impossible Crime'" is a story about the seemingly impossible murder of one of two geologists spending the winter in a cabin in northern Canada to study the permafrost. "Ring the Bell Softly" shows Hoch's interest in religion and evil, already evident in his Simon Ark stories and the anthology of Catholic stories he edited. A mysterious stranger named Chance visits a priest in a valley from which almost everyone else has moved. Three stories in this collection explore the reasons behind war. "I'd Know You Anywhere" is about a soldier whose love of killing is born during World War II and follows him through Korea, Vietnam, and beyond. "Another War" tells of the dangerous, gun-oriented recreational activities of a group of veterans who miss their wartime experiences. "Festival in Black," a Cold War spy story set against the background of a movie festival, deals with the nature of patriotism.

Although in general, recognition is less likely to be accorded to short-story writers than to novelists, Hoch is proving to be the exception to this rule. Since 1985, *EQMM* has polled its readers annually regarding their favorite author and story. Hoch has proved to be their favorite writer, though he has never won their Readers Award for any individual story in a given year, since the votes are divided among his tales, which appear in every issue of the magazine. He received an Edgar nomination for "The Most Dangerous Man Alive" (*EQMM,* 5 May 1980). More recently, he won Bouchercon Anthony Awards (named after Anthony Boucher) for "One Bag of Coconuts" (*EQMM,* November 1997) and "The Problem of the Potting Shed" (*EQMM,* July 2000). In 1991 Hoch was guest of honor at the twenty-second annual Bouchercon, held in Pasadena, California. Private Eye Writers of America selected him for its lifetime achievement award in 2000, as did Bouchercon in 2001. Also in 2001, MWA pre-

sented him with its most coveted award, that of Grand Master.

Edward D. Hoch is one of the most recognized and honored of mystery short-story writers partly because of his prolificacy and longevity. In writing of Hoch's receiving MWA's Grand Master Award, moreover, Janet Hutchings, editor of *EQMM,* pointed out, " . . . Ed Hoch could not have maintained his unbroken streak of publication in *EQMM,* or held his place of esteem with readers and other writers had he failed to provide, with each tale, the brilliant plotting, the sleight of hand, and the full cast of characters that are his trademarks. The almost legendary nature of his achievement derives from the merging of quantity with quality."

Interviews:

John Kovaleski, "Shortcut to Murder," *Armchair Detective,* 23 (Spring 1990): 152–169;

Brad Skillman, "Edward Hoch: Master in His Own Write," *Drood Review,* 11 (October 1991): 4–5;

J. Alec West, "An Interview with Ed Hoch," *Murderous Intent Mystery Magazine,* 3 (Spring 1997): 14–16;

Steve Lewis, "An Interview with Edward Hoch," *Mystery,* 45 (August 2004): 37–40.

Bibliography:

June M. Moffatt and Francis M. Nevins Jr., *Edward D. Hoch Bibliography (1955–2004),* thirteenth edition (Downey, Cal.: Moffatt House, 2004), pp. 1–2.

References:

Mark Hare, "Hoch Writes a Life of Mystery," *Rochester Democrat and Chronicle,* 4 March 2001, pp. 1, 8–9;

Janet Hutchings, "Edward D. Hoch: Grand Master," *Edgar Allan Poe Awards: Millennium Edition* (New York: MWA, 2001), p. 14;

Marvin S. Lachman, "Edward D. Hoch: A Brief Biography," *Bouchercon .22 Souvenir Program Book* (Pasadena, Cal.: Bouchercon .22, n.d.), pp. 6–7;

Lachman, "Edward D. Hoch: An Appreciation," *Bouchercon 2001: A Capital Mystery* (Washington, D.C.: Bouchercon, 2001), pp. 9–10;

Lachman, "Introduction," in *Edward D. Hoch Bibliography,* eleventh edition (Downey, Cal.: Moffatt House, 2001), pp. 1–2.

Evan Hunter
(Ed McBain)
(15 October 1926 –   )

Martin Kich
Wright State University–Lake Campus

See also the Hunter entry in *DLB Yearbook: 1982*.

BOOKS: *The Big Fix* (New York: Falcon, 1952); republished as *So Nude, So Dead,* as Richard Marsten (New York: Fawcett, 1956);

The Evil Sleep (New York: Falcon, 1952);

Find the Feathered Serpent (Philadelphia: Winston, 1952);

Danger: Dinosaurs, as Marsten (Philadelphia: Winston, 1953);

Don't Crowd Me (New York: Popular Library, 1953; London: Consul, 1960); republished as *The Paradise Party* (London: New English Library, 1968);

Rocket to Luna, as Marsten (Philadelphia: Winston, 1953; London: Hutchinson, 1954);

The Blackboard Jungle (New York: Simon & Schuster, 1954; London: Constable, 1955);

Cut Me In, as Hunt Collins (New York: Abelard-Schuman, 1954; London: Boardman, 1960); republished as *The Proposition* (New York: Pyramid, 1955);

Runaway Black, as Marsten (New York: Fawcett, 1954; London: Red Seal, 1957);

Murder in the Navy, as Marsten (New York: Fawcett, 1955; London: Muller, 1956); republished as *Death of a Nurse,* as McBain (New York: Pocket Books, 1968; London: Hodder & Stoughton, 1972);

Cop Hater, as Ed McBain (New York: Permabooks, 1956; London: Boardman, 1958);

The Jungle Kids (New York: Pocket Books, 1956);

Second Ending (New York: Simon & Schuster, 1956; London: Constable, 1956); republished as *Quartet in "H"* (New York: Pocket Books, 1957);

The Mugger, as McBain (New York: Permabooks, 1956; London: Boardman, 1959);

The Pusher, as McBain (New York: Permabooks, 1956; London: Boardman, 1959);

The Spiked Heel, as Marsten (New York: Holt, 1956; London: Constable, 1957);

Evan Hunter (photograph by Drasica Dimitrijevic-Hunter; from The Last Dance, *2000; Richland County Public Library)*

Tomorrow's World, as Collins (New York: Avalon, 1956); republished as *Tomorrow and Tomorrow* (New York: Pyramid, 1956); republished as *Tomorrow and Tomorrow,* as McBain (London: Sphere, 1979);

The Con Man, as McBain (New York: Permabooks, 1957; London: Boardman, 1960);

Killer's Choice, as McBain (New York: Permabooks, 1957; London: Boardman, 1960);

Vanishing Ladies, as Marsten (New York: Permabooks, 1957; London: Boardman, 1961);

The April Robin Murders, by Hunter (as McBain) and Craig Rice (New York: Random House, 1958; London: Hammond, 1959);

Even the Wicked, as Marsten (New York: Permabooks, 1958); republished as by McBain (London: Severn House, 1979);

I Like 'Em Tough, as Curt Cannon (Greenwich, Conn.: Fawcett, 1958);

I'm Cannon—For Hire, as Cannon (Greenwich, Conn.: Fawcett, 1958; London: Fawcett, 1959);

Killer's Payoff, as McBain (New York: Permabooks, 1958; London: Boardman, 1960);

Lady Killer, as McBain (New York: Permabooks, 1958; London: Boardman, 1961);

Strangers When We Meet (New York: Simon & Schuster, 1958; London: Constable, 1958);

Big Man, as Marsten (New York: Pocket Books, 1959); republished, as by McBain (Harmondsworth, U.K.: Penguin, 1978);

Killer's Wedge, as McBain (New York: Simon & Schuster, 1959; London: Boardman, 1961);

King's Ransom, as McBain (New York: Simon & Schuster, 1959; London: Boardman, 1961);

A Matter of Conviction (New York: Simon & Schuster, 1959; London: Constable, 1959); republished as *The Young Savages* (New York: Pocket Books, 1966);

'Til Death, as McBain (New York: Simon & Schuster, 1959; London: Boardman, 1961);

Give the Boys a Great Big Hand, as McBain (New York: Simon & Schuster, 1960; London: Boardman, 1962);

The Heckler, as McBain (New York: Simon & Schuster, 1960; London: Boardman, 1962);

The Last Spin and Other Stories, as McBain (London: Constable, 1960);

See Them Die, as McBain (New York: Simon & Schuster, 1960; London: Hodder & Stoughton, 1960);

Lady, Lady, I Did It! as McBain (New York: Simon & Schuster, 1961; London: Boardman, 1963);

Mothers and Daughters (New York: Simon & Schuster, 1961; London: Constable, 1961);

The Remarkable Harry (London & New York: Abelard-Schuman, 1961);

The Wonderful Button (London & New York: Abelard-Schuman, 1961);

Like Love, as McBain (New York: Simon & Schuster, 1962; London: Boardman, 1964);

The Birds (London: Hollywood Scripts, 1962);

The Empty Hours, as McBain (New York: Simon & Schuster, 1962; London: Boardman, 1963);

Happy New Year, Herbie, and Other Stories (New York: Simon & Schuster, 1963; London: Constable, 1965);

Ten Plus One, as McBain (New York: Simon & Schuster, 1963; London: Hamilton, 1964);

Ax, as McBain (New York: Simon & Schuster, 1964); republished as *Axe* (London: Hamilton, 1964);

Buddwing (New York: Simon & Schuster, 1964; London: Constable, 1964);

Doll, as McBain (New York: Delacorte, 1965; London: Hamilton, 1966);

He Who Hesitates, as McBain (New York: Delacorte, 1965; London: Hamilton, 1965);

The Sentries, as McBain (New York: Simon & Schuster, 1965; London: Hamilton, 1965);

Eighty Million Eyes, as McBain (New York: Delacorte, 1966; London: Hamilton, 1966);

The Paper Dragon (New York: Delacorte, 1966; London: Constable, 1967);

A Horse's Head (New York: Delacorte, 1967; London: Constable, 1968);

Fuzz, as McBain (Garden City, N.Y.: Doubleday, 1968; London: Hamilton, 1968);

Last Summer (Garden City, N.Y.: Doubleday, 1968; London: Constable, 1969);

Shotgun, as McBain (Garden City, N.Y.: Doubleday, 1969; London: Hamilton, 1969);

Sons (Garden City, N.Y.: Doubleday, 1969; London: Constable, 1970);

Jigsaw, as McBain (Garden City, N.Y.: Doubleday, 1970; London: Hamilton, 1970);

The Beheading and Other Stories (London: Constable, 1971);

Hail, Hail, the Gang's All Here, as McBain (Garden City, N.Y.: Doubleday, 1971; London: Hamilton, 1971);

Nobody Knew They Were There (Garden City, N.Y.: Doubleday, 1971; London: Constable, 1971);

The Easter Man: A Play and Six Stories (Garden City, N.Y.: Doubleday, 1972);

Every Little Crook and Nanny (Garden City, N.Y.: Doubleday, 1972; London: Constable, 1972);

Sadie When She Died, as McBain (Garden City, N.Y.: Doubleday, 1972; London: Hamilton, 1972);

Seven (Garden City, N.Y.: Doubleday, 1972; London: Constable, 1972);

Come Winter (Garden City, N.Y.: Doubleday, 1973; London: Constable, 1973);

Hail to the Chief, as McBain (New York: Random House, 1973; London: Hamilton, 1973);

Let's Hear It for the Deaf Man, as McBain (New York: Doubleday, 1973; London: Hamilton, 1973);

Bread, as McBain (New York: Random House, 1974; London: Hamilton, 1974);

Streets of Gold (New York: Harper & Row, 1974; London: Macmillan, 1975);

Blood Relatives, as McBain (New York: Random House, 1975; London: Hamilton, 1976);

Doors, as Ezra Hannon (New York: Stein & Day, 1975; London: Macmillan, 1976);

Where There's Smoke, as McBain (New York: Random House, 1975; London: Hamilton, 1975);

The Chisholms: A Novel of the Journey West (New York: Harper & Row, 1976; London: Hamilton, 1976);

Guns, as McBain (New York: Random House, 1976; London: Hamilton, 1976);

Me and Mr. Stenner (New York: Lippincott, 1976; London: Hamilton, 1977);

So Long as You Both Shall Live, as McBain (New York: Random House, 1976; London: Hamilton, 1976);

Goldilocks, as McBain, Matthew Hope series (New York: Arbor House, 1977; London: Hamilton, 1978);

Long Time No See, as McBain, 87th Precinct series (New York: Random House, 1977; London: Hamilton, 1977);

Calypso, as McBain (New York: Viking, 1979; London: Hamilton, 1979);

Walk Proud (New York: Bantam, 1979);

Ghosts, as McBain (New York: Viking, 1980; London: Hamilton, 1980);

Heat, as McBain (New York: Viking, 1981; London: Hamilton, 1981);

Love, Dad (New York: Crown, 1981; London: Joseph, 1981);

Rumpelstiltskin, as McBain (New York: Viking, 1981; London: Hamilton, 1981);

Beauty and the Beast, as McBain (London: Hamilton, 1982; New York: Holt, Rinehart & Winston, 1983);

The McBain Brief, as McBain (London: Hamilton, 1982; New York: Arbor House, 1983);

Far from the Sea (New York: Atheneum, 1983; London: Hamilton, 1983);

Ice, as McBain (New York: Arbor House, 1983; London: Hamilton, 1983);

And All Through the House, as McBain (Garden City, N.Y.: Doubleday, 1984);

Jack and the Beanstalk, as McBain (New York: Holt, Rinehart & Winston, 1984; London: Hamilton, 1984);

Lightning, as McBain (New York: Arbor House, 1984; London: Hamilton, 1984);

Lizzie (New York: Arbor House, 1984; London: Hamilton, 1984);

Eight Black Horses, as McBain (New York: Mysterious Press, 1985; London: Hamilton, 1985);

Snow White and Rose Red, as McBain (New York: Holt, Rinehart & Winston, 1985; London: Hamilton, 1985);

Another Part of the City, as McBain (New York: Mysterious Press, 1986; London: Hamilton, 1986);

Cinderella, as McBain (New York: Holt, 1986; London: Hamilton, 1986);

Poison, as McBain (New York: Arbor House, 1987; London: Hamilton, 1987);

Puss in Boots, as McBain (New York: Holt, 1987; London: Hamilton, 1987);

Tricks, as McBain (New York: Arbor House, 1987; London: Hamilton, 1987);

The House That Jack Built, as McBain (New York: Holt, 1988; London: Hamilton, 1988);

McBain's Ladies: The Women of the 87th Precinct, as McBain (New York: Mysterious Press, 1988; London: Hamilton, 1988);

Downtown, as McBain (New York: Morrow, 1989; London: Heinemann, 1989);

Gangs, as McBain (New York: Avon, 1989);

Lullaby, as McBain (New York: Morrow, 1989; London: Hamilton, 1989);

McBain's Ladies, Too: More Women of the 87th Precinct, as McBain (New York: Mysterious Press, 1989; London: Hamilton, 1990);

Three Blind Mice, as McBain (New York: Arcade, 1990; London: Heinemann, 1991);

Vespers, as McBain (New York: Morrow, 1990; London: Heinemann, 1990);

Widows, as McBain (New York: Morrow, 1991; London: Heinemann, 1991);

Kiss, as McBain (New York: Morrow, 1992; London: Heinemann, 1992);

Mary, Mary, as McBain (New York: Warner, 1992; London: Heinemann, 1992);

Scimitar, as John Abbott (New York: Crown, 1992; London: Heinemann, 1992);

Mischief, as McBain (New York: Morrow, 1993; London: Hodder & Stoughton, 1993);

Criminal Conversation (New York: Warner, 1994; London: Hodder & Stoughton, 1994);

There Was a Little Girl, as McBain (New York: Warner, 1994; London: Hodder & Stoughton, 1994);

Romance, as McBain (New York: Warner, 1995; London: Hodder & Stoughton, 1995);

Gladly, the Cross-Eyed Bear, as McBain (New York: Warner, 1996; London: Hodder & Stoughton, 1996);

Privileged Conversation (New York: Warner, 1996; London: Hodder & Stoughton, 1996);

Me and Hitch (London & Boston: Faber & Faber, 1997);

Nocturne, as McBain (New York: Warner, 1997; London: Hodder & Stoughton, 1997);

The Last Best Hope, as McBain (New York: Warner, 1998; London: Hodder & Stoughton, 1998);

The Big Bad City, as McBain (New York: Simon & Schuster, 1999; London: Hodder & Stoughton, 1999);

Driving Lessons, as McBain (London: Orion, 1999; New York: Carroll & Graf, 2000);

Barking at Butterflies, and Other Stories (Unity, Me.: Five Star, 2000; London: Allison & Busby, 2003);

The Last Dance, as McBain (New York: Simon & Schuster, 2000; London: Hodder & Stoughton, 2000);

Running from Legs and Other Stories, as McBain (Unity, Me.: Five Star, 2000; London: Allison & Busby, 2003);

Candyland: A Novel in Two Parts, as Hunter and McBain (New York: Simon & Schuster, 2001; London: Orion, 2001);

Money, Money, Money, as McBain (New York: Simon & Schuster, 2001; London: Orion, 2001);

Fat Ollie's Book, as McBain (New York: Simon & Schuster, 2002; London: Orion, 2002);

The Moment She Was Gone (New York: Simon & Schuster, 2002; London: Orion, 2003);

The Frumious Bandersnatch, as McBain (London: Orion, 2003; New York: Simon & Schuster, 2004).

PLAY PRODUCTIONS: *The Easter Man,* Birmingham, England, Birmingham Repertory Theatre, 1964; revised as *A Race of Hairy Men!* New York, Henry Miller's Theater, April 1965;

The Conjuror, Ann Arbor, Mich., Lydia Mendelssohn Theatre, 5 November 1969;

Stalemate, New York, 1975.

PRODUCED SCRIPTS: *Strangers When We Meet,* motion picture, based on Hunter's novel, Columbia Pictures, 1960;

The Birds, motion picture, Universal Pictures, 1963;

Fuzz, motion picture, United Artists, 1972;

Walk Proud, motion picture, Universal Pictures, 1979;

The Chisholms, television, CBS, 1979–1980.

OTHER: *Crime Squad,* edited as Ed McBain (London: New English Library, 1968);

Homicide Department, edited as McBain (London: New English Library, 1968);

Downpour, edited as McBain (London: New English Library, 1969);

Ticket to Death, edited as McBain (London: New English Library, 1969).

During a career spanning more than fifty years, Evan Hunter has written more than 125 books, including 37 under his own name and 14 under the pseudonyms Richard Marsten, Hunt Collins, Curt Cannon, Ezra Hannon, and John Abbott. He has written general fiction, juvenile fiction, plays, and scripts for motion pictures and television. He is best known, however, for his crime fiction, written as Ed McBain. As McBain, he has written nearly 80 books, including more than 50 87th Precinct novels, one of the finest police procedural series in the mystery genre.

The 87th Precinct series differs from earlier procedurals by Hillary Waugh and John Creasey in an emphasis on a "group" protagonist. McBain has acknowledged that his conception of the 87th Precinct was most influenced by the television series *Dragnet.* The 87th Precinct series itself clearly has provided a model for such ensemble television police series as *Barney Miller, Hill Street Blues, NYPD Blue,* and *Homicide.* Among mystery novelists and readers, McBain's series has achieved such stature that many continue to assume that McBain is the originator of the police-procedural mystery. Certainly, because of the critical reception and longevity of the series, one would be hard-pressed to identify an author of police procedurals in the last four decades who has neither imitated some essential aspects of McBain's approach nor tried pointedly to distinguish his or her work from McBain's by bringing other fictional elements into the genre. For instance, for all of their stylistic distinctiveness, the novels in James Ellroy's "L.A. Quartet" feature ensembles of detectives individualized in the McBain mode. On the other hand, in his series featuring Isaac Sidel, Jerome Charyn has given the police procedural such an idiosyncratically postmodern turn that many critics and reviewers have questioned whether the novels can even be categorized with the 87th Precinct novels as procedurals.

Evan Hunter was born Salvatore Albert Lombino on 15 October 1926 in New York City to Charles and Marie (Coppola) Lombino. One of his aunts, a midwife, delivered him on a kitchen table. Lombino grew up in the Italian neighborhood of East Harlem and in the North Bronx. His grandfather operated a tailor's shop blocks from Lombino's boyhood home in "Italian Harlem." His father was a mail carrier and musician. In an interview with Ronald Kovach, which appeared in the March 2002 issue of *The Writer,* Hunter recounted how his father enthusiastically supported his efforts and inventiveness as a child, once helping him to start a neighborhood newspaper and in another instance helping him to construct a stage set and the figures for a puppet show. Lombino attended Evander Childs High School in the Bronx and later studied art at the Art Students League of New York. While an art student, he worked mornings at the New York Public Library.

In 1943–1944 Lombino attended The Cooper Union for the Advancement of Science and Art and, exposed to the work of many other young artists, came to recognize that he was probably not talented enough to pursue a career as an artist. From 1944 to 1946 he served in the United States Navy. Requisitioning a radioman's neglected typewriter for his own use, he began writing in earnest–but without success–for the pulp magazines. Still, one of his shipmates, who had been a writing instructor at the University of Wisconsin, provided constructive criticism of the stories, and Lombino felt that he was making great progress toward his goal of becoming a published writer.

After his discharge from the armed services, Lombino attended Hunter College (now a part of the City University of New York) on the GI Bill. He has credited English professor Francis Kolars with both encouraging him and offering useful criticism of his writing. On 17 October 1949, Lombino married a fellow student, Anita Melnick, with whom he had three sons–Ted, Mark, and Richard–all born after he legally changed his name to Evan Hunter but before he achieved his first big success as a writer with the publication of *The Blackboard Jungle* in 1954. During his college years, Lombino papered an entire bathroom with rejection slips.

In 1950, Lombino graduated Phi Beta Kappa from Hunter College with a B.A. in English. He then taught for six months at a vocational high school in New York City. His teaching experience provided much of the background for *The Blackboard Jungle*. Later, he was an emergency telephone operator for the American Automobile Association, played piano in a jazz band, and sold lobsters for a wholesaler.

In 1951, Lombino answered an advertisement in *The New York Times* for an editor's position with the Scott Meredith Literary Agency. Although initially disappointed that the position was not with a newspaper or a magazine, he became more enthusiastic about the possibilities in the work when he learned that the editor whom he was replacing had resigned to pursue a full-time career as a writer. After several months on the job, Hunter showed some of his own work to Scott Meredith, who suggested markets that might be interested in several of the stories and actually arranged McBain's first sale to a pulp magazine. Although McBain received just $12 for the story, "Reaching for the Moon," which appeared in the November 1953 issue of *Science Quarterly Fiction,* the occasion was momentous in his perception of himself as a writer. The story was the only work published under his birth name. From his experiences with the staff and clients of the agency, he acquired much of the professionalism that has marked his varied career as a writer.

Evan Hunter, the name Lombino chose for himself, was the name under which his first three books

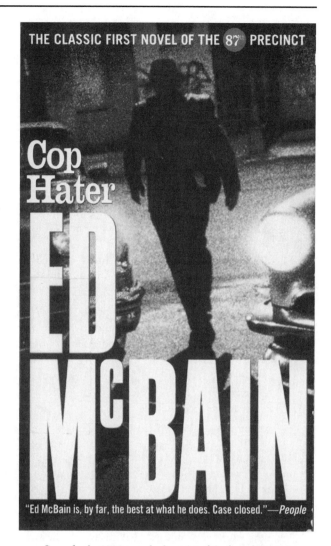

THE CLASSIC FIRST NOVEL OF THE 87 PRECINCT

Cop Hater

ED McBAIN

"Ed McBain is, by far, the best at what he does. Case closed."—*People*

Cover for the 1999 paperback reprint of the first of Hunter's novels published under the pseudonym Ed McBain, featuring the police officers of the 87th Precinct in the fictional northeastern city of Isola (Richland County Public Library)

were published in 1952: *The Evil Sleep,* a science-fiction novel; *The Big Fix,* a mystery-suspense novel later republished as *So Nude, So Dead* (1956) under the pseudonym Richard Marsten; and *Find the Feathered Serpent,* a science-fiction tale about a time traveler. Some writers have reported that Hunter took his first name from Evander Childs High School and his surname from Hunter College; however, Sarah Booth Conway reported in a 1990 article in *The Washington Post* that Hunter claimed the name had other sources: "I thought Hunter was a good name–aggressive, ambitious, hungry." He knew casually a writer called Evan who looked "mysterious, confident, daring, like a gambler. I liked that." In a 2002 interview with Anne Simpson of *The Herald* (Glasgow), he described his father's reaction to his legally changing his name:

I tell you, in 1952 Italians were way down the pecking order of immigrants. When I told my father I was changing my name he said: "Great idea." Next day he gave me a list of 200 choices all resonant of the name he'd given me at birth. I said: "That's fine but I can't use them." He didn't mind.

Before Hunter left the Scott Meredith agency in May 1953, he not only was a published novelist but also had made his first nonpulp sale to *Discovery* magazine, which was edited by novelist Vance Bourjaily. The story, "To Break the Wall," was the genesis of what became *The Blackboard Jungle.* Living off $3,000 in savings, Hunter was determined to try to succeed as a full-time writer. In 1953 he published *Don't Crowd Me,* his fourth novel published as Evan Hunter, as well as *Rocket to Luna* and *Danger: Dinosaurs,* both juvenile titles that he published under the pseudonym Marsten.

In 1954, Hunter published three books, *The Blackboard Jungle* under his own name and two "genre" works—*Cut Me In,* as Hunt Collins, and *Runaway Black,* as Marsten. Hunter chose to write under the pseudonyms to separate formally his "genre" work from his "serious" novels written as Hunter. A chase novel featuring a murder suspect who is trying to slip out of sight, *Runaway Black* is notable for its grimly vivid detailing of its Harlem setting. Because his earlier four novels as Hunter had garnered little notice, critics and readers treated *The Blackboard Jungle* as if it were a first novel. The book, which Hunter wrote in just two months, created a sensation and was regarded as an exposé of the failings of the public school system. *The Blackboard Jungle* brought Hunter a notoriety with which he was sometimes uncomfortable and also gave him instant stature. After the book was adapted into a critically and commercially successful movie starring Glenn Ford in 1955, it remained in print for decades. Also in 1955, *Murder in the Navy,* his second crime novel, was published under the name Marsten; thirteen years later it was republished as *Death of a Nurse* under the pseudonym Ed McBain, a name that by then had equaled or even outstripped the fame of Evan Hunter.

Because by 1956 Erle Stanley Gardner was clearly entering the later stages of his career, Herb Alexander, editor in chief at Pocket Books, asked Hunter to consider developing a mystery series. Given the literary legitimacy that accrued to the Hunter byline after the success of *The Blackboard Jungle,* the author decided to avoid further genre confusion involving his other pseudonyms and settled on the name Ed McBain (a Scottish name to go with the WASP name Evan Hunter) for the new series.

In the more than four decades that have followed since Hunter's creation of Ed McBain the writer, the two names have evolved as contrasting personae, to the point that in 2001, *Candyland: A Novel in Two Parts* was published as by Hunter and McBain. In her review of the book for the 16 June 2001 issue of *Weekend Australian,* Julie Lewis succinctly described the difference between the Hunter and McBain personae: "Hunter is intellectual, literary, inclined to write about families, relationships and social issues. . . . McBain is best known for his supremely well-crafted and solid-selling police procedurals." She ties in the double dust-jacket photo for "jointly authored" *Candyland,* quoting the author himself: "'That was a fun thing,' says Hunter, chuckling. 'We decided what Evan Hunter would look like and we dressed him. In one of the pictures we took that day I was wearing a bow tie, a bit more like a college professor. McBain we thought should look like an undercover cop.'" In a 1993 interview for *The Scotsman,* Alan Taylor commented on the range of accents and inflections in McBain's own voice: "The accent veers from the Bronx to upper crust English, from the low purring of a garrulous Godfather to that of a Hollywood butler played by John Gielgud." Writing under several pseudonyms seems to have been more than a matter of expediency in the marketing of his books.

In his 30 July 1997 interview with Clyde Haberman in *The New York Times,* Hunter described how his first success as Hunter complicated his primary research for the 87th Precinct series: "The cops were suspicious. I had just come off *The Blackboard Jungle,* which was looked upon as an attack on the New York school system. They said, 'He did a number on them, and now he's going to do one on us.'"

Cop Hater (1956), the first 87th Precinct novel, opens with a description of the city that immediately emphasizes the setting of the series:

> The city lay like a sparkling nest of rare gems, shimmering in layer upon layer of pulsating intensity. The buildings were a stage set. They faced the river, and they glowed with man-made brilliance, and you stared up at them in awe, and you caught your breath. Behind the buildings, behind the lights, were the streets. There was garbage in the streets.

McBain has said of the 87th Precinct series: "I think of the 87th as one big book, a changing portrait of a big city and of crime and punishment in our time."

Looking back to *Cop Hater* in her review of *The Last Dance* (2000) in the 30 January 2000 issue of *The New York Times Book Review,* Marilyn Stasio describes the elements that have characterized the series, noting that setting is integral to its distinctive success:

> In creating an entire precinct of working-stiff police officers to man these gritty novels, McBain also demys-

tified the traditional detective hero and brought him down to earth. His vision, he says, was of "a squad room full of cops, each with different traits, who when put together would form a conglomerate hero." The final stroke was setting the stories in New York (reconfigured as a mythical metropolis called Isola) and making the city a central character.

Stasio also identifies the "stylistic ground rules" of the series: "multiple story lines, split-focus action, rotating ensemble players, street-savvy dialogue and soul-of-the-city settings."

In his book *The Boys from Grover Avenue: Ed McBain's 87th Precinct Novels* (1985), George N. Dove provides a primer on the novels up to *Ice* (1983). He meticulously describes how McBain has disguised the geography of New York City by rotating the boroughs roughly ninety degrees along the line of the Hudson River to create the fictional Isola ("island" in Italian), and he locates most of the landmarks specified in the course of the events of the novels. Likewise, Dove details how McBain has distorted temporal relationships to sustain the credibility of the series for four and a half decades. The story lines have reflected current events and changes in the popular culture, and the police procedures and techniques have remained cutting-edge. Almost all of the novels have been precisely dated, so Dove can provide a detailed time line of the cases that the detectives have investigated as well as the significant events in the detectives' personal lives. Yet, the detectives themselves have aged only gradually, remaining middle-aged and vital when, by chronology, they should have become gray-haired and been long retired. In fact, when the plots have not called for some recognition of aging, the detectives and their families have remained happily stalled at certain stages of their lives. As a result, the earlier books in the series seem much less dated than one might reasonably expect them to be. As a result, they have been republished regularly and have had good sales.

Of the detectives in the 87th Precinct, Steve Carella comes closest to being a conventional protagonist. Generally even-tempered, fair-minded, and professional in his investigations, Carella is an admirable character, if not quite a paragon. He approaches his work rationally, but he is also capable of intuitive insight and imaginative strategies. He is dependable and adheres to a fairly high code of professional and personal conduct, but he is not inflexible, not a stuffed shirt. He is good-looking without being vain, physically capable without being hard, and educated without being bookish. His happy marriage to Teddy, a beautiful deaf woman, provides a personal complement to his professional life.

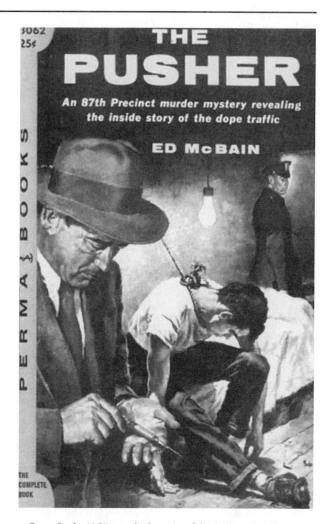

Cover for the 1962 paperback reprint of the third novel in Hunter's 87th Precinct series, originally published in 1956 (from Richard A. Lupoff, The Great American Paperback [Portland, Ore.: Collectors Press, 2001]; Bruccoli Clark Layman Archives)

The other detectives can also be described in terms of how their personalities complement or provide contrasts with Carella's. Despite his eccentrically redundant name, Carella's partner, Meyer Meyer, is to all appearances almost remarkably unremarkable—an ordinary-looking man in early middle age whose manner might suggest that he is a bookkeeper for a small firm. But Meyer Meyer is an effective detective precisely because he is so low-key, because he is almost unfailingly objective, thorough, and patient. Not only can he be relied on to apply himself steadily to the more pedestrian aspects of police work, but he can also be counted on to maintain a certain necessary distance in the course of emotionally charged cases. Like Carella, Meyer has a stable home life and a supportive wife.

On the other hand, the youngest detective in the precinct, Bert Kling, becomes involved in a series of highly charged relationships with women that end badly, leaving him feeling alternately disillusioned and cursed. Despite the turmoil in his personal life, however, Kling proves a fairly competent, if sometimes autonomous, investigator. In some respects, Kling seems perpetually naive; yet, the experiences that test his resiliency seem to provide him with a demeanor that encourages a sense of connection. Those who work with him or who come into contact with him during the course of his investigations ultimately trust his perceptions and his reliability.

In contrast with the almost careless boyishness of Bert Kling, Cotton Hawes comes across as extremely polished. He is physically well-proportioned, innately intelligent, and self-assured. The one suggestion that his self-confidence has not made him invulnerable is a jagged white streak in his full head of auburn hair. Hawes's complement is Arthur Brown, an African American detective whose truly imposing size belies a great deal of self-control and a considerable capacity for empathy.

As foils to the professionalism of these five detectives, three other detectives have provided increasingly comic illustrations of unprofessional behavior. Roger Haviland seems to embody the stereotype of the hard-nosed, heavy-fisted detective. After Haviland is killed off, McBain replaces him with Andy Parker, who is more burly than hard but indulges in racial, ethnic, and sexual stereotypes with an amazing lack of self-consciousness. Finally, McBain introduces Fat Ollie Weeks, whose obnoxious personality and equally unprogressive attitudes are emphasized by his almost incredible slovenliness.

In a brief review in the 29 April 1956 issue of *The New York Times,* Anthony Boucher described *Cop Hater* as "a tough, sexy novel with inherent honesty and decency." In quick succession, in 1956 McBain published the second and third novels in the series, *The Mugger* and *The Pusher.* Boucher included both books in his list of the most notable mystery-detective novels of 1956 and thereby did much to bring the series to critical notice.

In 1957, *The Con Man* and *Killer's Choice* extended the series to five novels in just two years. As Marsten, the author also published two other mystery-suspense novels, *The Spiked Heel* (1956) and *Vanishing Ladies* (1957). In 1957 he garnered his first formal recognition for his work as McBain; his short story "The Last Spin," originally published in the September 1956 issue of *Manhunt,* was nominated for Best Short Story by the Mystery Writers of America (MWA). Although he wrote many stories in the 1950s and has continued to write short stories under both the Hunter and McBain bylines, and although some of the stories have demon-

strated a skillfulness and even an ease with the form, his efforts in the short story have clearly become peripheral to his concentration on the novel.

McBain's experiments with pseudonyms reached their apogee in 1958. In addition to two more entries in the 87th Precinct series, *Killer's Payoff* and *Lady Killer,* he published *Strangers When We Meet,* his seventh novel as Hunter; *Even the Wicked,* his fifth novel as Marsten; *I'm Cannon—For Hire,* the first Curt Cannon novel, featuring a hard-boiled detective who was also featured in the short-story collection *I Like 'Em Tough* (1958); and *The April Robin Murders* (1958), McBain's completion of an unfinished novel by the recently deceased Craig Rice.

In 1959, the 87th Precinct series reached ten novels, with the publication of *Killer's Wedge, 'Til Death,* and *King's Ransom.* Attesting to the growing popularity of the series, *Killer's Wedge* was the first novel in the series to be published in hardcover. Boucher described it as "an unusually taut and tense novel, and a tour de force of mystery-suspense construction." In 2001, Marcel Berlins of *The Los Angeles Times* chose *Killer's Wedge* as one of the twenty best mystery-detective novels of the twentieth century. In the novel, a woman who wants to kill Carella comes to the precinct house with a bottle of nitroglycerin. But Carella is out investigating a case, and his progress on that case is juxtaposed against the increasing tension among the detectives facing an increasingly taut situation in the squad room. In 1962, Japanese movie director Akira Kurosawa used *King's Ransom,* a novel about a perfectly executed kidnapping of the wrong child, as the basis for his critically acclaimed motion picture *High and Low,* which starred Toshiro Mifune, an actor described as both the Japanese John Wayne and a prototype for Clint Eastwood's screen persona. *A Matter of Conviction,* the eighth Evan Hunter novel (republished as *The Young Savages* in 1966), and *Big Man,* the sixth and last Marsten novel, were also published in 1959. The steadily expanding popularity of the 87th Precinct novels led the author to publish almost all of his subsequent mysteries under the name Ed McBain.

The year 1960 was the last year in which McBain published three 87th Precinct novels: *Give the Boys a Great Big Hand, The Heckler,* and *See Them Die.* The titles were becoming more ironic, playing off familiar phrases rather than simply indicating the type of criminal or crime featured in the main story line. For instance, in *Give the Boys a Great Big Hand,* the detectives pursue a murderer who amputates his victims' hands. The reviewer for *The New Yorker* remarked, "Mr. McBain tells his story with his usual strident authority."

During the rest of the 1960s, McBain added ten more novels to the 87th Precinct series, from *Lady, Lady, I Did It!* (1961) to *Shotgun* (1969). In *He Who Hesi-*

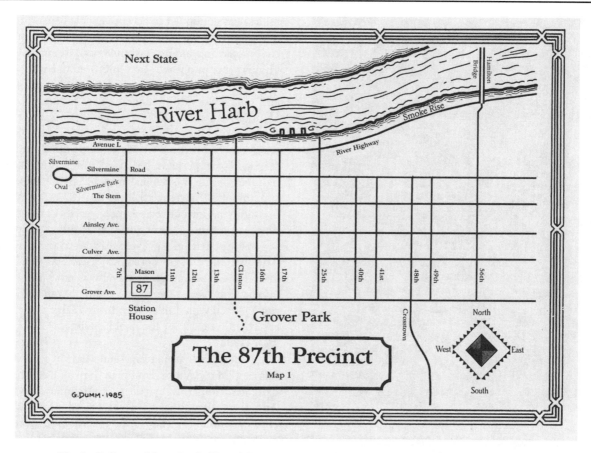

Map by G. Dumm of the setting for Hunter's long-running series of police procedural novels (from George N. Dove,
The Boys from Grover Avenue: Ed McBain's 87th Precinct Novels, *1985;*
Thomas Cooper Library, University of South Carolina)

tates (1965), McBain tried to experiment somewhat with the narrative pattern of the series, relating the action through the point of view of a visitor to New York City who turns out to be a criminal, and most reviewers, other than Boucher, felt that the experiment was largely unsuccessful. The judgment of Sergeant Cuff in the October 1965 issue of *The Saturday Review* was typical: "87th Precinct personnel supply little action or dialogue to this latest of the 87th Precinct murder yarns, wherein the reader is present at the crime. The story is grindingly slow-motion. May the author return to the old formula, one of the few authentic police-in-action series left in this virtuous world." On the other hand, the most critically well-received of these novels was probably *Fuzz* (1968). Reviewing the novel in the 20 October 1968 issue of *The New York Times,* A. J. Hubin praised the atypical style of the novel: "That part of Evan Hunter who writes as Ed McBain has become a wag. . . . His new novel is the tale of a city full of comedians, not all of them funny. . . . I don't know when I've enjoyed the 87th Precinct as much."

In the 1961–1962 television season, *87th Precinct* was aired, starring Robert Lansing as Steve Carella and

costarring Gena Rowlands and Robert Fell. In several interviews, Hunter commented on how the television series quickly used up the plots from his McBain novels, despite his great productivity. In 1965, Hunter, as McBain, published *The Sentries,* the first nonseries McBain novel, which Earl Tannenbaum of *Library Journal* called "a fast-paced, realistic doomsday novel full of suspense and sharp characterizations." During the 1960s, the author also produced six more novels, two collections of short stories, and two juvenile books under the name Evan Hunter. *Sons* (1969), a multigenerational story of Italian Americans from World War I to Vietnam, was critically praised for its handling of broad and difficult themes and its realistic detailing of the often difficult process by which immigrants have become assimilated into American society.

In the 1970s, McBain added ten more novels to the 87th Precinct series, from *Jigsaw* in 1970 to *Calypso* in 1979. Almost two decades after its publication in 1972, *Sadie When She Died,* which treats the brutal murder of a housewife who led a double life, was voted one of the Independent Mystery Booksellers Association's "100 Favorite Mysteries of the Century" and was also

Cover for the fiftieth novel in the 87th Precinct series, published in 2000 (Richland County Public Library)

midcareer, continued to accept new challenges. In addition to writing six more novels, three more short-story collections, and another juvenile book under the name Hunter, he published two more nonseries novels—*Where There's Smoke* (1975) and *Guns* (1976)—as McBain, and one, *Doors* (1975), under a new pseudonym, Ezra Hannon. All three are suspenseful crime novels told from the criminals' points of view. Although all received fairly favorable reviews, none developed into a series—in part, perhaps, because Hunter as McBain recognized that he was mining ground already staked out superbly by Lawrence Block. In 1977, the McBain pseudonym introduced a new series character, a divorced defense attorney named Matthew Hope who has relocated from the Northeast to Calusa, Florida. The first entry in the series was *Goldilocks* (1977), and although the second Hope novel was not published for another four years, the series eventually ran to fourteen novels, each with a title taken from a fairy tale or nursery rhyme, except for the final installment, *The Last Best Hope* (1998).

After his first marriage ended in divorce, Hunter married Mary Vann Finley in June 1973. His stepdaughter from this marriage is Amanda Eve Finley. Author of the critically well-received novel *Sassafras* (1980), Hunter's second wife eventually concentrated on managing his career. They have divided their time between homes in New York City and Sarasota, Florida—the model for the fictional Calusa of the Matthew Hope series.

Beginning with *Calypso* the McBain 87th Precinct novels began to have single-word titles with multiple levels of meaning. In fact, the author's conception of a novel in the series usually started with finding a title and inventing details connected to it. In his interview with Kovach for *The Writer,* McBain explained that the single-word title *Ice* suggested the winter setting, a situation concerning show business (*ice* is a specialized slang term for a certain type of scam involving inflated ticket prices for theatrical shows), and a plot involving both diamonds and cocaine (*ice* has been street slang for both).

In 1981, *Hill Street Blues,* an ensemble television drama about a police precinct, debuted to critical acclaim on NBC. Hunter as McBain felt that the show was so clearly modeled on his 87th Precinct series that he publicly considered bringing a lawsuit against the creators of the show. He told Haberman of *The New York Times:* "The lawyer thought I had a case, but he asked if I had $500,000 to lose, because it could go either way. I did not have $500,000 I was willing to lose, and I was going up against NBC. So, we let it drop." Hunter has since admitted that his response to the show was a mixture of disappointment and admira-

included in H. R. F. Keating's *Crime and Mystery: The 100 Best Books.* Also in 1972, the movie *Fuzz* was released. The most successful adaptation of a McBain novel, *Fuzz* starred Burt Reynolds, Tom Skerritt, Raquel Welch, Yul Brynner, and Jack Weston.

Two reviews of *Hail, Hail, the Gang's All Here* (1971), which presents a single day's events in the precinct house, suggest that for some readers the middle novels in the series became somewhat predictable. The reviewer for the 15 March 1971 issue of *Best Sellers* wrote, "McBain, as usual, displays his competent grasp of the multifaceted life of an average American police precinct, but somehow the story seems to lack spontaneity; perhaps it is one too many in a long and successful series." Similarly, in a review for the 30 May 1971 issue of *The New York Times Book Review,* Newgate Calendar observed, "Another skillful writer who has been writing essentially the same book for a long time . . . McBain has the police routine down very well, and he writes about it in a sober, unsentimental style. But this particular McBain novel is too superficial, slick, and tricky."

The diversity of the writing projects that Hunter as McBain took on in the 1970s shows that the author, perhaps recognizing the need to rejuvenate himself in

tion: he was in the process of trying to develop another series based on the 87th Precinct novels and recognized that *Hill Street Blues* was so good that it made any other series in the same vein look like a knockoff.

In 1986, a feature story on the Hunters' Connecticut home appeared in *Architectural Digest*. They had spent a decade and a half remodeling it. Almost a decade later, Michael Blowen visited the residence to interview Hunter (McBain) for the *Boston Globe,* saying that the residence, a "reconstructed Revolutionary-era sawmill, snuggles along the banks of the Silvermine River in the rural Connecticut hills."

In the 1980s and 1990s, the 87th Precinct novels became thicker, more complex works in which McBain developed and varied multiple plotlines with facility. He extended the series to forty-nine novels, and the critics typically found each new book more effective on some level than any previous effort. For instance, the reviewer for *Magill Book Reviews* said of *Poison* (1987): "The plot is tautly paced and sometimes brutally explicit, although McBain's descriptions are always based in authenticity rather than shock value, and the balance between action and character development is well maintained throughout the book." In the late 1980s, McBain published three nonseries novels—*Another Part of the City* (1986), *Downtown* (1989), and *Gangs* (1989). The last two are crime novels told by the criminals, but *Another Part of the City* focuses on a police detective named Reardon from New York's 5th Precinct.

In 1986 McBain received the Grand Master Award for lifetime achievement from the MWA, and in 1998, he became the first American to receive the Diamond Dagger lifetime achievement award from the British Crime Writers Association. These honors are indications of a critical consensus that he has managed to enrich his series dramatically and thematically. In his review of *Widows* (1991) for the 13 May 1991 issue of *New Republic,* Luc Sante offered one of the most serious, extended commentaries on the popularity and significance of the 87th Precinct series:

> While it may be said that mere entertainments are under no obligation to confront the loaded issues of the day, such a thing is simply not possible in the minefield terrain of inner-city crime drama. Racism, sexism, economic inequality are ingrained in the topic, and to ignore them would be to treat them derisively. On the other hand, to take them on fully is to risk a great deal, especially within the enveloping context of a series. The major characters cannot be challenged very deeply without risking their moral authority and, by extension, the stability of the narrative machine that will engender future installments.

Sante closed by comparing McBain's novels to *Hill Street Blues* and observing that the effect they provide is "more than just a matter of fleeting diversion":

> The multicharacter, multiplot constructions of these cop sagas not only make vehicles for the kind of all-around entertainment that movies used to provide but seldom do anymore—you get bathos here, comedy there, a bit of folk wisdom, some armchair psychology, some romantic byplay, maybe a song-and-dance routine. Their apparently collagiste approach also seems consistent with the improbable juxtapositions of urban life. . . . The messes of real life are displayed and then blanketed; bombs go off, but under the eye of the bomb squad. . . . The series is more than just a tale of police detectives; it is, in its way, a traffic cop of urban chaos.

Hunter evidently became so satisfied with his work as McBain that after the publication of *Lizzie* in 1984, he did not publish another novel as Hunter until *Criminal Conversation* in 1994 and *Privileged Conversation* in 1996. Both are suspenseful crime novels with strong psychological elements that distinguish them from the McBain novels, even though they explore similar terrain to that covered in the 87th Precinct novels. In addition, Hunter felt comfortable pulling the plug on the Matthew Hope series with *The Last Best Hope* in 1998. He offered this explanation to Michele Ross in the 31 July 1997 issue of *Christian Science Monitor:* "I'm going to stop this series, because it's become too difficult to write, with always having to check legal facts." That the series had perhaps run its course is evident in Stasio's review in the 22 March 1998 issue of *The New York Times Book Review:* "With its disorienting procedures, the double investigation [by Hope and by some of the 87th-Precinct detectives] also adds more convolutions to a story already snarled in double-crosses, disguises, role-playing and mistaken identity—much of it hilariously inept."

In his one experiment with writing under a new pseudonym in the 1990s, Hunter published the thriller *Scimitar* (1992) as John Abbott. On the back cover of the novel is a photo of the author in silhouette, and the biographical note on the back flap rather coyly notes that "John Abbott is the pseudonym of a world-famous novelist." Despite favorable reviews, the novel was a commercial disappointment. The novel, which details a terrorist attack using nerve gas, became controversial at about the same time that it was being remaindered, as some readers thought it might have inspired the 1993 sarin gas attack on a Tokyo subway. Hunter responded by declaring that the formulas offered in the book were harmless—precisely because he did not want to be held responsible for any copycat crimes.

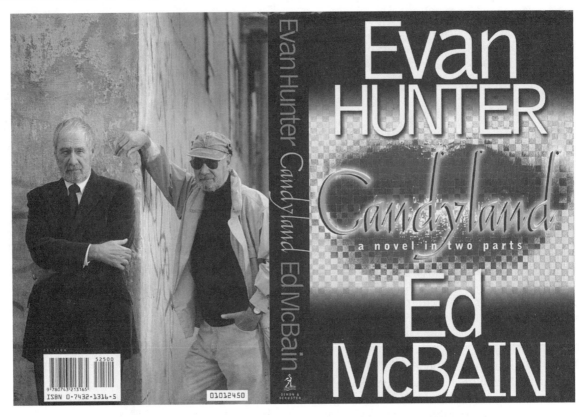

Dust jacket for Hunter's 2001 "collaboration" with his pseudonymous alter ego; the photograph depicts him
as both personae (photograph by Robert Clark; Richland County Public Library).

In 1995, *Ed McBain's 87th Precinct,* a made-for-television movie based on the novel *Lightning* (1984), was aired on NBC. Starring Randy Quaid as Steve Carella, it disappointed the author, who felt that the producers had diluted the grittier aspects of the story too much and had moved the emphasis too far away from the nuts and bolts of police work to the development of rather predictable melodrama exploring facile themes. It was one of the few disappointments Hunter as McBain experienced during this period.

His personal life, however, was more tumultuous. In the decade between 1987 and 1997, Hunter suffered three heart attacks. After his second marriage ended in divorce, he married Yugoslavian Drasica Dimitrijevic on 9 September 1997, in the garden of the Hotel Cipriani in Venice.

In 2000, the 87th Precinct series reached fifty novels with the publication of *The Last Dance,* which was chosen as a Notable Book of the Year by *The New York Times.* In her review for the 30 January 2000 issue of the *Times,* Stasio commented on the author's artistic development:

> McBain has always had a keen ear for the vernacular, but nowadays his dialogue is so sharp you could cut your wrists on it. Doesn't matter whether it's a weary

waitress mopping the counter in an all-night diner, a theatrical producer smugly puffing on a Havana cigar or some punk killer who resents being arrested before he can finish his breakfast, the citizens of Isola are fearless back-talkers who use language to paint their naked faces and cover their guilty tracks. That is why it's worth paying attention, as Carella does, to the pent-up outburst of 'a woman who has nobody to talk to.' That is also why the scenes between Carella and Teddy, his deaf-mute wife, who has no words to hide behind, are always so tender—and so telling.

Like most other reviewers, Sybil Steinberg of *Publishers Weekly* (18 October 1999) concurred with Stasio's judgment: "The 50th novel of the 87th Precinct is one of the best, a melancholy, acerbic paean to life—and death. . . ."

In 2001 McBain published the fifty-first novel in the series, *Money, Money, Money.* The reviewer for *Publishers Weekly* remarked, "The minor characters are sketched as vividly as a Hirschfeld drawing, and McBain's mordant humor keeps the violence somewhat balanced." Dick Lochte in *The Los Angeles Times* concurred that this novel "is funnier than the usual 87th-Precinct tale," and Peter Millar in *The Times* (London) praised the "finely tuned prose and wittily ironic characterization." He describes Ollie Weeks as "perhaps the most politically incorrect character in modern American fiction."

In 2001, Hunter joined the personae that he had attempted for so long to keep separate. *Candyland* was presented as a "collaboration" between Hunter and McBain, with each writing half of the novel in his "characteristic" style. In his review in *The New York Times Book Review* (4 February 2001), Bruce DeSilva observed, "The novel is a gimmick, and it is a surprise that it works at all. That it works so superbly is a tribute to the skills of this great storyteller."

In 2001 McBain underwent surgery to repair an aneurysm, but the operation seems hardly to have slowed him down. In 2002, his twenty-sixth novel as Evan Hunter, *The Moment She Was Gone,* was published. He and his wife have been collaborating on a libretto for a stage adaptation of Rowland Barber's *The Night They Raided Minskys* (1960). McBain's fifty-second 87th Precinct novel, *Fat Ollie's Book* (2002), expands on the segment of the "book" presented at the end of *Money, Money, Money.* He has commented in several interviews that he would like his last McBain novel to be called "Exit" but wonders if he will ever have the courage or foresight to begin writing it.

Certainly, when his career does come to an end, Hunter as McBain will be remembered for the 87th Precinct series because of its breadth and its influence. The attention to his work as McBain may eventually provoke some long-overdue recognition of his achievement in the "serious" novels he has written as Hunter. This possibility is clearly the opposite of what he expected more than a half century ago, at the beginning of his prolific career. But he could not have anticipated the increased critical appreciation for work in the "popular" genres or the diminished interest in "conventional" novels, regardless of their subjects or the craft evident in their telling.

Interviews:

Alan Taylor, "On the Case," *Scotsman,* 19 September 1993;

Michael Blowen, "Ed McBain, Inc.," *Boston Globe,* 19 March 1996, p. 35;

Clyde Haberman, "At Lunch with Evan Hunter: Why Shouldn't a Writer Have Several AKA's?" *New York Times,* 30 July 1997, p. C1;

Selwyn Raab, "Writing under an Assumed Name," *New York Times Book Review,* 30 January 2000, p. 13;

Jeff Zaleski, "PW Talks with Evan Hunter," *Publishers Weekly,* 248 (1 January 2001): 68;

Anne Simpson, "An Identity Parade with Crime's Mr. Big Mac," *Glasgow Herald,* 21 January 2002, p. 11;

Ronald Kovach, "Urban Legend," *Writer,* 115 (March 2002): 24–28.

References:

George N. Dove, *The Boys from Grover Avenue: Ed McBain's 87th Precinct Novels* (Bowling Green, Ohio: Bowling Green State University Press, 1985);

H. R. F. Keating, "Ed McBain: *Sadie When She Died,*" in *Crime and Mystery: The 100 Best Books* (New York: Carroll & Graf, 1987), pp. 155–156;

Julie Lewis, "Stunned into Silence," *Weekend Australian,* 27 October 2001, p. R12;

E. E. Macdonald, "Genre and Masculinity in Ed McBain's 87th Precinct Novels," *Journal of the American and Comparative Cultures,* 25 (Spring 2002): 47–50;

John Pescatore, "Evan Hunter on Writing Mysteries," in *The Fine Art of Murder: The Mystery Reader's Indispensable Companion,* edited by Ed Gorman, Martin H. Greenberg, and Larry Segriff (New York: Galahad, 1993), pp. 214–216.

Papers:

Evan Hunter's papers are held by the Mulgar Memorial Library, Boston University.

Emma Lathen
(Mary Jane Latsis)
(12 July 1927 – 27 October 1997)

and

(Martha Henissart)
(4 June 1929 –)

Marcia B. Dinneen
Bridgewater State College

BOOKS:
By Latsis and Henissart as Emma Lathen

Banking on Death (New York: Macmillan, 1961; London: Gollancz, 1962);

A Place for Murder (New York: Macmillan, 1963; London: Gollancz, 1963);

Accounting for Murder (New York: Macmillan, 1964; London: Gollancz, 1965);

Death Shall Overcome (New York: Macmillan, 1966; London: Gollancz, 1967);

Murder Makes the Wheels Go 'Round (New York: Macmillan, 1966; London: Gollancz, 1966);

Murder Against the Grain (New York: Macmillan, 1967; London: Gollancz, 1967);

Come to Dust (New York: Simon & Schuster, 1968; London: Gollancz, 1969);

A Stitch in Time (New York: Macmillan, 1968; London: Gollancz, 1968);

Murder to Go (New York: Simon & Schuster, 1969; London: Gollancz, 1970);

When in Greece (New York: Simon & Schuster, 1969; London: Gollancz, 1969);

Pick Up Sticks (New York: Simon & Schuster, 1970; London: Gollancz, 1971);

The Longer the Thread (New York: Simon & Schuster, 1971; London: Gollancz, 1972);

Ashes to Ashes (New York: Simon & Schuster, 1971; London: Gollancz, 1971);

Murder without Icing (New York: Simon & Schuster, 1972; London: Gollancz, 1973);

Sweet and Low (New York: Simon & Schuster, 1974; London: Gollancz, 1974);

By Hook or by Crook (New York: Simon & Schuster, 1975; London: Gollancz, 1975);

Double, Double, Oil and Trouble (New York: Simon & Schuster, 1978; London: Gollancz, 1979);

Going for the Gold (New York: Simon & Schuster, 1981; London: Gollancz, 1981);

Green Grow the Dollars (New York: Simon & Schuster, 1982; London: Gollancz, 1982);

Something in the Air (New York: Simon & Schuster, 1988; London: Simon & Schuster, 1988);

East Is East (New York: Simon & Schuster, 1991; London: Gollancz, 1991);

Right on the Money (New York: Simon & Schuster, 1993; London: Gollancz, 1993);

Brewing Up a Storm (New York: St. Martin's Press, 1996);

A Shark out of Water (New York: St. Martin's Press, 1997; Bath: Chivers, 1998).

By Latsis and Henissart as R. B. Dominic

Murder, Sunny Side Up (London & New York: Abelard-Schuman, 1968);

Murder in High Place (London: Macmillan, 1969; Garden City, N.Y.: Doubleday, 1970);

There Is No Justice (Garden City, N.Y.: Doubleday, 1971);

Murder out of Court (Garden City, N.Y.: Doubleday, 1971; London: Macmillan, 1971);

Epitaph for a Lobbyist (Garden City, N.Y.: Doubleday, 1974; London: Macmillan, 1974);

Murder out of Commission (Garden City, N.Y.: Doubleday, 1976; London: Macmillan, 1976);

The Attending Physician (New York: Harper & Row, 1980; London: Macmillan, 1980);

A Flaw in the System (London: Macmillan, 1983);

Unexpected Developments (New York: St. Martin's Press, 1984).

Emma Lathen mysteries are highly literate, well crafted, and often comic. Each centers on the world of business—from commerce to finance, from service industries to sports. Subjects include fast-food franchises, the Oriental-rug business, car manufacturers in Detroit, and the vacation-condominium business. Social satire figures prominently in each book. Every novel begins with an observation on Wall Street that soon leads to an introduction of the Sloan Guaranty Trust and to some type of disruption in an aspect of business involving the Sloan. This difficulty includes at least one murder that will, by the end of the novel, be resolved. The detective-hero who solves the murders in each book is banker John Putnam Thatcher, senior vice president and head of the trust department at the Sloan. Thatcher believes that passion never causes murder. The motive is always money: Who will gain or lose the most? Thatcher was the first fictional detective from the world of finance and business, and although the concept of a banker-hero may strike many as dull, the intricately plotted, quick-moving Lathen novels captivate readers.

Emma Lathen is actually two authors—Mary Jane Latsis and Martha Henissart. They combined their names to form a pen name: M (Mary) and Ma (Martha) resulted in Emma, and Lat (Latsis) plus Hen (Henissart) equals Lathen.

Latsis, the daughter of Greek immigrants, was born 12 July 1927 in Oak Park, Illinois, a suburb of Chicago where her father was a druggist. She graduated from Wellesley College in 1949 with a major in economics. Latsis worked for the government in Washington, D.C., and abroad, including a stint with the Central Intelligence Agency (CIA) during the Korean War. She returned to school and earned a master's degree in Public Administration from Harvard in the early 1950s. More work for the government, both at home and abroad, followed. Latsis also worked as an agricultural economist for the United Nations and was an economics instructor at Wellesley College.

Martha Henissart was born 4 June 1929 in New York City and grew up in Inwood Park, Manhattan, the daughter of a French parfumier. She learned English in the New York public schools. Henissart graduated from Mount Holyoke College in 1950 with a major in physics. She earned a law degree from Harvard in the mid 1950s and went to work for the Raytheon Company. Subsequently, she practiced law in New York and Boston.

Latsis and Henissart met in 1952 while both were at Harvard; they discovered a common interest in mysteries. In a 1975 interview in *Harvard Magazine,* Henissart said that she had read "just about every mystery in the

Dust jacket for the 1967 novel, written by Mary Jane Latsis and Martha Henissart under the pen name Emma Lathen, featuring banker-detective John Putnam Thatcher of the Sloan Guaranty Trust (Richland County Public Library)

New York Public Library." Both "consumed" the huge collection of "whodunits" in Harvard's Widener Library. After working in New York for several years, in 1960 Henissart took a corporate legal position in Boston. While looking for a house, she stayed with Latsis. During a conversation about the dearth of good mysteries, they decided to collaborate and write one. The prospect of "an independent income" was also attractive. They planned to create a character who would be involved in situations in which they could use their strengths in business and law and decided on a banker as the main character "because there is nothing on God's earth a banker can't get into." Their immediate incentive was a Macmillan-sponsored contest with a $3,000 prize. Latsis said in a 20 August 1978 interview with Margo Miller of the *Boston Globe,* "I don't say we wrote the first book as a joke, but we were casual about it," even sending it off wrapped in a plain brown wrapper. Although they did not win the prize, Macmillan accepted *Banking on Death* (1961) for publication.

This novel sets the pattern for subsequent novels describing Wall Street and the Sloan, headquartered in the heart of the financial district. In the novel, Lathen describes the Sloan as "far too important to concern itself with, say, Christmas Savings Clubs; you go to an uptown branch for that. The Sloan invests, underwrites, finances." Initial comments on Wall Street immediately focus the novels on the world of money and power. This introduction is followed by some type of crisis in the banking world or a particular industry. Jane S. Baker-man, in her 1976 article "A View from Wall Street: Social Criticism in the Mystery Novels of Emma Lathen," states that Lathen does "a masterful job of walking that thin line between reassuring predictability and boring facility." Lathen varies the topics of the novel as well as location. What keeps the novels lively is Lathen's "stringent comments about American life." Bakerman believes that the social criticism in the Lathen novels saves them from "formalism."

Banking on Death involves the murder of a "supposedly" missing heir to a trust administered by the Sloan. This novel introduces the main series character, John Putnam Thatcher. Thatcher—a sixty-something widower, born in Sunapee, New Hampshire, and Harvard educated—is urbane and witty, insightful and generous; he does not age or change. His consistency provides stability to the bank; his curiosity provokes his interest in solving the crimes; and his dry humor provides the fun. Thatcher is not a "tough guy," but he is unyielding when it comes to protecting the interests of the bank. Different novels give center stage to other employees of the Sloan, but Thatcher is always instrumental in finding the murderers. Although the background and industries focused upon show that time does not stand still, greed, the prime motive for murder, remains a constant in Thatcher's world, as it does in the "real" world.

John Thatcher, eminently sensible, intelligent, and logical, is surrounded by a cast of supporting characters who have certain foibles. The president of the Sloan, Bradford Withers, spends little time at the Sloan; his chief interest in the bank is redecorating his office and arranging the staff Christmas party. As pointed out in *Going for the Gold* (1981), Withers, a "man of many enthusiasms, did not number banking among them." His role is "largely" ceremonial, and his remarks are "clueless." Withers is described in *A Place for Murder* (1963) as "an amiable, diffuse man who wisely delegates the nonceremonial aspects of his august position to subordinates." He has a "well bred, vacuous face" and reserves "his enthusiasm for his quite remarkable series of athletic feats, performed at great cost in inaccessible areas of the world." Withers reappears throughout the series.

Everett Gabler, a bank officer in charge of Rails and Industrials, is another regular. Gabler is always apt to see the negative and is known as being cantankerous, conservative, and pompous. He is frugal and has a notoriously weak stomach; yet, he is tough when the interests of the Sloan are involved. Easygoing Charlie Trinkam, a bachelor with a consuming interest in beautiful women, is Thatcher's second in command.

Miss Rose Theresa Corsa, Thatcher's secretary, is a paragon. In *Green Grow the Dollars* (1982), she is said to possess the ability to "reduce Armageddon to manageable proportions." She knows everything that is going on at the bank and often despairs of her boss's tendency to pursue interests beyond what she believes is bank business. Thatcher fears that she could do his job better than he does. She has the ability to keep Thatcher and almost everyone else in line. The chairman of the board of Sloan and the president of the United States are the only exceptions.

Each Lathen novel also includes an additional cast of characters central to the action. In *Banking on Death,* other characters involved are Arthur Schneider, a businessman with a temper; his sister Grace, a spendthrift and closet alcoholic; and Martin Henderson, whose less-than-prudent investments are not going to sustain his lifestyle. Introduced in this novel as well is junior trust officer Kenneth Nicolls, who appears in several subsequent novels. In addition to the plot, the novel provides a peek into New York and Boston during the 1960s, with references to such sites as the Sheraton Plaza in Boston, Ken's Steak House in Framingham, and Bonwit Teller in New York. *Banking on Death* was an immediate success, and Anthony Boucher, book reviewer for *The New York Times* (10 December 1961), stated that the murder puzzle was "sound and well-clued" and continued, "Addicts of violent action may be bored, but for others, Miss Lathen is a find." The book was republished in 1994 as a selection of mystery expert and publisher Otto Penzler in his Classic American Mystery Library series. A favorable review of the republished novel appeared in the *Wilson Library Bulletin* (March 1994); in it Gail Pool notes that "Lathen's sense of comedy is superb," proving that she is not "dated."

During the 1960s, Latsis and Henissart continued to work in their respective professions, dividing their time between writing and careers. Latsis became a consultant, and Henissart a freelance lawyer for mutual funds. For years the authors carefully protected their identities. Neither wanted to have clients wondering if they might be future characters in a mystery novel. By the 1980s, Latsis and Henissart's novels had become so successful that they devoted themselves full-time to writing, and their identities were revealed. Latsis lived in Brookline, Massachusetts, and Henissart in Wellesley

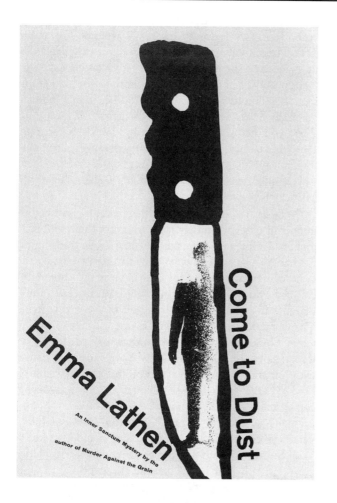

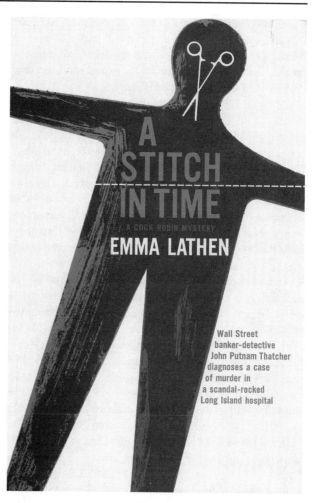

Dust jackets for Lathen's two John Putnam Thatcher novels published in 1968
(Richland County Public Library)

during the winter months. During the summer, they both lived in Warren, New Hampshire. To write the twenty-four Emma Lathen novels (and the nine novels they wrote under the pen name R. B. Dominic), they developed a method.

First they outlined a plot. In a 1 December 1977 *Forbes* magazine article, they explained, "The basic plot of everything we do is a fraud of some sort. We like to take an industry and find out what wriggles in it." Then each wrote alternate chapters simultaneously. When they first started writing, the outline was detailed, a whole page for each chapter, but as they wrote more of the novels, they just agreed on general ideas. Once they decided on the business they would like to write about and the people involved, they created a plot and decided who was going to be murdered and by whom. Then they determined how Thatcher could catch the murderer. In a 1975 *Harvard Magazine* interview, they confessed, "A couple of times we created a foolproof murder that not even

Thatcher could solve, and we had to go back and put in a mistake or two on the part of the murderer." After each wrote her chapters, they assembled them, and each author rewrote her chapters as needed. Then they got together, looked over the book as a whole, and created a clean copy for the typist. This step entailed going over the manuscript word by word. A book typically took them six or seven months; some more than a year.

They were meticulous in their attention to style. In a 1983 interview with John C. Carr, Latsis stated, "We have reintroduced the colon, the semicolon and the exclamation mark"; Henissart added, "We were able to reintroduce the complex sentence." The end result, enhanced with an extensive vocabulary, is an engaging, literate style. However, the tight plotting, the difficulty of discovering "whodunit," and the comedy are what make the novels so popular. Their comedy is based on wit, verbal irony, situations, and many characters. Their wit can be seen readily in the Lathen novels and is often apparent in the chapter headings that, in various guises, are variations on the subject of the novel. For example, in *Murder to Go* (1969), a novel on the fast-food industry, the first chapter is "Prepare for Cooking," and the final chapter is "Take a Disjointed Tale."

Puns abound in the books. An example occurs in the title of the final chapter for *Pick Up Sticks* (1970), set in the woods of New Hampshire–"His Last Bough." In some novels, comic situations become farce, as in *Death Shall Overcome* (1966), when a variety of "lunatic fringe" groups march on Wall Street, and the staid Thatcher leads the impromptu Sloan choir in a hymn, and again in *Murder Against the Grain* (1967), when the Cuban navy tries to blockade the New York harbor, and diplomats from the Soviet Union are introduced to gourmet potato chips.

Each novel opens with a description of the power and activities of Wall Street and ends with Thatcher's often detailed explanation of the crime and the motivation. The only motivation in the Lathen novels, however, is money. Thatcher, using the same abilities that made him a successful banker, spots the murderers. His trained intelligence, broad business experience, and insight into human nature enable him to put together the clues that lead to the murderers and their motives.

The 1960s were the most productive decade for Lathen, ten novels. They vary in location from New York City to Detroit and from rural Connecticut to Greece. Changes in venue enable the exploration not only of different businesses but also of other cultures.

Banking for Death is amusing, but *A Place for Murder,* the second Lathen novel, is highly comic. The setting is Shaftsbury, Connecticut, peopled by the affluent and those who serve them. Thatcher becomes involved at the request of Sloan president Bradford Withers, whose sister Olivia Austin is getting a divorce and for whom Thatcher is to "handle" delicate property and financial concerns. Thatcher discovers a body, allegedly killed by a set of antlers belonging to Withers. While Withers is being investigated by the police, business at the Sloan must continue, so Sloan principals come to Shaftsbury. Also arriving are the people taking part in the Housatanic Dog Show and their dogs, several with pedigrees and names longer than their bodies. *The New York Times* book reviewer Boucher notes that the book is a "more than worthy second novel" and "a shrewd and humorous social study."

Accounting for Murder (1964) takes place back in New York City with problems at the National Calculating Company. Some stockholders have revolted because there were no dividends and have hired a famous accountant, Clarence Fortinbras (the novel is filled with puns relating to *Hamlet*), to discover what is rotten in the company. Just when he appears to have discovered

major fraud, he is murdered by someone who wraps the cord from his adding machine around his neck. Thatcher is involved since the Sloan has invested heavily in National Calculating. Various suspects include the inept president of the company, whose major strength is his reputation as a player on the 1929 Harvard football team. Boucher, reviewing the novel for *The New York Times,* comments, "Emma Lathen and her detective John Putnam Thatcher . . . are among the strongest contributors of the 1960's to the pure detective story." The book was republished in 1995 in Penzler's Classic American Mystery Library series.

Death Shall Overcome, published in 1966, is a comic treatment of a then timely topic: the proposal of a black millionaire for a seat on the all-white New York Stock Exchange. The novel is developed through the machinations of various groups for and against the candidate, Edward Parry: these ploys involve death threats, sit-ins, marches in support, and the murder of the wrong man. Thatcher becomes an unwilling member of the Committee of Three, trying to diffuse an explosive situation that threatens to shut down the New York Stock Exchange with a march on Wall Street to protest the exclusion of blacks. Lathen also diffuses a "touchy" subject by using comedy in her descriptions of the various groups involved, such as the White Association for Civic Intervention, "known as 'Whacky' the length and breadth of Wall Street." Thatcher is forced to attend interminable meetings. When he learns that the guest speaker for one meeting has the reputation of being an intellectual, Thatcher gives him "precisely three minutes." Then he chooses the "course of prudence," suspending "all thought entirely." Critic Boucher of *The New York Times* described this novel as the best Lathen novel thus far.

The fifth Lathen novel, *Murder Makes the Wheels Go 'Round* (1966), takes Thatcher to Detroit. The Sloan is encouraged to buy stock in Michigan Motors, a company that has survived an antitrust, price-fixing incident and appears to be on the right track. Although several executives spent time in jail, some of them feel they should get their old jobs back, and one is discovered murdered inside a Super Plantagenet, the premier line of Michigan Motors. Thatcher survives boardroom politicking, executive wives, and too many company functions and puts together the clues to discover both motive and murderer. In reviewing the novel, *New York Times* critic Boucher makes a comment that is true of all the Lathen novels: "skill in making big-business intricacy clear and plausible."

World and national events are often reflected in Lathen novels. *Murder Against the Grain* has as its background the United States sale of wheat to the Soviet Union in 1963 and 1964. The Sloan is involved with the financing, but forged papers result in a loss of $1,000,000 for the bank. The courier of the forged papers is murdered, and several government agencies become involved: the Federal Bureau of Investigation (FBI), the CIA, and the State Department. Groups protesting the wheat sale gather, including the Cuban navy, the French Canadians, and the Free Ukrainians. The longshoremen go on strike to further complicate the matter. Lathen draws a particularly comic character in flamboyant entrepreneur Abe Baranoff, a thinly disguised portrait of Sol Hurok–Russian immigrant, impresario, and producer. As Hurok did, Baranoff brings various Soviet attractions to the United States, such as the Leningrad Symphony and Plomsky's Otter Ensemble, trained otters that can sing "'The Volga Boatman,' dance a rousing mazurka, and assemble a three-stage rocket."

The title of the seventh Lathen novel, *Come to Dust* (1968), is from Shakespeare's play *Cymbeline:* "Golden lads and girls all must, as chimney sweepers, come to dust." The novel focuses on those golden lads privileged to be considered for admission to prestigious Brunswick College, a highly competitive, Ivy League men's college in New Hampshire. A respected alumnus and member of the admissions committee, Elliot Patterson, has disappeared, and so has a $50,000 bearer bond (which is equivalent to cash) he has received as a donation to the college. Thatcher's involvement is through his "boss" at the Sloan, George Lancer, chairman of the board and an alumnus of Brunswick. The disappearance of the admissions folders of the applicants from New York City and the murder of one of these applicants add to problems at Brunswick.

The novel is full of humor, ranging from the sight of ancient alums trying to out-drink the undergraduates, to Thatcher's description of his evening at a museum reception. The modern-style art museum, the Gary (surely a parody of the Guggenheim Museum), and the works of modern artists are of no interest to Thatcher, who describes the event as resembling a "debutante cotillion in a reformatory." Remarking on the humor in the novel, *New York Times* book critic Allen J. Hubin states, "it's her mischievous, sometimes biting choice of just the right word that elevates the commonplace to the sublime."

A second novel published in 1968, *A Stitch in Time,* initially focuses on Miss Corsa, described as "a young woman clearly designed by nature for the motto: We are not amused." Her belief in decorum and propriety and her ability to keep Thatcher in line are stressed. Despite Miss Corsa's best efforts, Thatcher gets distracted from "bank business," this time by a case of medical malpractice at Southport Hospital, on Long Island. Lathen focuses on the medical industry and its abuses. An arrogant surgeon, Wendell Martin, has left seven hemostats in a patient who dies. Southport Hospital has other problems as well, and when Martin is murdered, supposedly

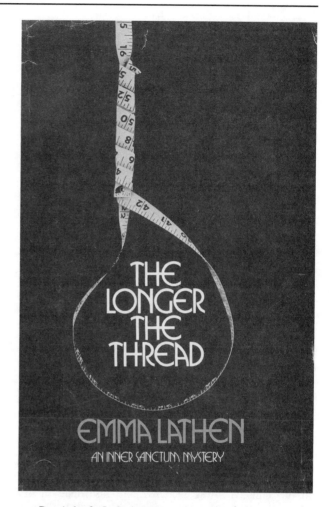

Dust jacket for Lathen's 1971 novel in which Thatcher travels to Puerto Rico for Sloan Guaranty and solves a mystery involving kidnapping and murder (Richland County Public Library)

by a mugger, Thatcher senses something deeper is amiss. Following the money trail, his investigation unearths a massive case of price-fixing for prescriptions drugs, involving many of the doctors at the hospital.

Lathen's next area to write about was the franchise industry, specifically fast food, in *Murder to Go.* Chicken Tonight has become a hugely successful franchise and, to diversify, is contemplating buying Southeastern Insurance. The proposal is halted by the poisoning of hundreds of people and the death of one man. Someone has added zinc, a lethal ingredient, to the Chicken Mexicali, the newest and most popular item on the menu. Chicken Tonight is shut down, and the hunt is on for the poisoner. By asking himself some key questions, such as Why does anyone want to destroy Chicken Tonight and hundreds of franchise owners? Thatcher discovers the answers.

Because of her roots in Greece, Latsis was consumed by the 1967 Greek colonel's coup; she and Henissart interrupted their current project and wrote *When in Greece* (1969) in six weeks. The novel is located, for the most part, in Greece, during a coup and an earthquake. Initially, the focus is on junior trust officer Kenneth Nicolls, who is representing the Sloan, which is financing a major project in Greece. Following a coup, Nicolls is arrested by the military but escapes and goes into hiding. The Sloan sends Everett Gabler to represent the bank and push the search for Nicolls, but Gabler is kidnapped. The conservative, often prissy, Gabler drives his kidnappers crazy with his constant talking; yet, he is aware that he must escape since he "would not trust the Greek police to locate the Mediterranean Sea."

This novel has suspense, an intricate plot, humor, as well as several interesting characters. A chase scene and sleights of hand at a number of shops provide fun, as do Lathen's descriptions. An example of the humor in the novel is this passage about German tourists: "But no power on earth can keep Germans in Germany. Primal forces as powerful as those impelling lemmings to the sea put bibulous Bavarians into lederhosen and deliver them to the Cote d'Azur, Port 'Ercole, and the kingdom of the Hellenes."

During the 1970s the Lathen novels continued what had become a successful format. Writing as Emma Lathen, Latsis and Henissart wrote seven novels; they also wrote four novels under their other pseudonym, R. B. Dominic. Again varying the locations of the novels, *Pick Up Sticks,* the eleventh Lathen novel, is set in the United States. Thatcher and his friend Henry Morland, on vacation, plan to walk the New Hampshire segment of the Appalachian Trail. What should have been a holiday becomes involvement in a crime. While attempting to rescue two lost and extremely amateur trail walkers, Morland, going for help, finds a body. The background for the novel is the vacation-condominium industry. Developers are promoting Fiord Haven in the White Mountains by inviting prospective buyers to visit the site and giving them a weekend of hard-sell, all expenses paid, at the White Mountains motel. One of the prospects has been killed by a hammer. When one of the developers is murdered, Thatcher marshals the resources of the Sloan by recruiting Sloan executives to pose as buyers and discovers what is so amiss at Fiord Haven as to provoke murder.

In *The Longer the Thread* (1971), Thatcher once more leaves the United States, this time for Puerto Rico. He is to assess the Sloan investment in Slax Unlimited, a garment factory in Puerto Rico, but he finds sabotage and murder. With the vote imminent to decide if Puerto Rico remains a "commonwealth" of the United States or becomes independent, all sorts of political activities and factions are fighting against United States companies. As usual, the chapter headings reflect the subject matter—for

example, "Pinking Shears" and "Pins and Needles." Sabotage at the Slax factory is just the beginning; the kidnapping and murder of the company president provokes a manhunt that ends at El Morro, the fortress that once protected the harbor of San Juan.

Ashes to Ashes (1971) again shows use of current material in a Lathen novel. This novel concerns the efforts of a group of parents in Queens to save their beloved parish school, St. Bernadette's. The Archdiocese of New York has sold the property to Unger Realty Corporation, which plans to build a twenty-two-story apartment house on the site. The Sloan is providing the $4,000,000 mortgage to Unger, an "old and valued" customer. The murder of the head of the parent group fighting for the school stalls the movement. Thatcher, currently acting president of the Sloan, spends much time in Queens. Looking for the most basic motive for murder, greed, Thatcher asks, Who will benefit most "financially" if the school is demolished?

Studying the background, always part of Latsis and Henissart's technique in developing a Lathen storyline, prompted them to buy season tickets to see the Boston Bruins, a hockey team. In *Murder without Icing* (1972), the city of New York is in a frenzy because the hockey team is having a winning season for the first time and has made the playoffs. The Sloan is a major advertiser. When a creditor proposes to buy out one of the owners of the team, he is murdered. The season continues its winning pace, thanks to star player Billy Siragusa. The description of his skating and puck handling is a fictional sketch of Boston Bruin star Bobby Orr. Thatcher had "avoided seventy-seven games of the hockey season to date. But all winning streaks come to an end." He attends a game, but the star collapses on the ice, victim of a cyanide-laced cold tablet. The chapter headings indicate the author knows hockey.

Thatcher goes from hockey to chocolate in the next Lathen novel, *Sweet and Low* (1974). He has been appointed to the Board of Directors of Dreyer Chocolate, and during the weekend of his first board meeting in upstate New York, an employee is murdered. The action shifts to New York City and the activities of super trader Amory Shaw, king of the buyers on the New York Cocoa Exchange. Lathen, drawing on her background, provides insight into the world of commodities—buying, selling, making money, and losing it. *The New York Times* reviewer Newgate Callendar remarked on Lathen's deftness in weaving the information about futures trading into the "fabric" of the story. After Shaw is murdered, the president of Dreyer is arrested, and Thatcher's task is to find a lawyer over the Columbus Day Weekend. He asks, "Is the whole New York Bar on Fire Island?"

The Oriental-rug business is the background for *By Hook or by Crook,* the 1975 Lathen novel. A long-lost aunt who has shares in the business of the Parajian family comes to New York City to meet with these purveyors of Oriental rugs and is almost immediately the victim of a lethal poison. The Sloan has been overseeing her interests, and the first question is whether the dead woman is the real aunt who disappeared into Russia in the early 1930s.

The novel provides a wealth of information about the Oriental-rug business and changing methods of rug production. British mystery author P. D. James, in a review in *TLS: The Times Literary Supplement,* notes that readers are "agreeably instructed in the production, marketing and cost of antique carpets." With increased industry in their countries, weavers no longer wish to spend their lives at the loom when they can work for good money in an oil field. Who would want to sit, they ask, "hunched over a loom, tying eight hundred knots an hour"? Everett Gabler, who has been taking care of the trust on behalf of the missing aunt, plays an important part in this book. "When Everett called for help, the wolf was not at the door, he was moving into the guest room." When the company agent flies in from Iran, he, too, is poisoned. *Christian Science Monitor* reviewer J. G. Harrison remarked that the novel is distinguished by a "high order of literate writing, and psychology, strong character drawing, trustworthiness of background, and subtle humor."

Double, Double, Oil and Trouble (1978) provides a timely look at the oil business. Having experienced the various gasoline shortages of the 1970s, caused in part by embargoes by oil-producing countries, Latsis and Henissart as Lathen focus on companies looking for new sources of oil. The site to be developed is offshore at Noss Head, Scotland. The Sloan is backing Macklin Company, which appears certain to get the bid from the British Department of Energy because of the work of Davidson Wylie, Macklin's chief negotiator, but Wylie is kidnapped. John Thatcher and Charlie Trinkam carry the ransom money to a bank in Switzerland, and the wait begins. Although Wylie is not released, Macklin does get the contract, and Thatcher and his group begin finalizing the financing. Shortly after Wylie appears, he is murdered, as is his estranged wife. Thatcher sets up a scenario to catch the conspirators involved in the kidnapping and, consequently, in murder.

During the 1980s, only three Lathen novels were written. *Going for the Gold* is set at the 1980 Olympics in Lake Placid. Bradford Withers has been appointed to the International Olympic Committee, and Thatcher is present to oversee Withers and the Sloan branch offices. As usual, chapter titles reflect the action. The first chapter, "Barometer Falling," describes the death of a French ski jumper who is shot, mid flight, by a sniper. In addition to murder, the Sloan is stuck with $500,000 in coun-

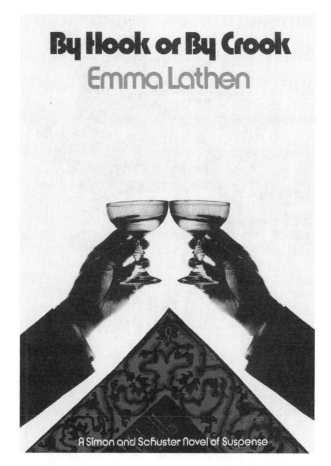

Front cover of Lathen's 1975 novel, in which John Putnam Thatcher investigates a series of murders involving a family's oriental-rug business (Richland County Public Library)

terfeit Euro-checks. The novel goes inside the Olympic village, focusing on several competitors and a variety of activities in addition to the competitions, ranging from meals to discos. Thatcher, at Withers's insistence, finds himself at a disco: "He accepted the need for disco in the modern world. War, pestilence and fever exist. Why not disco." The United States victory over the U.S.S.R. hockey team is not forgotten, as Lathen blends a true event with fiction.

From the thrilling events of Olympic competition, Lathen shifts to the tomato. In *Green Grow the Dollars,* Vandam Nursery and Seed Company, the largest mail-order-nursery business in the world, has developed a blockbuster of a tomato plant that will produce great-tasting tomatoes for six full months. Because of this discovery, Vandam has been purchased by Standard Foods, a Sloan client. Then a small, unheard-of company claims to have discovered the super tomato first and halts the publication of the Vandam annual catalog, an event eagerly awaited across America. Matters come to a head in Chicago during a convention when an employee of

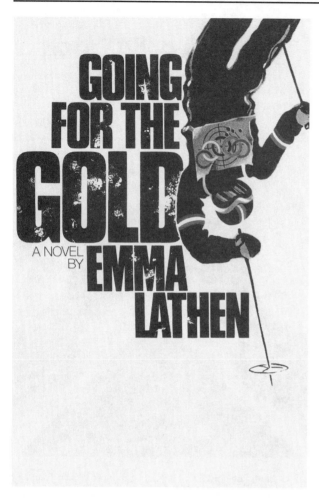

Dust jacket for Lathen's 1981 John Putnam Thatcher mystery,
set at the 1980 Winter Olympics in Lake Placid, New York
(Richland County Public Library)

the "upstart" company is murdered. Thatcher's secretary, Miss Corsa, an avid gardener anxious to receive her Vandam catalog, provokes Thatcher into solving the crime.

After a five-year absence, John Thatcher and the Sloan return in *Something in the Air* (1988), set in Boston and again focusing on a current financial topic. Airline deregulation has spawned Sparrow Flyways, a no-frills airline. The employees are not happy with the proposed expansion of routes to the West Coast and delegate a pilot to be their spokesperson at a meeting with management. The pilot is murdered, and the employees propose a job action: to cancel all flights to and from Pittsburgh the Wednesday before Thanksgiving. Lathen writes, with her typically dry humor, "The Wednesday before Thanksgiving proves that mass evacuation is really possible. Within hours, eighty percent of the population relocates to distant feeding grounds, in a migration with predictable characteristics." The action closes down the

entire east coast. Everett Gabler's accounting reveals the financial motives behind the murder, enabling Eleanor Gough, one of Lathen's strong female characters, an owner, to take charge of the airline. Wendy Wasserstein, Pulitzer Prize–winning playwright, reviewed the novel for *The New York Times,* describing it as "an observant tale of financial and criminal intrigue," but was particularly impressed with the portrayal of a businesswoman and saw the novel as "quite a feminist tale."

As Lathen, Latsis and Henissart collaborated on four novels in the 1990s. They show that time does not stand still in business and finance. In *East Is East* (1991), the Sloan is no longer the third-largest bank in the world, having been nosed out by "some behemoths in Tokyo." Thatcher has traveled to Japan to oversee the activities of Lackawanna, an American company emerging out of bankruptcy and proposing to sell electronics products to Japan. Lackawanna seems about to succeed until a clerk in Japan's Ministry of Trade and Investment is found murdered. Suspected of bribery, the principals of Lackawanna are expelled from Japan. Behind-the-scenes groups are for or against the president of Lackawanna, who has created an economic miracle in restoring the company to financial stability; some want to draft him for president of the United States. Marilyn Stasio, reviewing the novel for *The New York Times,* stated that Lathen "has a wonderful knack for turning the driest, most complicated corporate maneuvers into high drama, and occasionally burlesque."

Typically, Lathen shifts her focus from major financial issues to a smaller concern—in this instance, kitchen appliances. In *Right on the Money* (1993), the plan of ASI, a large manufacturer of water fixtures, to acquire Ecker, a small, family-run company, goes awry when an engineer from ASI is skewered at a trade show. The Sloan is banker for Ecker, and Thatcher works closely with the police, finally solving the murder. *Time* magazine book reviewer William A. Henry III praised Lathen for conveying "the general corporate mindset and the nubby details of an industry."

Brewing Up a Storm (1996) focuses on the beer industry and the problem of teenagers drinking. Kischel Brewery has created a nonalcoholic alternative to its popular beer, Kix. The new drink is named Quax and is sold in nearly identical bottles. No Beer-Buying Youngsters (NOBBY), a group headed by indomitable and abrasive Madeleine Underwood, has sued Kischel as being responsible for the drunk-driving death of a seventeen-year-old. Underwood is murdered after inciting a riot against a fast-food restaurant (the chain is a Sloan client) selling Quax. In addition to the serious issues of suggestive advertising and teenage addictions, Lathen has some fun satirizing the American penchant for gigantic shopping malls. Mohawk Crossing, in upstate New York, starts with the plans by a small Indian reservation for a gambling casino. An entrepreneur increases the scope to "the world's largest shopping center." Lathen notes, "Through some weird process of divination he spied a correlation between acquiring consumer goods and touring the land of Natty Bumpo."

In *A Shark out of Water* (1997), the twenty-fourth Lathen novel, Thatcher is now CEO of the Sloan, "in all but name," and the Sloan is "flourishing." When Walter Bowman, the Sloan's chief of research, alerts Thatcher to the possibility of a massive project to rebuild the Kiel Canal, Thatcher heads for Europe. The action of the novel focuses on the Baltic Area Development Association (BADA), headquartered in Gdansk, and the conflict between development and environmental concerns. Disaster strikes in the form of an unusually severe fog, which backs up shipping through the Kiel Canal, causing collisions, explosions, and loss of life. The canal is shut down. Those in favor of rebuilding the canal see the event as an opportunity, and the Sloan will be involved in the financing. When the chief of staff of BADA, who had publicly announced he had evidence of fraud, is murdered, Thatcher and Everett Gabler, who find the body, start their search for a killer. A second murder forces Thatcher to enlist the help of a Greek shipping magnate whose hobby is creating scenarios for fraud. Using the example of the United States case against Billy Sol Estes, Lathen combines an actual case of fraud with fiction.

On 27 October 1997, Mary Jane Latsis died of a heart attack and stroke in Plymouth, New Hampshire. At the time of her death another novel, using the Persian Gulf War as a backdrop, was 80 percent completed. Although Henissart planned to complete the book, she did not know whether John Thatcher would continue. The novel has not been finished.

Novelist C. P. Snow, in London's *Financial Times,* described Emma Lathen as "probably the best living writer of American detective stories" and suggested reading Lathen books to discover "what working America is like." Lathen has also been called the Agatha Christie of Wall Street. Like Christie's, Lathen's novels are tightly plotted and do not include lengthy descriptions of the murders. Sex is practically nonexistent in the novels. According to the *St. Louis Post Dispatch,* the central character of each novel, John Thatcher, should be placed "permanently and deservedly alongside Nero Wolfe, Philip Marlowe and Sam Spade at the summit of American detective heroes." Lathen won several awards, including

Gold and Silver Daggers from the British Crime Writers Association for *Murder Against the Grain* and *Accounting for Murder* respectively. Lathen was nominated for an Edgar for *When in Greece.* At the 1983 Edgar Awards of the Mystery Writers of America, a new award was introduced in honor of Ellery Queen, to be given whenever the Awards Committee felt such distinction was warranted. The first Ellery Queen Award was presented in May 1983 to Emma Lathen. In 1997 the Agatha Award for Lifetime Achievement was presented to Emma Lathen.

Interviews:

Max Hall, "The Case of the Wall Street Murder Mysteries; an Interview with Emma Lathen," *Harvard Magazine* (July–August 1975); reprinted in *Mount Holyoke Quarterly* (Winter 1977): 15–17;

Margo Miller, "White collar life and a bit of murder; Two women merge their talents as mystery writer Emma Lathen," *Boston Globe,* 20 August 1978, pp. B1, B5;

John C. Carr, "Emma Lathen," in *The Craft of Crime; Conversations with Crime Writers* (Boston: Houghton Mifflin, 1983), pp. 176–201.

References:

Jane S. Bakerman, "A View from Wall Street: Social Criticism in the Mystery Novels of Emma Lathen," *Armchair Detective,* 9 (1976): 213–217;

Bakerman, "Women and Wall Street," *Armchair Detective,* 8 (1974): 36–41;

Jeanne F. Bedell, "Emma Lathen," in *10 Women of Mystery,* edited by Earl F. Bargainnier (Bowling Green, Ohio: Bowling Green State University Popular Press, 1981), pp. 248–267;

David Brownell, "Comic Construction in the Novels of Emma Lathen and R. B. Dominic," *Armchair Detective,* 9 (1976): 91–92;

John G. Cawelti, "Emma Lathen: Murder and Sophistication," *New Republic,* 31 (July 1976): 25–27;

Barbara Lawrence, "Emma Lathen: The Art of Escapist Crime Fiction," *Clues,* 3, no. 2 (Fall–Winter 1982): 76–82;

"Mary Jane Latsis," *Boston Herald,* 2 November 1997, p. 80;

"Masters of White-Collar Homicide," *Forbes* (1 December 1977): 89;

William A. S. Sarjeant, "Crime on Wall Street," *Armchair Detective,* 21, no. 2 (Spring 1998): 128–145;

"Two Lady Writers Make a Killing," *Business Week* (9 May 1970): 48.

Frances Lockridge

(10 January 1896 – 17 February 1963)

Richard Lockridge

(25 September 1898 – 19 June 1982)

Marvin S. Lachman

BOOKS: *How to Adopt a Child,* by Frances Lockridge (New York: New York Children, 1928); revised as *Adopting a Child* (New York: Greenberg, 1948);

Darling of Misfortune: Edwin Booth 1833–1893, by Richard Lockridge (New York: Century, 1932);

Mr. and Mrs. North, by Richard Lockridge (New York: Stokes, 1936; London: Joseph, 1937);

The Norths Meet Murder (New York: Stokes, 1940; London: Joseph, 1940); republished as *Mr. and Mrs. North Meet Murder* (New York: Avon, 1952);

Murder Out of Turn (New York: Stokes, 1941; London: Joseph, 1941);

A Pinch of Poison (New York: Stokes, 1941; London: Hutchinson, 1948);

Death on the Aisle (Philadelphia: Lippincott, 1942; London: Hutchinson, 1948);

Hanged for a Sheep (Philadelphia: Lippincott, 1942; London: Hutchinson, 1944);

Death Takes a Bow (Philadelphia: Lippincott, 1943; London: Hutchinson, 1945);

Killing the Goose (Philadelphia: Lippincott, 1944; London: Hutchinson, 1947);

Payoff for the Banker (Philadelphia: Lippincott, 1945; London: Hutchinson, 1948);

Death in the Mind, by Richard Lockridge and G. H. Estabrooks (New York: Dutton, 1945);

Death of a Tall Man (Philadelphia: Lippincott, 1946; London: Hutchinson, 1949);

Murder within Murder (Philadelphia: Lippincott, 1946; London: Hutchinson, 1949);

Untidy Murder (Philadelphia: Lippincott, 1947; Sydney: Phantom, ca. 1953); republished as *The Case of the Untidy Murder* (New York: Avon, 1950);

Think of Death (Philadelphia: Lippincott, 1947);

Murder Is Served (Philadelphia: Lippincott, 1948; London: Hutchinson, 1950);

I Want to Go Home (Philadelphia: Lippincott, 1948);

The Dishonest Murderer (Philadelphia: Lippincott, 1949; London: Hutchinson, 1951);

Spin Your Web, Lady! (Philadelphia: Lippincott, 1949; London: Hutchinson, 1952);

A Matter of Taste, by Richard Lockridge (Philadelphia: Lippincott, 1949; London: Hutchinson, 1951);

Cats and People (Philadelphia: Lippincott, 1950);

Murder in a Hurry (Philadelphia: Lippincott, 1950; London: Hutchinson, 1952);

Foggy, Foggy Death (Philadelphia: Lippincott, 1950; London: Hutchinson, 1953);

The Proud Cat (Philadelphia: Lippincott, 1951);

Murder Comes First (Philadelphia: Lippincott, 1951);

A Client Is Cancelled (Philadelphia: Lippincott, 1951; London: Hutchinson, 1955);

Dead as a Dinosaur (Philadelphia: Lippincott, 1952; London: Hutchinson, 1956);

Death by Association (Philadelphia: Lippincott, 1952; London: Hutchinson, 1957); republished as *Trial by Terror,* with an introduction by Anthony Boucher (New York: Mercury, 1954);

The Lucky Cat (Philadelphia: Lippincott, 1953);

Death Has a Small Voice (Philadelphia: Lippincott, 1953; London: Hutchinson, 1954);

Stand Up and Die (Philadelphia: Lippincott, 1953; London: Hutchinson, 1955);

Curtain for a Jester (Philadelphia: Lippincott, 1953);

The Nameless Cat (Philadelphia: Lippincott, 1954);

A Key to Death (Philadelphia: Lippincott, 1954);

Death and the Gentle Bull (Philadelphia: Lippincott, 1954; London: Hutchinson, 1956); republished as *Killer in the Straw* (New York: Mercury, 1955);

Frances and Richard Lockridge (photo by Conrad Eiger, from A Key to Death, 1954;
Richland County Public Library)

The Cat Who Rode Cows (Philadelphia: Lippincott, 1955);

Death of an Angel (Philadelphia: Lippincott, 1955; London: Hutchinson, 1957); republished as *Mr. and Mrs. North and the Poisoned Playboy* (New York: Avon, 1957);

Burnt Offering (Philadelphia: Lippincott, 1955); as Francis Richards (London: Hutchinson, 1957);

The Faceless Adversary (Philadelphia: Lippincott, 1956); republished as *Case of the Murdered Redhead* (New York: Avon, 1957);

Let Dead Enough Alone (Philadelphia: Lippincott, 1956); as Richards (London: Hutchinson, 1958);

Voyage into Violence (Philadelphia: Lippincott, 1956; London: Hutchinson, 1959);

Practise to Deceive (Philadelphia: Lippincott, 1957); as Richards (London: Hutchinson, 1959);

The Tangled Cord (Philadelphia: Lippincott, 1957; London: Hutchinson, 1959);

The Long Skeleton (Philadelphia: Lippincott, 1958; London: Hutchinson, 1960);

Accent on Murder (Philadelphia: Lippincott, 1958); as Richards (London: Long, 1960);

Catch as Catch Can (Philadelphia: Lippincott, 1958); as Richards (London: Long, 1960);

The Innocent House (Philadelphia: Lippincott, 1959); as Richards (London: Long, 1961);

Murder and Blueberry Pie (Philadelphia: Lippincott, 1959); republished as *Call It Coincidence,* as Richards (London: Long, 1962);

Murder Is Suggested (Philadelphia: Lippincott, 1959; London: Hutchinson, 1961);

Show Red for Danger (Philadelphia: Lippincott, 1960); as Richards (London: Long, 1961);

The Golden Man (Philadelphia: Lippincott, 1960; London: Hutchinson, 1961);

The Judge Is Reversed (Philadelphia: Lippincott, 1960; London: Hutchinson, 1961);

With One Stone (Philadelphia: Lippincott, 1961); republished as *No Dignity in Death,* as Richards (London: Long, 1962);

The Drill Is Death (Philadelphia: Lippincott, 1961); as Richards (London: Long, 1963);

Murder Has Its Points (Philadelphia: Lippincott, 1961; London: Hutchinson, 1962);

And Left for Dead (Philadelphia: Lippincott, 1962; London: Hutchinson, 1962);

First Come, First Kill (Philadelphia: Lippincott, 1962); as Richards (London: Long, 1963);

Night of Shadows (Philadelphia: Lippincott, 1962); as Richards (London: Long, 1964);

The Ticking Clock (Philadelphia: Lippincott, 1962; London: Hutchinson, 1963);

The Distant Clue (Philadelphia: Lippincott, 1963); as Richards (London: Long, 1964);

Murder by the Book (Philadelphia: Lippincott, 1963; London: Hutchinson, 1964);

The Devious Ones (Philadelphia: Lippincott, 1964); republished as *Four Hours to Fear*, as Richards (London: Long, 1965);

Quest for the Bogeyman (Philadelphia: Lippincott, 1964; London: Hutchinson, 1965);

Murder Can't Wait, by Richard Lockridge (Philadelphia: Lippincott, 1964); as Richards (London: Long, 1965);

The Empty Day, by Richard Lockridge (Philadelphia: Lippincott, 1965);

Squire of Death, by Richard Lockridge (Philadelphia: Lippincott, 1965); as Richards (London: Long, 1966);

Encounter in Key West, by Richard Lockridge (Philadelphia: Lippincott, 1966);

Murder Roundabout, by Richard Lockridge (Philadelphia: Lippincott, 1966); as Richards (London: Long, 1967);

One Lady, Two Cats, by Richard Lockridge (Philadelphia: Lippincott, 1967);

Murder for Art's Sake, by Richard Lockridge (Philadelphia: Lippincott, 1967); as Richards (London: Long, 1968);

With Option to Die, by Richard Lockridge (Philadelphia: Lippincott, 1967); as Richards (London: Long, 1968);

Murder in False-Face, by Richard Lockridge (Philadelphia: Lippincott, 1968; London: Hutchinson, 1969);

A Plate of Red Herrings, by Richard Lockridge (Philadelphia: Lippincott, 1968); as Richards (London: Long, 1969);

Die Laughing, by Richard Lockridge (Philadelphia: Lippincott, 1969); as Richards (London: Long, 1970);

A Risky Way to Kill, by Richard Lockridge (Philadelphia: Lippincott, 1969); as Richards (London: Long 1970);

Troubled Journey, by Richard Lockridge (Philadelphia: Lippincott, 1970; London: Hutchinson, 1971);

Twice Retired, by Richard Lockridge (Philadelphia: Lippincott, 1970; London: Long, 1971);

Inspector's Holiday, by Richard Lockridge (Philadelphia: Lippincott, 1971; London: Long, 1972);

Preach No More, by Richard Lockridge (Philadelphia: Lippincott, 1971; London: Long, 1972);

Death in a Sunny Place, by Richard Lockridge (Philadelphia: Lippincott, 1972; London: Long, 1973);

Something Up a Sleeve, by Richard Lockridge (Philadelphia: Lippincott, 1972; London: Long, 1973);

Write Murder Down, by Richard Lockridge (Philadelphia: Lippincott, 1972; London: Long, 1974);

Not I, Said the Sparrow, by Richard Lockridge (Philadelphia: Lippincott, 1973; London: Long, 1974);

Death on the Hour, by Richard Lockridge (Philadelphia: Lippincott, 1974; London: Long, 1975);

Or Was He Pushed? by Richard Lockridge (Philadelphia: Lippincott, 1975; London: Long, 1976);

Dead Run, by Richard Lockridge (Philadelphia: Lippincott, 1976; London: Long, 1977);

A Streak of Light, by Richard Lockridge (Philadelphia: Lippincott, 1976; London: Long, 1978);

The Tenth Life, by Richard Lockridge (Philadelphia: Lippincott, 1977; London: Long, 1979);

The Old Die Young, by Richard Lockridge (New York: Lippincott & Crowell, 1980; London: Hale, 1981).

Edition and Collection: *Murder! Murder! Murder!* (Philadelphia: Lippincott, 1956)–comprises *The Norths Meet Murder, Murder Out of Turn,* and *A Pinch of Poison;*

Death on the Aisle, introduction by Robert E. Briney (New York: Bantam, 1986).

OTHER: *Murder Cavalcade,* preface by Richard Lockridge (New York: Duell, Sloan & Pearce, 1946); abridged as *Great Murder Stories* (New York & Harmondsworth, U.K.: Penguin, 1948);

Crime for Two, edited by Frances and Richard Lockridge (Philadelphia: Lippincott, 1955; London: Macdonald, 1957);

"Mr. and Mrs. North," by Richard Lockridge, in *The Great Detectives,* edited by Otto Penzler (Boston: Little, Brown, 1978), pp. 155–163;

"Pattern for Murder," in *Detective Duos,* edited by Marcia Muller and Bill Pronzini (New York: Oxford University Press, 1997), pp. 135–148.

SELECTED PERIODICAL PUBLICATIONS–UNCOLLECTED:

FICTION

"Death on a Foggy Morning," *This Week* (1955); republished as "Hit-and-Run," *Ellery Queen's Mystery Magazine,* 34 (July 1959): 106–112;

"Too Early for Murder," *This Week* (1956); republished as "Nobody Can Ask That," *Ellery Queen's Mystery Magazine,* 29 (May 1957): 36–40;

"The Cat and the Killer," *This Week* (1956); republished as "The Searching Cats," *Ellery Queen's Mystery Magazine,* 31 (February 1958): 40–46;

"Boy Kidnapped," *This Week* (1957); republished as "Dead Boys Don't Remember," *Ellery Queen's Mystery Magazine,* 32 (July 1958): 49–55;

"Murder by the Clock," *This Week* (1957); republished as "If They Give Him Time," *Ellery Queen's Mystery Magazine,* 35 (February 1960): 48–54;

"Death and the Fiery-Eyed Cat," *This Week* (1958); republished as "Cat of Dreams," *Ellery Queen's Mystery Magazine,* 35 (May 1960): 104–111;

"All Men Make Mistakes," *Ellery Queen's Mystery Magazine,* 32 (November 1958): 32–37;

"Allergic to Murder," *This Week* (1959); republished as "The Accusing Smoke," *Ellery Queen's Mystery Magazine,* 38 (August 1961): 18–25;

"Captain Heimrich Stumbles," *Ellery Queen's Mystery Magazine,* 34 (November 1959): 22–28;

"The Scent of Murder," *Ellery Queen's Mystery Magazine,* 36 (August 1960): 5–9;

"A Winter's Tale," *Ellery Queen's Mystery Magazine,* 37 (February 1961): 5–13;

"Flair for Murder," *Ellery Queen's Mystery Magazine,* 46 (October 1965): 6–13.

NONFICTION

"The Nathan Phenomenon," by Richard Lockridge, *Saturday Review of Literature,* 25 (24 January 1942): 12–13;

"Some Like It Crude; Some Like It Subtle," by Richard Lockridge, *Writer,* 74 (October 1961): 10.

Though Dashiell Hammett's Nick and Nora Charles came first, Frances and Richard Lockridge were most responsible for the popularity in the 1940s and 1950s of a subgenre of mystery fiction in which a husband and wife are series characters. Their Mr. and Mrs. North series went beyond print to success on the stage, screen, radio, and television. Prolific writers, they created other series characters and a fictional universe in which their sleuths often intersected. The Norths' world was centered in an orderly, middle-class New York City that their creators turned into an American version of the British village–the prototypical closed society of the mysteries of Agatha Christie and other Golden Age writers. The popularity of the Lockridges with readers was equaled by the esteem of most influential critics of their day.

Frances Louise Davis was born on 10 January 1896 in Kansas City, Missouri, the daughter of Laura Saunders Hunt Davis and William Wynn Davis. She attended the University of Kansas at Lawrence but did not graduate

and was a reporter, feature writer, and music critic for the *Kansas City Post* from 1918 to 1922. Richard Orson Lockridge was born on 25 September 1898 in St. Joseph, Missouri, to Mary Olive Notson Lockridge and Ralph David Lockridge. He attended Kansas City Junior College from 1916 to 1918, then served one year as a seaman in the U.S. Navy, mostly aboard the *USS North Dakota* at the Brooklyn Navy Yard. After the war, Richard attended the University of Missouri at Columbia in 1920 but did not earn a degree. While working for the *Kansas City Kansan* and then the *Kansas City Star,* he met fellow journalist Davis. The couple were married on 4 March 1922 and soon left for New York City.

In an October 1961 article for *Writer,* Richard Lockridge said, "We were, I guess, typical of youngish people who came to New York in the twenties, and lived in the Village and scrambled for a living with typewriters." They lived in a Greenwich Village studio apartment that had no refrigerator. Frances wrote publicity for the New York State Charities Aid Association, eventually becoming assistant secretary of that organization, with which she was associated from 1922 through 1943. She used her experience to write *How to Adopt a Child* (1928). Richard became a reporter for the *New York Sun* in 1923. Before being hired, he published humorous sketches for the paper about the survival efforts of an unnamed New York couple, clearly based on the Lockridges, whom he called "Babes in the Studio." As a reporter for the *Sun,* his assignments included covering some of the best-known criminal trials of the 1920s. He also worked as a "rewrite man" and had a reputation for being one of the fastest in the business.

In 1928 Richard became drama critic for the *Sun.* As his interest in theater heightened, he began research into the life of the most famous American actor of the nineteenth century, publishing *Darling of Misfortune: Edwin Booth 1833–1893* in 1932. It received favorable reviews, with H. I. Brock in *The New York Times* (11 September 1932) calling it the best book written about Booth.

In 1932 Richard, building on his earlier newspaper sketches, created Mr. and Mrs. North in a series of vignettes for *The New Yorker.* The characters, who had no first names, were again based on the Lockridges and episodes from their marriage. Though these sketches were virtually plotless, they proved popular with readers who enjoyed the humor and identified with the Lockridges' insights into marriage. In 1936 they were collected and published as *Mr. and Mrs. North,* though, to the annoyance of Lockridge, the book was promoted as a novel. In his 20 September 1936 *New York Times* review, E. H. Walton suggested readers expecting a novel would be disappointed, whereas "The secret of the Norths' charm is that they are not entangled in plot."

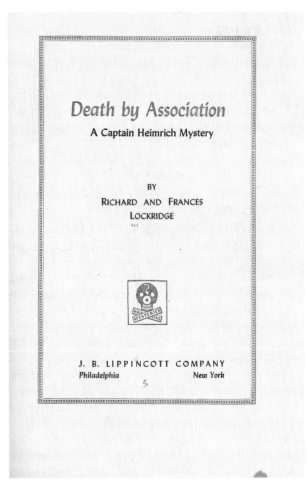

Death by Association

A Captain Heimrich Mystery

BY
RICHARD AND FRANCES
LOCKRIDGE

J. B. LIPPINCOTT COMPANY
Philadelphia   New York

Title page for the Lockridges' 1952 mystery featuring Captain Merton Heimrich of the New York State Police, whom they introduced in their 1947 novel Think of Death *(Richland County Public Library)*

The Lockridges had been inveterate mystery readers when Frances decided, in 1939, to write a mystery novel herself. She became bogged down and turned to Richard for help, thus beginning the collaborative pattern that served them throughout their career. Richard quoted Frances's summary of their writing process in *The Great Detectives* (1978): "I think up interesting characters and Dick kills them off." Frances devised plots and characters that they discussed together and prepared outlines, from which Richard wrote the books.

The result of their first writing partnership was *The Norths Meet Murder,* published in January 1940. The protagonists were named Pamela and Gerald "Jerry" North. He is a publisher, and she is a homemaker who is active in charitable work. The novel was an immediate success, going into five printings in hardcover. The formula that led to the success of the series was established in this book and retained, with few changes, for twenty-five additional titles.

A feature of the series is the Norths' habit of stumbling over bodies. In their initial outing, Pam plans to hold a party and rents a vacant studio in the Greenwich Village apartment building in which they live. They visit the studio and find a corpse in the bathtub. The policemen who investigate become important characters in the series. They are Homicide Lieutenant (later Captain) Bill Weigand, who becomes a close friend of the Norths. His assistant, Detective (later Sergeant) Aloysius Mullins, also likes them, though he constantly complains that the cases in which they are involved are "screwy." Also on hand is Pete, the first of the Norths' cats, all based on cats the Lockridges owned. In a prefatory disclaimer, the Lockridges demonstrate their attitude toward cats: "With the exception of Pete, the characters in this novel are fictional and have no counterparts in life. Pete is real; the authors live in his house."

Weigand, unlike other police friends of amateur sleuths, does a great deal of the detecting. He respects Pam's hunches and is better than anyone else at understanding "Pamese," the elliptical language she speaks. (Jerry North's reaction is to run his fingers through his hair in exasperation.) For example, referring to people having acquaintances in common, Pam says, "People overlap." In *The Dishonest Murderer* (1949) she refers to a conniver "not letting her face show what her right hand's doing." In *Death Takes a Bow* (1943), she calls grown-ups "children who have begun to wear out." Regarding her intuitive approach to solving crimes, Pam says in *Murder Is Served* (1948), "Logic is wrong . . . if it's too logical."

With Weigand's consent, Pam holds a "suspects party" in *The Norths Meet Murder,* at which she discovers the murderer's identity. Her facial expression reveals that she knows, and she is barely rescued from the murderer's clutches by Mullins. Weigand, independently, has arrived at the same solution. During the series, Pam and Weigand often separately arrive at the correct solution, she by intuition, he by police procedures.

On 12 January 1941 *The Norths Meet Murder,* dramatized by Owen Davis, opened on Broadway as *Mr. and Mrs. North,* with Peggy Conklin and Albert Hackett as Pam and Jerry, along with Philip Ober as Weigand and Millard Mitchell as Mullins. It had a successful run of 163 performances and was selected by Burns Mantle as one of the ten best plays of the 1940–1941 season. M-G-M bought the rights and made a movie of it in 1941, with Gracie Allen and William Post Jr. as Pam and Jerry. Paul Kelly was Weigand, and Mitchell again played Mullins. Also in 1941 *Mr. and Mrs. North* became a popular radio show. It lasted thirteen years, with various actors in the main roles. The Lockridges won a Mystery Writers of America Edgar Award for one of the few scripts they wrote themselves for this series in 1945. A television series, with Barbara Britton and Richard Denning as the Norths, played from 1952 through 1954.

Though most of the North books are set in Manhattan, the second, *Murder Out of Turn* (1941), begins at the Norths' vacation cottage in Putnam County, New York. Weigand visits, and a murder occurs. Lockridge's description of Weigand's response to the murder is an example of the succinct language he uses to convey character: "Weigand was a man on vacation in the country when he knelt beside the body, but he was a policeman when he stood up." In this book Weigand meets Dorian Hunt, who becomes an important part of the series as the future Mrs. Weigand. *Murder Out of Turn,* like most Lockridge books, has a suspenseful ending. In this case, there is a car chase—one of the earlier ones in crime fiction, before they became clichés—after the killer, who has kidnapped Dorian. After Weigand rescues her, they realize that, despite their early antagonism because of her suspicion of the use of police authority, they really care for each other.

The Norths regularly drink and eat with the Weigands, first at Charles Restaurant in Greenwich Village and later at the Hotel Algonquin. The Lockridges' indulgent attitude toward social drinking is clearly conveyed as both Norths claim they drive better after a cocktail. Alcohol is regarded as almost medicinal. For instance, Weigand, tired and in a bad mood, perks up in *Murder Out of Turn* after a martini. "The bartender . . . smiled and was clearly pleased with Weigand's progress. The bartender was a physician, surveying convalescence."

A Pinch of Poison (1941) and *Death on the Aisle* (1942), the third and fourth of the North books, were early examples of the authors incorporating their backgrounds into the plots. The former is about the poisoning of a woman who works as a volunteer in an adoption agency. The latter has a theatrical background and involves the murder of an "angel," the theatrical term for the financial backer for a show. Weigand attends a well-described rehearsal in order to check on the timing of the killing and becomes so enthralled by the play that he almost forgets the murder.

Richard served as the drama critic for the *New York Sun* until 1942, when the forty-four-year-old returned to the U.S. Navy as a lieutenant, serving as a public relations officer. He spent most of his time at navy headquarters in New York, so the Lockridges were not forced to abandon the Norths during World War II, though they published fewer books than previously.

The aspect of the North series most criticized was the recurring device of placing Pam in danger at the end of an adventure. For example, in *Death on the Aisle,* her habit of talking out loud while speculating about the murder makes the killer think she knows the truth. Jerry is along on her detecting adventures in the early books and often rescues her when he is not the one in danger. In the fifth North novel, *Hanged for a Sheep* (1942), the climax

takes place in the dark, with Pam pursued by the killer and Jerry trying to find her. Pam mistakenly hits her husband on the head with a vase. Howard Haycraft wrote in *Ellery Queen's Mystery Magazine* (April 1946), "Someday . . . I'd like to read a North story in which Mrs. N. does *not* wander alone and unprotected into the murderer's parlor in the last chapter."

Other North novels of the 1940s are *Killing the Goose* (1944), *Payoff for the Banker* (1945), *Death of a Tall Man* (1946), *Murder within Murder* (1946), *Untidy Murder* (1947), and *The Dishonest Murderer*. In them the friendship between the Norths and the Weigands deepens, and in *Murder within Murder* Weigand is willing to risk his job to protect Pam when he thinks she is unfairly considered a suspect.

Despite the success of the North series, Richard was anxious to experiment. In 1945, with psychology professor G. H. Estabrooks, he published *Death in the Mind,* an espionage thriller about Nazis in the United States in 1942. The anonymous reviewer for *The New Yorker* (25 August 1945) found it exciting, but most other critics were unimpressed. Will Cuppy, in *The New York Times Book Review* (26 August 1945), informed readers that there were "so many foreign agents popping up in disguise that you haven't a chance of keeping them straight."

In *Think of Death* (1947) the Lockridges introduced a new series character, Captain Heimrich of the New York State Police, who appears in sixteen books co-authored by the couple, plus another eight written by Richard alone after Frances died. Heimrich is described in *Accent on Murder* (1958) as "a solid man with a square face—a face which appeared to have been carved from some dark wood." Early in his career he is a lonely man, first living in police barracks and then in a suburban hotel room. He seldom speaks more than he has to, making him seem less articulate than Bill Weigand. He is stationed in Putnam County, and his cases are usually set there or in neighboring Westchester—an area the Lockridges knew well because they maintained a home there, near the Connecticut border. Without the emphasis on Pam and her idiosyncrasies, there is more room for character development in this series. The frequent presence of young lovers in danger turns many Heimrich books into highly suspenseful romantic thrillers.

Making Heimrich a series character might well have been an afterthought. The viewpoint in *Think of Death* is that of Martin Brooks, a former Office of Strategic Services major, now a lawyer, called to the suburban home of his former wife, Ann, and her second husband. The victim in the first of two murders is her new husband, and the possibility that love between Martin and Ann has been rekindled makes them prime suspects. Heimrich is known as Captain P. T. Heimrich in this book, and he does not even solve the murders. In fact, he is about to arrest the wrong person when good guesswork by Brooks solves the mystery, with Heimrich fortunately present.

Think of Death received outstanding reviews. Isaac Anderson in *The New York Times* (30 March 1947) said, "Seldom have we read a detective story so expertly integrated or with characters so skillfully portrayed." In the *San Francisco Chronicle* (13 April 1947), Anthony Boucher mentioned "Full-bodied characters and a convincingly delicate sense of the impact of murder." Jacques Barzun and Wendell Hertig Taylor, in *A Catalogue of Crime* (1989), thought this book the best of all the Lockridges' books.

Heimrich returns as Captain Merton Heimrich in *I Want to Go Home* (1948), in which he proves to be a better detective. The new first name appears to have been used to inject humor into the series, since Heimrich is annoyed when people use it. The Lockridges also gave him mannerisms that proved annoying to reviewers. Heimrich has a habit of closing his eyes while he interrogates suspects. He also has distracting speech patterns.

Heimrich became almost as popular as the Norths, and most years the Lockridges alternated North and Heimrich books, though their prolificity and popularity allowed them to publish more than two books in many years. In 1949, *A Matter of Taste,* the third Lockridge novel of that year, was a solo effort by Richard that delves into abnormal psychology. It tells of a middle-aged epicure whose only motive for committing murder is to enjoy the sensation of it.

During the 1950s the Lockridges averaged almost three books a year, publishing ten novels about the Norths, nine featuring Heimrich, and one, *The Tangled Cord* (1957), in which Weigand appears without the Norths, though he is teamed with Nathan Shapiro, a New York City police detective the Lockridges introduced in *The Faceless Adversary* (1956). Shapiro had another solo novel in 1959, *Murder and Blueberry Pie.* They also published two nonseries mysteries, books about cats, and short stories for *This Week.*

During the early 1950s the Lockridges published several books about cats. *Cats and People* (1950) is a nonfiction work based on the Lockridges' three Siamese cats, Martini, Gin, and Sherry—they also appear in the North books—and was an anecdotal history and guide to the relationships between cats and people. Four later books, *The Proud Cat* (1951), *The Lucky Cat* (1953), *The Nameless Cat* (1954), and *The Cat Who Rode Cows* (1955), were children's fiction.

The Lockridges often tried to vary the backgrounds of their novels. *Dead as a Dinosaur* (1952) is about paleontology and, with typically subtle humor, comments about financing an expedition: "Ancient bones are most readily uncovered by modern dollars." It concludes with what Boucher described in *The New York Times Book Review* (25 May 1952) as "a strange elaborate chase scene in a

dark museum which keeps verging on farce while remaining strictly chilling." *Curtain for a Jester* (1953), about the murder of a cruel practical joker, has a similarly wild ending, with the suspects appearing at a Long Island novelty factory.

In *Death Has a Small Voice* (1953) Pam is endangered for virtually the entire book. She is kidnapped by a killer because she receives a recording that she thinks is from Jerry but is actually of a murder taking place. Much of the book is about her efforts to escape and those of Jerry and Weigand to find her. In the book section of the *New York Herald Tribune* (31 May 1953) James Sandoe wrote: "as a thriller . . . it is especially commendable for the ingenuity of its postponements and the feverish sustenance of its fear."

Death of an Angel (1955) returns the Norths to the milieu that Richard Lockridge knew best, the Broadway theater. It was one of their best books, featuring what an unsigned review in *The New Yorker* of 19 March 1955 called "the humor and literacy that makes them almost unique." In *Voyage into Violence* (1956), the Norths and the Weigands take a cruise ship to the Caribbean. When a private detective onboard is murdered, Weigand agrees to spend part of his vacation investigating. Pam tries to help and trails a suspect from the ship in Havana, but because of her unfamiliarity with the city she has to rely on the suspect as her guide. Other North novels of the 1950s are *Murder in a Hurry* (1950), *Murder Comes First* (1951), *A Key to Death* (1954), *The Long Skeleton* (1958), and *Murder Is Suggested* (1959).

Heimrich's forte is as a catalyst, gathering the suspects at the end and applying pressure until one says or does something that leads to the killer revealing guilt. This process often confirms suspicions he has but for which he has insufficient evidence. In *Death by Association* (1952), he says, typically, "The point is to have the character fit the crime." While he makes use of physical evidence in this book and others, he more often solves cases by empathy, "the ability to absorb somebody else's mind and use it to think with." Boucher gave an especially astute and balanced evaluation of Heimrich in his introduction to *Trial by Error,* the paperback reprint of Death by Association: "if he indulges to excess in the habit of beginning sentences with 'Now . . .' and ending them with '. . . naturally'—well, putting up with such tics is a small price to pay for his astute thinking, his adroit analysis of evidence, his acute perception of the fact that all crimes have their root in character."

The Lockridges featured Heimrich in other novels of the 1950s: *Foggy, Foggy Death* (1950), *A Client Is Cancelled* (1951), *Stand Up and Die* (1953), *Death and the Gentle Bull* (1954), *Let Dead Enough Alone* (1956), *Practise to Deceive* (1957), and *Accent on Murder.* They reduced the character's verbal tics and gave him more depth, beginning in *Burnt*

Offering (1955) with the introduction of Susan Faye, a widow and young mother whom he courts and later marries after a romance that extends through several books. Reviewing *Show Red for Danger* (1960) in *The New York Times Book Review* (21 February 1960), Boucher praised the Lockridges' handling of what he called the always tricky problem of the series detective in love.

Beginning in the mid 1950s, the Lockridges also wrote crime short stories. Eight were published in *This Week* and reprinted in *Ellery Queen's Mystery Magazine*. Another five were written originally for the latter periodical. Twelve of these stories are about Heimrich, and while they are too short to be complex mysteries, they are strong on suburban details such as gardening. The most compelling, about the kidnapping of a ten-year-old after he gets off a school bus, is "Boy Kidnapped" (*This Week*, 1957), reprinted in *Ellery Queen's Mystery Magazine* as "Dead Boys Don't Remember" in July 1958.

The longest—and arguably the best—Lockridge short story is the only one they wrote about the Norths: "There's Death for Remembrance," first published in 1955 and republished as "Pattern for Murder" in *Ellery Queen's Mystery Magazine* (October 1957). It was also included under the latter title in Marcia Muller and Bill Pronzini's 1997 anthology, *Detective Duos*. It begins with the type of opening sentence Richard Lockridge often used to capture readers' attention: "Fern Hartley came to New York to die, although that was far from her intention." Pam and Jerry attend an informal reunion of her Midwestern high-school classmates who are now in New York, and one is murdered. Searching for the crucial clue in the case, she says in typical "Pamese," "It's on the tip of my mind."

In *The Faceless Adversary* the Lockridges introduced another new series character, Nathan Shapiro, who appears in ten subsequent books. Shapiro is described as tall, thin, and rumpled in appearance. He is a New York police detective who is best remembered for his inferiority complex; he frequently claims he is not up to the assignments he is given. In his first case he has a minor but important role. As in many non-North stories, the official detective is not introduced until after the reader has had the opportunity to identify with a young couple in love. In *The Faceless Adversary* the happiness of John Hayward and his fiancée, Barbara Phillips, is dashed on the night of their engagement when Hayward becomes a murder suspect. The victim was a woman Hayward claims he never knew. Shapiro's superiors are sure of Hayward's guilt, but he retains an open mind, leading a fellow detective to deride him as "Benefit-of-the-doubt Shapiro." The detective work he does is minimal, consisting mainly of following suspects. Though he does not know who is guilty, he appears in time when Hayward confronts the killer.

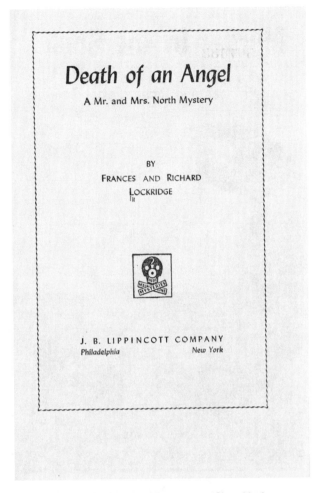

Title page for the Lockridges' 1955 Pam and Jerry North mystery, set in the Broadway milieu familiar to Richard Lockridge from his years as drama critic for the New York Sun *(Richland County Public Library)*

In *The Tangled Cord* Weigand has his only case without the Norths, and it was generally greeted without enthusiasm. Even Boucher, perhaps the greatest fan of the Lockridges, said in *The New York Times Book Review* (5 May 1957) that it was written "with all the professional ease one expects of the Lockridges, but one sees no compelling reason for it having been written at all."

Catch as Catch Can, the third book the Lockridges published in 1958 and the first nonseries suspense thriller they wrote together, concerns an international spy ring. They wrote three other nonseries thrillers: *The Innocent House* (1959), *The Golden Man* (1960), and *The Ticking Clock* (1962). Alone, Richard wrote three more after the death of Frances. In these books, the protagonist is generally a young woman in danger, but one who shows more intelligence than the heroines of typical romantic thrillers.

Frances Lockridge died at the age of sixty-seven, on 17 February 1963, shortly after the Lockridges celebrated

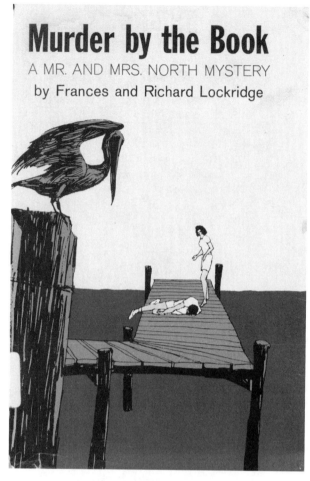

*Dust jacket for the last of the Lockridges' Pam and Jerry
North mysteries, published in 1963, the year of Frances
Lockridge's death (Richland County Public Library)*

the publication of their fiftieth mystery. During the early
years of the decade she worked on twelve books with
Richard, four of which were published posthumously. In
two 1960s books they created new series characters, Paul
Lane and Bernie Simmons. Another was the final book in
the North series, *Murder by the Book* (1963). Richard wrote
no additional North books, saying in an October 1978
interview in *The Armchair Detective*, "I couldn't write Mrs.
North after Frances died. Frances was to a considerable
degree Mrs. North." He published twelve books in the
1960s under his own name.

Lane, another New York police detective, is introduced in *Night of Shadows* (1962). Evans Parten meets Alison Kent, whom he has not seen for years. Before they
can renew their friendship, she is kidnapped. Parten has
trouble convincing the police (including Lane) of what
has happened, so he turns detective himself and finds Alison is innocently involved with a Latin American dictator
and the political exiles who oppose him. Lane, the bland-
est of all Lockridge series characters, plays a minor role.

He returns in *Quest for the Bogeyman* (1964), where his
work is overshadowed by Eleanor Howell, a cat-owning
social worker for an adoption agency, then disappears
from the Lockridge canon except for occasional cameo
appearances, as in *Murder in False-Face* (1968).

A more successful series character, Bernie Simmons, an assistant district attorney in Manhattan, also
makes his debut in 1962, in *And Left for Dead*. He eventually appears in seven novels. An especially strong Simmons book is *The Devious Ones* (1964), the second in the
series. Though Simmons is important to the novel, it is
about Loren Hartley, the typical Lockridge heroine in
danger through no fault of her own. Loren meets a high-
school chum who drugs her. She awakens in the middle
of Manhattan, in Bryant Park, with no memory of the
previous four hours of her life. Her uncle was murdered
during the hours she lost, and, as his only heir, she is suspected.

In addition to Simmons, Shapiro plays a lesser, but
important, part in *The Devious Ones*. Heimrich is also mentioned, since part of the action takes place in Putnam
County as well as in Connecticut at Loren's family home.
Simmons goes there to question her, and, feeling herself
to be the hostess, she wonders, "What do you offer quiet
men who have come to arrest you for murder?" Additional books with Simmons are *Squire of Death* (1965), *A
Plate of Red Herrings* (1968), *Twice Retired* (1970), *Something
Up a Sleeve* (1972), and *Death on the Hour* (1974).

One of the strengths of the Lockridges' books is the
way their many series characters interact, stepping into
each other's series and each time in the process adding a
little more depth to themselves. According to Richard, he
deliberately did not describe his characters in great detail,
allowing readers to imagine for themselves their appearance.

Richard continued to write prolifically in the years
following Frances's death, publishing twenty-one books
between 1964 and 1974. Two, *The Empty Day* (1965) and
Encounter in Key West (1966), were not crime novels, and
neither attracted praise, though the former was applauded
for Lockridge's authentic use of newspaper background.
Lockridge admitted to feeling depressed after Frances's
death, and he conceded that a feeling of the "uselessness
of living" was present in *The Empty Day*.

In 1965 Lockridge married Hildegarde Dolson, a
writer who had written novels and nonfiction, but no
mysteries. She helped Lockridge with *One Lady, Two Cats*
(1967), his nonfiction book about their marriage and her
introduction to Siamese cats. She also turned to writing
mysteries, publishing four in the 1970s.

One of the best of Lockridge's nonseries suspense
thrillers is *Murder in False-Face*. In it Joan Mead, a Manhattan attorney, goes to Connecticut to visit her wealthy
aunt. She finds the aunt murdered and becomes the lead-

ing suspect—she inherits under her will—because the police will not believe her story about a stranger who has a face that looks "as if it could be taken off and put back on again." The plot is more appropriate to a shorter work, but several exciting chases make the novel especially suspenseful.

Richard and Frances Lockridge were politically liberal, inserting criticisms of McCarthyism in some of their 1950s books. In a similar spirit, Richard's *With Option to Die* (1967) is about the racial conflicts that result from African Americans attempting to buy homes in suburbia. Reviewing the novel favorably in *The New York Times Book Review* (29 October 1967), Boucher said that Lockridge "deals more acutely and perceptively with our interracial problems than a large number of Serious Writers."

Reviews of Lockridge's solo writing continued to be generally favorable, though critics increasingly found faults, especially noting predictability and a lack of complexity in plotting. Reviewing *A Risky Way to Kill* (1969), one of several books Lockridge wrote about practical jokers, in *The New York Times Book Review* (12 October 1969), Allen J. Hubin said: "The resulting case can hardly be described as baffling—but it is agreeably fleshed out with sharply observed detail." In *Inspector's Holiday* (1971) Heimrich and his wife take a Mediterranean cruise, making a ship the setting for murder as the Lockridges had done for the Norths in *Voyage into Violence*. Newgate Calendar, in *The New York Times Book Review* (11 July 1971), wrote: "There are no surprises here. Lockridge is not going to disturb a winning formula. But his book, like all his others, is easy to read, gracefully written, a lot of fun."

Lockridge and his wife moved to North Carolina around 1970. His only mystery set there—the nonseries *Death in a Sunny Place* (1972), about a murder at a country club—drew the poorest reviews he received for his crime fiction, with Callendar in *The New York Times Book Review* (30 January 1972) judging the story "limp and predictable," and Barzun and Taylor, in *A Catalogue of Crime*, calling it "absolute drivel."

Lockridge found renewed approval when he returned to his series characters and their New York City and suburban settings. In *1001 Midnights* (1984) Karol Kay Hope praises a Simmons book, *Death on the Hour* (1974), and writes of *Dead Run* (1976), a Heimrich mystery: "This is an easygoing small-town story with good characterization and with images of the countryside that are so well drawn they will stay with you for a long time." Writing in *The Mystery Fancier* (January 1977), Steve Lewis thought that *Dead Run* was "quite comfortable" and likened reading it to relaxing with old friends.

Having suffered a stroke in the early 1970s, Lockridge was confined to a wheelchair and wrote less than previously. In the last decade of his life he published only seven books. Hildegarde Dolson died on 15 January 1981, and Lockridge died the following year, in Tryon, North Carolina, on 19 June 1982. He was eighty-three years old.

Two separate attempts to reprint Frances and Richard Lockridge's Mr. and Mrs. North books in paperback, in the 1980s and 1990s, were not successful. The combination of mystery puzzle and sophisticated comedy of manners in the Lockridge books, and their New York City settings, perhaps no longer resonated with younger readers. Yet, those same elements have ensured their continued popularity with readers who appreciate what Boucher called "that wonderful effortless readability which is the Lockridges' trademark."

Interview:

Chris and Janie Filstrup, "An Interview with Richard Lockridge," *Armchair Detective,* 11 (October 1978): 382–393.

References:

Gail Adams, "Double Jeopardy: Husband and Wife Teams in Detective Fiction," *Armchair Detective,* 8 (August 1975): 251–256;

R. Jeff Banks, "Mr. and Mrs. North," *Armchair Detective,* 9 (June 1976): 182–183;

Jane Merrill Filstrup, "Cats in Mysteries," *Armchair Detective,* 11 (January 1978): 58–62; (April 1978): 134–138;

Filstrup, "Murder for Two: Richard Lockridge," *New Republic,* 22 (July 1978): 35–38;

Frederick Isaac, "Looking Glass Detection: The Norths and Bill Weigand Speak," *Mystery Fancier,* 8 (September–October 1986): 18–22;

Isaac, "Out on a Spree: Lockridges, Norths and Others," *Mystery Readers Journal,* 14 (Spring 1998): 3–4;

Steve Lewis, "Mystery Dial IV: Mr. and Mrs. North," *Poisoned Pen,* 2 (July–August 1979): 25–26;

William A. S. Sarjeant, "Crime Novelists as Writers of Children's Fiction XXIV: Frances and Richard Lockridge," *Crime and Detective Stories,* no. 38 (November 2000): 29–31;

Carolyn Wheat, "The First Felines of Mystery," *Mystery Readers Journal,* 14 (Winter 1998–1999): 3–5;

Dilys Winn, "Till Death Do Us Part: Nick & Nora, Pam & Jerry, Tommy & Tuppence," in her *Murderess Ink: The Better Half of the Mystery* (New York: Workman, 1979), pp. 136–138.

Dennis Lynds
(Michael Collins)
(15 January 1924 –)

Ward B. Lewis
University of Georgia

See also the article by Lynds in the *Dictionary of Literary Biography Yearbook: 1985*.

BOOKS: *Combat Soldier* (New York: New American Library, 1962);

Uptown Downtown (New York: New American Library, 1963);

The Shadow Strikes, as Maxwell Grant (New York: Belmont Books, 1964);

Cry Shadow! as Grant (New York: Belmont Books, 1965);

Shadow Beware, as Grant (New York: Belmont Books, 1965);

The Shadow's Revenge, as Grant (New York: Belmont Books, 1965);

Mark of the Shadow, as Grant (New York: Belmont Books, 1966);

Shadow–Go Mad! as Grant (New York: Belmont Books, 1966);

The Night of the Shadow, as Grant (New York: Belmont Books, 1966);

Act of Fear, as Michael Collins (New York: Dodd, Mead, 1967; London: Joseph, 1968);

The Shadow–Destination: Moon, as Grant (New York: Belmont Books, 1967);

A Dark Power, as William Arden (New York: Dodd, Mead, 1968; London: Hale, 1970);

The Mystery of the Moaning Cave, as Arden, Alfred Hitchcock and the Three Investigators series (New York: Random House, 1968; London: Collins, 1969);

Deal in Violence, as Arden (New York: Dodd, Mead, 1969; London: Hale, 1971);

Lukan War, as Collins (New York: Belmont Books, 1969);

The Brass Rainbow, as Collins (New York: Dodd, Mead, 1969; London: Joseph, 1970);

The Mystery of the Laughing Shadow, as Arden, Alfred Hitchcock and the Three Investigators series (New York: Random House, 1969; London: Collins, 1970);

Night of the Toads, as Collins (New York: Dodd, Mead, 1970; London: Hale, 1972);

The Falling Man, as Mark Sadler (New York: Random House, 1970);

The Planets of Death, as Collins (New York: Berkley, 1970);

The Secret of the Crooked Cat, as Arden, Alfred Hitchcock and the Three Investigators series (New York: Random House, 1970; London: Collins, 1971);

Here to Die, as Sadler (New York: Random House, 1971);

The Goliath Scheme, as Arden (New York: Dodd, Mead, 1971; London: Hale, 1973);

Walk a Black Wind, as Collins (New York: Dodd, Mead, 1971; London: Hale, 1973);

Another Way to Die, as John Crowe (New York: Random House, 1972);

A Touch of Darkness, as Crowe (New York: Random House, 1972);

Die to a Distant Drum, as Arden (New York: Dodd, Mead, 1972); republished as *Murder Underground* (London: Hale, 1974);

Mirror Image, as Sadler (New York: Random House, 1972);

Shadow of a Tiger, as Collins (New York: Dodd, Mead, 1972; London: Hale, 1974);

The Mystery of the Shrinking House, as Arden, Alfred Hitchcock and the Three Investigators series (New York: Random House, 1972; London: Collins, 1973);

Circle of Fire, as Sadler (New York: Random House, 1973);

Deadly Legacy, as Arden (New York: Dodd, Mead, 1973; London: Hale, 1974);

The Mystery of the Blue Condor, as Arden (Lexington, Mass.: Ginn, 1973);

Dennis Lynds (photograph © by Christopher Gardner; from the dust jacket of Cassandra in Red, *1992; Richland County Public Library)*

The Secret of Phantom Lake, as Arden, Alfred Hitchcock and the Three Investigators series (New York: Random House, 1973; London: Collins, 1974);

The Silent Scream, as Collins (New York: Dodd, Mead, 1973; London: Hale, 1975);

Woman in Marble, as Carl Dekker (Indianapolis: Bobbs-Merrill, 1973);

Bloodwater, as Crowe (New York: Dodd, Mead, 1974);

Charlie Chan Returns (New York: Bantam, 1974);

The Mystery of the Dead Man's Riddle, as Arden, Alfred Hitchcock and the Three Investigators series (New York: Random House, 1974; London: Collins, 1975);

The N3 Conspiracy, as Nick Carter (New York: Award, 1974);

Blue Death, as Collins (New York: Dodd, Mead, 1975; London: Hale, 1976);

Crooked Shadows, as Crowe (New York: Dodd, Mead, 1975);

S.W.A.T.–Crossfire (New York: Pocket Books, 1975);

The Blood-Red Dream, as Collins (New York: Dodd, Mead, 1976; London: Hale, 1977);

The Green Wolf Connection, as Carter (New York: Award, 1976);

The Mystery of the Dancing Devil, as Arden, Alfred Hitchcock and the Three Investigators series (New York: Random House, 1976; London: Collins, 1977);

Triple Cross, as Carter (New York: Award, 1976);

The Mystery of the Headless Horse, as Arden, Alfred Hitchcock and the Three Investigators series (New York: Random House, 1977; London: Collins, 1978);

When They Kill Your Wife, as Crowe (New York: Dodd, Mead, 1977);

The Mystery of the Deadly Double, as Arden, Alfred Hitchcock and the Three Investigators series (New York: Random House, 1978; London: Collins, 1979);

The Nightrunners, as Collins (New York: Dodd, Mead, 1978; London: Hale, 1979);

Close to Death, as Crowe (New York: Dodd, Mead, 1979; London: Hale, 1983);

The Secret of the Shark Reef, as Arden, Alfred Hitchcock and the Three Investigators series (New York: Random House, 1979; London: Collins, 1980);

The Slasher, as Collins (New York: Dodd, Mead, 1980; London: Hale, 1981);

Why Girls Ride Sidesaddle (Chicago: December Press, 1980);

Touch of Death, as Sadler (Toronto: Raven House, 1981);

The Mystery of the Purple Pirate, as Arden, Alfred Hitchcock and the Three Investigators series (New York: Random House, 1982);

Freak, as Collins (New York: Dodd, Mead, 1983; London: Hale, 1983);

The Mystery of the Smashing Glass, as Arden, Alfred Hitchcock and the Three Investigators series (New York: Random House, 1984; London: Collins, 1985);

Deadly Innocents, as Sadler (New York: Walker, 1986);

Mercenary Mountain, as Carter (New York: Charter, 1986);

The Samurai Kill, as Carter (New York: Charter, 1986);

The Mystery of Wreckers Rock, as Arden, Alfred Hitchcock and the Three Investigators series (New York: Random House, 1986; London: Collins, 1987);

Minnesota Strip, as Collins (New York: Fine, 1987; London: Oldcastle, 1990);

Red Rosa, as Collins (New York: Fine, 1988; London: Oldcastle, 1990);

Castrato, as Collins (New York: Fine, 1989);

Hot Wheels, as Arden [The Three Investigators, Crimebusters series] (New York: Random House, 1989);

Chasing Eights, as Collins (New York: Fine, 1990);

The Irishman's Horse, as Collins (New York: Fine, 1991);

Cassandra in Red, as Collins (New York: Fine, 1992);

Crime, Punishment, and Resurrection, as Collins (New York: Fine, 1992);

The Cadillac Cowboy, as Collins (New York: Fine, 1995);

Talking to the World and other Stories (Santa Barbara, Cal.: Daniel, 1995);

Fortune's World: Stories, as Collins (Norfolk, Va.: Crippen & Landru, 2000);

Spies and Thieves, Cops and Killers, Etc., as Collins (Waterville, Me.: Five Star, 2002);

Charlie Chan in The Temple Of The Golden Horde, as Collins (Holicong, Pa.: Wildside Press, 2003).

OTHER: "Yellow Gal," in *New World Writing,* volume 11 (New York: New American Library, 1957), pp. 246–256;

"Death My Love," as John Douglas, in *Mink is for a Minx,* edited by Leo Margulies (New York: Dell, 1964), pp. 123–136;

"Man on the Run," in *Mink is for a Minx,* edited by Margulies (New York: Dell, 1964), pp. 109–122;

"A Blue Blonde in the Sky over Pennsylvania," in *The Best American Short Stories 1965,* edited by Martha Foley (New York: Houghton Mifflin, 1965), pp. 233–239; republished in *The Short Story: Fiction in Transition,* edited by J. Chesley Taylor (New York: Scribners, 1969), pp. 277–293;

"Freedom Fighter," as Collins, in *Crime Without Murder,* edited by Dorothy Salisbury Davis (New York: Scribners, 1970), pp. 35–45;

"No One Likes to Be Played for a Sucker," as Collins, in *All but Impossible!* edited by Edward D. Hoch

(New Haven, Conn.: Ticknor & Fields, 1981), pp. 245–272; republished in *First Cases. First Appearances of Classic Private Eyes,* edited by Robert J. Randisi (New York: Dutton, 1996), pp. 3–20;

"Scream All the Way," as Collins, in *Alfred Hitchcock's Tales to Make You Quake and Quiver,* edited by Cathleen Jordan (New York: Dial, 1982), pp. 66–80;

"Who?" as Collins, in *Alfred Hitchcock's Death-Reach,* edited by Jordan (South Yarmouth, Mass.: Curley, 1982), pp. 1–19;

"The Oldest Killer," as Collins, in *The Year's Best Mystery and Suspense Stories 1984,* edited by Hoch (New York: Walker, 1984), pp. 27–39;

"Eighty Million Dead," as Collins, in *The Eyes Have It,* edited by Randisi (New York: Mysterious Press, 1984; London: Severn House, 1988), pp. 45–62;

"Why I Write Mysteries: Night and Day," as Collins, in *Dictionary of Literary Biography Yearbook: 1985,* edited by Jean W. Ross (Detroit: Gale, 1986), pp. 58–61;

"The Motive," as Collins, in *A Matter of Crime,* volume 2, edited by Matthew J. Bruccoli and Richard Layman (San Diego: Harcourt Brace Jovanovich, 1987), pp. 68–97;

"Black in the Snow," as Collins, in *An Eye for Justice,* edited by Randisi (New York: Mysterious Press, 1988), pp. 53–66;

"Crime and Punishment," as Collins, in *The Year's Best Mystery and Suspense Stories 1989,* edited by Hoch (New York: Walker, 1989), pp. 1–10;

"The Chair," as Collins, in *Justice for Hire,* edited by Randisi (New York: Mysterious Press, 1990), pp. 63–76;

"Still Life with Doc Holliday," in *New Frontiers,* volume 2, edited by Martin H. Greenberg and Bill Pronzini (New York: Tor, 1990), pp. 179–184;

"Brett Halliday," as Collins, in *Twentieth-Century Crime and Mystery Writers,* edited by John M. Riley, third edition (Chicago & London: St. James Press, 1991), pp. 489–491;

"Role Model," as Collins, in *Deadly Allies,* edited by Randisi and Marilyn Wallace (New York: Doubleday, 1992), pp. 116–136;

"Angel Eyes," as Collins, in *Deadly Allies II,* edited by Randisi and Susan Dunlap (New York: Doubleday, 1994), pp. 399–425;

"A Matter of Character," as Collins, in *Partners In Crime,* edited by Elaine Raco Chase (New York: Signet, 1994), pp. 68–99;

"The Chocolate Cat," as Collins, in *Cat Crimes Takes A Vacation,* edited by Greenberg and Ed Gorman (New York: Fine, 1995), pp. 64–88;

"Can Shoot," as Collins, in *Private Eyes*, edited by Mickey Spillane and Max Allan Collins (New York: Signet, 1998), pp. 215–244;

"Part of History," as Collins, in *Death By Espionage*, edited by Martin Cruz Smith (Nashville, Tenn.: Cumberland House, 1999), pp. 60–75;

"The Horrible, Senseless Murders of Two Elderly Women," as Collins, in *Fedora I*, edited by Michael Bracken (Doylestown, Pa.: Wildside Press, 2001), pp. 225–232;

"Twilight's Last Gleaming," as Collins, in *Flesh & Blood: Dark Desires*, edited by Max Allan Collins and Gelb (New York: Mysterious Press, 2002), pp. 339–358;

"A Delicate Mission," as Collins with Gayle Lynds, in *Flesh & Blood: Guilty As Sin*, edited by Max Allen Collins and Gelb (New York: Mysterious Press, 2003), pp. 110–126.

SELECTED PERIODICAL PUBLICATIONS–
UNCOLLECTED: "The Island," *Interim*, 4 (1954): 57–63;

"Rites of Spring," *Prairie Schooner*, 28 (Spring 1954): 33–37;

"Marriage and Death, Solitude and Confusion," *Western Humanities Review*, 35 (Winter 1981): 331–343;

"Triptych," *Western Humanities Review*, 35 (Summer 1981): 135–142;

"The Country of the Southern Ute," *South Dakota Review*, 20 (Autumn 1982): 65–72;

"In Memoriam," for Ross Macdonald, *Armchair Detective*, 16 (Summer 1983): 227;

"The Girl in White," *South Dakota Review*, 22 (Autumn 1984): 86–94;

"Expanding the *Roman Noir*: Ross Macdonald's Legacy to Mystery/Detective Authors," *South Dakota Review*, 24 (Spring 1986): 121–124;

"Harlot's Cry," as Collins, *South Dakota Review*, 24 (Spring 1986): 125–128;

"Takeda Shogun," *South Dakota Review*, 26 (Spring 1986): 10–17;

"The Mexican Waiter," *Carolina Quarterly*, 38 (Winter 1986): 77–86;

"After Auschwitz," *South Dakota Review*, 25 (Spring 1987): 17–59;

"Albert Magnus, Father Vitanza, and the Hammer," *Puerto Del Sol*, 23 (Spring 1987): 136–147;

"Charles Ives and the President of the United States," *South Dakota Review*, 27 (Winter 1990): 156–161;

"The French Revolution," *South Carolina Review*, 26 (Fall 1993): 115–124;

"Disney World," as Collins, *Ellery Queen's Mystery Magazine*, edited by Janet Hutchings (May 2002): 42–54;

"Next Door Dave," as Collins, *Ellery Queen Mystery Magazine*, edited by Hutchings (July 2004): 41–53.

In a comment he provided for *Twentieth-Century Crime and Mystery Writers* (1985), Dennis Lynds–writing as Michael Collins, his best-known pseudonym–explains his interest in the crime novel:

> I write about people driven to violent actions by forces from inside and outside. The forces of the world in which they live. A real world. Our world. If anything distinguishes my books particularly from other books, it is that I write what could be called *sociodramas*. I want to understand and show what made these people as they are, what created the pressures that will explode within them. What made them, then, act in a crisis as they acted, and what made violence their ultimate solution.

Lynds believes that focusing on crime affords the writer the opportunity to reveal a society and its people in "sharp outline"; he hopes to excite, thrill, and entertain by allowing the reader to live "a real experience with real people" in order to understand "what makes our world tick."

Dennis John Lynds was born 15 January 1924 to Archibald John Douglas and Gertrude (Hyem) Lynds in St. Louis, Missouri. His parents were both English actors who happened to be playing winter stock in St. Louis when he was born but returned to England within six months, where he grew up in and around London. In 1930, when he was six, his parents returned to New York and then went back to St. Louis to do summer stock at an outdoor theater. From there they moved to Hollywood, where Lynds attended the Vine Street School at Sunset and Vine, but his father hated the movies and the Hollywood English colony, some of whose members he knew quite well, notably Herbert Marshall and Stanley Ridges. A stage offer came from Denver, and Lynds went to school there for a few months, until the family returned to New York and settled in Sheepshead Bay, Brooklyn, where he spent the rest of his childhood and adolescence. He attended Brooklyn public schools and Brooklyn Technical High School, a competitive-admission, all-city school.

Lynds served from 1943 to 1946 with the United States Army Armored Infantry in Europe, where he was decorated with the Combat Infantry Badge, Bronze Star, Purple Heart, and three battle stars. In 1949, Lynds received a B.A. in chemistry from Hofstra University, and in 1951 he took an M.A. in journalism from Syracuse University. His first career was as a chemist with Charles Pfizer and Company, and during the 1950s he edited several industrial publications in New York, among them *Chemical Week* and *Chemical Engineering*

 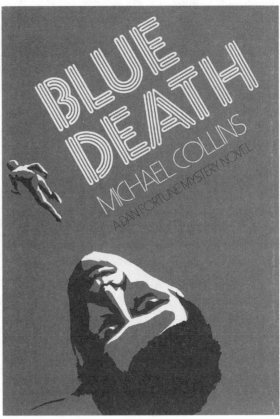

*Dust jackets for two of the seven Dan Fortune novels that Dennis Lynds published as Michael Collins
in the 1970s (Richland County Public Library)*

Progress. Lynds has married three times: in 1949 to Doris Flood (divorced 1956); in 1961 to Sheila McErlean, with whom he raised two daughters, Katherine and Deirdre (divorced 1985); and in 1986 to Gayle Hallenbeck Stone. In 1965, Lynds moved to Santa Barbara, California, a small city ninety miles north of Los Angeles he had visited and decided to settle in, where he writes and enjoys avocational interests such as theater, fishing, wine, music, and poker.

In an article written for *DLB Yearbook: 1985,* "Why I Write Mysteries: Night and Day," Lynds—again writing as Collins—describes how he made the transition to full-time writer: "I began to write in the army, continued in college, and [starting in 1948] published poetry and stories in the smaller literary magazines. After college I published stories in the larger literary quarterlies, and two mainstream novels. By 1960 I felt established enough on the edges of literature to quit my editorial job and work on my fourth novel full time."

In explaining how he began writing detective fiction, Lynds quotes Henry James the elder, who told his sons, "The natural inheritance of everyone who is capable of spiritual life is an unsubdued forest where the wolf howls and the obscene bird of night chatters" (*Substance

and Shadow, 1866). Although he had published two non-detective novels—*Combat Soldier* (1962) and *Uptown Downtown* (1963)—and had worked on two more, Lynds realized he was not then ready to write novels that addressed the questions of the spiritual life as he wanted to write them:

> I could not write a novel that dealt with that dark bird, the metaphysical, the night, with the vision and tools I had found up until then.

> I needed a new way of writing, of seeing, of painting that obscene bird. I could grope toward that in short stories, but not yet in the novel. I could not write novels the way I had written the first four and deal with my bird of night. That was going to take time and searching. And while I searched, how was I to live?

> The answer for Lynds was the American detective novel.

Lynds writes that thinking people have two sets of concerns: "the ethical and the metaphysical; the social and the transcendental; the mind and the soul; the day and the night. Part of a whole, yes; but separate too." He decided to write detective fiction because he realized there "were other birds, other beasts, to wonder about, to understand, to question":

> The ethical not the metaphysical. The mind not the soul. The social not the transcendental. The day not the night. I had many ideas, questions, stories to write that dealt not with the obscene bird or the internal wolf, but with very external wolves and the vultures of broad daylight. The way man lives not so much with himself as with other men. Obviously, man is a unit. Psychology is part of day and night. But art is not life, art can be only partial, and in art there is a matter of emphasis. Man is in the end, alone with his obscene bird, but along the way he lives with many other men and he must deal with that too.

For Lynds, the detective novel "is built around an observer, a questioner, a searcher. One who watches the events and tries to understand." He finds it "a form almost perfectly suited" to asking ethical and social questions.

Beginning in 1962, Lynds wrote detective stories for magazines, and in 1964 he was hired to write novels featuring The Shadow under the house name of Maxwell Grant used by Walter Gibson since 1931 for stories and novels dealing with the heroic exploits of the crime fighter with the hypnotic power to cloud minds and so make himself invisible to those around him. The character had become popular on the radio in the 1930s, and listeners from the 1930s into the 1950s recall the sinister voice at the beginning of broadcasts, "Who knows what evil lurks in the hearts of men? The Shadow knows!" When Lynds took on the task, he inherited the requisite features for the hero—the great black cloak, the slouch hat, the fire-opal ring, and the burning eyes. He wrote eight novels in the series for Belmont publishers, beginning with *The Shadow Strikes* (1964) and ending with *The Shadow—Destination: Moon* (1967).

The same year he published his last Shadow novel as Grant, Lynds published his first novel as Michael Collins, *Act of Fear* (1967). According to Robert A. Baker and Michael T. Nietzel in *Private Eyes: One Hundred and One Knights* (1985), the work "marked the initiation of a private eye renaissance." A significant contribution to the hard-boiled genre, *Act of Fear* introduced investigator Dan Fortune, who has been featured in eighteen novels. The search for a missing person and/or the investigation of a messy problem, such as a murder, are the typical elements of a Collins novel. In *Act of Fear,* Fortune is faced with a case in which a policeman is mugged on his daylight beat, a neighborhood youth disappears, and several deaths ensue.

In the first paragraphs of the novel, Fortune sets the locale in the Chelsea district of Lower West Side Manhattan, where Lynds once lived. (The first thirteen Dan Fortune novels are set there, with many trips to other places, including Santa Barbara; two Mark Sadler novels, three William Arden novels, both early non-genre novels; and many short stories.) Fortune alludes to his woman, Marty Adair, and his best friend, Joe Harris, the bartender at Packy Wilson's Pub. The reader learns that Fortune's name is a derivational legacy of his grandfather:

> The Fortune was once Fortunowski, and there used to be a *T* in the middle for Tadeusz. That was the name my grandfather carried off the boat: Tadeusz Jan Fortunowski. When I was a boy the old men told me that my grandfather carried that name with pride, even with arrogance. Like most middle and east Europeans, his pedigree was a chaos of history. He was born in Lithuania, under a Russian government, of Polish parents who spoke German. But he was proud that he was a Pole, and the name was all he had to prove what he was. My father was born here. Chelsea was a world of Americans and Irish then, and a man needs to belong. My father became *Fortune.* The old men told me that my grandfather had refused to speak to anyone named Fortune, son or no son.

Dan Fortune, 5' 10" tall and of average weight, was forty-one in 1967 when the series debuted with *Act of Fear* and is limited by the absence of a left arm, which at age seventeen he lost in an accident when he fell into the hold while looting a ship. Fortune concocts stories about his missing arm—variously explaining that he lost it at Normandy Beach, in an assassination attempt on Adolf Hitler, or during escape from a sinking submarine. He avoids operations that are "big or dangerous" in favor of small jobs for small- and medium-sized businesses (such as catching pilferers, inside thieves, and shoplifters), divorce cases, armed-guard jobs at $2.00 an hour, and delivering subpoenas for $5.00 apiece. He describes his work as dealing mostly with "the personal problems of small people who want to apply a little pressure on someone but don't want the police." He continues, "It's not work I especially like, but a man must eat, and it's work I know how to do." Because of his work, Fortune is regarded as a cop in Chelsea, but the nickname Danny the Pirate from his youth has helped to remove "the cop-taint." Nevertheless, he is not completely accepted in Chelsea, since he has been away, read books, and enjoyed some education.

Fortune's lack of an arm and imposing size reinforce his strategic inclinations to duck punches and run. Such a mode of operation is grounded in a strong survival instinct: "I don't carry a gun. It's too dangerous. . . . Sooner or later you will use it. A man with a gun is a

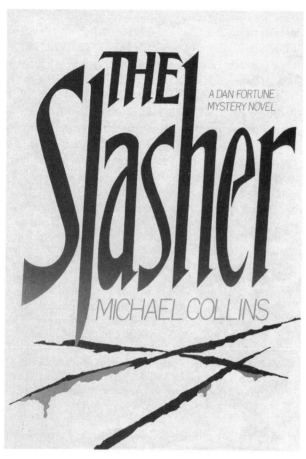

Dust jacket for Collins's 1980 novel in which Dan Fortune travels from New York to Los Angeles to investigate a murder for his friend Marty (Richland County Public Library)

marked man. I'm a fair shot, but I don't want to prove it and find out the hard way that the other man is better." He also has a fine sense of what is and is not required of him: "It's not so important to win a fight, but it is important to not let the other man win." Nevertheless, he demonstrates perseverance in the face of danger. In his entry on Collins for *Twentieth-Century Crime and Mystery Writers* (1980), Richard C. Carpenter argues that Fortune's single arm is the key to his character:

> He is the wounded man whose wound makes him fearful—the thought that something might happen to his remaining arm fills him with dread—yet conversely makes him expose himself to danger in order to prove he exists. And he is the determined man bent on carrying out his mission no matter what the cost. This exposure and this determination lead to insult, injury, loneliness solaced only by brief love affairs, and the risk of sudden death. In every novel he is beaten, harassed or sometimes shot.

An ethical man who must face ambiguous moral circumstances, Fortune is upright in his own behavior

and reluctant to pass judgment on others. In his 1984 essay for *Clues: A Journal of Detection,* "Dennis Lynds and the Social Conscience," Carpenter describes Fortune as "an old-fashioned liberal humanist who sees people less as intrinsically wicked than as warped and deluded by social forces beyond their control." In *Act of Fear* the example of Andy Pappas, a school chum who became a boss of the rackets and thus inspires fear and respect in Chelsea, invokes in Fortune a feeling of self-reproach and a sense of collective responsibility: "A man like Andy Pappas is where we all went off the track."

Fortune expresses his observations on human behavior, often philosophical or sociological in nature, in a spare style in which possible exceptions or contradictions are usually represented in parentheses in the earlier books:

> We don't admit it, but we consider a successful man a better man. A prince of success, an inevitable winner. Maybe it's only that we never lost our need for princes, and if we don't have an aristocracy, we make one. An aristocracy is comforting. It takes us off the hook—we never really had a chance to make it big. At the same time, of course, since an aristocracy of success isn't really closed to us we can all dream. A contradiction, sure, but logic has never bothered people's attitudes much.

> The big houses. A car for each day. The real mark of success since our history began—to have a great deal more than you, or anyone, needed. Someday the mark of success will be to have *almost* as much as you need. It will be better, but a lot will be lost, and I don't think there'll be a place for a man like me. A new world with a different dawn and different birds singing a different song.

While some readers find him humorless, Fortune's interior comments are often acute and amusing, as when he describes the remodeling involved in the top floor of a six-story tenement, where the adjoining walls had been knocked out: "The place was not lack-of-money ugly; it was plain rotten-taste ugly. The whole place shouted of money made too late to know how to spend it."

The descriptions of sex and violence in *Act of Fear* are restrained. Although Marty, an aspiring actress and exotic dancer, employs her beauty to support herself, the book includes only the most general descriptions of her appearance. The author provides no titillating verbal foreplay to acts of sexual intercourse nor descriptions of the acts themselves. The novel includes neither brutality nor bloody gore. The only descriptions of violence are in another character's attack upon Fortune and Fortune's self-defense. This pattern remains true for the first few books, but slowly the novels open into more explicit and graphic sex and violence as American society itself opened in the same way from the early 1960s through the mid 1990s.

Act of Fear earned Lynds the Edgar Allan Poe Award of the Mystery Writers of America for the best first novel of a new author in 1967. As Collins, Lynds published one more Fortune novel in 1969, *The Brass Rainbow,* and in the same year published a science-fiction novel, *Lukan War.* Meanwhile, in 1968, under the pseudonym William Arden, he published *A Dark Power,* a stand-alone short story, "Success of a Mission" (*Argosy,* April 1968), and *The Mystery of the Moaning Cave.* "Success of a Mission" won Lynds his second Edgar nomination.

The novels by Arden initiated two separate series that were published by Dodd, Mead and Random House, respectively. *A Dark Power,* an economical third-person narrative, centers on the character Kane Jackson, an industrial consultant in Santa Barbara, California, where Lynds had moved in 1965. Jackson serves as a specialist in the practice and investigation of industrial espionage, a subject that Lynds no doubt was familiar with from his experiences as a chemist and as an editor for the chemical-industry press. Four more books appeared in this series: *Deal in Violence* (1969), *The Goliath Scheme* (1971), *Die to a Distant Drum* (1972), and *Deadly Legacy* (1973). Jackson is a harder, higher paid, more sophisticated, and more cynical persona than Fortune, as befits the ruthless corporate world in which he works and lives. The series was critically well received, but not commercially successful—perhaps, as some critics have suggested, it was ahead of its time—and Lynds abandoned it after *Deadly Legacy.*

Lynds also used the Arden pseudonym for the books he wrote for Random House in its series of juvenile mysteries, Alfred Hitchcock and the Three Investigators. Over eighteen years Lynds wrote fourteen novels in the series, beginning with *The Mystery of the Moaning Cave* (1968) and ending with *Hot Wheels* (1989).

The 1970s were Lynds's most productive decade, as he never published fewer than two novels in any year; published four novels in 1970, 1974, and 1976; and published six novels in both 1972 and 1973. In 1970 Lynds began a new detective series for Random House, writing as Mark Sadler. The six Sadler novels, beginning with *The Falling Man,* feature Paul Shaw as a modern professional private eye with the firm of Thayer, Shaw, and Delaney Security and Investigations, based in its New York office on Madison Avenue. The firm is run in a business-like way with an image tailored to business clients. Shaw carries a six-shot Colt Agent, drives a Ferrari, and lives with his successful actress wife in a penthouse on Central Park South.

Under the Sadler pseudonym, Lynds assumes an authorial stance reflecting the outlook of his central character. The Shaw novels pose a conflict between those on the fringe—hippies, environmentalists, black militants, and students—and the police, politicians, and capitalists who govern this society with corrupt brutality. Lynds wrote three more Shaw novels in the 1970s: *Here to Die* (1971), *Mirror Image* (1972), and *Circle of Fire* (1973). According to Francis M. Nevins Jr. in "Private Eye in an Evil Time: Mark Sadler's Paul Shaw," a 1978 article in *Xenophile,* no other private-eye novels capture so well the nightmare America suffered through during the Vietnam and Nixon years. These Sadler novels were also well received by the critics but were not financially successful, a circumstance Nevins attributes to Lynds's "uncomfortable reminders of current horrors" being unwelcome in the domain of the private-eye novel.

In 1972 Lynds initiated a second series for Random House, writing as John Crowe, with *Another Way to Die* and *A Touch of Darkness.* He wrote four more novels in this series, all published in the decade: *Bloodwater* (1974), *Crooked Shadows* (1975), *When They Kill Your Wife* (1977), and *Close to Death* (1979). All of these novels are set in fictional Buena Costa County, California. Continuity in the works is provided by the site rather than by the adventures of a central character; Lynds focuses instead on the local police investigators doing their duty under grisly circumstances. In this decade, Lynds also published *Woman in Marble* (1973), his only novel under the pseudonym Carl Dekker; three novels under the house name of Nick Carter—*The N3 Conspiracy* (1974), *The Green Wolf Connection* (1976), and *Triple Cross* (1976); and two novelizations of television plays under his own name, *Charlie Chan Returns* (1974) and *S.W.A.T.—Crossfire* (1975).

As Collins, Lynds continued the adventures of Dan Fortune in the 1970s with *Night of the Toads* (1970), *Walk a Black Wind* (1971), *Shadow of a Tiger* (1972), *The Silent Scream* (1973), *Blue Death* (1975), *The Blood-Red Dream* (1976), and *The Nightrunners* (1978). His third Fortune novel, *Night of the Toads,* is a pivotal work. It is the first of his detective novels to develop what he and others have called the "sociodrama" core of his fiction, a core he slowly expanded and deepened over the years as Collins and incorporated into his Sadler, Crowe, and Arden novels. It takes place mainly in the world of the New York theater and involves the questions of abortion, un-American inquisitions, and moral cowardice.

In *Blue Death,* another key novel in the early Fortune books, for the first time Fortune clearly shows that his problem with his world is not a matter of aberrant individuals but of the society itself. The other Fortune novels of the 1970s continue the sociological pattern. *Walk a Black Wind* involves the plight of the American Indian; *Shadow of a Tiger* considers the dark guilts of

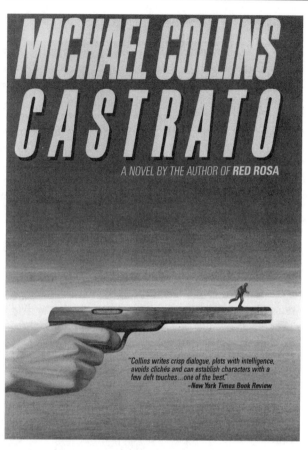

Dust jacket for Collins's 1989 novel in which Dan Fortune contends with the inteference of the CIA and the FBI as he searches for a missing man (Richland County Public Library)

World War II and colonialism; *The Silent Scream* investigates the peacetime consequences of training men to kill in war, the corruptions of a fast-buck society, and the Mafia; *The Blood-Red Dream* examines modern "tribalism" and the difference between a "freedom fighter" and a "terrorist"; and *The Nightrunners* pictures the devastating results of the clash of morality, self-interest, and profit (all timeless subjects, the essence of literature).

As these novels progress, society changes, and Fortune changes with it. He still does not carry a gun habitually or as a matter of course, but he carries it more often and eventually abandons his "old cannon" for a more modern, convenient, and efficient weapon. After the first three or four novels, he does not noticeably age. The subject never comes up. As with those of the Private Investigators (PIs) of Dashiell Hammett, Raymond Chandler, and Ross Macdonald before him, and unlike more recent PIs in fiction, Fortune's personal life plays only a minor part in the novels. In a definition of his private-eye hero, Chandler said, "I don't care about his private life." The lives at the core of each novel are those of the other people in the book, as seen through the eyes and mind and voice of the detective.

Yet, the Fortune books are rooted in contemporary events beginning with World War II, and by 1992 he should be sixty-six years old. That is one reason Lynds has not written a Fortune novel since 1992, and he has said that when he does write a new one, it will have to be set in the past. The short stories are written as essentially timeless.

In 1981 the Collins novels received international recognition from the Arbeitsgemeinschaft Kriminalliteratur (Crime Literature Association) of West Germany. The association commended the Collins novels as a contribution to mystery fiction as literature: "The break in private eye novels started with Michael Collins. At the end of the 1960's, he gave the private eye novel something new and a human touch needed for years. They are much more than entertainment. There is a philosophy behind the detective. In each book we take a look at a special section of American society."

From 1980 onward, Lynds has written mainly as Collins and focused on Fortune, though he has also employed the Arden, Sadler, and Carter pseudonyms. Among his non-Collins works are two story collections written under his own name, *Why Girls Ride Sidesaddle* (1980) and *Talking to the World and Other Stories* (1995), and the last two novels in the Shaw series, *Touch of Death* (1981) and *Deadly Innocents* (1986). In *Private Eyes: One Hundred and One Knights,* Baker and Nietzel compare Lynds's most acclaimed detectives, asserting that Shaw is "as good as, if not better than Dan Fortune." The *San Francisco Chronicle* joined in, saying that Lynds was "As good a writer of the hard-boiled novel as Elmore Leonard, and a better one than Robert B. Parker," and *The New York Times* added, "Sadler achieves something beyond an action story. He is a novelist as well as a writer of whodunits." Nevertheless, once again, Lynds eventually had to abandon the series because of lack of commercial success.

In the 1980s, Lynds was honored by the Private Eye Writers of America, who elected him as the president of the organization in 1985 and presented him with its Award for Lifetime Achievement in 1988. Well aware of the tradition of the American detective novel, Lynds memorialized his friend Macdonald, who died on 11 July 1983, in *Armchair Detective.* In "Expanding the *Roman Noir:* Ross Macdonald's Legacy to Mystery/Detective Authors," an essay he wrote for *South Dakota Review* (Spring 1986), Lynds appraises the genre and the contribution of Macdonald to its development. Lynds credits Macdonald with bringing crime "from Hammett's dark and bloody ground, from Chandler's Outsider on the mean streets to the people next door, the neighbor up the block." Lynds then explains how in his own work he seeks to continue the development of the form:

For me, there is at least one more step–to bring the detective novel into the living room of the reader himself. To make him see the violence and darkness as his own. Make him see, when he looks at killer and victim alike, that it is not the problem of the police, of one man of honor in an alien world, of the man in the house next door or the neighbor down the street–it is his problem.

Since 1980 Lynds as Collins has published two story collections featuring Fortune–*Crime, Punishment, and Resurrection* (1992) and *Fortune's World* (2000)–and written seven novels featuring the detective: *The Slasher* (1980), *Freak* (1983), *Minnesota Strip* (1987), *Red Rosa* (1988), *Castrato* (1989), *Chasing Eights* (1990), *The Irishman's Horse* (1991), and *Cassandra in Red* (1992).

These later novels mark some sharp shifts in Lynds's work. Three of them– *The Slasher, Red Rosa,* and *Castrato*–are crucial. In *The Slasher,* Fortune is briefly reunited with Marty, now in her second marriage and living in Malibu, California, and meets Kay Michaels. In *Red Rosa,* Lynds first employs third-person scenes from points of view other than Fortune's, while maintaining first person for Fortune. Part of the book again takes place in Santa Barbara, and at the end, his New York building burns down, and he is planning to move to Santa Barbara with Kay Michaels. In *Castrato,* Fortune has moved to Santa Barbara, where he lives in a Spanish Colonial–style rambler in a beach area known as Summerland.

In *Castrato,* Lynds's stylistic devices have become more sophisticated as he has developed as a writer. He employs short chapters in the novel, organized into the three sections–"Santa Barbara," "New York," and "The Valley"–as Fortune's locale of operations changes. The first chapter serves as an introduction, narrated in the third person, present tense, to the four main characters: Frank Owen and his former wife, Diane, and Billy Owen and his wife, who must scramble to feed her children, about whom the novel turns. The following chapter switches to the first-person narration of Fortune as he clings to cover under rifle fire. Italics are used to represent flashbacks, and additional third-person scenes, just as related short stories do, reenact scenes in which Fortune is not present, but he has learned about. Such innovations drastically reduce the number of static "interview" scenes so prevalent in mystery novels, and both compactly and dramatically reveal the histories and personae of other characters. (In the next novel, *Chasing Eights,* Lynds uses three points of view: an authorial voice in the present tense for a pair of hired killers; an authorial close-third, present-tense voice for a major antagonist; and Fortune's first person.)

In *Castrato,* Fortune must face the violent interference of both the CIA and FBI as he searches in rural California for Frank Owen's missing brother, Billy, a John Wayne wannabe who is allegedly involved in gun-running and drug smuggling in Central America. The violence and profanity that became noticeable in *Freak* continue to be more explicit and realistic. Fortune's new love interest, Kay Michaels, is a model and sometime actress as well as a businesswoman and agent for other models in Los Angeles. Marty was attractive, bright, and capable of straightening out Fortune's sometimes fuzzy and twisted logic; they went to bed as a matter of course. Kay Michaels, on the other hand, is not as well developed as a character and has her own life separate from Fortune's. Lynds is more frank and graphic in his depictions of sex than he was in his earlier novels.

As they search for Billy, Fortune and Frank Owen discuss the idea of manhood in the modern West. Owen manifests the macho mystique reinforced by the Western stereotype of the strong, heroic man. "A cowboy without a frontier, a hunter with nothing to hunt," he represents a false ideal of rugged individualism. For Owen, *huevos* (balls), signify manly independence. Insecure yet holding to the belief that males are superior to females, Frank sees taking responsibility in a relationship as undermining his manhood: "Cut off our balls to make us good husbands, fathers, providers, baby sitters. The women and society."

Through Fortune, Lynds questions the myth of the Old West, which is associated with features of male chauvinism and egocentrism in the novel. The belief that the West was an empire established by rugged individualism and the virtues of hard work, honesty, and integrity is discounted by Fortune, who argues that the West was built upon the bodies and the land of Indians, Mexicans, and Chinese coolies. The land was preserved for the privileged in rights of way for the railroads, federal grazing land, and water rights. The gunslinger, sheriff, or United States Marshal, Fortune maintains, was employed by the railroads, cattle barons, and town builders to mask their world and power so as to better manipulate others. For Fortune, the CIA and sham patriotism are manifestations of continued American policies of ruthless self-aggrandizement and rapacity.

Social issues–in this case tenants' rights and discrimination against minorities–are again paramount in *Cassandra in Red,* a novel that is nevertheless full of action, suspense, and violence. Set in Santa Barbara, the novel shares with *Castrato* a tripartite structure, each section of which is prefaced with the italicized dialogue of clandestine military figures moving stealthily through the night. After the corpse of a militant street advocate is found in a park, masked men in black attempt to discourage Fortune's investigation. A suicide impels the police to close the case, but not before Fortune is attacked again by seven masked men who are ultimately traced to the Western Service Institute, a training center for the armed

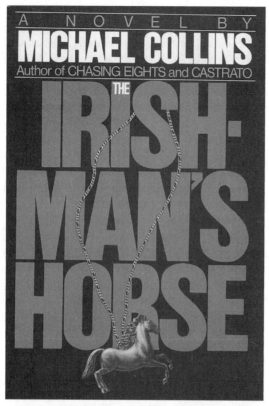

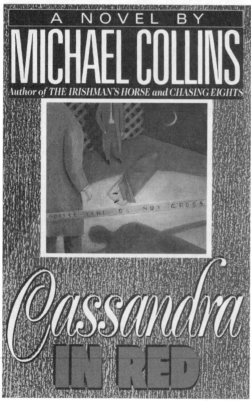

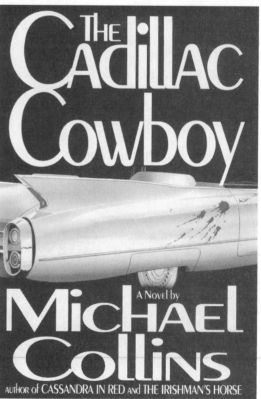

Dust jackets for the four Dan Fortune novels Lynds published in the 1990s (Richland County Public Library)

services. These men use a bigoted ideology to justify murder: "We had to take back our country from the bums and foreigners and liberals." Lynds makes extensive use of his new techniques and strategies in the novel, the most interesting of which reveal the sociopolitical attitudes of Fortune as an inheritance of the socialist background of his immigrant forebears.

After eighteen Dan Fortune novels, Lynds in 1995 broke from the mold that brought him success and under the pseudonym Michael Collins introduced Langford (Ford) Morgan as the hero of *The Cadillac Cowboy*. Not a detective, Morgan at forty-six is a former soldier and CIA agent who now tends to an export-import business in Costa Rica. He is a wealthy man who was engaged in essentially illegal endeavors while in the CIA, who drives a BMW, and who carries no gun until he acquires a Czech Vz70 for reasons of self-defense. Asked by his former wife to look into the attempted murder of one of her former husbands, tycoon Ralph Baliol, Morgan shows that, like Fortune, he is a determined investigator with his own code of ethics. Lynds in this novel employs close third-person narration to carry the action and makes wide use of his new techniques to present the genealogy of the characters and the history of forebears reaching back to Europe, an approach that suggests that contemporary violence is comprehensible in an historical context.

In "Why I Write Mysteries: Night and Day," which he wrote at the height of his career, Lynds shows the stubborn independence of a writer who is willing to take chances, to go against any expectation other than his own:

> What began as a split in my needs as a writer seems to be coming back together. Ethical and metaphysical, night and day, mainstream and detective are merging. The social and ethical is surfacing in my short stories, and in my last detective novels I find myself grappling with that obscene bird of night, the howling wolf inside. (Not always to the delight of my agent, or publishers, or even readers, I'm afraid.)

While some reviewers and readers have objected to the social analysis and introspection evident in Lynds's later novels in the Fortune series, critics such as Baker and Nietzel argue that Lynds has made an original contribution to the genre. Dan Fortune is the worthy successor to Hammett's Sam Spade, Chandler's Philip Marlowe, and Macdonald's Lew Archer, "the culmination of a maturing process that has transformed the private eye from the naturalistic Spade through the romantic Marlowe and the psychological Archer to the sociological Fortune."

Since 1995, Dennis Lynds has continued to write Dan Fortune short stories, with four pieces published in 2004. An interesting development is a group of stories involving Fortune's father and grandfather and their influence on him. But Lynds's activities in the novel have turned back to the nongenre mainstream, although in 2002 he received the Marlowe Award of Mystery Writers of America SoCal Chapter for Life Achievement, and some indications suggest he will return to the crime field.

References:

Mike Ashley, *The Mammoth Encyclopedia of Modern Crime Fiction* (New York: Carol & Graf, 2001), pp. 102–105;

Robert A. Baker and Michael T. Nietzel, *Private Eyes: One Hundred and One Knights* (Bowling Green, Ohio: Bowling State University Popular Press, 1985), pp. 176–182;

Richard C. Carpenter, "Dennis Lynds and the Social Conscience," *Clues: A Journal of Detection*, 5, no. 1 (Spring–Summer 1984): 36–57;

John Conquest, *Trouble Is Their Business: Private Eyes in Fiction, Film, and Television 1927–1988* (New York & London: Garland, 1990);

William L. DeAndrea, *Encyclopedia Mysteriosa* (New York: Prentice Hall, 1994), pp. 70, 124;

David Geherin, *The American Private Eye: The Image in Fiction* (New York: Ungar, 1985), pp. 155–162;

Joseph Green and Jim Finch, *Sleuths, Sidekicks, and Stooges: An Annotated Bibliography of Detectives, Their Assistants, and Their Rivals in Crime, Mystery, and Adventure Fiction* (Aldershot, U.K.: Scolar Press/ Brookfield, Vt.: Ashgate, 1997);

Leslie Henderson, *Twentieth-Century Crime and Mystery Writers,* 3rd edition (London & Chicago: St. James Press, 1991), pp. 233–237;

Francis M. Nevins Jr., "Private Eye in an Evil Time: Mark Sadler's Paul Shaw," *Xenophile,* no. 38 (March–April 1978): 11;

Jay P. Pederson, *St. James Guide to Crime and Mystery Writers* (Detroit: New York, Toronto & London: St. James Press, 1996), pp. 218–221;

Bill Pronzini and Marcia Muller, *1001 Midnights: The Afficionado's Guide to Mystery and Detective Fiction* (New York: Arbor House, 1986), pp. 25, 157–158, 176, 704–705;

John M. Reilly, *Twentieth-Century Crime and Mystery Writers* (New York: St. Martin's Press, 1980), pp. 339–344;

Reilly, *Twentieth-Century Crime and Mystery Writers,* second edition (New York: St. Martin's Press, 1985), pp. 187–190.

Papers:

Dennis Lynds's papers are held in the Special Collections, Davidson Library, University of California at Santa Barbara.

John D. MacDonald

(24 July 1916 – 28 December 1986)

Matt Theado
Gardner-Webb University

and

Tim Cummings

See also the MacDonald entries in *DLB 8: Twentieth-Century American Science-Fiction Writers* and *DLB Yearbook: 1986.*

BOOKS: *The Brass Cupcake* (New York: Fawcett, 1950; London: Muller, 1955);

Murder for the Bride (New York: Fawcett, 1951; London: Muller, 1954);

Judge Me Not (New York: Fawcett, 1951; London: Muller, 1964);

Weep for Me (New York: Fawcett, 1951; London: Muller, 1964);

Wine of the Dreamers (New York: Greenberg, 1951); republished as *Planet of the Dreamers* (New York: Pocket Library, 1953; London: Hale, 1955);

Ballroom of the Skies (New York: Greenberg, 1952);

The Damned (New York: Fawcett, 1952; London: Muller, 1964);

Cancel All Our Vows (New York: Appleton-Century-Crofts, 1953; London: Hale, 1955);

The Neon Jungle (New York: Fawcett, 1953; London: Muller, 1954);

Dead Low Tide (New York: Fawcett, 1953; London, 1953);

All These Condemned (New York: Fawcett, 1954; London: Hale, 2001);

Area of Suspicion (New York: Dell, 1954; London: Hale, 1956);

Contrary Pleasure (New York: Appleton-Century-Crofts, 1954; London: Hale, 1955);

A Bullet for Cinderella (New York: Dell, 1955; London: Hale, 1960); republished as *On the Make* (New York: Dell, 1960);

Cry Hard Cry Fast (Greenwich, Conn.: Fawcett, 1955; London: Hale, 1969);

John D. MacDonald (courtesy of Matt Theado)

You Live Once (Greenwich, Conn.: Fawcett, 1956; London: Hale, 1976);

April Evil (New York: Dell, 1956; London: Hale, 1957);

Border Town Girl (Greenwich, Conn.: Fawcett, 1956; London: Hale, 1970);

Murder in the Wind (New York: Dell, 1956; republished as *Hurricane* (London: Hale, 1957);

Death Trap (New York: Dell, 1957; London: Hale, 1958);

The Price of Murder (New York: Dell, 1957; London: Hale, 1958);

The Empty Trap (Greenwich, Conn.: Fawcett, 1957; London: Magnum Books, 1980);

A Man of Affairs (New York: Dell, 1957; London: Hale, 1959);

The Deceivers (New York: Dell, 1958; London: Hale, 1968);

Clemmie (New York: Fawcett, 1958);

Soft Touch (New York: Dell, 1958; London: Hale, 1960);

The Executioners (New York: Simon & Schuster, 1958; London: Hale, 1959); republished as *Cape Fear* (New York: Fawcett, 1962);

Deadly Welcome (New York: Dell, 1959; London: Hale, 1961);

The Beach Girls (New York: Fawcett, 1959; London: Muller, 1964);

Please Write for Details (New York: Simon & Schuster, 1959; London: Hale, 1962);

The Crossroads (New York: Simon & Schuster, 1959; London: Hale, 1961);

The End of the Night (New York: Simon & Schuster, 1960; London: Hale, 1964);

The Only Girl in the Game (New York: Fawcett, 1960; London: Hale, 1962);

Slam the Big Door (New York: Fawcett, 1960; London: Hale, 1961);

Where Is Janice Gantry? (New York: Fawcett, 1961; London: Hale, 1963);

One Monday We Killed Them All (New York: Fawcett, 1961; London: Hale, 1963);

The Girl, the Gold Watch, and Everything (New York: Hodder Fawcett, 1962; Sevenoaks, U.K.: Coronet, 1968);

A Key to the Suite (New York: Fawcett, 1962; London: Hale, 1968);

A Flash of Green (New York: Simon & Schuster, 1962; London: Hale, 1971);

I Could Go On Singing (New York: Fawcett, 1963; London: Hale, 1964);

On the Run (New York: Fawcett, 1963; London: Hale, 1965);

The Drowner (New York: Fawcett, 1963; London: Hale, 1964);

The Deep Blue Good-By, Travis McGee series (New York: Fawcett, 1964; London: Hale, 1965);

Nightmare in Pink, Travis McGee series (New York: Fawcett, 1964; London: Hale, 1966);

A Purple Place for Dying, Travis McGee series (New York: Fawcett, 1964; London: Hale, 1966);

The Quick Red Fox, Travis McGee series (New York: Fawcett, 1964; London: Hale, 1966);

A Deadly Shade of Gold, Travis McGee series (New York: Fawcett, 1965; London: Hale, 1967);

Bright Orange for the Shroud, Travis McGee series (New York: Fawcett, 1965; London: Hale, 1967);

The House Guests (Garden City, N.Y.: Doubleday, 1965; London: Hale, 1966);

Darker Than Amber, Travis McGee series (New York: Fawcett, 1966; London: Hale, 1968);

One Fearful Yellow Eye, Travis McGee series (New York: Fawcett, 1966; London: Hale, 1968);

End of the Tiger and Other Stories (New York: Fawcett, 1966; London: Hale, 1967);

The Last One Left (Garden City, N.Y.: Doubleday, 1967; London: Hale, 1968);

Pale Gray for Guilt, Travis McGee series (Greenwich, Conn.: Fawcett, 1968; London: Hale, 1969);

The Girl in the Plain Brown Wrapper, Travis McGee series (New York: Fawcett, 1968; London: Hale, 1969);

No Deadly Drug (Garden City, N.Y.: Doubleday, 1968);

Dress Her in Indigo, Travis McGee series (Greenwich, Conn.: Fawcett, 1969; London: Hale, 1971);

The Long Lavender Look, Travis McGee series (New York: Fawcett, 1970; London: Hale, 1972);

S*E*V*E*N (New York: Fawcett, 1971; London: Hale, 1974)—comprises "The Random Noise of Love," "Dear Old Friend," "The Willow Pool," "Quarrel," "Woodchuck," "Double Hannenframmis," and "The Annex";

A Tan and Sandy Silence, Travis McGee series (New York: Fawcett, 1972 [i.e., 1971]; London: Hale, 1973);

The Scarlet Ruse, Travis McGee series (New York: Fawcett, 1973; London: Hale, 1975);

The Turquoise Lament, Travis McGee series (Philadelphia: Lippincott, 1973; London: Hale, 1975);

The Dreadful Lemon Sky, Travis McGee series (Philadelphia: Lippincott, 1975 [i.e., 1974]; London: Hale, 1976);

Condominium (Philadelphia: Lippincott, 1977; London: Hale, 1977);

The Empty Copper Sea, Travis McGee series (Philadelphia: Lippincott, 1978; London: Hale, 1979);

Other Times Other Worlds (New York: Fawcett, 1978; London: Hale, 1979);

The Green Ripper, Travis McGee series (Philadelphia: Lippincott, 1979; London: Hale, 1980);

Free Fall in Crimson, Travis McGee series (New York & San Francisco: Harper & Row, 1981; London: Collins, 1981);

Nothing Can Go Wrong, by MacDonald and John Kilpack (New York & San Francisco: Harper & Row, 1981);

Cinnamon Skin: The Twentieth Adventure of Travis McGee (New York & San Francisco: Harper & Row, 1982; London: Collins, 1982);

The Good Old Stuff: 13 Early Stories, edited by Martin H. Greenberg and others (New York & San Francisco: Harper & Row, 1982; London: Collins, 1982);

More Good Old Stuff (New York: Knopf, 1984);

One More Sunday (New York: Knopf, 1984; London: Hodder & Stoughton, 1984);

The Lonely Silver Rain, Travis McGee series (New York: Knopf, 1985; London: Hodder & Stoughton, 1985);

Barrier Island (New York: Knopf, 1986; London: Hodder & Stoughton, 1987);

Reading for Survival (Washington, D.C.: Library of Congress, 1987);

Meditations on America: John D. MacDonald's Travis McGee Series and Other Fiction, by MacDonald and Lewis D. Moore (Bowling Green, Ohio: Bowling Green State University Popular Press, 1994);

Film Classic: Cape Fear (London: Bloomsbury, 1997).

OTHER: *Mystery Writers of America Anthology,* edited by MacDonald (New York: Dell, 1959);

Richard Riley, *The Gulf Coast of Florida,* introduction by MacDonald (Skyline Press, 1984).

SELECTED PERIODICAL PUBLICATIONS–
UNCOLLECTED: "Cash on the Coffin," *Detective Tales* (May 1946);

"A Handful of Death," as Peter Reed, *Doc Savage* (June 1946);

"Blame Those Who Die," *Short Stories* (25 June 1946);

"Bury the Pieces!" *Dime Mystery* (July 1946);

"Get Dressed for Death," *Mammoth Mystery* (October 1946);

"The Scarred Hand," as John Farrell, *Doc Savage* (November 1946);

"The Startled Face of Death," as Scott O'Hara, *Doc Savage* (November 1946);

"Oh, Give Me a Hearse!" *Dime Detective* (October 1947);

"My Mission Is Murder," *Dime Detective* (November 1947);

"The High Walls of Hate," *Dime Detective* (February 1948);

"With Soul So Dead," *Dime Detective* (March 1948);

"One Vote for Murder," *New Detective* (March 1948);

"Her Black Wings," *Shock* (March 1948);

"High Dive to Oblivion," *Dime Detective* (April 1948);

"Red-Headed Bait," *Detective Tales* (September 1948);

"Scene of the Crime," *Detective Tales* (September 1948);

"Just a Kill in the Dark," *New Detective* (September 1948);

"Trial by Fury," as O'Hara, *New Detective* (September 1948);

"Tune in on Station Homicide," as Reed, *New Detective* (September 1948);

"Killing All Men!" *Black Mask* (March 1949);

"Kiss the Corpse Goodbye," as O'Hara, *Black Mask* (March 1949);

"I'll Drown You in My Dreams," *Dime Detective* (March 1949);

"Danger–Death Ahead!" *New Detective* (March 1949);

"A Corpse in His Dreams," *Mystery Book* (Spring 1949);

"The Widow Wouldn't Weep," *All-Story Detective* (April 1949);

"His Own Funeral," as John Lane, *Detective Tales* (April 1949);

"The Corpse Belongs to Daddy," *Dime Detective* (April 1949);

"Loot for the Unlucky Lady," *FBI Detective* (April 1949);

"Run, Sister, Run!" *Detective Tales* (July 1950);

"Dead Men Don't Scare," *Dime Detective* (July 1950);

"Five-Star Fugitive," as O'Hara, *Dime Detective* (July 1950);

"His Fatal Fling," *Dime Detective* (August 1950);

"The Lady Is a Corpse!" *Detective Tales* (September 1950);

"Exit Smiling," *Dime Detective* (September 1950);

"The Homesick Buick," *Ellery Queen's Mystery Magazine* (September 1950);

"Get Thee Behind Me," *Detective Fiction* (March 1951);

"Case of Nerves," *Detective Tales* (March 1951);

"The Deadliest Game," *Detective Tales* (April 1951);

"Death Is My Comrade," *New Detective* (April 1951);

"Introduction and Comment," *Clues: A Journal of Detection,* 1 (Spring 1980): 63–74.

Author of sixty-seven published novels, more than five hundred short stories, and four nonfiction volumes, John D. MacDonald was one of the most prolific popular writers of the twentieth century. At the time of his death, his novels had sold more than eighty million copies. His works continue to sell briskly in reprints, particularly the twenty-one novels of the Travis McGee series.

In a writing career spanning thirty-six years, MacDonald wrote books classifiable as horror, comedy, corporate drama, and science fiction. The bulk of his books are crime fiction—stories involving suspense, mystery, sudden violence, and the need for solving a puzzle. Few of McDonald's novels can be categorized as "detective fiction" in the strictest sense, as his protagonists are rarely law enforcement agents or private detectives. Indeed, of all his heroes, only Paul Stanial of *The Drowner* (1963) is an authentic private investigator. Fenn Hillyer of *One Monday We Killed Them All* (1961) identifies himself as a detective lieutenant, but his investigative powers go mostly untested in a novel more reminiscent of the Western movie *High Noon* (1952) than of a classic detective novel such as Raymond Chandler's *The Big Sleep* (1940).

MacDonald's first novel, *The Brass Cupcake* (1950), is clearly recognizable as a hard-boiled crime thriller in the traditional mold. He later enlarged the scope of his material with his series protagonist, Travis McGee, who after his debut in *The Deep Blue Good-By* in 1964 occupied most of MacDonald's production. The thoughtful and often damning observations of his contemporary American culture woven into MacDonald's work led critic Anthony Boucher in *Encyclopedia of Mystery and Detection* (1976) to label him "the John O'Hara of the crime suspense story." With McGee, MacDonald reinvigorated what was in the mid 1960s a tired genre; he applied a businessman's method to production and a moralist's approach to theme.

John Dann MacDonald was born 24 July 1916 in Sharon, Pennsylvania. His parents, Eugene Andrew and Marguerite Grace (Dann) MacDonald, had moved from the Bronx a short time before. At age ten, Jack, as he was known in childhood, moved to Utica, New York, with his family, which by then included his younger sister and only sibling, Doris. His father was, by MacDonald's accounts, a reserved man with whom John had a rather emotionally distant, respectful relationship. Throughout MacDonald's youth, his father pursued a career that led him from blue-collar factories to the executive offices of the arms industry. Eugene's work ethic, which included strict adherence to a daily regimen, was a model for the habits MacDonald later developed as a writer.

At age twelve, MacDonald contracted scarlet fever, and, along with it, mastoiditis. His convalescence required bed rest for more than a year, during which he became an avid reader. His taste for books was eclectic; he read great works of literature as well as works by contemporary authors and pulp writers. Forever changed by the experience, he continued to consume books almost obsessively. As reported in Hugh Merrill's *The Red Hot Typewriter: The Life and Times of John D. MacDonald* (2000), MacDonald recalled that as a teenager in Utica he read his way "through library shelves, one book after another, going at the rate of a couple a day for years, making myself myopic and astigmatic."

Despite his love for reading, MacDonald in his youth did not think himself capable of becoming a writer. His education indicates that he was preparing himself for a future in business, perhaps for a career not unlike his father's. He graduated from Utica Free Academy in 1933, an undistinguished student who excelled at touch-typing. After traveling through Europe at age seventeen with an older friend, MacDonald enrolled in the

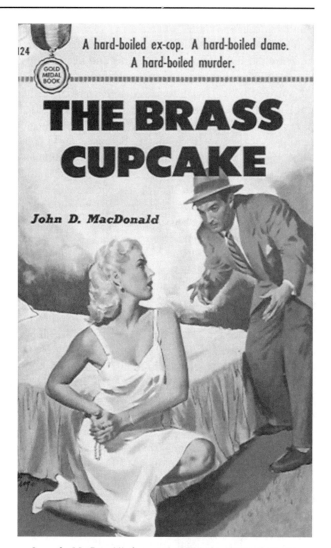

Cover for MacDonald's first novel, published in 1950, inspired by the works of Dashiell Hammett and Raymond Chandler (Collection of Matt Theado)

Wharton School of Business at the University of Pennsylvania but dropped out after three semesters. He then worked odd jobs for three months in New York City and returned to college at Syracuse University, where he graduated in 1938 with a bachelor of science degree in business administration. During his time at Syracuse, he met Dorothy Mary Prentiss, an artist. They married secretly in 1937, officially in July 1938. Their only child, Maynard John Prentiss MacDonald, was born in March 1939, when the MacDonalds were living in Cambridge, Massachusetts. MacDonald received his M.B.A. from Harvard Graduate School of Business Administration in June of that year.

Following graduation from Harvard, MacDonald briefly worked in jobs he was unable or unwilling to hold, including insurance salesman and collection agent. In 1940 he accepted a commission as a first lieutenant in the United States Army Ordnance Department, but he found his military duties only slightly more satisfying than his experiences in the business world. His years in the army did teach him about firearms and manufacturing—knowledge that he put to use in his fiction.

In 1943 MacDonald was ordered overseas to the China-Burma-India theater and was promoted to captain; in 1944 he was recruited by the Office of Strategic Services and promoted to major. Because of the top-secret nature of his assignments, his correspondence home was heavily censored. His creative response to the limits imposed by censorship was to write his wife a letter that included a short story he had written called "Interlude in India" to portray some scenery of his daily life. Dorothy MacDonald, having more confidence in her husband's talents than he did, typed the story and sent it to several publishers. *Esquire* rejected it, but the rejection included a brief note of encouragement. *Story* magazine accepted and paid $25 for the piece. This minor accomplishment had a profound impact on MacDonald, who learned of it only upon his reunion with his wife. As reported by Edgar W. Hirshberg in *John D. MacDonald* (1982), MacDonald recalled, "I did not think of myself as a writer, only one who wished that he were one. . . . When I found out my words had actually sold . . . I felt as if I were a fraud, as if I were masquerading, as if I were trying to be something I wasn't."

Like tens of thousands of veterans returning stateside in 1945, Lieutenant Colonel MacDonald was faced with the necessity of finding work quickly. The sale of his first story energized him to try the writer's trade. In the manner one might expect of a Harvard M.B.A., he approached writing as a business. He went to his typewriter as the businessman goes to the office, beginning early in the morning, breaking for lunch, and returning to work for the remainder of the afternoon. He adhered to this schedule throughout his career, despite his awareness that it was distinctly "unwriterly": "It wasn't until my habit patterns were firmly embedded that I discovered that writers tended to work a couple of hours and then brood about it the rest of the day," he told Joseph Haas of the *Chicago Daily News* in September 1969.

MacDonald considered the postwar years a time of apprenticeship, the first four months of which, as he recalled in a stylized memoir, *The House Guests* (1965), he spent turning out "800,000 words of unsalable manuscript." He kept dozens of stories in the mail to publishers at all times, only retiring a story after it had received a sufficiently discouraging number of rejections. Without Dorothy's support, he might have conceded what others were insisting—namely, that he was a "readjustment problem." In 1946, after five months of hard work, MacDonald sold his second story, "Female of the Species," to *Dime Detective* magazine for $40. By the end of 1946, his stories were selling consistently. Although he wrote

mainly for pulp magazines, such as *Doc Savage* and *The Shadow,* he occasionally did place a piece in the more esteemed and better-paying slicks, such as *Esquire, Cosmopolitan,* and *Liberty*.

As was the case with other pulp writers of his time, MacDonald wrote in several genres, not only police and crime stories but also Westerns, science fiction, and tales based on his experiences in World War II. He knew intuitively how to satisfy the pulp audience's appetite for tight, compelling fiction and soon learned the techniques of effective storytelling. He became a master at quickly setting the scene for crime, as in "You Remember Jeannie," published in *Crack Detective* in May 1949:

> For many years Bay Street was the place. Bar whiskey for thirty cents a shot, or a double slug for fifty. A waterfront street, where dirty waves slapped at the crushed pilings behind the saloons. A street to forget with. A street which would close in on you, day to day, night to night, until the wrong person saw some pitying old friend slip you a five. They would find you at dawn, and an intern from City General would push your eyelid up with a clean pink thumb and say, "More meat for the morgue."

But even though MacDonald became a popular contributor to magazines, he sometimes had to accept tampering with his words. Magazine editors changed many of his original titles, apparently to make them more lurid. *Dime Detective* published thirty-nine of MacDonald's stories over the next five years and changed the titles of all but six of them. He had titled his first professional publication "Paint on Her Hair." His titles "Death for Sale," "A Place To Live," "State Police Report That . . . ," and "Unmarried Widow" were changed to "My Mission Is Murder" (November 1947), "Oh, Give Me a Hearse!" (October 1947), "You'll Never Escape" (May 1949), and "A Corpse-Maker Goes Courting" (July 1949), respectively.

The pulps were harmed by the advent of paperback novels and television. Nonetheless, from 1946 to 1950, MacDonald published more than two hundred short stories in their pages, under both his own name and various pseudonyms: John Lane, Henry Reiser, John Wade Farrell, Robert Henry, Peter Reed, and Scott O'Hara. He accepted the use of pseudonyms to accommodate pulp editors who wished to conceal that one author had written more than one story for a particular issue. For example, MacDonald published three stories in *The Shadow* in December 1946; editors gave two of the stories to "house name" authors Peter Reed and Robert Henry. While this practice was acceptable to MacDonald at the time, he later objected to the use of pen names. He told Merrill in *The Red Hot Typewriter* that "the writer is in the business of dropping his trousers in the town square, and it is unfair to wear a mask while doing so."

By 1950 MacDonald had proven his ability to produce impressive quantities of salable fiction for the short-story market. As an indication of the prolific output MacDonald achieved once he was under way, he published eleven stories in a two-month period during the winter of 1946–1947, and in 1949, he published seventy-three stories. When Fawcett Publishing commissioned its new line of paperback originals, Gold Medal Books, MacDonald was perfectly suited to the needs of a quickly expanding niche in the novel-publishing market. The Gold Medal line was Fawcett's attempt to join the increasingly lucrative paperback market. Instead of merely reprinting novels from the hardcover publishers, Gold Medal Books brought out paperback originals. At that time, the company was distributing The New American Library of World Literature (NAL), and by contractual arrangement was proscribed from competing for reprint rights.

For the first few years after the war, the MacDonalds lived in New York State, then spent a year in Mexico, where they found living far more affordable. Inspired partly by their mutual admiration of Malcolm Lowry's novel *Under the Volcano* (1947), they chose to live in the town of Cuernavaca. The year provided MacDonald with experiences and ideas he explored in several later works. The MacDonalds returned briefly to New York in fall 1949. Then, in what was their nomadic fashion at the time, they moved to Florida, ultimately settling for good in Sarasota in 1951.

MacDonald made his first foray into the traditional world of the crime detective novel long before the advent of Travis McGee. Of all MacDonald's work, his first published novel, *The Brass Cupcake,* owes the greatest debt to the detective fiction of Dashiell Hammett and Raymond Chandler. The first edition of the book employs the phrase "hard-boiled" three times in cover blurbs, lest the casual book shopper mistake it for anything else. Cliff Bartells, the protagonist of *The Brass Cupcake,* is a former cop who turns in his badge after being demoted to foot patrolman because he refuses to "play ball" with the local crime syndicate. He explains, "The process tagged me once and for all a square cop—a Christer who couldn't be made." He describes his policeman's brass badge in jailhouse language:

Anything you got by guile—extra cigarettes, more food, a pint bottle—was called a cupcake. You could lose a cupcake the same way. So when they took it away from me, it wasn't even a badge any more. Just another cupcake. Something I chiseled and then got chiseled out of. A brass cupcake. Something of no importance. No importance at all. Yet I cried into my pillow like a fool kid that night.

Bartells takes a job as an insurance investigator and uncovers a murder-for-profit scheme. He solves the

Cover for MacDonald's 1952 novel, one of several inspired by his time spent living in Mexico in 1948–1949 (Collection of Matt Theado)

crime, exposes the depth of local police corruption, wins the girl, and is rehired, this time as deputy chief.

MacDonald continued the same high production rate in the paperback-novel business as he had in the pulps. Fawcett published seven MacDonald novels by the end of 1953: *The Brass Cupcake, Murder for the Bride* (1951), *Judge Me Not* (1951), *Weep for Me* (1951), *The Damned* (1952), *The Neon Jungle* (1953), and *Dead Low Tide* (1953). While MacDonald avoided the conventional hero of detective fiction in subsequent novels, *The Brass Cupcake* provides a glimpse of narrative conventions he employed in much of his later mystery fiction. Primarily, he established a distinct narrative voice, which conveyed an unabashedly moralistic tone.

In "A Letter from JDM," first published in the March 1972 issue of *JDM Bibliophile,* MacDonald unapologetically maintained that moral concerns were at the heart of his work: "To many tastes, I am and shall remain a writer of less than genuine literary merit because I am, at the heart of it all, a moralist. I believe people must accept responsibility for those acts which affect the lives of others." Nearly every novel MacDonald wrote is an exploration of human behavior in the face of difficult ethical quandaries. The reader can clearly tell what the author sees as the proper choice for the characters; yet, when they fall, MacDonald makes their missteps understandable and believable in light of their human frailties, vanities, and appetites. Up until the adventures of Travis McGee, rarely is moral ambiguity found in the costly and dangerous consequences of their follies.

Another of MacDonald's principal aims is to tell a good story. "My purpose is to entertain myself first and other people secondly," he told an interviewer in the 10 March 1975 issue of *Newsweek*. "If you can make a living doing this, it's like a license to steal." In the 23 June 1982 *Washington Post*, book reviewer Jonathan Yardley claimed that one of MacDonald's "most admirable qualities as a novelist is that he almost unfailingly manages to deliver precisely the pleasure that his readers anticipate–a quality too-little noticed and remarked upon among writers whose principal business it is to entertain. But also as usual, MacDonald provides a good deal more than mere diversion." MacDonald has the ability to hold the reader's attention with fast-paced action and intriguing, if rather hastily sketched, characters.

The well-constructed first chapter of MacDonald's second novel, *Murder for the Bride,* exemplifies his ability to engage the reader. It opens with oilman Dil Bryant looking for petroleum reserves in the swamps of Mexico. Bryant's first-person narration vividly evokes in only three brief paragraphs the jungle surroundings and its inherent hardships; then Bryant confesses to being distracted by reveries of his recent honeymoon with the lovely and mysterious Laura Rentane. Mail call brings a letter from a friend back home, urging him to return, asserting that Laura is in trouble, "probably the worst kind." Bryant decides to leave immediately, but not before an old friend and coworker reveals his disapproval of Laura and his opinion that she is "an international tramp." A brief fistfight ensues, but even as Bryant defends his bride's honor, the flavor of desperation is in his words and thoughts–a hint of a man in the thrall of the femme fatale. Bryant describes his return to New Orleans, where he discovers that Laura has been murdered. The first chapter ends with a police interrogation, a scene that serves to expose unsavory and suspicious aspects of Laura's character and to reveal how little Bryant actually knows about her beyond her irresistible sexuality. The final paragraph of the twelve-page chapter sets the hook, as he remembers hearing Laura talk in her sleep: "It sounded like German. She said that was silly because she couldn't speak German."

At this point MacDonald's main character makes the transformation to crime detective. The shock of Laura's murder is compounded by the realization that everyone near to him believed her to be "cheap," "hard-eyed," "ruthless," or worse. Determined to prove them wrong, he tells his boss he is quitting to find the murderer. His boss replies, "You gotta be heroic, eh? Go plunging around and make like catching murderers. A movie boy. Amateur cop." Thus, *Murder for the Bride* is the first of many MacDonald mysteries featuring ordinary men caught in situations that compel them to act in the capacity of private investigators. MacDonald had perfected this pattern in the short stories of the pulp-fiction market. For example, his story "A Corpse-Maker Goes Courting" opens with Max Raffidy, a newspaper reporter whose paper has just folded, sitting alone in a bar drinking not enough to drown his misery, but just enough "to make it swim a little." A lovely but thoroughly dazed young woman bursts into his gloom, mistaking him for her fiancé, who, it turns out, has disappeared mysteriously. Raffidy appreciates two reasons for helping out the girl: she is a damsel in distress, and he might be able to use her plight for a feature story that would get him hired by the other newspaper in town. At first his cause is noble enough: "Sir Raffidy rears in on his white horse," the knight-errant that Travis McGee became fifteen years later. Raffidy's naiveté nearly undoes him and the girl. While under his care, the girl is kidnapped by the same thugs who killed her fiancé, and now Raffidy, the erstwhile hero, is "alone with his enormous guilt." Guilt is another element for later novel heroes, culminating in McGee.

Drawing from his experiences with arms and his business education, MacDonald often chose to give his able but untrained heroes professions from the private sector–executives or managerial types in manufacturing industries; architects and construction contractors; or insurance men. Such characters allow MacDonald to enrich his stories with the arcana of American business and the dynamics of men in positions of power.

As he was establishing his name in the paperback-novel market, MacDonald was developing a signature convention, well known to his fans and critics alike. Labeled variously as digressions, musings, dissertations, rants, sermons, lectures, commentary, or proselytizing, these passages are found with increasing frequency and length as one traces the history of MacDonald's work, finding their most expansive expression in the Travis McGee series. Encompassing such diverse topics as customer service, medicine, sex, juvenile delinquency, drugs, economics and finance, urban decay, the credit-card industry, and (perhaps the one most dear to him) development and its impact on the environment, MacDonald's "sociological asides" (his description in the spring 1980

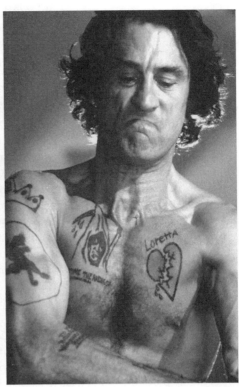

Robert Mitchum (left) as the sadistic villain Max Cady in Cape Fear, *the 1962 motion-picture adaptation of MacDonald's 1958 novel* The Executioners. *Robert De Niro played the role in the 1991 remake (left: AP Wide World; right: Corbis).*

issue of *Clues: A Journal of Detection*) afford him an opportunity to relate his moral vision more explicitly. For example, in *The Turquoise Lament*, McGee presents his view on the Fort Lauderdale Christmas scene:

> The unaffiliated, unfamilied, uninvolved make the obligatory comments about Christmas being the Great Retailers' Conspiracy. Buy now. You don't owe a dime until February. The Postal Service gets their big chance to screw up the delivery of three billion cards. Urchins turn the stores into disaster areas. Counter clerks radiate an exhausted patience leavened with icy flashes of total hate. The energy crisis is accelerated by five billion little colored light bulbs, winking on and off in celebration. Amateur thieves join the swollen ranks of the professionals in ripping off parked cars loaded with presents, in picking pockets, prying sliding doors open, shoplifting and mugging the ever-present drunk. Bored Santas jingle their begging bells and the old hymns blur loudly through the low-fidelity speakers of department-store paging systems.

McGee's screed veers from the usual Scrooge rant, though, when he segues to the topic of air conditioning. McGee outlines the violations of common sense by merchants and hotel managers who, by turning the thermostats low, become "the unknowing victims of a long-term conspiracy" run by architects and building contractors who pocket kickbacks by pushing larger-than-needed air-conditioning units. McGee concludes that if all thermostats were blocked to prevent such low indoor temperatures, then the power companies would burn less fuel for electricity and people would be healthier. McGee closes his sermon by pointing out an ironic twist as he returns to the narrative: "So it was a reversal of the Christmas temperatures of the remembered childhood in northern places. Lauderdale was steamy hot on the outside, achingly frigid on the inside." Nonetheless, in *A Bibliography of the Published Works of John D. MacDonald* (1980), he recognizes the split reaction among readers: "I get as many letters from people saying, 'Get off your damn soapbox and get on with the story,' as I get letters from people who say, 'Gee, I love all those asides. I don't like the plots and I don't like all that violence. I just read the books because I like what you say about things.'"

MacDonald also incorporated more-traditional genre conventions into his writing. Regardless of their occupations, but in keeping with their circumstantial status as detectives, MacDonald's crime-fiction protagonists embody traits typical of the private investigator. They work alone, often pitted against the evil principals of the story as well as the local law enforcement apparatus, which at times are one and the same. Any cooperation they receive is given grudgingly and only when the abilities of the hero have earned the respect of a good cop. They may use violence to further their ends, reluctantly or in self-defense, and their involvement, while sometimes professional at the outset, inevitably evolves into a personal stake.

MacDonald held dear the belief that good can conquer evil; however, his conviction may have been reinforced by how well the axiom served him in the marketplace. MacDonald admitted a weakness for tidy conclusions. The tendency certainly did not harm him as a popular writer. If sales figures are any measure, his readership never tired of his version of the rewards of righteousness. Most of the early MacDonald mysteries conclude with the hero emerging unscathed, notwithstanding a random gunshot wound or facial contusion. Waiting for him, sometimes in a hospital bed of her own, is the love interest. This pattern, however, like many of MacDonald's other narrative conventions, became less predictable in the Travis McGee books.

In May 1955 MacDonald published "The Bear Trap" in *Cosmopolitan,* for which he won the Ben Franklin Award for best short story in an American popular magazine. Also that year MacDonald left Gold Medal Books to work for his friend Knox Burger, an editor at Dell First Editions. *Soft Touch* (1958), a Dell book, provides an early example of MacDonald's experimentation with his popular formula. An atypical protagonist, Jerry Jamison of *Soft Touch* is a man who believes in his own essential decency. Dissatisfied working for his incompetent father-in-law, he tells his wife, Lorraine, that he is ready to quit. However, Lorraine, a shallow, vulgar alcoholic, refuses to cooperate with his plans to rebuild their lives. When former army buddy Vince proposes to hijack the payoff in an illegal arms deal, Jamison's domestic malaise and the apparent moral ambiguity of the crime lead him to join the scheme. After this first fateful decision, Jamison gradually compromises his standards further, committing adultery and, finally, murder. MacDonald builds a character who could have saved himself had he shown real moral conviction. After giving in to the lure of easy money, though, Jamison finds reversing course increasingly more difficult, until he is virtually forced to commit the next crime to hide the last. In keeping with MacDonald's vision of justice, Jamison is the instrument of his own undoing. In the madness brought on by his descent into evil, he leads the authorities to where he remembers burying the loot. In fact, it is where he has buried his wife. *Soft Touch* is a MacDonald morality tale with a twist; none of the three principal characters has a happy ending. They all must suffer the consequences of their venality.

Lorraine Jamison is a familiar type among MacDonald's characters. Women of her ilk provide a necessary stress on the lead male characters. A few deft narrative strokes paint a coarse, fading beauty, once lush in appearance, but now simply a lush. She is first described seated at the vanity in yellow bra and panties, "doing her nails, half an old fashioned handy at her elbow." Spoiled, vain, and driven by material desires, Lorraine and other such figures in MacDonald's fictional world represent the worst in womanhood. They are unable to support or empathize with the noble impulses of the hero because nobility is foreign to their primitive mentalities. Accustomed to a world of quid pro quo, these women are prostitutes in all but name, capable of instantly transferring their loyalties to the highest bidder or the strongest beast. They function to demonstrate how worthless the human condition becomes when reduced to an economic equation. MacDonald returns to the type often in the McGee series, creating situations in which Travis can exercise his brute appeal to use such women as tools in his investigations.

Savvy in matters of business, MacDonald artfully controlled the publication of his novels. Although he forfeited a degree of critical consideration in so doing, he continued having his books published in paperback form through the 1950s and 1960s, even when the option of hardback became available to him. He believed the volume of softcover copies he could sell would net far more than hardbacks, which he viewed as prohibitively expensive to the general public. His latest releases and reprints filled the racks of magazine stands in bus and train stations and drugstores nationwide. By the late 1950s, confident of his reputation, he began to allow the initial publication of some, though not all, of his books in hardback. *The Executioners* (1958) was the first he wrote with the hardback market in mind. It brought him many reviews, his first book-club deal, and the adaptations of his book for the movie *Cape Fear* (1961 and 1991). In June 1958 *The New Yorker* declared *The Executioners* a "competently written and ingenious story" and concluded that "altogether the effect is unusually chilly." The critic for *The New York Herald Tribune* took notice of MacDonald's narrative strengths while still describing him with the usual caveats reserved for the genre writer, proclaiming in an 8 June 1958 review that MacDonald "tells an exciting story which keeps you reading from start to finish. He is no practitioner of the distinguished style or the sensitive detail, but he can spin an expert yarn." *The Saturday Review* and *The San Francisco Chronicle* acknowledged MacDonald's capacity for maintaining suspense (1 July and 6 July 1958, respectively), and *The New York Times* critic, Anthony Boucher, himself a prizewinning crime and science-fiction writer, glowingly reviewed *The Executioners* in a 1 June 1958 piece: "MacDonald not only tells, with quiet realism, a powerful and frightening story; he takes a deeper look than most suspense novelists at the problem of private and public justice."

In the late 1950s MacDonald returned to his original publisher, Fawcett, when Burger left Dell to take a job with Fawcett. *Where Is Janice Gantry?*, published by Fawcett in 1961, features another often repeated MacDonald prototype, the sadistic cop. In this case, Sheriff Millhaus uses physical force on suspects and witnesses to intimidate or extract information. Millhaus is the local law enforcement apparatus with whom Brice runs afoul. In MacDonald's moral cosmos, sadists who abuse their authority always receive retribution. At the least, they are exposed for the savages they are and lose their positions; when their crimes are egregious, they may pay for them with their lives. Implicit in the denouement is MacDonald's faith in the ultimate triumph of what is right, while a character such as Millhaus may believe his brutality is excusable when it furthers the interests of justice—or, more accurately, his twisted view of justice. MacDonald makes the hubris of a character such as Millhaus blatant; thus, he allows his reader to anticipate the character's eventual downfall, which is invariably the result of the superior performance and morality of the amateur detective. MacDonald employs cops in various ways throughout the Travis McGee series, from those who defend their turf—and with whom McGee must contend, as his meddling often convinces the cops that he himself is a suspect in the crime—to the truly brutal and sadistic cops, most notably deputies Lew Arnstead and King Sturnevan of *The Long Lavender Look* (1970).

In MacDonald's good-versus-evil moralistic universe, the villains are a breed apart. They appear frequently in the company of the good guys, but before long they make themselves known through their vindictive actions. Once revealed, they stalk about with neither guile nor remorse. Fenn Hillyer, the detective lieutenant hero of *One Monday We Killed Them All*, begins his adventures when he picks up his brother-in-law from prison. Dwight McAran clearly has not been reformed. Hillyer's police background equips him with the ability to perceive McAran's "innate capacity for lawless violence. It is idiotic to use a word like psychopath. That is a wastebasket word, a receptacle for all those people in whom we detect a kind of strangeness with which we can make no valid contact." McAran is incapable of empathy but expert at mimicking it, knowing it is useful in deceiving others. McAran also represents various other traits that characterize MacDonald's villains as Hillyer states:

> They are overly plausible. Their eyes seem to have a curious opacity. They laugh too quickly at your first joke, and wander away in the middle of your second one. Their smiles are practiced in front of mirrors. Any concern seems faked. There is never any evidence of anxiety. To them the great sin is not in sinning but in being caught at it. Add a constant need for and carelessness with money, plus a ruthless use of women, and the

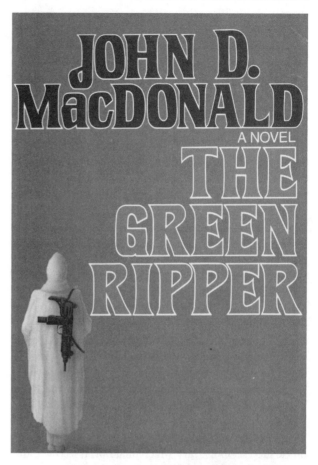

Dust jacket for MacDonald's eighteenth novel featuring "salvage consultant" Travis McGee, published in 1979 and winner of the American Book Award in 1980 (Richland County Public Library)

proficient cop begins to tighten up a little, because it is a pattern he has seen before.

In addition, McAran's appearance is physically deceptive. Like other MacDonald villains, initially he seems weaker and smaller than he later proves to be: "He is one of those men who do not seem particularly big until you notice some small detail, such as the great thickness of wrist." Junior Allen in *The Deep Blue Good-By* is a typical MacDonald villain. Strong beyond his girth, violent and sadistic, he can be shrewdly calculating when plotting evil and then cat-like in his quickness when fighting. When McGee finally kills Junior in a gruesome finale, McGee is surprised by his triumph: "I kept looking for him. I couldn't believe that anything had ended him." In a sense, nothing had "ended him," for he reappears in various guises throughout the series.

Just as MacDonald's efforts as a short-story writer in the 1940s had prepared him for his career as a novelist, his work in the 1950s and early 1960s served as preparation for the even greater popular success of the Travis

McGee series. By the early 1960s, MacDonald was receiving critical notice, particularly from his champion at *The New York Times,* Boucher. On 9 August 1959, Boucher wrote that *The Crossroads* "is one of John D. MacDonald's suspense-stories-that-approach-straight-novels, devoted less to theft and murder (though these are ingenious) than to an examination of a complex family enterprise . . . and the people in the family who run it." Boucher continued his careful reading and effulgent praise of MacDonald's work in his 4 September 1960 review of *The End of the Night,* calling it "a serious examination of a socio-psychological problem" and at the same time "an irresistibly readable suspense story."

In 1962, MacDonald was elected president of the Mystery Writers of America, and the French translation of *A Key to the Suite* (1962) earned him the Grand Prix de Littérateur Policiere. Also that year, Burger proposed the idea of a serial character to MacDonald. As the result of a dispute, Burger had allowed Richard Prather, author of the Shell Scott mystery series, to leave Fawcett, and Burger asked MacDonald to provide a replacement series. MacDonald had rejected a similar proposition earlier in his career, fearing it would limit his range. (Prather later parodied the philosophical ramblings of MacDonald's series hero, Travis McGee, with the villain Burper McGee in his 1969 novel *The Cheim Manuscript.*)

McGee was introduced in four novels released in quick succession in 1964. MacDonald produced and discarded two versions of the first installment, *The Deep Blue Good-By,* before hitting upon the McGee characteristics that satisfied him. A blurb on the 1986 reprint of this first novel of the series identifies Travis as "part rebel, part philosopher, and every inch his own man . . . the rugged, sexy Florida boat bum with a special genius for helping friends in trouble." The second novel in the series, *Nightmare in Pink* (1964), was published simultaneously with *The Deep Blue Good-By. A Purple Place for Dying* (1964), *The Quick Red Fox* (1964), and *A Deadly Shade of Gold* (1965) followed, all five having been in progress or near completion before the first novel was published. MacDonald recalls that he considered various methods of identifying his McGee books as a series, including numbers, musical terminology, and days of the week. Burger suggested that MacDonald use colors, and he approved of the idea. Readers could identify the series easily but not feel compelled to read the books in any predetermined order.

MacDonald established McGee's reluctant-hero traits in *The Deep Blue Good-By;* McGee describes himself as "that big brown loose-jointed boat bum, that pale-eyed, wire haired girl-seeker, that slayer of small savage fish, that beach-walker, gin-drinker, quip-maker, peace-seeker, iconoclast, disbeliever, argufier, that knuckly, scar-tissued reject from a structured society. . . ." When the first novel opens, McGee simply cannot ignore a young woman's call for help: "But now Cathy had created the restlessness, the indignation, the beginnings of that shameful need to clamber aboard my spavined white steed, knock the rust off the armor, tilt the crooked old lance and shout huzzah." A Korean War veteran and former football player who keeps himself fit and trim, McGee generally impresses women with his size but is sometimes underestimated by foes. He describes himself before a fight: "I am tall, and I gangle. I look like a loose-jointed, clumsy hundred and eighty. The man who takes a better look at the size of my wrists can make a more accurate guess."

McGee ages as the series goes on—from approximately thirty-eight years old to forty-three, over the publishing history of twenty years—though he shows remarkably few handicaps from the physical wounds inflicted on him during his adventures. He does not escape so easily from the emotional wounds, though, and this vulnerability endeared him to readers. He emerges as the "knight-errant," the wounded hero who grows wiser but more jaded and embittered, gathering his courage and strength one more time—for each novel—to take on the forces of injustice. As a novel progresses, McGee's reflexes quicken; his reasoning grows crisper; all of his senses intensify until he is fully charged, a relentless pursuer of evildoers. But then each novel typically ends with him wounded anew, bearing physical scars outwardly and emotional scars inwardly.

Beyond his ability as a yarn spinner and master of his trade—each novel presents a "whodunit" that unfailingly involves lavish sex and brutish violence—MacDonald succeeded in his series through making McGee an engaging and memorable character. He is both savage and sentimental, capable of mercilessly torturing a thug to gain information and then lovingly preparing tea and hot soup for a sick girlfriend. In the 10 March 1975 issue of *Newsweek,* Arthur Cooper identifies the split in the hero: "a cynic who knows that man is base and a romantic who wants to believe he isn't." Newgate Callendar in the 7 October 1979 issue of *The New York Times Book Review* proclaimed that MacDonald's hero "is what every man dreams of being: tall, strong, honest, indestructible, a demon with the ladies (but only one at a time, please) and—above all—a man with an aura that makes everybody look at him with a combination of respect and fear. . . . Yet the author also wants us to believe that Travis McGee is a pussycat."

Other of McGee's qualities doubtless appealed to readers as well. McGee lives on a fifty-two-foot houseboat that he won in an all-night poker game, in a story appropriately named "The Busted Flush." Moored at Slip F-18, Bahia Mar, in Fort Lauderdale, this floating bachelor pad features a king-sized bed and gigantic shower, as well as a series of gimmicks and special features that become apparent when the plot requires them. His only drug is alcohol, preferably Plymouth gin, and he offsets its effects by maintaining his physical stamina with long stints repairing his boat and punishing runs through knee-deep surf. He drives an electric blue Rolls Royce converted into a pickup truck, modified for style and usefulness. Though technically unemployed, he supports himself by helping his friends—and friends of friends—who find themselves in trouble in ways that make them hesitant to go to the police for assistance. McGee's usual fee is half of whatever the victims hope to recover. This self-described "salvage consultant" is essentially an unlicensed detective, and his amateur status frees him to choose his work and his methods. While going about his salvage work, he spouts his particular brand of philosophical musings, battles corruption and villainy, and beds women. He enjoys more than fifty bedmates in twenty-one novels.

McGee not only solves crimes, he usually aids in the redemption, when possible, of the young women victims, often leading to a sexual relationship. The McGee women are frequently the "broken birds," beaten down or cowed by their pasts or by the brutal villain whom McGee is after. The happy ending (beyond the brief sun- and love-filled cruise), as far as the love interest is concerned, is precluded by the serial formula. MacDonald could not carry over characters often, as that would limit his possibilities in the next book and go against McGee's essential nature as a loner. The women are part of temporary relationships by mutual understanding. Cathy Kerr in *The Deep Blue Good-By* and Isobel Webb in *A Purple Place for Dying* are conveniently killed; Nora Gardino in *A Deadly Shade of Gold* and Cindy Birdsong in *The Dreadful Lemon Sky* (1975) are not up to a permanent relationship; Puss Killian in *Pale Gray for Guilt* (1968) presumably dies of cancer after the book ends but lives long enough to bear McGee's daughter, who finds him in the final book, *The Lonely Silver Rain* (1985). Some women in the novels—the prostitutes-in-all-but-name type—are not capable of being redeemed. Two notable variations on the type are Vangie Bellemer in *Darker Than Amber* (1966) and Mary Alice in *The Scarlet Ruse* (1973).

More so than in his earlier novels, MacDonald invests his hero with many of his own concerns, his so-called sociological asides. At times, McGee is clearly MacDonald's mouthpiece, venting or holding forth, rallying or decrying. In *Dress Her in Indigo* (1969), for example, McGee notices "a tragic flaw in the narcotics laws—that possession of marijuana is a felony. Regardless of whether it is as harmless as some believe, or as evil and vicious as others believe, savage and uncompromising law is bad law. . . ." McGee gives his reasoning:

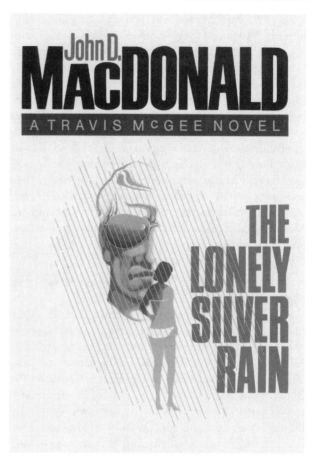

Dust jacket for MacDonald's last Travis McGee novel,
published in 1985 (Richland County Public Library)

Let's say a kid in Florida, a college kid eighteen years old, is picked up with a couple of joints on him. He is convicted of possession, which is an automatic felony, and given a suspended sentence. What has he lost? The judge who imposes sentence knows the kid has lost the right to vote, the right to own a gun, the right to run for public office. He can never become a doctor, dentist, C.P.A., engineer, lawyer, architect, realtor, osteopath, physical therapist, private detective, pharmacist. . . . It slams too many doors. It effectively destroys the kid's life. It is too harsh a penalty for a little faddish experimentation. The judge knows it. So he looks for any out, and then nothing at all happens to the kid. Too many times harsh law ends up being, in effect, no law at all.

Such digressions serve to fill out McGee's character, and MacDonald is careful not to allow what may be considered an indulgence to derail his story.

Although McGee is essentially a loner, his stalwart friend and confidant, Meyer, plays an important role in the series. An independently wealthy, highly intelligent, semiretired economist in his early fifties, Meyer lives near McGee on a boat of his own; unlike McGee he is content to stay out of trouble and lead a much calmer life. Unfortunately, as with McGee's women, Meyer at times is all too close to the action for his own safety. In addition to being a generally chummy companion and chess partner for McGee, Meyer provides a conversational foil when McGee needs to sort out his motivations. In the November 1986 issue of *Psychology Today,* Raymond D. Fowler compared the sides of MacDonald's personality with those of his fictional creations, McGee and Meyer. Fowler determined that if McGee is an alter ego for MacDonald, the Harvard M.B.A. who would rather type all day than seek adventure, then Meyer is much more like his creator. He represents a sane, reasoned center in the midst of McGee's violence-rocked world. In terms of structure, Meyer provides readers with insights into McGee's ethical rationale and emotional depths.

In the last year of his life, MacDonald wrote an essay on the importance of books, "Reading for Survival." In the introduction, MacDonald told his editor that he had much difficulty producing a successful essay: "I could not make the essay work, and I could not imagine why. I must have done two hundred pages of junk. Then Jean Trebbi [director of The Florida Center for the Book] wrote asking me why didn't I use the device of a conversation between McGee and Meyer. Why indeed?" One last time, MacDonald brought out his fictional team for a verbal slugfest of conversation and camaraderie, to exhort his audience to read and to show that reading is vital to the survival of the species.

John D. MacDonald is best known today for his accomplishments in the Travis McGee series, a run of publishing successes that broke the mold MacDonald had fashioned for himself as a writer of pulp fiction and a genre novelist. From 1964 until his death from complications following open-heart surgery 28 December 1986, MacDonald published only four non-McGee novels. *The Last One Left* (1967) was nominated for an Edgar Award as the best mystery of the year. In 1971, Syracuse University presented MacDonald the Pioneer Medal, an honor given their most prominent alumni. In 1972 the Mystery Writers of America presented him with their highest honor, the Grand Master Award. In 1980, he received the American Book Award for McGee's eighteenth adventure, *The Green Ripper* (1979).

MacDonald excelled in the crime and suspense genre even as he transcended the limits critics often associate with it. Praise for his work often came wrapped in the qualification that he was a mystery writer—or a science-fiction writer—and then, despite the categorization, a good writer. Novelist Jim Harrison wrote in the 23 February 1975 *New York Times Book Review* that "MacDonald could never be confused with the escapism that dominates the suspense field." Harrison admitted that

although generally he is not appreciative of what he calls lightweight books, he was impressed that his literary friends, who, while not making "extravagant critical claims" for MacDonald's work, "all readily admit that MacDonald is a very good writer, not just a good 'mystery writer.'" Harrison details one quality of the Travis McGee series that elevates it beyond those of other series sleuths: "McGee has all the grief of a moralist. He simply can't stand the way things in our republic have gone from awful to worse, but he hesitates to preach about it. His morals, in short, are not 'situational.'" When Harrison wrote these words, MacDonald was in complete command of his craft. His profundity at times matched his literary fertility, and he always rewarded his readers, whether they came in search of a dash of philosophy or a boatload of guns, thugs, girls, and cash—all swathed in McGee's blend of muscles and sighs, granite vengeance and tender remorse.

Letters:

A Friendship: The Letters of Dan Rowan and John D. MacDonald 1967–1974 (New York: Knopf, 1986).

Interview:

Joseph Haas, "Maestro of the Mystery," *Panorama–Chicago Daily News,* 6–7 September 1969, p. 4.

Bibliography:

Jena Shine and Walter Shine, *A Bibliography of the Published Works of John D. MacDonald* (Gainesville: University of Florida Libraries, 1980).

References:

Raymond D. Fowler, "The Case of the Multicolored Personality," *Psychology Today,* 20 (November 1986): 38–42, 46–47, 49;

David Geherin, *John D. MacDonald* (New York: Ungar, 1982);

Edgar W. Hirshberg, *John D. MacDonald* (Boston: Twayne, 1982);

Hugh Merrill, *The Red Hot Typewriter: The Life and Times of John D. MacDonald* (New York: St. Martin's Minotaur, 2000);

Herbert Mitgang, "Behind the Best Sellers: John D. MacDonald," *New York Times Book Review,* 15 May 1977, p. 42;

Walter Shine, *Rave or Rage: The Critics and John D. MacDonald* (Gainesville: University of Florida Libraries, 1993).

Papers:

The John D. MacDonald Manuscript Collection is held by George A. Smathers Libraries at the University of Florida.

F. van Wyck Mason
(Geoffrey Coffin, Frank W. Mason, Ward Weaver)
(11 November 1901 – 28 August 1978)

Peter Kenney

BOOKS: *Seeds of Murder* (Garden City, N.Y.: Doubleday, Doran, 1930; London: Eldon, 1937);

Captain Nemesis (New York & London: Putnam, 1931);

The Vesper Service Murders (Garden City, N.Y.: Doubleday, Doran, 1931; London: Eldon, 1935);

The Fort Terror Murders (Garden City, N.Y.: Doubleday, Doran, 1931; London: Eldon, 1936);

The Yellow Arrow Murders (Garden City, N.Y.: Doubleday, Doran, 1932; London: Eldon, 1935);

The Branded Spy Murders (Garden City, N.Y.: Doubleday, Doran, 1932; London: Eldon, 1936);

Spider House (New York & London: Mystery League, 1932);

The Shanghai Bund Murders (Garden City, N.Y.: Doubleday, Doran, 1933; London: Eldon, 1934); revised as *The China Sea Murders* (New York: Pocket Books, 1959; London: Consul, 1961);

The Sulu Sea Murders (New York: Doubleday, Doran, 1933; London: Eldon, 1936);

The Budapest Parade Murders (Garden City, N.Y.: Doubleday, Doran, 1935; London: Eldon, 1935);

Murder in the Senate, by Mason and Helen Brawner as Geoffrey Coffin (New York: Dodge, 1935; London: Hurst & Blackett, 1936);

The Washington Legation Murders (Garden City, N.Y.: Doubleday, Doran, 1935; London: Eldon, 1937);

The Forgotten Fleet Mystery, by Mason and Brawner as Coffin (New York: Dodge, 1936); as F. van Wyck Mason (London: Jarrolds, 1943);

The Seven Seas Murders (Garden City, N.Y.: Doubleday, Doran, 1936; London: Eldon, 1937);

The Castle Island Case (New York: Reynal & Hitchcock, 1937; London: Jarrolds, 1938); revised as *The Multi-Million Dollar Murders* (New York: Pocket Books, 1960; London: Hale, 1961);

The Hong Kong Airbase Murders (Garden City, N.Y.: Doubleday, Doran, 1937; London: Jarrolds, 1940);

The Cairo Garter Murders (Garden City, N.Y.: Doubleday, 1938; London: Jarrolds, 1938);

F. van Wyck Mason (courtesy of F. van Wyck Mason Jr.)

Three Harbours (Philadelphia: Lippincott, 1938; London: Jarrolds, 1939);

The Singapore Exile Murders (New York: Doubleday, Doran, 1939; London: Jarrolds, 1939);

Stars on the Sea (Philadelphia: Lippincott, 1940; London: Jarrolds, 1940);

The Bucharest Ballerina Murders (New York: Stokes, 1940; London: Jarrolds, 1941);

Hang My Wreath, as Ward Weaver (New York: Funk, 1941; London: Jarrolds, 1942);

The Rio Casino Intrigue (New York: Reynal & Hitchcock, 1941; London: Jarrolds, 1942);

Rivers of Glory (Philadelphia: Lippincott, 1942; London: Jarrolds, 1944);

Q-Boat, as Frank W. Mason (Philadelphia: Lippincott, 1943);

End of Track, as Weaver (New York: Reynal & Hitchcock, 1943);

Pilots, Man Your Planes! as Mason (Philadelphia: Lippincott, 1944);

Flight into Danger, as Mason (Philadelphia: Lippincott, 1946);

Saigon Singer (Garden City, N.Y.: Doubleday, 1946; London: Barker, 1948);

Eagle in the Sky (Philadelphia: Lippincott, 1948; London: Jarrolds, 1949);

Cutlass Empire (Garden City, N.Y.: Doubleday, 1949; London: Jarrolds, 1950);

Dardanelles Derelict (Garden City, N.Y.: Doubleday, 1949; London: Barker, 1950);

Valley Forge: 24 December 1777 (Garden City, N.Y.: Doubleday, 1950);

Proud New Flags (Philadelphia: Lippincott, 1951; London: Jarrolds, 1952);

Himalayan Assignment (Garden City, N.Y.: Doubleday, 1952; London: Hale, 1953);

The Winter at Valley Forge (New York: Random House, 1953); republished as *Washington at Valley Forge* (Eau Claire, Wis.: E. M. Hale, 1953);

Golden Admiral: A Novel of Sir Francis Drake and the Armada (Garden City, N.Y.: Doubleday, 1953; London: Jarrolds, 1954);

Wild Drum Beat (New York: Pocket Books, 1953);

The Barbarians (New York: Pocket Books, 1954; London: Hale, 1956);

Blue Hurricane (Philadelphia: Lippincott, 1954; London: Jarrolds, 1955);

Two Tickets for Tangier (Garden City, N.Y.: Doubleday, 1955; London: Hale, 1956);

Silver Leopard: A Novel of the First Crusade (Garden City, N.Y.: Doubleday, 1955; London: Jarrolds, 1956);

Captain Judas (New York: Pocket Books, 1955; London: Hale, 1957);

Our Valiant Few (Boston: Little, Brown, 1956); republished as *To Whom Be Glory* (London: Jarrolds, 1957);

Lysander (New York: Pocket Books, 1956; London: Hale, 1958);

The Gracious Lily Affair (Garden City, N.Y.: Doubleday, 1957; London: Hale, 1958);

The Young Titan (Garden City, N.Y.: Doubleday, 1959; London: Hutchinson, 1960);

Return of the Eagles (New York: Pocket Books, 1959);

Secret Mission to Bangkok (Garden City, N.Y.: Doubleday, 1960; London: Hale, 1961);

The Battle of Lake Erie (Boston: Houghton Mifflin, 1960);

Manila Galleon (Boston: Little, Brown, 1961; London: Hutchinson, 1961);

The Sea Venture (Garden City, N.Y.: Doubleday, 1961; London: Hutchinson, 1962);

Trouble in Burma (Garden City, N.Y.: Doubleday, 1962; London: Hale, 1963);

The Battle for New Orleans (Boston: Houghton Mifflin, 1962);

Zanzibar Intrigue (Garden City, N.Y.: Doubleday, 1963; London: Hale, 1964);

Rascals' Heaven (Garden City, N.Y.: Doubleday, 1964; London: Hutchinson, 1965);

Maracaibo Mission (Garden City, N.Y.: Doubleday, 1965; London: Hale, 1966);

The Battle for Quebec (Boston: Houghton Mifflin, 1965);

Wild Horizon (Boston: Little, Brown, 1966);

The Deadly Orbit Mission (Garden City, N.Y.: Doubleday, 1968; London: Hale, 1968);

The Maryland Colony (New York: Crowell-Collier / London: Collier-Macmillan, 1969);

Harpoon in Eden (Garden City, N.Y.: Doubleday, 1969; London: Hutchinson, 1970);

Brimstone Club (Boston: Little, Brown, 1971; London: Hutchinson, 1972);

Roads to Liberty (Boston: Little, Brown, 1972);

Log Cabin Noble (Garden City, N.Y.: Doubleday, 1973); republished as *Stand before Kings* (London: Hutchinson, 1974);

Trumpets Sound No More (Boston: Little, Brown, 1975; London: Hutchinson, 1976);

Guns for Rebellion (Garden City, N.Y.: Doubleday, 1977; London: Hutchinson, 1978);

Armored Giants: A Novel of the Civil War (Boston: Little, Brown, 1980; London: Hutchinson, 1981).

Collections: *Captain North's Three Biggest Cases* (New York: Grosset & Dunlap, 1932)—comprises *The Vesper Service Murders, The Yellow Arrow Murders,* and *The Branded Spy Murders;*

Military Intelligence—8 (New York: Stokes, 1941)—comprises *The Washington Legation Murders, The Hong Kong Airbase Murders,* and *The Singapore Exile Murders;*

Oriental Division G-2: Captain North's Three Famous Intrigues of the Far East (New York: Reynal & Hitchcock, 1942)—comprises *The Sulu Sea Murders, The Fort Terror Murders,* and *The Shanghai Bund Murders;*

The Man from G-2: Three of Major North's Most Important Adventures (New York: Reynal & Hitchcock, 1943)—comprises *The Cairo Garter Murders, The Yellow Arrow Murders,* and *The Rio Casino Intrigue.*

OTHER: *The Fighting American: A War-Chest of Stories of American Soldiers, from the French and Indian Wars through the First World War,* edited by Mason (New

York: Reynal & Hitchcock, 1943; London: Jarrolds, 1945);

American Men at Arms, edited by Mason (Boston: Little, Brown, 1964).

SELECTED PERIODICAL PUBLICATIONS—UNCOLLECTED: "The Repeater," *Ellery Queen's Mystery Magazine* (February 1947);
"The Port of Peril," *The Saint* (August 1955);
"The Plum-Colored Corpse," *The Saint* (September 1956);
"Port of Intrigue," *The Saint* (January 1957);
"An Enemy at the Dinner Table," *Mike Shayne Mystery Magazine* (February 1965).

Although F. van Wyck Mason wrote many historical novels and books for older juveniles, he is known primarily by mystery and detective readers for his twenty-seven books featuring Hugh North. He also wrote four mysteries using three other protagonists. Mason's main concerns, besides family and work, were his military career, outdoor life, wide travel, and a love of history. He put all of these interests and passions together in the North series, in which a military career man finds high adventure amid political intrigues in exotic locations around the world. Mason was particularly proud of his extensive travels, and on the occasion of his fiftieth anniversary report to his Harvard class of 1924 he wrote: "My principal recreation is traveling, which has been too extensive to enumerate here, and, I have visited all the continents in connection with research or military duties."

Francis van Wyck Mason was born in Boston on 11 November 1901 to Francis Payne Mason and Erma (née Coffin) Mason. He was descended from an old Nantucket family. During the first eight years of his life Mason lived abroad while his grandfather Francis Paine Mason, was American consul in Munich and Paris. He had one younger brother, Charles Caffin Mason.

Mason's military experience—which included a total of eighteen years, counting both active service and reserve duty—had a profound effect on his writing, especially the development of the North series. At the age of sixteen he served briefly as an ambulance driver in the Verdun region of France during World War I. Later, in 1918–1919, he secured a commission as a second lieutenant in the American Expeditionary Force of the U.S. Army. Mason's duties were primarily as an interpreter since he was fluent in both French and Spanish. For this service he received the Medaille de Sauvetage.

After the war Mason spent one year at Berkshire School in Massachusetts before going to Harvard,

Dust jacket for Mason's 1952 novel, in which spy Hugh North foils Russian and Chinese agents who are trying to gain influence in a small country between Nepal and Tibet (Richland County Public Library)

from which he graduated in 1924. Mason next settled in New York City, where he became a sergeant in the 101st Cavalry of the New York National Guard, from 1924 to 1929. This unit was long associated with the polo-playing elite of the city. He then moved to Baltimore, where he served as a first lieutenant in the 110th Field Artillery of the Maryland National Guard, from 1930 until 1933. Mason married Dorothy Louise Macready on 19 November 1927 in New York City. They had two sons: Francis van Wyck Jr., born in 1928, and Robert Ashton, born in 1930.

Mason was a full-time writer during most of his adult life, except for brief stints in the wallpaper business and then as an importer of antiquarian books, maps, rugs, and embroideries. Writing was his only occupation after 1928 other than World War II military service. The earlier part of his writing career was dominated by mystery and detective novels. The latter part was devoted mostly to historical novels, although he continued to produce Hugh North stories until

1968. Commenting on Mason's mystery novels in *The St. James Guide to Crime & Mystery Writers,* J. Randolph Cox remarked: "Stripped to their essential detective structure, the novels involve a problem for North to solve which includes a series of murders and a puzzle to unravel. This may be a message to be deciphered, the true meaning of a word or phrase, or the location of a treasure, all of which become keys to the larger mystery. The vivid background based on careful research and Mason's own travels is part of the appeal of the stories."

Mason describes North's background in the foreword to the ninth novel in the series, *The Washington Legation Murders* (1935). North was born in 1883 in New Hampshire; because his father, a former U.S. attorney general, was investigating corruption in the consular service, North spent his early years in Europe before returning to the United States to attend West Point. After graduating with honors, he became an assistant military attaché at Vienna: "There his taste for criminal investigation soon became apparent, and he spent much time with the criminologists who were then making Vienna famous in police circles throughout the world." During World War I he was in charge of army counterespionage in France and foiled a plot to assassinate the representatives at the Versailles Conference. After the war he was permanently assigned to the Department of Criminal Investigations of G-2, "whose functions include the investigation of the most delicate matters of state."

North makes an inauspicious debut in Mason's first novel, *Seeds of Murder* (1930). The important clues in the story are three datura seeds placed in the form of a triangle beneath the bodies of two murder victims. North is a houseguest and is invited to investigate because of his fame as a World War I investigator. Reviewing the novel in *Books* (27 July 1930), Will Cuppy called it "fast, furious and thoroughly readable." The reviewer for the *Bookman* (November 1930) concurred, calling the novel "a right smart story of what happened to a wealthy Wall Street broker who defrauded his friends and subjected his wife to endless cruel indignities." The reviewer for the *New York Post* (2 August 1930), however, expressed a contrary opinion: "So inexpertly treated that none of it becomes even momentarily convincing or exciting."

In *The Vesper Service Murders* (1931) North is invited to take part in the investigation of a series of murders in the city of Deptford, Massachusetts, again because of his reputation as a World War I investigator. This time the invitation comes from the local police. He is already famous because of newspaper publicity about previous cases he has solved, dating back to his World War I army service in Europe. He

employs a knowledge of American Morse code as a tool of detection in this case. The book is written in the style of a police detective story, with North's friend Walter Allan, a doctor, narrating, as he does in *Seeds of Murder. The Vesper Service Murders* is the last mystery book in which Mason employs a narrator.

Reviewing *The Vesper Service Murders* in *Books* (24 May 1931), Cuppy showed reservations about the novel: "The tale is marred in spots by awkward plotting, ectoplastic characters and dialogue that is not a bit like it." Bruce Rae, in *The New York Times Book Review* (24 May 1931), was more positive: "Aside from his failure to sustain suspense, Mr. Mason has done well in other departments. He draws a fine picture of corruption in a small city and of the efforts of the moral elements to stamp it out." W. R. Brooks, in the 3 June 1931 issue of *Outlook,* called the novel "a swift and consistent yarn."

North is a guest at a dinner party at the residence of Colonel Peter Andrews in *The Fort Terror Murders* (1931). The colonel is the commanding officer of Fort Espanto in the Philippines. At the party Inez Sarolla tells the other guests a legend about hidden treasure in the fort that has been passed down through generations of local residents. Several men have died mysteriously in pursuit of it. A search party for the treasure is spontaneously organized, led by Inez's cousin Ricardo Mendez and her fiancé, Lieutenant Dale Bowen. Mendez and Bowen disappear into the old ruins of the fort. Later a scream is heard. Mendez is found dead from a knife wound, but Bowen is missing. Andrews asks North to conduct an investigation of the murder. North's only clues are two rosaries and a little piece of sheepskin. The solution to the puzzle will lead to the treasure. Cuppy, writing in *Books* (27 December 1931), found the novel lacking: "Those who undertake this quest must be prepared for more childishness than usual." Isaac Anderson, in *The New York Times Book Review* (27 December 1931), noted: "The entire action of the story takes place during two nights and a day, but more things happen during that short time than are usually crowded into a year. An unusually good mystery thriller."

In *The Yellow Arrow Murders* (1932) North is sent to Cuba to either buy or steal advanced torpedo plans that are being sold in Cienfuegos by the inventor of the new weapon. The seller of the plans calls himself Alvarado, but his real name is Doelger. He is a disgruntled American who was discharged from the U.S. Navy for dereliction of duty in 1918. When North arrives in Cienfuegos, he finds plenty of competitors already there seeking the prize. Some are agents of their governments, while others are adventurers in the game for profit. In one role or another there are representatives from England, France, Japan, Germany, Russia, Portugal, and Italy. *The Yellow Arrow Murders* is the first novel in the series in which North operates in a foreign country under orders from G-2, the intelligence division of the U.S. Army.

Mason followed up *The Yellow Arrow Murders* by sending North to Honolulu in *The Branded Spy Murders* (1932). North's mission is primarily to prevent a war from breaking out between Japan and the United States. A Japanese naval squadron is headed toward Honolulu with unknown intent. North attends a party at the home of Abner Polk, owner of a large American steel company. The other guests at the party include intelligence operatives from Russia, France, England, and Japan as well as steel barons from France and Germany. All have an interest in either starting or preventing the war. Before the evening is over a dead woman is found floating near Polk's dock. She has a strange design on her shoulder, perhaps a tattoo that has been erased. North must identify the dead woman and uncover how her death fits into a plot to start war. The toughest obstacle he faces in this adventure is his attraction to Nadia Stefan, a beguiling Russian agent. Considering the fact that the story was written in 1932, Mason showed apparent prescience in depicting a near attack by Japanese naval ships on Honolulu. William C. Weber, reviewing the book in the *Saturday Review of Literature* (21 January 1933), noted: "This happens in Honolulu and is an international affair, in which a United States secret service man finally defeats the plotters who would plunge America and Japan into warfare. Quite a few people are dispatched in various unpleasant ways before the heroine dies and saves the game." A reviewer for the *Boston Transcript* (28 December 1932) wrote: "Perhaps the author has never been anywhere near Hawaii, but he sounds convincing."

Mason interrupted the Hugh North series at this point in his career to write *Spider House* (1932), in which the protagonist is Janos Catlin, a state police captain. Catlin is called to the house of Ezra Boonton, who used to run a shady brokerage firm on Wall Street. Boonton is receiving threatening letters from dissatisfied clients who have lost money from investments sold by his company. Boonton is known as "the spider of the street" because of his many crooked deals.

When Catlin arrives at the house he finds a paranoid Boonton, who is being attended by Dr. George Lawes and nurse Dora Delray and guarded by an oversized butler named Kelly. Also at the house are a male nurse named Gruber and Boonton's younger brother, Juan. Before long Kelly is murdered. Later, Ezra is killed, and Catlin has to find the murderer, who is thought to be still in the house. The plot is compli-

Dust jacket for Mason's 1960 novel in which Hugh North is assigned to protect an American rocket scientist traveling to Thailand to search for his missing wife (Richland County Public Library)

cated by the presence of a blackmailer and a drug ring whose main operative is Gruber. After some solid detective work, Catlin solves the murder cases by proving that Lawes killed both Kelly and Boonton. Lawes is in turn murdered by Delray, who slits his throat with a scalpel while he tries to implicate her in his crimes. The book ends with an inexplicable scene wherein Catlin promises to visit Delray in prison.

Mason returned to his series protagonist with *The Shanghai Bund Murders* (1933), in which North is on a riverboat heading toward Shanghai during a time when there is much fighting and turbulence surrounding that city. On the trip a young Englishman named Trenchard is murdered. North is joined on the boat by his friend from British military intelligence, Bruce Kilgour. North learns that Trenchard was a British agent trying to get information on an arms shipment being sent to General Wang, a warlord with ties to French and Italian interests. Wang is now threatening Shanghai, which is defended by General Yuan, who is backed by England and the United States. A third army planning to attack Shanghai is led by an American soldier of fortune named Sam Steel.

North's mission is to locate an arms shipment before either Wang or Steel can seize it and cause disaster for the American and English residents of Shanghai. Almost every country with a political or economic interest in Shanghai has a representative engaged in the search. As usual North finds that the lines between friend and foe often seem blurred. The tale takes place after Japan seized Manchuria and set up the puppet state of Manchukuo in 1931. The Chinese warlords and not the Japanese are presented as the main villains in the story, however.

In his next adventure, *The Sulu Sea Murders* (1933), North is investigating a shooting in a bar in Zamboanga in the Philippines. A pearl diver named George Lee is dying from a wound inflicted by an unidentified American soldier. The murderer is probably from Fort Winfield on the nearby island of Sanga Sanga. North proceeds to Fort Winfield, and finds that the killings seem to be tied to a valuable collection of pearls lost with the recent sinking of the junk *Chu Shan*. *The Sulu Sea Murders* is not a spy story; in fact, North is sometimes referred to in the novel as a detective. Anderson, writing in *The New York Times Book Review* (15 October 1933), reviewed the novel enthusiastically: "There is no lack of excitement in this swiftly moving yarn of murder in the tropics." The reviewer for the *Saturday Review of Literature* (14 October 1933) agreed that the novel offered "excitement and lucid action amidst squalid surroundings."

North goes to Hungary in *The Budapest Parade Murders* (1935) to investigate the murder of Sir William Woodman, a famous pacifist. He must also recover certain letters stolen from Woodman, which provide proof that the munition manufacturers of the world are conspiring to create a war. Anderson, in writing in *The New York Times Book Review* (6 January 1935), commented on Mason's characteristically complicated plotting: "There are plots and counter-plots without number, and so many persons are interested in securing the letters for one purpose or another that North's task seems almost impossible."

In a change of pace, Mason introduced Scott Stuart, an inspector for the Department of Justice and a new protagonist, who solves the poisonings of an attaché and a senator in *Murder in the Senate* (1935). Stuart is described as having a stocky build, in contrast to North's tall and fairly lean physique. Stuart is also more blunt and aggressive in manner than North. *Murder in the Senate* was written by Mason and Helen Brawner under the pseudonym George Coffin and was generally well received. Anderson, for example, wrote in the 10 November 1935 issue of *The New York Times*

Book Review: "The story is loaded with propaganda, which will please or displease the reader according to his political opinions and affiliations, but the author has contrived to weave all this into a story brimful of excitement and suspense."

North works on a counterintelligence assignment in *The Washington Legation Murders*. A recent wave of spying has resulted in the loss of American tank designs and other valuable military secrets to several foreign powers. Much of the spying has been attributed to a mastermind called simply the Guardsman. North and Count Erich Oxenstahl of the Swedish Legation devise a plan to trap the Guardsman. A rendezvous is arranged, and Oxenstahl goes to the designated meeting spot with $50,000 to buy secrets about U.S. cruiser torpedo protection. Oxenstahl and his bodyguard, Sergeant Baker, are both found murdered, however, and Senator Freeman, who is sponsoring a bill providing severe penalties for those caught spying against the United States, is also killed.

Construction of five new cruisers and two dreadnoughts is to begin soon in various American shipyards. North and his British ally Kilgour must solve the murders and put a stop to the Guardsman before more military secrets are stolen. To assist them North enlists the services of Vanessa Byrne, who is temporarily out of work after being fired from her job at the Baltic Legation. Vanessa seems innocent enough, but she is descended from a long line of Irish soldiers of fortune, and her allegiance is always in doubt.

This story was written after Adolf Hitler rose to power and Germany, Japan, and Russia had all become possible adversaries in any future conflict. Top-secret weapons mentioned by the author include the stratosphere bomber and the antitorpedo machine gun. C. W. Morton Jr., in the *Boston Transcript* (7 December 1935), wrote that the novel "belongs in the upper middle class of secret service fables." Anderson agreed in *The New York Times Book Review* (8 December 1935): "In short, the story has everything that a novel of international intrigues should have."

Scott Stuart makes another appearance in *The Forgotten Fleet Mystery* (1936), also written by Mason and Brawner as Coffin. The inspector is on the trail of Ernst Marwitz, who has been trying to sell stolen military secrets to Italy and Japan. Stuart is particularly interested in preventing a formula for a new type of fuel from falling into the hands of any potential enemy. The trail leads to the site of some old German liners maintained as reserve transports after World War I off Maryland. Traveling in disguise, Stuart manages to get a job as a watchman on one of the ships. His employer is Geneva Bennet, who is trying to recover some jewels that she believes are hidden on one of the vessels. The jewels were stolen from her late father, who was convicted of insurance fraud and later sent to prison as a result of the crime. There is a connection between the mystery of the missing jewels and the theft of military secrets. In order to discover the truth, Stuart has to determine the identity of Marwitz among the many different people he meets on his new job, as well as expose the international jewel thief known to the police as Baron Hermann Von Ehrenbreit. Anderson, in the 18 October 1936 edition of *The New York Times Book Review,* wrote that *The Forgotten Fleet Mystery* "is packed with excitement and swift action from the first page to the last."

After a collection of four North novellas, *The Seven Seas Murders* (1936), Mason published one of his most unusual books, *The Castle Island Case* (1937), in collaboration with Henry Clay Gipson, a photographer. The text of the novel is interspersed with photos depicting incidents in the story, sometimes including clues. The models for the photos were selected mostly from local Bermudians, and Mason himself was used for photos of Inspector Boyd of the Bermuda police force.

Major Roger Allenby travels on the *Bermuda Clipper* to investigate the disappearance of Judy Fortier. Miss Fortier left a convincing suicide note, but her body has never been found. She is insured by Inter-Ocean Life Assurance Company, for which Allenby is an investigator. Similar to both Mason and North, Allenby has a military background of service during World War I. Otherwise, Mason provides little personal information about his protagonist. After Allenby arrives in Bermuda, he goes as a guest to the house of Barnard Grafton. He is posing as a potential investor in Grafton's latest project, the Rio Loia Power Company in Ecuador. Other houseguests include Grafton's partner, Townley Ward, and Patricia Fortier, the sister of the missing girl. Judy had been Grafton's secretary and lover for the past two years. Judy had remained Grafton's secretary after he had unexpectedly married a wealthy widow from Boston, but she had been obviously depressed about this betrayal.

During Allenby's first evening in Bermuda a dinner party is hosted by Grafton. Early the following morning Patricia Fortier is found slain. Before this murder can be solved, Grafton's wife is also killed. The mystery is then further complicated by the discovery of Judy Fortier, who is found alive and in hiding on the island. The leading murder suspects include Grafton's boatman, Creepy, and Ward. A crucial clue turns out to be a granny knot tied by the killer, which leads Allenby to conclude that Ward is the villain, since all of the other suspects have significant boating experience and are not likely to use such a knot.

Mason uses a trip on a flying boat to introduce some of the major characters of *The Castle Island Case,* a device he also employs two years later in *The Singapore Exile Murders* (1939). Cuppy expressed his approval of *The Castle Island Case* in the 10 October 1937 issue of *Books:* "The story is fast and full of shudders—a welcome travel-mystery. It's also a splendid ad for Bermuda and a certain camera." A reviewer in the 9 October 1937 issue of the *Saturday Review of Literature* also liked the new format, asserting that the "plentitude of candid camera shots (by Gipson) add zest to a thriller more highly seasoned than most." Anderson, however, writing in *The New York Times Book Review* (14 November 1937), disagreed: "As for us, we'll take our Van Wyck Mason straight, if he doesn't mind."

Mason next resumed the North series with *The Hong Kong Airbase Murders* (1937). Trans-Pacific Airways has developed an emergency fuel formula that can provide clipper ships with a greatly increased flying range of up to six thousand miles. The formula, however, has not yet been perfected. When the operations manager of Trans-Pacific commits suicide, he leaves a note mentioning the secret formula and its amazing possibilities. The suicide note is published in a newspaper, giving the secret formula wide publicity. North is sent to Hong Kong to keep the formula away from any potential enemies in a future war. He quickly learns that there are several operatives seeking the formula. There is also a rival airline, Air Oriental, which is planning a Pacific route and wants to have the advantages of the new fuel. Air Oriental is registered as a Chinese corporation but uses German pilots and equipment.

Sam Patterson, the chief engineering officer of Trans-Pacific, is murdered; the company safe is broken into; and the formula is stolen. North believes that the murder of Patterson and the theft of the formula are connected. The leading suspects are Patterson's former and current girlfriends. Also under suspicion are the new operations manager of Trans-Pacific and the Macao manager of Air Oriental. In addition, North must consider representatives of Japanese, Russian, and French interests. North pursues his investigation at a time when tensions are heating up before World War II in both Europe and the Far East. Germany in particular is singled out as a threat. He is aided by Sir George Amberson and Inspector Yu Shih of the Royal Victoria Police.

Kay Irvin reviewed *The Hong Kong Airbase Murders* positively in *The New York Times Book Review* (12 September 1937): "The story races from adventure to adventure, from one puzzling detail to another, but the suspense of the main theme is well sustained." Cuppy, writing in *Books* (26 September 1937), was also enthusi-

Cover for a 1967 paperback reprint of Mason's 1965 novel in which Hugh North travels to Venezuela to prevent Russian agents from using a newly developed secret weapon (Collection of Mark McEwan)

astic: "Our author, who has been favorably compared with E. Phillips Openheim, does wonders with the secret process and the spies, adding plenty of good Hongkong color to the mix-up."

Mason next sent North to Africa in *The Cairo Garter Murders* (1938). North assists Kilgour on a case involving a series of murders in Cairo. The killer leaves a woman's red and black garter fastened about the left arm of each victim. The murders are somehow linked with the recent supplying of Arab tribes with modern weapons, which has led to trouble brewing in Palestine. Solution of the crimes is aided by the ability of North and his allies to decode messages, including one written in hieroglyphics. The book was praised by several critics. Cuppy, in *Books* (8 May 1938), called it "both meaty and exciting—a spring bargain for brows of any height," while the reviewer for the *Saturday Review of Literature* (30 May 1938) judged it "topnotch."

Set in Southeastern Asia before the outbreak of World War II, *The Singapore Exile Murders,* another North novel, is a fast-paced story involving the struggle for a secret formula for making more effective steel for military armor. Most of the countries striving for power in the region at that time have an agent searching for the prize. North, who early in the novel is promoted to the rank of major, represents the United States. Writing in *Books* (11 June 1939), Cuppy observed that the novel includes "one of Mr. Mason's snappiest climaxes."

After the outbreak of World War II in Europe, North is sent to Romania in *The Bucharest Ballerina Murders* (1940). Most critics were lukewarm about this effort, as exemplified by the reviewer in *The New Yorker* (2 November 1940), who wrote: "This story, centered in Cernauti, Rumania, combines authentic sounding atmosphere with weakish melodrama." In *The New York Times Book Review* (3 November 1940), however, Anderson was more enthusiastic: "This is as lively an adventure as Hugh North has ever encountered in his long and colorful career."

North makes his last appearance before the United States entered World War II in *The Rio Casino Intrigue* (1941). In this novel he is in Brazil investigating the activities of the Americus Arms Corporation, which employs several fascist and Nazi sympathizers. After he moves his investigation from São Paulo to Rio de Janeiro, North learns of an unidentified ship that is headed to an unknown Brazilian port carrying Axis saboteurs, technicians, and gold to help fifth columnists in their efforts to gain a foothold in Brazil and surrounding countries. North's mission is to find out the identity and destination of the ship and prevent its reaching Brazil.

Using friends and contacts in Rio, North arranges a party, to which are invited leading members of the local Patriotistas movement. All are suspected of being supporters of the Axis cause, and most are either of Spanish, German, Italian, or Japanese ancestry. At the party Luis da Evarista, president of Americus Corporation, is murdered. North decides that the solution of the murder may lead to the information he needs to stop the unidentified ship. He receives help from Aurora Morrow, niece of a shipping magnate. The most interesting character in the novel, however, may be Paula Harte, who was born in Chile but whose father was a German subject who died during World War I. Paula is now acting as a freelance agent, trying to sell information to the highest bidder.

Charlotte Dean, in *The New York Times Book Review* (2 November 1941), wrote that *The Rio Casino Intrigue* "is all very exciting, full of greed, passion and murder, and the solution is sad but satisfactory." The reviewer in the *Springfield Republican* (30 November 1941) noted that it leaves a "lasting impression . . . less . . . of high entertainment than of stern warning."

In January 1942 Mason went on active duty with the U.S. Army as a major. Promoted to lieutenant colonel in December 1942 and later to colonel in May 1945, he served in Europe at the General Staff Corps of the Supreme Headquarters Allied Expeditionary Force from October 1944 until July 1945. His duties there were primarily as chief historian of the civil and military government section. Mason's military honors in World War II included the croix de guerre with two palms. He was also made an officer in the French Legion of Honor.

Saigon Singer (1946) is the first North mystery Mason wrote after World War II. North returns to Asia, where he was last seen in *The Singapore Exile Murders*. He goes to Saigon to track down a tangled web of traitors, blackmailers, and smugglers, including a Swiss banker, a beautiful singer, and at least one impostor. In addition to writing a good mystery story, Mason offers a look at a slice of Saigon life before the postwar troubles in Indochina began in earnest. A reviewer in the 30 November 1946 issue of *The New Yorker* wrote: "North accomplishes his mission and clears up a couple of murders as well. Just the thing for those who like a neat plot, accompanied by incense, eggplants, and other Oriental trimmings." Hoffman Birney, in *The New York Times Book Review* (24 November 1946), described the novel as "a slam-bang, slap-dash tale of brawls and boudoirs, magnates and mistresses, guns, poison, grand opera." Anthony Boucher, writing in the *San Francisco Chronicle* (15 December 1946), observed: "The gallant major's return is highly welcome after five years; the Annamite local color is fascinating; and even howlers in opera and chemistry do not keep this from being one of the best of the North novels."

Dardanelles Derelict (1949) is the first Hugh North novel to present a Cold War adventure. North is in Turkey pretending to be drunk and disillusioned, but he is really trying to penetrate a network of communist spies. The goal is to obtain a certain microfilm with secrets that will allow the United States to regain the lead from Russia in the development of missiles and bacteriological weapons. As usual, Mason's plot accurately reflects the tensions of the times.

North's female helper in this adventure is Haidi Lawson, a newspaper reporter of part Turkish ancestry. At the end of the story North proposes marriage to Haidi, who is hospitalized with the flu. Readers learn later in *Two Tickets for Tangier* (1955), however, that Haidi never recovered from her illness and died in Istanbul. The reviewer for *The New Yorker* (26 November 1949) did not have high praise for *Dardanelles Dere-*

lict: "The descriptions of life in Turkey, social and military, seem valid, but beyond that there's very little to recommend the book." Beatrice Sherman, in the 20 November 1949 edition of *The New York Times Book Review*, gave the novel a mixed review: "The style is corny, the adventure is rip-roaring, the death rate high, and victory for our side sure in the finish, let the bodies fall where they may."

In *Himalayan Assignment* (1952) North is sent to the semi-independent state of Jonkhar, which acts as a buffer zone between Nepal and Tibet. His mission is to defeat attempts by Russia and China to gain influence in the tiny territory and control over its strategic location. North's chief allies are Ad Delahanty and Subnadar Thopa. Delahanty is a former U.S. Army sergeant who was dishonorably discharged for desertion. He is currently the owner of a business that outfits hunting and mountaineering expeditions. Thopa is a Ghurka mountain guide whose skills are indispensable during North's long trek overland to Jonkhar.

The opposition includes Russian and Chinese agents, who are also competing against each other. Members of the Jonkhar royal family have their own personal agendas based mostly on the struggle for succession to the throne of the Sri Rajah. The one loose cannon in the whole mix is Baroness Atossa Frederika Matala. Although she is an Estonian and allied with the Russians, the baroness is also a liberated lady who is capable of making her own deals. North is promoted to colonel.

James Kelly mentioned the limitations of *Himalayan Assignment* in *The New York Times Book Review* (20 January 1952), judging the novel "a medium-grade North adventure which will not be likely to disappoint regular fans or cast a spell over newcomers." E. J. Fitzgerald noted the complexities of the plot in his review in the *Saturday Review of Literature* (9 February 1952): "The complications get a little thick at times, and sometimes it's hard, even with a scorecard, to tell which side the players are on." The reviewer for the *Springfield Republican* (17 February 1952) gave a more positive assessment: "It's a very timely story and a remarkably fine adventure yarn."

In *Two Tickets for Tangier* North is sent to Africa. His mission is to locate a German scientist named Franz Vogel, who has been working in Russia since the end of World War II. Vogel has invented a deadly new gas called "thulium-X," the formula for which he carries only in his head. Since escaping from Russia, he has been hiding in Tangier. Marya Bessemer, a German whose main occupation has been dealing in forged passports, has been acting as a broker for Vogel. She plans to make as much money as possible for herself on any transaction involving the formula.

VAN WYCK
MASON

THE DEADLY
ORBIT MISSION

A new
Colonel North
adventure

Dust jacket for the last of Mason's Hugh North novels, published in 1968 (Richland County Public Library)

North is delayed en route from London to Tangier because of a plane crash at sea. He survives the crash and recuperates in Paris. Meanwhile, someone impersonating him arrives in Tangier and negotiates with Bessemer for the formula. The impostor is really Major Reginald Travis, formerly of Her Majesty's Grenadier Guards, now working as a spy for Moscow. Travis gets the formula from Vogel, then kills the scientist and goes undercover in Tangier to wait for a meeting with notorious Russian agent Ilya Kyushev.

North's challenges once he arrives in Tangier are to convince the local authorities that he is the real Colonel North and to track down Travis before he hands over the formula to Kyushev. He gets help on the case from Lady Angela Forrester, a British intelligence operative.

L. G. Offord, writing in the *San Francisco Chronicle* (10 April 1955), considered the novel "routine, perhaps, but expert and readable, uncluttered by ideologies." In *The New York Times Book Review* (6 March 1955), Henry Cavendish praised Mason's eye for exotic atmosphere: "Proper amounts of cocktail drink-

ing and love making are pleasantly blended with a whole welter of other shenanigans against the chromatic backdrop of Tangier, which Mr. Mason has painted with a loose but wonderfully picturesque brush."

North solves his twentieth case in *The Gracious Lily Affair* (1957), which bears the usual Mason trademarks of thorough research—exotic locales, a smorgasbord of intriguing characters, a series of murders, and a puzzle to solve within the larger riddle. The case begins in Bermuda, where a Portuguese plane carrying a courier crashes offshore. As always, Mason's attention to detail stands out, with North in this case traveling to more than sixty locales between Bermuda and the Far East. Along the way Mason also offers interesting tidbits on local ethnic customs. Richard Match, writing in *The New York Times Book Review* (20 October 1957), praised Mason's "smooth brand of tongue-in-cheek melodrama" but noted that it "played out according to rules as stylized and artificial as a game of chess." James Sandoe, in the *New York Herald Tribune Book Review* (20 October 1957), was less complimentary: "About half of Van Wyck Mason's new thriller is reasonably amusing but inflation sets in, excitement is not really multiplied by multiple corpses and nothing ever lifts Mr. Mason's prose off dead level."

Mason's first wife died on 17 March 1958. He then married his secretary, Jeanne-Louise Hand, on 3 October 1958 in Boston. The couple moved to Bermuda in 1963, where they lived luxuriously at "Hampton Head" in Southhampton. Mason was a longtime president of the American Society of Bermuda and a member of the Royal Bermuda Yacht Club. He was also a member of the Harvard Club (New York City), the Army and Navy Club (Washington, D.C.), and the Devonshire Club (London) and was a fellow of both the Society of Collectors and Historians and Boston University Libraries.

Mason completely rewrote *The Shanghai Bund Murders* and published the substantially altered version of the story as *The China Sea Murders* in 1959. The names of some of the characters were retained, but the plot was entirely revised to reflect the changing politics of East Asia. Chinese warlords were replaced as villains by Chinese Communists, and much of the action takes place aboard a ship traveling from Formosa to Korea rather than on a riverboat going to Shanghai. Similarly, *The Castle Island Case* was revised as *The Multi-Million Dollar Murders* (1960). In this instance, however, Major Roger Allenby is replaced as the protagonist by North.

In *Secret Mission to Bangkok* (1960) North is traveling from Honolulu to Bangkok under the assumed name of Charles Boyden. His mission is to protect Dr.

Hans Bracht, who is aboard the same airplane but unaware of North's identity. Bracht is a U.S. rocket scientist who has come to Thailand to search for his missing wife; North has been assigned to follow him and make sure he does not fall into Russian hands before returning to the United States.

The two men stay at the Imperial Hotel in Bangkok, and North has to identify the Russian agents among the hotel guests, including an American movie crew filming in Thailand. He is also interested in the owner of the hotel, Chu Hoong, the millionaire manufacturer of a potent drink called Dragon's Tooth Elixir. North as usual is pursued by beautiful women but is invariably interrupted during any promising romantic interludes by circumstances beyond his control. Offord, writing in the *San Francisco Chronicle* (6 March 1960), likened the characters in *Secret Mission to Bangkok* to "brightly colored puppets" but asserted that "Mason fans won't care," while the reviewer in the *New York Herald Tribune Book Review* (13 March 1960) suggested that the novel "adds up to a standard fare perhaps, but of a very superior brand."

In *Trouble in Burma* (1962) North is sent to Burma on a secret mission. His assignment is to locate and destroy a vital U.S. rocket capsule that has accidentally fallen somewhere deep in the jungle east of Mandalay. The pretext for the search is that an American plane has crashed on a flight from Karachi to Bangkok. The trip from Rangoon to Mandalay will be made by boat up the Irrawaddy River. On the boat with North are a Chinese army colonel, an American expatriate pilot, two beautiful Burmese women, and a female American archaeologist. North and the Chinese colonel are of course in search of the capsule. The three women are on a quest for a rare ruby, which is known to be in the vicinity of the crash. One of the women is also acting as a secret agent for Moscow, while the American pilot is offering his services to the highest bidder.

In *Zanzibar Intrigue* (1963) North and his aide, Captain Kenny Trotter, are sent to Zanzibar to rescue a CIA agent who is being used by the Russian KGB in East Africa. The agent is really Master Sergeant Willie Bonhart, who defected from the army to East Berlin several years ago, posing as a disgruntled soldier. As a black man and a soldier, he is a useful symbol for the Russians as they strive to gain influence in Zanzibar and nearby territories that are seeking independence.

North and Trotter go to Africa disguised as employees of a spice company. At their first stop in Nairobi they learn that the East African Liberation Party is also interested in Bonhart. The leader of the party is James Mnoyah, who used to be a Mau Mau member. Both Bonhart and Mnoyah have a potential enemy in Tommy Henderson, a white settler who lost his wife and children to Mau Mau terrorists. All of these forces have to be taken into account as North and Trotter proceed to Zanzibar and attempt to free Bonhart from the KGB officers who are holding him hostage before his appearance at a mass rally for African independence.

Zanzibar Intrigue utilizes a wealth of background information on East African politics. Much is made of the 1961 murder of Patrice Lumumba and of the Russian involvement at that time in the former Belgian Congo. As in past North adventures, the use of coded messages is a key ingredient in the success of his mission. D. B. Hughes, in *Book Week* (24 November 1963), wrote that the novel "has a special quality that may surprise even his most fervid admirers." Boucher, writing in *The New York Times Book Review* (29 September 1963), judged it "a sketchy and oversimplified approach to the African problem; but it's a good competent thriller, with some unexpected switches."

In *Maracaibo Mission* (1965) North is briefed in Florida about a new weapon under development in Russia. The new military hardware uses a lightning ball as an innovative way to harness hydrogen energy. The Russians plan to use it to destroy oil derricks and refineries in the vicinity of Lake Maracaibo in Venezuela, thus toppling the shaky democratic regime in that country in favor of a communist dictatorship. North's mission is to locate the weapon and destroy it within ten days. He begins his work at the Hotel Fountainbleu in Miami Beach, where he picks up the trail of two Russian agents on the way to Lake Maracaibo. North's contact person in Venezuela is an Irish Venezuelan named McJuan Kelley. North is also equipped with the latest gadgets in this novel, perhaps in a nod to Ian Fleming's James Bond books of the same era.

The Deadly Orbit Mission (1968), Mason's final North adventure, is vintage North, with lots of close combat featuring knives and blunt instruments. North's comrades for this adventure include an expatriate nightclub operator and diamond smuggler, a local thief, a madame, and an infamous masseuse. The villains are led by recruits from the depths of Tangier society. Tangier itself is described in detail, reflecting the benefits of Mason's earlier research for *Two Tickets for Tangier*. Allen J. Hubin, reviewing the novel in *The New York Times Book Review* (19 May 1968), acknowledged that "captain, major and now Colonel North must be our oldest fictional spy—at least in years of service."

Mason imagined North in his own likeness. Like his creator, North was descended from an old New England family, educated abroad in boyhood, attended New England boarding schools, and had forebears with distinguished U.S. government service. They also shared extensive military service beginning with World War I in Europe. Mason's background bred in him, and thus in North, a sense of responsibility to preserve and pass to future generations the legacy of the early American settlers. Mason saw himself to be performing this function as a writer, and North serves in the same role by defending American interests against a variety of enemies.

F. van Wyck Mason died on 28 August 1978 while swimming in the Atlantic Ocean near his home at Southampton, Bermuda. He was seventy-six years old and had lived in Bermuda for fifteen years at the time of the accident. An inquest jury of nine men ruled that Mason died as a result of a heart attack while swimming. In all he wrote twenty-five historical novels, four anthologies, eight juvenile books (including three written under a pseudonym), and two mystery novels under another pseudonym, in addition to the twenty-seven books in the Hugh North series. In his fiftieth anniversary report to his Harvard classmates, Mason summed up his own opinion of his writing career: "I have attempted through my books to make Americans more conscious of their heritage by entertaining, as well as instructing, readers as to why various events have occurred and what the result was, rather than by writing straight histories, which are largely composed of dates."

Bibliography:

Allen J. Hubin, *The Bibliography of Crime Fiction, 1749–1975: Listing All Mystery, Detective, Suspense, Police and Gothic Fiction in Book Form Published in the English Language* (San Diego, Cal.: University of California, San Diego, 1979), p. 286.

References:

Jacques Barzun and Wendell Hertig Taylor, *A Catalogue of Crime,* revised and enlarged edition (New York: Harper & Row, 1989), p. 388;

Peter Kenney, "F. Van Wyck Mason and the Hugh North Series of International Intrigue," *Crime and Detective Stories,* 10 (January 1994): 19–20;

Ellen Nehr, *Doubleday Crime Club Compendium, 1928–1991* (Martinez, Cal.: Offspring, 1992), pp. 29, 44, 55, 67, 92, 108, 127, 142, and 156;

Chris Steinbrunner and Otto Penzler, *Encyclopedia of Mystery and Detection* (New York: McGraw-Hill, 1976), pp. 282–283.

Papers:

The papers of F. van Wyck Mason are held at the Howard Gotlieb Archival Research Center at Boston University.

Helen McCloy

(6 June 1904 – 8 December 1992)

Anita G. Gorman
Slippery Rock University of Pennsylvania

BOOKS: *Dance of Death* (New York: Morrow, 1938); republished as *Design for Dying* (London: Heinemann, 1938);

The Man in the Moonlight (New York: Morrow, 1940; London: Hamilton, 1940);

The Deadly Truth (New York: Morrow, 1941; London: Hamilton, 1942);

Cue for Murder (New York: Morrow, 1942);

Who's Calling? (New York: Morrow, 1942; London: Nicholson & Watson, 1948);

Do Not Disturb (New York: Morrow, 1943);

The Goblin Market (New York: Morrow, 1943; London: Hale, 1951);

Panic (New York: Morrow, 1944; London: Gollancz, 1972);

The One That Got Away (New York: Morrow, 1945; London: Gollancz, 1954);

She Walks Alone (New York: Random House, 1948; London: Coker, 1950); republished as *Wish You Were Dead* (New York: Spivak, 1958);

Better Off Dead (New York: Dell, 1949);

Through a Glass, Darkly (New York: Random House, 1950; London: Gollancz, 1951);

Alias Basil Willing (New York: Random House, 1951; London: Gollancz, 1951 [i.e., 1952];

Unfinished Crime (New York: Random House, 1954); republished as *He Never Came Back* (London: Gollancz, 1954);

The Long Body (New York: Random House, 1955; London: Gollancz, 1956);

Two-Thirds of a Ghost (New York: Random House, 1956; London: Gollancz, 1957);

The Slayer and the Slain (New York: Random House, 1957; London: Gollancz, 1958);

The Last Day, as Helen Clarkson (New York: Torquil, 1959);

Before I Die (New York: Dodd, Mead, 1963; London: Gollancz, 1963);

The Singing Diamonds and Other Stories (New York: Dodd, Mead, 1965); republished as *Surprise, Surprise* (London: Gollancz, 1965);

Helen McCloy (from Burn This, *1980; Richland County Public Library)*

The Further Side of Fear (New York: Dodd, Mead, 1967; London: Gollancz, 1967);

Mr. Splitfoot (New York: Dodd, Mead, 1968; London: Gollancz, 1969);

A Question of Time (New York: Dodd, Mead, 1971; London: Gollancz, 1971);

A Change of Heart (New York: Dodd, Mead, 1973; London: Gollancz, 1973);

The Sleepwalker (New York: Dodd, Mead, 1974; London: Gollancz, 1974);

Minotaur Country (New York: Dodd, Mead, 1975; London: Gollancz, 1975);

The Changeling Conspiracy (New York: Dodd, Mead, 1976); republished as *Cruel as the Grave* (London: Gollancz, 1977);

The Impostor: A Novel of Suspense (New York: Dodd, Mead, 1977; London: Gollancz, 1978);

The Smoking Mirror: A Novel of Suspense (New York: Dodd, Mead, 1979; London: Gollancz, 1979);

Burn This: A Novel of Suspense (New York: Dodd, Mead, 1980; London: Gollancz, 1980).

Collection: *The Pleasant Assassin and Other Cases of Dr. Basil Willing* (Norfolk, Va.: Crippen & Landru, 2003).

OTHER: *20 Great Tales of Murder by Experts of the Mystery Writers of America,* edited by McCloy and Davis Dresser as Brett Halliday (New York: Random House, 1951; London: Hammond, 1952);

The Second Book of Crime-Craft: A Selection from 20 Great Tales of Murder, edited by McCloy and Dresser as Halliday (London: Transworld, 1958);

Murder, Murder, Murder: 10 Tales from 20 Great Tales of Murder, edited by McCloy and Dresser as Halliday (New York: Hillman-Curl, 1961).

SELECTED PERIODICAL PUBLICATIONS–UNCOLLECTED: "Whodunits–Still a Stepchild," *New Republic,* 56 (31 October 1955): 29;

"The Pleasant Assassin," *Ellery Queen's Mystery Magazine* (December 1970): 134–148;

"A Case of Innocent Eavesdropping," *Ellery Queen's Mystery Magazine,* 71 (March 1978): 6–19;

"Murphy's Law," *Ellery Queen's Mystery Magazine,* 73 (April–June 1979): 77–91;

"That Bug That's Going Around," *Ellery Queen's Mystery Magazine,* 74 (July–September 1979): 127–141.

Although Helen McCloy's popularity has waned in the last thirty years, she contributed a large body of still enjoyable and engrossing fiction. Believing that the "true detective story is fun to write and fun to read," she concluded that contemporary readers had become more interested in detective fiction "because there is some lack in the accepted literary diet, some nutritional imbalance or vitamin deficiency" that they are "subconsciously trying to correct" (*St. James Guide to Crime and Mystery Writers,* 1991). Always interesting, erudite, aware of political, sociological, and scientific trends,

McCloy wrote in a highly readable, fluent style. Although she repeats certain motifs, her novels and short stories vary in theme and plot; she was not afraid to experiment with point of view and to tackle contemporary problems while providing entertainment for the literate reader.

Born in New York City on 6 June 1904, Helen Worrell Clarkson McCloy was the daughter of writer Helen Clarkson, who wrote short stories under her maiden name, and William Conrad McCloy, managing editor of *The New York Evening Sun.* Educated at the Friends School in Brooklyn, McCloy received her first check when at fourteen she wrote a literary essay for the *Boston Transcript;* her second check, for a poem published in *The New York Times,* arrived a year later. McCloy went to Europe in 1923; studied at the Sorbonne; worked as a reporter for Hearst's Universal News Service (1927–1932); as an art critic for *International Studio* (1930–1931); as London art critic for *The New York Times* (1930–1931); and as a freelance contributor to the *London Morning Post* and *Parnassus,* returning to the United States in 1932.

In the 1930s McCloy began writing mysteries. In 1938 she published her first novel, *Dance of Death,* which introduces Dr. Basil Willing, an urbane psychiatrist-detective who relies in part on Freudian psychology to trap his criminals via their mistakes. "Blunders, like dreams," he states, "are messages in code. By decoding them we are able to eavesdrop on the unconscious and get at the truth." The "tall and lean" Willing, who lives "in an antiquated house at the unfashionable end of Park Avenue, below Grand Central," had a Russian mother, "and that accounted for many things–among them his thin-skinned temperament, more sympathetic, irritable and intuitive than that of races on whom the shell of civilization has had time to harden." Written from the third-person point of view, *Dance of Death* makes frequent use of dialogue and allows readers to know from time to time what Willing is thinking. Called "a truly exceptional bit of mystery writing" by *The New York Times* (27 February 1938), the novel deftly conveys the atmosphere of Manhattan in 1938. Kitty Jocelyn is found dead in the snow, her body inexplicably hot. That guests at her debutante party saw her dancing even while she was evidently lying in the snow is explained when her cousin Ann Jocelyn Claude admits to changing places with Kitty. The victim, who, though naturally slender herself, had appeared in ads endorsing Sveltis, a reducing drug, was murdered by someone avenging the death of another from the same drug.

Dance of Death uses humor and references to both Freudian and Jungian psychology; the unraveling of "this unhappy case," in Dr. Willing's judgment, "demonstrates the value of psychology in criminal investigation." McCloy told *St. James Guide to Crime and Mystery Writers* that in this first of thirteen Basil Willing novels she was consciously beginning a series, "trying to write the classic detective story with a detective who appears in each book, a startling or puzzling beginning followed by twists and turns in the plot, including hidden clues to the murderer and a surprise ending in which those clues are shown to lead rationally to one guilty person." Anthony Boucher, in his introduction to McCloy's *Cue for Murder* (1942), relates that reviewers of *Dance of Death* called McCloy "a genuine find" and compared her to Margery Allingham and Ngaio Marsh. According to Boucher, the book would have won an Edgar award if the Mystery Writers of America (MWA) had been in existence at the time.

McCloy's second novel, *The Man in the Moonlight* (1940), begins with Patrick Foyle, assistant chief inspector of the New York Police Department, a character introduced in *Dance of Death*, looking at bulletins from the dean on the campus of Yorkville University in Manhattan. McCloy gracefully sets the scene:

> Foyle's pipe was drawing evenly, the western sun was genial against his back and the east wind fresh against his cheek with a tang of salt and tar. The lawn at his feet sloped down to the East River where the water reflected the innocent blue of the sky. A string of coal barges was moving ponderously upstream with the drowsy deliberation of a slow-motion picture. Beyond, the Long Island shore looked flat, diminished and still as a colored photograph. To the right, the granite clock-tower of the University library rose above a grove of elms that swayed and rustled in ladylike protest at the rudeness of the breeze. There was no other sound but the thud of tennis balls on the University courts beyond the trees.

For the first, but not for the last time, a McCloy protagonist spots a note with a cryptic and deadly message, this time a carbon copy of a typed message that "floated before the wind like a kite, twisting, rising and falling, until it came to rest on the grass a few yards from the bench where he [Foyle] was sitting." The note announces that the recipient has been "chosen as murderer for Group No. 1." Although Foyle plays a role in the plot, which involves Nazis, Dr. Basil Willing unmasks the murderer, in part through logic and hard evidence and in part through his insights into human behavior: "whenever you lied," he tells the culprit, "you told the truth, for the creative imagination must always suggest the true emotional state of the creator." *The Man in the Moonlight* introduces Gisela von Hohenems, an Austrian refugee and secretary to researcher Franz Konradi, the murder victim; she becomes

Cover for a 1944 paperback reprint of McCloy's first novel, originally published in 1938, which introduces Freudian psychiatrist and sleuth Basil Willing (from Piet Schreuders, *Paperbacks, USA: A Graphic History, 1939–1959* [San Diego: Blue Dolphin, 1981]; Richland County Public Library)

engaged to Willing in a later novel, *Through a Glass, Darkly* (1950) and appears as his wife in *Alias Basil Willing* (1951). Though American reviewers tended to like the book, Ralph Partridge in *The New Statesman and Nation* (7 December 1940) offered a dissenting voice: "The motive for the crime proves to be such an outrage to reason that even the preceding psychological mumbo jumbo has not prepared one for it. As for the man in the moonlight, he was just the criminal whom everyone was being too psychological to recognise."

McCloy's 1941 novel, *The Deadly Truth*, opens with Claudia Bethune's visit to Dr. Roger Slater, inventor of a truth serum. She steals some tablets that are later used on guests at a house party on a Long Island estate, where Dr. Basil Willing is renting a guesthouse. At close to four in the morning, Basil spots a flickering light from the main house. Investigating, he sees a dying fire in a fireplace and a woman with her head in her hands; he hears footsteps. The unconscious Claudia has been choked by her own emerald necklace, twisted into a sort of tourniquet and held in place by a fruit knife. Moments later, Claudia dies. Willing identifies the murderer by means of the killer's acute sense of hearing; he is the only one to hear the deliberate rustling of leaves by a state trooper, and earlier the murderer had heard the faint sounds made by Willing at the murder scene. In *The Deadly Truth,* McCloy offers a clever way to describe Willing—state troopers stop him for speeding, ask him questions, and read the details on his driver's license: he is forty-three, just under six feet, with brown eyes, dark brown hair, and a weight of 164 pounds. When the police ask his business address, he ponders whether to tell them that he works at a psychiatric clinic or at the office of the district attorney, who employs him as a consultant.

Though Willing is seeing Gisela von Hohenems during the novel, not much attention is given to their relationship. Critic Will Cuppy in *Books* (15 June 1941) called attention to McCloy's "combining sensational ingredients with all-around erudition in about equal parts and stirring with fundamental brainwork." The reviewer for *The New York Times* (15 June 1941) reported that "the novel as a whole is handled with a wit and suavity which are nothing short of fascinating."

Dr. Basil Willing continued to use his knowledge of human perception and motivation in the 1942 mystery *Cue for Murder,* praised by Anthony Boucher for its intricate clues. A premeditated murder onstage during a Broadway performance of Victorien Sardou's *Fédora* (1882) causes Willing to philosophize that the motive "'must be unusually compelling. Almost anyone may kill on impulse, but premeditated murder must have a motive strong enough to sustain a mood of cold fury that nullifies all fear of punishment. It must be a motive that makes every alternative to murder seem intolerable." The title of the novel, from *Othello* (1604?), cleverly connects the plot of the novel—about marital discord, jealousy, and murder—with William Shakespeare's play. Kay Irvin, writing in *The New York Times* (11 October 1942), offered praise: "Helen McCloy can not only make up a good mystery tale: she can write it as a good novel, with lively characterization, logical reasoning and satiric wit."

Who's Calling?, also published in 1942, begins with a telephone call to Frieda Frey from an anonymous caller who warns her not to go to Willow Spring, home of former senator Mark Lindsay. The poisoning of Chalkley V. Winchester during a dance at Willow Spring eventually leads to a Hollywood contract for Frey, a former nightclub singer. When Basil Willing enters the conflict in the middle of the novel, a woman weeding a garden observes him: "He was tall and lean with brown hair bared to the sun. She thought he looked younger than he actually was. As he drew nearer she became aware of a thoughtful face and a certain slow grace in gait and gesture." *Who's Calling?* is one of a few McCloy novels in which the guilty person—whose modus operandi is revealed at length toward the end of the novel—is not apprehended, but commits suicide. *The New Yorker* (11 April 1942) called the novel a "neatly told story that has almost everything, and it may make you wonder what your subconscious is up to."

McCloy's sixth book, *Do Not Disturb* (1943), more a suspense than a detective novel, does not include Basil Willing and experiments with point of view; the story is told in the first person by a young woman, Edith Talbot, who checks into a New York hotel and hears screams in the next room. Informed that the room is occupied by a doctor and his son, who is recovering from an operation, Edith is later told that police are in the room giving a suspect the third degree. More bizarre situations occur: Edith is run down on the street, but recovers; she discovers a dead man in her room and is later followed; suspecting her former husband, she uses her wits and courage to unmask a Nazi. McCloy captures the flavor of wartime America throughout the novel, increases suspense through first-person narration, and creates realistic settings without elaborate or distracting descriptions.

The Goblin Market (1943) also uses wartime spying and secret codes, this time cablese, the jargon journalists sent to their editors. Basil Willing now works for Naval Intelligence. McCloy borrowed her title and the epigraph from Christina Rossetti:

We must not look at Goblin men,
We must not buy their fruits:
Who knows upon what soil they fed
Their hungry, thirsty roots?

The book uses the poem to suggest "all forms of evil contraband trade from cocaine and slaves to gunrunning and black-market bootlegging." Though governments attempt to oppose these goblin markets, Willing argues that the "goblins are elusive, hard to catch or control, men without a country or a conscience"; yet, they are the same people who say that "human nature is too nationalistic to prevent future wars by international agreement." McCloy hated fascism as well as jingoism and more than once used the vehicle of detective fiction to critique the barbarism of her century.

With *Panic* (1944), McCloy continued to combine mystery with wartime concerns and her fascination with secret codes—for the second time without the presence of Basil Willing. Ronnie Mulholland (who notifies his cousin Alison of the apparently sudden death of her uncle, Felix Mulholland) is a member of the League of Super Americans, "one of those economists who are attracted by the symmetry of collectivism, particularly the authoritarian, undemocratic collectivism we call Fascism today. He believed it was coming and he wanted to be in on the ground floor." Uncle Felix, on the other hand, was working for the War Department. Fascism continues to be McCloy's concern in *The One That Got Away* (1945), a Basil Willing novel narrated by psychiatrist Peter Dunbar, which includes effective description of Scotland and postulates the intriguing theory that fascism derives in part from a hatred of women and rejection of motherhood. Using the Hitler Youth movement as an example, McCloy shows how Nazis wanted to replace motherhood and family with government control. In the words of one character, "Though no one could ever call me a Nazi, or even a Nazi sympathizer, I must say there was one thing about the Nazis I admired—the Nazi ideals of the Youth Movement. Hitler took male children away from the suffocating featherbed of mother love and started molding them into hard, ruthless men at the age of seven or eight."

On 13 October 1946 McCloy married Davis Dresser—writer of romances, Westerns, and detective fiction—who under his best-known pseudonym, Brett Halliday, produced the hard-boiled detective Mike Shayne. Together, McCloy and Dresser founded Torquil Publishing Company and the Halliday and McCloy Literary Agency (1953–1964) and edited *20 Great Tales of Murder by Experts of the Mystery Writers of America* (1951), which includes McCloy's "Chinoiserie" as well as her postscript to the collection. Davis (as Halliday) and McCloy also edited *The Second Book of Crime-Craft: A Selection from 20 Great Tales of Murder* (1958) as well as *Murder, Murder, Murder* (1961). They had one daughter, Chloe, on 29 March 1948 and divorced in 1961.

McCloy's 1948 novel, *She Walks Alone,* her third novel without Basil Willing, begins with the intriguing assertion, "The following pages are to be read only in the event of my death by violence. . . ." Addressed to the Commissioner of Police, Puerta Vieja, Santa Teresa, the first pages report an odd request by a gardener, Leslie Dawson, that the narrator, a woman employed by Rupert Lord, write a letter to the gardener's wife in New York. The narrator later sees the supposedly illiterate gardener, who is unknown to Lord, writing in the post office. Later, on a ship bound for New York, the still unidentified narrator discovers that she is carrying a great deal of money in a package given to her. This

Cover for the 1949 paperback edition of McCloy's 1943 novel, in which Basil Willing, a Naval Intelligence officer during World War II, thwarts black marketeers (from Geoffrey O'Brien, Hardboiled America: The Lurid Years of Paperbacks [New York: Van Nostrand Reinhold, 1981]; Richland County Public Library)

section ends with an incomplete sentence: "as you may have guessed already, I hid the money in. . . ." The novel then continues via third-person narration, relating the efforts of the police chief, Urizar (who also appeared in *The Goblin Market*), to determine who wrote the previous "script" and who killed a woman onboard the ship. Urizar and Lars Lindstrom, the ship's captain, conclude that Nina Keyes must be the writer of the script. The third section is another letter by Nina addressed—from Washington, D.C.—to Urizar; the final section returns to third-person narration. With murders, a deadly snake, exotic settings, and a surprise ending, the book features characters who are not what they seem. A suspense novel rather than a novel of detection, *She Walks Alone* cleverly experiments with point of view and confounds the reader with an array of suspects and suspicious acts until, finally, the guilty person is unmasked, in part by certain omissions in testimony, omissions that function, in the words of the police chief, as the primary "method of distortion." *She Walks Alone* was greeted with mixed reviews; Isaac Anderson in *The New York Times* (2 May 1948) called it "first-rate" and "spine-tingling," whereas the critic for *The New Yorker* (8 May 1948) labeled it "not a very sensible story, on the whole."

Through a Glass, Darkly expanded from a 1949 short story of the same name, was McCloy's personal favorite as well as the book some critics consider her masterpiece. Dedicated to her daughter, Chloe, "little green shoot that came up in the Spring," this eighth Basil Willing novel concerns a teacher, Faustina Crayle, who is dismissed from the Brereton School for Girls, seemingly for no reason. Willing, who is brought into the case by his fiancée, Gisela, learns that Faustina has irrefutably been seen in two different places at the same time and was dismissed for the same eerie reason from a previous position at the Maidstone School in Virginia. When Gisela finds Alice Aitchison, the drama teacher, dead, Beth Chase, a fourteen-year-old student, claims that Faustina pushed Alice backward down the steps of the summerhouse, but Faustina declares that she was telephoning Gisela from New York at the time. Basil Willing's sleuthing uncovers that Faustina will inherit valuable jewels when she turns thirty; if she dies earlier, the jewels are to go to the heirs of the original owners, who were generous clients of Faustina's mother, a prostitute. The theme of the doppelgänger is cleverly solved in the end, though the murderer does not accept Willing's explanation of the crime, and the novel ends ambiguously, with the accused declaring, "'You don't believe me. . . . Neither you nor I nor anyone else will ever know the whole truth about this. Or anything else. It's all mystery. One more little puzzle can't add or detract much.' He looked out at the stars and smiled secretly. 'God knows what's up there anyway!'"

In 1950 McCloy became the first woman president of the Mystery Writers of America. During the 1950s and 1960s she co-authored a review column for Connecticut newspapers. In 1953 she received an Edgar award from the MWA for her criticism.

In the beginning of McCloy's novel, *Alias Basil Willing,* Willing, having married Gisela von Hohenems between novels, sees a man hail a cab and identify himself as Dr. Basil Willing. After following in another cab, the real Willing enters a house in Greenwich Village and finds a lively party. The impostor, hired by Katherine Shaw, an elderly blind woman, to attend the party and investigate the host, Dr. Zimmer, later dies while having a drink with the real Willing at a bar. Katherine Shaw also dies of poisoning. Half the guests

at Dr. Zimmer's party are potential murderers and half potential victims; Zimmer himself is a psychiatrist who finds out the unconscious desires of his patients, shows them what they were thinking, then offers murder "committed vicariously—at a price." Dr. Zimmer, a Nazi sympathizer, "sells extermination at a very high price to anyone who wanted to get rid of anyone else for whatever reason." In Zimmer's garden, "No birds sang," because of the unused poison buried there.

McCloy's next two novels following *Alias Basil Willing* were nonseries works. McCloy's 1949 novella, *Better Off Dead,* appeared first as a short story in *The American Magazine.* In it, fifteen years earlier, Frank Bly had been accused of stealing $5,000 and had later been identified as a murder victim. Now he returns to his hometown (Yarborough, Pennsylvania) under a new identity, Stephen Longworth. As Frank Bly, he had been befriended by Tess Vanbrugh and her family and was fond of little Nan, Tess's daughter. He had been building a dollhouse for Nan when accused of the theft. The attempt on Frank's life, the killing of a stranger, and, finally, the murder of Tess's husband are connected to a cabinet sent over from France and wrapped in newspapers telling a story of guilt.

McCloy's 1954 novel, *Unfinished Crime,* is set in New York City. The novel begins with Peter Moxon, in possession of a rare ruby, being followed. To hide the jewel, he places it in a ten-cent store among some cheap costume jewelry on sale for twenty cents each. Intent on buying the ruby necklace the next day, Moxon thinks it unlikely that anyone will have bought the jewel before he returns the next day, since the store is about to close. Moments later, Moxon is killed by a car, and the ruby is purchased by Sara Dacre, who recognizes a young man in the store as her neighbor, Gerry Hone. When Gerry later disappears from the Automat, Sara becomes involved in a series of scary incidents and meetings with suspicious people who want the ruby, including a man with a tattoo of a cat on his wrist as well as Gerry Hone's double. Part of the attraction of the novel lies in the budding romance between Sara Dacre and Gerry—or is it his double? Although McCloy manages to keep the suspense building throughout the novel, she employs too much coincidence to move her plot toward its climax. "A bit thinnish," wrote Sergeant Cuff in *The Saturday Review* (27 November 1954).

McCloy returns to Basil Willing in *The Long Body* (1955), which begins with the widowed Alice Hazard going through her husband's desk after his accidental death. After opening a locked drawer, she finds a green envelope marked "Papers Pertaining to Miss Lash"; yet, the envelope contains nothing. Christina Lash turns out to be a friend of Alice Hazard's son. Christina

Lash's death and her connection to the late Mr. Hazard are exposed in part by the scent of perfume on the green envelope. The climax of *The Long Body* reveals that Lash was killed to keep Alice Hazard from becoming a killer; Lash's murderer, in turn, is killed in a car accident, an event that leads Basil Willing to say, "Thank God!" Boucher, writing in *The New York Times* (16 October 1955), thought the conclusion "awkward, anticlimactic and (astonishing from so meticulous a technician as McCloy) inconsistent," with Dr. Willing "wasted on an almost unnecessary bit-role."

In a short essay for *The New Republic* (31 October 1955), "Whodunits—Still a Stepchild," McCloy describes two noticeable trends in mysteries: "the increasing internationalism that appears in scenes, in characters, and even in authors" and "the blurring of all distinctions between detective stories, mystery stories and suspense novels, and, what is more important, a blurring of the distinction between the suspense novel and the so-called straight novel." Yet, though she maintains that the best suspense novels "are on the same plane" as the best straight fiction, McCloy notes that suspense novels are sold for less money and not as actively promoted by the book industry. Suspense novels are also less likely to be reviewed individually by critics and more likely to be considered with other books in a column by a critic who evaluates all of the books "largely by the logic of their plots, treating the well-plotted story, told in deplorably pedestrian style, and peopled with types instead of characters, on exactly the same plane as the well-plotted story, told with literary art, by a mind capable of reflection as well as observation."

McCloy also chose to examine the world of books in her fiction with *Two-Thirds of a Ghost* (1956), a witty and satiric treatment of the New York publishing scene, centered on the death of a writer at a publisher's party. In what was her last Basil Willing novel before a twelve-year hiatus for the series, McCloy contrasts serious and popular literature, with one of the characters, a critic, stating, "Today a plot is indecent anywhere outside a mystery, the last refuge of the conservative writer." Critic James Sandoe, writing in *The New York Herald Tribune* (7 October 1956), stated that *Two-Thirds of a Ghost* "is all done with elegance, a dash of pastiche here and acid flick of parody there."

In *The Slayer and the Slain* (1957), McCloy explores the phenomenon of split personality. When Harry Deane inherits a good deal of money from his uncle, he retires from his teaching job in New England and returns to Virginia, where Celia, the love of his life, lives with her husband, Simon. Strange events—a missing driver's license, a hostile note, a forged check—eventually make sense as actions caused by the other half of

THE ONE
THAT GOT AWAY

by Helen McCloy

WILLIAM MORROW & COMPANY
New York - - - 1945

Title page for McCloy's Basil Willing novel in which the psychiatrist postulates a link between fascism and a lack of maternal affection (Richland County Public Library)

a split personality. That the narrator is one half of a personality and his adversary the other half is explored through written correspondence between the two, which strains credibility, while paving the way for a logical, though tragic, conclusion.

Always interested in the events of the day, McCloy often aired contemporary concerns in her novels. During the war years, she wrote about fascism, and in the late 1950s, when many were concerned about the possibility of nuclear war, she departed from detective fiction to treat the threat posed by the atomic bomb in *The Last Day* (1959), a book she wrote under her mother's maiden name, Helen Clarkson. McCloy's first-person narrator, Lois, and her husband, Bill, on an island without a car radio or newspapers, are unaware of a developing international crisis that leads to Armageddon. Although at first they have difficulty finding people on the island, eventually they become part of a group of citizens who see "far across the dunes, on the horizon—the vast, idiot glare, more blinding than the sun itself." One by one, the residents die of radiation sickness, including Bill and his friend Eric, who had been colleagues at the Atomic Energy Commission.

Although not a detective story, *The Last Day* has affinities with McCloy's suspense fiction in its tension and its concern with human motivation. McCloy offers more philosophy in this novel than she usually does. In an extended discussion toward the end of the novel, she examines the causes of nuclear war, and one of the characters likely speaks for the author:

> . . . any culture dominated by science tends to be inaesthetic and immoral. Science has no conscience. It's neither good nor bad. It's neutral like all tools. It can be put to good uses or bad uses, but the choice of the uses to which it is put cannot be made scientifically for that choice must be governed by the unscientific values of morals and aesthetics.

Each chapter in the novel covers one day, with the last chapter titled "The Last Day." In a poignant reversal of the Genesis account of creation, the world slowly dies in six days. McCloy explicitly alludes to Genesis in a comment by the doctor on the island:

> Time is the great deceiver. The Garden of Eden story was not history, but prophecy. This was Eden and we didn't know it. The atomic cloud is the angel with the flaming sword that will keep us out forever more. And the knowledge of good and evil was our downfall. We knew the difference and yet we chose evil.

In *Before I Die* (1963) McCloy explores not only the meretriciousness of Hollywood and the advertising world but also the devastating effects of an extramarital affair. Bob Lundy, who works for an advertising agency, wants an adventure "Before I die," and gets what he desires in an affair with Kyra Novacz, seemingly the daughter of a United Nations translator, Dada Novacz; Dada, however, is Kyra's husband. Dada's murder leads two women to save their marriage via crime or deceit, as McCloy once again explores moral ambiguity.

McCloy's collection *The Singing Diamonds and Other Stories,* published in 1965, includes eight stories, four of which are prize-winning mysteries that appeared in *Ellery Queen's Mystery Magazine.* The diamonds in the title story are a type of flying saucer, "nine flat, elongated squares, like the pips on a nine of diamonds, flying in V-formation at 1,500 miles per hour"; as witnesses of the sighting begin to die, one of them calls upon Basil Willing to solve the mystery. Of the origin of the first story, McCloy said, "It was through MWA that I met Fred Dannay. He told me that *Ellery Queen's Mystery Magazine* was starting a mystery short-story contest and asked me if I would submit a story. I sent him 'Chinoiserie,' which has now been republished more than anything else I ever wrote. It was even made into a radio play in the largely Chinese city of Singapore. I owe all this to MWA, through whom we met, for the story had been rejected previously by every other magazine in New York and London." The collection includes "Number Ten Q Street," "Silence Burning," "The Other Side of the Curtain," "Surprise, Surprise!," "Through a Glass, Darkly," and "Windless," an early version of *The Last Day.*

McCloy's *The Further Side of Fear* (1967) takes place in London, where the protagonist, Lydia Grey, wakes up "to darkness" and hears a prowler in her room. Two men, an Englishman and an American, are both suitors, and both become suspects with the revelation that Lydia's apartment has been the site of espionage. A visit from her two daughters and their friendship with two young men both complicate and lead to the resolution of the plot. When the daughters are kidnapped, Lydia decides to play along with the criminals. The climax at an Italian inn is enjoyable despite its improbability. Though lacking the psychological speculation of some of her other novels, *The Further Side of Fear* shows McCloy's interest in motivation and in personality. Lydia "was aware of a change in Gerald. Now he was the man she had rather liked on shipboard. Apparently it was Alan's presence that had brought out another side of his personality. After all, what we call personality is a process, not a thing. What another thinks of as my personality is really an interaction between my personality and his. Each time one is with a different person, one becomes a different person." The title is explained when Lydia sees the perpetrator act at the end: "She thought: 'He, too, has passed to the further side of fear. He doesn't really care what becomes of him any more.'"

In *Mr. Splitfoot* (1968), Basil Willing and his wife must seek refuge during a snowstorm when their car breaks down. Finding a house where a party is in progress, they also find what seems to be a rapping poltergeist, talk about a haunted bedroom, and later, a dead body in that same room. McCloy often fills her books with literary allusions, as in this work, in which characters have the names of the Fates—Clotho, Atropos, and Lachesis—and a parakeet bears the name Tobermory, derived no doubt from H. H. Munro's story. Basil Willing sees in the adulterous murderer's charges of adultery against his wife "delusional jealousy. It's a common failing of a certain type of human male. He's almost promiscuous to the point of satyriasis but he is prey to unconscious guilt and, in our jargon, he projects this repressed guilt on his wife. She is the one he sees as unfaithful as if she were a glass in which he could see nothing but his own face." In *The New York Times Book Review* (17 November 1968), A. J. Hubin commented, "The story is nicely structured, neatly misdirected, and abounds with fine distinct characterizations"; the *TLS: The Times Literary Supplement* critic (1 May 1969), on the other hand, praised "this good story" but called the ending "careless," complaining as well that "the characters who have evoked our sympathy too rudely dropped out of notice."

In 1971 McCloy helped to found a New England chapter of the Mystery Writers of America in Boston and published *A Question of Time,* the first of seven non-series novels, largely ignored by the critics. The novel dabbles in precognition, déjà vu, and a third theory: "It's Nietzche's eternal recurrence modified by Einstein and Vedanta. Time is curved as well as space. When we die, we are reborn, but not as others, always as ourselves in the same time and place as before." *A Change of Heart* (1973) is about two school friends, Lee and Laurie, who made a promise to meet again on Lee's fiftieth birthday in the Small Bar of the Crane Club in New York. The novel includes a jewel thief and an impostor. A 1974 novel, *The Sleepwalker,* depicts a woman who lost her memory when her husband and baby were killed after the family witnessed a Mafia murder. *Minotaur Country* (1975) involves a newspaper reporter, Tash Perkins, who interviews the wife of the governor, then has an affair with the governor after his wife dies in a suspicious fire. The governor himself is shot to death, and Tash is almost killed as well, but she is rescued by her managing editor, Bill Brewer. Although she has lost the great love of her life, the prediction is that "she'll marry and live happily ever after. She's the marrying kind." More a romance than a mystery, the novel failed to win the approval of Newgate Callendar, whose review in *The New York Times* (11 May 1975) dismissed *Minotaur Country* in a few words: "A pretty newspaper girl goes to work in the Governor's office, gets a crush on him, finds something venomous pursuing the Governor and his family. Junk. On page 156, incidentally, we meet our old friend Lady MacBeth."

The Changeling Conspiracy (1976) does not feature Basil Willing, though it does deal with terrorism, kidnapping, and psychology. In *The New York Times* (2 January 1977) Callendar wrote, "The author has taken elements from the Patricia Hearst affair; a kidnapped girl lets her family know that she agrees with the ideals of the activists who have abducted her. There is a good deal of talk about brainwashing. The girl's boyfriend goes underground to solve the case.

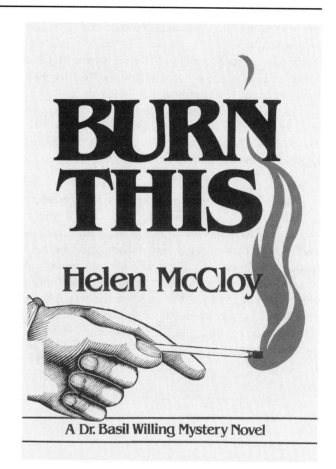

Dust jacket for McCloy's last novel, published in 1980, in which a Boston boardinghouse full of writers provides the setting for a murder mystery (Richland County Public Library)

At the end everything is resolved, but in a mechanical, artificial manner." *The Impostor* (1977) features an accident victim, a stranger claiming to be her husband, a secret code, and the return of both the protagonist's memory and her real husband. Published in 1979, *The Smoking Mirror* is set in 1940 France, with gambling, murder, romance, clairvoyance, and antifascism all playing roles.

In McCloy's last published novel, *Burn This* (1980), Harriet Sutton has bought a house in an historic Boston neighborhood on the advice of her lawyer. A writer herself, Harriet has rented out rooms in the house to other writers. One day she sees a letter float down and land at her feet. The note says "BURN THIS" and seems to have been written by someone who knows the identity of Nemesis, the pseudonym of a literary reviewer. Not only does the novel include an array of literary eccentrics, but it also involves murder, seemingly by an attack dog, and the return of Basil Willing. The murderer and Nemesis are cleverly unmasked, with suspicion initially falling on several people, including Harriet Sutton's disturbed son, a Vietnam veteran. The book is interesting in part for its evocation of Boston, where McCloy spent her final years, and its discussion of literary matters—copyright, ghostwriting, reviews, writer's block, and plagiarism. McCloy also shows an awareness of opposing trends in psychiatry; Dr. Willing tells Harriet Sutton, "After years of neglecting emotional causes for physical causes, they began neglecting physical causes for emotional causes."

McCloy suffered a broken leg in a car accident circa 1980, mentioned in a draft of a letter to a friend: "I had to spend six weeks in bed or in an armchair and I think this enforced rest did me good because usually I go from one thing to another and never stop to rest at all." The same letter reveals her pessimism about current events: "The state of the world is so appalling I cannot let myself think about it . . . Poor old human race, struggling along from one crisis after another!"

In 1990 the MWA presented McCloy with the Grand Master Award, a prize given to those who have made significant contributions to detective fiction. McCloy enjoyed giving and attending parties, and she cherished her many friends. For years, she lived in an apartment on Beacon Hill in Boston, a setting used in several of her works. She died on 8 December 1992. Although her death went unnoticed—no obituaries appeared—and her books are out of print, she contributed to twentieth-century detective fiction by writing literate, readable books that focus on motivation, depict the ambiguities of life, and emphasize the use of psychology to solve crime.

Reference:

John McAleer, "The Grand Master: Helen McCloy," in *Mystery Writers of America Annual* (1990).

Papers:

Helen McCloy's papers are at the Mugar Memorial Library, Boston University.

Sharyn McCrumb

(26 February 1948 –   )

Marcia B. Dinneen
Bridgewater State College

BOOKS: *Sick of Shadows* (New York: Avon, 1984; Wallington, U.K.: Severn House, 1992);

Lovely in Her Bones (New York: Avon, 1985; Sutton, U.K.: Severn House, 1993);

Highland Laddie Gone (New York: Avon, 1986; Wallington, U.K.: Severn House, 1993);

Bimbos of the Death Sun (Lake Geneva, Wis.: TSR, 1987; London: Penguin, 1989);

Paying the Piper (New York: Ballantine, 1988; London: Severn House, 1991);

If Ever I Return, Pretty Peggy-O (New York: Scribners, 1990; London: Coronet, 1995);

The Windsor Knot (New York: Ballantine, 1990);

Missing Susan (New York: Ballantine, 1991);

The Hangman's Beautiful Daughter (New York: Scribners, 1992; London: Hodder & Stoughton, 1996);

MacPherson's Lament (New York: Ballantine, 1992);

Zombies of the Gene Pool (New York: Simon & Schuster, 1992);

She Walks These Hills (New York: Scribners, 1994; London: Coronet, 1995);

If I'd Killed Him When I Met Him (New York: Ballantine, 1995);

The Rosewood Casket (New York: Dutton, 1996; London: Hodder & Stoughton, 1996);

Foggy Mountain Breakdown and Other Stories (New York: Ballantine, 1997; London: Hodder & Stoughton, 1998);

The Ballad of Frankie Silver (New York: Dutton, 1998; London: Hodder & Stoughton, 1998);

The PMS Outlaws (New York: Ballantine, 2000);

The Songcatcher (New York: Dutton, 2001; London: Hodder & Stoughton, 2001);

Ghost Riders (New York: Dutton, 2003).

Sharyn McCrumb (photograph by D. D. Galyean, VPI & SU; from If Ever I Return, Pretty Peggy-O, *1990; Richland County Public Library)*

With her knowledge of folklore, botany, geology, and history, Sharyn McCrumb has made the Appalachian Mountain region of eastern Tennessee come alive for her readers. McCrumb also writes mysteries; some include incidents that took place during the Civil War; others relate true stories about happenings before the Revolutionary War; and some focus on the present. Unlike some mystery writers, McCrumb does not start out with a murder in chapter 1. Sometimes, one hundred pages later a person will die, and both reader and characters in the novel can share or celebrate the loss, depending upon the identity of the deceased. Occasionally, McCrumb's murderers are quite likable. Her tales of mystery are less about "whodunit" and more a psychological exploration of why a person would kill. In a 1990 interview in *Clues* magazine, McCrumb stated that she uses murder "as a catalyst" to demonstrate how people react to real or imagined threats to their social positions. To McCrumb, "the murder is always committed to protect an assumed cultural identity. It's not committed for money, for revenge, or for love. It is always 'This is who I have chosen to be and you're threatening my identity.'"

To show a variety of characters, events, and places, McCrumb has written three series of novels: the Elizabeth MacPherson mysteries, described by McCrumb as "Jane Austen with an attitude," are predominantly social satires of a Southern society in which appearance and social position are of prime importance. The Jay Omega novels, also satires, are centered on the world of science-fiction writers and their fans. McCrumb's "serious novels" form the "ballad" series, set in fictional Wake County, in eastern Tennessee. The novels are so named because of the titles and the use of the lyrics of ballads throughout the books, as well as their being written in the ballad tradition themselves, with stories of love and hate and encounters with the supernatural. These novels focus on the importance of the past to the present and include multiple story lines as well as time frames.

Sharyn Elaine Arrowood was born on 26 February 1948 in Wilmington, North Carolina. Central to her childhood was listening to her father's bedtime stories, which ranged from *The Iliad* to tales of Civil War soldiers. In the introduction to *Foggy Mountain Breakdown and Other Stories* (1997), she states, "I come from a race of storytellers." Her great-grandfathers were circuit preachers in the Smoky Mountains, collecting stories as they distributed the word of God. McCrumb attributes her love of storytelling and mountain culture to them. She grew up listening to her father's tales of his life and background. He was born in the mountains of western North Carolina and grew up in eastern Tennessee. His stories supplied the "mountain influence" in her writing. Her mother, a "flatlander" who grew up around New Bern, North Carolina, contributed stories from the other side of the family, the Southern, "genteel" tradition.

Since the age of seven, McCrumb has wanted to be a writer, and, like the Brontë children, did her share of juvenile writing. Her first "work," written in the second grade, was a poem, "The Gypsy's Ghost," and at age nine she wrote a story to "explain" the song "Danny Boy." In an interview with Charles L. P. Silet, published in the fall 1995 issue of *The Armchair Detective,* she remarked that such early writing taught her where to place her commas. During high school she developed the character Elizabeth MacPherson in a draft of a short story later published as "Love on First Bounce" in her collection *Foggy Mountain Breakdown and Other Stories.*

Elizabeth grew into the main character in a series of novels.

In 1970, McCrumb graduated from the University of North Carolina with a B.A. in communications and Spanish. Uncertain about a career choice, she worked at a variety of jobs, including teaching at the Forsythe Technical Institute in Winston-Salem, North Carolina, and at Virginia Polytechnic Institute and State University, in Blacksburg, Virginia, and as a reporter for the *Smoky Mountain Times* in Bryson City, North Carolina. On 9 January 1982 she married David Kenneth McCrumb, a corporate environmental director; they have two children, Spencer and Laura.

McCrumb's first novel, *Sick of Shadows* (1984), begins the Elizabeth MacPherson series. The novel is set in Georgia as the Chandler family gathers for a wedding that will shortly become a funeral. Newly graduated from college with a degree in sociology and no idea what to do with her life, Elizabeth, whose mother is a Chandler, has been invited to be a bridesmaid. Elizabeth comments on the prewedding activities in a tongue-in-cheek style that has become characteristic of her commentary throughout the series. Writing to her brother, Bill, Elizabeth remarks, "Plans for the wedding occupy Aunt Amanda's every waking moment. It's like watching Eisenhower plan D-Day." Physically, Elizabeth is "that pretty little gal with the dark hair" who looks "a little like Linda Ronstadt." In *Paying the Piper* (1988), Elizabeth describes herself as "neither wholesome or ordinary" with "too much imagination." In the series her imagination is what enables Elizabeth to put together disparate elements in order to discover murderers and motives.

In *Sick of Shadows,* McCrumb paints a detailed picture of the preparations for the wedding and the characters involved. The book, described by McCrumb as a "comedy of manners," is a social satire of genteel Southern families and is peopled with some remarkable characters, described as "individualists" by "Captain Grandfather" Chandler, a retired admiral who still wears his uniform and runs the house "like a destroyer." Geoffrey Chandler, Elizabeth's cousin, is introduced and appears in subsequent books. Always well-dressed and quoting William Shakespeare, Geoffrey provides humor in the novel through his biting wit as do the author's comments on Southern stereotypes. For example, the bride, another of Elizabeth's cousins, has "graduated" from Cherry Hill, known as a finishing school to the deluded and as a mental institution to the informed. On the surface, Aunt Amanda Chandler is a Southern lady of charm, well taught in the arts of setting a proper table and writing notes; she is also a closet alcoholic. The sheriff affects the demeanor of a "good ol' boy" with his "folksy" conversation and accent, but he has a degree from Georgia Tech and can discuss wave-particle duality with Charles Chandler, a pretentious intellectual and yet another of Elizabeth's cousins.

After the bride is murdered, Elizabeth's brother, Bill, who has avoided the wedding, claiming too much work at law school, is prompted by clues embedded in Elizabeth's letters to set up a scenario to reveal the murderer. Bill appears briefly at the end of the novel but plays a bigger part in other novels in the series. Originally published as a paperback, the book was favorably reviewed by Kathleen Maio in the *Wilson Library Bulletin* (8 September 1984); she called it "an unusual and very promising debut."

A second Elizabeth MacPherson novel, *Lovely in Her Bones* (1985), shows Elizabeth, still searching for a career, enrolled in a folk-medicine class at a Virginia university. Characters include Bill and his roommate, Milo, a graduate student and research assistant to Dr. Lerche, a forensic anthropologist. While looking for medicinal herbs, Elizabeth finds a skull that she is certain is a murder victim's. The simpler explanation, provided by Milo at the site, is that the skull washed down from a grave situated at the edge of an eroded cliff. The skull of the Confederate soldier sparks Elizabeth's interest in archaeology and the study of bones, which becomes her vocation.

The novel is about the Cullowhees, an isolated group of people in the mountains of North Carolina who are trying to save their land from strip miners by getting Dr. Lerche to prove they are an Indian tribe. Their land is on tribal grounds and, therefore, inviolable. Lerche needs volunteers to dig in the old Cullowhee cemetery to prove their claim, and Elizabeth volunteers. Like all of McCrumb's novels, the plot is enhanced with background information on a variety of subjects, including folk medicine—specifically various plants and what they will cure, such as ginseng as a cure for some allergies. Some individuals in the novel, who will make a fortune if the land is sold to strip miners, try various ways to halt the work of the scientists and their crew. Lerche is murdered, and Elizabeth actively investigates. She puts together the clues, discovers an unlikely suspect as the murderer, and is almost a third murder victim herself after drinking a potentially lethal cup of tea. *Lovely in Her Bones* was voted the Best Appalachian Novel of 1985.

In the third Elizabeth MacPherson novel, *Highland Laddie Gone* (1986), McCrumb indulges in some delightful satire of ancestor-worshiping Americans of Scottish descent, who gather each year at Glenco Mountain in western Virginia for the annual Highland Games. Accompanied by her fun-loving cousin, Geoffrey, Elizabeth is Maid of the Cat for this year's Highland Games. The weekend is one of celebrating

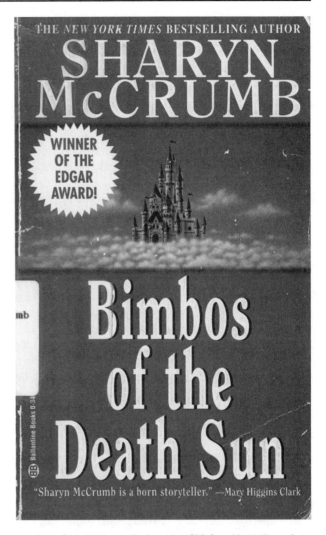

THE *NEW YORK TIMES* BESTSELLING AUTHOR
SHARYN McCRUMB
WINNER OF THE EDGAR AWARD!
Bimbos of the Death Sun
"Sharyn McCrumb is a born storyteller." —Mary Higgins Clark

Cover for a 1997 paperback reprint of McCrumb's 1987 novel, judged best paperback mystery of the year by the Mystery Writers of America, in which the protagonist attempts to solve a murder at a convention of science-fiction fans (Richland County Public Library)

Scottish-American history, as people come, wearing their clans' tartans, despite the heat, and reliving the battle of Culloden. Geoffrey is there to get "atmosphere" for his little theater's production of *Brigadoon*. Elizabeth's role is to parade around, showing off Cluny, a bobcat, Clan Chattan's mascot.

Amid the Parade of Clans, the piping competitions, the throwing of the caber, and dancing, two murders take place that Elizabeth, who is now working toward a degree in forensic anthropology, is determined to solve. However, she is newly in love with Cameron Dawson, a Ph.D. marine biologist, just arrived from Scotland, who would rather hunker down in front of a large-screen television in an air-conditioned room than try to explain that he knows precious little about the minutiae of Scottish history with which the

Americans are so besotted. Conspiracies abound, ranging from the activities of the SRA (Scottish Revolutionary Army), which expects to free Scotland from the English, to the plots of James Stuart MacGowan, a precocious ten-year-old, whose main objective is to escape his doting parents. Despite the ninety-degree heat, the heavy wool of the costumes, and the general confusion, romance blossoms for Elizabeth and Cameron.

While writing, McCrumb was working on an M.A. in English with a focus on Appalachian literature and culture from Virginia Polytechnic Institute and State University; she completed the degree in 1987. At Virginia Tech, she taught journalism and was a film librarian. Since 1988, she has worked as a full-time novelist, lecturer, and writer in residence at King College, Tennessee, and Shepherd College, West Virginia. She lives in Shawsville, Virginia.

The genesis of McCrumb's fourth novel, *Bimbos of the Death Sun* (1987), was a practical joke. When she was a graduate student at Virginia Tech, McCrumb slipped a manuscript into a pile of short-story entries for a contest sponsored by the university science-fiction club. One of the judges was English instructor John Nizalowski. In her story, she portrayed his dog and his office mate as evil aliens in a spoof of *Moby-Dick* (1851). As cited in the Author's Note to *Bimbos of the Death Sun,* Nizalowski, after he had stopped laughing, told her, "You know, that title is really too good to waste on a practical joke." The novel that bears this title, a spoof of science-fiction writers and their fans, won an Edgar Award from the Mystery Writers of America for the best paperback mystery of 1988. McCrumb, having attended several science-fiction conventions and witnessed fans idolizing their hero-writers, had plenty to work with in this tale. Set at a science-fiction convention, the hero, Dr. Jay O. Mega, a professor of electrical engineering, is invited as a "guest writer" because of his book *Bimbos of the Death Sun.* However, Jay is not the principal guest; that honor is given to Appin Dungannon, a miserable, despotic author whose creation Tratyn Runewind, a Viking hero, is widely popular. Dungannon, described as "a malevolent elf with a drinking problem," is renowned for making enemies, but at this convention someone actually murders him instead of just threatening to kill him.

Dr. Mega, known as Jay Omega, his nom de plume, finds himself thrust into the role of Dungeon Master. With the help of his significant other, Dr. Marion Farley, and her background in folklore, Jay scripts the game during which the killer, one of the players in this "real life" Dungeons and Dragons game, is played out. The book is peopled by several fan types: those into war games, fantasy, and *StarTrek.* McCrumb's writing is full of funny one-liners, and her descriptions of the participants, wearing outlandish costumes at the "con," show her sense of the absurd.

Following the success of *Bimbos of the Death Sun,* McCrumb returned to heroine Elizabeth MacPherson in *Paying the Piper.* Continuing her infatuation with all things Scottish, including Cameron Dawson, Elizabeth signs up for an archaeological dig on a remote island in the Hebrides. Cameron will be studying seals on a nearby island. Elizabeth's expedition will measure the standing stones of the island of Banrigh and hopes to find Celtic treasure. Before leaving Edinburgh, Elizabeth and Cameron take a tour of famous murder sites. Someone is actually murdered during the tour, but Elizabeth puts the occurrence behind her in anticipation of her search for Celtic treasure. The expedition, however, turns lethal as people begin dying from a mysterious illness.

As is typical with McCrumb, she includes some ancient lore in the novel. One story is the Celtic myth of the selkie, that seals are really the souls of men who died; another is the story of the Tarans, unbaptized children who "were put in unmarked graves" set high between heaven and earth. According to the legend, they can be heard crying in the wind. Elizabeth, however, did not hear the voices of dead children but the sound of a piper heralding his own death, alone on a remote island. A combination of Elizabeth's curiosity and intelligence and Cameron's concern for her safety unmasks the murderer.

In 1990, *If Ever I Return, Pretty Peggy-O* was published, the first of McCrumb's ballad novels. The old stories and ballads that were part of McCrumb's heritage and the myths, folktales, and history of the Appalachian region give these novels a depth the other books lack. In the journal *Now and Then* (Fall 1993), McCrumb claims she began the series because "I was tired of hearing the stereotypes of Appalachia, and so I decided to set a series in East Tennessee so that people could see the culture there and realize that it's not Bo Duke" (from the popular television series *The Dukes of Hazzard*). McCrumb is particularly proud of these novels, some of which have become required reading in regional history classes. To categorize these novels as mysteries is, according to McCrumb, not appropriate since she sees the novels as "serious explorations of the politics and culture of the mountain south." However, each of the ballad novels includes at least one murder, and the plot of the novel unveils not only the killer or killers but the "rationale" for the murder.

Each ballad novel also includes a subplot that either obliquely or in a straightforward manner addresses a contemporary issue, such as the effects of child abuse in *The Hangman's Beautiful Daughter* (1992) or the negative effects of land development in *The Rose-*

wood Casket (1996). In addition, the ballad series has a core of continuing characters. Three are introduced in the first ballad novel: Spencer Arrowood (named for McCrumb's paternal grandfather), sheriff of Wake County, Tennessee; his deputy, Joe LeDonne; and Martha Ayers, police dispatcher. A fourth continuing character, Nora Bonesteel, is introduced in *The Hangman's Beautiful Daughter*.

Spencer Arrowood is a local boy, born and raised in fictional Hamelin, Tennessee; he attended the local schools, left town to serve in the army in Germany, "pushing paperclips," and returned home after a failed marriage. Because of his low-key charm and his previous service under the former sheriff, he is elected sheriff. Contrasted to Arrowood is deputy Joe LeDonne, an uptight veteran of Vietnam who is unable to leave the war behind and is haunted by memories. A passage in *The Hangman's Beautiful Daughter* concerns his one-year tour of duty in Vietnam: "He didn't so much survive it as mutate to accommodate its demands." McCrumb describes him as "a thin crust of snow over a pit of ice water" who is always taking chances. According to LeDonne, the only "safe people are the dead ones." Martha Ayer, in her forties, survivor of two marriages, is an efficient dispatcher but believes she needs more in her personal and professional life. Over the course of the ballad novels, she proves her ability and is promoted to deputy.

The principal setting for the ballad novels is in the town of Hamelin, population nine hundred. Although the town is fictional, in an interview for WDBJ radio, McCrumb stated that she pictures Newcastle, Virginia, when describing Hamelin. The small town has a main street, a local newspaper, a popular diner. It is a place where families have lived for generations, and neighbors know each other.

In *If Ever I Return, Pretty Peggy-O*, the first two words introduce the sheriff, who is visiting the cemetery on Memorial Day. The note of remembrance and war is struck with the beginning quote from Edgar Lee Masters's *Spoon River Anthology* (1915). The voice is that of Harry Wilmans, a soldier who followed the flag and died, "shot through the guts," in a foreign war (the Spanish American). Arrowood is remembering his brother, Cal, who died in 1966 in Vietnam.

Vietnam and its aftermath play a central role in this novel. The major plotline concerns Peggy Muryan, a famous folk singer who has moved to town and is trying to write new material for a comeback. The past intrudes with memories of her former singing partner, Travis Perdue, whom Peggy left behind on her climb to fame. He was drafted during the war in Vietnam and, supposedly, died there. His letters to her, which are interspersed throughout the narrative, re-create the hor-

Cover for McCrumb's 1990 novel, the first of her mysteries based on the songs and folklore of rural Appalachia (Richland County Public Library)

ror of the war. The mystery begins with the arrival of postcards, sent to Peggy and written in the style of Travis Perdue, full of information that only Travis could know. Then her dog is hanged, butchered, and mutilated with a mark used by a Vietnam armed forces unit. Some sheep are savagely slaughtered, and a teenage girl who has a remarkable resemblance to the younger Peggy is murdered.

The mystery is the identity of the killer: Is it Travis Perdue, lost in Vietnam and returned to get even with Peggy for her success without him? Or is it the crazy Vietnam vet who lives back in the woods in a cabin? Central to the novel is the effect of war not only on those who fight but on families and friends. A subplot concerning a high-school reunion reinforces the effect of Vietnam on a generation that lost not only friends and family but innocence. In an interview with Rebecca Sexton, published in *Clues* in 1990, McCrumb describes the book as a study of the 1960s generation. As in all her novels, she does extensive research. To get background for this novel, she talked to hundreds of people, eliciting their reflections on those turbulent years.

During the course of the novel, LeDonne has been focusing on clues that do not gel with his experience in Vietnam. However, the mystery is solved when the killer at last confronts Peggy. The novel won the MacCavity Award and was on the *New York Times* list of Notable Books of 1990. *New York Times* book reviewer Marilyn Stasio applauded McCrumb's "strongly individualized characters" in the "tightly plotted mystery" (20 May 1990).

After this novel, McCrumb returned to the Elizabeth MacPherson series in *The Windsor Knot* (1990). Set in Scotland and Georgia, the novel focuses on the upcoming wedding of Elizabeth and Cameron. Although both had relished a long engagement, Elizabeth puts the marriage plans into overdrive when she discovers that the queen is having her annual garden party in Edinburgh, and Elizabeth can only attend if she is married to Cameron. McCrumb's off-the-wall characters, including the Chandler family from *Sick of Shadows,* a missing garden gnome that appears to be sending postcards from various locations around the world, and a murder that is solved by cousin Geoffrey complete the picture of wedding mayhem.

In *Missing Susan* (1991), the sixth novel in the Elizabeth McPherson series, Elizabeth, now married and living in Scotland, is bored. Cameron has planned a six-week trip with his marine biologist friends to the North Atlantic to study sea lions. Elizabeth, armed with a new Ph.D. in forensic anthropology, cannot find a job, so she decides to join a Murder Tour group in England, looking at historic sites of past murders and mysteries, culminating in a Jack the Ripper Tour in London. The tour is led by Rowan Rover, an expert on nonfictional murders, from the death of Amy Robsart in Queen Elizabeth I's time to the Yorkshire Strangler. However, Rowan has serious financial problems and has agreed to murder Susan Cohen, a member of the tour group, in return for a sizable amount of cash provided by her uncle, who has initiated the contract. The title of the novel, *Missing Susan,* is made ironic by Rowan's continual failed attempts to murder Susan. The only murders in the novel are those studied throughout the Murder Tour.

The book satirizes the crime genre by making the reader sympathize with the murderer and hope he is successful in killing the odious Susan. Another target of McCrumb's satire is the tourists who go from site to site taking pictures but not taking in the historical significance of what they are "seeing." The novel is full of background information on the history and culture of southern England and Wales, focusing on Stonehenge, Bath, Oxford, the New Forest, and several sites in Cornwall.

McCrumb's second ballad novel, *The Hangman's Beautiful Daughter,* begins with an in-depth portrait of Nora Bonesteel, a woman well past seventy years old who lives alone on Ashe Mountain, on land that has belonged to her family since 1793. She also sees ghosts, and, like her grandmother and Scottish ancestors, she has "The Sight," the unsought "gift" of seeing tragedy before it occurs. At the beginning of the novel, Bonesteel is stitching a dark quilt with four coffins in the center, and two to the side. The quilt signifies the deaths that occur in the novel. Nora Bonesteel is described in a 12 April 1992 article by *Los Angeles Times* book critic Charles Champlin as a "dominating figure" who becomes "a kind of Celtic chorus," commenting on the action and characters. A repository of mountain lore, Bonesteel appears in subsequent ballad novels.

The main story line of the novel is the murder of Mr. and Mrs. Underhill and their youngest son, Simon, by their oldest son, Josh, who then kills himself. Two teenage children are left and placed under the guardianship of Laura Bruce, the minister's pregnant wife, whose husband is serving as chaplain to troops in Iraq, left behind after the Gulf War. Additional characters are Tavy Annis and Taw McBryde, who were boys together. Taw went to Detroit for work, married, and stayed. Tavy remained on the family farm in Wake County, Tennessee. Fifty years later Taw, widowed, comes home to find his old friend dying of cancer.

With this set of characters McCrumb explores environmental issues. The Little Dove River that has supplied the community with water for years is full of carcinogens from a paper company upriver in North Carolina. Tavy and Taw's fight against the paper company and the working out of the reason the Underhills were murdered are the principal focuses of the novel. Although Sheriff Arrowood and others regard the murders as a solved crime, Deputy LeDonne is not so sure. He suspects that the deaths had a cause not discovered in the initial investigation. During the climax of the novel, the truth of the murders is revealed by one of the remaining children, who tells what happened the night the Underhill family died.

In addition to the narrative, McCrumb enriches the novel with lore about quilting, legends, holiday traditions, and folk remedies. As all the ballad novels do, this one includes song. McCrumb discusses the hymn "I Wonder as I Wander" and its Celtic roots. The book was awarded Best Appalachian Novel in 1992 by the Appalachian Writers Association and was on the *New York Times* Notable Books list. Reviewing the book on 19 April 1992, *New York Times* book critic Stasio focuses on the character of Nora Bonesteel and equates

McCrumb to Nora in that "she plucks the mysteries from people's lives and works these dark narrative threads into Appalachian legends older than the hills."

After the intensity of this ballad novel, McCrumb returned to light-hearted satire with Elizabeth MacPherson in *MacPherson's Lament* (1992). The object of the satire is the stereotype of the genteel Southern old lady and the "land grabbing" Yankees, still trying to take the South by buying up property. Most of this book centers on Elizabeth's brother, Bill, just graduated from law school and trying to establish a practice with a friend from law school, A. P. Hill, named for her ancestor, a Civil War general. Five feet two with blue eyes and tough as nails, Hill is a female who dislikes the establishment, those law firms of "good ol' boys" and her cousin Stinky, the attorney general of Virginia. She has decided to practice law with the kind but innocent MacPherson.

Bill becomes involved with selling an antebellum home for eight old ladies, the last residents of a mansion for widows and daughters of the Confederacy. However, like many little old ladies, these women are astute, but unlike most, they develop a criminal plan to defraud the state of Virginia, which is in the process of taking the home by eminent domain, by selling the house to a "Yankee." The old ladies employ the most gullible lawyer they can find, Bill MacPherson, to take care of the bill of sale. Then they disappear.

It appears as if Bill has not only taken the money but killed the old ladies. To aid her brother, Elizabeth returns from Scotland to search for the ladies who are, in turn, looking for buried Confederate gold. A second story line, set in 1865, is that of two Confederate soldiers who are guarding the Confederate treasury. The last reported location of the treasury is Danville, Virginia, the final capital of the Confederacy. Each soldier takes some gold bars and returns home. One buries his portion in South Carolina. This buried gold is what the ladies, one a descendant of this soldier, are searching for. McCrumb effectively separates the two time frames by chapters: those chapters concerning 1865 are introduced with quotations from "John Brown's Body". The contemporary chapters are headed by excerpts of Civil War songs.

In her next novel, McCrumb returned to Jay O. Mega and Marion Farley in *Zombies of the Gene Pool* (1992). This novel is another spoof of science-fiction writers and fans as well as editors and journalists. Jay and Marion are invited to accompany a fellow professor, Dr. Erik Giles, who once wrote science fiction, but "grew up" and turned to the study and teaching of English literature, to an unusual science-fiction event: the recovery of a pickle jar buried more than thirty years ago, containing never-published manuscripts and

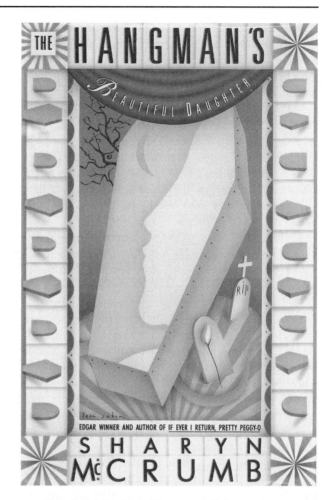

Cover for McCrumb's 1992 mystery novel, her second one set in the Appalachian Mountains (Richland County Public Library)

memorabilia from a group of writers who called themselves the Lanthanids. Some of these writers have become famous, and their early work is expected to bring a huge price at an auction to be held once the pickle jar is recovered. Because the jar was buried, it has become more inaccessible since the farm on which it was buried is now on the bottom of Lake Breedlove, created by the Tennessee Valley Authority.

However, the dam needs repairing, and engineers are draining the lake. Ruben Mistral, a Hollywood big shot, orchestrates a reunion of the old members of the Lanthanids for the purpose of recovering the pickle jar. Then the unexpected happens: the long-dead Pat Malone, bane of the group for his vicious tongue, appears, determined to ruin the reunion and the chance for the authors to make some major money. But Pat Malone is killed before he reveals everyone's hidden secrets.

This novel is full of humor. It pokes fun at the pretension of the writers, the journalists, and the publishers, all gathered for the opening of the pickle jar. McCrumb balances the fun with sadness at the failing memory of a formerly great writer. The ending raises the questions: was an impostor posing as Malone, and is Malone really alive after all?

McCrumb's next novel, *She Walks These Hills* (1994), a ballad novel, is a story of journeys. Set in 1779, it is the story of Katie Wyler, whose parents were killed by the Shawnee. She was captured and taken away from her father's farm in Mitchell County, North Carolina. Her story is her journey home from Ohio, following the rivers, over hundreds of miles of wilderness.

The novel also includes journeys taken in the present time. Jeremy Cobb, a Ph.D. candidate, is focusing his dissertation in ethnohistory on the old stories of Appalachia and is consumed by the story of Katie Wyler. His attempt to replicate her journey is his story. Another journey, set in the present, is that of sixty-three-year-old Harm Sorley, who is confused about time. He has Korsakoff's syndrome, a disease that distorts his memory. Harm, living in the 1960s when he last saw his wife and baby, has such a desire to be with them again that he escapes from prison to journey home. A disc jockey, Hank the Yank (from Connecticut), is captivated by the story of Harm Sorley and mounts a radio crusade to "save" him. Hank also begins his own investigation of why Harm took an ax to Claib Maggard, because "something about that original case just doesn't make sense." After reading old newspapers, provoking people's memories of the murder, and talking to Nora Bonesteel, Hank begins to uncover the mystery. Part of the explanation of the "bad blood" between the Sorleys and Maggard includes the historic facts of the establishment of the Cherokee National Forest in the 1930s and the turning of people off their land as a result.

Chapter headings are verses from an 1885 *Tennessee Methodist Hymnal* that, according to *Los Angeles Times* book critic Champlin (9 October 1994), are "movingly apt underscorings for a story in which the persistence of the past is so strong an element." The novel includes legends, folklore (such as how to make bees stay once the owner of the hive is gone), and true stories (such as the hanging of Mary the elephant in 1916 in Erwin, Tennessee). All enrich the book, as does the information on the geology of the mountains and their connections to European mountains and on the Celtic people who settled in the United States, attracted to the area because of its resemblance to home.

Like the previous ballad novels, characters include Sheriff Arrowood, Deputy Joe LeDonne, Martha Ayers (now advancing in her career as a deputy), and Nora Bonesteel. The setting is the mountains of North Carolina and Tennessee. All the travelers are heading toward Mitchell County. The novel includes details of events on their travels and what happens when they meet. In *She Walks These Hills*, an old murder is explained; an even older murder is revealed; and a murder takes place in the present time. The book won the 1994 Anthony and the 1995 Agatha Awards.

McCrumb's next Elizabeth MacPherson novel, *If I'd Killed Him When I Met Him* (1995), focuses on a variety of dysfunctional marriages. Like the previous MacPherson novels, this one includes a murder from the past that haunts the present. After the Civil War, a former major in the Union Army, Philip Todhunter, dies from arsenic poisoning. Todhunter had been accepted into Southern society, despite the "Late Unpleasantness," because of his money and marriage to an impoverished Southern belle, Lucy. Everyone suspects his wife of the murder, but no one can determine how she did it or why. Consequently, she is acquitted.

In the present time, another murder takes place, but with no mystery of who killed attorney Jeb Royden. Eleanor Royden (based on the true-life story of Betty Broderick of San Diego), long married to attorney Royden, is divorced by him and persecuted in a divorce described as "a blood sport." She loses everything—home, money, position, and friends. One day she murders him and the new (and much younger) Mrs. Royden. None of her dead husband's lawyer friends will represent her, so she hires A. P. Hill, Bill MacPherson's law partner. Bill has his own case. A married woman, Donna Jean Morgan, wants to sue her husband, a carpet layer and minister of his own church, who has taken another wife. The "voice of God" instructed him to do so. The other Mrs. Chevry Morgan, Tanya Faith, is barely sixteen.

When Chevry is found dead of arsenic poisoning, people recall that Donna Jean's ancestress is Lucy Todhunter. Bill contacts his sister, Elizabeth, for help, since she is a forensic anthropologist. Elizabeth has been living in Danville, Virginia, since her husband Cameron was lost at sea. To keep busy, she works as a private investigator for MacPherson and Hill. After a near-death experience with arsenic poisoning herself, Elizabeth solves the old mystery of how Todhunter died as well as the new case of how Chevry Morgan was poisoned.

The novel is full of humor, some of it dark, verging on the macabre. Eleanor Royden's remarks about her marriage are so similar to many modern-day marriages that the humor stings. In another case, Miri Malone hires Bill so that she can legally marry a dolphin. She drowns in the dolphin's tank; dolphins mate underwater. The marriages in this book are, in several ways, deadly; if not terminated by actual death, they end by disappearance, drowning, and sheer boredom. *Washington Post* Book World critic Pat Dowell describes the novel in a 18 June 1995 article as a "seriocomic fugue on the feminist theme of mid-life sexual politics." Dowell notes that the title refers to a comment overheard from a battered woman: "If I'd killed him when I met him, I'd be out of prison now."

The Rosewood Casket, another ballad novel, begins with a poem by Jim Wayne Miller, Kentucky poet laureate, titled "Small Farms Disappearing in Tennessee." This poem sets the stage for a novel about the land. Currently, the farms are disappearing because of the younger generation's lack of interest, taxes, land developers, the encroachment of civilization in the form of subdivisions and strip malls, and the wealthy newcomers who pay for scenic views. The past is also a part of the novel—the stories of Daniel Boone, his adventures and his words, and of Nancy Ward, a Cherokee wise woman who advised her people to learn to live with the whites. She died before realizing that the settlers wanted all the land.

This novel involves the dying Randall Stargill and his four living sons, a secret from the past, a murder, and a lost child. Chapter headings include the words of Daniel Boone, as a reminder of what was lost in the past, and one chapter introduced by a quote from English dramatist Arthur Wing Pinero, describing the future as the past "entered through another gate." Throughout the novel the past intrudes and clashes with the present. The concept of the difficulty of "going home again" is developed through the stories of the four sons who, at their dying father's request, return home to make a Rosewood coffin for him.

A major theme in the novel is "ruthless invaders" who take the land. To the Cherokee, they were the white men, the settlers. To those early settlers, they were people who took the land through land grants. Today, they are the developers, who are taking the old farms. Trees, animals, birds, and clean air are being lost. As in her other ballad novels, McCrumb enriches her text with old legends and even a recipe for making a scripture cake. *New York Times* book critic Stasio described the novel as a "magical mountain tale" (19 May 1996). *Washington Post* Book World critic Maureen Corrigan commented in a 21 April 1996 review that "In an earlier life, McCrumb must have been a balladeer, singing of restless spirits, star-crossed lovers and the consoling beauty of nature. Here, that older folk material acts as a refrain to the more realistic narrative about farmers clashing with newcomers who want their land at any cost."

McCrumb's next publication is a collection of twenty-four short stories, *Foggy Mountain Breakdown and Other Stories.* The stories include "Happiness Is a Dead

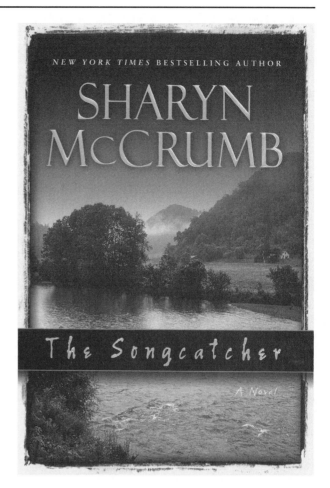

Dust jacket for McCrumb's 2001 novel, inspired in part by the experiences of her Scottish immigrant ancestor (Richland County Public Library)

Poet" and "Nine Lives to Live." In this story, Philip Danby has been joking that when he dies he wants to come back as a cat. After he is murdered, he gets his wish and comes back as a cat with a mission: to murder his murderer. The story "A Wee Doch and Doris" won the 1990 Agatha Award. It is not a mystery since there is little suspense that Louis the burglar will be "done in" by a little old lady. His plan to rob the house on New Year's Eve is derailed as the lady offers hospitality and a "wee doch and dorris," a Scottish expression for last drink of the evening. He has the drink and then is confronted with Doris, the old lady's daughter, a policewoman who captures him.

McCrumb's next book is *The Ballad of Frankie Silver* (1998), based on the true story of the hanging in 1833 of a woman, not yet twenty, the first woman hanged in North Carolina, for the murder, dismemberment, and burning of her husband, Charlie. In an Author's Note, McCrumb states that the case became to her about poor people as defendants and rich people as officials of the court, about Celtic versus English values in developing

America, and about mountain people versus the "flat-landers" in any culture. In this story about "equal justice under the law," McCrumb remarks that "not much has changed." The story includes background about the times, the law, and actual historic personalities.

The parallel plot is a present-time case and the execution of Fate Harkryder, whose background, dress, and lifestyle help to convict him of a murder he did not commit. Both Frankie and Fate are portrayed as victims of a legal system through their own ignorance of how the system works and a built-in fear of the ways of "flatlanders." As in the other ballad novels, the characters include Sheriff Arrowood, recovering from a nearly fatal gunshot wound, who is facing his own mortality and reminiscing about his predecessor, Sheriff Nelse Miller, who questioned whether Frankie Silver was, in fact, guilty of murder. Miller also had a gut feeling about Harkryder's innocence.

During his convalescence, Arrowood begins a study of the Silver case and then is summoned to witness the execution of Fate Harkryder, since he was the arresting officer some twenty years ago. Uncovering the truth about Frankie reveals the truth about Fate. In a 3 May 1998 review *New York Times* book critic Stasio commented, "By working in two time frames and alternating the narrative voice, McCrumb threads both stories into a single pattern, a dense and lovely but very dark design that illustrates the social hypocrisy of the legal system as much as the harshness of mountain justice then and now."

Following the serious ballad novel, McCrumb returned to Elizabeth MacPherson with *The PMS Outlaws* (2000). The novel is another social satire, focusing on beauty used as currency and also as a weapon. The novel is also about how men perceive women as objects, their worth determined by face and figure.

Elizabeth has committed herself to a mental hospital in hopes of curing her depression over her husband's death at sea. The people she meets at Cherry Hill develop the theme that physical beauty is all-important in society. One of the patients is part of a mystery. Elizabeth's brother, Bill, buys a mansion, a "real steal," for more upscale law offices. He and his partner, A. P. Hill, can live on the second floor and save rent money. One problem is that the former owner, ninety-four-year-old Jack Dolan, refuses to vacate. Hill has her own problems. A former undergraduate and law-school classmate, Patricia Perdue, has helped a criminal, Carla Larkin, escape from jail, and Perdue and Larkin are on a rampage—conning men, stealing their money, and leaving the victims handcuffed and naked. The rub is that Hill had the idea years ago when she and Patricia did the same to avenge a classmate's humiliation. The classmate was invited to a frat party, which turned out to be a "pig" party: whoever brings the ugliest girl wins.

Hill and Perdue got even; dressed to the nines and loaded with makeup, they snagged the frat brother and stripped him, leaving him naked and humiliated. The novel also includes a murder that took place some years ago, and cousin Geoffrey reappears to provide comedy and help the newly functioning Elizabeth solve an old crime.

McCrumb discovered Malcolm McCourry, a Scottish ancestor, while researching *The Ballad of Frankie Silver*. McCourry, her four times great-grandfather, was originally from Scotland and eventually came to Morristown, New Jersey, when he was nearly twenty years old and was apprenticed to become a lawyer. In 1794 he left home and family to journey down the Wilderness Road and homestead in the mountains of North Carolina. Intrigued by McCourry's life and the history of the times, McCrumb combined her other passion, folk songs and their origin, and wrote *The Songcatcher* (2001), another ballad novel.

The title reflects those who, like Cecil Sharpe, came from England and traveled over the country to write down the old songs before they were lost. An "ancient" ballad, "The Rowan Stave," which unites the different elements in the story, was, in fact, written by McCrumb herself. The music was by a friend. The novel includes a story line from the past, detailing the life of McCourry, and one from the present, involving a famous folk singer, Lark McCourry. The setting is Hamelin, Tennessee, with the usual characters as supporting cast: Sheriff Arrowood, Deputy LeDonne, Deputy Martha Ayes, and Nora Bonesteel. The principal part of the narrative is the story of Malcolm McCourry who, at age nine, was kidnapped from his home island of Islay in the Hebrides. The novel follows him to America, details his career and his raising a family in New Jersey and his second family in the mountains. McCrumb also traces the lives of his descendants, and their stories are accompanied by actual historical events, including the Revolutionary War and the Civil War. True accounts of life in Hart's Island Prison in New York City for captured Confederate soldiers and even the story of Colonel John T. Wilder, the Union commander who asked the enemy for advice, enhance the novel. The present-time story line concerns Lark McCourry, whose plane crashes in the mountains as she is returning home to her dying father. The search for Lark and her search for a lost song, "The Rowan Stave," flesh out the novel. Book reviewer Judith Warner of the *Washington Post* found the novel to be "plodding" and Lark McCourry an "ill-tempered prima donna" in a 15 July 2001 review.

Although *Ghost Riders* (2003) makes fun of Civil War re-enactors, it also provokes the ghosts of "real" Civil War participants to stir the observers. McCrumb's point is that the Civil War did not end in 1865. There was so "much sorrow and ruin and hatred among neighbors" during the war years that the past was never over. "They will not turn loose of that war."

The novel focuses on an area in North Carolina and Tennessee, the mountain region of Appalachia, where families were torn with loyalties to the Union and the Confederacy; the "wrong side was to take a side." Principal historic characters are Zebulon Vance—lawyer, congressman, and governor of North Carolina during the war years—and Malinda "Sam" Blalock, who cut her hair and followed her husband to war, enlisting as a Confederate soldier. Later, she and her husband were discharged from the army and engaged in guerrilla fighting in the mountains for the Union army. McCrumb spent four years doing research for the book, which received mixed reviews.

Ghost Riders is one of McCrumb's ballad novels, but the series characters of Nora Bonesteel and Sheriff Spencer Arrowood have little more than minor appearances. The major focus is the continuing effect of war. Sheriff Arrowood is investigating an ancestor who was the last man killed east of the Mississippi in the Civil War, and the reenactors are trying to relive a battle that had little consequence. What had consequence was the divided family loyalties that resulted in long-standing feuds in the mountain regions.

Sharyn McCrumb's focus on the area and people of Appalachia earned her the Outstanding Contribution to Appalachian Literature Award in 1997. For the most part, McCrumb's novels are set in Appalachia. They delve into the history of the mountain regions of North

Carolina and Tennessee and the flatlands. The more serious ballad novels can be contrasted with the social satire of a more genteel Southern tradition in the Elizabeth MacPherson series and the general hilarity of the Jay Omega books. McCrumb was asked in a 1993 interview published in the journal *Now & Then* whether it was difficult to write three different series. McCrumb replied that it was a challenge; "I like the opportunity to change moods and tell different stories." Her books are best described, by McCrumb herself in the biography on her website, as "Appalachian quilts," pieced together with legends, ballads, history, and her own family stories.

Interviews:

Rebecca Sexton, "The Art of Writing Intelligent Fiction: An Interview with Sharyn McCrumb," *Clues,* 11, no. 2 (1990): 95–101;

Jeffrey Marks, "Sharyn McCrumb's Ballad of the Beautiful Appalachian Death Sun," *Now & Then,* 10, no. 3 (Fall 1993): 31–33;

Charles L. P. Silet, "She Walks These Hills: An Interview with Sharyn McCrumb," *Armchair Detective,* 28, no. 4 (Fall 1995): 368–380;

Rebecca Laine, "Telephone Interviews with Sharyn McCrumb" (8 July 1997) <www.sharynmccrumb.com>.

Reference:

Meredith Sue Willis, "The Ballads of Sharyn McCrumb," *Appalachian Journal,* 25, no. 3 (Spring 1998): 320–329.

Ralph McInerny

(24 February 1929 –)

Anita G. Gorman
Slippery Rock University of Pennsylvania

BOOKS: *The Logic of Analogy: An Interpretation of St. Thomas* (The Hague: Nijhoff, 1961);

A History of Western Philosophy, volume 1: *From the Beginnings of Philosophy to Plotinus* (Chicago: Regnery, 1963);

Thomism in an Age of Renewal (Garden City, N.Y.: Doubleday, 1966; Notre Dame, Ind. & London: University of Notre Dame Press, 1968);

Jolly Rogerson (Garden City, N.Y.: Doubleday, 1967);

Studies in Analogy (The Hague: Nijhoff, 1968 [i.e., 1969]);

A Narrow Time (Garden City, N.Y.: Doubleday, 1969);

A History of Western Philosophy, volume 2: *Philosophy from St. Augustine to Ockham* (Notre Dame, Ind.: University of Notre Dame Press, 1970);

The Priest (New York: Harper & Row, 1973; London: Souvenir, 1974);

The Gate of Heaven (New York: Harper & Row, 1975);

Rogerson at Bay (New York: Harper & Row, 1976);

Her Death of Cold, (New York: Vanguard, 1977; London: Hale, 1979);

The Seventh Station, A Father Dowling Mystery (New York: Vanguard, 1977; London: Hale, 1979);

St. Thomas Aquinas (Boston: Twayne, 1977);

Spinnaker (South Bend, Ind.: Gateway, 1977);

Bishop as Pawn, A Father Dowling Mystery (New York: Vanguard, 1978; London: Hale, 1980);

Quick as a Dodo (New York: Vanguard, 1978);

Romanesque (New York: Harper & Row, 1978; London: Hale, 1979);

Abecedary (Notre Dame, Ind.: Juniper, 1979);

Lying Three, A Father Dowling Mystery (New York: Vanguard, 1979; London: Hale, 1980);

Second Vespers, A Father Dowling Mystery (New York: Vanguard, 1980; London: Hale, 1981);

Not a Blessed Thing! as Monica Quill, A Sister Mary Teresa Mystery (New York: Vanguard, 1981);

Rhyme and Reason: St. Thomas and Modes of Discourse (Milwaukee: Marquette University Press, 1981);

Thicker Than Water, A Father Dowling Mystery (New York: Vanguard, 1981; London: Hale, 1982);

Ralph McInerny (from Rogerson at Bay, *1976; Richland County Public Library)*

Ethica Thomistica: The Moral Philosophy of Thomas Aquinas (Washington, D.C.: Catholic University of America, 1982; revised, 1997);

The Frozen Maiden of Calpurnia (Notre Dame, Ind.: Juniper, 1982);

Let Us Prey, as Quill, A Sister Mary Teresa Mystery (New York: Vanguard, 1982);

A Loss of Patients, A Father Dowling Mystery (New York: Vanguard, 1982);

Connolly's Life (New York: Atheneum, 1983);

The Grass Widow, A Father Dowling Mystery (New York: Vanguard, 1983);

Getting a Way with Murder, A Father Dowling Mystery (New York: Vanguard, 1984; Bath: Chivers, 1986);

And Then There Was Nun, as Quill, A Sister Mary Teresa Mystery (New York: Vanguard, 1984);

The Noonday Devil (New York: Atheneum, 1985);

Nun of the Above, as Quill, A Sister Mary Teresa Mystery (New York: Vanguard, 1985);

Rest in Pieces, A Father Dowling Mystery (New York: Vanguard, 1985; Bath: Chivers, 1991);

Being and Predication: Thomistic Interpretations, Studies in Philosophy and the History of Philosophy, volume 16 (Washington, D.C.: Catholic University of America Press, 1986);

Leave of Absence (New York: Atheneum, 1986);

Miracles: A Catholic View (Huntington, Ind.: Our Sunday Visitor, 1986);

Sine Qua Nun, as Quill, A Sister Mary Teresa Mystery (New York: Vanguard, 1986);

The Basket Case, A Father Dowling Mystery (New York: St. Martin's Press, 1987; London: Boxtree, 1992);

Cause and Effect (New York: Atheneum, 1987);

Art and Prudence: Studies in the Thought of Jacques Maritain (Notre Dame, Ind.: University of Notre Dame Press, 1988);

The Veil of Ignorance, as Quill, A Sister Mary Teresa Mystery (New York: St. Martin's Press, 1988);

Abracadaver, A Father Dowling Mystery (New York: St. Martin's Press, 1989); republished as *Sleight of Body* (London: Macmillan, 1989);

Body and Soil (New York: Atheneum, 1989);

Four on the Floor (New York: St. Martin's Press, 1989);

Frigor Mortis (New York: Atheneum, 1989);

Boethius and Aquinas (Washington, D.C.: Catholic University of America Press, 1990);

A First Glance at St. Thomas Aquinas: A Handbook for Peeping Thomists (Notre Dame, Ind.: University of Notre Dame Press, 1990);

Savings and Loam, An Andrew Broom Mystery (New York: Atheneum, 1990);

Easeful Death (New York: Atheneum / Toronto: Maxwell Macmillan Canada / New York: Maxwell Macmillan International, 1991);

Judas Priest, A Father Dowling Mystery (New York: St. Martin's Press, 1991; Bath: Chivers, 1992);

The Nominative Case, as Edward Mackin (New York: Walker, 1991);

The Search Committee (New York: Atheneum / Toronto: Collier Macmillan Canada / New York: Maxwell Macmillan International, 1991);

Sister Hood, as Quill, A Sister Mary Teresa Mystery (New York: St. Martin's Press, 1991);

Aquinas on Human Action (Washington, D.C.: Catholic University of America Press, 1992);

Desert Sinner, A Father Dowling Mystery (New York: St. Martin's Press, 1992; Sutton, U.K.: Severn House, 1994);

Infra Dig (New York: Atheneum / Toronto: Maxwell Macmillan Canada / New York: Maxwell Macmillan International, 1992; Bath: Chivers, 1993);

Aquinas Against the Averroists: On There Being Only One Intellect (Lafayette, Ind.: Purdue University Press, 1993);

Nun Plussed, as Quill, A Sister Mary Teresa Mystery (New York: St. Martin's Press, 1993);

The Question of Christian Ethics (Washington, D.C.: Catholic University of America Press, 1993);

Seed of Doubt, A Father Dowling Mystery (New York: St. Martin's Press, 1993);

A Cardinal Offense, A Father Dowling Mystery (New York: St. Martin's Press, 1994);

The God of Philosophers (Salt Lake City: Westminster-McMurrin Lectures, 1994);

Modernity and Religion (Notre Dame, Ind.: University of Notre Dame Press, 1994);

Mom and Dead, An Andrew Broom Mystery (New York: Atheneum / Toronto: Maxwell Macmillan Canada / New York: Maxwell Macmillan International, 1994);

The Case of the Constant Caller, A Father Dowling Mystery for Young Adults (New York: St. Martin's Press, 1995);

The Case of the Dead Winner, A Father Dowling Mystery for Young Adults (New York: St. Martin's Griffin, 1995);

Law and Ardor, An Andrew Broom Mystery (New York: Scribners, 1995);

Let's Read Latin: Introduction to the Language of the Church (South Bend, Ind.: Dumb Ox Books, 1995; revised, 2000);

Aquinas and Analogy (Washington, D.C.: Catholic University of America Press, 1996);

The Tears of Things, A Father Dowling Mystery (New York: St. Martin's Press, 1996);

Half Past Nun, as Quill, A Sister Mary Teresa Mystery (New York: St. Martin's Press, 1997);

On This Rockne, A Notre Dame Mystery (New York: St. Martin's Press, 1997);

The Lack of the Irish: A Mystery Set at the University of Notre Dame (New York: St. Martin's Press, 1998);

The Red Hat (San Francisco: Ignatius, 1998);

What Went Wrong with Vatican II: The Catholic Crisis Explained (Manchester, N.H.: Sophia Institute Press, 1998);

Irish Tenure: A Mystery Set at the University of Notre Dame (New York: St. Martin's Press, 1999);

A Student's Guide to Philosophy (Wilmington, Del.: ISI Books, 1999);

The Book of Kills: A Mystery Set at the University of Notre Dame (New York: St. Martin's Press, 2000);

Grave Undertakings, A Father Dowling Mystery (New York: St. Martin's Press, 2000);

Heirs and Parents, An Andrew Broom Mystery (New York: St. Martin's Minotaur, 2000);

Still Life (Unity, Me.: Five Star, 2000);

Characters in Search of Their Author: The Gifford Lectures Glasgow 1999–2000 (Notre Dame, Ind.: University of Notre Dame Press, 2001);

Death Takes the Veil and Other Stories, as Quill, with an introduction by Ralph McInerny (Waterville, Me.: Five Star, 2001);

The Defamation of Pius XII (South Bend, Ind.: St. Augustine's Press, 2001);

Emerald Aisle: A Notre Dame Mystery (New York: St. Martin's Press, 2001);

Shakespearean Variations (South Bend, Ind.: St. Augustine's Press, 2001);

Sub Rosa, An Egidio Manfredi Mystery (Waterville, Me.: Five Star, 2001);

Triple Pursuit, A Father Dowling Mystery (New York: St. Martin's Press, 2001);

As Good As Dead (Waterville, Me.: Five Star, 2002);

Celt and Pepper (New York: St. Martin's Minotaur, 2002);

Prodigal Father, A Father Dowling Mystery (New York: St. Martin's Minotaur, 2002);

The Ablative Case (Waterville, Me.: Five Star, 2003);

Aquinas (Oxford, U.K.: Polity, 2003; Malden, Mass.: Blackwell, 2003);

Irish Coffee (New York: St. Martin's Minotaur, 2003);

Last Things, A Father Dowling Mystery (New York: St. Martin's Minotaur, 2003);

The Very Rich Hours of Jacques Maritain: A Spiritual Life (Notre Dame, Ind.: University of Notre Dame Press, 2003);

Green Thumb (New York: St. Martin's Minotaur, 2004);

Requiem for a Realtor, A Father Dowling Mystery (New York: St. Martin's Minotaur, 2004);

Slattery: A Soft-Boiled Detective (Waterville, Me.: Five Star, 2004);

The Soul of Wit (South Bend, Ind.: St. Augustine's Press, 2004).

OTHER: *Kierkegaard: The Difficulty of Being Christian,* translated by McInerny and Leo Turcotte, edited by Jacques Colette (Notre Dame, Ind. & London: University of Notre Dame Press, 1968);

New Themes in Christian Philosophy: Papers Presented at a Conference Held at the University of Notre Dame September 1966, edited by McInerny (Notre Dame, Ind. & London: University of Notre Dame Press, 1968);

Angelo Paredi, *A History of the Ambrosiana,* by translated by McInerny and Constance McInerny (Notre Dame, Ind.: University of Notre Dame Press, 1983);

The Catholic Woman: Papers Presented at a Conference Sponsored by the Wethersfield Institute, New York City, September 28, 1990, edited by McInerny (San Francisco: Ignatius Press, 1991);

"Saints Preserve Us: The Catholic Mystery," in *The Fine Art of Murder: The Mystery Reader's Indispensable Companion,* edited by Ed Gorman and others (New York: Carroll & Graf, 1993), pp. 148–150;

Thomas's Commentary on the Ethics, edited by McInerny (Notre Dame, Ind.: Dumb Ox Books, 1993);

Thomas's Commentary on De Anima, edited by McInerny (Notre Dame, Ind.: Dumb Ox Books, 1994);

The Collected Works of Jacques Maritain: Volume 3, The Degrees of Knowledge, edited by McInerny (Notre Dame, Ind.: University of Notre Dame Press, 1995);

Thomas Aquinas, *Selected Writings,* translated and edited by McInerny (London: Penguin, 1998);

The Aquinas Catechism: A Simple Explanation of the Catholic Faith by the Church's Greatest Theologian, foreword by McInerny (Manchester, N.H.: Sophia Institute Press, 2000);

Murder Most Divine: Ecclesiastical Tales of Unholy Crimes, edited by McInerny and Martin H. Greenberg (Nashville: Cumberland House, 2000);

Murder Most Catholic: Divine Tales of Profane Crimes, edited by McInerny (Nashville: Cumberland House, 2002);

Yves René Marie Simon, *A Critique of Moral Knowledge,* translated, with an introduction, by McInerny (New York: Fordham University Press, 2002).

A professor of philosophy, journalist, translator, editor, writer of theological and philosophical works, short-story writer, and novelist, Ralph McInerny has produced more than sixty works of fiction, the majority of which have been mysteries featuring amateur detectives Andrew Broom, Sister Mary Teresa Dempsey, and the best known, Father Roger Dowling. Immersed in the work of Boethius, Søren Kierkegaard, and especially Thomas Aquinas, McInerny does not hesitate to label himself as an orthodox Roman Catholic. His faith impels him—whether in his scholarly work, his serious fiction, or his popular fiction—to deal with the moral choices human beings make daily and the consequences of those choices in both time and eternity. Even detective fiction, McInerny asserted in the April 2000 issue of *Crisis* magazine, "conveys a sense of what life is about, the often-unstated criteria by which the actions depicted are to be judged."

Born in Minneapolis on 24 February 1929 to Austin Clifford McInerny, an engineer, and Vivian Gertrude Rush McInerny, Ralph Matthew McInerny attended elementary school at St. Helena Parish; he then studied at Nazareth Hall, a minor seminary, interrupting his studies to serve in the U.S. Marine Corps in 1946–1947. After completing his work at Nazareth Hall, he earned a B.A. degree in 1951 from St. Paul Seminary in St. Paul, Minnesota, majoring in philosophy. He completed an M.A. degree in philosophy and classics at the University of Minnesota in 1952 and a Ph.D. in philosophy in 1954 at Laval University, Quebec. In 1953, he married Constance Terrill Kunert; they are the parents of four daughters and two sons. McInerny began his academic career in 1954–1955 as an instructor in philosophy at Creighton University; since 1955 he has taught at the University of Notre Dame.

McInerny's first published works were scholarly articles and books, including *The Logic of Analogy: An Interpretation of St. Thomas* (1961), the first volume of *A History of Western Philosophy* (1963), and *Thomism in an Age of Renewal* (1966). During the 1960s he began writing short stories for such magazines as *Redbook* and *Ladies' Home Journal*, choosing pseudonyms such as Ernan Mackey and Harry Austin because this sort of popular writing deviated so dramatically from his scholarly pursuits. While he was writing *Thomism in an Age of Renewal*, his editor at Doubleday asked McInerny to show him the manuscript, should he ever write a novel. Inspired by his editor's interest, he wrote *Jolly Rogerson* (1967), the eponymous protagonist of which suffers through marital difficulties, campus politics, and theological doubts. D. E. Thompson in *Library Journal* (1 October 1967) called attention to the "great deal of soul searching and personal recrimination" in the novel, and he thought the plot twists sometimes "difficult to understand." *Studies in Analogy,* a philosophical work, followed in 1968, and that book was followed in 1969 by a second novel, *A Narrow Time,* which details the personal conflicts of the protagonist regarding such matters as sex, death, and religion.

In the 1970s, McInerny continued his two-track career, following his second volume of *A History of Western Philosophy* (1970) with his third novel, *The Priest* (1973), a best-seller that delineated the confusion in the Catholic Church after the Second Vatican Council through the experiences of Frank Ascue, who satisfies neither the conservative nor the liberal elements of his parish in Fort Elbow, Ohio. Raymond A. Schroth, writing in *Common-*

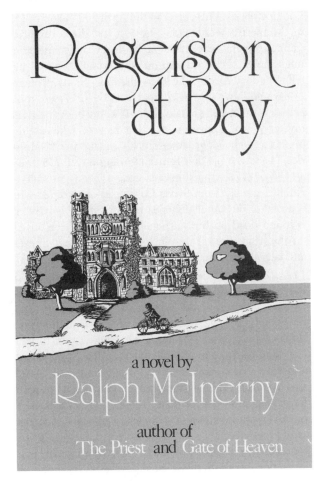

Dust jacket for McInerny's 1976 sequel to his Jolly Rogerson *(1967), about the worries of a middle-aged academic (Richland County Public Library)*

weal (10 August 1973), said that one of McInerny's "central themes is the intellectual sterility of American Catholic culture and he develops it by introducing recognizable characters with funny names who once dazzled the 1960s lecture circuit . . . and having them talk like fools." McInerny's 1975 novel, *The Gate of Heaven,* one of the author's personal favorites, focuses on a retirement community named Porta Coeli (Latin for Gate of Heaven), which consists of priests of the Society of St. Brendan. The oldest building of Porta Coeli, Little Sem, is to be demolished to make way for a girls' dormitory at the college run by the society. In 1975, McInerny also began his fifteen-year tenure as editor of *New Scholasticism.* *Rogerson at Bay* (1976), a sequel to McInerny's first work of fiction, brings back Matthew Rogerson, who in this new book contends with a prostate condition, a wife who has enrolled in college and become more independent, his belated circumcision, and a romantic interest.

In the summer of 1976, McInerny's agent suggested a mystery series with a priest as protagonist.

Looking back on his career in the April 2001 issue of *Crisis*, McInerny recalled that he foresaw three obstacles standing in his way: he thought that writing mysteries might be "a backward step on what I imagined was my rising literary career"; he knew that his priestly protagonist would inevitably be compared to G. K. Chesterton's Father Brown; and "Finally, I didn't know how to write a mystery," an admission that led him to take up the project as a challenge. After quickly selling two "trial stories," he wrote his first Father Dowling novel, *Her Death of Cold* (1977), which begins with a late-night call to Father Dowling from Sylvia Lowry, an old woman who is afraid to die. After disappearing for three days, Sylvia is found dead on her kitchen floor, having been struck on the head, then frozen in her own basement freezer, and later thawed and moved.

Her Death of Cold introduces most of the residents of Fox River, Illinois, who reappear in later Dowling books: Dowling, pastor of St. Hilary's, a pipe-smoking, thin, recovered alcoholic, orthodox in belief; his middle-aged housekeeper, Marie Murkin; Dowling's good friend Captain Phil Keegan of the Fox River Police, a widower and fellow Chicago Cubs fan, whose work and friendship with the priest fill the void left by his wife's death; Edna Hospers (a married parishioner with a husband in prison), who in subsequent novels supervises programs at the parish center; and the competent Lieutenant Cy Horvath of the Fox River Police. *Her Death of Cold* ends ambiguously—as do many later novels—in this case with two would-be murderers but no clear act of murder. *The Critic* (Summer 1977), a liberal Catholic magazine, urged the author to "stick to philosophy and academia. He is hopelessly out of his element, if this mystery debut is a fair sample of his talents." H. C. Veit in the *Library Journal* (1 February 1977) thought the novel "interesting but readily understandable only by Roman Catholics."

The second Dowling novel, *The Seventh Station* (1977), explores a recurring McInerny concern—murder motivated by revenge and fueled by an inaccurate understanding of the demands of religious faith. Posing as a Franciscan, the murderer, whose ideal is the fanatic fifteenth-century Dominican monk Girolamo Savonarola, gathers at a retreat house a group of men, all of whom had a connection to the suicide of his sister, and begins killing them, one at a time. When the phony monk catches his foot in his robe and is then caught by the police, McInerny merges poetic with legal justice and adds a pun, a union he employs in other novels as well: "Blaise would have been wiser to have remained defrocked." Though the murderer believes his sister suffers in hell, Dowling responds with orthodox Catholic theology: "We can never know what passes between a soul and God at the moment of death." Blaise gives his own victims the chance to repent before death, lest he

"have their damnation on my conscience." Newgate Calendar in *The New York Times* (11 December 1977) called this novel "a well-written mystery, tight in its organization, real in its characters."

In the last years of the 1970s, McInerny's varied writing projects included *St. Thomas Aquinas* (1977), a volume in the Twayne Authors Series; the nonmystery novel *Spinnaker* (1977), a work set in the 1960s at a college campus in conflict with the Ephchoke Indian nation over land claims; and two books for children, *Quick as a Dodo* (1978) and *Abecedary* (1979). McInerny's academic career also continued to progress. In 1978, he was named the Michael P. Grace Professor of Medieval Studies at Notre Dame and director of the Medieval Institute at the university. In 1979, he became director of the Jacques Maritain Institute at Notre Dame.

In the last years of the decade, he also wrote three novels with mystery themes. *Bishop as Pawn* (1978), a Dowling novel, begins with the abrupt return of Billy, husband of rectory housekeeper Marie Murkin, fifteen years after he had abandoned her. Billy is promptly and mysteriously murdered in the rectory. Meanwhile, Eunice Flanagan has been visiting the rectory for premarital counseling but failing to bring along her fiancé. The bishop, who stays overnight at St. Hilary's after a confirmation ceremony, is kidnapped, though Dowling, who physically resembles the bishop, was the intended victim. The kidnapping, Eunice Flanagan's duplicity, and Billy Murkin's murder all turn out to be connected.

In *Romanesque* (1978), a young scholar encounters terrorists in Rome, and in his fourth Dowling book, *Lying Three* (1979), McInerny depicts the near assassination of the Israeli consul, the successful murder of a Fox River Zionist during a Chicago Cubs game, arms sales to Arabs, and a woman who has left her previous role as member of an American terrorist group to forge a new identity. The book ends with Father Dowling's musings: "Danger did lurk in unexpected places: Cub Park, the Stratton Bridge, the fifteenth hole of the Fox River Country Club. It was an odd thought that a golf course too lies in the Vale of Tears. Where else? It is the only real estate there is."

McInerny continued to be productive in the 1980s, publishing twenty-seven books in the decade. Scholarly work included *Rhyme and Reason: St. Thomas and Modes of Discourse* (1981), *Ethica Thomistica: The Moral Philosophy of Thomas Aquinas* (1982), *Being and Predication: Thomistic Interpretations* (1986), *Miracles: A Catholic View* (1986), *Art and Prudence: Studies in the Thought of Jacques Maritain* (1988), and *A First Glance at St. Thomas Aquinas: A Handbook for Peeping Thomists* (1990). In 1981, he founded, with Michael Novak, *Crisis*, a conservative Catholic magazine, to which McInerny still contributes a monthly column, "End Notes." He combined fiction with theological commentary in *The Frozen Maiden of Calpurnia,* a fairy tale with a moral (1982); *Connolly's Life* (1983), about a priest who returns from the dead; *The Noonday Devil* (1985), which focuses on the death of a conservative New York cardinal and the subsequent intrachurch intrigue to replace him; and *Leave of Absence* (1986), a book that revisits the dislocations in the Catholic Church after the Second Vatican Council.

More Father Dowling mysteries appeared during the 1980s as well. *Second Vespers* (1980) concerns a Fox River bookstore, a diary written by local author Francis O'Rourke, and some supposed letters by the same writer. *Thicker Than Water* (1981) begins with Marie Murkin's discovery that the offering box near the magazines and pamphlets lacks the right amount of money; the pork chops she has been defrosting are gone; and her jams and jellies are missing from the basement freezer. Murder soon follows, and when all is sorted out, Father Dowling muses on the conflict between justice and mercy. Consistent with their vocations, Dowling leans toward mercy; Keegan the policeman, toward justice. In *A Loss of Patients,* published in 1982, Father Dowling investigates the suspected suicide of the athletic and affluent Barbara Rooney, killed, it turns out, by an oral surgeon who commits multiple murders in an effort to avoid getting caught. Though overpowered by the murderous dentist and injected with sodium pentathol, Dowling still sees the culprit's humanity: "Now that Olson's punishment was assured, he was that much readier for mercy. Not human forgiveness—who could extend that to a man who had murdered four fellow human beings? But there is One who is the union of justice and mercy and it was before His bar that he hoped to bring Martin Olson."

The Grass Widow (1983) begins with a visit to Father Dowling by Clare O'Leary, who tells him her husband, radio personality Larry O'Leary, has talked on the air about killing her; she is later found dead. In *Getting a Way with Murder* (1984), another Dowling mystery, suspicion initially points to a seemingly guilty party—Howard Downs—who denies killing his wife but later confesses to killing an attorney; the plot details a series of complicated relationships, including the revelation that Downs is the father of a young woman working in his own office. As *Rest in Pieces* (1985) opens, Father Dowling is perusing a recent issue of *The New Scholasticism,* a journal that McInerny himself edited at the time. The priest's quiet study is interrupted by a visitor wanting to confess his sins. Claiming to be Pat Gallagher, an old friend, the visitor is blown up when he later starts his car. Latin American politics, liberation theology, and terrorism all play roles in the complications and resolutions of the plot. In *The Basket Case* (1987), Dowling finds a baby in the church, but the baby's mother, Constance Farley

Dust jacket for McInerny's 1977 novel that introduces his priest-detective, Father Dowling (Richland County Public Library)

Rush, who has placed the baby there, tells him not to contact the police. Of interest is that Rush's father, a faithful Catholic, an usher, a pillar of the community and church, never received communion, a memory that leads Dowling and Keegan to unearth Farley's life with a mistress. When Dowling deduces that Peter Rush, the baby's father, has been killed by his elderly mother-in-law, no trial is necessary: "A second stroke took the old lady and she departed this vale of tears with the grim satisfaction of knowing that no one else would be blamed—or given credit—for killing Peter Rush." Dowling must reveal to Keegan what he has learned in order to establish the innocence of other suspects, but in this work, as in other McInerny novels, only divine justice prevails.

Abracadaver (1989) begins with a magic show performed for the senior citizens at St. Hilary's by one of Dowling's seminary classmates. The magician-priest, Don, says he needs some "precious jewelry," and Aggie

Miller offers a ring, which turns out to be the motivation for Aggie's murder soon after. When the murderer dies in a confrontation with Father Dowling, after falling and being pierced by a "bloody pointed stick," Dowling decides not to reveal the man's guilt, since little would be gained by the publicity, and the killer's widow would suffer from the knowledge: "it was far from the first time that he had had to carry in silence knowledge of the sins of others."

After the Father Dowling series was well underway, McInerny's agent, Theron Raines, suggested, perhaps as a joke, a series about nuns, so McInerny began the Sister Mary Teresa novels, writing as Monica Quill (a pun on *pen name*). The first book, *Not a Blessed Thing!* (1981), introduces Sister Mary Teresa Dempsey, a scholarly, fat nun in full habit, member of the almost defunct Order of Martha and Mary, now presiding over a Chicago convent housed in a Frank Lloyd Wright house. Two younger nuns–Sister Kim Moriarity, whose brother Richard is a police officer, and Sister Joyce–complete the members of the convent. Richard Moriarity asks the sisters to provide sanctuary for Cheryl Pitman, a socialite whose life has been threatened. Murders follow, and Emtee (the nickname used by the other sisters) Dempsey uses her formidable wits to solve the crimes. In "How I Took the Veil," the introduction to a 2001 collection, *Death Takes the Veil and Other Stories,* McInerny reveals that the Sister Mary Teresa Dempsey series was "deliberately modeled" on Rex Stout's Nero Wolfe novels. Emtee Dempsey is McInerny's Wolfe; graduate student Sister Kim is "more or less" Archie Goodwin, the narrator of the Nero Wolfe mysteries. Like Nero Wolfe, Emtee Dempsey almost never leaves her home and yet invariably identifies the murderer. This parallel with Rex Stout's work was "crucial" for McInerny when he began the series, though over time he moved from a single narrative point of view to multiple viewpoints.

The second novel in this series, *Let Us Prey,* was published in 1982. Sister Mary Teresa Dempsey and her two nuns reappeared in *And Then There Was Nun* (1984) and in *Nun of the Above* (1985), which begins with the visit to the convent of the father of Sarah Pinking, a woman who supposedly wants to be a nun. When Sarah is strangled while sunbathing on the roof of her apartment building, the stage is set for Emtee to solve this crime and two others. *Sine Qua Nun* (1986) begins with Emtee's visit to a television studio, where she is to converse with a radical nun; the nun does not appear, and a conversation ensues instead with the cleverly named Geoffrey Chaster, creator of pornographic novels. Murders lead Sister Mary Teresa to intuit the identity of the murderer, though she does not want to take credit since she did not use correct reasoning to determine guilt. Echoing Thomas à Becket in T. S. Eliot's *Murder in the Cathedral* (1935),

she concludes, "To point to the right person for the wrong reason is no cause for pride." In *The Veil of Ignorance* (1988), another Sister Mary Teresa mystery, Lydia Hopkins, convicted of murdering her husband and daughter, seeks sanctuary in the convent after being temporarily released from prison on a technicality. Emtee Dempsey's confidence in Lydia's innocence is tested when Lydia disappears and other deaths occur. Through Emtee's detective work, Lydia is not only found innocent but also is restored to her previously unknown father, a reunion that echoes that in the earlier *Getting a Way with Murder.*

With *Cause and Effect* (1987), McInerny introduces a new series set in Wyler, Indiana, and featuring lawyer Andrew Broom. McInerny states, "I began the Andrew Brooms to get out of church, so to speak, wanting a series without nuns and priests, but not because I lost my zest for Father Dowling and Sister Mary Teresa." *Cause and Effect* begins with Andrew's learning that he is dying of cancer, a false diagnosis deliberately given by the doctor, who happens to be Andrew's wife's lover, and continues with a hired killer, some clever sleuthing by Andrew's nephew Gerald, and an ending marked by poetic justice. A novel lacking in overt Catholic themes, it nonetheless mirrors McInerny's moral stance. *Body and Soil* (1989), the second Andrew Broom mystery, concerns a messy divorce, the murder of the husband, and the fleeing of the wife to the home of her best friend, her husband's mistress. *Frigor Mortis* (1989) begins with the murder of George Arthur while ice fishing and continues with the murder of his murderous widow.

Since writing his first short stories in the 1960s, McInerny has continued to publish stories in various magazines, including one Father Dowling story for every issue of *Catholic Dossier,* a magazine McInerny founded in 1995. A collection of Dowling stories, *Four on the Floor: A Father Dowling Mystery Quartet,* appeared in 1989. "The Ferocious Father" concerns a fund-raiser, a dead body found in a car trunk, and an adulterous love affair. In "Heart of Gold," Ray Phillips, an old man, gives Edna Hospers a statue of St. Anthony of Padua that he says he made in prison; Phillips is later murdered. With "The Dead Weight Lifter," a wealthy man is found on the steps of the senior center at St. Hilary's. In "The Dutiful Son," Dowling is told by Francis Stendall that he had promised to exhume a body buried in the yard of the house where his family lived years before. The story ends with the sort of ambiguity McInerny uses from time to time. Dowling will not tell the police what he knows: "If a crime was committed, it was not by you. Unless the burial was a crime, and that has been rectified now."

McInerny was even more prolific in the 1990s, producing more than thirty books, among them such scholarly works as *Boethius and Aquinas* (1990), *Aquinas on*

Human Action (1992), *Aquinas Against the Averroists: On There Being Only One Intellect* (1993), *The Question of Christian Ethics* (1993), *The God of Philosophers* (1994), *Modernity and Religion* (1994), *Let's Read Latin: Introduction to the Language of the Church* (1995), *Aquinas and Analogy* (1996), *What Went Wrong with Vatican II: The Catholic Crisis Explained* (1998), and *A Student's Guide to Philosophy* (1999).

Five more Dowling novels appeared in the 1990s, beginning with *Judas Priest* in 1991. In many of his writings, McInerny alludes to the period of turmoil within the Catholic Church after the Second Vatican Council. Though he acknowledges the ambiguities of the world and of the Church, he constructs plots in which deviation from orthodoxy often leads to social disintegration. In *Judas Priest,* the defections of a priest, Chris Bourke, and a nun, Janet Gray, twenty years before continue to spawn evil. They married, formed the Enlightened Hedonism movement, and had a child—though Janet said on television that if abortion had been legal, she would have aborted her child. By the end of the book, Janet Gray has returned to her religious community; the daughter, Sonya, who expressed an interest in the religious life, is found dead; and so is Craig Wilhelms, who worked for Chris Bourke and who also had become interested in the Church. The murderer, who sees himself as an instrument of God, turns out to have been influenced by fundamentalist television evangelists. As in *Bishop as Pawn,* Dowling is lured into a warehouse, where he traps the murderer by putting epoxy glue on his chair. When later the culprit is confined to a mental hospital, the inmate sends Dowling "lamentations, anathemas," and messages from God, concerning the latest of which Dowling remarks, "He made more sense before he became unglued."

In *Desert Sinner* (1992), Stacey Wilson, a former Las Vegas showgirl jailed for her husband's murder, insists on her innocence but fails to reveal where she was on the day of the murder. Having solved the crime, the priest-detective muses on the ways in which secular patterns parallel the religious: "That night Father Dowling sat up late in his studio, smoking his pipe and considering the odd shrines and patrons and rituals that defined the life of Tyrone Pajakowski's mother. Roulette and baccarat were her rites, Las Vegas her place of pilgrimage, celebrities her saints. And greed had made the desert bloom."

Another Dowling mystery, *Seed of Doubt* (1993), opens with the suspicious death of Margaret Sinclair, owner of an important collection of landscapes by American artist Clayton Ford. In addition to the mystery of Margaret's connection to Ford and the circumstances of her short-lived marriage, the book focuses on Margaret's granddaughter and her romance with Joel Cleary, a lawyer who has left his wife and child. Characters are more

Dust jacket for McInerny's 1987 novel, the first of his mysteries featuring Indiana lawyer and detective Andrew Bloom (Richland County Public Library)

fully developed in this novel, and the love depicted is more tender than in previous novels.

A Cardinal Offense (1994) takes Father Dowling to the Notre Dame versus University of Southern California football game at the same time as a conference on annulment practices in the Church is meeting on campus. Present at the conference is Cardinal Hildebrand, perhaps modeled on the Vatican's Cardinal Joseph Ratzinger.

In 1995, McInerny brought out *The Case of the Constant Caller,* billed as a "Father Dowling Mystery for Young Adults" and featuring many of the same Fox River inhabitants but with the addition of two teen sleuths, Janet Hospers and Gerry Krause. In *The Tears of Things* (1996), which borrows its title from Virgil's *Aeneid,* the reunion of high-school sweethearts eventually leads to murders as well as to revelations about parentage. The novel includes one of McInerny's more explicit descriptions of Dowling's vocation: "To be a pastor, to be the priest for the members of his own parish, to be in the arena where he would save or lose his own soul in administering to others, had brought a new clarity of mind and satisfaction of soul. One of the great truisms of spiritual conferences finally became a truth for him. It is in our failures that God can speak to us most directly."

Under the pseudonym Monica Quill, McInerny continued to produce mysteries starring Sister Mary Teresa Dempsey, including *Sister Hood* (1991), featuring the daughter of gangster Iggie Moran, now Sister Mary Magdalene, a Carmelite nun who seeks refuge with the Order of Martha and Mary. Toward the end of the novel, Sister Kimberly tells Emtee Dempsey not to brood or to blame herself for what has happened. Sister Mary Teresa responds, "I never brood, Sister Kimberly. I would consider myself deficient in trust in God's providence should I give myself up to brooding. Nonsense. I have been reviewing the events of the past weeks." The old nun-detective reappears in *Nun Plussed* (1993), which involves the murder of Margaret Nelson Doyle, who has left her husband, and a suspicious confession by Gregory Doyle, a dealer in rare books and manuscripts. In still another Sister Mary Teresa Dempsey mystery, *Half Past Nun* (1997), she is intent on finding not only a serial killer pursued by Richard Moriarity but also the killer of Mitzi Earl, a woman attacked outside of Emtee's convent.

In the 1990s, McInerny continued to write novels featuring Andrew Broom: *Savings and Loam* (1990), *Mom and Dead* (1994), and *Law and Ardor* (1995). Nonseries novels also appeared, including *The Search Committee* (1991), a campus mystery featuring Matthew Rogerson, McInerny's first protagonist. *The Nominative Case* (1991), written under the pseudonym Edward Mackin, again explores the seamy side of academia. Stanley Bledsoe, informed that one of his poems has been accepted for publication, must suffer the indignity of a further letter from the publisher: "Disregard letter accepting 'Fronds.' Your attempted plagiarism caught in time. Submit nothing further here." The poem in question, penned by Henry VIII, had been sent in Bledsoe's name by two other faculty members. Bledsoe's body is found later in a stolen car. *The Nominative Case* mixes mystery with a satire of the battles fought in minor institutions of learning, in this case New York City's Lyndon Johnson Community College, peopled with cleverly named academics: Stanley Bledsoe, Pregunta, Hackis, James B. Cable, and Larry Gridiron. Another mystery of the 1990s, *Easeful Death* (1991), is about Howard Webster, a poet and teacher tired of life who laments that his accomplishments have not been recognized. When a derelict commits suicide in his Wisconsin barn, Webster trades identities. While in Italy, he hears that the seemingly dead Webster is now praised as a great poet. Returning to the United States in disguise, he learns that a curator is

in charge of the farm and cataloguing his papers; his daughter Felicia is making money from her father's reputation; and his former wife wants some of the profit. Philip Knight and his obese, brilliant brother Roger are drawn into solving mysteries of murder and authorship. With *Infra Dig* (1992), McInerny explores the efforts of a Wisconsin widow, Susan Nebens, to hide that she has accidentally run over and killed her nasty father-in-law, for whom she was caring. When her station wagon containing the body is stolen, the car thieves Lorch and Casey are blamed for the old man's death. The thieves' attempt to blackmail Susan leads to mayhem. Justice is not quite served in this book, but on the other hand, fitting punishment is, more or less, allotted to the deserving.

On This Rockne (1997), set at the University of Notre Dame, brings back detective Philip Knight and his brilliant brother Roger, now a member of the faculty. *The Lack of the Irish* (1998) opens with joint events on the same weekend—a football game between Notre Dame and Baylor and a conference of their faculties. The Reverend Edwina Marciniak, pastor of the Independent Protestant Church of Jesus Christ and His Almighty Parent, a former Catholic, decides to lead a boycott of the football game.

With *The Red Hat* (1998), McInerny reverted to a serious treatment of church politics. A newly designated cardinal, Thomas Lannan, archbishop of Washington, D.C., must face a scandal from his own past. His boyhood friend, Jim Morrow, author of *The Decline and Fall of the Catholic Church in America,* is named American ambassador to the Vatican. The Pope dies before Lannan and other nominees are inducted into the College of Cardinals, and so they are excluded from the conclave choosing the Pope's successor. With threatened schism, an antipope in Avignon, and Lannan's scandal, the novel was called Manichaean by reviewer John Christie in *Commonweal* (14 August 1998), a charge, he wrote, that "may not matter to one segment of his veteran readership which will relish the book precisely for its absolutes."

Irish Tenure (1999), set on the Notre Dame campus, pits against each other two philosophy professors vying for the same tenured position; the more liberal candidate, Amanda Pick, is found dead, as is, later, her housemate. Professor Roger Knight and his detective brother perform the investigation, which concerns not only murder but also a manuscript by Chesterton, who had visited the campus years before. In a climactic scene, the manuscript is found in a quite ordinary place, like "the Invisible Man" in one of Chesterton's Father Brown stories, where the plot "turns on the omnipresent invisibility of the mailman."

With the new century, McInerny continues to produce both scholarly works and fiction. Two theological works were published in 2001—*Characters in Search of Their Author,* a defense of natural theology, and *The Defamation of Pius XII* (2001), an exoneration of the Pope's conduct during the Holocaust. In *Shakespearean Variations,* published in the same year, McInerny addresses the subject of aging, using the same first and last lines of Shakespeare's sonnets as well as his rhyme scheme, while changing the bodies of the poems. McInerny has continued to produce detective fiction in the new millennium. The Knight brothers reappear in *The Book of Kills* (2000), another mystery in the Notre Dame series, this one focusing on the kidnapping of administrators, the desecration at Cedar Grove Cemetery, and a claim by Orion Plant, a history scholar, that the land belonging to Notre Dame was actually stolen from Native Americans. Because of these events, a half-time prank broadcast on national television, and a potential lawsuit, Father Bloom, chancellor of the university, asks the help of detectives Philip and Roger Knight. When Orion Plant is murdered, his head decorated with an Indian headdress, the Knight brothers recognize an important lesson: "A case is always difficult when you have so many people with good reason to have done the deed." *Emerald Aisle: A Notre Dame Mystery* (2001) continues the Roger and Philip Knight series with a plot having to do with missing rare literary documents and the on-again, off-again romances between Larry Morton and two women—Nancy Beatty and Dolores Torre, his freshman sweetheart. Murder complicates wedding plans until everything is sorted out by the Knight brothers. At the end of the novel, Roger Knight muses on the moral maxims of Father Carmody: "A person can be guilty of something he did not do. And innocent of what he did." Reviewers Jeff Zaleski and Peter Cannon wrote in *Publishers Weekly* (24 September 2001) that "McInerny makes the improbable credible"; his "proven track record of mysteries light on violence but freighted with humor and wisdom should guarantee an eager reception for this fifth book in the series."

Father Dowling continues to thrive in the new century. In *Grave Undertakings* (2000), he visits gangster Vincent O'Toole, who apparently makes an act of contrition just before he dies from a gunshot wound. O'Toole's grave is later desecrated, and a woman believes she has heard the voice of the Virgin Mary from a statue. Mrs. O'Toole decides to reinter her husband near the statue. Much mayhem takes place in this novel, and one anomaly: Marie Murkin's husband is described as missing, when, in fact, he was murdered in the 1978 novel *Bishop as Pawn. Triple Pursuit* (2001), the twentieth Dowling mystery, focuses on conflict at St. Hilary's: the possible murder of a woman who has been attending mass at the parish and the rivalry over a younger woman between two old men attending the senior center. Remarking on

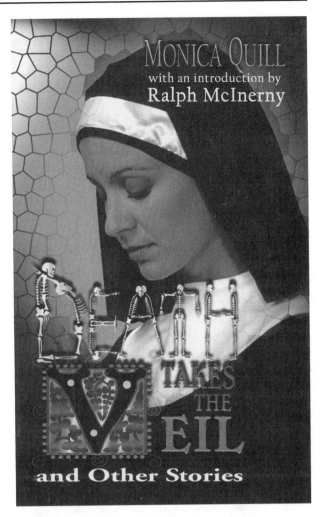

Cover for McInerny's 2001 collection, published under the pseudonym Monica Quill, featuring the mystery-solving nun, Sister Mary Teresa Dempsey (Richland County Public Library)

the murderer's plea of insanity, lawyer Amos Cadbury tells Roger Dowling that "the evil men do is now taken to be the result of illness. Is Original Sin an illness?" Dowling replies, "Not in that sense, Amos." As housekeeper Marie Murkin dances with Cadbury at a wedding reception, Dowling retreats to the comfort of his study, his pipe, and his favorite poet: "An hour with Dante and a renewed perspective on the human comedy seemed called for." *Publishers Weekly* (26 February 2001) gave McInerny credit for "his dry wit and realistic depiction of the elderly, as well as his all too human characters" but termed the book a "predictable entry in a generally lackluster series" that "should still please the older audience who are Dowling's principal fans, but it will take a miracle for this novel to increase McInerny's reader base." In spite of mixed critical reaction, the Dowling books have sold well and were even the inspiration for a television series starring Tom Bosley as Dowling and Tracy Nelson as a nun, his sidekick in detection, a character not appearing in the novels (McInerny did not write the screenplays for the series). Musing on his Dowling books, McInerny wrote for the April 2001 issue of *Crisis* magazine: "How much longer will the series run? I am aiming for 30 novels, *Deo volente*. Father Dowling, who isn't a day older than when I met him, is of course always on call. I thank God that I was that fateful day in 1976." In 2002 still another Dowling novel was published, *Prodigal Father,* which takes the priest to a retreat, an earlier murder, and a drowning. *Kirkus Reviews* (15 May 2002) termed the book "not as sharp as McInerny's best, or as plodding as his worst, but comfortably enough in the middle to keep the Dowling faithful from bolting the flock."

Emtee Dempsey returned in 2001 with *Death Takes the Veil and Other Stories,* a Monica Quill book, once again featuring the sisters of the Order of Martha and Mary in seven cleverly plotted short works—four novellas and three short stories. In *Heirs and Parents* (2000) Helga Bjornsen, a college student and summer intern at Andrew Broom's law office in Wyler, Indiana, is murdered, and Broom competes with rival attorney Frank McGough over the will of local millionaire Stanley Waggoner. McInerny introduces in *Still Life* (2000) Egidio Manfredi, a detective nearing retirement, and Noonan, his younger associate in Fort Elbow, Ohio, who are contacted by a graduate student working on the papers of a poet, the missing wife of a professor. *Library Journal* (1 November 2000) praised the book: "Clever repartee, hidden alliances both present and past, false claims of guilt, pointed observations on aging, and surprising marriage plans underscore the author's talents."

In 2000, McInerny collaborated with Martin H. Greenberg on a collection of short stories, *Murder Most Divine: Ecclesiastical Tales of Unholy Crimes,* featuring such writers as G. K. Chesterton, Charlotte Armstrong, and Antonia Fraser. McInerny contributed two stories to the collection, one under the name Monica Quill. In the introduction to the book, McInerny writes,

> No literary genre exhibits art's dependence on a moral point of reference more strikingly than the murder mystery. To take the life of another is wrong; the murderer must be discovered and suitably punished. That is the rock bottom assumption of the murder mystery. In an age when commonly shared moral beliefs are increasingly atrophying, the murder mystery continues in popularity, perhaps as the last refuge of the reader who wants to see good triumph and evil punished, at least on the printed page.

In the same introduction, McInerny contends that in "a morally disintegrating society . . . any appeal to what

had once been the common morality is more easily made through a clerical or religious figure"; a character such as a "nun or priest or monk represents right and wrong more dramatically than an officer of the law or ordinary private detective."

No doubt Ralph McInerny will continue to write scholarly books, novels featuring Father Roger Dowling, Sister Emtee Dempsey, the Knight brothers, and Egidio Manfredi, as well as mysteries set on the University of Notre Dame campus, and other nonseries novels. In his 1993 essay "Saints Preserve Us: The Catholic Mystery," McInerny argues that the identifying marks of this subgenre are not the presence of a priest or authorship by a Catholic, or even treatment of "Catholic" themes, but rather that they imitate Dante's *La Divina Commedia* (circa 1313–1321), which views "human action through the lens of the eternal stakes involved." All of imaginative literature, McInerny asserts, has to do with human beings making choices that either strengthen or weaken character; they "instinctively turn to imaginative reenactments of human action for some sense of what it all means." Detective fiction accomplishes this goal on what he terms "a fairly superficial level"; still, it accomplishes the goal, and that is the author's intention. Even when he laces his plot with humor and wit, as he frequently does, McInerny sees the sadness of life, the tragedies of so many human choices, but above all, the hope of redemption and the infinite mercy of God. All of his detectives combine rectitude with cleverness and compassion, and of these detectives, Roger Dowling no doubt will live the longest.

References:

Ray B. Browne, "Ralph McInerny: Religious Detective Fiction in Chicago," in *Heroes and Humanities: Detective Fiction and Culture* (Bowling Green, Ohio: Bowling Green State University Popular Press, 1986), pp. 105–111;

Ross Labrie, "Ralph McInerny," in *The Catholic Imagination in American Literature* (Columbia, Mo.: University of Missouri Press, 1997), pp. 233–247;

William David Spencer, "The Scholastic World of Ralph McInerny's Father Dowling and 'Monica Quill's' Sister Mary Teresa," in *Mysterium and Mystery: The Clerical Crime Novel* (Ann Arbor: University of Michigan Research Press, 1989), pp. 133–146.

Papers:

Ralph McInerny has donated his papers to the University of Notre Dame Archives.

Walter Mosley

(12 January 1952 –   )

John L. Cobbs
Montgomery County Community College

BOOKS: *Devil in a Blue Dress* (New York: Norton, 1990; London: Serpent's Tale, 1991);

A Red Death (New York: Norton, 1991; London: Serpent's Tale, 1992);

White Butterfly (New York: Norton, 1992; London: Serpent's Tale, 1993);

Black Betty (New York: Norton, 1994; London: Serpent's Tale, 1994);

RL's Dream (New York: Norton, 1995; London: Serpent's Tale, 1995);

A Little Yellow Dog (New York: Norton, 1996; London: Serpent's Tale, 1996);

Gone Fishin' (Baltimore: Black Classic Press, 1997; London: Serpent's Tale, 1997);

Always Outnumbered, Always Outgunned: The Socrates Fortlow Stories (New York: Norton, 1997; London: Serpent's Tale, 1997);

Blue Light (Boston: Little, Brown, 1998; London: Serpent's Tale, 1999);

Walkin' the Dog (Boston: Little, Brown, 1999; London: Serpent's Tale, 2000);

Workin' on the Chain Gang: Shaking Off the Dead Hand of History (New York: Random House, 2000);

Fearless Jones (Boston: Little, Brown, 2001; London: Serpent's Tale, 2001);

Futureland: Nine Stories of an Imminent World (New York: Warner, 2001);

Bad Boy Brawly Brown (Boston: Little, Brown, 2002; London: Serpent's Tale, 2002);

Six Easy Pieces (New York: Atria Books, 2003; London: Serpent's Tale, 2003);

What Next? A Memoir Toward World Peace (Baltimore: Black Classic Press, 2003; London: Serpent's Tale, 2003);

Fear Itself: A Mystery (Boston: Little, Brown, 2003; London: Serpent's Tale, 2003);

The Man in My Basement (Boston: Little, Brown, 2004; London: Serpent's Tale, 2004);

Little Scarlet (New York & Boston: Little, Brown, 2004).

Walter Mosley (photograph by Chip Cooper; from the dust jacket for Little Scarlet, *2004; Collection of George and Julie Anderson)*

OTHER: "Fearless," in *Spooks, Spies, and Private Eyes: Black Mystery, Crime and Suspense Fiction,* edited by Paula L. Woods (New York: Doubleday, 1995), pp. 135–157;

Black Genius: African-American Soulutions to African-American Problems, edited by Mosley and others, introduction by Mosley (New York & London: Norton, 1999);

The Best American Short Stories 2003, edited by Mosley and Katrina Kenison (New York: Houghton Mifflin, 2003);

"Bombadier," in *Shades of Black,* edited by Eleanor Taylor Bland (New York: Berkley, 2004), pp. 297–302.

In 1992, when President Bill Clinton was asked who his favorite mystery writer was, he replied, "Walter

Mosley." Although Mosley had already won critical acclaim, the president's endorsement brought him to the attention of a larger public. His next book, *Black Betty* (1994), the third in the Easy Rawlins series, sold one hundred thousand copies in hardback. His Easy Rawlins books, as well as his novels featuring Fearless Jones, are set in the African American community of Los Angeles, from the immediate post–World War II years into the turbulent 1960s. His two books about former convict Socrates Fortlow, *Always Outnumbered, Always Outgunned* (1997) and *Walkin' the Dog* (1999), are set in the same locale in the 1990s.

Mosley has been praised for his evocative style and for staking out new territory for the hard-boiled genre. "Mosley's L.A.," writes David L. Ulin in the 6 August 1995 issue of *The Los Angeles Times Book Review*, "is not that of Raymond Chandler, where tycoons and hoodlums cross paths on gambling boats anchored off the Santa Monica coast. Rather it is a sprawl of black neighborhoods largely hidden from the history books, a shadow community within the larger city, where a unique, street-smart justice prevails." More than just a genre writer, Mosley in his Easy Rawlins books is presenting a social history of the black experience in America at a crucial period in the struggle for civil rights. As critic Marilyn C. Wesley notes in her 2001 essay "Power and Knowledge in Walter Mosley's *Devil in a Blue Dress*," the writer's real objective is not the resolution of the crime narrative or of the problems of society: "In *Devil in a Blue Dress* and the other Easy Rawlins novels, Walter Mosley represents rather than resolves complicated historical issues of the multiracial society Easy uncomfortably inhabits."

Born on 12 January 1952 in Watts–a poor inner-city section of South Central Los Angeles–Mosley was the only son of a custodian, LeRoy Mosley, whom the writer has frequently named as the most important influence in his childhood and in shaping his career as an artist. His father had drifted west to California from Louisiana, as his son says, "riding the freights." He became the partial model for Mosley's best-known fictional detective, Easy Rawlins, as well as for Socrates Fortlow. Mosley's mother, Ella, who worked for the Los Angeles Department of Education, was the decendent of Jews. In growing up Mosley experienced cross-cultural influences that became the focus of his life and novels. He is acutely conscious of the traditions and the history of the oppressed peoples that were his legacy through his parents. For both mother and father, stories were important. Mosley maintains that his father was by far "the best storyteller on both sides of the family." "When I was a child," Mosley recalled, "I believed that there was all sorts of magic in books." He told interviewer Maya Jaggi of *The Guardian* (2003) that his parents paid $9.50 for him

to attend the Victory Baptist day school, a private African American elementary school.

Mosley's family left Watts, the locus of the notorious 1965 race riots, for "more affluent, working-class" West Los Angeles when he was twelve. His parents were able to buy two duplexes and began renting out three of the four apartments–an important event for Mosley's later novels as Easy Rawlins similarly becomes a property owner. Meanwhile, Mosley enrolled at Louis Pasteur Junior High School and then Hamilton High School, from which he graduated in 1970. In the early 1970s Mosley grew long hair and, he says, "hung out" with hippies in Northern California and traveled in Europe.

A determined Mosley worked his way to a higher education, going to school in Vermont, first at Goddard College and then at Johnson State College, where he earned a bachelor of arts degree in political science. Seeing the future importance of computers in American life, he trained as a computer programmer. In 1981 he moved to New York City, where he met the dancer and choreographer Joy Kellman, whom he married in 1987 (divorced in 2001). His interest in technology forecast the books he has written in the science-fiction genre, *Blue Light* (1998) and *Futureland: Nine Stories of an Imminent World* (2001).

Although his technical training led to a position with Mobil Oil, Mosley found his work as a programmer tedious and pursued means of self-expression, including painting and pottery. Inspired by having read Alice Walker's *The Color Purple* (1982), he tried writing. In a December 1995 interview for *Ebony,* he recalls being excited by a sentence he wrote one Saturday at work– "On hot sticky days in southern Louisiana the fire ants swarmed." He says he "stumbled onto writing somewhere around 33 or 34 and I went, 'Oh, this is interesting. This is kind of fun.'" At first he studied poetry because he "believed that you really can't write fiction unless you know poetry in some way or another. . . . You don't necessarily have to have a classical relationship to it but you have to understand the music of poetry to write good fiction." In 1985 he began to take night classes in the graduate writing program of the City University of New York.

Mosley was unable to find a publisher for his first novel, *Gone Fishin'* (1997)–about a young Easy Rawlins coming of age in the borderland between Texas and Louisiana–because, as he told Jaggi, "they said, 'white people don't read about black people, black women don't like black men, and black men don't read. So who the hell is going to read this book?'" Mosley credits the success of Terry McMillan's best-selling books *Disappearing Acts* (1990) and *Waiting to Exhale* (1992) with changing the perceptions of publishers. When *Devil in a Blue Dress* was published in 1990, critics compared Mosley's writing to the work of Chandler, whose cynical portrait of Los Angeles set the tone for hard-boiled urban detective fiction, and to the hardened voice and style of Chester Himes, the African American detective writer. The reviewer for *The New York Times* noted that Mosley's novel marked "the debut of a talented author with something vital to say about the distance between the black and white worlds, and with a dramatic way to say it." Mosley's fiction reflects the mixing of cultures that is characteristic of his life. A man who has lived in worlds often considered black (Watts) or white (college in Vermont, computer programmer in a corporation), Mosley has chosen to write about the interaction between the races.

Devil in a Blue Dress introduces Ezekiel "Easy" Rawlins, an unemployed black veteran returned from World War II who finds America just as racist as it was when he left to fight for it. Determined not to be ground down by the social, political, and economic system that crushes so many black men before they have a chance to succeed, Easy has a canny business sense and a willingness to do what he has to do to survive. At first, his only refuge from his brutal world is his house, and he understands the importance of the property to his sense of identity. Having been laid off at Champion Aircraft, Easy is desperate to avoid foreclosure on his home, and he agrees, against his better judgment, to track down Daphne Monet, a white woman who has a fondness for hanging out in black bars, for a white "businessman," DeWitt Albright.

Devil in a Blue Dress is representative of Mosley's writing in that he portrays both white and black worlds, neither in a particularly flattering way. Among the white characters in this novel are Albright—whose handshake is "strong but slithery, like a snake coiling around my hand"—who fires Easy because he won't be a "Step 'n Fetchit" kind of black man. Then there are the Los Angeles police who are eager to pin a list of murders on Easy or any other black man they can find. Easy, though, is not without guile, and he uses his ability to lie and manipulate to get the information he wants.

In her 2001 essay "Invisible Detection: The Case of Walter Mosley," Helen Lock discusses how Mosley's books revise the figure of the traditionally white hard-boiled detective, a man who operates in the borderland between good and evil and who, as John G. Cawelti argues in *Adventure, Mystery, and Romance: Formula Stories as Art and Popular Culture* (1977), must define his own moral position in "a complex process of changing implications":

> The ambivalence and duality necessarily inherent in such a detective's perception both of society and of himself take on a more profound significance in Walter

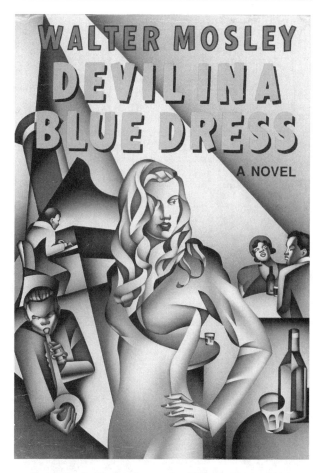

Dust jacket for Mosley's first novel, published in 1990, which is set in post–World War II Los Angeles and introduces his best-known character, African American veteran and reluctant detective Easy Rawlins (Richland County Public Library)

Mosley's novels, where they become a powerful metaphor for the African American experience of "double-consciousness" (in W. E. B. Du Bois's phrase), especially in the urban America of the period. The "changing implications" of the investigative process become infinitely more complex, and painful to negotiate, when a black detective finds himself haunting an additional borderland, that where the interests of his own community and those of the broader, predominantly white, society uneasily co-exist and frequently collide. Mosley's protagonist, Easy Rawlins, is in fact characterized and motivated most centrally by his experience of duality and by a resultant ambiguity of attitude toward the cases he investigates, often reluctantly. At the same time, however, it is this very duality that facilitates the functional invisibility that he exploits to his advantage, making his detective work possible.

Critic Scott Bunyon argues that in his first adventure Easy is "naive" and does not realize "how vulnerable he is." In "No Order from Chaos: The Absence of Chandler's Extra Legal Space in the Detective Fiction

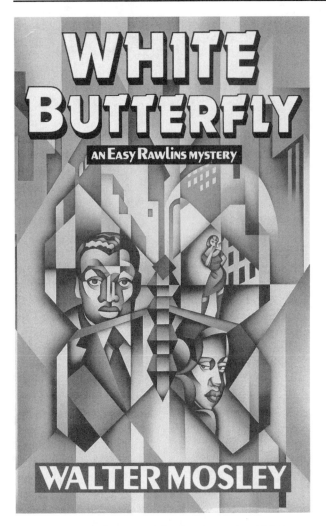

Dust jacket for Mosley's third Easy Rawlins novel, published in 1992, in which Rawlins's new life as a family man is disrupted by his investigation of a series of murders of prostitutes (Richland County Public Library)

The only time in my life that I had ever been completely free from fear was when I ran with Mouse. He was so confident that there was no room for fear. Mouse was barely five-foot-six but he'd go up against a man Dupree's size and you know I'd bet on the Mouse to walk away from it. He could put a knife in a man's stomach and ten minutes later sit down to a plate of spaghetti.

Mouse's only virtue is loyalty, but it is crucial for Easy that when he needs help, Mouse provides it. He is far more dangerous than Easy can bring himself to be, and his brutality is useful to Easy in his investigations.

At the end of *Devil in a Blue Dress,* Easy's efforts result in a kind of rough justice, and he finds himself with an unexpected financial windfall as well as the responsibility for a small Mexican boy, Jesus, who had been kept by a pederast. He is the first of two children Easy unofficially adopts as he creates a patchwork family for himself over the course of the series. Easy remains troubled by the murders Mouse has committed on his behalf. As critic Wesley observes, the novel closes with Easy submitting "his own evolving ethics to the wisdom of his moral mentor":

> "Odell?"
> "Yeah, Easy."
> "If you know a man is wrong, I mean, if he did somethin' bad but you don't turn him in to the law because he's your friend, do you think that's right?"
> "All you got are your friends, Easy."
> "But then what if you know somebody else who did something wrong but not so bad as the first man, but you turn this other guy in?"
> "I guess you figure that other guy got ahold of some bad luck."
> We laughed for a long time.

Easy thus chooses to reject "the premise of 'law' for the practice of loyalty which adjusts to changing circumstances." With the excellent reviews the novel received–it was made into a 1995 movie starring Denzel Washington–Easy Rawlins's life on the tenuous edge of the American dream was launched. Through nine books to date, Easy has walked the line between racism and capitalism. When forced to, he lies, cheats, and steals, but he is fundamentally decent and kind as well.

Mosley's second novel, *A Red Death* (1991), is perhaps the most rooted in historical time of all the Easy Rawlins tales, set as it is in 1953, during the era of McCarthyism and Cold War paranoia. Easy has invested the money he ended up with in *Devil in a Blue Dress* in property but is so wary of drawing attention to himself that he pretends to be only the handyman and employs a shady businessman named Mofass to act as the landlord. As in the first novel Easy's financial situation–in this case

of Chester Himes and Walter Mosley" (2003), Bunyon notes that Easy is unaware that his search for Monet is being monitored by Albright, the gangster Frank Green, and his murderous friend Mouse: "Easy's realization of his visibility and vulnerability in the liminal spaces frequented by criminals comes when Frank Green holds him at knifepoint in Easy's own house, a house that symbolizes independence for Easy. Easy is only saved by the intervention of Mouse."

Rodent-faced Raymond "Mouse" Alexander, Easy's boyhood friend from Houston, is one of the most memorable antiheroes in detective literature. Although Easy "ran away from Mouse and Texas to go to the army and then later to L.A.," his old friend remains the most powerful figure in his life, more formidible in his way than the six-foot-five-inch Dupree Bouchard:

his acquisition of the apartments with off-the-books money–makes him vulnerable. He is threatened by two conflicting elements of white oppression: a racist IRS agent looking for money and an even more dangerous FBI agent who wants to use Easy to frame suspected communist sympathizers–whether they are actually communists or not. In the complex plot, Easy becomes involved with the African American church, a return-to-Africa group, and again runs afoul of the police. Chaim Wenzler, the Jewish union organizer who works at First African Baptist, is shot, as are the pastor of the church and a female parishioner with whom he is having sex. And one of Easy's tenants appears to have hanged herself. In the course of his investigation he becomes estranged from his friend Odell, who blames Easy for the death of his pastor, and loses EttaMae to Mouse, whom he had planned on betraying. Aware of his own guilt, he forgives Mofass for trying to cheat him. "I ain't got no friends," he tells Mofass at the conclusion. "I want you to keep workin' fo' me, William. I want you to be my friend."

In *White Butterfly* (1992), set in 1956, Easy is living a settled life; he has a wife, Regina, a new baby daughter, and is the owner of several buildings. In Easy's world and time, however, no black man can be secure in his life. As critic Angela Morrison asserts, "Mosley has shown how the myth of the American Dream was peddled to the whole nation as something to search for; but for blacks it is kept out of reach." In *White Butterfly* this unequal system for whites and for blacks is conspicuous because, as Easy is well aware, the police do not bother investigating a string of murders of black "party girls" until Robin Garnett–a white University of California Los Angeles coed, the daughter of a prosecuting attorney for the city, who leads a double life as a stripper–joins the list of victims.

After the police are able to coerce Easy's assistance by threatening to investigate Mouse for the murders, Easy's pursuit of the case ends up costing him his marriage, which has been based in part on his keeping much of his identity hidden from his wife:

> I had lived a life of hiding before I met Regina. Nobody knew about me. They didn't know about my property. They didn't know about my relationship to the police. I felt safe in my secrets. I kept telling myself that Regina was my wife, my partner in life. I planned to tell her about what I'd done over the years. I planned to tell her that Mofass really worked for me and that I had plenty of money in back accounts around town. But I had to get at it slowly, in my own time.
>
> The money wasn't apparent in my way of living. So there was no need for her to be suspicious. I intended to tell her all about it someday. A day when I felt she could accept it, accept me for who I was.

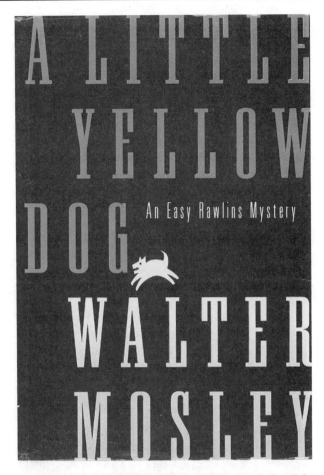

Dust jacket for Mosley's 1996 novel in which Easy Rawlins's settled life as supervising senior head custodian at Sojourner Truth Junior High is disrupted by a desperate teacher and her Chihuahua-sized dog (Richland County Public Library)

As critic Lock notes, "Who he is, however, proves to be a vexed question, and Regina's suspicions drive her away before he can satisfactorily answer it." At the end of the book, she has run off with their daughter to be with Dupree Bouchard, and Easy moves to a new home with Jesus and his second adopted child, Feather, the half-black baby daughter of the murdered Robin Garnett.

At the beginning of *Black Betty*, set in 1961, Easy awakes from a distubing dream memory of Mouse murdering Big Hand Bruno Ingram in a dispute over a twenty-five-cent bet:

> I sat up trying to throw off the nightmare. It had been almost five years, but Bruno died in my dreams at least once a month–more often recently. I'll never forget him being nailed to the wall by my best friend's gun.
>
> I tried to think of better things. About our new young Irish president and Martin Luther King; about how the world was changing and a black man in America had the chance to be a man for the first time in hun-

 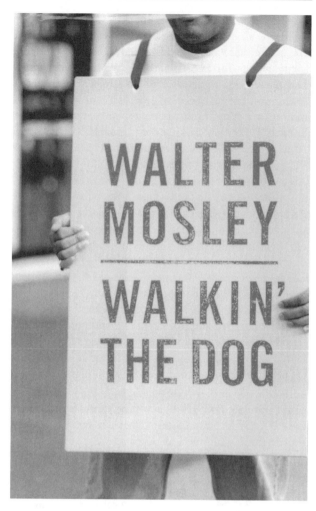

Dust jackets for Mosley's two books about the former convict Socrates Fortlow, published in 1997 and 1999 (Richland County Public Library)

dreds of years. But that same world was being rocked almost daily by underground nuclear explosions and the threat of war.

Easy's financial situation is again tenuous, for his once-profitable real estate investments have crashed, and he needs money to support Jesus and Feather. When he is approached by private investigator Saul Lynx to locate Elizabeth Eady, the maid for a wealthy white family, he has little choice but to take the case. He is also intrigued at the prospect of finding "Black Betty," whom he remembers from Houston's Fifth Ward as "a great shark of a woman. Men died in her wake." The murder-strewn search is complicated by Mouse, recently released from prison, who is bent on finding the man who betrayed him to the authorities. For a time, Mouse even suspects Easy of having informed on him.

Black Betty was praised by reviewers for its action and style and also for its compelling portrayal of its set-

ting. As Bill Ott noted in his review in *Booklist,* "the case at hand is never really the center of attention" for Mosley:

> Just as he did with the war and the McCarthy era, Mosley gives us a recognizable moment in American history viewed through the eyes of a single black man. This perspective, rare in crime fiction, vivifies not only the black experience but the larger event as well. Here we feel the hot winds that would eventually ignite the Watts riots not as abstract issues in race relations, but as emotions in the hearts of individuals we have come to know and care about. In Easy's bitterness and in the bone-weary fatigue with which he greets each new act of senseless violence—whether the weapon is a white cop's fists or Mouse's Colt-.45—we feel the ineffable sadness that has come to envelop our urban landscape.

The novel was chosen by *Publishers Weekly* as one of the best books of 1994.

Mosley's first departure from detective fiction, *RL's Dream* (1995), is the story of a black blues player, Atwater "Soupspoon" Wise. Soupspoon, evicted from his apartment and dying of cancer, is taken in by a neighbor, Kiki Waters, a young white woman. Set in contemporary Manhattan, the novel traces their developing relationship as they share brutal memories of their lives in the South and Soupspoon recalls the blues legend Robert (Leroy) Johnson. Jaggi reports that "Mosley started the novel when his father was diagnosed with cancer and finished it after he died on New Year's day 1993." Mosley told Jaggi that Soupspoon's remission from cancer allows him to "recapture who he was" in a way his own father was unable to do.

Mosley returned to Easy Rawlins in *A Little Yellow Dog* (1996). Set in 1963, the novel shows Easy trying to lead a reformed life. He no longer drinks and has a "respectable" job as director of the custodial staff at Sojourner Truth Junior High School in Watts, a position he was able to land by doing a "favor" for a member of the Board of Education who was being blackmailed. On his staff are EttaMae and Mouse, once again together. Mouse, who in a fight over a woman had killed Sweet William Dokes—a friend and a man who may have actually been his father—is in his own way trying to lead a better life. Still viciously amoral at heart, he evidently does have a confused love for LaMarque, his son by EttaMae, whom he cautions, "Don't you never kill a man don't deserve to die."

In the main plot of the novel Easy tries to help Idabell Turner, a teacher at the school who wants to get away from her husband, and through her he becomes involved in uncovering a heroin-smuggling scheme organized by her brother-in-law Roman Gasteau. Drugs, which Mosley had not dealt with in his earlier fiction, are a significant theme in the novel. More troubling to Easy than his discovery of the "reefer parties" some teachers attend or even the heroin is the damage he sees kids doing to themselves. Early in the novel he describes how the "oleander bushes along the front of the old school were decorated with white flags. T-shirts, handkerchiefs, corners torn from old sheets. They were hung from branches and spread out over the grass." Easy speaks of these "glue sniffers' rags" when Sergeant Sanchez tells him that the murders of the Gasteau brothers indicated a serious drug problem:

> "Naw, man. What's serious is you got four or five dozen kids in the neighborhood climbin' up under the bushes in front'a the school ev'ry night disintegratin' their brains on airplane glue." I was mad. "Every mornin' you walk right over the rags. You see the kids stalkin' an' staggerin' around and what you do? You come in here an' try'n scare me because of somethin' that happened years ago. I don't know nuthin' 'bout no heroin. I do know about glue though. You wanna hear about that?"

> "That's just penny-ante," Sanchez said. He was dead serious.
> "So what you worried 'bout is how much the drugs cost, you don't care about what they do."

For Easy the efforts of the authorities—brown, black, or white—are always misplaced, their values at odds with the realities of the street and the welfare of its people.

At the heart of *A Little Yellow Dog* as well as in most of Mosley's other work lies Los Angeles—colorful, varied, and culturally rich—full of contradictions and untold stories:

> Southeast L.A. was palm trees and poverty, neat little lawns tended by the descendents of ex-slaves and massacred Indians. It was beautiful and wild; a place that was almost a nation, populated by lost peoples that were never talked about in the newspapers or seen on the TV. You might have read about freedom marchers; you might have heard about a botched liquor store robbery (if a white man was injured)—but you never heard about Tommy Jones growing the biggest roses in the world or how Fiona Roberts saved her neighbor by facing off three armed men with only the spirit of God to guide her.

The novel concludes on an ominous note as Mouse, who has spent his life ignoring conventional morality, apparently dies defending Easy—on the same day that Easy learns of President Kennedy's assassination. But in the ending there is also hope for new beginnings. His daughter Feather has adopted the murdered Idabell's little yellow dog, rechristening him "Frenchie," and Easy reaches out to Bonnie Shay, a Caribbean stewardess friend of Idabell's who was unwittingly involved in the heroin scheme. In a final phone conversation Easy suggests that they "get together": "When I hung up I felt as if I was an astronaut who had completed his orbit of the earth and now I was pulled by some new gravity into a cold clean darkness."

Mosley published his next book, *Gone Fishin'*—the first Easy Rawlins novel he wrote, which had been rejected by publishers in the late 1980s—with a small black publishing house, Black Classic Press in Baltimore. A stew of sex, voodoo, and death, the novel takes Easy back to his early manhood in Houston in 1939 when he accompanies Mouse on a journey to the Louisiana bayou town of Pariah to get money from his stepfather, Reese Corn. Mouse's murder of his stepfather foreshadows his later taste for amoral violence and leads Easy to the realization that he "couldn't live with those people anymore." Although *Gone Fishin'*, like the previous Easy Rawlins novels, generally received excellent reviews, with comparisons made between Mosley and William Faulkner, Charles Taylor in the on-line magazine *Salon* maintained that Mosley's books

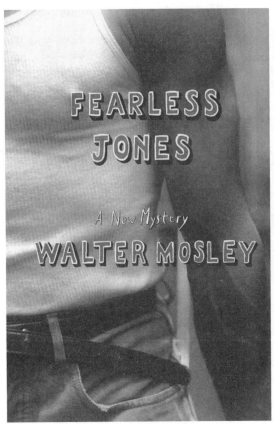 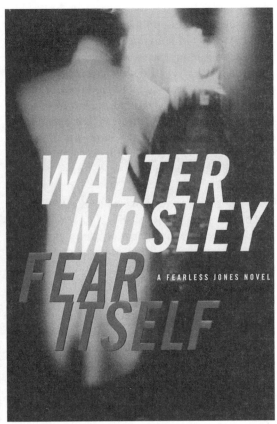

*Dust jackets for Mosley's novels, published in 2001 and 2003, that feature tough guy Fearless Jones
and bookstore owner Paris Minton (Richland County Public Library)*

"aren't much more than the usual hardboiled fantasy, masochistic and narcissistic in equal measure." He derided Mosley's admirers by asking: "Do people fall for this stuff because the idea of a black writer of hardboiled fiction is a novelty, or because that clipped, faux Hemingway prose makes Mosley's phony hard truths go down easier?"

Later in 1997 Mosley published *Always Outnumbered, Always Outgunned,* a book set in contemporary Los Angeles featuring Socrates Fortlow, a former convict who spent twenty-seven years in an Indiana penitentiary for rape and murder. Eight years out of prison and living in a shack in Watts, the nearly sixty-year-old Socrates strives to overcome the angry legacy of hatred from his prison days. In the novel—more accurately, a collection of connected stories—Socrates accepts his painful life, thinks about it, and tries to improve it. Terrified of reverting to the violence that led to his imprisonment, he never carries a gun. "I either committed a crime or had a crime done to me every day I was in jail," he says. "Once you go to prison you belong there."

Fortlow has hands that are able to "crush rocks," but he becomes a bagger at a local supermarket and vows to avoid trouble, regardless of the misery of his present condition. But of course, trouble finds him, and each of the fourteen stories is about his reaching out to do what he perceives to be the "right thing." He helps throw a crack dealer out of his neighborhood, confronts an arsonist, helps an old man dying of cancer, and becomes a father figure to a twelve-year-old boy, Darryl, who he learns has participated in the killing of a retarded boy.

Socrates Fortlow is an inquiring man trying to figure out not only himself but also the world in which he finds himself. In a rough way he represents the Socratic method of coming to the truth. In each story "the truth" is not simply something that he takes for granted, as it often seems to be for Easy Rawlins, but something that Fortlow must slowly come to understand. He broods upon the corruption—particularly crime and drugs—that he sees as destroying the black community of America. As Mosley said of this character: "As a teacher he is also a student. He's learning. So in some of the stories you'll find he's actually taking somebody and teaching them what's right, or he's giving them a lesson or showing them something."

Always Outnumbered, Always Outgunned was a great critical success. Writing in the 9 November 1997 issue of *The New York Times,* Sven Birkerts praises the believability of the character:

> Mosley models Socrates from all sides, many unflattering, yet he manages to leave us with the impression of a man whose soul is tuned to the pain of others. Socrates acts decently not because he hews to a code of right action, but because decency follows from this susceptibility. His decency is a force. Over time, and not always easily, Socrates brings Darryl around. He has searched out the wounded soul, not the felon, and the wounded soul eventually answers. But credibly–Mosley has not appliquéd his morality; he has located its deep coiled root and tracked it up to the surface.

"Mosley's style," Birkerts asserts, "suits his subject perfectly. The prose is sandpapery, the sentence rhythms often rough and jabbing. But then–sudden surprise–we come upon moments of undefended lyricism. This, too, belongs to the character portrait."

After *Blue Light,* a work of science fiction that received mixed reviews, Mosley published his second Socrates Fortlow book, *Walkin' the Dog,* a collection of twelve stories. For Peter McCarthy in the *Boston Review,* the key question raised in the book is asked by Socrates of a group of friends at the beginning of the penultimate story, "Rascals in the Cane": "What I wanna know is if you think that black people have a right to be mad at white folks or are we all just full 'a shit an' don't have no excuse for the misery down here an' everywhere else?" McCarthy asserts that through Socrates, Mosley is getting at "nothing less than the fundamental questions of being black and living in an inner city today. Socrates, in plain terms, gets to the heart of what he experiences as a black man: namely, a persistent sense of frustration, and an ever-present anger that stems from that frustration. From finding and keeping an apartment, to getting a job, Socrates never quite gets a fair shake. Mosley shows how that burns while skillfully leaving self pity out of the equation." Adam Goodheart in *The New York Times* (7 November 1999) also has praise for the collection, which he calls "as much moral fable as social fiction," but wonders whether Socrates' "rigidity"–his tendency to fall back into his prison self when he is pressed–might limit the character's further development: "This rigidity of character rings absolutely true in Mosley's telling, but it also means that Fortlow's story starts to lose steam once he has been pushed down and pulled up a certain number of times. By the time you reach the last few chapters of 'Walkin' the Dog,' you start to wonder whether there's enough to its hero to make another installment."

After publishing a nonfiction work of social analysis, *Workin' on the Chain Gang: Shaking Off the Dead Hand of History* in 2000, Mosley returned solidly to the detective genre with his next novel, *Fearless Jones* (2001). Mosley calls this violence-filled book an experiment in "comic noir": "Even though these terrible things happen, very often you end up laughing." Set in Watts in 1954, the novel is narrated by the decidedly unhard-boiled Paris Minton, the owner of a bookstore and a compulsive reader. Minton's alter ego is the title character, Fearless Jones: "Tall and slender, darker than most Negroes in the American melting pot, he was stronger than tempered steel and an army-trained killing machine." A World War II veteran, who, like Mouse, fears nothing, Fearless is loyal and proud as well as being a genuinely kind man.

In "The Writing of Fearless Jones," an essay posted on his website, Mosley explains that he began the novel "simply to get involved once again with the characters Paris Minton and Fearless Jones," whom he had introduced in a story included in the anthology *Spooks, Spies, and Private Eyes: Black Mystery, Crime and Suspense Fiction* (1995). Mosley found Paris and Fearless interesting "because of what their characters reveal about intelligence." A logical thinker who loves chess, Paris "would be a top ranked student but on the street he has serious limitations. That's because Paris is a normal every day kind of Joe. He's afraid of violence and trouble." Mosley hoped that having Paris as the narrator of the tale would "allow the reader a different kind of entrée into this story of mayhem, doublecrosses, and corruption." In contrast to Paris, Fearless has "a brave and smart heart. Fearless has trouble with the logic of checkers but he can read what's going on deep in a man's soul."

The plot of this novel is reminiscent of *A Little Yellow Dog* in that it begins with a beautiful woman in need of help. Within a day after Elana Love enters Minton's bookstore in an obviously agitated state, Paris finds himself beaten up, shot at, and robbed by Elana of his car and his money. Worse, for him, his beloved bookstore is burned to the ground. Paris bails Fearless out of jail, and the two begin a search for Elana and a missing Swiss bond that the thug who beat up Paris believed she had. In due course the two come to the aid of an elderly Jewish couple, Fanny and Sol Tannenbaum, and become involved with Israeli agents and a Nazi commandant. Corrupt, racist police and a gang of savage former convicts complicate Fearless and Paris's search for what seems to be a fortune in stolen goods.

Fearless Jones generally received good reviews. Jesse Berrett in *The New York Times* (10 June 2001), however, found the novel less compelling than Mosley's work in the Easy Rawlins series. For Berrett "the central mystery" of the novel "is why Mosley has chosen to begin a new series, set in the same place and at the same time, with a new character." He argues that the new novel

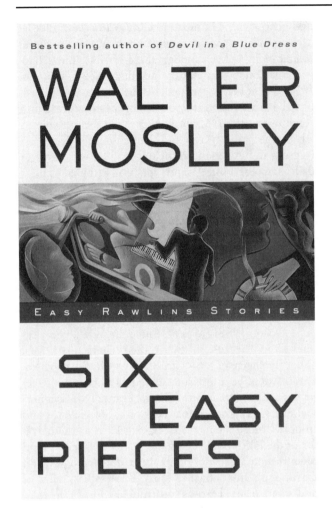

Dust jacket for Mosley's 2003 collection of stories featuring Easy Rawlins, in which Rawlins's psychopathic friend Mouse returns, despite his presumed death in A Little Yellow Dog *(Richland County Public Library)*

"trolls the same waters Mosley has previously explored: the arbitrariness of a police system that relies on racial terror as a substitute for justice, the dovetailing of anti-Semitism and racial prejudice and the tenuous necessity of interracial collaboration and perhaps occasional friendship. . . . Even the best parts of the book feel like diminished versions of what he has previously done more powerfully."

After *Futureland,* his second work of science fiction, Mosley returned to Easy Rawlins in *Bad Boy Brawly Brown* (2002), the seventh in the series. As a black man in "a world where the white man's de facto king" and a man with the skills and occasionally the instincts of a criminal, Easy understands and in some measure is sympathetic to those who call for revolution. On the other hand, as a father, a reasonable middle-aged man, having a stake in the economic structure of that imperfect society, he often finds himself committed to the values of the status quo. He is divided in character if not in personal-

ity, and in none of the books of the Easy Rawlins series is this split more dramatic than in *Bad Boy Brawly Brown.*

The novel is set in early 1964, a few months after the events concluding *A Little Yellow Dog.* Bonnie Shay and the dog Frenchie have become part of Easy's family, though Frenchie is always snarling at Easy: "He was the love of my little girl's life, so I accepted his hatred. He blamed me for the death of Idabell Turner, his first owner; I blamed myself for the death of my best friend." The novel begins with Easy's memory of Mouse:

> MOUSE IS DEAD. Those words had gone through my mind every morning for three months. *Mouse is dead because of me.*
>
> When I sat up, Bonnie rolled her shoulder and sighed in her sleep. The sky through our bedroom window was just beginning to brighten.
>
> The image of Raymond, his eyes open and unseeing, lying stock-still on EttaMae's lawn, was still in my mind.

Easy's grief over Mouse's death is a recurring theme; Easy often hears Mouse's voice in his mind, pushing him and reassuring him throughout.

When Easy's old friend John asks him to find and talk sense to Brawly Brown, the son of his girlfriend Alva, Easy is drawn into the disastrous politics of the period. He quickly finds that Brawly is deeply involved in the confused morass of the Urban Revolutionary Party, an organization with a peaceful agenda but also with a violent radical element. In the end Easy resorts to violence himself to prevent Brawly's participation in a dangerous plot. In the 10 July 2002 issue of the *Washington Post,* Bill Kent writes: "despite a meandering plot, too many violent males and sultry females and a discomfiting resolution, the book's a winner. We can forgive an awkwardly constructed plot in a mystery tale—we all know the hero has to solve the crime and, at its least, a plot is a variation on a familiar theme. What keeps us turning the pages is a realistic, believable, compelling hero using his wits, his fists, good luck and bad to explore an equally realistic, compelling setting."

A major theme in *Bad Boy Brawly Brown*—and one that runs through the series and is central as well in the Socrates Fortlow books—is the relationship between a father figure and a potentially wayward son. As Mosley says of the novel, it "talks about black men and their sons and their friends' sons." In addition to trying to save Brawly, Easy throughout the novel must contend with Jesus' desire to drop out of school and build a boat. Actually, as *Library Journal* notes, *Bad Boy Brawly Brown* could be another book in a series that might be called "Easy Rawlins's Family Values," for in novel after novel the meaning of domestic values are explored, through Easy's caring for his adopted children and his loving but rocky relationships with women.

In 2003 Mosley brought out two mystery books—the eighth book in the Easy Rawlins series, *Six Easy Pieces,* and the second novel about Paris Minton and Fearless Jones, *Fear Itself*—as well as his response to the events of 11 September 2001 and the war on terror, *What Next? A Memoir Toward World Peace.* The stories of *Six Easy Pieces* detail some important plot developments for Easy and his associates, as his friend Mofass commits suicide; his relationship with Bonnie is tested when he suspects she has had an affair; and he is surprised by the miraculous return of Mouse:

> The knocking was soft and unhurried. Whoever it was, he, or she, was in no rush.
> When I pulled the door open I was looking too high, above the man's head. And then I saw him.
> He pushed me aside and went past saying, "If it wasn't for ugly, Easy, I woulda never even seen you again."
> "Raymond?" I could feel the tears wanting to come from my eyes. I was dizzy too. Torn between the two sensations I couldn't go either way.

Although *Fear Itself* was praised by many, some reviewers, including Judith Wynn in the 27 July 2003 *Boston Herald,* criticized the characterization of the title character: "Fearless Jones has evolved from a mere mortal into a comic book-style superhero, able to read minds and run 'faster than Jesse Owens at a Nazi barbeque.'" In his 16 August 2003 review of *Six Easy Pieces* and *Fear Itself* for *Shaking Through.Net,* Kevin Forest Moreau, while recommending both books, faults Mosley for his handling of Mouse and Fearless. The return of Mouse, he argues, is handled in a "doggedly anticlimactic fashion," and he finds the relationship between Paris and Fearless too unbalanced: "Trouble is, while Minton is a fully fleshed-out character, Fearless never becomes more than a cipher." In both works "the important role of the powerful friend is lessened."

One notable aspect of Mosley's Easy Rawlins series is his treatment of color. Blue, red, white, black, yellow, and brown are used in the titles of the first six novels of the series. In the collection *Six Easy Pieces,* the title of each story includes a color word: "Smoke," "Crimson Stain," "Silver Lining," "Lavender," "Gator Green," "Gray-Eyed Death," and "Amber Gate." Mosley interweaves various images of color, particularly for "black" people. Characters aren't simply "black." But they are "coffee-colored," "pale brown," "ebony," "chocolate," and dozens of other colors. Mosley has said that his purpose is twofold: to counter the white stereotype that blacks all look alike and also to stress the variety of humanity.

In 2004 Mosley published two works, the nongenre novel *The Man in My Basement* and his ninth book about Easy Rawlins, *Little Scarlet.* Set in 1965, the novel presents a picture of Watts after the riots. As Gary Dretzka notes in his review for the 18 July 2004 *Chicago Sun-Times,* "Mosley doesn't bother to re-create—or even allude to—the incident that lit the fuse of the insurrection (a routine arrest for drunken driving outside a liquor store)." Mosley does, however, in Easy's colloquy with Bonnie, offer an explanation for how such riots begin. "Pain has a memory of its own," he tells her. When Bonnie asks, "Shouldn't we decide at some time to let it go and move on?" Easy feels compelled to answer fully:

> "You can't ever leave something like that behind. You go to sleep with it and you wake up with it too." I was looking her in the eye then. She wanted to turn away but would not.
> "But it's worse than that," I said. "For most people the pain they experience is just inside them. I hit you in the head but that's you and me. You could leave, find another man. You could go to work and none of the other women got a big knot on their heads. But if you come from down in Watts or Fifth Ward or Harlem, every soul you come upon has been threatened and beaten and jailed. If you have kids they will be beaten. And no matter how far back you remember, there's a beatin' there waiting for you. And so when you see some man stopped by the cops and some poor mother cryin' for his release it speaks to you. You don't know that woman, you don't know if the man bein' arrested has done something wrong. But it doesn't matter. Because you been there before. And everybody around you has been there before. And it's hot, and you're broke, and people have been doin' this to you because of your skin for more years than your mother's mother can remember."

John Burdett in the *Washington Post* (25 July 2004) asserts that "the true protagonist of the book is collectively the riots and their aftermath. Mosley is considerably more interested in the ambiguous state of mind of the black citizenry, the disorientation of the cops and the looted, shambolic condition of Watts itself than he is in the adventures of his hero. Watts, in truth, is a world turned upside down, and Mosley simply points his hero at it and rolls the camera."

Easy Rawlins's involvement in the Little Scarlet case begins when he is approached by Detective Melvin Suggs at his office, which he obtained as the result of a favor he did in *Six Easy Pieces.* Suggs asks him to investigate the murder of Nola Payne, aka Little Scarlet, the unreported thirty-fourth victim of the riots. The police believe she was killed by a white man and are hoping for a quick, quiet investigation and an arrest, but as Suggs states, "a white policeman looking into anything down in Watts right now will only draw attention to something we need to keep quiet."

Little Scarlet has received overwhelmingly positive reviews. Harper Barnes in the 11 July 2004 issue of the *St. Louis Post-Dispatch* writes that at times, "as their number rose to eight, the Rawlins novels came to seem a tad

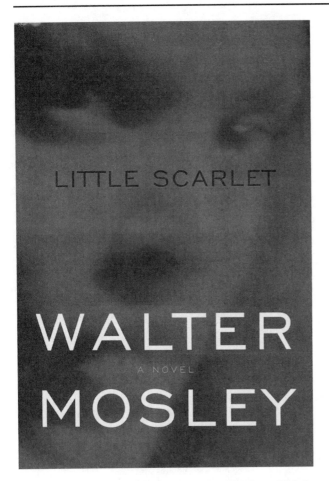

Dust jacket for Mosley's eighth novel about Easy Rawlins, published in 2004, set in the aftermath of the 1965 Watts riots (Collection of George and Julie Anderson)

ment of 'Chinatown'-like eeriness for its secrets and its deadly self-deceptions. What makes it more than a genre piece is Easy's insight into how the world is changing around him. 'The morning air still smelled of smoke,' the book begins, but before it is over, there is a clearing of the air."

At fifty-two, Walter Mosley is respected as a writer beyond genre. He was named the first Artist-in-Residence at the Africana Studies Institute of New York University, where he directs a lecture series titled "Black Genius." He is a director on the board of the National Book Awards, the Poetry Society of America, a member of the executive board of PEN American Center (and founder of its Open Book Committee), and a past president of the Mystery Writers of America.

In his review of *Little Scarlet* for the *Chicago Sun-Times,* Dretzka suggests that the next logical step for Mosley may involve Easy and Mouse with "the Bloods and Crips, vicious and highly organized gangs that filled the void left when the LAPD effectively relinquished control of Watts and South Central." But it is pure speculation to try to predict a versatile writer. Whatever directions Mosley takes in the future, his novels so far stand as a distinguished contribution to detective fiction.

Interviews:

"The Mystery of Walter Mosley," *Ebony* (December 1995);

Maya Jaggi, "Socrates of the Streets," *Guardian,* 6 September 2003, pp. 7, 20.

References:

Roger A. Berger, "'The Black Dick': Race, Sexuality and Discourse in the L.A. Novels of Walter Mosley," *African American Review,* 31 (Summer 1997): 281–295;

Scott Bunyon, "No Order from Chaos: The Absence of Chandler's Extra Legal Space in the Detective Fiction of Chester Himes and Walter Mosley," *Studies in the Novel,* 35 (2003);

John G. Cawelti, *Adventure, Mystery and Romance: Formula Stories as Art and Popular Culture* (Chicago: University of Chicago Press, 1977);

Helen Lock, "Invisible Detection: The Case of Walter Mosley," *MELUS,* 26 (2001);

Marilyn C. Wesley, "Power and Knowledge in Walter Mosley's *Devil in a Blue Dress,*" *African American Review,* 35 (2001).

forced and perfunctory, with languorous plots and occasionally murky writing," but asserts that the new novel "would be hard to put down if your house was on fire":

> "Little Scarlet" is so strongly plotted and so cleanly and evocatively written that it never even hints of being a polemic. At the same time, through a hero who is far from perfect but whose key existential decisions reflect a passionate morality, Mosley sheds more light than any number of official reports on what it was like to be a thoughtful black man in post-World War II Los Angeles, scene of two of the most devastating race riots in American history.

In *The New York Times* (5 July 2004) Janet Maslin found "Easy's repetitively bitter talk of oppression" superfluous: "This book needs no excess baggage. Its plot explores the riots' irrevocable consequences and builds up to a denoue-

Michael Nava

(16 September 1954 –   )

Karl L. Stenger
University of South Carolina Aiken

BOOKS: *The Little Death* (Boston: Alyson, 1986);

Goldenboy (Boston: Alyson, 1988);

How Town: A Novel of Suspense (New York: Harper & Row, 1989);

The Hidden Law (New York: HarperCollins, 1992);

Created Equal: Why Gay Rights Matter to America, by Nava and Robert Dawidoff (New York: St. Martin's Press, 1994);

The Death of Friends (New York: Putnam, 1996);

The Burning Plain (New York: Putnam, 1997);

Rag and Bone (New York: Putnam, 2001).

OTHER: "Street People," *Finale: Short Stories of Mystery & Suspense,* edited by Nava (Boston: Alyson, 1989), pp. 193–241;

"Grief," in *Certain Voices: Short Stories about Gay Men,* edited by Darryl Pilcher (Boston: Alyson, 1991), pp. 207–222;

"Gardenland, Sacramento, California," in *Hometowns: Gay Men Write about Where They Belong,* edited by John Preston (New York: Dutton, 1991), pp. 21–29;

"Abuelo: My Grandfather, Raymond Acuña," in *A Member of the Family: Gay Men Write about Their Families,* edited by Preston (New York: Dutton, 1992), pp. 15–20;

"The Marriage of Michael and Bill," in *Friends and Lovers: Gay Men Write about the Families They Create,* edited by Preston and Michael Lowenthal (New York: Dutton, 1995), pp. 111–124;

"Coming Out and Born Again," in *Wrestling with the Angel: Faith and Religion in the Lives of Gay Men,* edited by Brian Bouldrey (New York: Riverhead, 1995), pp. 175–182;

"Boys Like Us," in *Boys Like Us: Gay Writers Tell Their Coming Out Stories,* edited by Patrick Merla (New York: Avon, 1996), pp. 154–166;

"Journey to 1971," in *Gay Travels: A Literary Companion,* edited by Lucy Jane Bledsoe (San Francisco: Whereabouts Press, 1998), pp. 130–137;

"Charity," in *Las Christmas: Favorite Latino Authors Share Their Holiday Memories,* edited by Esmeralda Santi-

Michael Nava (photograph © Jerry Bauer; from The Hidden Law, *1992; Richland County Public Library)*

ago and Joie Davidow (New York: Knopf, 1998), pp. 51–57.

SELECTED PERIODICAL PUBLICATIONS–
UNCOLLECTED: "Magical Thinking," *James White Review,* 15 (Fall 1998): 19;

"Rat," *Harrington Gay Men's Fiction Quarterly,* 1 (1999): 113–129.

Michael Nava, the author of a completed cycle of seven mystery novels, is considered the best contemporary gay mystery writer and the worthy successor to his mentor and model Joseph Hansen, the originator of the gay mystery novel. Henry Rios, Nava's Chicano lawyer and sleuth, is as unabashedly and unapologetically homosexual as Dave Brandstetter, Hansen's insurance investigator and detective. The trials and tribulations both protagonists undergo provide the reader with an accurate chronicle of gay life in post-Stonewall (time since a 1969 riot in Greenwich Village between gays and police that provided the spark for the gay rights movement) America. In Etelka Lehoczky's 2001 article "Building a Mystery," Nava acknowledges the unbroken thread that connects him to Hansen:

> He used the mystery to actually explore what it means to be gay. In the classic American mystery, the private investigator is an outsider who's generally viewed [as] fairly disreputable by the people who hire him. So if you are in fact an outsider because you're gay or a woman or African-American, it's a very interesting vehicle to explore the whole issue of being on the fringe.

That Nava's protagonist is not only openly gay but also Chicano makes him a double outsider. In his dissertation treating Nava as well as Oscar Zeta Acosta and Arturo Islas, Enrique G. López points out that Nava's hero "is really a member of an outgroup within an outgroup in society. . . . Rios must learn to juggle these two aspects of his self-identity, not an easy task." The tension between Rios's sexuality and ethnicity intensifies throughout the cycle of seven novels and gives his story additional depth and complexity.

Miguel Angel Nava was born 16 September 1954 in Stockton, California, the second of six children, and grew up in a poor Mexican neighborhood in Sacramento called Gardenland. As Nava reveals in the 1992 essay "Abuelo: My Grandfather, Raymond Acuña," one of several autobiographical pieces he has written, it "was no secret in my family that I did not have a father." Although Michael and his older brother Tommy shared the name of their mother's first husband, whom she divorced shortly after Michael's birth, his natural father was a man "with whom my mother, then married, had had an affair, to the lasting shame of her Mexican-Catholic family." Nava saw his father only once, briefly, when he was five years old, and he was always ashamed when his natural father's name was mentioned.

Nava's estrangement from his family increased when his mother married Butch, an alcoholic construction worker who beat his wife, spent time in prison, and showed little paternal interest in the boy. When the eleven-year-old was sexually molested by his uncle Frankie, he felt cast off completely. The only person Nava felt a kinship with was his maternal grandfather, Raymond Acuña, "a solitary, secretive man," in whom Nava could discern his potential adult self. Whenever the fights between Nava's mother and stepfather escalated, he slipped out of the house and sought refuge at his grandparents' home, where he curled up on their sofa.

While biding his time to escape the barrio of Gardenland for good, Nava developed survival strategies. As he recalls in his 1999 essay "Rat," he became furtive and quiet at home, creeping "along the walls trying not to be noticed," a behavior that earned him the nickname "Rat." Nava excelled in school, where he was able to receive the attention and praise that was lacking in his home: "the quieter I got at home, the more voluble I became at school, an attention-seeker desperate, particularly, for the approval of my teachers." In "Rat" Nava relates a poignant story of how he and Yolanda, an African American classmate, were taken out to dinner by their teacher and her husband as a reward for having won a spelling bee: "for that moment at the coffee shop of the bowling alley she and I were brother and sister in the aristocracy of intellect and Mrs. Baptiste and her husband were our parents."

When Nava attended Norte del Rio High School, he became a "frenetic overachiever," as he told Robert Burke in a 1991 interview, serving as student body president, captain of the debating team, and class valedictorian. Being aware of his homosexual tendencies since the age of twelve, Nava developed several unrequited crushes on male schoolmates. As he writes in his 1995 essay "The Marriage of Michael and Bill," the first boy he fell in love with was David, "an ordinary fellow fourteen-year-old with pale skin, green eyes, and the wiry build of a runner." Being too timid to reveal his affection, Nava poured his feelings into the poem "For David," imitating William Shakespeare's sonnets, and, in an act of despair, swallowed a handful of phenobarbital. His suicide attempt failed, however, because the dose was too small.

In 1971, when Nava was about to turn seventeen, he was introduced to a boy he calls "Joey Spencer," a transfer student who was half Anglo, half Mexican and with whom Michael sensed a kinship. In his 1996 essay "Boys Like Us," Nava writes, "He was a boy like me, from a poor family, ambitious but diffident, hungry for encouragement but fearful of being mocked." The two were paired up as debate partners, and soon they were inseparable. In his 1998 autobiographical essay "Journey to 1971," Nava admits that he "fell as deeply in love with him as I have ever loved anybody in my life." Joey, however, was straight and unable to return Nava's affection.

Nava has given two different versions of the end of their friendship. In "Boys Like Us," he states that the two shared a sexual encounter during a trip to a speech tournament in San Francisco. When Joey felt ashamed afterward and asserted defensively that he was not "queer," Nava felt rejected and isolated: "The fabric of our friendship began to unravel, and this led to awkwardness, misunderstandings, tension, silence." Writing about his friendship with Joey in "Journey to 1971," Nava denies that any sexual encounter took place: "Sometimes, that year, I slept over and we shared his bed. No, nothing ever happened. I was too repressed to make a move on him, but even the remote possibility, not to mention the incidental touching of our bodies, made those nights more erotic for me than most of my sexual encounters have been since." Joey's reaction to Nava's confession that he was in love with him appears kinder in this version: "I'm not a homosexual, Michael." No matter which of the two versions comes closer to the truth, clearly Nava's friendship with Joey represented a defining event in his life; even after the two separated to attend different colleges, years passed before Nava stopped missing his friend.

When Nava entered Colorado College to major in history on a full scholarship, he sublimated his sexual longings and emotional needs into intellectual accomplishment, a strategy his friend Robert Dawidoff is quoted as calling "ambition disorder" in Philip Gambone's *Something Inside: Conversations with Gay Fiction Writers* (1999). Nava was asked to join Phi Beta Kappa Honor Society and graduated with honors in 1976. He then received a Watson Fellowship for a one-year stay in Buenos Aires, where he was to study and translate the work of Rubén Darío, a Nicaraguan poet. In the interview with Gambone, Nava admitted that he conned his way there "because I was the golden boy at the school where I went."

Being thrown into a foreign city of nine million people while barely being able to speak Spanish represented a formidable challenge for Nava. He had a hard time meeting people because Americans were regarded with suspicion and a gay subculture did not exist. Nava told Gambone that it "was the loneliest year of my life. I spent a lot of time in bed reading Charles Dickens." By surviving this difficult year, he realized that "loneliness wouldn't kill me." When he returned to the United States in 1977, Nava decided to go to law school, since he did not want to become a teacher and since his science background was insufficient for medical school. He passed the law boards and was accepted by Stanford University. Nava admits that he was not a good law student and did not like law school because it lacked reality: "I thought about dropping out, but I didn't know what else to do, so I stuck with it." He had started writing poetry while in college, setting out to be "the great American poet," and even had some of his work published around 1983, but he knew that he would not be able to support himself writing poetry.

Stanford provided a tolerant and sophisticated environment that allowed Nava to be open about his sexual orientation. As he recounts in "The Marriage of Michael and Bill," he hung out at the Gay People's Union looking for possible partners, and, while his dates never resulted in much more than sex, he was not unhappy. Together with his best friend, Susan, he devised a contest called "Find Mr. Stanford," the goal of which was "to identify the one male classmate who epitomized the bourgeois

Dust jacket for Nava's 1992 novel, the fourth to feature gay Chicano lawyer and sleuth Henry Rios (Richland County Public Library)

conventionality we pretended to disdain." They decided to bestow this title upon Bill Weinberger, a friendly and studious Clevelander who was so neat "his jeans were creased." Much to Nava's surprise, a year later he was approached by Weinberger, who was just coming out of the closet. Their first intimate encounter changed their lives and led to an intense relationship that lasted for nine years. Nava explains, "When we found each other it was as if, in an alien country, each of us had found someone who spoke his native language." He admits that their years together were not always easy or happy ones, partly because the two men had no blueprint or model for a gay marriage and partly because of the baggage each of them brought to the relationship. When the final breakup took place in 1989, the two men remained close friends. Nava gratefully acknowledges that Weinberger gave him permission to have a normal life and to leave the hurts of his childhood behind: "Bill was not the first family I ever had, but he was the first family I chose."

Nava was not only happy in his private life in the early 1980s but also successful professionally. He graduated from Stanford with a law degree in 1980, passed the bar exam, and was immediately offered a position as deputy city attorney in Los Angeles. Being openly gay turned out to be an advantage for Nava, because, as he told Gambone, the city attorney "wanted the office to reflect the community" and was actively recruiting gay lawyers. Although Nava initially enjoyed the job, he gradually became disillusioned with the justice system and resigned from his position in 1984 to join a private law firm in Encino. That same year he finished his first mystery novel, *The Little Death* (1986), which he had started four years earlier while working the graveyard shift at the Palo Alto jail.

Nava recalls the genesis of *The Little Death* in the preface to the fifteenth anniversary edition of the novel. At the jail it was his job "to interview arrestees after they were booked to determine whether they should be released on their own recognizance or held overnight until a judge could set bail." Since his clients consisted primarily of drunk drivers, inept burglars, or unlucky prostitutes, Nava quickly became bored and, instead of concentrating on his impending bar exam, jotted down his impressions of the goings-on in the jail. This "literary doodling" formed the core of the novel that Nava completed in August 1984. Having been rejected by thirteen publishers, the manuscript was eventually accepted by Sasha Alyson, the owner of a small, Boston-based gay publishing company. The novel was published in 1986, its jacket carrying a laudatory blurb by Joseph Hansen: "Nava takes his work seriously. Dark and tangled as is the plot of *The Little Death,* it is about unmistakably real people, living in the real world, and coping with real problems. His mystery is more than that—it is a genuine novel."

In his 1991 interview with Burke, Nava characterized his first novel "as a sort of Raymond Chandler with a gay Philip Marlowe." When readers first meet Henry Rios, Nava's gay version of Marlowe, he is thirty-three and in the midst of a professional and personal crisis. He has been a public defender for ten years and, having recently lost a big case and having been demoted as a result, he is disillusioned and burned out. Relegated to a branch office, he feels as if he is being put out to pasture. Since law has always been the center of Rios's life and since he has always taken refuge in his profession, his demotion has resulted in a profound identity crisis. Even though he is offered a position training new lawyers, he decides to hand in his resignation: "I don't see myself as a teacher. . . . I'm not ready to sit on the veranda and tell war stories." When his best friend, Aaron Gold, offers him a prestigious job with his law firm, Rios rejects the offer. He is not interested in defending the rich, because he feels a kinship with outcasts of society: "if they're out-

siders, so am I." He decides to strike out on his own instead and to open a small law office.

Rios's first case involves Hugh Paris, a troubled young gay man from an extremely wealthy and politically influential family. Rios first encounters Hugh in the county jail after his arrest on drug charges. Rios is immediately drawn to the young man, who reminds him of a saint "being led off to his martyrdom. There was a glint of purity in Hugh Paris's eyes completely at odds with everything that was happening around him." When Paris shows up at Rios's doorstep several weeks later, claiming that his grandfather, who controls his money and who hates him, is planning to have him killed, Rios offers him his bed and his affection. While sex for him in the past had largely been a matter of one-night stands, the intimate encounter with Paris awakens in Rios the possibility of an emotional bond: "Now that my career had come to an abrupt halt, there was a lot of time . . . Enough time to go crazy, or fall in love again." The two men start seeing each other, but their chance at happiness comes to a sudden end when Paris is found dead of a drug overdose.

When the death is ruled accidental, Rios decides to uncover the true cause: "I was now his advocate, not his lover." While delving into Hugh's background and untangling the complex relationships of the Linden/Smith/Paris family, Rios comes across two additional murders camouflaged as accidents. His attempt to uncover the buried secrets of the powerful clan threatens his own personal safety. Rios's apartment is ransacked, and he is abducted by four thugs and almost framed for the murder of Aaron Gold. Eventually, the villains are exposed. As Dawidoff points out in his April 2001 article for the *San Francisco Bay Guardian* website, "The Education of Henry Rios: Why Michael Nava's Seven-volume Bildungsroman Is a New American Classic," a characteristic of the entire cycle of novels is that "the bad guys are the privileged and corrupt who think that because they own the world and are in the habit of running it that they are above its laws." For Rios the resolution of the case is a hollow victory: the truly evil villain dies of a stroke before he can be brought to justice while "a moderately good man who chose expediency over justice the one time it really mattered" has to bear the brunt of the law.

Since *The Little Death* sold reasonably well, Sasha Alyson requested a sequel, and Nava obliged. He admits in his preface to *The Little Death* that his career as a mystery writer was inadvertent: "I had never intended to start a series, but I was still interested in the character and the possibilities of crime fiction, so I obliged him with *Goldenboy* and thus became a full-fledged mystery writer." While homosexuality serves as a minor theme in *The Little Death,* it takes center stage in Nava's second novel.

In *Goldenboy* (1988), Rios, now thirty-six and devastated by Paris's death, has succumbed to alcoholism and landed in a hospital. After drying out, he channels his energies into political activism by helping his friend Larry Ross, a gay L.A. lawyer, to mount a campaign to defeat the move to reinstate the sodomy statutes in California. At the opening of the novel, Ross asks Rios to represent Jim Pears, a young gay busboy who is accused of stabbing a coworker to death. Brian Fox, the murder victim, had caught Jim having sex with a man behind the restaurant and supposedly threatened to expose Jim's sexual escapade to his parents. Rios is initially reluctant to take on the seemingly open-and-shut case, but when Ross, who is dying of AIDS, appeals to Rios's solidarity as a gay man by claiming that it was society's bigotry that drove Jim to murder, Rios relents. His client insists that he is innocent, and, when he is not believed, overdoses on barbiturates in prison. As he has sustained serious and irreversible brain damage, the case against him is dismissed, and he is remanded to the custody of his parents.

Rios now feels more driven than before to prove the young man's innocence, and his investigation leads him to a famous and charismatic actor, whose double life he exposes. He also meets and falls in love with Josh Mandel, one of Jim's coworkers. Despite the fact Josh is HIV positive, they embark on a relationship that provides a major theme of the next four novels. Dawidoff points out that "through the shifts and transformations of their relationship Henry experiences AIDS at the shortest remove." As was the case in *The Little Death,* justice is only partially served. When Josh is recruited to expose the villain in a sting operation, the undercover plan goes awry, and Josh shoots and kills him in self defense. Evil has touched the innocent, and the novel ends on a disquieting note that is only slightly alleviated by the possibility of a loving relationship between Rios and Josh.

Nava told Burke in his 1991 interview that in *Goldenboy* "I started to sneak in a lot of my rage." While his rage is directed in this novel against homophobia and self-hate, Nava's ire focuses on pedophilia and child abuse in his next novel, *How Town* (1989), a title he took from a poem by E. E. Cummings. The shift in focus may in part be related to Nava's move from a small gay publishing company to the major mainstream publisher Harper & Row. In Anthony Slide's *Gay and Lesbian Characters and Themes in Mystery Novels: A Critical Guide of Over 500 Works in English* (1993), Nava conceded that he felt an implicit onus writing for the gay market: "There is a certain amount of internal pressure to write affirmatively about gay relationships. With *Goldenboy* especially, I think I was affected by it."

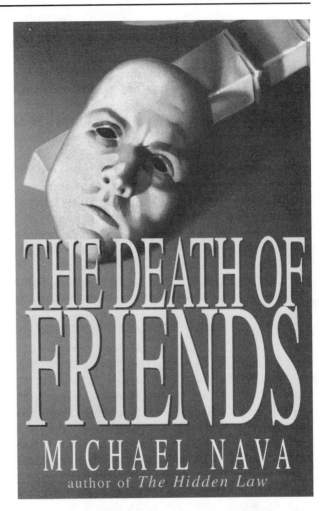

Dust jacket for Nava's 1996 novel, in which Rios investigates the murder of a closet homosexual judge and attempts to come to terms with a former lover's illness (Richland County Public Library)

At the beginning of *How Town,* Rios, now thirty-seven, has set up house with Josh in Los Angeles so that his young lover can attend UCLA, receive the medical treatment necessary to maintain his health, and be close to his parents. Rios has considered shutting down his law practice and teaching at a local law school instead so that he can spend more time with his friend. Rios is contacted by his older sister, Elena, who still lives in Los Robles, the small Northern California town in which they grew up. Although the two siblings are estranged, Elena asks her brother to defend heterosexual pedophile Paul Windsor, a childhood friend, who has been accused of murdering John McKay, a peddler of child pornography.

During Rios's investigation, which reveals that the actual murderers had been molested by their victim when they were children, Rios is forced to confront his past. He and his sister grew up in a dysfunctional family: "There had been little about our childhood that could be described as paradisical. Our alcoholic father was either brutal or sullenly withdrawn. Our mother retaliated with religious fanaticism." Instead of seeking refuge in each other's company, the siblings grew apart and developed separate coping strategies. Elena entered a teaching order of nuns after high school in order to defy their father. After his death, she obtained an M.A. in American literature and accepted a teaching position at a women's college. Even though she is a lesbian, she keeps her distance from her gay brother, despite his attempts to forge a bond. Rios recognizes that "the past was a thin layer of ash over embers that could still burn." Not until Nava's seventh and last novel, *Rag and Bone* (2001), do the siblings come to terms with their past and begin "to master the paradox of family."

As in his two previous novels, Nava not only reverses "the pluses and minuses of the traditional dichotomies between good and evil" but also complicates them, as Michael R. Hames-García argues in his essay "Subverting Noir: Chicano/Joto Integrity and Morality in the Mystery Novels of Michael Nava" presented in April 1999 at the National Association for Chicana and Chicano Studies. While Rios is initially repulsed by the pedophile, who is innocent of the murder, he feels sympathy for the murderers. Rios's moral certainties, moreover, are challenged when he realizes that his "values were acquired through trial and error . . . they were learned, not given, and came out of experience." When he is unexpectedly attracted to a policeman who, despite his bodybuilder's bulk, "had a child's round, large-eyed, pretty face," Rios comes close to understanding the pedophile's urges: "I was not a pedophile, nor had I ever consciously entertained those fantasies, but I was a sexual being and for a moment in the jail I'd felt Paul's excitement and it terrified me." The novel, which, according to *Booklist,* "stretches the psychological and emotional boundaries of the genre," ends on a disquieting note of moral ambiguity, and its last ominous scene also sets the stage for Nava's next novel: Josh's T-cell count has dropped, and he finds himself in the hospital for a new treatment.

The Hidden Law (1992), with its title taken from a poem by W. H. Auden, represents a significant step in Nava's development as a writer. While the mystery elements are still important and expertly handled, the themes of sexual and ethnic difference become more important. Slide asserts that *The Hidden Law* "is a transitional novel, moving Nava away from the mystery genre to the personal, testamentary novel." One major theme is Josh's deteriorating health and its deleterious effect on his relationship with Rios. That Rios is HIV negative drives a wedge between the two lovers, and Josh adopts an us-versus-them mentality,

accusing Rios of acting "like a true neggie." Feeling that his HIV-negative lover is unable to understand his fears and needs, Josh turns to a seropositive support group for help and even becomes "an AIDS guerrilla," joining ACT UP. Eventually, he leaves Rios for Stephen, a fellow AIDS sufferer and activist.

Being deserted by his lover awakens sleeping demons in Rios and opens old wounds. He tries to come to terms with the impact his father, "a great and impartial hater," had had on his life: "He was a whirlwind, like the Old Testament God, or something, ripping through my life, uprooting me, tossing me around." During several therapy sessions, Rios realizes that not only is he still living with his father's judgments of him but he is also living out those judgments. He finally acknowledges that nothing is wrong with being the kind of man he is, and he lays his demons to rest. He also makes his peace with Josh, whose mind has been affected by AIDS. Rios helps Josh draft his last will and testament and make plans for his memorial service.

The second major theme of the novel is Rios's Chicano background. Whereas Nava had already touched upon it briefly in the previous novels, he now trains the spotlight on the question of how, as Hames-García puts it, "Henry negotiates and renegotiates the gay and Chicano spaces of community and familia." At the center of the murder mystery is Senator Agustin Peña, the ranking Latino officeholder in California, who has his sights set on becoming mayor of Los Angeles. His candidacy is severely jeopardized when he kills a man while driving under the influence of alcohol. Rios initially resents Peña for betraying his roots by becoming "tainted by his success, . . . arrogant in the pursuit of his objectives" and is reluctant to represent him. After Peña is shot to death by an unknown assailant, Rios comes to the realization that the successful politician had never forgotten his roots, and having "traversed the same trajectory," he feels a kinship with Peña. Rios's image of Peña, however, is altered once more when he learns that the senator not only had cheated on his wife with every woman who would have him but also had assaulted her and had driven his own son to patricide.

Rios's realization that part of the tragedy was caused by Peña's ethnic background strikes close to home. Peña, like Rios's father and Rios himself, had never been able to overcome the contempt and slights he had to suffer as an outsider in the Anglo world nor to suppress his anger and hurt caused by his mistreatment. Rios recognizes that Peña's "spectacular success had not been enough to break the circuits of resentment, any more than my fine academic degrees had, and we had both ended up like our fathers, seething alcoholics. There was a crucial difference though–I had not had a son to visit this fury on. He had." The other crucial difference between the two men is Rios's homosexuality, which aggravates his outsider status. López writes that Rios "is trying to survive between two social determinates usually at loggerheads with each other—as an ethnic minority in a predominately Anglo culture, and as a gay person in a mainly heterosexual society. . . . Henry Rios eventually becomes an 'other' and is thus caught in the middle of two social groups leading to the inevitable clash between ethnic group allegiance and sexual self-acceptance." This conflict almost tears Rios apart, and at the end of *The Hidden Law,* he decides to stop taking cases.

Rios's gradual and arduous healing process is documented in Nava's most poignant novel, *The Death of Friends* (1996), which opens with an earthquake shaking Los Angeles. Not only has Rios's life been shaken by the Peña case but also by the devastation AIDS has caused in the gay community. Josh's health has deteriorated, and his lover, Steven, as well as a dozen of Rios's friends, has succumbed to the disease. L.A. has become the city of death for Rios, and he is deeply affected by the carnage that surrounds him: "there were rips in the fabric of my reality that could not be mended by grieving or the passage of time." At the beginning of the novel, he gradually resumes his practice on a small scale, having taken a sabbatical from the law and gone into therapy. The murder of Chris Chandler, a closeted Superior Court judge and Rios's close friend with whom he had had a brief affair while in law school, confirms in Rios the belief that he chose the right path when he decided to acknowledge and embrace his homosexuality. A quote from the Gospel of Thomas, which Nava uses as one of the epigraphs for the book, states the premise: "Jesus said, 'If you bring forth what is inside you, what you bring forth will save you. If you don't bring forth what is inside you, what you don't bring forth will destroy you.'" By hiding his true self and living in a closet in order to further his career, Chandler eventually destroys his family and precipitates his own death.

Recognizing that his closeted friend was a kind of doppelgänger, the ghostly reverse image of himself, Rios finds new resolve to live an authentic life: "I didn't think my life was a failure. It was different from the lives of most people, and for that reason often more difficult than I observed their lives to be, but it was a life largely without regrets or fear. I knew I had done, was doing, the best I could." Rios's newly found resolve and strength is sorely tested when his former lover Josh succumbs to AIDS in the final pages of the novel.

In his conversation with Gambone, which took place in Boston in 1993 after a reading from his novel in progress, then titled "The Last Days," Nava revealed that he had changed the original first-person narration of the book to a third-person point of view. Nava based this change on his need to grow as a writer and to open up his novels: "I wanted to be able to follow the lives of other characters and I can't do that through Rios's eyes because his perspective is by necessity limited to what he knows or what he can intuit or what he can infer. And that's just not enough." Nava, however, eventually changed his mind and kept the first-person narrator for this as well as subsequent novels.

Rios's voice and perspective provide authenticity and poignancy in the novels of the series. The reviewer for *The San Francisco Chronicle* compared Nava's protagonist favorably to those of Walter Mosley and Sara Paretsky: "Like Easy Rawlins or V. I. Warshawski, Henry Rios is a fully developed human and humane character with a private life and personal relationships with loved ones that inform the very sleuthing that creates the foundation for a fast-paced and intense novel of contemporary life." Nava conceded to Gambone that little distance exists between who he is and what he writes: "Frequently the veil of fiction is gossamer thin. . . . I'm the kind of writer who writes very close to the bone. That's my strength. It's also my struggle." By employing a first-person narrator, who is, to a certain extent, the author's alter ego, Nava is able to give impassioned voice to the outrage over life's injustices that drives him to write. As Rios says succinctly at the beginning of *The Burning Plain* (1997): "Hell is other people."

The Burning Plain, Nava's sixth novel, is his most ambitious and most intricately plotted work. It also boasts the largest body count, with at least five murders and two suicides figuring in the story. Having successfully fought Josh's parents in court because they want to ignore their son's final wish to be cremated, Rios, now forty-five, has trouble coming to grips with his friend's death: "I buried myself in work, suffered my aging, lustful body and waited for it all to go away." When his path crosses with Alex Amerian, a young hustler/aspiring actor who resembles Josh as he first knew him, Rios is unwittingly drawn into a serial murder case. After Alex is brutally killed, Rios becomes the prime suspect in Alex's murder because Rios had slept with him. When additional victims are found, and the police seem disinterested in solving the murders of these gay men, Rios takes on the task. He is motivated not only by the need to clear his name but also by a gay man's sense of obligation to bring the perpetrator or perpetrators of the apparent hate crimes to justice. His investigation exposes the sometimes deadly machinations of the Hollywood movie industry and corruption and homophobia within the police force.

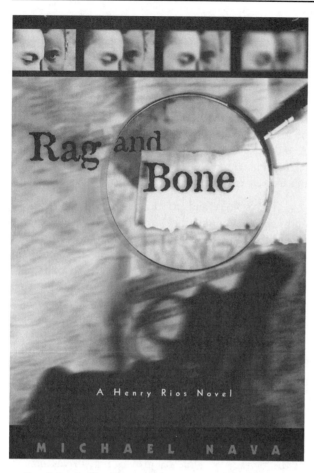

Dust jacket for Nava's 2001 novel, with which the author, as he writes in an afterword, "brings to an end . . . my career as a mystery writer" (Richland County Public Library)

In this novel as in his others, Nava paints a searing and unforgettable picture of Los Angeles, comparing the city to Dante's Inferno:

> By mid-May, the city was drifting into summer, a season of muggy, overcast mornings followed by days of asphalt-melting heat and nights when the air was filled with grit and smelled of gasoline. From the parched hills, the houses of the rich looked down upon a burning plain, where the metallic flash of sunlight in the windshields of a million cars was like a frantic signaling of souls.

Dawidoff writes that perhaps no other writer "has caught the shifting scenes and characters of Los Angeles in the last decade as Nava has." J. A. Reed of *People* magazine compares Nava's vivid depiction of Los Angeles with that of one of the writer's literary idols: "In the tradition of Raymond Chandler, Nava finds L.A. guilty as charged—a place where greatness is measured by greenbacks and lives are tossed aside like so many rejected movie scripts. And like Chandler's better work, *Plain* pushes at the edges of the genre, turning a crime novel into a morality play."

Having painted on a large canvas in *The Burning Plain,* Nava returns to a more intimate subject in his last novel in the Rios series, *Rag and Bone,* revisiting the theme of familia that he had first explored in *Goldenboy.* At the beginning of *Rag and Bone,* Rios, at forty-nine, only two years older than his creator, suffers a serious heart attack while arguing a case. He recovers but finds difficulty in coming up with reasons to be alive: "I didn't feel needed." This feeling of redundancy, however, dissipates when his sister, Elena, turns to him again for help. She reveals that thirty years earlier she had secretly had a daughter, whom she gave up for adoption. Vicky, the daughter, has suddenly and unexpectedly surfaced with her young son, Angel, seeking refuge from her abusive husband, Pete Trujillo. When Pete is shot to death, Vicky admits to killing him in self-defense. Rios, however, suspects that Vicky's confession is bogus and serves to protect her son. He uncovers that Pete had informed on a Latino gang that brought heroin into the country from Mexico and that the turncoat had been punished for his betrayal. Rios takes Angel under his wing because, as he observes, Vicky "reminds me of Mom, Angel is like me, and I see history repeating itself." By letting his sister and niece into his life, Rios finally begins to master the paradox of family: "loving without liking." He even forms a family of sorts with John DeLeon, a grounded and mature man "who was pretty much what he appeared to be." After much searching, Rios has finally found his soul mate, with whom he plans to stay. He tells John, "It is like we grew up together and then found each other again years later." Not only is personal happiness finally in Rios's grasp but also professional fulfillment: at the end of the novel, he is about to be named trial-court judge. Jane Adams stresses in her review of *Rag and Bone* for amazon.com the importance of character development: ". . . it's the multidimensionality of his central characters rather than the mysteries they're caught up in that drive [sic] Nava's perceptive, brilliantly explicated novels."

Nava's revelation in the postscript to *Rag and Bone* that it "brings to an end this series of mysteries and my career as a mystery writer" came as a shock to his readers. In interviews, Nava has given several reasons for his decision. In 2001 he told his friend and fellow mystery-writer Katherine V. Forrest that he was not interested in writing mysteries any longer because "over time the constraints imposed by the mystery form have been harder and harder to transcend without ignoring them altogether" and because the mystery form "increasingly gets in the way of the stories I really want to tell." Nava also conceded that he had said all he had to say about the experience of being gay in a predominantly heterosexual culture, "for now at least." More bluntly he told Charles Hix:

I'm not interested in writing about being a homosexual any more. . . . I'm older. I'm now 46. There are other more meaningful things to think about. I've returned to the Catholic Church. I'm a practicing Catholic again. From 1986 to 1992 was really a high point for our generation in terms of writing and readership. That period coincided with AIDS activism. It was exciting to be a writer then, despite the horror. Now the belief that AIDS is a containable disease (which I'm not sure is true) has made it a less compelling topic.

In addition, the pressures of working full-time as an appellate lawyer in the California Supreme Court have left him exhausted, as he conceded to Gerald Bartell of *The Washington Blade*. Nava has left the possibility of future novels open: "Eventually there will be more books. I want to do some living. Living will fill me up with ideas." Asked by Hix what subject matter might attract him if and when he returns to writing, Nava answered: "I'd like to write about baseball. I love baseball."

While Nava's achievement as a gay mystery writer is unquestionable—he was awarded Lambda Literary Awards in 1989, 1991, 1993, 1997, and 2002, and received the Lifetime Achievement Award of the Publishing Triangle in 2001—his importance as a gay Chicano writer is less settled. Alan West-Duran neglected to include Nava in his otherwise comprehensive two-volume survey, *Latino & Latina Writers* (2004). In his article on Mexican American literature in *Recovering the U.S. Hispanic Literary Heritage* (1993), Raymund A. Paredes criticized Nava for his depiction of Rios in *Goldenboy*, asserting that the character "inhabits the novel as a Chicano in name only; there is no significant presentation of Chicano culture and no supporting Chicano characters." However, critics such as Ricardo Ortiz, López, and Hames-García—the last asserting that Nava is "perhaps the most widely read contemporary Chicana/o writer"—have argued for the important role ethnicity plays in Nava's mysteries. Dawidoff has called Henry Rios "one of the best-delineated and most interestingly explored Mexican American protagonists in contemporary American fiction," and López has shown that "Nava explodes any myths, misconceptions, or stereotypes concerning Chicano/as in his murder mysteries." One can only hope that Nava, whether he writes more mysteries or turns in a different direction, will choose to give readers and critics more to argue about.

Interviews:

Robert Burke, "Brains & Rage: A Talk with Michael Nava, Creator of Henry Rios," *Bloomsbury Review,* 11 (June 1991): 25;

Burke, "Slumber Party: An Interview with Mystery Writers Ellen Hart, Michael Nava & Sandra Scop-
pettone," *Bloomsbury Review,* 16 (January/February 1996): 14–15;

Stephen M. Murphy, "'The Burning Plain' and Other Stories: An Interview with San Francisco attorney/ writer Michael Nava," *San Francisco Attorney Magazine,* 24 (October/November 1998): 35–36; reprinted in abbreviated form in *Mystery Review,* 8 (Fall 1999): 45–47;

Philip Gambone, "Michael Nava," in *Something Inside: Conversations with Gay Fiction Writers* (Madison: University of Wisconsin Press, 1999), pp. 123–141;

Katherine V. Forrest, "Adios, Rios. Katherine V. Forrest Talks to Michael Nava about the Finale of His Award Winning Series," *Lambda Book Report,* 9 (March 2001): 8–10;

Charles Hix, "Final Chapter," *Publishers Weekly,* 248 (23 April 2001): 31.

References:

Scott Brassart, "Foreword," in Michael Nava, *Goldenboy* (Los Angeles: Alyson, 1999), pp. 3–4;

Robert Dawidoff, "The Education of Henry Rios: Why Michael Nava's Seven-volume Bildungsroman Is a New American Classic," *San Francisco Bay Guardian* website (April 2001) <http://www.sfbg.com/lit/ apr01/>;

Michael R. Hames-García, "'Who Are Our Own People?': Challenges for a Theory of Social Identity," in *Reclaiming Identity: Realist Theory and the Predicament of Postmodernism,* edited by Paula M. L. Moya and Hames-García (Berkeley, Los Angeles & London: University of California Press, 2000), pp. 102–129;

Etelka Lehoczky, "Building a Mystery," *Advocate* (19 June 2001): 82–84;

Enrique G. López, "The Intersection of Ethnicity and Sexuality in the Narrative Fiction of Three Chicano Authors: Oscar Zeta Acosta, Arturo Islas, and Michael Nava," dissertation, Ohio State University, 1998;

Ricardo L. Ortiz, "Sexuality Degree Zero: Pleasure and Power in the Novels of John Rechy, Arturo Islas, and Michael Nava," in *Critical Essays: Gay and Lesbian Writers of Color,* edited by Emmanuel S. Nelson (New York: Haworth, 1993), pp. 111–126;

José R. Santana, "Fictions of Masculinity in the Novels of John Rechy and Michael Nava," *Berkeley McNair Journal,* 4 (Winter 1996): 145–153.

Papers:

Some of Michael Nava's papers are housed in the Charles E. Young Research Library Department of Special Collections at the University of California, Los Angeles.

Sara Paretsky

(8 June 1947 –)

Peter Dempsey
University of Sunderland, U.K.

BOOKS: *Indemnity Only* (New York: Dial, 1982; London: Gollancz, 1982);

Deadlock (New York: Dial, 1984; London: Gollancz, 1984);

Killing Orders (New York: Morrow, 1985; London: Gollancz, 1986);

Bitter Medicine (New York: Morrow, 1987; London: Gollancz, 1987);

Blood Shot (New York: Delacorte, 1988); published as *Toxic Shock* (London: Gollancz, 1988);

Burn Marks (New York: Delacorte, 1990; London: Chatto & Windus, 1990);

Guardian Angel (New York: Delacorte, 1992; London: Hamilton, 1992);

Tunnel Vision (New York: Delacorte, 1994; London: Hamilton, 1994);

Windy City Blues (New York: Delacorte, 1995); published as *V. I. for Short* (London: Hamilton, 1995);

Ghost Country (New York: Delacorte, 1998; London: Hamilton, 1998);

Hard Time (New York: Delacorte, 1999; London: Hamilton, 1999);

Total Recall (New York: Delacorte, 2001; London: Hamilton, 2001);

Blacklist (New York: Putnam, 2003; London: Hamilton, 2003).

OTHER: *Beastly Tales: The Mystery Writers of America Anthology,* edited by Paretsky (New York: Wynwood, 1989);

A Woman's Eye, edited by Paretsky (New York: Delacorte, 1991; London: Virago, 1991);

Women on the Case: Twenty-Six Original Stories by the Best Women Crime Writers of Our Time, edited by Paretsky (New York: Delacorte, 1996; London: Virago, 1996).

Sara Paretsky (from Blacklist, *2003; Richland County Public Library)*

Sara Paretsky is one of the most critically and commercially successful of contemporary urban crime novelists. She is arguably the most prominent of a group of women crime writers who began publishing in the early 1980s and who both used and challenged the conventions of hard-boiled detective fiction by producing politically committed, feminist private investigators, women who were neither victims nor predators, the roles familiar from classic hard-boiled fiction. Paretsky's first novel, *Indemnity Only* (1982), like the laconically two-word-titled novels that followed it, adheres to the conventions of the hard-boiled crime story, but these conventions are largely undercut because the protagonist is a woman.

Since the publication of John Cawelti's pioneering *Adventure, Mystery and Romance: Formula Stories as Art and Popular Culture* (1976), critics have discussed the profoundly masculine worldview of the hard-boiled crime story, but Paretsky's fiction challenges this orthodoxy. Not only is her detective, V. I. (Victoria Iphigenia) Warshawski, a woman in a man's world, but also Paretsky herself is a woman writing in a genre dominated by men. On publication, *Indemnity Only* was seen as a reinvention of the hard-boiled genre from a liberal, feminist perspective, a self-conscious intervention into the field. Paretsky has written, "My work developed as a reaction to [Raymond] Chandler. I found myself wishing for a woman hero. I spent many years working on different ways in which a woman could play a stronger, less sexual role and finally, in 1979 came up with V. I. Warshawski."

All hard-boiled fiction deals with death; murder and its investigation form the driving force of most of the plots of mystery novels. While Paretsky's work certainly conforms to the hard-boiled genre in this respect, death also plays an important part in the psychic life of Warshawski. For a hard-boiled private investigator (P.I.), she is unusually concerned with forms of loss—of parents, individuality, and personal autonomy—as many commentators on her work have noted. Central to her world are concepts of personal responsibility and community, and her sympathy for the poor and oppressed is a hallmark of the series.

While firmly grounded in contemporary reality, Paretsky's fiction achieves a mythic and symbolic dimension rarely found in the genre. Throughout the series, she works carefully with the elemental images of fire and water. In three novels the plot turns on a death by fire, and in another four books Warshawski narrowly avoids drowning. The most significant image of water in the Chicago-set series is Lake Michigan. The lake becomes a powerful and ambiguous presence precisely because it is a place of rejuvenation where Warshawski seeks escape and where she exercises and swims in an attempt to regain a sense of selfhood and autonomy. At the same time, the lake conjures up fearful images of death by drowning. For Warshawski, the lake represents both the possibility of annihilation and the attraction of death, the surrender of responsibility. Paretsky develops the complex character of her detective and the dangerous world she explores through twelve increasingly subtle and well-wrought volumes.

Sara Paretsky was born into a comfortable middle-class family on 8 June 1947 in Ames, Iowa. Daughter of David Paretsky, a scientist, and Mary Edwards Paretsky, a librarian, Paretsky was a bright child who wrote her first story at age seven in a family environment in which, she said speaking to Stephanie Merritt in *The Observer*, 13 August 2000, "they didn't think it was really worth educating girls." In an interview with British crime critic John Williams for his book *Badlands*

(1990), Paretsky described the attitude in her hometown toward a woman who wanted to pursue a writing career: "As a woman your creativity should be confined to the making of cakes and babies." This world is the one from which both Paretsky and her creation Warshawski escape, and as a P. I. from an ethnic background, Warshawski encounters the attitude throughout the books that feature her. Paretsky attended a little two-room school in Kansas and went on to earn a B.A. degree from the University of Kansas in 1967. She then moved to Chicago, where she went to secretarial school. In 1971 she became publications manager for the Chicago-based Urban Research Corporation, and then in 1974, a freelance business writer. Paretsky married Courtney Wright, a professor at the University of Chicago, 19 June 1976, and in 1977 she earned an M.B.A. and a Ph.D. in history from the university. The couple have raised their three children—Kimball, Timothy, and Philip—in Chicago. From 1977 through 1986 Paretsky worked as a marketing manager for the insurance company Continental National America, giving up her work there to become a full-time writer after having published three novels.

Indemnity Only was the result of a New Year's Day resolution Paretsky made in 1979—to write a book "or die trying." In beginning and in developing her series, she worked with the knowledge she had gained of the business world. She differs from most hard-boiled writers in her focus on "white-collar" crime. Paretsky's detective seeks out, as Ralph Willett says in *The Naked City* (1997), "white-collar criminals, not only financial crooks but also those who prey on the marginalized, needy, and elderly." In an interview Paretsky explained her concern with this sort of crime: "A shooting is a tragedy, but it doesn't affect thousands of people. Fraud can." Her books have given her the chance "to nail the bad guys who ordinarily get away with it in the courts."

The character who "nails the bad guys" is V. I. Warshawski—called by the androgynous names "Vic" or "V. I." by her friends, never the obviously female "Vicky." Daughter of a Polish policeman father and Italian former singer mother, she was brought up in Hegewisch, a working-class district on the south side of Chicago. Though both parents are dead before the first novel opens, theirs is a continuing presence throughout Paretsky's fiction, and V. I. measures herself against their hopes and fears for her. Her mother, Gabriella—whose olive skin and love of music V. I. has inherited—encouraged her daughter to seek a career. In *Indemnity Only,* she imagines her mother's voice saying "Yes, Vic, you are pretty—but pretty is no good. Any girl can be pretty—but to take care of yourself you must have brains. And you must have a job, a profession. You must work."

Dust jacket for Paretsky's 1990 novel, in which Chicago private detective V. I. Warshawski investigates the destruction by fire of a hotel owned by her aunt (Richland County Public Library)

Vic studied law at the University of Chicago and with high hopes afterward went to work at the public defender's office. She became a P. I. because of her unhappiness there, a decision she explains in the first novel: "I got disillusioned with working for the Public Defender–the setup is pretty corrupt–you are never arguing for justice, always on points of law. I wanted to get out of it, but still wanted to do something that would make me feel that I was working on my concept of justice." This speech is repeated and refined in most of the novels that follow *Indemnity Only*. In the second novel, *Deadlock* (1984), Warshawski says that she "got tired of sending poor innocent chumps off to Stateville because the police wouldn't follow up our investigations and find the real culprits. And I got even more tired of watching clever guilty rascals get off scot-free because they could afford attorneys who know how to tap-dance around the law." In the third novel in the series, *Killing Orders* (1985), she says that "you'd leave

court every day feeling that you've just helped worsen the situation."

Although an orphan, an only child, and a divorcée, Warshawski builds a network of friends and colleagues around her that function as "a surrogate family," an alternative community of her own choosing that provides her with emotional and intellectual support. In an important sense, the novels are the story of the growth and development of this community and the toll V. I.'s dangerous occupation takes upon it. Throughout the series, Paretsky is concerned with the public and the private, with the community and the individual's responsibility within it.

Indemnity Only begins with Warshawski's arrival one hot July evening at her modest office in an unfashionable part of the Chicago Loop, where she is met by a man who says he is John L. Thayer, a leading Chicago banker. (He is actually union official Andrew McGraw, the father of the girl he asks V. I. to find.) "Thayer" picked V. I.'s name from the phone book, presuming she would be a man. He asks if V. I. has a partner and asserts that "this really isn't a job for a girl to take on . . . things may get heavy." V. I. says that she is "a woman" and can look after herself. In this opening conversation of the novel, V. I. experiences the first of many encounters with patriarchal attitudes. "Thayer," desperate to employ someone not familiar to his business associates on La Salle Street, gives V. I. the job of finding Anita Hill, whom he identifies as the girlfriend of his son, Peter Thayer. The classically episodic hard-boiled plot of the novel allows the reader to see the world from V. I.'s perspective, that of a woman whose politics were shaped by the student demonstrations and civil rights movements of the 1960s, and to see how those values operate in the much-changed world of the early 1980s. This theme is developed in later novels, especially in *Hard Time* (1999).

Warshawski's investigation into the disappearance of Hill (actually McGraw), an idealistic young student at the University of Chicago, leads to the discovery of the murdered body of Peter Thayer and ultimately to the disclosure of white-collar crime. After finding the body, V. I. reports the murder to the police anonymously. Homicide Lieutenant Bobby Mallory, a close friend of V. I.'s late father, suspects the report came from her and warns her off the case: "Being a detective is not a job for a girl like you, Vicki–it's not fun and games." Throughout the series, Warshawski receives similar advice from male friends and foes alike. As Ralph Willett notes, most male characters "are unable to reconcile her profession and life style with their simplistic categories of female sexuality."

Mallory's prediction that V. I. is antagonizing "organized crime, organized labor, a whole lot of organizations that you shouldn't mess with" proves true. V. I. is attacked by two heavies on the stairs of her apartment. In the episode V. I. shows herself to be a physically skillful fighter, but she is finally beaten and taken to Earl Smeisson, a notorious Chicago mobster, who tells her to "lay off the Thayer case." Later her apartment is wrecked in the search for an incriminating document. A visit to Peter Thayer's father introduces his fourteen-year-old daughter, Jill, one of many lonely, neglected children of the rich and powerful, who are at odds with their parents' values and who appear regularly in Paretsky's novels. Devoted to her brother, Peter, Jill wants to know who killed him. Taken off the search for Anita by her client, McGraw, Warshawski accepts a $1 fee from Jill to solve the murders of her brother and father, who also turns up dead. Attempts to bribe or threaten V. I. to forgo an investigation only make her more determined to solve it. "You can fire me," she tells McGraw, "but you can't get rid of me." Like Chandler's P. I. Philip Marlowe, V. I. cannot be intimidated or bought off.

Warshawski takes Jill to stay with her good friend Doctor Lotty Herschel, a kind of surrogate mother figure whom V. I. worked with as a student when the doctor performed abortions through an underground referral service before abortion was legalized. Toward the end of the novel, Lotty says, "Vic, be careful: you have no mother, but you are a daughter of my spirit." The tension between Lotty's concerns over her friend's life-threatening work and V. I.'s need to live independently become important in later novels. In all subsequent novels but one, Warshawski takes cases because they involve a member of her "extended family," from an old aunt in *Killing Orders* to an old friend who works with Lotty at her clinic in *Hard Time*. While Jill Thayer is not a relation, V. I. sees her in that way: "Something about her pierced my heart, made me long for the child I'd never had."

The majority of V. I.'s extended-family relationships are with women. Briefly married to Richard Yarborough, a fellow law student, now a partner at one of the leading law firms in Chicago, V. I. in *Indemnity Only* explains to insurance man and love interest Ralph Devereux that "my first marriage fell apart because I'm too independent. . . . I have some close women friends because I don't feel that they are trying to take over my turf. But with men, it always seems, or often seems, as though I'm having to maintain who I am." Devereux is the first of many men who want to get close to Warshawski but who break off with her because they cannot cope with her independence or fear for her life and wish to protect her, something she cannot allow and

maintain her personal and professional integrity. Ralph says, "I've been falling in love with you, Vic, but you don't need me." Earlier she had told him, "I'm a good detective . . . it's not a job that's easy to combine with marriage," a speech that echoes the sentiments of a long line of male P. I.s. V. I. does occasionally long for protection, but for her the cost in personal terms would be too great. She sometimes wishes she was doing "the middle-class family thing. But that's a myth, you know. . . . I know I'm longing for a myth, not the reality."

When Warshawski returns to the University of Chicago to attend a women's group meeting as part of her search for Anita, the episode allows Paretsky to present the variety of political positions the women hold regarding their oppression. The group debates issues arising out of the exclusion of women from positions of power in both the business world and the organized labor movement and considers whether they should adopt a reformist or revolutionary stance on women's liberation: "do you concentrate on equal pay and equal rights, or do you go off and try to convert the whole of society to a new set of sexual values?" V. I. has a sympathetic but wry attitude toward the debate and clearly criticizes the radicals at the meeting, seeing them as paranoid. Accused of being a cop, a stooge of the forces of oppression, she makes a speech in which she sees her status as a self-employed woman as central to her political integrity and fundamentally different from that of a paid officer of the state: "It makes an enormous difference. I'm the only person I take orders from, not a hierarchy of officers, aldermen, and commissioners." As she leaves the meeting, she gives out her calling card in the hope that someone's concern over the fate of a female colleague will triumph over their suspicion of her.

Indemnity Only ends with the telling of the myth of King Midas, an exemplary tale for those in the story who, as Andrew McGraw says of himself, "only saw the money." While Warshawski remembers that the gods restored King Midas's daughter to him as a result of his repentance, Paretsky leaves the conclusion of her novel more open, with the reconciliation of the McGraws uncertain. References to myth are found throughout Paretsky's work, and a fruitful tension exists between the realism of the setting and the mythic and symbolic resonances in the psychic life of Paretsky's heroine.

What is remarkable about Paretsky's first book is that it establishes plot elements and patterns that are repeated with variations in her subsequent work. The action of the Warshawski novels is instigated by a friend or family member. Despite being warned off the case, V. I. continues with the investigation. When she endures a beating, her doctor friend Lotty patches her up, but such occurrences increase the tension between the two and between V. I. and other friends. Her cases also complicate her relationship with a current lover, who departs at the conclusion. Each investigation of corporate crime reveals a little more about V. I.'s past and the ghosts that haunt her and shape her notions of social justice and personal responsibility. Paretsky is able to enrich and deepen her detective's relationship with her friends, colleagues, various public institutions such as the police, and with her own past, while all the time developing her political analysis and making it more complex and subtle.

Paretsky's first novel received favorable reviews. *Publishers Weekly* called *Indemnity Only* "the start of a very promising new mystery series," while *Chicago Magazine* compared Paretsky's integration of character and environment to past masters of the genre Dashiell Hammett and Chandler. In the 3 March 1982 issue of *The New Republic,* crime-fiction critic Robin W. Winks described the novel as "thoroughly convincing."

The background for Paretsky's second novel, *Deadlock,* is Great Lakes shipping, another industry run by men. The novel was praised by a wide variety of specialist and general publications, including *TLS: The Times Literary Supplement,* the *New York Daily News,* the *Times* (London), and *Publishers Weekly,* which called it a "top-notch mystery." *Deadlock,* which began to solidify Paretsky's reputation as an author of tough, carefully researched, and exciting mystery thrillers, eventually won an award from the Friends of American Writers in 1985.

In *Deadlock,* Warshawski decides to investigate the suspicious death of her cousin, former hockey star Bernard "Boom Boom" Warshawski, who fell (or was pushed) into a ship propeller while working on the Chicago waterfront. Warshawski's friend Herschel suggests that to be totally sure about Boom Boom, V. I. could try investigating what happened. Her investigations at the Eudora Grain Company lead Warshawski to believe that Boom Boom was killed because of information he uncovered about grain shipments on the Great Lakes. As she investigates, she boards a giant $80,000,000-dollar grain carrier as it passes through the Soo locks, where sabotage causes the deadlock of the title. The descriptions of the grain elevators are breathtaking and, according to *The Chicago Sun-Times,* "rival Hitchcock's effects in *Vertigo.*" V. I. finally discovers that the mystery of Boom Boom's death is connected to the rivalry between two heads of shipping companies. The novel ends with the destruction by fire on water of the villain of the piece.

Many critics, most notably Guy Szuberla and Thomas S. Gladsky, have pointed out Warshawski's complex relationship to her ethnic background. War-

shawski is proud of her Polish Catholic and Italian Jewish provenance; yet, at Boom Boom's wake after his funeral, she is, in Szuberla's words, "reeling with a sense of suffocation among her aunts, uncles, and relatives from South Chicago." Her hostility to their conservative religiosity and narrow moral outlook is evident in every line. V. I. describes them dismissively as "Boom Boom's moist, indistinguishable aunts and cousins." Her most pressing need is to escape from the South Side, as in a sense she already has done, by getting a law degree and becoming a professional, independent woman.

A sense of grudging obligation usually motivates V. I.'s dealings with her blood relatives, but Boom Boom was something more to her. As she says, "With his death, I'd lost my whole family." Boom Boom , like Peter Thayer in *Indemnity Only,* was an intelligent and idealistic young man who died because he discovered wrongdoing and trusted the respected person to whom he revealed the information.

Midway through the novel when the case is going badly, V. I. describes how the ship walls "started to close in on me." Feeling desolate, she takes herself to Lake Michigan. She describes how "the water slapping at my feet seemed to call me to itself . . . think of infinite rest, no responsibilities, no need for control. Just perfect rest." Toward the end of the novel, V. I. responds much differently to the lake. Although she recalls, "I have always had a fear of death by drowning more than any other end," to escape being killed on board a yacht, she must jump overboard into the freezing water of Lake Michigan. Watching from the water, Warshawski sees the yacht explode. V. I. is pulled from the water "babbling of gods and dragon ships."

In Paretsky's third novel, *Killing Orders,* V. I. is called in by her great-aunt Rosa, who has been fired from her job as treasurer in a Dominican priory, where she is under suspicion of complicity in stock forgeries worth $5,000,000. Rosa and Warshawski hate each other, but V. I.'s mother, on her deathbed, had forced V. I. to make a promise about her aunt. Finding out where the forgeries came from and why they were made brings V. I. into contact with her most formidable opponents—a Catholic secret society, an important Chicago mobster, and the Catholic Church itself, as represented by the Vatican's director of financial affairs, Xavier O'Faolin. In the course of her investigation, Warshawski uncovers links between big business, organized crime, and the Church. Fire is the dominant element in this novel. Warshawski and her lover narrowly escape from her apartment when it is set ablaze. In the climax, the real villain is consumed by fire when his car is blown up by a bomb.

Paretsky tackles head-on the relationship of the Church and politics. Near the beginning of the novel, Warshawski goes to the priory to investigate the disappearance of the stock certificates and gets into a debate on the Church and politics. V. I. says,

> We could talk about the politics of abortion, for example. How local pastors try to influence their congregations to vote for anti-choice candidates regardless of how terrible their qualifications may be otherwise . . . we're never going to agree on whether abortion is a moral issue or a private matter . . . but one thing is clear—it is a highly political issue. . . . Now the tax code spells out pretty specifically how clear of politics you have to stay to keep your tax-exempt status.

She goes on to say that "So far no tax-court judge has been willing to take on the Catholic Church—which in itself argues some hefty clout." A monk explains that "two of our priests were shot in El Salvador last Spring; the government suspected that they were harboring rebels." V. I. stays silent, but thinks that whether the Church is working for the poor or not, "it was still, in my book, up to its neck in politics." Warshawski's attitude toward individual priests can be distinguished from her criticisms of the Catholic Church as an institution.

V. I.'s investigation draws in not just family, but old friends, with dreadful consequences, as V. I. uses private relationships to ferret out information in the public world. Lotty's engraver uncle, whom Warshawski asks for help, is stabbed and nearly dies. Stockbroker Agnes Paciorek, an old university friend of V. I.'s from a wealthy Catholic family, is murdered while looking into the finances of a shady company for V. I. This death has emblematic qualities. Vic and Agnes go back "to the Golden Age of the sixties, when we thought love and energy would end racism and sexism."

In a key scene in the novel, Warshawski is interviewed by Lieutenant Bobby Mallory about Agnes's death. An old-fashioned man, Mallory has accepted Agnes's mother's belief that Vic and Agnes had a lesbian relationship. Mallory is disgusted by the idea. V. I. is incensed, torn between denial of the lie, and the rejection of the idea of lesbianism as perversion. The scene allows Paretsky the chance to delineate different strands of feminist politics and to deliver the clearest statement yet on Warshawski's analysis of the fate of the post-1960s women's movement. More importantly, through Mallory's private and sincerely held (though not carefully thought out) beliefs on gay relationships, Paretsky is able to show the way Catholic, conservative values have public and political consequences. The way sexism constricts the lives and opportunities for women

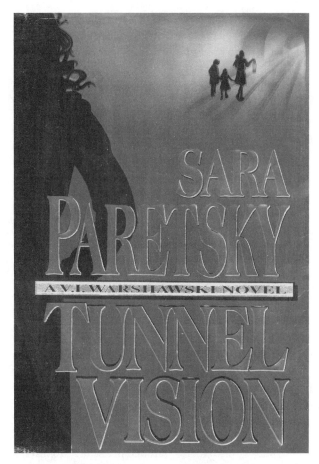

Dust jacket for Paretsky's 1994 novel, in which Warshawski's investigations lead her into a network of tunnels underneath Chicago (Richland County Public Library)

gives Warshawski her only pang of sympathy for her despised aunt Rosa and Agnes's bigoted mother. Both women had enormous energy, which because of the stereotypical roles available to them, remained largely unused.

Warshawski describes to Mallory how the dreams of the 1960s began to fall apart: "We had Watergate and drugs and the deteriorating economy, and racism and sexual discrimination continued despite our enthusiasm. So we all settled down to deal with reality and earn a living. You know my story. I guess my ideals died the hardest. It's often that way with the children of immigrants. We need to buy the dream so bad we sometimes can't wake up." She says that the older she gets "the less politics means to me. The only thing that seems to matter is friendship." As she says later, "we all have to listen to the voice within us, and how easily you can look at yourself in the mirror depends on whether you obey that voice or not." V. I. has that opportunity soon after when she is warned off the case by mobster Don Pasquale. Continuing the case also means surrendering her lover, Roger, who wants her to give up the case because of its risks. "No one protects me, Roger. I don't live in that kind of universe," she replies.

Warshawski finally gets to the bottom of the conspiracy behind the forged stock certificates and ends the corruption that involved the Church, business, and organized crime. But as Richard E. Goodkin notes in his 1989 essay for *Yale French Studies,* the novel places just as much emphasis on the personal and private ramifications of the inquiry. By the end of the novel, certain debts are paid, though in an unconventional fashion. Don Pasquale sends V. I. $25,000, which allows her to buy a new apartment on Racine Avenue. Aunt Rosa reveals the reason for her hatred of V. I.'s mother. Agnes's mother commits suicide because of guilt she feels over her unwitting part in her daughter's death. Lotty seeks a reconciliation with V. I. As in the two previous novels, *Killing Orders* ends with reference to a myth. V. I. tells Lotty her middle name is Iphigenia, the same as the daughter Agamemnon sacrificed for a fair wind to sail for Troy. V. I. feels her mother, by making her give the promise of help to Rosa, made her a victim of the past, as critic Katy Emck says, of "having become the sacrificing mother's own sacrifice." Lotty dispels the thought by telling V. I. that "in Greek legend Iphigenia is also Artemis the huntress."

Killing Orders met with much praise on publication. *The New York Times Book Review* (15 September 1985) admired the way Paretsky wrote about church corruption, suggesting that she "seems willing to take on any institution, no matter how sacred." Paretsky was interviewed on the front page of *The New York Times Review of Books,* coverage that indicated her arrival as one of the most significant contemporary crime writers in the United States. Feminist writer Joan Smith in *New Statesman* argued that the novel "is not only a joy to read; it restores politics to its rightful place in the mainstream private eye novel."

One of Paretsky's most overtly political novels, *Bitter Medicine* (1987) begins with Warshawski giving her pregnant friend Consuelo and her sullen young husband, Fabiano Hernandez, a lift to a job interview that has been arranged for him. The young woman goes into premature labor, and V. I. takes her to a nearby for-profit hospital, Friendship Five. Malcolm Tregiere, Lotty Herschel's associate, arrives to help in the treatment, but to no avail. When both Consuelo and her baby die, the deaths seem like an unavoidable tragedy. Later, when Tregiere is found brutally murdered in his apartment, apparently the victim of a gang-related robbery-homicide, Lotty asks, "Vic, do me a favor: look into it." Warshawski, who doubts that she has any better chance of solving the crime than the

police, is reluctant to get involved: "Lotty, this is like–like trying to cure a cholera epidemic." Lotty counters, "maybe you can't solve the crime, maybe the epidemic of gang violence is too big for anyone, even the state, to solve. But I am asking you, friend to friend, for a friend." With friendship at the center of her political beliefs, V. I. cannot refuse.

Warshawski also becomes interested in the circumstances of Consuelo's death. Consuelo's sister Carol says to V. I., "You are almost family," and V. I. dreams of the stillborn infant, which, as Sally Munt in *Murder by the Book?* (1994) argues, "haunts her subconscious as her own baby." Warshawski finds that the small-time hood who was the father of Consuelo's baby has been bought off and something about the deaths of the mother and child is being covered up.

While V. I. is investigating Dr. Tregiere's death, Lotty's Damen Avenue storefront clinic is the focal point of an antiabortionist protest. As the demonstration mounts during the day, Lotty and her colleagues, including V. I., are called Nazis and murderers. For Lotty, who escaped from the Nazis in prewar Vienna, the experience recalls troubling memories: "I'm telling you Vic–I'm scared. . . . I watched them burn our house to the ground. Never did I expect to feel that same fear in America." Lotty's receptionist says, "I raised six children . . . some of these women who come in–they're no more than little girls themselves. No one to help them feed themselves, let alone a child. And now I'm a murderer?" When the television cameras turn up in time to see the clinic go up in smoke, V. I. tells the journalists, "This is where poor women and children come to be treated for nominal fees by one of Chicago's top physicians. Make sure your viewers see that these righteous people have destroyed a major source of health care for Chicago's poor." As it turns out, the clinic was destroyed to cover for men working for Friendship Hospital who were trying to steal Dr. Tregiere's notes, the key to the mystery. V. I, searching on her own, breaks into the offices of the antiabortionists, eventually discovering the evidence that links Consuela's death and the destruction of Lotty's clinic.

During the course of her involvement in Consuela's tragedy, V. I. begins a relationship with Peter Burgoyne, the ambitious and talented doctor at Friendship who treated Consuela and her baby. V. I. eventually discovers that he is criminally implicated in their deaths. After she exposes him, she learns that he had been instructed by the director of the hospital to stay close to her. Wracked with guilt over the deaths for which he feels responsible, Burgoyne commits suicide in front of V. I. and the police. Warshawski berates herself for her poor judgment in men, but takes in Burgoyne's golden retriever, Peppy. V. I. and Mr.

Contreras, V. I.'s new neighbor, form a bond by sharing the dog between them. At the end of the novel, V. I.'s surrogate family has been extended by two.

The Toronto Globe and Mail called *Bitter Medicine* "a finely crafted and immensely readable book," while in the United Kingdom the *Daily Telegraph* called it "an exciting and thought-provoking thriller." *Time Out* described Paretsky as "bringing new sensibilities and insights to the genre . . . assured, gripping, and convincing."

In *Blood Shot* (1988)—published as *Toxic Shock* in the United Kingdom, where the British Crime Writers Association awarded it a Silver Dagger—Warshawski returns to her roots in South Chicago when childhood friend Caroline Djiak asks her to search for the father she has never known and whose identity her mother refuses to reveal. The investigation leads to the Xerxes chemical plant, "the malign center which Warshawski must expose," where Caroline's invalid mother, Louisa, had worked before falling ill. A generation before, V. I.'s mother had taken in Louisa when she had been thrown out of her own home for being pregnant with Caroline.

At the Xerxes plant, V. I.'s questions about Caroline's paternity meet with the kind of silence that leaves the detective in no doubt that something much more serious is being concealed. As in her previous novels, Warshawski soon reaches the point at which the only way she can stay alive is to bring the secret into the light. Once again, the obligations of the past involve V. I. in a personal quest that has important public consequences. V. I. is also again asked to abandon the case when the body of another old friend, Nancy Cleghorn, turns up in a polluted Dead Stick Pond. "Who are you working for?" an attorney asks her. "Myself. Myself, myself, it is enough, or so Medea said," she replies. Eventually, the reasons for Louisa's illness become clear to V. I., and she finds Caroline's father, quite the nastiest public official Paretsky has created.

One of the most terrifying scenes in Paretsky's fiction occurs after V. I. first begins stirring up trouble both in her old neighborhood and at the chemical plant. As she is taking Peppy for a walk by Lake Michigan, she is abducted, tied up, and dumped where her murdered friend's body was found, the marshland of the chemically toxic Dead Stick Pond: "Alone in this dark cocoon, I was going to drown, black swamp water in my lungs, my heart, my brain. The blood roared in my head and I cried tears of utter helplessness." She is rescued by her protective neighbor, Mr. Contreras, who was alerted to her absence when the dog returned without her. The episode makes V. I. ask herself if she is a fearless champion of truth, or, as Lotty says, "in love with danger and death."

Blood Shot is about the poisonous effects of the past, and for Louisa in particular, they are both chemical and familial. After Caroline decides to leave Chicago to study forestry in Montana, she tells V. I., ". . . I wanted to tell you in person, and I hope you meant it, that you'll always be my sister, because, well, anyway, I hope you meant it." Munt in *Murder by the Book?* observes that *Blood Shot* exhibits Warshawski's concepts of the good and the bad family. The bad one is the biological one, exemplified in Louisa's abusive and suffocating childhood. The good family is a chosen one, exemplified by V. I.'s mother's "adoption" of the abandoned and pregnant Louisa and V. I.'s "sisterhood" with Caroline.

Blood Shot was published to excellent reviews. Paul Johnson in *The Chicago Tribune* (29 September 1988) described Warshawski as "one of the finest, if not the finest, of the female first-person shamuses," while Marilyn Stasio in *The New York Times Book Review* (9 October 1988) called Paretsky's novel "her best and boldest work to date in creating a criminal investigation that is a genuine heroic quest." *Newsweek* called it "her best book yet" (26 September 1988). From *Blood Shot* onward, Paretsky's novels have become more complex and ambitious.

In *Burn Marks* (1990), a novel about the intersection of crime and city politics, Warshawski's aunt Elena's SRO (single-room occupancy) hotel burns down, and the hard-drinking and importunate old woman turns up on V. I.'s doorstep. The insurance firm hires V. I. to investigate the fire at Elena's hotel as suspicious. Elena then disappears, and her young friend is found dead. In the course of her investigation V. I. is pursued by the police, crooked developers, and politicians on the take. Subplots include Warshawski's tense romantic relationship with a policeman, Michael Furey, the son of an old friend of Bobby Mallory, the beginnings of the "yuppification" of Warshawski's apartment block, and trouble with some young neighbors. Once again Paretsky is able to combine an action-filled plot touching on important social issues with thoughtful material on the clash between family loyalty and trust and more-general concepts of social justice.

A new note enters Paretsky's fiction in *Burn Marks* as Warshawski begins to notice signs of aging, and the decay of the body becomes a theme in this and subsequent novels. At thirty-seven, V. I. wonders "if I was doomed for an old age of crabby isolation." With little time to worry about it, she throws herself back into the arson case. Called for help by Aunt Elena, she goes to meet her and is knocked out. She wakes up to find herself and her aunt in a burning building. Through tremendous effort, they escape, though injured. V. I. is attended in the hospital by Lotty. While such a scene is

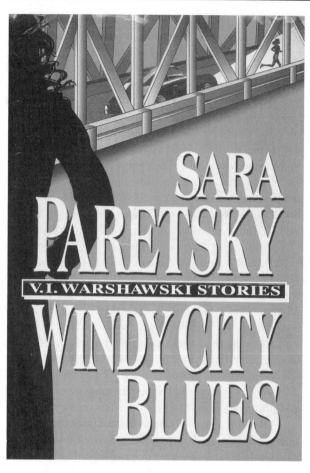

*Dust jacket for Paretsky's 1995 collection of short stories
(Richland County Public Library)*

familiar to Paretsky's readers, Lotty on this occasion warns V. I. of the physical toll her profession is taking on her: "This is the third time you've been hit hard enough to knock you out. I don't wish to spend my old age treating you for Parkinson's or Alzheimer's—which is exactly where you're heading with your reckless attitude."

The novel ends with V. I. reluctantly accepting Eileen Mallory's invitation to her husband's sixtieth birthday party. Angered by his own misjudgment of Furey, to whom he had tried to be a mentor, Bobby Mallory had earlier verbally abused V. I. At the party Bobby apologizes and agrees to accept V. I. the way she is: "you're the daughter of the two people I loved best, next to Eileen, and you can't do things different than you do, shouldn't do them different, not with Gabriella and Tony bringing you up." V. I. then presents him with a small package that she had brought "just in case I felt like giving you a present." Bobby is then moved to tears when he finds Tony Warshawski's shield in the little box. Paretsky has not only developed V. I.'s char-

acter but also has developed an understanding of her in others, notably Bobby.

Burn Marks was generally seen to be yet another advance in Paretsky's career, another well-researched and well-constructed story that deepened the development of her P.I. The *Atlanta Journal-Constitution* is representative in its comment that Paretsky "just keeps getting better," while reviewers in the *The Sunday Times* in the United Kingdom claimed that "Warshawski . . . bristling with feminist wit has transformed a genre sinking under its own clichés," while the daily London *Times* suggested that "feisty private eye Vic Warshawski grows more interesting, quirky, and admirable with every story."

The structure of *Guardian Angel* (1992) is contrapuntal, as Paretsky traces two major stories that are brought together at the conclusion. The first deals with Warshawski's attempts to look after the interests of Hattie Frizell, an old woman whose refusal to tidy her garden and keep her five dogs leashed raises the ire of a young lawyer, Todd Pichea, and his wife, Chrissie, who have recently moved into V. I.'s Racine Avenue neighborhood—so much so that when the old woman is unexpectedly taken to hospital, they manage to get themselves made her legal guardians and have her dogs destroyed. V. I. suspects that there is more to their interest in the guardianship than the dogs, and eventually she is proved right. The second thread involves V. I.'s investigation of the murder of Mitch Kruger, Mr. Contreras's oldest friend. He had claimed to have some information about the steel manufacturing company that employed both him and Mr. Contreras, and V. I. discovers that Kruger's death is linked to this information. Warshawski's dealings with her friends and neighbors lead into a larger tale of skulduggery involving an industrial family, fraudulent union officials, and an important bank.

Over the years, Paretsky's novels have charted the changes in the Chicago skyline—the mocking of Helmut Jahn's architecture is a minor theme—and the growing economic success of a group of young, middle-class Chicagoans. *Guardian Angel* deals directly with this phenomenon by addressing the yuppification of Warshawski's previously "quiet, blue-collar" district. "Rehab mania," as V. I. calls it, "had hit. While house prices trebled the traffic had quadrupled." The concomitant hike in property taxes is something Warshawski and Mr. Contreras can ill afford. Paretsky's novel also examines the value system of these successful young professionals and offers a glum critique of their superficial obsession with style and status as well as their individualistic materialism.

In *Guardian Angel,* V. I.'s investigations put her friends in serious danger, especially Lotty, who is badly beaten after being mistaken for the detective. When V. I. is reluctant to spend the night alone and asks to stay at Lotty's, she replies, "I wish I could help you put your pieces back together again, but I'm in too many pieces myself to help you." In the last pages of the novel, the two friends have not reconciled. V. I. understands that Lotty's "injuries, or her fear, had given her a repugnance to my work." V. I. confesses to her policeman lover that she dreads Lotty leaving her: "I'm so scared—scared she's going to leave me the way my mother did. It didn't matter that I loved my mother, that I did what I could to look after her. She left me anyway. I don't think I can bear it if Lotty abandons me too." As the novel concludes on a bleak note, the reader is left to consider at what cost V. I.'s autonomy is bought. The dark themes of the novel, touching on love, loss, and aging, give it an even greater emotional range and depth than Paretsky's previous work.

While some critics attacked the complexity of the plot, *Guardian Angel* garnered favorable reviews in *The New York Times Book Review* and *The Chicago Tribune*. *The San Francisco Chronicle* described the V. I. of *Guardian Angel* as "refreshingly introspective, and uncharacteristically vulnerable," while Christopher Lehmann-Haupt in *The New York Times* praised Warshawski's "extreme sensitivity to injustice" in "the richest and most engaging yet of Ms. Paretsky's thrillers" (31 March 1992).

Paretsky's next novel, *Tunnel Vision* (1994), a mystery story on an epic scale, takes the flooding of the Chicago tunnels in 1992 as its starting point. The dangerous maze of underground tunnels operates as a powerful metaphor for the sinister workings of the various plots against V. I.'s life, an index of the life-threatening, complex world in which she works. V. I. encounters a homeless mother and children in the basement of her office building. They soon disappear into the tunnels under V. I.'s building. One of the board members is found dead in V. I.'s office, and the detective becomes the chief suspect. V. I. turns up a financial scandal involving industry and banking and a chilling case of child abuse, not among the poor, but in one of the most respected Chicago families. Two dramatic set pieces are the action highlights of the story; one involves fire (a gunfight and a huge explosion at an airfield); the other, water (a breathtaking escape from the flooding tunnels). But at the heart of the tale is another vulnerable, bright teenager who turns to Warshawski for help. Emily Messenger's story is more shocking than the financial skulduggery V. I. unearths.

The novel is given an extra dimension of realism through Paretsky's exploration of V. I.'s isolation and aging. Lotty is still cool toward V. I.: "I worry, Vic, when you intervene in other people's lives. Someone usually suffers." V. I. explains, "Her anger and my remorse cut a channel between us that we rebridged only after months of hard work. Every now and then it gapes open again." V. I. is approaching forty and observes that "a circle of small broken veins near my left kneecap was an early sign of age"; a friend points out the flecks of white that are beginning to appear in V. I.'s hair. More seriously, Mr. Contreras worries about the lack of stability in her life: "living by yourself without any proper furniture? What's your life going to be like when you're my age?" Her investigation drives her and her lover Conrad apart because V. I. is forced to choose between him and protecting Emily: "To dig a channel between us would be like cutting off a piece of my heart. But to abandon Emily to salvage my life with Conrad would mean cutting off a piece of my soul."

Eventually, V. I. manages to link together two groups of the suffering—the children of a poor abused woman and the children of a rich abusive father—and brings some comfort and stability into the lives of both. The case is successfully concluded, but at great personal cost. In the final chapter, however, at V. I.'s moment of greatest isolation, she returns to her apartment to a surprise birthday party with all her friends, including Lotty. Like the end of a Shakespeare comedy, evil is expelled; all the players return to the stage; and isolation vanishes, at least for the moment. V. I. muses, "What else can I say except that good friends are a balm to the bruised spirit?"

Reviewers of *Tunnel Vision* responded to its ambition; it was probably the most highly regarded of Paretsky's novels until *Total Recall* (2001). *Booklist*, *The St. Louis Post-Dispatch*, *The Rocky Mountain News*, and many other papers saw it as Paretsky's best work to date. Lehmann-Haupt of *The New York Times* (12 June 1994) found much to admire in *Tunnel Vision*, especially Warshawski herself, but criticized its political stereotyping—Paretsky's representing the poor and other marginalized groups as good and the rich and powerful as evil. Reviews in the United Kingdom were positive, *The Sunday Telegraph* claiming that "Paretsky is a great story-teller."

After the lengthy *Tunnel Vision*, Paretsky rested V. I. for her next novel, the remarkable *Ghost Country* (1998), in which the author continued her examination of the lives thrown aside in the quest for material success, but in a literary style beyond the reaches of the predominantly realist detective novel. *Windy City Blues* (1995) is a collection of short stories originally published between 1983 and 1992. They are all traditional puzzle stories, and though they are successful at that level, they lack the quality most readers enjoy in the novels, the development of the character of V. I. through her relationships with her friends. The exception is "Grace Notes," a moving story involving family

Dust jacket for Paretsky's 1999 novel, in which Warshawski goes inside a women's prison to solve a murder related to a media tycoon (Richland County Public Library)

honor and trust that was written especially for the collection.

Paretsky returned to a novel-length treatment of V. I. Warshawski in *Hard Time,* a book that examines the increasing power of the media moguls who dominate the information and entertainment industries by buying up television stations, movie companies, and newspapers. After V. I. finds an escapee from a women's prison dying in the road after a hit-and-run accident, her investigations link the owner of the women's prison and a media tycoon. To discover the truth about the woman's death, V. I. spends a month in Coolis prison, and the harrowing chapters set there are central to the power of the novel. The women's prison run by men is an emblem of the worst possible relations between the sexes, an exploitative, patriarchal dystopia that contains a disproportionate percentage of poor immigrants. Paretsky's portraits of the wives of powerful men and women executives who work for the media mogul and the prison boss, ambitious and complicit in the exploitation of other women, are withering. The

novel also features some particularly vicious and corrupt policemen and another neglected child of rich parents, Robbie Baladine, who helps V. I. crack the case. The conclusion, like that of *Killing Orders,* is set in a Catholic church, but in this work, the Church, in the person of benevolent and virtuous Father Lou, is a force for good. He looks after Robbie and gives him some much-needed self-respect by coaching him in boxing.

At forty-four, V. I. continues to age and find the routines of breaking and entering and enduring beatings more difficult to take. Patching her up once again, Lotty remarks, "You are foolhardy, which in case you didn't know, means to be daring without judgment." With a flash of insight that illuminates Warshawski's behavior in many of the previous books, Lotty asks V. I., "how old was your mother when she died?" V. I. confirms that her mother was forty-four. Lotty suggests that V. I. is unconsciously guilty both for living while her mother died and for having the opportunity to live longer than her. V. I.'s death wish, as Lotty sees it, is intimately linked to her mother's life and death. Paretsky's detective is a complex enough creation to have inspired many critical articles dealing with Warshawski's feminism and her ethnicity as well as the relationship of her works to the hard-boiled tradition.

Compared to *Tunnel Vision, Hard Time* brought a generally more muted response from the critics. Plenty of warm praise for the book came from *The Los Angeles Times* ("Returns in great form") and *The Chicago Tribune* ("Paretsky has no peer"), particularly for the realism and sympathy of the portrayal of the female inmates in the terrifying section in which Warshawski is in prison for a month. Paretsky, while denied access to a women's prison, interviewed former prisoners and lawyers as part of her research for the novel and was appalled at what she found. In an interview published in *The London Observer* on 13 August 2000, she said, "The average age of a woman in an American prison is 20, 60% are illiterate and 80% are black or Hispanic. There is a tremendous amount of sexual assault." With the publication of the ambitious *Total Recall,* many critics suggested that *Hard Time* was a novel that trod water in terms of the development of the Warshawski series. Maxim Jakubowski, in *The London Guardian* of 1 December 2001, for example, described *Total Recall* as "a return to form."

Early in *Total Recall,* Warshawski is hired by Isaiah Sommers, the nephew of a recently deceased black factory worker, Aaron Sommers, who had a fully paid-up life insurance policy. However, when Aaron's widow, Gertrude, attempts to collect on the policy to pay for her husband's funeral, she is told by the Midway Insurance Company that the policy had been cashed a decade earlier. Midway is owned by Ajax Life Insurance Company, where Ralph Devereux (V. I.'s lover in her first novel, *Indemnity Only*) is now Head of Claims. V. I.'s investigations trace an insurance fraud involving the new owners of Ajax, the Swiss company Edelweiss, back to Nazi occupied Europe, where the other major narrative thread of the novel originates. This story begins in contemporary Chicago. V. I.'s friend, hospital administrator Max Loewenthal, is a guest at a conference that has set up a dialogue between Christians and Jews. Max is to speak about his efforts in Europe in 1947 to track down his and his friends' relatives, most of whom, he discovered, died in the concentration camps, including Lotty's family. He was also looking for their assets, which have disappeared. Lotty is critical of Max taking part in the conference as she sees it as confirming the two dominant stereotypes of Jews—that they are victims and that they are only interested in money. Max feels that the Swiss banks are the ones that really care about money, as they refuse to return assets pilfered from European Jews under the Nazis.

Outside the conference, two sets of protestors harangue one another; the first is led by Joseph Posner, orthodox Jewish leader of a group known as the Maccabees, who are calling for the State of Illinois to pass a law forbidding insurance companies from doing business in the state unless they can prove that they were not sitting on any life or property claims from Holocaust victims. On the other side is African American community leader Alderman Louis Durham, whose demonstrators oppose the passing of a Holocaust asset recovery act unless it includes a clause granting reparations from companies who profited from slavery in the United States.

The media reporting of the conference is overshadowed by the appearance of a shabby and mentally fragile character, Paul Radbuka, who has, with the help of controversial therapist Thea Weill, seemingly recovered memories of being a child survivor of the Holocaust. These memories lead him to claim kinship with Max. But Paul Radbuka has the greatest effect on V. I.'s best friend and mentor, Lotty Herschel. In the prewar Vienna of her childhood, Lotty had some dealings with the Radbuka family, but they were so traumatic that she will not reveal what they were to either V. I. or Max, who has become her lover. As V. I. uncovers the insurance fraud at Ajax, she begins to find Paul Radbuka's life entangled with it. Most disturbing for V. I. is the eventual disappearance of Lotty and a set of Paul Radbuka's father's notebooks, which eventually reveal the heart of the mystery.

If ever a book bore out Gavin Stevens's famous comment in act 1, scene 3 of William Faulkner's *Requiem for a Nun* (1951), then *Total Recall* is it: "The past is never dead. It's not even past." Two voices narrate the novel. Readers are familiar with V. I.'s wisecracking first-person narratives, but at regular intervals another voice takes over—Lotty's story in her own words, from her escape from prewar Vienna as a ten-year-old, to her training in London, and to an event that forms the denouement of the novel. This novel is Paretsky's most ambitious, moving, and structurally exhilarating. As V. I. learns about Lotty's life in Vienna and London from her friends, Lotty's own narrative fills in the details with dizzying shifts in time and place. The interleaving of Lotty's narrative with V. I.'s investigations give a sense of the simultaneity of past and present.

Paretsky's use of the Holocaust might be seen as inappropriate, too serious a subject for a mystery story, wildly overbalancing a novel whose other element is little more than a small-time insurance fraud. Paretsky is clearly aware of the possibility of trivializing the subject. The novel escapes this criticism because she has alluded to Lotty's history from her first novel and in many since and has, in a sense, earned the right to tell Lotty's story. Also, the novel comments on victimhood, history, and memory through a complex series of moral oppositions. In a book that pushes the boundaries of what subject matter a mystery novel can encompass, Paretsky has produced, through an act of imaginative sympathy, the best work of her career. *Total Recall* was seen by the critics as a daring, risk-taking project. In the United Kingdom, *The Guardian* of 1 December 2001 said that Paretsky "finds a subject that justifies her anger and packs a mighty punch," while *The Observer* of 20 January 2002 called the novel "Utterly absorbing." The December 2001 *Publishers Weekly* echoed the majority of other reviews when it said that "Paretsky's novel explores the complex web of degrees of guilt and complicity surrounding the fate of Holocaust victims with compelling, terrible clarity and inevitability."

Though set, like its predecessor, in contemporary times, *Blacklist* (2003) is in an important sense an historical novel, dealing with the legacy of the 1950s, the McCarthy years of blacklists, witch-hunts, and red scares. It is also a post–11 September 2001 novel in two senses. First, Paretsky gives a sense of the effect the destruction of the Twin Towers had on her detective; "Right after the Trade Center, I'd been as numbed and fearful as everyone else in America," V. I. says on the first page of the novel. Second, it is a post–11 September novel because an important element in the book is an account of the climate of fear that existed in the United States post–11 September, a fear of terrorism and the subsequent eroding of civil rights under the Patriot Act, passed by Congress forty-five days after 11

September. "We are living in paranoid times," says Warshawski, "times of fear and brutality." The novel intends to draw a parallel between the paranoia and restrictions on liberty experienced by Americans in the 1950s and after 11 September.

Many parts of this sweeping legislation take away checks on law enforcement. For example, when the Federal Bureau of Investigation (FBI) supposes Warshawski has had contact with a suspected terrorist, an agent says to the angry detective demanding a warrant, "Ma'am, under the Patriot Act, if we believe there is an emergency situation we are permitted to bypass the warrant process." Paretsky has appeared in a series of national advertisements for The American Civil Liberties Union (ACLU) implicitly condemning the Patriot Act as being against the spirit of the First and Fourth Amendments to the United States Constitution and has written a thoughtful and carefully argued essay, "Truth, Lies and Duct Tape," on the Patriot Act itself, available on her website (http://www.saraparetsky.com).

However, as she says in her 25 September 2003 essay for *The New York Times* series "Writers on Writing," "I don't sit down to write books of social or political commentary. I am pulled by stories, not ideas." The story of *Blacklist* is a typically complex one, though it begins simply enough, as many mystery stories do. V. I. is employed by her oldest client, Darraugh Graham, to investigate his mother's complaint that she sees lights in the attic at night in Larchmont Hall, a dilapidated mansion that was once the Graham family home. Mrs. Graham, now ninety-one, lives opposite the old house. Police have dismissed her complaint as the imaginings of a lonely old woman, but when V. I. searches the grounds of the old place at night, she finds a body in the pond and catches sight of a teenage girl running from the scene. Larchmont Hall is in New Solway, a wealthy suburb forty-five miles west of Chicago, and the story centers on the lives and secrets of the rich who have lived there for nearly a century and on some powerful individuals whose careers were shaped by the politics of the United States in the 1950s.

The body in the pond belongs to Marc Whitby, a promising black journalist, and the police are quick to dismiss the death as a suicide. V. I. is employed by Whitby's sister, Harriet, to find out how and why Whitby died. V. I.'s dogged pursuit of Whitby's killer brings her into conflict with police from three jurisdictions and raises the ire of the some of the wealthiest and most powerful families in Illinois. With the help of Harriet and Amy Blount, the historian and researcher from *Total Recall,* V. I. discovers that Whitby was writing a book about Kylie Ballantine, an African American choreographer, dancer, and anthropologist. Ballantine was encouraged and financially supported by liberal pub-

lisher and New Solway resident Calvin Bayard, who became famous during the 1950s witch-hunts for standing up to the House Un-American Activities Committee (HUAC). The handsome, charismatic Bayard was idolized by Warshawski when he came to talk to her law class at the University of Chicago.

Bayard's tormentor at the time was his New Solway childhood friend, the recently deceased Olin Taverner, himself a legendary hate figure for liberals, someone who persecuted homosexuals, blacks, and suspected communists. V. I. says, " I couldn't think of one thing about Olin Taverner that I didn't despise." Yet, for some reason, Taverner did not destroy his old enemy Bayard at the HUAC hearings in the 1950s. Eventually, V. I. discovers that the two political opponents had a pact. V. I. finally tracks down the teenager she saw in the grounds of Larchmont Hall just before she found Whitby's body. She is Calvin Bayard's granddaughter, Catherine, who has inherited her grandfather's politics: the lights Mrs. Graham had seen in the attic of the mansion were real. The idealistic Catherine had been hiding a teenage Egyptian dishwasher who worked at her school. The FBI suspects he may have links to a terrorist organization at his mosque. To V. I., he is just a frightened boy who wants to work to send money home to his desperately poor family. The various plots are brought together in the shape of Calvin Bayard's formidable wife, Renee.

Larchmont Hall itself has the flavor of the Gothic about it, and it functions to give a further texture to the realistic surface of the novel. Darraugh Graham says of his old childhood home at the end of the book, "Larchmont is a terrible house—it sucks the life out of everyone who comes near it." To some extent it represents the dead hand of the past upon the present, the function old houses have in the Gothic tradition.

Blacklist was well received by the critics. The Associated Press reviewer in *The Columbia Daily Tribune* of 12 October 2003 was typical of many: "Paretsky's novels not only entertain us but they also make us think. Paretsky has an affinity for solid storytelling with a social agenda without sacrificing plot." *The Pittsburgh Tribune* of 23 November 2003 commented, "Paretsky has crafted a complex, disturbing thriller. . . . *Blacklist* is a story of youth and innocence, sex and betrayal, the McCarthy era and its blacklisting process, and anti-Arab sentiments and racial stereotyping in the aftermath of Sept. 11." However, against the grain of the majority of opinion, crime-fiction critic for *The Chicago Sun-Times,* Connie Fletcher, found "the latest entry in Sara Paretsky's groundbreaking, often compelling series . . . a clunker . . . the plot, filled to the gills as it is, advances by fits and starts and remains as murky as the weed-choked pond in which it begins." Fletcher's complaint points up a thematic element in the novel to be found in many of Paretsky's novels—the association of water with death. The pond, like Dead Stick Pond in *Blood Shot* and Lake Michigan in *Deadlock,* signifies a danger to the detective's life; when she falls into the pond before finding the body of Whitby, she describes her "clothes so heavy with the brackish water that they pinned me like an iron shroud." Later in the novel, the image of the pond is used as a metaphor by Llewelyn, an important publisher, to warn Warshawski off; "Get your stick out of that old pond you're stirring. The stench from the rot on the bottom could rise up and choke you."

Paretsky's V. I. Warshawski series traces the life of a woman whose politics was formed in the heat of the civil rights and women's rights struggles of the 1960s. Both movements had utopian and radical political goals that were under attack and largely in retreat during the conservatism prevalent in the 1980s and the 1990s. Paretsky's novels offer both a reflection and a critique of Chicago and the United States in the past two decades. V. I. often claims that she abandoned her more-radical beliefs as the 1970s began. In *Tunnel Vision,* she remarks, "The amount of misery is overwhelming and I'm not brave enough, smart enough, or rich enough to know what to do about it."

V. I. has changed less than many of her contemporaries. While she was initially interested in expensive clothes and cars, and in being professionally successful, her relatively modest apartment and income, similar to those of Philip Marlowe, signify her integrity in a world based on greed, not need. V. I. took part in the Freedom Rides and saw Martin Luther King Jr. speak in Chicago in 1966. In 1992, in *Guardian Angel,* while in Atlanta for a Cubs game, she makes a pilgrimage to King's birthplace. She is still connected to that radical tradition, though of course in a much-changed political environment.

Hard Time gives an example of what happened to the politics of V. I.'s contemporaries in the character of Alexandra Fisher. Once a radical friend of V. I., whom she remembers as "always on my butt for not joining protest movements," Fisher has "left the barricades for the boardroom" and is part of the legal team of a global media corporation. Critical of what she sees as V. I.'s old-fashioned, confrontational politics, Fisher says to her, "You have to learn to move on from those old battles. These are the nineties, after all." For V. I., the mass movement that formed the base for political change may have abated, but the principles are still in place.

The V. I. Warshawski novels are a rich contribution to the hard-boiled genre in large part because V. I.'s social relations are delineated in such great detail and deepened with each new novel. Many critics have

Dust jacket for Paretsky's 2003 novel, in which the author draws comparisons between the political climate of the United States during the McCarthy era and the period after 11 September 2001 (Richland County Public Library)

commented on this distinguishing feature of Paretsky's work. While Emck suggests that "Paretsky's achievement is to excavate and legitimate the presence of women within the hard-boiled genre," she goes on to say that Warshawski "undermines the separation between professional and personal worlds." In an important sense, the novels also explore the possibility of community in a modern metropolis, an environment traditionally hostile to such forms of social organization. Thomas S. Gladsky uses Werner Sollers's categories of *consent* and *descent* in his reading of the series. He sees the novels as about the "elimination of the biological ethnic family," a community based on descent, and the creation of a new consensual extended family of like-minded friends and neighbors. As Gladsky says, "Her new family is as much a political coalition as it is an intimate support group."

Sara Paretsky has often said that before she began to write, she needed to find a voice. Once she had it, her first novel became possible. Giving V. I. a voice, however, has allowed Paretsky to do much more than make her mark on hard-boiled detective fiction. The creation has also given her creator a means to speak boldly. As she has said, "V. I. has given me a voice, given me the courage to say a lot of things I wouldn't say in my own voice." That voice has produced a body of compelling, resonant, and socially conscious popular fiction.

References:

Jane S. Bakerman, "Living 'Openly and with Dignity'– Sara Paretsky's New-Boiled Fiction," *Mid-America: The Society for the Study of Midwestern Literature,* 12 (1985): 120–135;

Katy Emck, "Feminist Detectives and the Challenge of Hardboiledness," *Canadian Review of Comparative Literature,* 21 (September 1994): 383–398;

Thomas S. Gladsky, "Consent, Descent, and Transethnicity in Sara Paretsky's Fiction," *Clues: A Journal of Detection,* 16 (Fall/Winter 1995): 1–15;

Richard E. Goodkin, "Killing Order(s): Iphigenia and the Detection of Tragic Intertextuality," *Yale French Studies,* 76 (1989): 81–107;

Margaret Kinsman, "A Question of Visibility: Sara Paretsky and Chicago," in *Women Times Three: Writers, Detectives, Readers,* edited by Kathleen Gregory Klein (Bowling Green, Ohio: Bowling Green State University Popular Press, 1995), pp. 15–27;

Patricia E. Johnson, "Sex and Betrayal in the Detective Fiction of Sue Grafton and Sara Paretsky," *Journal of Popular Culture,* 27 (Spring 1994): 97–106;

Louise Conley Jones, "Feminism and the P. I. Code; or, Is a Hard-Boiled Warshawski Unsuitable to be Called a Feminist?" *Clues: A Journal of Detection,* 16 (Spring/Summer 1995): 77–87;

Sally Munt, *Murder by the Book?* (New York & London: Routledge, 1994), pp. 41–47;

Bethany Perkins, "Sara Paretsky: An Annotated Bibliography," *Bulletin of Bibliography,* 56, no. 4 (1999): 225–233;

Rebecca A. Pope, "'Friends Is a Weak Word for It': Female Friendship and the Spectre of Lesbianism in Sara Paretsky," in *Feminism in Women's Detective Fiction,* edited by Glenwood Irons (Toronto: University of Toronto Press, 1995), pp. 156–170;

Guy Szuberla, "The Ties That Bind: V. I. Warshawski and the Burdens of Family," *Armchair Detective,* 27 (Spring 1994): 146–153;

Sabine Vanacker, "V. I . Warshawski, Kinsey Millhone and Kay Scarpetta: Creating a Feminist Detective Hero," in *Criminal Proceedings: The Contemporary American Crime Novel,* edited by Peter Messent (Chicago: Pluto Press, 1997), pp. 62–86;

Linda S. Wells, "Popular Literature and Postmodernism: Sara Paretsky's Hard-Boiled Feminist," *Proteus: A Journal of Ideas,* 6, no. 1 (1989): 5–56;

Ralph Willett, *The Naked City* (Manchester: Manchester University Press, 1997).

Robert B. Parker

(17 September 1932 –   )

Donna Waller Harper
Middle Tennessee State University

BOOKS: *Personal Response to Literature,* by Parker and others (New York: Houghton Mifflin, 1970);

Order and Diversity: The Craft of Prose, by Parker and Peter Sandburg (New York: Wiley, 1973);

The Godwulf Manuscript (Boston: Houghton Mifflin, 1974 [i.e., 1973]; London: Deutsch, 1974);

Sports Illustrated Training with Weights, by Parker and John Marsh (New York: Lippincott, 1974);

God Save the Child (Boston: Houghton Mifflin, 1974; London: Deutsch, 1975);

Mortal Stakes (Boston: Houghton Mifflin, 1975; London: Deutsch, 1976);

Promised Land (New York: Delacorte, 1976; London: Deutsch, 1977);

Three Weeks in Spring, by Parker and Joan Hall Parker (New York: Houghton Mifflin, 1978; London: Deutsch, 1978);

The Judas Goat (Boston: Houghton Mifflin, 1978; London: Deutsch, 1982);

Wilderness (New York: Delacorte/Lawrence, 1979; London: Deutsch, 1980);

Mature Advertising: How to Create and Approve Effective Ads by Using Guidelines Based on Research (Reading, Mass.: Addison-Wesley, 1980);

Looking for Rachel Wallace (New York: Delacorte/Lawrence, 1980; Loughton, U.K.: Piatkus, 1982);

Early Autumn (New York: Delacorte/Lawrence, 1981; London: Severn House, 1987);

A Savage Place (New York: Delacorte/Lawrence, 1981; Loughton, U.K.: Piatkus, 1982);

Ceremony (New York: Delacorte/Lawrence, 1982; Loughton, U.K.: Piatkus, 1983);

The Widening Gyre (New York: Delacorte/Lawrence, 1983; Harmondsworth, U.K.: Penguin, 1987);

Love and Glory (New York: Delacorte/Lawrence, 1983);

The Private Eye in Hammett and Chandler (Northridge, Cal.: Lord John Press, 1984);

Valediction (New York: Delacorte/Lawrence, 1984; Harmondsworth, U.K.: Penguin, 1985);

Parker on Writing (Northridge, Cal.: Lord John Press, 1985);

Robert B. Parker (photograph © John Earle; from the dustjacket of Family Honor, *1999; Richland County Public Library)*

A Catskill Eagle (New York: Delacorte/Lawrence, 1985; Harmondsworth, U.K.: Viking, 1986);

Taming A Seahorse (New York: Delacorte, 1986; Harmondsworth, U.K.: Viking, 1987);

Pale Kings and Princes (New York: Delacorte, 1987; Harmondsworth, U.K.: Viking, 1988);

Crimson Joy (New York: Putnam, 1988; Harmondsworth, U.K.: Penguin, 1989);

Playmates (New York: Putnam, 1989; Harmondsworth, U.K.: Penguin, 1990);

Poodle Springs, by Parker and Raymond Chandler (New York: Putnam, 1989; London: Macdonald, 1990);

Stardust (New York: Putnam, 1990; Harmondsworth, U.K.: Penguin, 1991);

A Year at the Races, by Parker and Joan H. Parker (New York: Viking, 1990);

Perchance to Dream (New York: Putnam, 1991; London: Macdonald, 1991);

Pastime (New York: Putnam, 1991; Harmondsworth, U.K.: Penguin, 1992);

Double Deuce (New York: Putnam, 1992; Harmondsworth, U.K.: Viking, 1992);

Paper Doll (New York: Putnam, 1993; Harmondsworth, U.K.: Viking, 1993);

Walking Shadow (New York: Putnam, 1994; Harmondsworth, U.K.: Viking, 1994);

All Our Yesterdays (New York: Delacorte, 1994; London: Viking, 1994);

Thin Air (New York: Putnam, 1995; Harmondsworth, U.K.: Viking, 1995);

Chance (New York: Putnam, 1996; Harmondsworth, U.K.: Viking, 1996);

Small Vices (New York: Putnam, 1997; London: Murray, 1998);

Night Passage (New York: Putnam, 1997; London: Murray, 1998);

Sudden Mischief (New York: Putnam, 1998; Harpenden, U.K.: No Exit, 2002);

Trouble in Paradise (New York: Putnam, 1998; London: Murray, 1999);

Hush Money (New York: Putnam, 1999; London: Murray, 2000);

Family Honor (New York: Putnam, 1999; London: Murray, 1999);

Boston: History in the Making (Memphis, Tenn.: Towery, 1999);

Hugger Mugger (New York: Putnam, 2000; London: Murray, 2000);

Perish Twice (New York: Putnam, 2000; London: Murray, 2000);

Death in Paradise (New York: Putnam, 2001; London: Murray, 2001);

Gunman's Rhapsody (New York: Putnam, 2001);

Potshot (New York: Putnam, 2001; London: Murray, 2001);

Shrink Rap (New York: Putnam, 2002; London: Murray, 2002);

Widow's Walk (New York: Putnam, 2002; London: Murray, 2002);

Back Story (New York: Putnam, 2003; London: Murray, 2003);

Stone Cold: A Jesse Stone Novel (New York: Putnam, 2003; London: Murray, 2003);

Bad Business (New York: Putnam, 2004; London: Murray, 2004);

Melancholy Baby (New York: Putnam, 2004; London: Murray, 2004);

Double Play (New York: Putnam, 2004; Harpenden, U.K.: No Exit, 2005).

Collection: *The Early Spenser: Three Complete Novels* (New York: Delacorte, 1989; London: Penguin, 1994).

PRODUCED SCRIPTS: "One for My Daughter," television, *Spenser: For Hire,* ABC, 1987;

"Homecoming," television, *Spenser: For Hire,* ABC, 1987;

Spenser: Ceremony, television, script by Parker and Joan H. Parker, A&E, 1993;

Spenser: Pale Kings and Princes, television, script by Parker and Joan H. Parker, A&E, 1994;

Spenser: Small Vices, television, A&E, 1999;

Thin Air, television, A&E, 2000;

Walking Shadow, television, script by Parker and Joan H. Parker, A&E, 2001.

SELECTED PERIODICAL PUBLICATIONS–
UNCOLLECTED: "The Grim Laughter: Hamlet and the Renaissance," *Lock Haven Review* (1971): 45–57;

"Dark Laughter: Hamlet and the Problem of Belief," *Lock Haven Review* (1971): 81–89.

Robert B. Parker's Spenser, a rugged Boston detective featured in more than thirty novels, is a worthy heir to the hard-boiled tradition pioneered and developed by Dashiell Hammett, Raymond Chandler, and Ross Macdonald. Parker studied these writers in graduate school and wrote a dissertation, "The Violent Hero: A Wilderness Heritage and Urban Reality," in which he examines the style and cultural significance of their work. While readers familiar with Hammett's Sam Spade, Chandler's Philip Marlowe, and Macdonald's Lew Archer note many corresponding characteristics in Spenser, Parker has succeeded in creating his own distinctive hero. As David Geherin asserts in his study *Sons of Sam Spade: The Private Eye Novel in the 70s* (1980), "with each novel Parker has exhibited growing independence from his predecessors, confidently developing his own themes, characters, and stylistic idiom."

Although he remains true to many of the conventions of the genre, Parker has expanded the boundaries of hard-boiled fiction and adapted its detective to modern times. Like the authors he studied, Parker writes about an urban reality, but that reality and the detective's attitude toward it are much different from those created by Chandler and Macdonald, whose heroes are in part alienated from their own worlds–appalled by what their California cities are becoming. By setting the series in Boston, a city Spenser knows well and with which he identifies, Parker creates a strong sense of place reminiscent of Hammett's evocation of Sam Spade in the San Francisco of *The Maltese Falcon* (1930). Parker's choice of Boston, a city that symbolizes the East and American history, provides a significant contrast with the cities of the West so prominent in the classic novels of the hard-boiled tradition.

Committed first to his clients and his ideals, Spenser—like Spade, Marlowe, and Archer—is decisive, fiercely independent, and true to his personal code. He has the requisite rebellious streak that makes his working within a bureaucratic organization impossible, but more than his predecessors he maintains some ongoing personal connections to the police. Spade, Marlowe, and Archer worked alone and were never shown to have deep friendships, but Spenser's long-term relationships, particularly with his friend and alter ego, Hawk, and his lover Susan Silverman, have added depth to his characterization and to the series. When, in a 1985 interview in *The New Black Mask,* Parker was asked about his contribution to the hard-boiled tradition, he responded, "Love. I write about love. . . . If I have changed the form, whatever that form quite is, I think it's because of the degree to which I use it as a vehicle to write about love, which certainly not many hard-boiled private detective writers do."

Robert Brown Parker was born 17 September 1932 in Springfield, Massachusetts, to Carroll Parker, a telephone executive, and Pauline Murphy Parker, a teacher; he received his undergraduate degree from Colby College in Waterville, Maine, in 1954. Volunteering for the United States Army in 1954, he served in the infantry in Korea and was discharged in 1956. He married Joan Hall on 26 August 1956.

Joan Hall Parker has been a guiding force in her husband's life and career. Her urging that he earn his advanced degree so that he could have more time to write prompted him to return to graduate school. The two have collaborated on one book, *Three Weeks in Spring* (1978), the story of her battle with breast cancer and its effect on their marriage and family. They also have collaborated on screenplays for the television series *Spenser: For Hire* as well as four made-for-television movies based on the series. The couple have two sons, Daniel and David.

In 1957 Parker earned his M.A. from Boston University. In the next few years he held several jobs, including management trainee for Curtiss-Wright, technical writer for Raytheon Corporation, and copywriter and editor for Prudential Insurance. In 1960–1962 he was an executive for his own advertising company, Parker-Furman. In 1962 he returned to Boston University to pursue his doctorate, which he earned in 1971. In the mid 1960s Parker taught English at various insti-

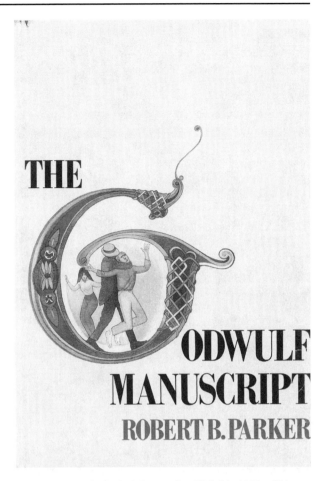

Dust jacket for Parker's first novel, published in 1973, which introduces Boston private investigator Spenser (Richland County Public Library)

tutions around Boston, including Massachusetts State College at Lowell as well as colleges at Suffolk and Bridgewater. In 1968 he accepted a position as an assistant professor at Northeastern; he retired as a full professor in 1979 to pursue his writing career full-time. In a *Toronto Globe and Mail* interview with Ian Brown, Parker expressed a dim view of his experience in academia:

> The academic community is composed largely of nitwits. If I may generalize. People who don't know very much about what matters very much, who view life through literature rather than the other way around. . . . In my fourteen or sixteen years in the profession, I've met more people that I did not admire than at any other point in my life. Including two years in the infantry, where I was the only guy who could read.

The writer's light regard for the academy is evident in the first scene of the first Spenser novel, *The Godwulf Manuscript* (1973). Spenser, the first-person narrator whose first name is never revealed, has a wisecracking style reminiscent of the speech of Philip Mar-

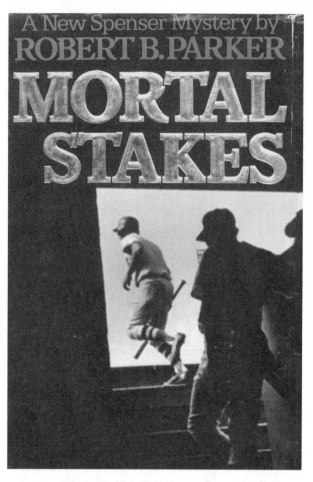

*Dust jacket for Parker's third novel, published in 1975
(Richland County Public Library)*

lowe. After his prospective client—a condescending university president whose office Spenser describes as looking "like the front parlor of a successful Victorian whorehouse"—notes that the assignment requires "restraint, sensitivity, circumspection, and a high degree of professionalism," Spenser interrupts him:

> Look, Dr. Forbes, I went to college once, I don't wear my hat indoors. And if a clue comes along and bites me on the ankle, I grab it. I am not, however, an Oxford don. I am a private detective. Is there something you'd like me to detect or are you just polishing up your elocution for next year's commencement?

Despite his effrontery, Spenser is hired to find a stolen medieval manuscript that is being held for ransom, a case that intertwines with a heroin operation on campus and leads to murder. In this initial adventure the reader learns of the detective's background: he is 6' 1" tall, a thirty-seven-year-old veteran of the Korean War, and a former professional boxer who works out with weights to stay in shape and relieve stress. Tenacious and ideal-

istic, Spenser continues the case even after the university fires him and forbids him to return to the campus.

In his habits as well as his ability to take punishment and bed women, Spenser in this first novel seems akin to a pulp adventure hero, but he is far more than a pastiche of hard-boiled traits. While he no longer smokes, he continues to drink hard liquor, especially in the early novels, and on occasion resorts to the bottle of bourbon in his desk drawer. Nothing can stop him once he takes on a cause: when he is shot and hospitalized, he drags himself from his bed to close the case; though weakened, he still manages to strangle a thug with his bare hands.

Uncharacteristic of his development in future novels, Spenser in *The Godwulf Manuscript* has few scruples about sexual relations: in this novel he has sex with both a mother and her daughter. But even in this novel Parker gives Spenser traits not commonly found among hard-boiled detectives. A college graduate with a literary mind—he sometimes introduces himself by saying his name is spelled with an *s* like the poet—Spenser is a sensitive man when he is not confronting criminals. He enjoys cooking, and conversations in *The Godwulf Manuscript* and the novels that follow often involve his preparation of meals. The literate nature of the series allows readers the pleasure of catching Parker's allusions to works of literature or movies. *The Godwulf Manuscript* includes references to Moloch of the Bible, to Robert Frost's poem "Birches," and to Joyce Carol Oates. Often the allusions are to history, as in descriptions of Boston when Spenser speaks of "Old Ironsides" and Bunker Hill.

The Godwulf Manuscript introduces characters that recur in the series; the most important are Lieutenant Martin Quirk and Sergeant Frank Belson. Initially, Spenser's relationship with Quirk is adversarial, while his relationship with Belson seems more tolerant because Belson apparently knew him earlier. Spenser's relationship with Quirk and Belson becomes more cooperative in later novels, but both cops sometimes resist and complain about what they often see as Spenser's interference in police business. Although Parker makes a point of having Spenser and other characters age and develop through the series, his initial characterization of Quirk does not jibe with his appearance in later books. If Quirk has served twenty-five years on the force, as is mentioned in *The Godwulf Manuscript,* then he would be well past retirement in some of Spenser's subsequent adventures were he to age at the same rate as the detective. Another recurring character introduced in the novel is gangster Joe Broz, who often plays a role in future novels when Spenser becomes involved with the organized-crime element in Boston.

The Godwulf Manuscript received mixed reviews. H. C. Veit in the *Library Journal* (1 January 1974) found

Dust jacket for Parker's 1983 novel, in which the detective attempts to come to terms with his separation from his lover, Susan Silverman (Richland County Public Library)

the novel "derivative," as did Newgate Callendar in *The New York Times Book Review* (13 January 1974). Veit suspected Parker of "a defective ear" because of what he considered the "faulty observations of *le high life*" in the novel. The reviewer for *Critic* (May/June 1974) welcomed Spenser as a "sterling private-eye in the tradition of Philip Marlowe, Lew Archer, and Archie Goodwin." Although he chided "Professor Parker" for sometimes straining "a little too hard to provide wisecracks," he concluded that the faults in the novel were not serious and did not detract from "a major achievement."

Parker often uses cultural references in his titles to suggest the themes of his novels, as in his second Spenser novel, *God Save the Child* (1974), in which the allusion to a well-known song performed by Billie Holiday fits with the focus on a runaway boy. Subsequent titles allude to the work of Robert Frost (*Mortal Stakes* [1975]), Samuel Taylor Coleridge (*A Savage Place* [1981]), William Butler Yeats (*Ceremony* [1982] and *The Widening Gyre* [1983]), John Donne (*Valediction* [1984]), Herman Melville (*A Catskill Eagle* [1985]), Robert Browning (*Taming a Seahorse* [1986]), John Keats (*Pale*

Kings and Princes [1987]), William Blake (*Crimson Joy* [1988]), William Shakespeare (*Walking Shadow* [1994] and *Small Vices* [1997]), and Edmund Spenser (*Sudden Mischief* [1998]). Shakespeare is also alluded to in non-Spenser novels, such as Parker's sequel to Raymond Chandler's *The Big Sleep* (1939), *Perchance to Dream* (1991), and his family saga of three generations, *All Our Yesterdays* (1994).

In *God Save the Child,* Spenser encounters an extremely dysfunctional family whose son Kevin has run away from home. Spenser is hired to find the fifteen-year-old and later to serve as bodyguard for Marge Bartlett, Kevin's mother. In the course of the investigation, during which the case of the runaway turns into a kidnapping, Spenser meets Smithfield High School guidance counselor Susan Silverman, a 5' 7" beauty with "shoulder length black hair and a Jewish face with prominent cheekbones" who shows an "intelligent maturity." Susan, who knows Kevin's personality better than his parents do, accompanies Spenser to the home of bodybuilder Vic Harroway, the man suspected of kidnapping the boy. In these novels, readers can

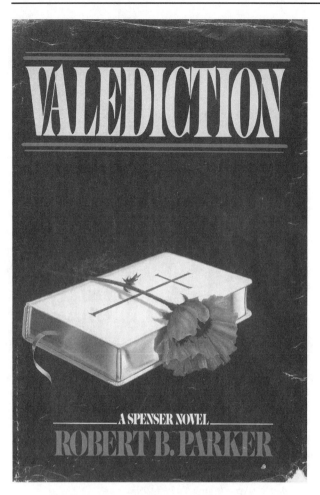

Dust jacket for Parker's 1984 novel, in which Spenser searches for a missing dancer and runs afoul of black mobster Tony Marcus, a recurring villain in the Spenser series (Richland County Public Library)

count on Parker's relating an exciting fight sequence between Spenser and an adversary, and in *God Save the Child,* Spenser fights Harroway to prove to Kevin that Harroway can be defeated so that the boy will return to his parents.

Reviews for Parker's second novel were more positive than those for his first. Veit in *Library Journal* (1 September 1974) criticized Parker's plotting but praised his characterizations of "disagreeable characters: the child's mother is unforgettable, a vain drunken fool; and the local police chief runs a close second." Other reviewers recognized the makings of a worthwhile series. Callendar in *The New York Times Book Review* (15 December 1974) wrote that "Parker must have learned a good deal from 'Godwulf'; his new book is more deft, smoother and sharper in characterization. Where 'Godwulf' read like a compilation of every private eye from Chandler on, 'God Save the Child' has a great deal more personality and character. . . ." In *Time* (10 Febru-

ary 1975), Martha Duffy asserted that on the evidence of the first two novels "this could well be a long-running series. Parker's writing is clear, his plots believable and uncluttered. In Spenser he has a malleable and therefore durable hero."

In the opening of *Mortal Stakes,* Parker shows his ability to set a scene and establish Spenser's voice as he describes one of the landmarks of Boston:

> It was summertime, and the living was easy for the Red Sox because Marty Rabb was throwing the ball past the New York Yankees in a style to which he'd become accustomed. I was there. In the skyview seats, drinking Miller High Life from a big paper cup, eating peanuts and having a very nice time. I wasn't supposed to be having a nice time. I was supposed to be working. But now and then you can do both.
>
> For serious looking at baseball there are few places better than Fenway Park. The stands are close to the playing field, the fences are a hopeful green and the young men in their white uniforms are working on real grass. . . .

Spenser is asked by a Red Sox official to investigate rumors that Rabb, a pitcher comparable to Sandy Koufax, has a gambling connection. While he pursues the case, the detective is romantically involved with both Susan Silverman and Brenda Loring, whom he met as a receptionist in *The Godwulf Manuscript,* but in the end he turns to Susan for solace after ambushing and killing the men who are blackmailing Rabb and his wife.

Critics gave *Mortal Stakes* mainly good notices. *Kirkus Reviews* (15 August 1975) recommended Spenser as "just about the best new private investigator in town": "Parker tells a fresh, funny, direct and different story—it's as tough as they come and spiked with a touch of real class." The reviewer for *Critic* (Spring 1976) criticized the plot as weak but praised Parker's gift for "vivid" writing and characterization: "There's even a plus in the form of wit and wisecracks scattered throughout." Veit in *Library Journal* (1 October 1976) wrote, "This one is first rate for sports fans and gambling freaks. It is pretty good even if you don't know anything about baseball." While not finding the novel "original," Callendar of *The New York Times Book Review* (4 January 1976) asserted that it was unquestionably entertaining: "'Mortal Stakes' never has a dull moment, and Spenser is the next best thing to Rex Stout's Archie Goodwin, on whom he is obviously patterned."

Parker's fourth novel, *Promised Land* (1976), which won the Edgar for the best mystery novel of the year, is pivotal in the series not only because Spenser and Susan enter into the monogamous relationship that is a major theme in many subsequent novels but also because the third main character of the series, Hawk, is introduced. Spenser's case begins when he is hired by Harv Shepard to find his wife, Pam, who after leaving her husband becomes involved with radical feminists and a bank robbery caper. At the same time Harv is being pressured by Hawk, a black man acting as an enforcer for the mob leader King Powers, about payback for a large loan he received for a real estate deal. The Shepards' marital problems arose because of an imbalance in their relationship, not from a lack of love: Harv had placed Pam on a pedestal and she felt stymied and unfulfilled. The Shepards' marriage serves as a foil to reveal the strengths of the vital relationship between Spenser and Susan.

While Spenser is trying to extricate the Shepards from their separate problems, he also struggles with Susan's desire to marry. This conflict is remedied, however, when Spenser proposes and Susan turns him down, deciding that their relationship is secure as it is, with both committed yet independent. In subsequent books, Spenser often calls on Susan—who later earns a doctorate in psychology from Harvard—for insights into people. She serves not only as a love interest but also as a sounding board. Many of his thoughts on the need for autonomy and proper conduct are expressed in dialogues with Susan. Geherin in *Sons of Sam Spade* argues that "Parker's handling of Spenser's relationship with Susan effectively disproves Chandler's assertion that the love story and the detective story cannot exist in the same book. Not only do they coexist in Parker's novel, the love story adds an element of tension by serving as a poignant reminder of the vast distance that separates the mean streets from the quiet ones."

The addition of Hawk to the cast of recurring characters is perhaps even more important to the success of the series than the evolving dynamic of Spenser's relationship with Susan. Spenser knows Hawk because they boxed together and because in his work he has encountered Hawk on the other side of the law. In a key scene in *Promised Land,* Hawk, trying to understand Spenser's involvement with Harv Shepard, takes Spenser and Susan for a ride in his car. Spenser explains to Susan that Hawk is "a free lance" who is hired by those who require his "kind of work":

> "And what is Hawk's kind of work?" Susan said, still to Hawk.
>
> "He does muscle and gun work."
>
> "Ah prefer the term soldier of fortune, honey," Hawk said to me.

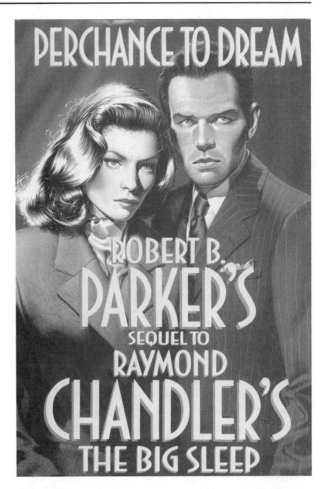

Dust jacket for Parker's 1991 novel. He completed Poodle Springs (1989), a novel begun by Raymond Chandler, before writing this novel alone (Richland County Public Library).

> "Doesn't it bother you," Susan said, "to hurt people for money?"
>
> "No more than it does him. . . ."
>
> "Not right," Hawk said. "Maybe he aiming to help. But he also like the work. . . . Just don't be so sure me and old Spenser are so damn different, Susan."

When Spenser arranges the arrest of Powers and the feminist terrorists during a gun deal, he warns Hawk and allows him to escape. Out on bail, Powers orders Hawk to kill Spenser, but Hawk refuses. At the conclusion, Susan kisses Hawk and asks why he did not shoot Spenser. He replies with a shrug and an assertion of a connection and a code of conduct the two men share that goes beyond the side of a conflict either chooses: "Me and your old man there are a lot alike. I told you that already. There ain't all that many of us left, guys like old Spenser and me."

According to Parker, his readers clamored for Hawk's return and involvement in novel after novel, and the repartee between Spenser and Hawk is one of the great strengths of the series. Parker discussed Hawk in a commentary on an excerpt published in the 1985 issue of *The New Black Mask:* "Hawk is, and the racial pun is intended, the dark side of Spenser. He is what Spenser might have been had he grown up black in a white culture." Parker continues, "His presence in the books provides me an opportunity to examine some aspects of the American Myth, and to comment, sometimes directly, sometimes obliquely, on racism." Besides his friendship with Spenser, Hawk is intensely loyal to Susan. He appreciates her style and character while she recognizes his innate sense of honor. She comes to trust him as much as Spenser does and relies on him to protect Spenser.

Hawk becomes less of an outlaw as the series proceeds and shares many of the same values Spenser as well as Quirk and Belson live by. Spenser tells Susan on more than one occasion that Hawk is a man who will not say "yes" and do "no." He can be trusted to keep his word and to be dependable. And yet Hawk, who epitomizes the ideal of autonomy, remains apart from the other characters. Whereas Spenser allows Susan, Quirk, Belson, and Hawk into his sphere of friends, Hawk allows only Spenser, and even that relationship is limited. Spenser knows little of Hawk's background and rarely ventures into Hawk's life—instead, allowing Hawk to come into his. Hawk changes little over the course of the series, keeping his sense of style, his fancy cars, and his Beacon Hill home; he dates frequently but not steadily.

Reviewing *Promised Land* in *The New Republic* (16 October 1976), Robin Winks questioned Spenser's reputation as a gourmet: "But does one really win a reputation for being a gourmet by drinking Amstel, eating soused shrimp, and telling us in some detail how the spaghetti sauce comes out of the can? Perhaps in Boston." She went on to make a more serious point about Parker's purpose: "In any event, *Promised Land* brings Spenser back for a fourth case, and while the mystery is slight, the straight-on examination of what breaks up marriages, and where Women's Lib fits into the scheme of things (or at least Spenser's scheme) is convincing, even informative reading." Callendar in *The New York Times* (31 October 1976), however, argued that the author is beginning to take his creation too seriously: "By now Spenser is an amalgam of Lew Archer, Travis McGee and, maybe, Hamlet. He does a lot of talking and philosophizing, this guy does. He tries to probe into people's motivations and minds. There is more navel-watching here than at a convention of gurus." The critique concluded with a sentiment that was often repeated, in one formulation or another, by many reviewers thereafter: "Spenser does talk too much, which is a pity because his fists are so much better than his mind."

Parker's first four novels established Parker as one of the leading hard-boiled writers of his generation and

created an audience for Spenser's continuing adventures. In the next dozen years he published twelve more Spenser novels—*The Judas Goat* (1978), *Looking for Rachel Wallace* (1980), *Early Autumn* (1981), *A Savage Place, Ceremony, The Widening Gyre, Valediction, A Catskill Eagle, Taming A Seahorse, Pale Kings and Princes, Crimson Joy,* and *Playmates* (1989)—as well as three nonseries novels: *Wilderness* (1979), *Love and Glory* (1983), and *Poodle Springs* (1989), a book begun by Raymond Chandler, who at his death had written drafts of four chapters, and completed by Parker, who wrote the subsequent thirty-seven chapters. In 1985 Parker sold his Spenser concept to television and the series *Spenser: For Hire* began. Parker served as consultant and occasional scriptwriter, sometimes collaborating with his wife. *Promised Land* served as the basis for the pilot episode. Parker maintained right of refusal for the stars, finally settling on Robert Urich as Spenser and Avery Brooks as Hawk.

Spenser's relationships with Susan and Hawk shaped the series as it evolved, and the novels frequently have some aspect of Spenser and Susan's development as lovers and lifetime companions as a theme. While Spenser and Hawk hunt down terrorists in London and other foreign cities in *The Judas Goat,* Susan remains in Boston to take graduate classes at Harvard. In *Early Autumn,* Spenser and Susan develop a surrogate parent relationship with fifteen-year-old Paul Giacomin, the pawn in an ugly custody battle between an unloving couple. In *A Savage Place,* Spenser has a brief affair with Candy Sloan, the California television reporter he is guarding—his only instance of unfaithfulness to Susan. The couple is separated in *The Widening Gyre,* when Susan is in Washington, D.C., completing an internship, and in *Valediction,* when she decides to take a job in San Francisco. In the latter of these two novels, after a workout session with Hawk, Spenser tells him that Susan has moved away. Hawk takes him to the bar in J. J. Donovan's Tavern:

> "She going to tell you where she lives?" Hawk said.
> "Maybe in a while."
> "Want me to find her?" he said.
> "No. She's got the right to be private."
> "She got somebody out there?" Hawk said.
> "I don't know."
> "If she got somebody, I can kill him," Hawk said.
> I shook my head again. "She's got a right to somebody else," I said. Hawk gestured another round at the bartender.
> "You too," Hawk said.
> "I don't want anyone else."
> "Thought you wouldn't."

Spenser's love for—some say, obsession with—Susan is unwavering after *A Savage Place.* In *A Catskill Eagle,* Spenser and Hawk are involved in rescuing Susan from a fortress hidden in a mine where she is being held by Russell Costigan, a man with whom she has had an affair. This novel reflects a basic difference between Hawk and Spenser: Hawk recognizes the need for violent action and takes it, while Spenser hesitates and worries even after he knows that they have taken the only course open to them. The novels after *A Catskill Eagle* focus in part on the redevelopment of Susan and Spenser's relationship.

One of the attractions of series fiction for many readers is their growing familiarity with the interconnected world the author is creating. Not only do readers get to know the major recurring characters, but they also recognize landmarks, settings, and minor characters who turn up more than once. A listing of a few of the interconnections in the novels might begin with Patricia Utley, the madam who tells Spenser about the pornographic movie used to blackmail Marty Rabb in *Mortal Stakes*. She appears again in *Ceremony* to take in April Kyle, the teen runaway who prefers a life of prostitution to living with her parents. In *Taming a Seahorse,* Utley hires Spenser to look for April when she returns to street prostitution. Introduced in *Early Autumn,* in which he learns lessons in autonomy from Spenser in a backwoods cabin, Paul Giacomin helps Spenser cope with Susan's absence in *The Widening Gyre* and provides the case of the missing dancer that occupies him in *Valediction.* Rachel Wallace, the lesbian feminist writer whom Spenser rescues in *Looking for Rachel Wallace,* refers Candy Sloan to Spenser in *A Savage Place* and helps with research about the Costigans in *A Catskill Eagle.* Readers also recognize recurring villains, such as Tony Marcus, a black mobster who in *Ceremony* is a purveyor of teen hookers. Among the novels in which he reappears are *Valediction, Taming a Seahorse,* and *Crimson Joy,* in which he helps Spenser when a serial killer of prostitutes interferes with his business. The villain who recurs most often is Joe Broz, introduced in *The Godwulf Manuscript.* In *Looking for Rachel Wallace,* Broz is mentioned only as the employer of a man Spenser encounters. After *The Widening Gyre,* some stories focus on Broz's inability to control his son, Gerry, who wants to impress his father so that he can take over the business but who lacks his father's skill or finesse. In *Playmates,* Gerry is involved with a small-town thug who hooks star basketball player Dwayne Woodcock into shaving points.

While reviewers in the 1980s continued to find strengths in Parker's writing, the consensus of opinion was that his work did not measure up to his earlier novels. For the first novel published in the decade, *Looking for Rachel Wallace,* Callendar in *The New York Times Book Review* (20 April 1980) praised his "crackling dialogue" and "expert writing" but also stated, "This is not one of the best Spenser books." *Kirkus Reviews* (15 January 1980)

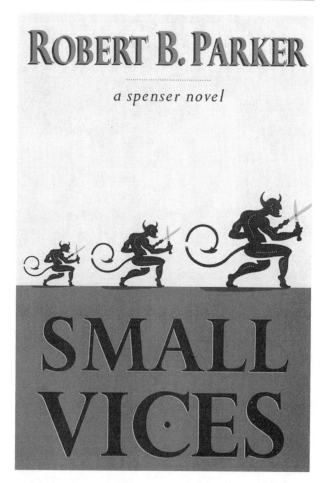

Dust jacket for Parker's twenty-fourth Spenser novel, published in 1997, in which he is almost killed by the "Gray Man"; much of the story concerns his recuperation (Richland County Public Library).

concluded that "the book too often resembles nothing so much as a trendy bull session. True, for every sententious line of dialogue, nine terrifically funny ones can be found, and the Boston atmosphere still rings true—so this little book is certainly painless." The comment by Robin Weeks in *The New Republic* (13 June 1983) about *Ceremony*—"Parker hasn't been this good since *Promised Land*"—was a variation of a sentiment expressed by other reviewers who praised particular novels. In the 1980s, however, reviewers did not think any Spenser novel was as good as Parker's first four books.

Published at the midpoint of the decade, *A Catskill Eagle* engendered wildly divergent opinions. The reviewer for *Time* (1 July 1985) praised it as Parker's "best mystery novel" and argued that he had successfully re-created a contemporary medieval quest by having Spenser rescue "a maiden imprisoned in a tower":

The "maiden" is Spenser's estranged girlfriend, Susan Silverman; her supposed captor is Spenser's rival for

Dust jacket for Parker's 1997 novel that introduces Jesse Stone, an alcoholic former Los Angeles policeman now serving as small-town Massachusetts police chief (Richland County Public Library)

her love; her disappearance may in fact be voluntary; her guards are also employees of an unscrupulous international arms dealer; the macho Spenser must rely on help from a lesbian journalist and a matronly psychotherapist; and the perilous rescue turns into a wantonly bloody and ignoble business, achieved with the connivance of morally dubious United States government agencies.

In *The New York Times Book Review* (30 June 1985), however, Callendar called it "a really silly book, impossible to take seriously, gooey and self-satisfied at the end, its heroism reminiscent of that of the heavily muscled characters in comic books." In *Newsweek* (17 June 1985), Peter S. Prescott preferred "the modest and affecting situations Parker once set forth in novels like 'Ceremony.'"

The harshest critical judgment on the series came from *Kirkus Reviews* (15 April 1986) in a critique of *Taming a Seahorse,* a novel that was published during the run of *Spenser: For Hire* on television:

Despite more than a few good one-liners, the Spenser of the 1980's continues to be a smug, self-righteous narcissist (as preoccupied with his outfits as any pimp), and not much fun. The hoary sentimentality about prostitution is slathered on extra-thick. But, with Parker's easy-read style and a bit less pretentiousness than some recent Spensers, this should do well commercially—thanks largely to heavy promotion, the TV tie-in, and the crest of Parker popularity that has coincided so ironically with his descent from genre artist to self-indulgent hack.

A far more positive assessment of Parker's career was offered by R. W. B. Lewis in *The New York Times Book Review* (23 April 1989). In his remarks on *Playmates,* the last Spenser novel of the 1980s, Lewis concluded,

Robert B. Parker established such an elevated standard with his first four novels, through "Promised Land" in 1976, that it would have been virtually impossible to keep it up. The level was impressively high, though, through five or six more titles, by which time it was clear that we were witnessing one of the great series in the history of the American detective story. But then, in the opinion of some, a decline set in. "A Catskill Eagle" in 1985 was an overlong chase-and-rescue story with a double-digit body count and Susan Silverman as the temporarily willful damsel in distress. Almost unthinkably for Mr. Parker and Spenser, last year's "Crimson Joy" barely escaped the banal. The striking recovery of power in "Playmates" is all the more a matter for wonder and rejoicing.

Most reviewers, however, were unwilling to call Parker a hack or to claim that he had recaptured past glory. In regard to *Playmates,* the reviewer for *Time* (15 May 1989) described how Spenser's investigation at Taft University involved academic integrity as well as the basketball team: "The reader puts up his feet and gets comfortable. That's a bad sign. Too much comfort, too little doubt. In the early Spenser books, everyone was edgy. Now hero, victim and villains fit their roles a trifle too cozily. Is it time for Spenser to retire and teach poetry at Taft?" The reviewer for the Canadian journal *Quill & Quire* (September 1989) called the novel "a better-than-average outing for one of the most popular series in the thriller sweepstakes."

In the 1990s Parker published ten Spenser novels—*Stardust* (1990), *Pastime* (1991), *Double Deuce* (1992), *Paper Doll* (1993), *Walking Shadow, Thin Air* (1995), *Chance* (1996), *Small Vices, Sudden Mischief,* and *Hush Money* (1999)—and two nonseries novels: *Perchance to Dream* and *All Our Yesterdays,* a family saga that traces three generations from 1920s Ireland to 1990s Boston. Parker also began two new series: the first is about Jesse Stone, an alcoholic former Los Angeles homicide detective who tries to rebuild his life as chief of police in Paradise, Massachusetts, in *Night Passage* (1997); the second introduces Sunny Randall, a female Boston P. I. divorced from her mob-connected husband in *Family Honor* (1999). During the decade, Parker collaborated with his wife on two Spenser movies for television, *Spenser: Ceremony* (1993) and *Spenser: Pale Kings and Princes* (1994), which were produced for the A&E network and starred Urich and Brooks as Spenser and Hawk. Later in the decade, he wrote a script for another A&E production, *Spenser: Small Vices* (1999), which starred Joe Mantegna as an older Spenser.

Parker continued to bring back characters who appeared in earlier novels and to introduce new characters as he advanced his series. Paul Giacomin is a presence in the books, for even when he does not have a major role, Spenser may mention Paul's picture or a letter received from him. In *Pastime* Spenser hunts for Paul's missing mother, Patty. His search for the mother, whose boyfriend, Richie Beaumont, has stolen money from Gerry Broz, leads Spenser again to interfere with the plans of the younger Broz. Joe Broz—who despite being a criminal possesses a sense of honor—has his right-hand man, Vinnie Morris, warn Spenser that Gerry plans to kill him. This action contributes to a decline in Broz's power and influence. *Pastime* introduces Pearl the Wonder Dog, a short-haired pointer patterned after Parker's own, who becomes an important part of Susan's and Spenser's lives. Morris, who possesses the same honor and integrity as do Hawk and Spenser and is purported to be a better shot than even Hawk, also becomes an important minor character.

Reviewers were more positive toward the Spenser novels after the 1980s. Michael Anderson, writing of *Pastime* in *The New York Times Book Review* (28 July 1991), argued that "Spenser's sagas are less tales of ratiocination than fables of exemplary conduct, the occasional violence or dubiety of the hero's actions is redeemed by the justice of his judgment and the righteousness of his character. Throughout the 18 novels, Mr. Parker has provided a continuing narrative on the refinement of a moral sensibility, Spenser's endeavors to act honestly and honorably." In the *Christian Science Monitor* (3 September 1991), Catherine Foster compared *Pastime* to *Early Autumn,* the novel that introduced the Giacomins to the series, and concluded that "the wit's more mature now, less forced . . . it's another good chapter in the continuing life of Spenser."

The attention Spenser lavishes on Susan—her appearance, which always takes his breath away, her mannerisms while thinking or working out, her work habits, her fashion sense, her shopping, and her dietary habits—sometimes sparked negative comments by reviewers, but the strengths of Parker's writing usually more than compensated for any perceived failings. In *Chance,* Susan accompanies Spenser and Hawk to Las Vegas,

Dust jacket for Parker's 1999 novel, the first to feature female Boston private investigator Sunny Randall, who has connections to organized crime through her former husband (Richland County Public Library)

where they search for a gangster's missing son-in-law. For reviewer Marilyn Stasio in *The New York Times Book Review* (19 May 1996), Susan's presence did not undermine Parker's accomplishment: "True, there's more talk than action in the story; but, with the exception of the arch banter between Spenser and Susan, his smug ladylove, the talk is golden. Besides supplying plenty of witty chitchat between Spenser and his alter ego, Hawk, Mr. Parker lavishes his attention on characters like Gino Fish, a mobster with diction so beautiful you could weep. Talk like this does not come cheap." Christopher Lehmann-Haupt, who also commented on the book in *The New York Times Book Review* (15 August 1996), asserted that "as always, Mr. Parker makes you laugh at the subtle variations he works on his politically incorrect themes" and praised its "pleasant glow of the familiar."

Parker's most interesting novel in the 1990s in terms of the development of Spenser's character is *Small Vices,* in which he is hired to investigate the possible framing of Ellis Alves, a black man and a career criminal, for the murder of a rich white coed. Among the obstacles to Spenser's search for the truth is the "Gray Man," a paid killer. As he is taking a late-afternoon run on a snowy day, crossing the Charles River—"the black water moved opaquely, patched with light and shadow"—on an arched footbridge, Spenser sees "a tall man in a gray overcoat" with a gun. The Gray Man shoots him three times. With great effort, Spenser heaves himself over the railing of the bridge and falls twenty feet. As Stasio observed in *The New York Times Book Review* (13 April 1997), "Spenser and his nemesis meet again, but not before an extraordinary 10-month hiatus, during which time the paralyzed detective (who sardonically refers to himself as Lazarus) hides out in California with his soul mate, Susan, and his friend Hawk, fighting his way back to life." Parker, she asserts, has written "a powerful piece about the defeat and reclamation of a hero." Calling the novel "the best for a long time," the reviewer for the *Seattle Post-Intelligencer* (12 April 1997) concluded, "The resolution will come as no surprise, but the aftershock of this story is more complex than the process of resolution: People have done bad things for good reasons, good things for bad reasons, and only Spenser's compass has held him true."

Parker, who turned seventy in 2002, has shown no sign of slowing down in the twenty-first century. Since the year 2000 he has published five new Spenser novels—*Hugger Mugger* (2000), *Potshot* (2001), *Widow's Walk* (2002), *Back Story* (2003), and *Bad Business* (2004). He has continued with his new series, publishing three Sunny Randall novels—*Perish Twice* (2000), *Shrink Rap* (2002), and *Melancholy Baby* (2004)—and two more Jesse Stone novels, *Death in Paradise* (2001) and *Stone Cold* (2003). He has also published *Gunman's Rhapsody* (2001), a Western about lawman Wyatt Earp, and *Double Play* (2004), a novel aboout Jackie Robinson's 1947 season with the Brooklyn Dodgers. Parker's books continue to please his audience and to garner respectful reviews.

A worthy heir to Hammett, Chandler, and Macdonald, Robert B. Parker in 2002 was named a Grand Master by the Mystery Writers of America. His influence on other writers is evident; many of them have followed Parker in writing about love in the hard-boiled novel. Also, as critic Keven Forrest Moreau observed on the website *Shaking Through Net* (16 August 2003), since Parker's introduction of "the impassive assassin Hawk to his Spenser series of detective novels, the chilling, competent sidekick has become a staple of modern crime fiction." In a 4 April 2000 interview with Bookreporter.com, Parker said he planned "to keep writing until I die." His

thirty-second Spenser novel, *Cold Service*, is scheduled for publication in spring 2005.

Interviews:

Anne Ponder, "A Dialogue with Robert B. Parker," *Armchair Detective,* 17 (Fall 1984): 340–348;

"Robert B. Parker: An Interview," *New Black Mask,* 1 (1985): 1–10;

Marilyn Kurata, "Interview: Robert B. Parker," *Clues,* 12 (Spring 1989): 1–31.

References:

Donna Casella, "The Catskill Eagle Crushed: The Moral Demise of Spenser in Robert B. Parker's *A Catskill Eagle," Clues,* 11 (Spring/Summer 1990): 107–117;

Casella, "The Trouble with Susan and Women in Robert B. Parker's Spenser Novels," *Clues,* 10 (Fall/Winter 1989): 93–102;

Herbert Fackler, "Dialectic in the Corpus of Robert B. Parker's Spenser Novels," *Clues,* 16 (Spring/Summer 1993): 13–24;

David Geherin, *Sons of Sam Spade: The Private Eye Novel in the 70s* (New York: Ungar, 1980), pp. 5–82;

Geherin, "Spenser," in his *The American Private Eye: The Image in Fiction* (New York: Ungar, 1985), pp. 164–166;

Russell Gray, "Reflections of Private Eyes: Robert B. Parker's Spenser," *Clues,* 5 (Spring/Summer 1984): 1–13;

Donald Greiner, "Robert B. Parker and the Jock of the Mean Streets," *Critique* (Fall 1984): 36–44;

Otto Penzler, "Robert B. Parker," *Armchair Detective,* 18 (Summer 1985): 258–261;

John W. Presley, "Theory into Practice: Robert B. Parker's Reinterpretation of the American Tradition," *Journal of American Culture,* 12 (Fall 1989): 27–30;

Louise Saylor, "The Private Eye and His Victuals," *Clues,* 5 (Winter 1982): 111–118;

Dennis Tallett, *The Spenser Companion: The Godwulf Manuscript to Hugger Mugger, A Reader's Guide* (Cal.: Companion Books, 2001);

Lonnie Willis, "Henry David Thoreau and the Hard-Boiled Dick," *Thoreau Society Bulletin,* 170 (Winter 1985): 1–3;

Robin Winks, "Robert B. Parker," in his *Colloquium on Crime: Eleven Renowned Mystery Writers Discuss Their Works* (New York: Scribners, 1986), pp. 189–203;

James Zalewski, "Rules for the Game of Life: The Mysteries of Robert B. Parker and Dick Francis," *Clues,* 5 (Fall/Winter 1984): 72–81.

George P. Pelecanos
(18 February 1957 –   )

Peter Gunn
University of Texas–Austin

BOOKS: *A Firing Offense* (New York: St. Martin's Press, 1992; London: Serpent's Tail, 1997);

Nick's Trip (New York: St. Martin's Press, 1993; London: Serpent's Tail, 1999);

Shoedog (New York: St. Martin's Press, 1994; London: Serpent's Tail, 2001);

Down by the River Where the Dead Men Go (New York: St. Martin's Press, 1995; London: Serpent's Tail, 1996);

The Big Blowdown (New York: St. Martin's Press, 1996; London: Serpent's Tail, 2000);

King Suckerman (Boston: Little, Brown, 1997; London: Serpent's Tail, 1997);

The Sweet Forever (Boston: Little, Brown, 1998; London: Serpent's Tail, 1999);

Shame the Devil (Boston: Little, Brown, 2000; London: Gollancz, 2000);

Right as Rain (Boston: Little, Brown, 2001; London: Gollancz, 2001);

Hell to Pay (Boston: Little, Brown, 2002; London: Orion, 2002);

Soul Circus (Boston: Little, Brown, 2003; London: Orion, 2003);

Hard Revolution (Boston: Little, Brown, 2004; London: Orion, 2004);

Drama City (Boston: Little, Brown, forthcoming 2005).

PRODUCED SCRIPTS: *Long Shots: The Life and Times of the American Basketball Association,* documentary, HBO, 1997;

Paid in Full, motion picture, script by Pelecanos (uncredited) and Matthew Cirulnick, Dimension, 2002;

"Cleaning Up," television, *The Wire,* episode 12, teleplay by Pelecanos, HBO, 2002;

"Duck and Cover," television, *The Wire,* episode 21, story by Pelecanos and David Simon, teleplay by Pelecanos, HBO, 2003;

George P. Pelecanos (from King Suckerman, *1997; Richland County Public Library)*

"Bad Dreams," television, *The Wire,* episode 24, story by Pelecanos and David Simon, teleplay by Pelecanos, HBO, 2003.

OTHER: "When You're Hungry," in *Unusual Suspects: An Anthology of Crime Stories from Black Lizard,* edited by James Grady (New York: Vintage, 1996), pp. 151–175;

Newton Thornburg, *Cutter and Bone,* introduction by Pelecanos (London: Serpent's Tail, 2001);

"The Dead Their Eyes Implore Us," in *A Measure of Poison,* edited by Dennis McMillan (Tucson, Ariz.: Dennis McMillan, 2002), pp. 1–20;

"Between Origins and Art," in *The Writing Life: Writers on How They Think and Work,* edited by Marie

Arana (New York: Public Affairs, 2003), pp. 85–89.

SELECTED PERIODICAL PUBLICATIONS–
UNCOLLECTED: "New Jack City," review of the
motion picture directed by Mario Van Peebles,
Cineaste, 18, no. 3 (1991): 49–50;

Review of *Night Squad* by David Goodis, *Armchair Detective*, 26, no. 1 (Winter 1993): 110;

Review of *Cropper's Cabin* by Jim Thompson, *Armchair Detective,* 26, no. 1 (Winter 1993): 110–111;

Review of *Berlin Noir* by Philip Kerr, *Your Flesh Quarterly,* 32 (1996): 49;

"What a Shamus; The Hard-Boiled Detective, Down but Not Out," review of *Never Street* by Loren D. Estleman, *Washington Post,* 24 March 1997, p. B2;

"Chili's on the Run," review of *Be Cool* by Elmore Leonard, *Washington Post,* 31 January 1999, p. X4;

"Night Shift: Washington Puts on a Different Face After Midnight," text by Pelecanos, photographs by Jim Saah, *Washingtonian Magazine,* 35, no. 1 (October 1999): 62–69;

"Action Films," *GQ,* 71, no. 3 (March 2001): 318–319;

"The Writing Life, by George P. Pelecanos," *Washington Post,* 27 January 2002, pp. T10+;

"Notes on Shoedog," *Time Warner Bookmark* (August 2004) <http://www.twbookmark.com/features/georgepelecanos/offthepage.html>.

George P. Pelecanos in his 1999 review of James Kelman's short-story collection *The Good Times* (1998) points to a distressing trend in American culture and society that motivates his own crime fiction: "Increasingly, blue-collar workers have become the new Invisible Man, and are no more visible in popular and literary fiction than they are in the minds of the privileged." Pelecanos's work attempts to rectify the situation by positioning the working class back at the center of American crime fiction. His novels essentially recast the origins of the genre from the 1930s, combining the violent physicality and masculine worldview of the hard-boiled tradition with the social concerns of proletarian realism to produce a fictional world inspired as much by Dashiell Hammett and the *Black Mask* Boys as by the bottom-dog school of Edward Dahlberg, Jim Tully, Richard Wright, and A. I. Bezzerides.

In keeping with the strong urban and regional accents of much 1930s fiction, Pelecanos's modern crime dramas are set in the working-class environs of Washington, D.C., where his family has lived and worked for several generations. Pelecanos sets out to chronicle the "invisible" side of the capital, juxtaposing the white domes and monuments of the federal government with the racial and ethnic diversity of the Wash-

ington working classes. "All of the novels, to some degree, attempt to humanize and illuminate the lives of people who are typically underrepresented in American fiction," Pelecanos explains in an autobiographical statement for *The Washington Post* (27 January 2002). "I mean to leave a record of this town, to entertain and to provoke discussion. My method is simple: to present the world as it is, rather than the way readers want it to be."

Pelecanos's grandfather (George Pelecanos) emigrated from Greece with Pelecanos's father (Peter G. Pelecanos) after World War I to escape the rural poverty and political turmoil brewing in the aftermath of the Greco-Turkish War. They settled in the Chinatown district of Washington, D.C., where George Pelecanos went to work in kitchens and sold fruit from a stand in the Southeast Market. Having left Greece when he was only a toddler, Peter Pelecanos grew up as an American youth–boxing, playing baseball, but also clashing with many of his father's Old World values. Peter enlisted in the United States Marines and saw action during World War II in the Pacific.

Pelecanos's maternal grandfather, Peter Frank, bought a little carryout kitchen in the Northwest district of the city–Frank's Carryout on 14th and R Streets. Peter settled down to work nights managing the new lunch counter. He married Frank's daughter, Ruby, who worked as an administrator, and together they had two daughters before their only son, George Peter Pelecanos, was born on 18 February 1957. Much of Pelecanos's youth was spent on 17th and Irving Streets in the Mount Pleasant district of D.C., where he grew up in a three-story brick row house with his two older sisters, his parents, and his grandparents.

Pelecanos's father purchased his own business in 1965–The Jefferson Coffee Shop on 19th Street between M and N Streets in Northwest–and moved his young family just over the district line to Silver Spring, Maryland. George worked as a delivery boy for his father, starting when he was eleven years old in the summer following the April 1968 riots sparked by Martin Luther King Jr.'s assassination and continuing throughout his teenage years. Despite spending much of his free time employed in his father's coffee shop and other jobs, Pelecanos still managed to engage in the petty criminal activities indicative of a rebellious teenager in the early 1970s–shoplifting, vandalizing, and experimenting with controlled substances. In *The Washington Post* on 27 January 2002, Pelecanos described his teen years as consisting of "Rec Department baseball, beer and fortified wine, girls, marijuana, pick-up basketball, muscle cars, Marlboros, rock and funk concerts at Fort Reno and Carter Barron, and stock-boy positions at

Dust jacket for Pelecanos's first novel, published in 1992, which introduces Nick Stefanos, advertising executive turned private investigator (Richland County Public Library)

now-shuttered retailers like Sun Radio at Connecticut and Albemarle. Occasionally, I found trouble. When things threatened to spin out of control, I remained grounded by my family and a martial, Greek-American work ethic I had absorbed, by example, from my parents."

The worst moment of his youth came when Pelecanos was seventeen years old. He and a sixteen-year-old friend were playing around in the house when they took down Peter Pelecanos's .38 special: "we started playing with it and put a round in," Pelecanos recalls. "We forgot about it and without thinking I pointed it in his face and pulled the trigger. Blew the side of his face off. Bullet went in, came out of his neck." Pelecanos's friend fortunately survived, and thanks to reconstructive surgery his face has apparently been left without a scar. Pelecanos's psychological scars have proven more difficult to repair, however, as evidenced by the number of people in his works who are shot in the face. One of the most autobiographical and graphic depictions comes near the end of *Down by the River Where the Dead*

Men Go (1995) when Jack LaDuke, Nick Stefanos's friend and partner, kills the drug kingpin Coley with a blast from his Ithaca shotgun, but takes a .38 round to the face in return:

> The right side of his jaw was exposed, skinless, with pink rapidly seeping into the pearl of the bone. You're okay, LaDuke, I thought. You turned your head at the last moment and Coley blew off the side of your face. You're going to be badly scarred and a little ugly, but you're going to be okay.
>
> And then I saw the hole in his neck, the exit hole or maybe the entry, rimmed purple and blackened from the powder, the hole the size of a quarter. Blood pumped rhythmically from the hole, spilling slowly over the collar of LaDuke's starched white shirt, meeting the blood that was the blow-back from Coley.

While quite graphic, the violence in Pelecanos's novels is never without consequence. "There's nothing funny about violence," Pelecanos assured Eric Brace of *The*

Washington Post in 1995. "Death is a real thing. I try to make it as horrible as possible because it is horrible." Pelecanos's intention is to shock readers and make them aware of the traumatic repercussions of violent acts.

Pelecanos enrolled as a freshman in the University of Maryland, College Park, in 1976 but soon dropped out to run the family business when his father suffered a heart attack. This event coincided with the U.S. bicentennial celebration in the summer of 1976, a time vividly evoked in *King Suckerman* (1997), and a period that Pelecanos fondly describes as "my time," when he cruised D.C. in a jacked-up 1970 gold Camaro, sporting an Afro, platform shoes, and a corduroy suit. Pelecanos eventually reenrolled in the University of Maryland as a film major, working his way through school by holding down a variety of jobs. Christmas break in 1978 found Pelecanos working the holiday rush at a women's shoe store–The Bootlegger on Connecticut and K–where he first met his wife, Emily Hawk. "He was very unusual," Emily recalled for Linton Weeks of *The Washington Post* (11 March 2004). "The way he dressed. He had this brown corduroy suit, very large hair and a goatee." Pelecanos's experience selling women's shoes on straight commission informs his 1994 novel *Shoedog,* just as all the other arcane knowledge and colorful anecdotes from Pelecanos's work history reappear in his novels, capturing a side of American life rarely seen in more-mainstream fiction.

Pelecanos's first novel, *A Firing Offense* (1992), documents the intricate workings of the retail electronics trade during the commission-driven hard-sell days before large corporate supercenters moved in. Pelecanos began working in retail electronics as a stock boy for Sun Radio when he was sixteen and worked in the profession for eight years. After graduating from the University of Maryland with a B.A. in film studies in 1980, Pelecanos worked as a salesman for a local retail chain–Luskin's–but devoted most of his attention to partying and seeing live music. In 1982 Pelecanos joined the local appliance dealer Bray & Scarff, and in six years found himself in the position of general manager; barely thirty, he was already running a major appliance chain with annual sales in excess of $30,000,000 and branch offices throughout the Washington area.

The stable income allowed Pelecanos to marry Hawk (who was then working at *Regardie's* magazine) on 26 October 1985, and together they adopted three children–Nick and Peter from Brazil, and Rosa from Guatemala. But domestic happiness could not compensate for a growing sense of alienation and stress at work. "At night, he came home and said he felt like someone was standing on his chest all day," Emily recalled in an interview with *CBS News Sunday Morning* (24 March 2002). "I used to sit in my pick-up truck at 7 o'clock in the morning outside my office," Pelecanos told Brace of *The Washington Post* (25 July 1995), "listening to the Replacements or something full blast thinking 'What am I doing here?'"

Suffering the full effects of an early midlife crisis, Pelecanos quit his job at Bray & Scarff to write a novel. In 1989, using several spiral-bound notebooks, he wrote by hand the first draft of *A Firing Offense*. Pelecanos knew the hard-boiled genre well from ten years of voracious reading, but otherwise he had no idea what he was getting himself into. Back in 1979 Pelecanos had taken a class on "Hard-boiled Detective Fiction" taught by Charles Misch at the University of Maryland. The class instilled a two-novel-per-week reading habit in Pelecanos and provided him with a perspective on hard-boiled fiction that related to his own experience: Misch "really got me amped about books, and these kinds of [hard-boiled] books in particular," he related to Jennifer Schuessler of *Publishers Weekly*. "I saw that they could be looked at as literature about working-class people. There were always lots of stories living in my head. But I thought writers were Waspy guys with Harris tweeds and suede patches on their elbows, not Greek kids like me who worked in carryout shops."

The proletarian accents of the hard-boiled genre got Pelecanos interested in books, but he took his greatest inspiration from the vibrant punk-music scene that swept through D.C. in the 1980s. In a review of Michael Azerrad's 2001 book *Our Band Could Be Your Life,* Pelecanos passionately describes the influence punk had on his artistic ambitions:

> I had never taken a writing class when I attempted to write my first book. Hell, I had never even met a novelist. To me, authors were 'other people.' But bands like Fugazi and The Mats and Husker Du told me, by example, that my lack of pedigree meant nothing relative to my potential for creativity. These people picked up guitars and played, and in the process made a kind of organic, volcanic art. . . . I thought I could do something similar with a pen. At the very least, these bands assured me I had the right to try.

The egalitarianism of the punk aesthetic fueled Pelecanos's ambitions and gave him the confidence to overcome his lack of formal training, but he was still naive when it came to the inner workings of the publishing industry. For example, he took *Writer's Market* (1997) at its word ("no simultaneous submissions") and sent *A Firing Offense* to only one publisher–St. Martin's Press. Without an agent or any significant prior publications,

Pelecanos's chances for publication were slim at best. He hedged his bet and secured employment at Circle Releasing (a movie studio) while waiting for a response from St. Martin's Press.

Circle Releasing (later, Circle Films) was a local production company owned and operated by Ted and Jim Pedas, two highly respected members of the Greek community in D.C. The company is best known for producing three early movies by Joel and Ethan Coen– *Blood Simple* (1984), *Miller's Crossing* (1990), and *Barton Fink* (1991)–but it was the Pedases' decision to pick up John Woo's *The Killer* (1989) for distribution in the United States that caught Pelecanos's attention. "I'd seen the film at the American Film Institute, at a Hong Kong film festival," Pelecanos recalls in an interview with *Mystery Scene* from 1998, "and I dug it to the degree that I was ready to come work for them [Circle Releasing] just to promote that one film, which is what I did." Pelecanos even wrote the tag line for the promotional poster for *The Killer*–"One bad hit man. One tough cop. And ten thousand bullets"–a description that he is proud to say earned him a place in Jeff Rovin's *The Book of Dumb Movie Blurbs* (1995). Pelecanos worked at Circle Films for ten years and was involved in the production of three movies: Robert M. Young's *Caught* (1996), Susan Skoog's *Whatever* (1998), and George and Mike Baluzy's *BlackMale* (2000). He left the company in 1999 to try writing for television in New York but only lasted two days before separation from his family brought him back to D.C.

Employment at Circle Films allowed Pelecanos to pursue a love of motion pictures that had been with him since childhood and that also plays a significant role in his fiction. "If it weren't for the crime and action films I saw over thirty years ago, I would not be a novelist today," Pelecanos states in an article for *GQ* (March 2001). "Filmmakers in the late 60s and early 70s consistently reached for the political subtext beneath the genre trappings . . . by contrasting their leading men's physical presence and anachronistic codes of honor against a rapidly changing, desk bound, mechanized world." This same code of masculinity is a common theme in Pelecanos's fiction. Most of his works explore the meaning of manhood in modern society, and the influences on this aspect of his fiction are generally more cinematic than literary: "the movies that left the most lasting impression on me were *The Magnificent Seven* and *The Great Escape* (both from John Sturges), *The Dirty Dozen* (Robert Aldrich), the Sergio Leone westerns, and [Sam] Peckinpah's *The Wild Bunch*," reports Pelecanos in an interview posted on his official website. "All describe a masculine world with codes of friendship, honor, and (bloody) redemption. Add to that my formative filmgoing years (the early to mid 70s), where I

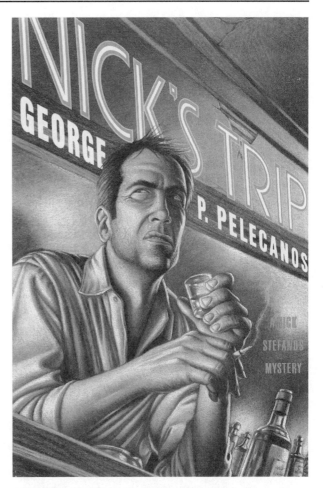

Dust jacket for Pelecanos's 1993 novel, in which Stefanos and an old friend from high school take to the road to find the friend's missing wife (Richland County Public Library)

got into the anarchic films of Don Siegel, [Martin] Scorcese, and others (and the entire exploitation, blaxploitation, and kung fu canon), and you pretty much have the setup for what I would explore in my novels."

The highly stylized action films, punk music, and hard-boiled fiction that influenced Pelecanos are deeply grounded in American popular culture. Indeed, one of the most distinctive features of Pelecanos's writing is the way he uses popular music, movies, sports, cars, and controlled substances to create a vivid sense of time, place, and characterization in his novels. "This may be a predictable sort of cultural accessorizing," as Ben Greenman points out in *The New Yorker* (8 April 2002), "but it's surprisingly effective as shorthand." Pelecanos typically avoids references to television, fast food, and brand-name commodities, but otherwise uses the narratives of popular culture as a way to update the hard-boiled genre for his generation.

Gordon Van Gelder was a twenty-four-year-old associate editor when he plucked *A Firing Offense* from the slush pile at St. Martin's Press. "I took it home one night and I was blown away by it," Van Gelder says, remembering the moment in the 1995 interview with Brace. "He knows the hard-boiled fiction genre inside and out, but brings a modern sensibility to it. . . . But without his incredibly descriptive writing that would be irrelevant." Van Gelder's advocacy was a key factor in getting Pelecanos's book into print: "Gordon was revered amongst writers," Pelecanos recalls. "If not for him, many risk-taking, ambitious genre novels would not have been published in the 90s." After one year of waiting, Pelecanos received an answering-machine message from Van Gelder offering a $2,500 advance to buy the manuscript.

A Firing Offense introduces Nicholas J. Stefanos, a recurring character in Pelecanos's fiction and the one modeled most directly after Pelecanos himself. After being fired from his job as advertising manager for Nutty Nathan's—a local chain of electronics stores modeled on Bray & Scarff—Stefanos applies for a D.C. private investigator's license and concentrates his energies on finding Jimmy Broda, a reckless kid who has disappeared after falling in with some local skinheads and cocaine dealers. Broda functions as Nick's doppelgänger in the novel, making Nick's investigation as much a quest to find his own lost youth as the missing stock boy. An opening comparison between a D.C. street and "a sodden butt drowning in the rot of a shot glass" captures the somber tone running throughout *A Firing Offense*. As first-person narrator, Stefanos describes the world through alcoholic eyes, and the narrative resolution arrives in the form of an apocalyptic shoot-out. The lightest and most interesting moments of the novel come during its strikingly authentic depictions of the retail electronics trade.

A Firing Offense received scant promotion from St. Martin's Press and sold fewer than one thousand copies during its initial publication. To help pay the bills, Pelecanos took a job bartending at My Brother's Place, a shot and beer joint catering to government workers and cops in D.C.'s federal district. Pelecanos's second novel, *Nick's Trip* (1993), opens with Stefanos pouring drinks at the Spot—"a bunker of painted cinder block and forty-watt bulbs at the northwest corner of Eight and G in Southeast." In an interview with *Mystery Scene* from 1998, Pelecanos cited Raymond Chandler's *The Long Goodbye* (1953) as the primary inspiration for *Nick's Trip*. Like Chandler, Pelecanos employs a dense and ambitious plot structure to explore issues of male friendship and trust.

Billy Goodrich, an old high-school friend and road-trip buddy, hires Stefanos to find his missing wife, April Goodrich, who left town with $200,000 of Joey DiGeordano's money. DiGeordano, a small-time numbers runner, is the son of crime boss Lou DiGeordano,

a friend of Stefanos's grandfather, Nicholas "Big Nick" Stefanos, whose story is told in Pelecanos's fifth novel, *The Big Blowdown* (1996). The friendship between Goodrich and Stefanos is shown in a series of flashbacks to the mid 1970s, evoking a time of male camaraderie infused with the popular culture Pelecanos found appealing as a D.C. youth:

> I had part-time work as a stock boy, but on the days I had off, Billy and I shot hoops. Every Saturday afternoon we'd blow a monster joint, then head down to Candy Cane City in Rock Creek Park and engage in pickup games for hours on end. The teams ended up being "salt and pepper," and the losers did push-ups. Billy had a cheap portable eight-track player, and on those rare occasions where we'd win, he would blast J. Geils's "Serve You Right to Suffer" over the bobbing heads of the losing team.

The height of their friendship comes during a cross-country road trip in the summer of 1976, but as the two start out on this excursion to find April Goodrich, they soon discover that fifteen years can create irrevocable differences in a friendship. Stefanos and Goodrich seem unable to interact with one another as adults, and the more they attempt to revert to their youth, the more they lament its passing. In a separate investigation, Stefanos briefly joins forces with Dan Boyle—a D.C. cop and regular Jack Daniels drinker at the Spot—to track down the killer of his journalist friend William Henry. Boyle's Colt Python and hard-boiled sensibilities come in handy during the resolution of the narrative. On a lighter note, some of the most enjoyable scenes in *Nick's Trip* occur when Stefanos interacts with Jackie Kahn, an accountant who moonlights as bartender for Athena's, a lesbian bar located a few blocks away from the Spot. The two strike up a humorous friendship that grows more mature and compassionate as the novel progresses. Jackie ultimately asks Nick to father a child for her and her partner, and their son appears in a cameo at the end of Pelecanos's eighth novel, *Shame the Devil* (2000).

After two first-person novels starring Nick Stefanos, Pelecanos departed from his series orientation to write a more experimental noir tale told from the perspective of criminals. "I was reading a lot of classic pulp/noir at the time, mainly David Goodis," Pelecanos recalled in an interview with Ali Karim of *Shotsmag* (May 2003). "I wanted to try to write one myself, knowing full well that there was no commercial potential whatsoever for a book of that kind in the modern market. Also, it was my first attempt at a third person novel. It would also give me an opportunity to write about two things very dear to me: women's shoes (and feet) and 60s American muscle cars. With a book of this kind there are no rules, and that was very appealing to me as well. No one read *Shoedog* in the States, but it got me some attention in France," where it was published in the prestigious Série noire.

Shoedog opens with a man named Polk pulling over in a souped-up 1969 Dodge to pick up Constantine, a drifter and former U.S. Marine about to return to D.C. after seventeen years of aimless exile. Polk is on his way to Florida, but first he needs to stop and collect a debt from an old service buddy named Grimes. Grimes plans heists for a hobby, then blackmails a crew of former convicts and wage laborers (including the philosophical black shoe salesman Shoedog) to carry them out. Lured by the bait of Grimes's sultry younger lover, Constantine signs on as a driver in Grimes's latest scheme to rob two liquor stores carrying large amounts of cash. A vicious double cross leaves Constantine and much of the crew on their own, but instead of running, they set out to hunt down the double-crossers with heavy firepower and a nihilistic attitude toward life.

Shoedog received high marks from reviewers, who generally highlighted the work's bleak but authentic tone. "Pelecanos has always been hard-boiled," said Pat Dowell of *The Washington Post* (19 June 1994), "but he aims straight and truly into the abyss with his noirish *Shoedog*." Emily Melton of *Booklist* (15 May 1994) praised the way "Pelecanos' haunting, gritty story works its way deep into his readers' collective psyches, simultaneously shocking, attracting, and repelling us with its unvarnished, unbeautiful realism and its explosive, stomach-churning violence." *Shoedog* remains Pelecanos's most experimental and anomalous novel, composed during a time of artistic freedom when the pressure to recoup a large advance was not yet present. Pelecanos recalls in the interview with Karim, "I felt like I could experiment and, as long as I delivered a 'good' book, could try anything in terms of bending the genre conventions." While formal experimentation in *Shoedog* comes across as overly self-conscious at times, the ambitions paid off in later works, when Pelecanos developed a cinematic and reportorial prose style able to match his content.

Down by the River Where the Dead Men Go—the dark final chapter in the Nick Stefanos series—was written in a fever after Pelecanos's return from Brazil in the winter of 1993–1994. "I saw kids literally starving in the street, just laying down and dying," Pelecanos recalled in an interview with *Publishers Weekly* (3 January 2000). "When you see that, it just rocks your world. Down there I was also reading in the American newspapers about Gingrich coming up, talking about ending welfare. People just don't realize what that invisible wall does. Since then all my books have been about class dif-

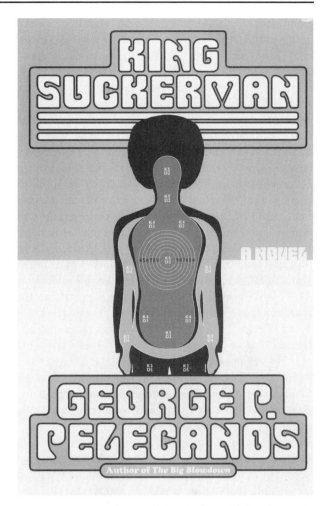

Dust jacket for Pelecanos's 1997 novel inspired by "blaxploitation" novels and movies (Richland County Public Library)

ferences and inequalities." Pelecanos translated the darkness of his Brazilian experience into a powerful and horrific work showing Stefanos's life spiraling out of control. The narrative opens with Stefanos careening wildly through the streets of D.C. in his 1966 Dodge Coronet 500. A long night of bourbons backed by beers causes multiple blackouts behind the wheel before Nick mercifully ends up facedown in his own vomit on the edge of the Anacostia River. Lying there in a semiconscious state with roaches biting his face, Stefanos overhears the murder of a young black teenager—Calvin Jeter—but is too immobilized to stop it. Wracked with the guilt brought on by sobriety, Stefanos sets out to find Jeter's killers and descends into a dank segment of the D.C. underworld rife with drugs, gay porn, and sleazy real-estate developers. The novel ends with Stefanos and his partner, Jack LaDuke, meting out extralegal justice on hoods and white-collar criminals in a shoot-out.

Reviews of the Stefanos books were unanimous in their praise and only grew in admiration as the series progressed. Pat Dowell of *The Washington Post* (19 April 1992) immediately called *A Firing Offense* a "contemporary classic" and referred to Pelecanos as "a fresh, new, utterly hard-boiled voice" that "writes tough guy talk for a younger generation, and knows the workaday world of Washington that the media ignores." *Publishers Weekly* (18 January 1993) gave *Nick's Trip* its highest grade, calling particular attention to a "cast of sharply etched minor characters, including a liquored-up, burned-out cop who plays a part in the credible, sobering conclusion, and adds to the pleasures offered by the offbeat Nick." The best reviews were reserved for *Down by the River Where the Dead Men Go,* which Melton of *Booklist* (15 April 1995) called "the ultimate in hard-boiled, hardcore fiction, with evil characters, graphic violence, and rough language." *Publishers Weekly* (24 April 1995) categorized *Down by the River Where the Dead Men Go* as "grunge crime fiction," adding, "Pelecanos joins company with James Ellroy, Andrew Vachss and Jack O'Connell in extending the noirest tones of crime fiction."

Pelecanos once described the Stefanos books as a "gradual, first-person journey into the abyss," but as the fictional life of his alter ego was deteriorating on the page, Pelecanos's own prospects were improving. "By the end of *Down by the River,* Nick's pretty much had it," Pelecanos admitted in the 25 July 1995 interview with Brace of *The Washington Post.* The novelty and youthful appeal of alcohol, drugs, and the nightlife were starting to wear off, replaced by family life and writing that was growing progressively more ambitious in scope with each new novel. In essence, the willful primitivism and raw emotion of Pelecanos's early punk aesthetic was starting to develop into a more mature style.

Pelecanos's next novel, *The Big Blowdown,* turns back the clock to tell the story of Nick Stefanos's grandfather and other Greek immigrant families from the 1930s to the 1950s. Pelecanos spent months interviewing D.C. elders and poring over periodicals in the Washingtoniana Room of the Martin Luther King Library; then he sat down and completed his "big, Warner Brothers-style crime novel," as he says in an interview with Ali Karim of *Shotsmag* (May 2003) in one four-month stretch. Pelecanos calls the novel in an online interview on his official website a "hard Valentine to my people," which is appropriate considering his parents and grandparents are interspersed throughout the narrative by name.

The Big Blowdown centers on Pete Karras—a Greek immigrant's son modeled after Pelecanos's father—who grows up on the mean streets of D.C. during the Prohibition era. Pete forges a strong friendship with Joey Recevo despite their differing ethnic backgrounds. When Karras returns from World War II in need of a job, Recevo helps him become an enforcer for Mr. Burke, a local mob boss who runs a protection racket extorting money from the lunch counters, vegetable stands, and small businesses of D.C. immigrants. When Karras is seen as going soft on some of his fellow Greeks, Burke's men come after him with baseball bats, and Recevo watches as they beat his friend senseless, turning Karras into a cripple with broken legs. Years pass as Karras limps around the streets despondent and depressed. He sires a son, Dimitri (who figures prominently in Pelecanos's next three novels), but regularly cheats on his wife. Big Nick Stefanos (father of the Nick Stefanos from earlier books) hires Karras as a short-order cook for his lunch counter. Meanwhile, Recevo has stayed loyal to the mafia, and when Mr. Burke asks him to shake down the lunch counter of a headstrong Greek who refuses to pay, the childhood friends are reunited under different circumstances to sort out violently the choices they have made and the loyalties they have kept.

For Pelecanos, writing *The Big Blowdown* was "a conscious effort to swing for the bleachers," and the novel received foreign acclaim, winning the Maltese Falcon Society's International Crime Novel of the Year Award in France, Germany, and Japan. Sales and a large audience in the United States lagged behind, however, and thus Pelecanos felt free to continue experimenting. "I was free to write virtually anything at that point in my career," he explained in a 2004 interview with Stacey Cochran: "I was not under contract to any publisher, and it's not as if I had a huge readership with preconceived expectations—and so I went full throttle into the world." His next novel, *King Suckerman,* is a freewheeling celebration of the 1970s—the rampaging decade of Pelecanos's teenage years—and the loving descriptions of the funky music, the movies with attitude, and the pimped-out style make it one of his most personal and engaging works.

King Suckerman is also a cautionary tale, and an opening epigraph with Curtis Mayfield expressing regret about the influence his *Superfly* soundtrack has had on the young sets the tone for the entire novel. All the characters in the book are eagerly anticipating the release of a fictional blaxploitation movie called *King Suckerman* (modeled after Iceberg Slim's 1967 novel, *Pimp*), including Marcus Clay, a black Vietnam veteran who owns and operates Real Right Records—an independent record store catering to the lower-income districts of D.C. Wilton Cooper, a brutal black former convict who likes smoking Kools and having sex with boys, picks up Bobby Roy Clagget at a drive-in movie theater. Clagget is a "white-boy-wanna-be-black-boy cracker" who sports an Afro, has horrendous acne, and is a stone-cold killer with a shotgun in his hands.

Together they head into D.C. to execute a drug deal. Clay and his buddy Dimitri Karras (son of Pete Karras from *The Big Blowdown*) mistakenly pick up a large sum of Cooper's cash when they stumble into the wrong warehouse looking for marijuana. Cooper and Clagget set out to recover the money, and a shoot-out along the rooftops of D.C. explodes together with the fireworks during the 1976 Bicentennial celebration.

Literary agent Sloan Harris of International Creative Management, who began representing Pelecanos with *Shoedog,* sold *King Suckerman* to Michael Pietsch at Little, Brown and Company for an advance approaching a high five figures for a two-book deal. The larger advance meant a larger publicity budget but also larger expectations. *King Suckerman* was on the shortlist for the 1998 Crime Writers' Association Golden Dagger Award, but United States sales remained mediocre. A cult following sprang up around the book, however, and Dimension Films, a division of Miramax, took an option on *King Suckerman* for Sean "Puffy" Combs. Combs was originally supposed to coproduce and star in an adaptation of *King Suckerman* for his Bad Boy Films production company, but after several years of development—including the writing of a screenplay by Pelecanos and Michael Imperioli (of *Sopranos* fame)—the rights were returned to Pelecanos.

The Sweet Forever (1998) jumps ahead ten years from where *King Suckerman* left off. Marcus Clay has just opened a branch of Real Right Records in a tough minority section of D.C. where most of the business has left because of the violence and death brought on by the epidemic crack cocaine trade. A car driven by a teenage drug courier crashes in front of Clay's new store, decapitating the driver, and a white suburbanite, Eddie Golden, pulls a pillowcase with $25,000 of Tyrell Cleveland's money out from the burning car. Eleven-year-old Anthony Taylor sees Golden take the money, but he does not fully trust the neighborhood cops and decides not to tell them, instead confiding in Clay. Cleveland, a street-savvy and vicious drug kingpin, wants his money back and comes calling at Clay's store with Short Man Monroe, a calm and deadly enforcer on Cleveland's payroll.

The majority of the narrative takes place over the course of three days in March 1986, when D.C. was on the verge of collapse from the corruption of Mayor Barry's Home Rule and the spread of crack throughout the city. The triumphs of Len Bias (a local high-school product and star basketball player for the University of Maryland) are chronicled throughout the novel, as is his death from a cocaine overdose after being signed to the Boston Celtics. "I cried the day he died," Pelecanos admitted in an interview with Eddie Dean from 1998. "It was a big thing here in Washington." Nick Stefanos

Dust jacket for Pelecanos's 1998 sequel to King Suckerman, *set in Washington during Mayor Marion Barry's Home Rule (Richland County Public Library)*

makes a brief cameo at the end of *The Sweet Forever,* this time as a young man on the street crying along with Dimitri Karras over the news of Len Bias's death.

All of Pelecanos's early novels end in some type of violent shoot-out, but *Shame the Devil* shifts perspective to look at the aftermath of violence. The novel opens with a horrific event and then traces the characters' attempts at healing and spiritual recovery. Pelecanos was now starting to rethink the hard-boiled genre and its pretense of detection, questioning whether murders can ever really be solved. The opening sequence of *Shame the Devil* is loosely based on an actual high-profile case from the mid 1990s in which all the employees at a D.C. Starbucks were killed during a botched heist. In the novel, Frank Farrow, Roman Otis, and Farrow's brother, Richard, rob May's Pizza Parlor, a D.C. restaurant doubling as a gambling front. The robbery goes horribly wrong, with four restaurant staffers killed and

Richard Farrow shot dead by the police. In the frantic getaway, Frank inadvertently runs over a young boy, Jimmy Karras, Dimitri Karras's son. Three years pass, and Karras is burned out, having turned to drugs in an effort to cope with his young son's death. Nick Stefanos comes back into the narrative as a major character, finding Karras a job as dishwasher at the Spot, which now serves as a neighborhood gathering place. A final shoot-out brings the narrative back to Haynes Point, where *The Big Blowdown* and the intertwined history of Nick Stefanos and Dimitri Karras began sixty years earlier.

The cycle of novels beginning with *The Big Blowdown* and ending with *Shame the Devil* have often been referred to as "The D.C. Quartet"–a title derived from James Ellroy's cycle of novels known as the "L.A. Quartet"–although Pelecanos prefers to call them his "Once Upon a Time in D.C." saga, a moniker bestowed by Jonathan Lethem when he compared *The Big Blowdown* to Sergio Leone's epic films. Lethem was not alone in his approval. *Publishers Weekly* (8 April 1996) praised how *The Big Blowdown* "lovingly re-creates old Washington with small details about soft-drink brands, tinned cars and cherished smokes. The ending is a haze of gunsmoke that drifts away to leave a mixed tableau of heroism and futility." Ben Greenman of *The New Yorker* (8 April 2002) called *King Suckerman* Pelecanos's "masterstroke: a revved-up, flashy tribute to the big-Afro seventies [with] characters, even the villains, motivated by a mixture of self-interest and existential despair which makes the battle between good and evil unusually compelling." Michael Connelly, quoted in *The Washington Post* (21 March 1999), called Pelecanos "the crime writer that other crime writers read for inspiration. His new book, *The Sweet Forever,* is the best book I've read, mystery or not, in years." Finally, in his glowing and perceptive remarks about *Shame the Devil,* Bill Ott of *Booklist* (15 November 1999) managed to encapsulate the critical response to Pelecanos's quartet by evoking mythic terms: "Pelecanos delivers a sort of summarizing chapter to what has become a magnificent serial novel depicting life on inner-city streets in the postwar era. . . . For mythic grandeur grounded in the gritty truth of the street, few contemporary novelists can top Pelecanos."

Pelecanos introduced a new cast of characters in *Right as Rain* (2001), an urban Western, set in D.C.'s Fourth District, that closely examines the racial divide in a contemporary setting. "It was time to get out of the small, insular world I had created and do something new," Pelecanos explained in a 2001 interview with *The Onion.* "I was trying to point the finger at all of us. We all have this problem, so why don't we admit it? The worst kind of novel is one that blames other people for

the racial problem in order to make the reader feel good about himself." To explore the issue of race from a multiracial and multigenerational perspective, Pelecanos created the unlikely partnership of Derek Strange, who is black, and Terry Quinn, an Irishman, two former cops who remain the protagonists in his next four best-selling novels.

In *Right as Rain,* fifty-year-old Derek Strange heads his own private investigation firm, Strange Investigations, and is hired by Leona Wilson to investigate the death of her son, Chris, an off-duty black police officer gunned down by Terry Quinn in a tragic mishap. Quinn, who quit the force to work in a used-book store, was legally cleared of any wrongdoing in the shooting–his actions deemed "right as rain" by the department–but he is still personally haunted by the thought that race was a subconscious motivator for his pulling the trigger. Strange interviews Quinn and believes his account; then he asks Quinn's help in investigating Chris's erratic behavior on the night of his death. Together they uncover a connection between the incident and the activities of a local drug dealer, which in turn leads them on a search for Wilson's sister–a young beauty now dying of malnutrition because of prostituting herself to feed a heroin habit.

The Strange and Quinn books mark the culmination of a trend in Pelecanos's fiction to become progressively less autobiographical in content. The sense of realism once derived from his prior work experience has gradually been replaced by field research with the D.C. police and private investigators. Pelecanos frequently rides with D.C. police on the midnight-to-dawn shift and knows several private investigators in Washington who put him in contact with prostitutes and other people who are out at night and see what is going on. Little, Brown seemed to like this new, less self-conscious approach and gave *Hell to Pay* (2002)–the second installment in the Strange-Quinn saga–a $100,000 ad campaign. The added publicity propelled *Hell to Pay* onto *The New York Times* extended best-seller list, and it even went on to win the 2003 *Los Angeles Times* Book Award. Pelecanos sees the changes as another part in his continued fight to keep his perspective in print: "After Springsteen wrote *Born to Run* he lost his old fans," Pelecanos explained to *Entertainment Weekly* (8 March 2002). "But to stay in this game, you got to make the publishers happy. All I want to do is shine a light on the working-class people of this city. The racial divide here is in your face. And that interests me, because I have three mixed-race kids. I worry about them. And I don't like the way the country is heading."

Like much of Pelecanos's more recent work, *Hell to Pay* focuses on the exploitation of disadvantaged children. Terry Quinn is now working part-time for Derek

Strange's detective agency, and both are coaching a pee-wee football team. Joe Wilder, their eight-year-old star quarterback, is shot and killed in a drive-by shooting at an ice-cream stand. Wilder's father, a well-connected criminal, contacts Strange and asks for his help in bringing the shooters to vigilante-style justice. Two other story lines run concurrently in the novel. Quinn is helping two female private investigators track down Jennifer Marshall, a runaway teen now a hooker for Worldwide Wilson, a ruthless pimp. In a separate investigation, a friend asks Strange to do a background check on his daughter's fiancé, Calhoun Tucker, a young black nightclub owner who seems too good to be true. Strange establishes Tucker as a legitimate young entrepreneur but also discovers he is being unfaithful with another woman. Strange is in no position to take the high road, however, and is forced to confront his own habit of massage-parlor sex and the repercussions it is having on his relationship with longtime lover and secretary Janine Baker.

Hell to Pay showcases Pelecanos's evolving prose style, which Ben Greenman of *The New Yorker* (8 April 2002) described as "telegraphic: a scaffolding of nouns and verbs, a few load-bearing adverbs, and a near-absence of adjectival frippery." Pelecanos's leaner prose and ear for realistic dialogue was also starting to catch the attention of some people outside the publishing industry. David Simon, the man behind "Homicide: Life on the Streets," approached Pelecanos to write for *The Wire,* an HBO crime drama set in Baltimore that conceptually attempts to bring a "visual novel" to television. Pelecanos started as a story editor, working alongside Ed Burns; then Pelecanos became a writer; and then he became the producer for the series, bringing in crime novelists Dennis Lehane and Richard Price to write for the third season. Pelecanos still applied himself to his novels, however, and with *Soul Circus* (2003), he produced a detached look at capital punishment and the rampant gun culture of D.C.

Soul Circus opens with Derek Strange married to Janine Baker and enjoying life with his stepson, Lionel, a high-school senior. Granville Oliver, a high-profile drug dealer and territorial gang leader in the southeastern part of D.C. known as Anacostia, has been arrested and faces the death sentence for murder under the federal RICO act. Oliver's lawyers hire Strange to locate a witness, Devra Stokes, whose testimony might be able to contradict Philip Wood, who is testifying to reduce his own stretch, and commute Oliver's sentence to life in prison. Strange feels an obligation to help Oliver, despite his reputation, largely because Strange killed Oliver's father decades earlier while serving as a police officer. Thus, Strange feels at least partially responsible for Oliver's upbringing and his resultant path toward

Dust jacket for Pelecanos's 2002 novel, his second to feature private investigators Derek Strange and Terry Quinn (Richland County Public Library)

drugs, gangs, and violence. Meanwhile, a gang war over control of Oliver's former territory looms. Any witness who can help the imprisoned kingpin's case ends up dead, as two rival up-and-coming drug lords kick off a turf war to fill the power vacuum created on the streets. The Anacostia section of D.C. turns into a war zone, and the only one who benefits is Ulysses Foreman, a former cop turned local gun dealer and expert in supply and demand.

In an interview with Karim from 2003, Pelecanos called *Soul Circus* "an almost reportorial look at the current situation in the American inner city." Like James Ellroy before him, Pelecanos was starting to push violently against the limitations of genre and bristle at the crime novelist label. As he told Robert Birnbaum in 2003: "It's an anti-detective novel. They are constantly one step behind the police throughout the book, as they would be. You know, private detectives don't solve murders. Police do." Pelecanos's constant quest for realism was moving his writing away from the set pieces of genre toward a journalistic form of historical ethnography—one that attempts to illuminate the present by interrogating the past. This trend is clearly showcased in Pelecanos's 2004 novel, *Hard Revolution,* which he calls in the interview with Karim his "*Big Blowdown* for the 1960s."

Hard Revolution is a prequel that opens in the spring of 1959, when Derek Strange is just entering his teenage years. Derek is caught shoplifting, but an adult gives him a break and teaches him a lesson that shapes his destiny as a man. Strange's family and upbringing remain the early focus of the novel, before the narrative jumps forward nine years to Lyndon Johnson's announcement that he will not seek a second presidential term. Derek has become one of the few black officers on the D.C. force, but he gets little respect from fellow blacks, many of whom feel he is working for the enemy. The ensuing plot involves two groups of criminals: a group of white racist thugs who drive custom cars while high on beer and amphetamines, and a group of blacks headed by Alvin Jones, a thieving pimp who carries a straight razor and has a pathological animosity toward women. A jaded white detective named Frank Vaughn tries to track down one of the thugs after he swerves his Ford Galaxie onto the sidewalk, killing a young black teenager. Meanwhile, Derek and his partner—the white Ivy League idealist Troy Peters—prowl the streets just as Dennis Strange, Derek's older brother, returns from Vietnam with a Black Power militancy and an addiction to painkillers that leads to harder drugs and a dangerous association with Alvin Jones. The last fifty pages of *Hard Revolution* capture Washington in flames, as the plotlines converge and explode when the assassination of Martin Luther King Jr. in Memphis triggers a weeklong wave of arson and riots that leave the city charred and divided.

Although Pelecanos's alter ego, Nick Stefanos, does not take center stage in the novel, *Hard Revolution* still resonates with strong autobiographical tones: "In a weird way, everything I've written about through my whole career has come out of that summer after the riots," Pelecanos said in an interview with Carol Memmott of *USA Today* (11 March 2004). "I always knew I wanted to write this book, but I didn't feel like I was ready and now I know why it's so important. All my obsessions, whether it's music, the race thing or the class divide, all these things come out of that summer."

Reviews of the Strange-Quinn books were again overwhelmingly positive. "To acclaim the urban thrillers of George P. Pelecanos as literary would be to falsify the very things that make them entertaining: exciting plots that unfold at a steadily accelerating pace; sharp, often funny dialogue; offhand references to movies and, especially, to music that reveal a writer attuned to pop culture," said Charles Taylor in his review of *Right as Rain* for *The New York Times* (25 March 2001). "But within the grubby and teeming territory he has staked out for himself, Pelecanos sketches a picture not so much of the dead end of inner-city life but of the inhabitants who refuse to give up the ghost." In her review of *Hell to Pay,* Ann Bruns of Bookreporter.com claimed "George Pelecanos has earned himself a permanent spot at the head of the table of *noir* writers." Memmott of *USA Today* (12 March 2003) said in her review of *Soul Circus:* "With every book Pelecanos takes his descriptive powers to a higher level of brilliance. Scenes of violence are reread for the beauty of the language and the cinematic quality that pushes readers to envision urban evil in all its forms." Bill Ott of *Booklist* (1 November 2003) started off a litany of great reviews for *Hard Revolution:* "Like Nathanael West describing the burning of Hollywood in *The Day of the Locust,* Pelecanos stage manages the conflagration [at the end of *Hard Revolution*] perfectly, capturing the personal tragedy and the metaphorical significance vividly and directly."

One has to look hard to find negative, or even mixed, reviews of Pelecanos's work, but *Hard Revolution* had at least a few dissenting opinions. For one, Edward Karam of *People Weekly* (15 March 2004) felt Pelecanos went overboard on the Washingtoniana this time: "The usually deft chatter about cars, movies and music that helps define Pelecanos's characters feels formulaic and overdone. And the riot scenes are like newspaper accounts, with characters tracked block by block. That minutiae may intrigue D.C. residents who remember the landmarks, but it stalls a good revenge story." Pelecanos's obsessive concern with period detail was taken to new heights when his publishers released a companion compact disc to *Hard Revolution.* Despite a few negative reviews, Little, Brown liked the work enough to offer Pelecanos a three-book contract for $1,500,000; his next novel, *Drama City,* looks at the brutal world of underground dogfighting, and is due out in 2005.

Beyond the best-seller lists, Pelecanos's popularity is now set to explode. Curtis Hanson, director of *L.A. Confidential* and *8 Mile,* has taken options on all the books featuring Derek Strange and plans to make a movie of *Right as Rain* using a script by David Benioff (of *Troy* fame). Whether Pelecanos's punk aesthetic can truly cross into mainstream popularity remains to be seen. His success, in both the marketplace and the genre, will ultimately depend on people's willingness to accept his technique, which employs a dark realism to frame fragmentary glimpses of hope. The principle of hope is at the core of Pelecanos's fiction.

Interviews:

Fred Blosser, "George P. Pelecanos," *Mystery Scene,* 60 (1998): 46–51;

Jennifer Schuessler, "Hard-boiled Family Values," *Publishers Weekly,* 247 (3 January 2000): 52–53;

Keith Phipps, "George P. Pelecanos," *Onion A. V. Club,* 37, no. 33 (19 September 2001) <www.theonion-avclub.com/feature/index.php?issue=3733&F=2>;

Tom Nolan, "George P. Pelecanos," *Mystery Scene,* 75 (2002): 56–58;

Bob Cornwell, "Hard-Boiled Heaven" (2002) <http://www.twbooks.co.uk/crimescene/pelecanosinterviewbc.htm>;

Anthony Mason, "Capital Crimes," *CBS News Sunday Morning* (24 March 2002);

Robert Louit, "George P. Pelecanos: Tempêtes á Washington," *Magazine Littéraire,* 411 (July–August 2002): 98–103;

Adam Dunn, "Gunplay: *PW* talks with George Pelecanos," *Publishers Weekly,* 250 (3 February 2003): 54;

Robert Birnbaum, "Robert Birnbaum Talks with the Author of *Soul Circus,*" *Identity Theory* (21 April 2003) <http://www.identitytheory.com/interviews/birnbaum100.html>;

Ali Karim, "George Pelecanos," *Shotsmag,* 18 (May 2003) <http://www.shotsmag.co.uk/SHOTS%2018/contents.htm>;

Steve Wynn and George P. Pelecanos, "Steve Wynn's Conversation with George Pelecanos," *Magnet Magazine,* 51 (September/October 2003);

Stacey Cochran, "George Pelecanos," *Plots with Guns,* 28 (March/April 2004) <http://www.plotswithguns.com/PelecanosIntv.htm>.

References:

Randall Bloomquist, "Confessions of a Consumer Electronics Salesman," *Washington Post,* 28 August 1996, p. R5+;

Eric Brace, "The Writer's Block: For Native George Pelecanos, Washington Is a Novel Setting," *Washington Post,* 25 July 1995, p. E1+;

Sean Daly, "Heavy Hitter: George Pelecanos Puts More Punch into Capital Crime," *Book Magazine,* 14 (January/February 2001): 18–20;

Eddie Dean, "Pulp Reality," *Washington City Paper,* 21 August 1998, cover story;

Daniel Fierman, "D.C. Confidential: Mystery Writer George Pelecanos Breaks Out of Washington's Mean Streets," *Entertainment Weekly,* 643 (8 March 2002): 36–38;

"George Pelacanos," *Time Warner Bookmark* (2004) <http://www.twbookmark.com/features/georgepelecanos>;

Ben Greenman, "Washington Wizard," *New Yorker,* 78 (8 April 2002): 90–92;

Natalie Hopkinson, "Eye on the Working Class: Local Novelist Depicts District's Blue-Collar Side," *Washington Post,* 15 March 2001: pp. T24+;

John-Ivan Palmer, "Roaches Ate My Face, Hard-Boiled Crime Novelist George Pelecanos," *Your Flesh Quarterly,* 34 (1996): 55–61;

Linton Weeks, "The Gumshoe's Guide to Washington, D.C.: Writer George Pelecanos Knows His Way around Town, and around a Detective Story," *Washington Post,* 11 March 2004, pp. C1+.

Rex Stout

(1 December 1886 – 27 October 1975)

Bobbie Robinson
Abraham Baldwin College

BOOKS: *How Like a God* (New York: Vanguard, 1929; London: Morley & Mitchell Kennerly, 1931);

Seed on the Wind (New York: Vanguard, 1930; London: Morley & Mitchell Kennerly, 1930);

Golden Remedy (New York: Vanguard, 1931);

Forest Fire (New York: Farrar & Rinehart, 1933; London: Faber & Faber, 1934);

Fer-de-Lance (New York: Farrar & Rinehart, 1934; London: Cassell, 1935);

The President Vanishes (New York: Farrar & Rinehart, 1934);

The League of Frightened Men (New York: Farrar & Rinehart, 1935; London: Cassell, 1935);

O Careless Love! (New York: Farrar & Rinehart, 1935);

The Rubber Band (New York: Farrar & Rinehart, 1936; London: Cassell, 1936);

The Hand in the Glove (New York: Farrar & Rinehart, 1937); republished as *Crime on Her Hands* (London: Collins, 1939);

The Red Box (New York: Farrar & Rinehart, 1937; London: Cassell, 1937);

The Nero Wolfe Omnibus (Cleveland: World, 1937);

Mr. Cinderella (New York: Farrar & Rinehart, 1938; London: Faber & Faber, 1939);

Too Many Cooks (New York: Farrar & Rinehart, 1938; London: Collins, 1938);

Double for Death (New York: Farrar & Rinehart, 1939; London: Collins, 1940);

Mountain Cat (New York: Farrar & Rinehart, 1939; London: Collins, 1940);

Red Threads, in *The Mystery Book* (New York: Farrar & Rinehart, 1939; London: Collins, 1941);

Some Buried Caesar (New York: Farrar & Rinehart, 1939; London: Collins, 1939);

Bad for Business, in *The Second Mystery Book* (New York: Farrar & Rinehart, 1940; London: Collins, 1945);

Over My Dead Body (New York: Farrar & Rinehart, 1940; London: Collins, 1940);

Where There's a Will (New York: Farrar & Rinehart, 1940; London: Collins, 1941);

Rex Stout (from Please Pass the Guilt, *1973; Richland County Public Library)*

Alphabet Hicks (New York: Farrar & Rinehart, 1941; London: Collins, 1942);

The Broken Vase (New York: Farrar & Rinehart, 1941; London: Collins, 1942);

Black Orchids: A Nero Wolfe Double Mystery (New York: Farrar & Rinehart, 1942; London: Collins, 1943);

Not Quite Dead Enough (New York: Farrar & Rinehart, 1944);

The Silent Speaker (New York: Viking, 1946; London: Collins, 1947);

Too Many Women (New York: Viking, 1947; London: Collins, 1948);

And Be a Villain (New York: Viking, 1948; London: Collins, 1948);

The Second Confession (New York: Viking, 1949; London: Collins, 1950);

Trouble in Triplicate (New York: Viking, 1949; London: Collins, 1949)–comprises "Before I Die," "Help Wanted, Male," and "Instead of Evidence";

In the Best Families (New York: Viking, 1950; London: Collins, 1951);

Three Doors to Death (New York: Viking, 1950; London: Collins, 1950)–comprises "Man Alive," "Omit Flowers," and "Door to Death";

Curtains for Three (New York: Viking, 1951; London: Collins, 1951)–comprises "The Gun with Wings," "Bullet for One," and "Disguise for Murder";

Murder by the Book (New York: Viking, 1951; London: Collins, 1952);

Prisoner's Base (New York: Viking, 1952; London: Collins, 1953);

Triple Jeopardy (New York: Viking, 1952; London: Collins, 1952)–comprises "Home to Roost," "The Cop Killer," and "The Squirt and the Monkey";

The Golden Spiders (New York: Viking, 1953; London: Collins, 1954);

The Black Mountain (New York: Viking, 1954; London: Collins, 1955);

Three Men Out (New York: Viking, 1954; London: Collins, 1955)–comprises "Invitation to Murder," "The Zero Clue," and "This Won't Kill You";

Before Midnight (New York: Viking, 1955; London: Collins, 1956);

Full House: A Nero Wolfe Omnibus (New York: Viking, 1955);

Might as Well Be Dead (New York: Viking, 1956; London: Collins, 1957);

Three Witnesses (New York: Viking, 1956; London: Collins, 1956)–comprises "The Next Witness," "When a Man Murders," and "Die like a Dog";

If Death Ever Slept (New York: Viking, 1957; London: Collins, 1958);

Three for the Chair (New York: Viking, 1957; London: Collins, 1958)–comprises "A Window for Death," "Immune to Murder," and "Too Many Detectives";

All Aces: A Nero Wolfe Omnibus (New York: Viking, 1958);

And Four to Go: A Nero Wolfe Foursome (New York: Viking, 1958); published as *Crime and Again* (London: Collins, 1959);

Champagne for One (New York: Viking, 1958; London: Collins, 1959);

Plot It Yourself (New York: Viking, 1959; London: Collins, 1960);

Murder in Style (London: Collins, 1960);

Three at Wolfe's Door (New York: Viking, 1960; London: Collins, 1961)–comprises "Poison à la Carte," "Method Three for Murder," and "The Rodeo Murder";

Too Many Clients (New York: Viking, 1960; London: Collins, 1961);

The Final Deduction (New York: Viking, 1961; London, Collins, 1962);

Five of a Kind: The Third Nero Wolfe Omnibus (New York: Viking, 1961);

Gambit (New York: Viking, 1962; London: Collins, 1963);

Homicide Trinity (New York: Viking, 1962; London: Collins, 1963)–comprises "Eeny Meeny Murder Mo," "Death of a Demon," and "Counterfeit for Murder";

The Mother Hunt (New York: Viking, 1963; London: Collins, 1964);

A Right to Die (New York: Viking, 1964; London: Collins, 1965);

Trio for Blunt Instruments (New York: Viking, 1964; London: Collins, 1965)–comprises "Kill Now, Pay Later," "Murder is Corny," and "Blood Will Tell";

The Doorbell Rang (New York: Viking, 1965; London: Collins, 1966);

Royal Flush: The Fourth Nero Wolfe Omnibus (New York: Viking, 1965)–includes *Fer-de-Lance* and *Murder by the Book;*

Death of a Doxy (New York: Viking, 1966; London: Collins, 1967);

The Father Hunt (New York: Viking, 1968; London: Collins, 1969);

Death of a Dude (New York: Viking, 1969; London: Collins, 1970);

Kings Full of Aces (New York: Viking, 1969)–includes "Home to Roost," "The Cop-Killer," and "The Squirt and the Monkey";

Three Aces: A Nero Wolfe Omnibus (New York: Viking, 1971);

Please Pass the Guilt (New York: Viking, 1973; London: Collins, 1974);

Three Trumps (New York: Viking, 1973);

Triple Zeck (New York: Viking, 1974);

A Family Affair (New York: Viking, 1975; London: Collins, 1976).

OTHER: *The Illustrious Dunderheads,* edited by Stout (New York: Knopf, 1942);

Rue Morgue No. 1, edited by Stout with Louis Greenfield (New York: Creative Age Press, 1946);

"Tough Cop's Gift," in *Christmas Annual* (New York: Abbott Laboratories, 1953);

Eat, Drink, and Be Buried, edited by Stout (New York: Viking, 1956);

"Cinderella Paperback," in *Writers Roundtable,* edited by Helen Hull and Michael Drury (New York: Harper, 1959);

The Nero Wolfe Cook Book, edited by Stout with the editors of Viking Press (New York: Viking, 1973).

SELECTED PERIODICAL PUBLICATIONS–
UNCOLLECTED: "Excess Baggage," *Short Stories,* 78 (October 1912): 26–32;

"The Infernal Feminine," *Short Stories,* 78 (November 1912): 88–91;

"A Professor's Recall," *Black Cat* (December 1912): 46–50;

"Pamfret and Peace," *Black Cat* (January 1913): 49–56;

"A Companion of Fortune," *Short Stories,* 79 (April 1913): 112–117;

"The Pickled Picnic," *Black Cat* (June 1913): 46–56;

"A White Precipitate," *Lippincott's Monthly Magazine,* 91 (June 1913): 730–734;

Her Forbidden Knight, All-Story Magazine, 26 (August 1913): 855–878; 27 (September 1913): 117–142; 27 (October 1913): 415–433; 27 (November 1913): 652–675; 27 (December 1913): 935–950;

"The Mother of Invention," *Black Cat* (August 1913): 27–33;

"Methode Americaine," *Smart Set,* 91 (November 1913): 129–134;

"The Pay-Yeoman," *All-Story Magazine,* 28 (January 1914): 186–192;

"A Tyrant Abdicates," *Lippincott's Monthly Magazine,* 92 (January 1914): 92–96;

Under the Andes, All-Story Magazine, 28 (February 1914): 241–380;

"Secrets," *All-Story Weekly,* 29 (7 March 1914): 208–216;

"Rose Orchid," *All-Story Weekly,* 30 (28 March 1914): 876–883;

"An Agacella Or," *Lippincott's Monthly Magazine,* 93 (April 1914): 465–473;

"The Inevitable Third," *All-Story Weekly,* 31 (25 April 1914): 886–892;

A Prize for Princes, All-Story Weekly, 31 (2 May 1914): 111–142;

"Out of the Line," *All-Story Cavalier Weekly,* 33 (13 June 1914): 886–892;

"The Lie," *All-Story Cavalier Weekly,* 33 (4 July 1914): 218–224;

"Target Practise," *All-Story Cavalier Weekly,* 40 (26 December 1914): 133–141;

"If He Be Married," *All-Story Cavalier Weekly,* 40 (16 January 1915): 762–768;

"Baba," *All-Story Cavalier Weekly,* 41 (30 January 1915): 351–356;

"Warner & Wife," *All-Story Cavalier Weekly,* 42 (27 February 1915): 222–242;

"A Little Love Affair," *Smith's Magazine,* 21 (July 1915): 615–626;

"Art for Art's Sake," *Smith's Magazine,* 21 (August 1915): 757–764;

"Another Little Love Affair," *Smith's Magazine,* 21 (September 1915): 1041–1052;

"Sanetomo," *All-Story Weekly,* 25 (September 1915): 717–723;

"Jonathan Stannart's Secret Vice," *All-Story Weekly,* 49 (11 September 1915): 236–242;

"Justice Ends at Home," *All-Story Weekly* (4 December 1915): 260–293;

The Great Legend, All-Story Weekly, 53 (1 January 1916): 225–261; 53 (8 January 1916): 444–473; 53 (15 January 1916): 717–745; 54 (22 January 1916): 138–171; 54 (29 January 1916): 342–360;

"It's Science that Counts," *All-Story Weekly,* 56 (1 April 1916): 468–478;

"The Rope Dance," *All-Story Weekly,* 59 (24 June 1916): 561–570;

"An Officer and a Lady," *All-Story Weekly,* 66 (13 January 1917): 610–616;

"Heels of Fate," *All-Story Weekly,* 77 (17 November 1917): 688–695;

"It Happened Last Night," *Canadian Magazine,* 85 (March 1936): 3–5;

"A Good Character for a Novel," *New Masses* (15 December 1936): 17–18;

"Bitter End," *American Magazine,* 130 (November 1940): 47–51, 127–147;

"Watson Was a Woman," *Saturday Review of Literature* (1 March 1941): 3–4, 16;

"Not Quite Dead Enough," *American Magazine,* 134 (December 1942): 131–151;

"We Shall Hate, or We Shall Fail," *New York Times Magazine* (17 January 1943): 6, 29;

"Grim Fairy Tales," *Saturday Review of Literature,* 32 (2 April 1949): 7–8, 34;

"Door to Death," *American Magazine,* 147 (June 1949): 146–160;

"The Cop-Killer," *American Magazine,* 151 (February 1951): 137–152, as "The Cop Killer";

"This Won't Kill You," *American Magazine,* 154 (September 1952): 131–143, as "This Will Kill You";

"Invitation to Murder," *American Magazine,* 156 (August 1953): 128–142, as "Will to Murder";

"The Zero Clue," *American Magazine,* 156 (December 1953): 119–133, as "Scared to Death";

"When a Man Murders," *American Magazine,* 157 (May 1954): 119–135;

"Die like a Dog," *American Magazine,* 158 (December 1954): 121–136, as "The Body in the Hall";

"His Own Hand," *Manhunt* (April 1955): 49–61;

"The Next Witness," *American Magazine,* 159 (May 1955): 121–136, as "The Last Witness";

"Christmas Party," *Collier's,* 139 (4 January 1957): 62–73, as "The Christmas-Party Murder";

"Easter Parade," *Look,* 21 (16 April 1957): 102–104, 106, 109–113, 115–118, 120;

"Fourth of July Picnic," *Look,* 21 (9 July 1957): 64–65, 67–68, 70, 73–76, 78–79;

"Blood Will Tell," *Ellery Queen's Mystery Magazine,* 241 (December 1963): 6–32, 79–98.

Rex Stout's creation of private detective Nero Wolfe and his assistant Archie Goodwin with their point-counterpoint relationship, their complementary but divergent approaches to solving appealing mysteries, and their straddling genres from the hard-boiled detective story to the novel of manners, secured Stout a place in American crime fiction. Finding the dark vision and penchant for unrelieved violence in the traditional hard-boiled novel too grim and the prissiness of contemporary stories of the "Great Detective" too limiting, Stout created a new self-contained and self-sustaining fictional world. Over a period of forty-two years and through seventy-two tales of Wolfe's and Archie's exploits, Stout's graceful blending of fictional orders reformed detective fiction and, according to his biographer John McAleer, "helped save the detective story from extinction."

Stout was born in Noblesville, Indiana, on 1 December 1886 to John Wallace Stout and Lucetta Todhunter Stout. From both the Stouts and the Todhunters he inherited five generations of Quaker ancestors. Rex was the sixth child and third son born into a family of four boys and five girls.

Drawn by Kansas having entered the Union as a free state, John Stout moved the family to Wakarusa, near Topeka, before Rex was a year old. He hoped to improve his financial situation and to raise his family in a friendly, moral environment. He was attracted to Kansas by the hordes of Mennonites, Quakers, and expatriated New Englanders who shared an antislavery goal and dominated Kansas Politics. Rex inherited intellectual gifts and good sense from both sets of ancestors.

Always a precocious child, he began to read at eighteen months; he read his father's Bible through at four, again at five, and by eleven had read John Stout's entire classical library of 1,126 volumes of history, poetry, essays, and English and American novels. When he was eleven, Stout became the spelling champion of Kansas, Nebraska, and Illinois. He developed a penchant and fascination for words at an early age from his grandmother Emily McNeal Todhunter, a voracious reader who kept a huge dictionary open next to her at all times and learned the meaning, pronunciation, and etymology of every word she did not know. Her talent with words complemented her talent with plants. More than likely, she in part fostered Stout's creation of the character of Nero Wolfe.

In mid September 1896 the Stout family moved from Wakarusa to Bellview, closer to Topeka. Six of the children enrolled in a district 61 school, where Stout excelled immediately. In addition to his spelling talent, the school principal discovered that Stout was a rapid calculator. Frequently, he stood Stout with his back to the board or blindfolded him while writing random numbers, four tiers of six across, on the board. He would show Stout the numbers, and within five seconds without fail Stout had the total. In the same year he won the spelling championship, school officials paraded him through a tour of Kansas schools to showcase his math talents. Stout was uncomfortable with the math ability and the tour; he hated to perform like a freak. The gift for calculating gradually disappeared, and he reported later to McAleer, "I think I consciously lost it because I didn't like it. I turned to words instead of figures. I'd always loved words."

Stout's reading during the years in Bellview continued in the vein he exhibited as a preschooler; it also presages the eclectic tastes and voracious reading habits of Nero Wolfe. Stout read Jonathan Swift, Alexander Pope, Samuel Johnson, George Eliot, Charles Dickens, Anthony Trollope, and the Brontë sisters; he devoured the works of Edgar Allan Poe, Wilkie Collins, and Sir Arthur Conan Doyle. By the time Stout was twelve, he had read many of William Shakespeare's works.

The Stouts moved into Topeka in January 1899. Stout and his sister Ruth entered Lincoln School, where he completed eighth grade as a twelve-year-old. Studying little, he finished high school in May 1903 without difficulty. In September, Stout went to the University of Kansas. Stout made little impression on the professors, and the college students made even less impression on him. He left with the strong sense that college offered him nothing; he believed he already knew more than most people he encountered there.

Stout returned to Topeka and took a job as usher at Crawford's Opera House, steeping himself in the culture of professional theater. Though he remained an usher for two years, he made little money and soon became a bookkeeper at the People's Ice and Fuel Company. At seventeen, Stout made his first money from writing when he sold a poem to *The Smart Set* for $12, though the magazine never published it. When he realized he would never see the poem in print, Stout burned all the poetry he had written up to that time and did not try writing again for several years.

In April 1905, shortly before Stout left Topeka, a robber stole his collection of nearly one hundred records and his Victor disk graphophone, carelessly leaving the crank behind. A month later an alert salesman remembered the theft and notified the police when a man came into his shop to order a crank for a Victor graphophone. For a brief time, the stolen goods resided at the police station, where Police Chief A. G. Goodwin treated the staff to a grand concert with Stout's records. Stout eventually retrieved his belongings from Chief Goodwin, who later became the model for Nero Wolfe's assistant Archie Goodwin.

In July, Stout decided to join the United States Navy and went to Pittsburg, Kansas, to enlist. After serving as a pay yeoman for two months, he was moved to President Theodore Roosevelt's yacht, the *Mayflower,* where he stayed for two years. Stout supplemented his navy pay of $26.20 per month by playing cards, adding to his income $150 a month on average. Stout's card skill got him invited to dinner and cards by his immediate supervisor, Lieutenant Graham Montrose Alvey, at the home of his bachelor uncle, Alvey A. Adee, second assistant secretary of state. Adee was addicted to exact word choice; precise linguistic economy was his standard for the State Department. His genius, reclusive lifestyle, vast knowledge, superb culinary taste, and expansive opinions and preferences impressed Stout. Along with his genius grandmother, Adee later informed Stout's creation of Nero Wolfe.

Having bought his discharge from the navy for $80 on 5 August 1907, Stout went to Cleveland, Ohio, determined to study law. After two months he gave up, finding law too undignified a profession for the honest man of integrity he considered himself. He then worked in a variety of jobs—tobacco-store salesman, railroad bookkeeper, bellhop, and tugboat worker. In the summer of 1909 he went to New York. Enthralled with the city, Stout wrote to Ruth suggesting that she, their mother, and youngest brother, Donald, join him. By Christmas most of the family were in the city living in two brownstones.

During the summer of 1910 Stout worked as a barker for a New York City tour bus and sold a four-line poem to *The Smart Set* for $10. It was published in November, and Stout quickly sent in two more poems that appeared in 1911. Feeling at loose ends, he undertook in 1911 a final year of wandering around the country seeking direction for his future. He worked in a dozen states, finding roots nowhere. He was always employed and always solvent. His jobs included shrimping, selling baskets and blankets on an Indian reservation, cooking, and managing a hotel. He told Alfred Bester in a 1969 interview for *Holiday,* "I never

had any adventures, but I had a lot of episodes. It was not only good preparation for a writer, but also for life." When he returned to New York, Stout took a job as a bookkeeper at Milbury Atlantic Supply Company; he wanted to earn enough money to take a room and write in earnest.

In early 1912 Stout quit his job to focus on writing. He quickly sold two stories to *Short Stories* magazine for $18 each and launched his writing career. "Excess Baggage" appeared in October. The narrator and central character, Frank Keller, is a brash womanizer who gets his comeuppance through a series of innocent but suspicious episodes that cause his wife to think he is unfaithful. The chief interests of the story are the pacing, economy, and idiom that anticipate the voice of Archie Goodwin. Stout published his first crime story, "A Professor's Recall," in December 1912 in *The Black Cat.* Between 1912 and 1917, he wrote four serialized novels and more than thirty short stories. *Her Forbidden Knight,* which began serialization in *All-Story Magazine* in August 1913 included some details that are precursors of the Wolfe saga. A detective crudely anticipates Inspector Cramer; Amanda Berry, a landlady, lives in an old brownstone; Pierre Dumain, a palmist and clairvoyant, gives lavish dinner parties with excellent fare; and a lawyer exhibits highly developed skill at cross-examination and staging charades. Clearly apprentice work, the novel nonetheless indicates Stout's skill with characterization among secondary ensemble characters.

In succession followed *Under the Andes* (published in *All-Story Magazine* beginning in February 1914), Stout's single attempt at a lost-world novel; *A Prize for Princes* (running in five issues of *All-Story Weekly* beginning May 1914), a prescient novel that ends with the assassination of a Balkan prince by an anarchist; and *The Great Legend* (published in *All-Story Weekly* beginning in January 1916), a tale set during the Trojan War. Interspersed among these novels was a series of short stories published in *The Black Cat, Lippincott's Monthly Magazine, All-Story Magazine,* and *The Smart Set* that continued until November 1917.

This writing was Stout's training ground, and in it he began to settle on the universal tensions created by the conflict of head and heart. He also augmented his understanding of fictional structure, characters, dialogue, pacing, and style. In effect, he served an apprenticeship that led him to Archie Goodwin and Nero Wolfe. Stout wrote all of the stories hastily, under pressure to make quick money. But considering that behavior a prostitution of talent, Stout gave up writing for a period, determined not to write again until he had sufficient money to turn to serious, careful writing, free from the distraction of supporting himself. The interlude lasted twelve years.

On 16 December 1916, Stout married Fay Kennedy, the younger sister of a childhood friend from Topeka, proposing to her one week after their meeting at a breakfast. They married in Chicago and traveled to Pittsburgh on a joint wedding and business trip. Stout's brother Bob had proposed a business venture he wanted to share with them. One of his clients, a superintendent of schools, had created a program to teach children thrift and money-management skills. Following the method he later employed in writing the Wolfe novels, Stout instantly conceived a fully realized plan for the Educational Thrift Service (ETS) that was economical, efficient, effective, and pleasing to all shareholders—depositors, schools, and bankers. Bob Stout became president of the ETS, but Stout ran the business with total control. The business quickly outstripped all other school savings programs, and by 1926 Stout was rich and free for other pursuits.

During this period, Stout's liberal leanings emerged publicly. In 1924 he invested $24,000 in a private printing of Giacomo Girolamo Casanova's *Memoirs,* barred from America because of erotic content. He was appointed to the board of the National Council on Censorship for the American Civil Liberties Union (ACLU) in the autumn of 1925, investing $4,000 of his earnings from the Casanova *Memoirs* to help launch *The New Masses,* a magazine that published articles, fiction, poetry, and art by radicals. Vanguard Press recruited Stout to become its president, a post he held until 1928. Of all these leftist affiliations made in 1925, his association with Vanguard alone lasted; there he could help shape policy, a role crucial to him. Though not approving of all the activities of the ACLU, Stout determined it had done little harm, but he believed *The New Masses* was, and intended to remain, communist, to him a vile persuasion. He tried to pull the magazine back to its original focus for six months but, with no success, he quit. However, he was not able to get his name removed from its listing of the executive board until July 1928.

During this time, Stout's circle of associates included most of the New York liberal and literary intelligentsia—Scott Nearing, Edmund Wilson, Bertrand Russell, Thorstein Veblen, Dorothy Parker, John Dos Passos, Max Eastman, Carl Van Vechten, Mark and Carl Van Doren, Joseph Wood Krutch, and Heywood Hale Broun. Stout's social life was full of frequent dinners and parties. All the while, he was collecting information, educating himself about the ills of modern society and the people who were trying to make it healthier. In all these relationships and activities, Stout probed the psyches of the participants, practiced his skill at thrust-and-parry conversation, and created skill-

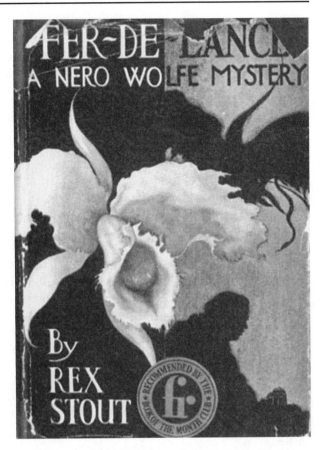

Dust jacket for Stout's 1934 novel, the first to feature the obese, beer-drinking, orchid-grower detective Nero Wolfe (Christie's New York, item number 217, 24 September 2004)

ful arguments that forced his friends to react to hypothetical situations and disclose their interior and intellectual lives.

Stout turned forty on 1 December 1926 and at last achieved the freedom to write he had sought for twelve years. On that day he sold his share of the ETS to his brother, agreeing to a percentage of the gross income of the business for twenty years; in an average year that brought him $30,000. In December 1927, the Stouts sailed for Europe and remained until November 1928. Determined to be a serious writer, he planned to write carefully and thoughtfully, not as a hack for the pulps.

After visiting England, Paris, Rome, Casablanca, Cairo, Belgium, Italy, and Spain, Stout returned to Paris ready to write. He began *How Like a God* (1929) in February 1929 and finished it in March. With that novel Stout instituted a practice that continued throughout his career; his first draft was always also his last. Writing rapidly in longhand, Stout had in mind the structure of the novel and names for the major characters before he began to write, but, according to McAleer, Stout "left it to his subconscious to work out the nuances of plot and characterization."

How Like a God is a psychological novel. At college Bill Sidney falls prey to the perverse sexual advances of the ten-year-old daughter of a campus laundrywoman. Millicent Moran, the young seductress, dominates Bill, who hates himself for being unable to detach her vulgar hold. When Millicent becomes an adult, she seeks him out again; though he tries to leave her several times, the sexual lure is too great, and he always returns. Finally, hating her and himself, he crushes her skull.

In *The Nation* (25 September 1929) Clifton Fadiman described the novel as having "an air of maturity about it few American first novels possess." Burton Rascoe in *Arts and Decorations* (November 1929) called Stout "a new novelist who is certain to command much attention from now on." Other reviewers focused on Stout's treatment of human psychoses and commented on his technical innovations, a pioneering method of handling interior monologue (narrating the story in second-person singular) and the narrative structure (Bill Sidney tells the story as he mounts the stairs to kill Millicent). Reviewers were reluctant to accept that so much could pass through a man's mind in so brief a time, and their mixed reviews focused on the psychological themes of the novel and shared a reluctance to deal with its sordid materials.

Having returned to New York in the late summer of 1929 and rented a place in Greenwich Village, Stout started another psychological novel, *Seed on the Wind,* in early October. When the market crashed at the end of the month, Stout lost most of the money he had earned at ETS. He told biographer McAleer, "It took me one bottle of wine to adjust to the news." *How Like a God* did not relieve Stout's financial straits either; after six months his royalties came to less than $700; he knew pressure was on him to make the second novel live up to the promise some reviewers saw in the first. He worked furiously and wrote to Egmont Arens, one of his closest friends, "I am rarely through before seven in the evening, including Sundays and holidays. Just a goddamn fiction factory."

He finished the book by March and began plans to build his dream house near Brewster, New York, on eighteen acres of land that straddled the New York–Connecticut border. In addition to masterminding the project and working with construction crews, he built bookshelves, kitchen cabinets, and much of the furniture. He built the house in seven months at a cost of $40,000. Quickly, High Meadow became the center of Stout's life and remained so until his death.

On 21 August 1930, with the building of High Meadow still under way, Stout received a note from William Soskin of *The New York Herald Tribune* praising

Seed on the Wind and congratulating him for evidence of "increasing maturity." A few days later Mrs. Bernard DeVoto wrote, "I think you have done a splendid piece of work. Your complete detachment from emotion pleases me very much. My husband, who is entirely too critical of American fiction, for once agrees with me." Nonetheless, reviews were mixed in America and abroad, and the book did not sell well.

Over the next several years, Stout published three more novels in the same psychological vein: *Golden Remedy* (1931), about an unmarried woman who has five children by five different men to spite her father; *Forest Fire* (1933), about a ranger who inadvertently and unknowingly falls in love with a man; and *The President Vanishes* (1934), about a notorious philanderer who is disgusted by women. Stout often heard his own name mentioned in the company of other major American writers of the 1930s, but he never broke into those circles. He told McAleer, "These four novels had demonstrated to my satisfaction two things, first—that I was a good storyteller, and second—that I would never be a great novelist." According to David R. Anderson, biographer and critic of the Nero Wolfe novels, "They experiment with point of view, narrative time, and psychology in fiction. But they have been overshadowed by the Nero Wolfe novels; nowadays, they are little read."

Though novels appeared regularly during the early 1930s, and Stout ordered his life further by moving from the city to High Meadow, his personal life was unstable. Fay Stout preferred the excitement of life in Manhattan and did not relish the quiet of High Meadow. According to McAleer, Stout "was bent now on realizing himself as a writer, and the new environment he was creating was an essential resource—a physical embodiment of the inner consistency he sought and advocated . . . establishing those routines which would supply verisimilitude to the scheduled existence of Nero Wolfe." Fay Stout saw no reason to sacrifice so much for Stout's literary ambitions, since his books were no source of income. An irreconcilable breach opened in the fourteen-year marriage, and they divorced in February 1931.

In short order, however, Stout met Pola Weinbach Hoffman, a designer of woolen fabrics well on her way to becoming famous in her field. Her own marriage was shaky, and when they met at High Meadow, both the place and its creator entranced Pola. They married there on 21 December 1932.

By early 1933, Pola was pregnant. Feeling the need of additional income, Stout consciously decided to shift the focus and tenor of his fiction. He told biographer McAleer: "To write profound things about the human soul, your feelings about it have to be very deep, very difficult." Stout did not see himself as that kind of person. He thought he could have joined the ranks of John Steinbeck or H. G. Wells but was unwilling to give up the part of his soul that he thought would be essential if he were to make serious observations about people and their behavior. He told McAleer, "I thought, if you're merely good and not great, what's the use of putting all that agony into it?" In the *Holiday* interview he told Bester, "I decided to write detective stories. You just tell stories and you don't have to worry about making new comments on life and human beings. That's when I started Nero Wolfe for *American Magazine*." In a 1946 interview with Robert Van Gelder for *Writers and Writing,* Stout said, "While I could afford to, I played with words. When I could no longer afford that I wrote for money." Detective stories sold better than any other kind of writing, so Stout tried his hand at them. Though years later, on 20 February 1963, he testified before the congressional Ways and Means Committee on copyright reform and the compromises many writers have to make because of financial need, he told McAleer he did not see himself compromising when he decided to write detective stories: "There was no thought of 'compromise.' I was satisfied that I was a good storyteller; I enjoyed the special plotting problems of detective stories; and I felt that whatever comments I might want to make about people and their handling of life could be made in detective stories as well as in any other kind."

On Wednesday, 18 October 1933, the day after Pola and their daughter Barbara came home from the hospital, Stout began his first detective story. He told McAleer he called the protagonist Nero Wolfe because the name was "simple but odd"; people would remember it. From childhood on Stout had read detective stories; his favorites were by Doyle and G. K. Chesterton, though he also liked Ronald Knox, Dorothy Sayers, Edgar Wallace, S. S. Van Dine, and Austin Freeman. He started to write without special preparation. He did not read criminology or detective science, visit police courts, or develop relationships with criminals, lawyers, or detectives.

Stout completed *Fer-de-Lance* (1934) before Christmas and delivered it to John Farrar. Later Farrar told McAleer, "Rex is the kind of author publishers dream about. He would block out a certain number of months in which to write a Nero Wolfe book. He would start work on a certain date. And with uncanny precision would finish the book on a specified date. And turn in a manuscript in perfect order." With publication of *Fer-de-Lance,* Nero Wolfe and Archie Goodwin almost immediately became part of the history of detective fiction. Though it is the first novel of the series, it is one of the best, and with it Stout carved out the tone, method,

and characters from which he never wavered. In addition, Stout initiated the standard details and circumstances of life in Wolfe's brownstone on West Thirty-fifth Street.

Fer-de-Lance concerns love, betrayal, violence, and revenge. Maria Maffei consults with Wolfe about her brother, who has been missing for several days. Wolfe doubts he will be interested in the case but, when Miss Maffei's devotion to her brother impresses him, agrees to Archie's conducting a preliminary investigation. Wolfe threads together coincidences that no one else sees and convinces officials to reinvestigate the case. According to a newspaper article, a university president died from a heart attack, but Wolfe is convinced he was poisoned. Events prove him correct. The president was accidentally murdered by a poisoned needle that was shot from a golf club and intended for someone else. A trail of deceit leads to a betrayed husband in the Argentine, who murdered his wife and his best friend, her lover, and left his infant son playing in their blood. The plot involves a patient attempt by the son to avenge his mother's murder and an attempt on Wolfe's life by the murderer, who plants a deadly snake, the fer-de-lance, in Wolfe's desk drawer. The novel ends with a fiery murder-suicide and Wolfe's having collected a $50,000 fee from the widow of the university president.

In evidence are all the conventions of the Wolfe saga—Wolfe's obesity and sloth, daily routines, and manner of conversing. The ensemble characters are in place. Archie Goodwin and Wolfe's cook, Fritz Brenner, inhabit the brownstone; Inspector Cramer of Manhattan Homicide, Saul Panzer, Fred Durkin, and Orrie Cather are the operatives on whom Wolfe depends, along with Archie, to do his investigative work outside the house.

From the beginning, readers wanted to know the source of the Wolfe character. Stout told McAleer, "I haven't the faintest idea where he came from. I can't answer 'why' questions about him." Despite his protests, most of Stout's literary friends believed that Wolfe is really Stout. Pola Stout maintained that through the years much in Wolfe and Archie assumed Stout's personality, and many particulars of their lives and habits parallel Stout's own. Like Stout, Wolfe breakfasts alone, prefers the feel of silver cutlery and the use of stainless steel at table, likes crosswords and chess, reads the books Stout read, and is liberal and agnostic. Archie has an excellent memory for details, is a flawless bookkeeper, likes opera and baseball, and dislikes Southern California. Many other preferences dovetail with Stout's. Physical characteristics of both characters resemble either Todhunter or Stout relatives, and dates often coincide with significant dates in Stout's family life.

Lionel Stander (left) as Archie Goodwin, Edward Arnold as Nero Wolfe, and Frank Conroy as Dr. Nathaniel Bradford in the 1936 Columbia motion picture Meet Nero Wolfe, *based on* Fer-de-Lance *(Columbia Pictures/The Kobal Collection)*

In March 1934, *The American Magazine* purchased serial rights to *Fer-de-Lance* for $2,500 and planned to bring out an abridged version in the fall in one installment. Columbia Pictures bought the screen rights for $7,500 and secured options for future stories in the series. *The American Magazine* published *Fer-de-Lance* under the title *Point of Death* on 24 October 1934 and as a book two days later to favorable reviews. *The Saturday Review* on 27 October called it "great stuff." Isaac Anderson in the Sunday *New York Times* on 28 October said, "The author has done a clever bit of work in making the narrative style employed by Archie correspond so exactly to his character and attainments as they are revealed in little touches here and there throughout the book." Carl Van Doren acquired a copy of *Fer-de-Lance* that Justice Oliver Wendell Holmes had read during the last year of his life; a marginal note read, "This fellow is the best of them all."

While good press built, Stout was already at work on his second Nero Wolfe novel. He began in October 1934 and delivered it to Farrar in six weeks. McAleer says that Stout "had found rhythms which would enable him, for many years, to produce a novel in thirty-eight days and a novella in a dozen days or less."

Almost immediately, Sumner Blossom, editor at *The American Magazine,* pushed Stout to create some shorter Wolfe pieces to "help build the character." Stout did not write those shorter pieces, however, until the advent of World War II.

The Saturday Evening Post began serialization of the second Wolfe novel on 15 June 1935; Farrar and Rinehart published it as *The League of Frightened Men* on 14 August. With its publication, Nero Wolfe became a de facto series. Stout was forty-eight years old when he wrote the first Wolfe novel, and though eventually he wrote several light novels and non-Nero Wolfe mysteries, the bulk of his fiction from 1934 throughout the rest of his long career focused on the Wolfe saga. In his *Rex Stout: An Annotated Primary and Secondary Bibliography* (1980), Guy M. Townsend observes that though Stout had already been a successful magazine writer and established a respectable though controversial place among mainstream novelists, his place as "the preeminent American mystery writer of the twentieth century" was earned through writing the Wolfe novels.

The League of Frightened Men is one of the best plotted of the Wolfe novels. Central figures are former Harvard classmates who participate in a hazing incident that leaves freshman Paul Chapin crippled. The upper-classmen form The League of Atonement and dedicate themselves to supporting Chapin financially. Twenty-three years after Chapin graduates and just three years after he has achieved success and independence by publishing a novel, two members of the League die violently. After each murder, Chapin sends each surviving member of the group a poem with the refrain, "Ye should have killed me." They quickly become The League of Frightened Men. After a Columbia University psychology professor, one of the League, requests help from Wolfe and then promptly disappears, Wolfe, eyeing a sizable fee, persuades the league to retain his services.

The climactic scene in which Wolfe reveals the murderer became a standard technique in future novels in the saga. Wolfe exposes the truth by gathering the principals in the case in his office and questioning them skillfully. Typically, Wolfe protests that revealing the murderer is of secondary importance to fulfilling his contract and receiving his fee.

The League of Frightened Men is a treatment of human psychology and the necessity of understanding it. The themes intertwine plots of thwarted love, obsession, and revenge. The plot turns on disguises, masks, and pretenses. Wolfe's initial move in the investigation is to read Chapin's book. When Chapin questions Wolfe's faith in his innocence, Wolfe replies, "I had read your books. I had seen you." In this book Stout enhances Wolfe's vision of himself as an artist and a psychologist. While in many of the novels the science of psychology comes under attack, Archie frequently calls Wolfe a psychologist. Wolfe's solving the crime most often stems from what he knows about human behavior, emotions, and the dynamics of human relationships.

The League of Frightened Men received favorable reviews from the critics, as Stout's friend Arens predicted. On 31 March 1934 he wrote to Stout, "I am quite excited about these books you are writing. There are rumors going around that the book that is now at Farrar & Rinehart is going to make a killing. When that kind of rumor gets around among the critics even before the book is printed, it is good news." In the period after the publication, Stout busied himself with the many avocations he could practice at High Meadow—gardener, cabinetmaker, landscaper, architect, cook, and iris fancier. He also wrote a non-Wolfe novel, *O Careless Love!* published 4 November 1935. It and another romance, "It Happened Last Night," published in *The Canadian Magazine* in March 1936, have more of the flavor of Stout's early apprentice work than the work of the mid 1930s.

Stout wrote the third Wolfe novel, *The Rubber Band* (1936), in the fall of 1935. By the spring of 1936, *The Red Box,* fourth in the saga, began serialization in *The American Magazine* in December and came out in hardcover on 15 April 1937. After its publication, Farrar suggested that Stout give Wolfe a rest and create a new detective. Farrar was afraid that giving the reading public two Wolfes a year would lead to market saturation and overexposure, but he also wanted to keep Stout active in the serial market. In the fall of 1936, Stout wrote *The Hand in the Glove* (1937), which introduced a woman detective, Theodolinda "Dol" Bonner, who in some respects is a female Nero Wolfe. The novel received generally weak reviews and is not memorable, but Dol appears in some later stories as one of Wolfe's operatives. Stout finished the fifth Wolfe novel, *Too Many Cooks* (1938), at High Meadow in the summer of 1937; serialization in *The American Magazine* began in March 1938. That same month Stout finished the next Wolfe novel, *Some Buried Caesar,* published in 1939. Both novels received rave reviews and established Stout as a literary figure.

Too Many Cooks takes place in a spa and is Stout's fullest treatment of Wolfe's gastronomic interests. Wolfe is invited as a guest of honor at a select convocation of a small group of master chefs. His motive for undertaking a rare absence from the brownstone is to secure a secret recipe for a sauce called *saucisse minuit.* One of the chefs is murdered, and the chef who created the dish is the chief suspect. In an attempted assassination, Wolfe receives a flesh wound from the murderer, whom he determines to unmask to save the innocent chef. Wolfe solves the crime and extorts the recipe from the accused chef as his only payment.

This novel is significant for its subtle treatment of race relations. While investigating the murder, Wolfe convinces the prosecutor that, rather than being a Negro, the killer wore blackface. Archie, the prosecutor, and the sheriff casually employ pejorative epithets and slurs, but Wolfe is no more condescending to the black wait staff than he is to the white staff. He even surprises one of the waiters by quoting a line of a Paul Laurence Dunbar poem. Both the prosecutor and the sheriff belittle Wolfe for his misguided courtesy.

When *Too Many Cooks* was published on 17 August 1938, Stout went on a fishing trip to the Adirondacks to celebrate. While he was away, a hurricane struck at High Meadow, but the house survived intact. Stout soon became embroiled in social and political turmoil. As he moved comfortably into the success and public notoriety that came with his Wolfe series, Stout assumed an active political role in promoting causes he believed in, most notably issues of human rights.

According to McAleer, Stout, having read *Mein Kampf* (1925) and believing it "the most immoral book ever written," became physically sick on 29 September 1939 when he learned of the German invasion of Czechoslovakia. Almost immediately, he learned that he had an ulcer; he quit smoking and went on a bland diet. Stout believed, however, that he would behave immorally to cloak himself in the sanctum of High Meadow and do nothing to bring down the forces of tyranny. He knew that Adolf Hitler must fall and committed his resources to help make it happen.

But as he was about to launch his career as a political activist, Stout achieved the unimaginable as a novelist. Between his birthdays in 1938 and 1939, he published five novels in hardcover–*Mr. Cinderella* (1 December 1938), *Some Buried Caesar* (2 February 1939), *Mountain Cat* (27 July 1939), *Double for Death* (3 October 1939), and *Red Threads* (1 December 1939). In addition, *Over My Dead Body* (1940), the seventh Wolfe novel, ran in *The American Magazine* beginning in September 1939. When he completed *Where There's a Will* in the fall of 1939 for a spring release in 1940, Stout had produced eight books in three years. In conversation with McAleer in 1973, Stout commented, "Eight books in three years? I'm surprised but not impressed. I must have needed money for something."

As the European situation deteriorated, Stout's political activities grew. He appeared frequently on "Information, Please!" a radio program hosted by Fadiman; together they explored their common animosity toward Hitler and ways to translate hatred into action. Stout's public outspokenness took many channels. He helped found the Friends of Democracy in 1937, the Committee to Defend America by Aiding the Allies in April 1940, and sponsored the Fight for Freedom Committee in 1940 to marshal public opinion against Nazi Germany.

After Farrar and Rinehart published *Where There's a Will* on 10 June 1940, it was the last Wolfe novel until the end of the war. During this period, Stout protected the routine of High Meadow–gardening, woodworking, and spending time with his two young daughters, Barbara and Rebecca (who had been born 4 May 1937). He also campaigned for Franklin Roosevelt's reelection during the summer.

In 1939 Stout had written *Double for Death,* a novel with a new detective, Tecumseh Fox. In the summer of 1940 he wrote a second Fox novel, *Bad for Business,* scheduled for publication in November 1940. When it was offered to *The American Magazine* for serialization, however, editor Blossom told Stout he would pay double if he rewrote it as a Wolfe novella. Stout produced the hybrid in eleven days. It appeared as "Bitter End" in the November issue. "Death Wears an Orchid," a second Wolfe novella–Stout wrote thirty-nine–appeared in *The American Magazine* in March 1940 and came out in hardcover as *Black Orchids* in May 1942.

Once America entered the war, Stout worked tirelessly as a propagandist for the war effort. In October he became a trustee of Freedom House, an alliance he maintained throughout his life. On 8 December 1941, *Alphabet Hicks,* another detective novel, was published. But with the entry of the United States into the war, Stout considered his fiction-writing career at a standstill. Unfazed by the poor reception of the novel, Stout focused almost exclusively on his political work. In addition to the "Speaking of Liberty" broadcasts, he made radio broadcasts for "Victory Volunteers" and wrote and conducted the series "Our Secret Weapon" for CBS from the summer of 1942 through the fall of 1943. In addition, he was elected president of the Friends of Democracy in October 1942; in 1944 he became a founder and the first president of the Society for the Prevention of World War III.

During the war years, Stout kept the Wolfe saga afloat through stories. In April 1942 the eleventh Nero Wolfe story, "Cordially Invited to Meet Death," appeared in *The American Magazine*. The majority of his energies went toward his work for the war effort, but he managed one Wolfe novella a year throughout the war. Stout had moved into New York to keep up his political activities, but he returned to High Meadow in August 1942 for a brief holiday and wrote "Not Quite Dead Enough" (published in *American Magazine,* December 1942). The next August at High Meadow he wrote "Booby Trap" (published in *The American* [August 1944]) and in June 1944 he returned to write "Help Wanted, Male" (published in *Trouble in Triplicate* [1949]). Almost immediately after the end of the war, in the fall of 1945, he wrote the fifteenth Wolfe story, "Instead of Evidence" (published in *Trouble in Triplicate*).

Within these stories Stout maintained his propaganda activities; Archie's and Wolfe's activities in support of the war provide background for the tales. In "Help Wanted, Male," Wolfe may be a spokesman for Stout; Wolfe wants to kill Germans personally. Stout had developed a strong antipathy for Germans, and in a major essay for *The New York Times* on 17 January 1943, "We Shall Hate, or We Shall Fail," he argued that to kill Germans was illogical unless people hated them; he also wanted the complete economic and industrial dismantling of Germany after the war.

On 8 June 1943, Avon Book Company approached Stout about lending his name and editorial expertise to a new periodical bearing his name, to be published in runs no smaller than one hundred thousand copies. On 5 December Stout became editor of *Rex Stout Mystery Quarterly* and agreed to write an introduction for each issue. The magazine appeared sporadically under a series of minor name changes from May 1945 through May 1947.

In the early years after the war, Stout channeled his efforts toward securing reprint royalties for authors. He was a member of the Author's League and the Author's Guild and was stunned to see publishers of hardcover books funneling their resources into paperback reprint houses. They could produce cheap reprints of an author's work and sell more copies more cheaply without paying appropriate royalties on the paperback sales. Stout argued that in an average year, publishers could make $6,720,000 from the cheap reprints, while the authors would receive only $600,000. He was determined that all authors receive a $.03 royalty on every $.25 paperback sold.

In the fall of 1944, Stanley Rinehart notified Stout that Farrar was not returning to the publishing business. Stout hoped that Farrar would set up his own publishing house. In October 1945, however, Stout gave up this hope and approached Harold Guinzburg of Viking; immediately Nero Wolfe had a new publisher. In March 1946 Stout started *The Silent Speaker,* the first Nero Wolfe novel in seven years, and finished it in April of that same year. From that point on, for nearly the next thirty years, Stout wrote only Wolfe stories. He spent six to eight weeks a year writing a novel and one or two novellas; the rest of the year he indulged himself in life at High Meadow or those public activities most interesting to him. After *The Silent Speaker* was published, Stout celebrated by finishing a novella, "Before I Die" (published in *Trouble in Triplicate*), which he had started on 12 October. On 20 October 1947, *Too Many Women* was published. Stout wrote "Man Alive" between 24 July and 3 August 1947; "Bullet for One" between 17 and 29 November, with two days off for Thanksgiving; and *And Be a Villain* between 19 March and 24 April 1948, published 27 September. This frenetic pace represents the manner of his writing during those six or eight weeks a year he devoted to the task. Stout wrote three more novellas the next year.

And Be a Villain opened the Zeck trilogy, which deals with Wolfe's death match with a master criminal, and for the first time in the saga the principals of West Thirty-fifth Street face a real threat from the outside. When Cyril Orchard, publisher of a horse-racing tip sheet, dies from poison in the middle of a live radio program, Wolfe gets himself hired by the radio host and her sponsors to investigate the murder as a publicity stunt. (He needs money to pay his federal income tax.) Because the clients are more interested in protecting a series of personal and professional secrets than in solving the murder, they withhold vital evidence. When another tip-sheet publisher is murdered, Wolfe discov-

ers that the two victims were part of a brilliant blackmail scheme and that one of their subscribers was buying their silence, not their information. He learns who the killer is, but a stunning, ominous event occurs during the investigation; a voice on the telephone orders him off the case. Arnold Zeck—a prominent friend of politicians, a city benefactor, and a well-known citizen of Westchester County—is displeased with Wolfe's activities.

This novel represents a change in Stout's interest; the novels of the middle period introduce politics, and Wolfe's general contempt of it, into the plots. In *The Second Confession* (1949), the second novel in which Zeck appears, Wolfe tangles with communism. A rich mine owner, James U. Sperling, hires Wolfe to prove that a young man with whom he fears his daughter is in love is a communist. Zeck again demands that Wolfe abandon the investigation and gives weight to his demand by having one of his henchmen invade Wolfe's brownstone, machine-gun Wolfe's orchids, shatter the rooftop greenhouse, and nearly kill Theodore Horstman, Wolfe's gardener. The culprit is the man whose communist leanings Wolfe is investigating. When the man is run over by a car, Sperling persuades one of his employees to sign a confession in order to protect his daughter from the publicity if news of her relationship with the murdered man comes out. Wolfe recognizes the confession as a fraud and continues the investigation. Because Zeck wants to know who murdered his protégé, he approves of Wolfe's persistence and pays him $50,000 for damage to the orchids. At the end of the novel, a shaky truce between Wolfe and Zeck is in place, but intimations of future conflict rumble.

As Stout's activities supporting the war effort began to wind down, he and others became convinced that the only way to eliminate the danger of future wars was to form a world government. In August 1944, he became a charter member of Americans United for World Organization, later the United World Federalists. After the Japanese surrender in August 1945, the Writers' War Board dissolved and reconvened itself as the Writers' Board, with Stout as chairman. In 1946 his term as president of the Society for the Prevention of World War III ended, but he remained active on the advisory council. In 1949 he helped found the Writer's Board for World Government. Stout was convinced that communism posed the same threat to world peace that fascism had in the previous decade, and he expended his public political energies toward fighting it.

Stout led the campaign for racial justice that the Writers' War Board began in 1944. A staunch defender of civil rights throughout his life, Stout dealt with social issues in several of his early novels; but in the middle of his detective-writing career they moved from the

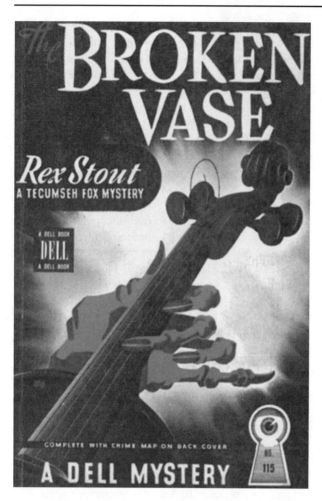

Cover for the 1946 paperback reprint of Stout's 1941 novel. Tecumseh Fox, a private investigator, was featured in three of the author's books (from Piet Schreuders, Paperbacks, U.S.A.: A Graphic History, 1939–1959 *[San Diego: Blue Dolphin, 1981]; Richland County Public Library).*

periphery. As the world political situation shifted after the war, and international realignment occurred, the view of the Wolfe novels turned outward. With *The Second Confession,* fighting the threat of communism centers Wolfe's conflict with Zeck. Wolfe apparently has an informer inside the American Communist Party. He uses clandestine information to publish an account of the communist conspiracy to influence the presidential campaign of 1948. Wolfe and Archie both detest the communists, and Wolfe actively supports the World Federalists, serving as a literary spokesman for Stout's own political activities of this period.

Viking brought out *Trouble in Triplicate,* the first of eleven volumes of Wolfe novellas, on 11 February 1949. On the same day, Stout began "Grim Fairy Tales," an article commissioned by Norman Cousins for *Saturday Review.* Stout's initial task was to explain the preeminence of Sherlock Holmes in the popular imagination, but he commented most fully, if uninten-

tionally, on his own creation of Wolfe. He argued that the most important hero of detective fiction is "reason" and said that the story ends "when reason's job is done." Ultimately, Stout wrote five articles dealing with detective fiction.

Three Doors to Death–which includes "Man Alive," "Omit Flowers," and "Door to Death"–was published in April 1950 as the second volume of Wolfe novellas. By this time, Stout had already been at work for a week on the final volume of the Zeck trilogy. *In the Best Families* (1950) completes the cycle of novels that forms the only series within the Wolfe saga and is a high point of the canon. Wolfe leaves the brownstone for an extended period of time and loses eighty pounds to prepare for a final showdown with Zeck, the master criminal.

The novel was published on 29 September 1950 to rave reviews. Julian Symons of the *Manchester Evening News* on 5 April 1951 wrote, "In the fight to the death between master-detective and master-criminal the most ingenious and unlikely subterfuges are used. . . . All this is very improbable. It is the art of Mr. Stout to make it seem plausible. . . . Holmes was a fully realized character. There is only a handful of his successors to whom that compliment can be paid. One of them, certainly, is Nero Wolfe."

In the Best of Families includes many elements that became typical of Wolfe mysteries. Wolfe accepts a case for a rich, ugly, neurotic woman, Mrs. Barry Rackham, who wants to know where her young, handsome husband gets his income. Having just paid his income tax, Wolfe needs money. The brownstone is invaded again, this time by a canister of tear gas disguised as Wolfe's favorite sausage; shortly, Wolfe receives another phone call from Zeck telling him to quit the case. Wolfe, of course, will not give up the case and sends Archie to investigate, assuming that Zeck is the source of the young husband's income. Mrs. Rackham is murdered while Archie is at her estate. Questioned by police and told to remain available, Archie quickly returns to West Thirty-fifth Street to find that Wolfe has disappeared without a trace.

After some time, Archie gets over Wolfe's disappearance and opens his own successful detective agency, making more money than Wolfe paid him. He continues his relationship with long-time girlfriend Lily Rowan. One of Zeck's minions hires Archie to tail young Rackham; in the process, Archie invades Zeck's operation. Soon Wolfe returns, and he and Archie orchestrate a situation that leads to the murder of Zeck and his cronies.

The novel is notable for the truths revealed about the relationship between Wolfe and Archie. Expressions of regard between the two are rare. Archie is most often flippant; Wolfe is taciturn. After the shock of Wolfe's disappearance has subsided, Archie says, "The hell of it wasn't how I felt, but that I didn't know how to feel. If I had actually seen the last of Nero Wolfe, it was a damn sad day for me, there were no two ways about that, and if I got a lump in my throat and somebody walked in I would just as soon show him the lump as not." Speaking to Zeck about Wolfe, he says, "I know he had his faults—God knows how I stood them as long as I did—but he taught me a lot, and wherever he is he's my favorite fatty." Archie's regard for Wolfe is deep and personal. Throughout the series Wolfe restricts his praise of Archie. But after Wolfe returns, he tells Archie, "I had gone as far as I could without you." He adds quietly, "It's vastly better this way."

With the trilogy, the professional and personal relationship between Wolfe and Archie reaches full maturity. They unite to defeat the ultimate opponent. Zeck identifies himself as a worthy challenger for Wolfe, whom he grudgingly admires. In the telephone calls through which he tries to control Wolfe's activities, Zeck maintains his superiority of mind, network, and influence. Because Wolfe admires Zeck's ingenuity and cunning, defeating him becomes the grand battle. For the first time in the series, Wolfe and Archie have been in mortal danger; the machine-gunning of the orchids, the exploding sausage, and Wolfe's exile underscore Zeck's invasion of Wolfe's private world. But Zeck's successful defeat cements Wolfe's and Archie's reputations as the best detectives anywhere and affirms their mutual regard.

Stout was at the top of his literary form in these novels. In discussing his writing habits with biographer McAleer, he outlined his typical approach and behaviors. Writing in a small L-shaped office at High Meadow, he was totally focused once he started writing. He told McAleer, "I can't stand distractions. I never even look out the window when I write." He wrote deliberately, with great surety: "The initial draft has always been the only draft, with an original and two carbons." He never revised, rarely even restructured a phrase. The Wolfe novels came from Stout's typewriter virtually flawless; he did no double-checking with earlier stories. He wrote at a rate of a page an hour, with his greatest output for any one day being twelve pages. He told McAleer, "None of them, either at Viking or at Farrar and Rinehart, has ever suggested changing a sentence."

On 5 November 1954 Stout stood next to President Dwight D. Eisenhower when he signed the Universal Copyright Convention into law. Stout had worked toward this event for years, believing strongly that all member nations should provide the same copyright privileges to foreign nationals that they guaranteed their own citizens. Stout had worked tirelessly behind the scenes to get this legislation through Congress; he instigated a letter and telegram campaign and arranged eight personal appearances at congressional hearings. For the next twenty years Stout channeled much of his energies toward the reform of domestic copyright laws. When President Gerald Ford signed into law the final version on 19 October 1976, Stout was already dead, but in conjunction with the event the Authors' Guild made its first presentation of the Rex Stout Award to Representative Robert W. Kastenmeier for his part in steering the legislation through Congress.

Stout published *The Black Mountain* on 14 October 1954; in this novel Wolfe ventures to his native Montenegro, searching for the killer of his oldest and closest friend, Marko Vukcic. The following June, Viking published *Full House,* the first of eight omnibus volumes. A year later, May 1956, *American Magazine* published the thirty-first and final Wolfe story. The short-story market was dying, and so was the magazine. When magazines stopped wanting stories, Stout no longer wrote them. Over the next six years, he wrote another nine novellas, three of which went directly to hardcover print.

In 1956 Stout published *Eat, Drink, and Be Buried* (an anthology of mystery stories in which each murder is achieved through the stomach), *Three Witnesses,* and *Might as Well Be Dead.* Archie takes center stage in *If Death Ever Slept,* published 25 October 1957; in the novel Stout explores industrial espionage. The Wolfe novels appeared regularly until the end of Stout's life: *Champagne for One* (1958), *Plot It Yourself* (1959), *Too Many Clients* (1960), *The Final Deduction* (1961), *Gambit* (1962), *The Mother Hunt* (1963), *A Right to Die* (1964), *The Doorbell Rang* (1965), *Death of a Doxy* (1966), *The Father Hunt* (1968), *Death of a Dude* (1969), *Please Pass the Guilt* (1973), and *A Family Affair* (1975). During these years several omnibus volumes and novella collections also appeared.

Stout had long used the Wolfe saga as a vehicle for strong social criticism. With *The Doorbell Rang* in 1965, Stout ventured into the political realm again. Wolfe's adversary in the novel is the Federal Bureau of Investigation and its director, J. Edgar Hoover. Hoover's ploy to shield himself and the agency from questioning or criticism disgusted Stout, and he takes both to task in the novel.

When Stout turned eighty on 1 December 1966, Jacques Barzun, dean of faculties and provost of Columbia University, commemorated the event with a scholarly monograph on the Wolfe saga. In it he wrote, "If he had done nothing more than to create Archie Goodwin, Rex Stout would deserve the gratitude of whatever assessors watch over the prosperity of American literature." With the stroke of an academic's pen, the saga received sanction as literature. From that time on, Stout's critical reputation grew, and he was rarely out of the public eye.

In November 1969 Stout began suffering from a series of blinding headaches that continued for two years and virtually paralyzed all his pleasurable activities. Biographer McAleer suggests that the headaches were spurred by the growing isolation Stout felt with his position on Vietnam; he supported President Lyndon Johnson's and later President Richard Nixon's war policies. But while Stout clung to his stance on the war, he realized that those who shared his view were dwindling.

Stout lived his last years at High Meadow peacefully and quietly, maintaining his active interest in politics. Though he had supported Nixon's Vietnam policy, he was seriously distressed by the Watergate affair. He told McAleer that Nixon "was unquestionably the greatest danger that ever occurred to American democracy." In his last few years, Stout's circle of lifelong friends constricted with their deaths, and Stout became feeble. But he continued to give interviews, read, keep up with his correspondence, and write. Though his body failed, his mind stayed keenly alert. When he died 27 October 1975, Harry Reasoner reported on the ABC Evening News: "Rex Stout was a lot of things during his eighty-eight years, but the main thing he was was the writer of forty-six mystery novels about Nero Wolfe and Archie Goodwin. A lot of more pretentious writers have less claim on our culture and our allegiance." *A Family Affair,* Stout's final novel, had appeared a month before he died. On the day of his death, *Time* magazine carried a review of *A Family Affair* that praised Stout's "elastic, contemporary mind" and his ability to "confound the actuarial tables." His family scattered his ashes at High Meadow.

By McAleer's count, when Stout died he had "fifty-seven books in print, more than any living American writer. These books had sold in excess of a hundred million copies and had been translated into twenty-six languages." His death was front-page news in *The New York Times.* His reputation as a writer and as a champion for human rights was already legendary. At the annual meeting of the Author's League, on 26 February 1976, John Hersey said of him, "In the entire history of the Authors' League, no single member has ever given so much lifetime and passion to the cause of the rights and well-being of writers as Rex Stout did."

Rex Stout's rank among the best writers of detective fiction is secure. The world he created and sustained flawlessly throughout the Wolfe saga remains unrivaled. He maintained the lives of his ensemble characters with an elegance that continues to set the standard for novelists of the genre. Stout once told McAleer that he had no intention of killing off his hero; "I hope he lives forever." So far, Stout's work continues to be widely read. A television series in the 1970s and a series for A&E television for the 2004–2005 season attest to Stout's durability.

Interviews:

Robert Van Gelder, *Writers and Writing* (New York: Scribners, 1946);

Alfred Bester, "Conversation with Rex Stout," *Holiday,* 46 (November 1969): 3–39, 65–67;

John McAleer, *Royal Decree: Conversations with Rex Stout* (Ashton, Md.: Pontes Press, 1983).

Bibliography:

Guy M. Townsend and others, *Rex Stout: An Annotated Primary and Secondary Bibliography* (New York: Garland, 1980).

Biography:

John McAleer, *Rex Stout: A Biography,* foreword by P. G. Wodehouse (Boston: Little, Brown, 1977).

References:

David R. Anderson, *Rex Stout* (New York: Ungar, 1984);

Jacques Barzun, *A Birthday Tribute to Rex Stout* (New York: Viking, 1965);

Ken Darby, *The Brownstone House of Nero Wolfe* (Boston: Little, Brown, 1983);

Mia I. Gerhardt, "Homicide West: Some Observations on the Nero Wolfe Stories of Rex Stout," *English Studies,* 49 (August 1968): 107–127;

Alva Johnston, "Alias Nero Wolfe," *New Yorker,* 25 (16 July 1949): 26–28, 30, 32, 37–41; 25 (23 July 1949): 30–32, 34, 39–43;

J. Kenneth Van Dover, *At Wolfe's Door: The Nero Wolfe Novels of Rex Stout* (San Bernardino, Cal.: Borgo Press, 1991).

Papers:

Rex Stout's manuscripts and papers are in the John J. Burns Library of Boston College.

S. S. Van Dine
(Willard Huntington Wright)
(15 October 1887 – 11 April 1939)

Marvin S. Lachman

See also the Van Dine entry in *DS 16: The House of Scribner, 1905–1930.*

BOOKS: *Europe After 8:15,* by Wright, H. L. Mencken, and George Jean Nathan (New York: John Lane, 1914);

Modern Painting: Its Tendency and Meaning, as Wright (New York & London: John Lane, 1915);

What Nietzsche Taught, as Wright (New York: Huebsch, 1915);

The Creative Will: Studies in the Philosophy and Syntax of Aesthetics, as Wright (New York & London: John Lane, 1916);

The Man of Promise, as Wright (New York & London: John Lane, 1916);

The Forum Exhibition of Modern American Painters, as Wright (New York: Anderson Galleries, 1916);

Mr. Masters' Spoon River Anthology, a Criticism, by Wright, Bliss Carman, William Stanley Braithwaite, and others (New York: Forum, 1916);

Misinforming a Nation, as Wright (New York: Huebsch, 1917);

Informing a Nation, as Wright (New York: Dodd, Mead, 1917);

The Future of Painting, as Wright (New York: Huebsch, 1923);

The Benson Murder Case (New York: Scribners, 1926; London: Benn, 1926);

The "Canary" Murder Case (New York: Scribners, 1927; London: Benn, 1927);

The Greene Murder Case (New York: Scribners, 1928; London: Benn, 1928);

The Bishop Murder Case (New York: Scribners, 1929; London: Cassell, 1929);

I Used to Be a Highbrow, but Look at Me Now (New York: Scribners, 1929);

The Scarab Murder Case (New York: Scribners, 1930; London: Cassell, 1930);

The Kennel Murder Case (New York: Scribners, 1933; London: Cassell, 1933);

Willard Huntington Wright (from The "Canary" Murder Case *[Boston: Gregg, 1980]; Richland County Public Library)*

The Dragon Murder Case (New York: Scribners, 1933; London: Cassell, 1934);

The Casino Murder Case (New York: Scribners, 1934; London: Cassell, 1934);

The Garden Murder Case (New York: Scribners, 1935; London: Cassell, 1935);

The President's Mystery Story, by Van Dine, Anthony Abbot, Samuel Hopkins Adams, John Erskine, Rupert Hughes, Rita Weiman, Fulton Oursler, and Franklin D. Roosevelt (New York: Farrar & Rinehart, 1935; London: Lane, 1936); revised and republished as *The President's Murder Plot* (New York: Prentice-Hall, 1967);

The Kidnap Murder Case (New York: Scribners, 1936; London: Cassell, 1936);

The Gracie Allen Murder Case (New York: Scribners, 1938; London: Cassell, 1938); republished as *The Smell of Murder* (New York: Bantam, 1950);

The Winter Murder Case (New York: Scribners, 1939; London: Cassell, 1939).

Collections: *Philo Vance Murder Cases* (New York: Scribners, 1936)–comprises *The Scarab Murder Case, The Kennel Murder Case,* and *The Dragon Murder Case;*

A Philo Vance Week-End (New York: Grosset & Dunlap, 1937–comprises *The "Canary" Murder Case, The Greene Murder Case,* and *The Bishop Murder Case.*

PRODUCED SCRIPTS: *The Clyde Mystery,* motion picture short, Warner Bros., 1931;

The Wall Street Mystery, motion picture short, Warner Bros., 1931;

The Week-End Mystery, motion picture short, Warner Bros., 1931;

The Symphony Murder Mystery, motion picture short, Warner Bros., 1931;

The Studio Murder Mystery, motion picture short, Warner Bros., 1932;

The Skull Murder Mystery, motion picture short, Warner Bros., 1932;

The Cole Case, motion picture short, Warner Bros., 1932;

Murder in the Pullman, motion picture short, Warner Bros., 1932;

The Side Show Mystery, motion picture short, Warner Bros., 1932;

The Campus Mystery, motion picture short, Warner Bros., 1932;

The Crane Poison Case, motion picture short, Warner Bros., 1932;

The Transatlantic Mystery, motion picture short, Warner Bros., 1932.

OTHER: *The Great Modern French Stories,* edited by Wright (New York: Boni & Liveright, 1917);

The Great Detective Stories: A Chronological Anthology, edited by Wright (New York: Scribners, 1927); republished as *The World's Great Detective Stories,* edited by Van Dine (New York: Blue Ribbon, 1931);

Fayette C. Ewing, *The Book of the Scottish Terrier,* introduction by Van Dine (New York: Orange Judd, 1932);

Alfred Morgan, *Tropical Fishes and Home Aquaria,* foreword by Van Dine (New York: Scribners, 1935);

"Twenty Rules for Writing Detective Stories," as Vance, in *Philo Vance Murder Cases* (New York: Scribners, 1936), pp. 74–83.

SELECTED PERIODICAL PUBLICATIONS–UNCOLLECTED: "The Detective Novel," *Scribner's Magazine,* 80 (November 1926): 532–539;

"I Used to Be a Highbrow, but Look at Me Now," as Wright, *American Magazine,* 106 (September 1928): 14–15, 118, 122, 124–131;

"The Scarlet Nemesis," *Cosmopolitan,* 86 (January 1929): 52–55, 167–170;

"A Murder in a Witches' Cauldron," *Cosmopolitan,* 86 (February 1929): 58–59, 140, 142, 144–146;

"The Man in the Blue Overcoat," *Cosmopolitan,* 86 (May 1929): 32–33, 126, 128–130;

"Poison," *Cosmopolitan,* 86 (June 1929): 56–57, 213–217;

"The Almost Perfect Crime," *Cosmopolitan,* 87 (July 1929): 66–67, 140, 142, 144;

"The Inconvenient Husband," *Cosmopolitan,* 87 (August 1929): 102–104, 107;

"The Bonmartini Murder Case," *Cosmopolitan,* 87 (October 1929): 92–94, 97–98;

"Fool!" *Cosmopolitan,* 88 (January 1930): 82–83, 114, 116.

An unsuccessful novelist and critic who derided detective fiction, Willard Huntington Wright turned to that genre when deeply in debt and became the best-selling American mystery author of the 1920s and 1930s. As S. S. Van Dine, he popularized the American detective novel at a time when English mysteries dominated the United States market. In addition to providing mysteries with intricately developed plots, Van Dine appealed to intellectuals and pseudointellectuals with the erudition of his detective, Philo Vance. At the same time, in *Black Mask Magazine,* such writers as Dashiell Hammett were creating a hard-boiled tradition of detective fiction, using overt violence and realistic private detectives to solve crimes.

Willard Huntington Wright was born 15 October 1887, in Charlottesville, Virginia, to Archibald Davenport Wright and Annie Van Vranken Wright. A brother, Stanton Macdonald Wright, who became an important painter, was born in 1890. The family moved to Lynchburg, Virginia, in 1894 and then to Los Angeles in 1901. Archibald Wright operated hotels, and Willard, who grew up living in them, was a voracious reader who early proclaimed that he wanted a life in the arts.

Beginning in 1903, Wright attended St. Vincent's College in California for one year. Later, he spent a term at the University of Southern California and a year at Pomona College. He never received a degree. In 1906, he entered Harvard as a nonmatriculating student, taking only two courses before he was dismissed for not doing his course work.

Traveling back to Los Angeles, Wright stopped to visit a family friend in Washington State. There he met Katharine Belle Boynton, who was impressed with his ambition to become a writer. They were married on 13 July 1907 in Seattle. Their only daughter, Beverly, was born in October 1908 in Los Angeles. Wright made attempts at business ventures, but none was successful because he was more interested in writing poetry and reading than in business.

While Wright was working as a railroad ticket taker in October 1908, a chance meeting with a reporter led to a trial position as a reporter and reviewer for *The Los Angeles Times*. He became a literary editor for the newspaper early in 1909 and became known for his acerbic criticism and scathing commentary in both *The Los Angeles Times* and *West Coast Magazine*, for which he wrote theater and book reviews and art criticism. In the 3 February 1912 issue of *The Los Angeles Times*, he wrote, "The woods are full of detective stories—most of them bad. In fact, any serious detective story is of necessity bad. It appeals to the most primitive cravings within us."

Wright admired H. L. Mencken—well-known writer, editor, and critic—and wrote many letters to Mencken praising his work. He also visited Mencken on trips to the East Coast. Abandoning *The Los Angeles Times* and his wife and child, Wright moved to New York City in December 1912. In January 1913, on Mencken's recommendation to the owner of *The Smart Set*, Wright at age twenty-five became the editor in chief for the magazine. His tenure was short, for he had ambitions of editing a far more radical magazine. He was fired in December 1913 after charging the publisher for the printing costs of the "dummy" issue of such a journal.

In the four years after leaving *The Smart Set*, Wright followed his interests and published eight books, none of which was a financial success. Two were about modern painting, and two were on Nietzschean philosophy; his interest in the latter reflected a pro-German attitude that made Wright unpopular even before the United States entered World War I. (His support for Germany—and a rumor that he was spying for that country—led to his being fired in 1917 as literary editor of *The New York Evening Mail*.)

Cover for the May 1926 issue of the magazine featuring the first appearance of Van Dine's erudite detective, Philo Vance (from Peter Haining, The Classic Era of Crime Fiction [Chicago: Chicago Review Press, 2002]; Bruccoli Clark Layman Archives)

One of his books, *Misinforming a Nation* (1917), was an attack on the *Encyclopedia Britannica*.

The Man of Promise (1916) is Wright's autobiographical novel about a rebellious writer who wants to write "big, radical and free work." His parents and wife try to convince him to do safer work, which he considers "petty and conventional." He leaves his wife for a series of affairs with other women but eventually, for the sake of his daughter, he unhappily returns to his family and a career as a professor. Reviews of the novel, with the exception of one by Mencken, were generally unfavorable and focused unsympathetically on the protagonist. In *The Dial* (8 June 1916), E. E. Hale said that Wright's hero "talked as if he had ideas, as if he were an intellectual giant; whereas he really was a muddle-headed sensualist."

In 1916 Wright was treated in New York for a nervous condition and for his addiction to cocaine and opium. The following year, broke and still sick, he returned to California for a temporary reconciliation with his wife. He reluctantly took a job copyediting for *The Los Angeles Times*. In 1919 he and his wife moved north, and he became cultural critic for *The San Francisco Bulletin*, but that position only lasted a few months. In poor health, he was unable to do the amount of writing the paper required.

Wright again abandoned his wife in 1920 and returned to New York. He was theater reviewer for *The Greenwich Villager*, a job that included no salary, only free tickets. He lived on loans and freelance assignments from movie magazines, including *Photoplay*. Wright continued this hand-to-mouth existence until 1923, when he decided on the course destined to change his life.

Helped by friends Jacob Lobsenz, who treated him for his addiction, and Norbert Lederer, who lent him detective stories, Wright set about investigating the genre and developing a "package" to take to a publisher. With new enthusiasm, inspired by being deeply in debt, he gave up what he still considered "serious" work and threw himself into writing outlines for three detective novels. Later, after achieving success, Wright claimed he was forbidden by his doctor, because of a mental and physical breakdown, to write for two years and was only allowed to read detective stories. In *Alias S. S. Van Dine: The Man Who Created Philo Vance* (1992), biographer John Loughery points out that during the period when Wright was allegedly forbidden to write, he must have started the outlines, since they were available to show publishers early in 1926.

Loughery reports that Wright was not ready to publish mysteries under his own name: "I saw no advantage, and even feared a certain disadvantage in wrenching my own name from its cultural moorings and setting it adrift upon the seas of popular fiction." He took the pseudonym S. S. Van Dine, fashioning it from a variation on a family name, Van Dyne, and the letters used in steamship names. He recalled that he only planned to write six detective novels and then return to his serious interests.

Maxwell Perkins, an influential editor at Scribners, had known Wright at Harvard. While Perkins knew of Wright's problems, he also knew of Wright's writing ability. Shown the detective story outlines after the publisher Horace Liveright had turned them down, Perkins was impressed and agreed to publish the books.

Philo Vance, the protagonist Wright chose, is based on himself as he was and as he wished to be. Vance is a cynical intellectual who is wealthy, handsome, and debonair. He is also a dilettante, knowledgeable in many fields, including art and psychology. Physically, Vance is described at his first appearance in *The Benson Murder Case* (1926): ". . . his mouth was ascetic and cruel . . . there was a slightly derisive hauteur in the lift of his eyebrows. His forehead was full and sloping. . . . His cold grey eyes were widely spaced. His nose was straight and slender, and his chin narrow but prominent, with an unusually deep cleft. . . . Vance was slightly under six feet. . . ." Van Dine likens Vance's appearance to that of John Barrymore in *Hamlet*. Vance's life of luxury, involving studying and collecting artwork, is only interrupted when his friend, Manhattan district attorney John F.-X. Markham, asks his aid in solving—or preventing—murder. Critics including T. J. Binyon in *Murder Will Out: The Detective in Fiction* (1989) and H. R. F. Keating in *Whodunit?* (1982) describe Vance as an American version of Dorothy L. Sayers's detective, Lord Peter Wimsey.

The first two Vance mysteries are based on actual murder cases that gained notoriety in the New York press. *The Benson Murder Case* parallels the 1920 murder of Joseph Elwell, a prominent stockbroker and bridge player, found shot to death in his brownstone apartment, as is Van Dine's fictional victim, Alvin Benson. Because he knows that Vance is interested in crime, Markham invites him to observe the investigation. Vance quickly displays the characteristics that led Keating, Anthony Boucher, and Francis M. Nevins to describe him as "insufferable." Five minutes after arriving at the Benson house, he claims to know the identity of the murderer, but he refuses to tell Markham or Sergeant Heath of the Homicide Bureau, allowing them to fix guilt at various times on five innocent people. Vance's speech is foppish. He calls Markham "Old Dear" and frequently omits letters—saying, for example, "don't y'know," "most amusin'," and "extr'ordin'rily simple."

The stories are told by a fictional character named S. S. Van Dine, who describes himself as Vance's "legal advisor, monetary steward, and constant companion." He is the most unobtrusive of narrators, playing no role in the stories. Boucher in the *San Francisco Chronicle* calls him "a character written in disappearing ink" (28 April 1946).

Beginning in his first book, Vance emphasizes psychological clues as the one infallible method of determining guilt; he minimizes the importance of physical clues. He finds a parallel between identifying an artist by brush strokes to distinguishing a murderer through a comparison between a psychological profile and the way a crime was committed. Vance says, "The only real clues are psychological—not material. Your truly profound art expert, for instance, does not judge and authenticate pictures by an inspection of the underpainting and a chemical analysis of the pigments, but by studying the creative personality revealed in the picture's conception and execution." Carrying the analogy further, Vance considers a crime that is well performed as a work of art, and in this and future books, he shows respect for the clever killer, bringing him or her to justice with reluctance. He claims not to be an avenger for society and prefers that murderers be allowed to commit suicide rather than be arrested.

From the start, Van Dine included many footnotes, often translating foreign phrases or expounding on art. These characteristics proved unpopular with some reviewers, who criticized them, even as they praised the mystery. In his review of *The Benson Murder Case* in the *New York Herald Tribune Books* (21 November 1926), Carty Ranck mentioned "many Latin and Greek quotations, all intended to show what a devil of a fellow is Philo Vance." In the *Saturday Review of Literature* for 15 January 1927, Hammett compared Vance's conversation in *The Benson Murder Case* to a student using the foreign words and phrases at the back of a dictionary.

Most reviews were favorable, however, and the air of erudition and Van Dine's storytelling appealed to readers. In *Murder for Pleasure* (1941), Howard Haycraft wrote of *The Benson Murder Case:* "Overnight, American crime fiction had come of age." He applauds Van Dine's decision to aim for a "higher stratum of the public than had previously been accustomed to read them," something that English writers, including Sayers, had been doing. The first edition of *The Benson Murder Case* went into eleven printings, and by early 1927 more than fifty thousand copies had been sold, a huge number for detective fiction at the time.

Having written outlines for two more Vance mysteries, Wright as Van Dine was in position to follow up his success with a second book, again recalling a real case. *The "Canary" Murder Case* (1927) is loosely based on the 1923 murder of "Dot" King, a promiscuous beauty of the Prohibition era. Van Dine fictionalizes her as Margaret Odell of the Ziegfeld Follies. Margaret is found strangled in her apartment, which is locked from the inside. Suspects include a prominent doctor, a businessman, a gambler, and various Broadway figures. Vance convinces Markham to agree to having the suspects play a poker game with him in the district attorney's office because he believes the card game will allow him to explore the psyche of the killer. Van Dine even has a footnote referring to an article by anthropologist George Dorsey calling poker the best psychological "laboratory." Though usually disdaining physical evidence, Van Dine also offers a plausible solution to the locked-room murder and includes a diagram in explanation. Heavily promoted by the publisher, *The "Canary" Murder Case* became an immediate best-seller, selling more copies than any previous mystery. Philo Vance had become the best-known American detective.

Reviews of *The "Canary" Murder Case* were highly favorable, though some critics complained about what they considered Vance's irritating personality. A. S. Pier in *Atlantic Bookshelf* (27 October 1927) called the plot ingenious, asserting that Van Dine writes with humor and "sketches character vividly and with deftness." Will Cuppy in the *New York Herald Tribune Books* (21 August 1927) wrote that Van Dine displays "such ingenious handling of clues and deft juggling of plot that even low brow readers must forgive him for his rather desperate display of culture." An unsigned review in *The New York Times Book Review* (2 October 1927), however, justly cites the author's apparent lack of familiarity with police techniques. Throughout the series, for example, the district attorney of Manhattan routinely conducts investigations himself—a highly unlikely procedure.

Using the reading he had done before outlining his first mysteries, Van Dine as Wright proved himself a notable historian in the field of mystery fiction. His introduction to the 1927 anthology *The Great Detective Stories: A Chronological Anthology* is considered by Haycraft and others an outstanding scholarly work. The book was originally published as edited by Wright, but it was reprinted as *The World's Great Detective Stories,* edited by Van Dine, after Wright had disclosed his pseudonym in *American Magazine* for September 1928 in an article titled "I Used to Be a Highbrow, but Look at Me Now."

Almost as popular as *The "Canary" Murder Case* was *The Greene Murder Case* (1928), in which someone tries to wipe out the Greene family in their mansion overlooking the East River. In his first novel not inspired by an actual crime, Van Dine has his narrator refer to "a hidden death-dealing horror [that] stalked through the grim corridors of that fated house." H. E. Dounce in the *New York Evening Post* (24 March 1928) said, "This is the best detective story of the season." An unsigned reviewer in *The Boston Transcript* (28 April 1928) opined, "Once again S. S. Van Dine has written a detective story that is inimitable and a joy to read. Even the most astute follower of the literature of mystery and crime will probably be unable to discover the culprit until the fifth from last page."

In 1928 Paramount began work on the movie *The Canary Murder Case* in both silent and sound versions for 1929 release. William Powell played Vance,

Wright (right) and actor William Powell, who played Philo Vance in five movies between 1929 and 1933 (from Jon Tuska,
The Detective in Hollywood [Garden City, N.Y.: Doubleday, 1978]; Bruccoli Clark Layman Archives)

repeating his role in *The Greene Murder Case,* also released in 1929, and *The Benson Murder Case* (1930). Van Dine as a character is omitted from all Vance movies. All the Vance books except *The Kidnap Murder Case* (1936) and *The Winter Murder Case* (1939) were made into movies at least once.

Beginning in January 1929, Van Dine published eight true-crime stories in *Cosmopolitan:* "The Scarlet Nemesis" (January 1929), "A Murder in a Witches' Cauldron" (February 1929), "The Man in the Blue Overcoat" (May 1929), "Poison" (June 1929), "The Almost Perfect Crime" (July 1929), "The Inconvenient Husband" (August 1929), "The Bonmartini Murder Case" (October 1929), and "Fool!" (January 1930). All are based on well-known European crimes, said to have been recounted to Van Dine by Philo Vance after Sunday night dinners at the latter's favorite club, the Stuyvesant.

The Bishop Murder Case (1929), considered by Nevins in an essay in *1001 Midnights* (1984) as the best of the Vance mysteries, has a murderer who taunts the police by leaving false clues in the form of Mother Goose nursery rhymes. Markham, turning to Vance for help, says, "we're confronted by something almost too diabolical to contemplate." The reviews were mixed, ranging from wild enthusiasm to one by W. R. Brooks in *Outlook* (27 February 1929) in which Brooks calls Vance "a long winded, pedantic bore." M-G-M outbid Paramount for the rights to *The Bishop Murder Case* and made a movie in 1930 with Basil Rathbone, who became the second of ten actors to play Vance on screen.

The success of the Van Dine books helped to save Scribners during the Great Depression and also permitted Van Dine to rid himself of old debts and to adopt a lifestyle similar to the one he gave Vance. In 1929 Van Dine met and fell in love with Eleanor Rulapaugh, known professionally as Claire de Lisle, an illustrator; their relationship raised the issue of how to dissolve Van Dine's first marriage. Van Dine used his money to secure a divorce: Katharine Wright agreed to the divorce in 1930, after he promised her and Beverly a year in Europe. Beverly had artistic ambitions and desperately wanted to study on the Continent. She maintained that her father had seldom shown her any affection or spent a significant amount of time with her. Van Dine married de Lisle in October 1930, and they were happy together: she shared his many expensive interests.

The fifth Vance novel, *The Scarab Murder Case* (1930), gave Van Dine a chance to incorporate one of his interests. He makes Vance such an expert in crime and Egyptian art that when the body of an art patron is found in a private museum, next to a rare blue gem in the shape of the beetle ancient Egyptians venerated, the person discovering the body calls Vance before notifying the police.

Critical reactions to *The Scarab Murder Case* were widely different. Hammett and Loughery asserted that its footnotes about Egyptian art and history slowed the plot. Yet, Eugene Reynal in the *Saturday Review of Literature* (24 May 1930) did not find the pace slow and praised it as "very close to the top of all detective stories. . . . The story rushes on to a series of exciting climaxes, carefully planned, artistically constructed, and ingeniously baffling."

A three-year gap elapsed before the publication of the sixth Vance mystery. In 1931 and 1932, Vance wrote screenplays for twelve movie shorts released by Warner Bros. as the "S. S. Van Dine Mystery Series." Philo Vance does not appear. Van Dine also wrote *The Blue Moon Murder Case* for First National, a subsidiary of Warner Bros.; the movie was released as *Girl Missing* (1933), again without Vance.

The Kennel Murder Case (1933) is about the locked-room murder of a noted collector of Oriental ceramics. It allows Vance to share another of his creator's interests, as dogs provide vital clues. Vance, like Van Dine at the time, breeds Scottish terriers in New Jersey. As in many of Vance's cases, the murderer is so clever that, though identified by Vance, the evidence is insufficient for conviction; a Doberman pinscher disposes of the killer. Reviews were generally favorable, and the movie version, starring William Powell, is regarded by movie historian William K. Everson as the best of the Vance movies.

His expensive way of living not only led Van Dine to take Hollywood money but also caused him to give up the idea of curtailing his career in mystery fiction after only six books. He provided Scribners with his seventh mystery, his second book to be scheduled for 1933 publication, *The Dragon Murder Case*. It employed still another of the expensive passions that were placing Van Dine in danger of going into debt again—tropical fish. According to Loughery,

Van Dine had enough tropical fish in his Manhattan apartment to fill sixty-eight tanks.

The Dragon Murder Case starts with a bizarre, seemingly impossible, murder. At the estate of a collector of unusual fish, a man dives into a pool and disappears, his body never rising to the surface. When the body is found, it is several miles away and has gashes that appear to have been made by a dragon-like monster. Van Dine had often contended that no author had more than six good mysteries within his capability, and Boucher in the *San Francisco Chronicle* seems to agree, asserting that *The Dragon Murder Case* "may well be the worst whodunit ever written" (25 June 1944). Others, however, found the novel one of the more logical and fairly resolved of all the Vance books. Norman Klein in the *New York Evening Post* (14 October 1933) praised its swift storytelling and readability.

The Casino Murder Case (1934) is the first of two mysteries to reflect Van Dine's growing addiction to gambling. After receiving a message warning of impending tragedy in the Llewellyn family, which owns a gambling den catering to Manhattan's wealthy, Vance goes to the casino but cannot prevent the first of two poisonings. Though some critics continued to find merit only in the first six Van Dine mysteries, Isaac Anderson in *The New York Times* (30 September 1934) called *The Casino Murder Case* as good as earlier books, saying, "The crime is an uncommonly subtle one, and the solution of it is one of the major triumphs of Vance's career."

Van Dine's favorite form of gambling was betting on horse races, and *The Garden Murder Case* (1935) includes much information on betting. A murder occurs as family and friends of Professor Ephraim Garden gather to listen to the radio broadcast of an important race. This novel is notable for being the only one in which Philo Vance shows an affection for a woman; his feelings for Zalia Graem almost cause Van Dine to violate one of the "Twenty Rules for Writing Detective Stories" that he had propounded in an article included in *Philo Vance Murder Cases* (1936). He had said the detective should never have a love interest. *The Garden Murder Case* has the most exciting ending of the series, with Vance plunging off a rooftop after a confrontation with the killer.

In "Collecting Mystery Fiction: S. S. Van Dine," an article in the fall 1982 issue of *Armchair Detective*, Otto Penzler wrote, "If there has been a fictional detective easier to parody than Vance, he remains undiscovered." Van Dine was not averse to the additional recognition that came from the many Vance parodies. The earliest was probably "The Pink Murder Case" by Christopher Ward, writing as "S. S.

Dust jacket for the fifth Philo Vance novel, published in 1930, in which the detective demonstrates his expertise in ancient Egyptian art (<home.comcast.net/~seriesauctions/images/VD_Scarab.jpg>)

Veendam," in the *Saturday Review of Literature* for 2 November 1929. Van Dine helped Corey Ford, writing as John Riddell, with *The John Riddell Murder Case,* a parody that Scribners published in 1930. In *The Garden Murder Case,* Van Dine even quotes Ogden Nash's famous couplet: "Philo Vance / Needs a kick in the pance."

When Franklin D. Roosevelt mentioned an idea for a mystery to Fulton Oursler, the latter solicited other writers for the project that eventually became *The President's Mystery Story* (1935). Roosevelt's idea involved a wealthy man disappearing with enough money to sustain him but without leaving a trace. In great need of money, Van Dine turned down few opportunities, and he joined six other authors who agreed to write a chapter each to flesh out Roosevelt's idea.

Some critics—including Jon L. Breen, in his review of Loughery's biography of Van Dine in *What About Murder?* (1993)—have called *The Kidnap Murder Case* Van Dine's weakest book, but contemporary reviews were kinder, praising its narrative power, though finding the plot not as carefully worked out as those in his previous works. Key evidence used for the solution is not shared with the reader, and much

depends on an unlikely theory connecting the perfume a woman wears to her hair color. It is largely set in "The Purple House," the strangely painted mansion built by Karl K. Kenting, a man obsessed with the letter "K." (He joined the Ku Klux Klan and named his sons "Kaspar" and "Kenyon.") When Kaspar is kidnapped, and a note written in Chinese ink and signed in cabalistic symbols is discovered, Markham asks Vance to help him investigate. Vance in this book is more physically active than in past books: he hides in a Central Park tree, invades a criminal's lair in the Bronx, and engages in a shootout. However, unlike hard-boiled heroes of the era, Vance continues to use precious language, referring to Markham as "Old Dear."

Increasingly desperate for money, Van Dine was using his fame to appear in magazine advertisements for liquor, radios, and automobile tires. He was receptive when late in 1937 Paramount Pictures offered him $25,000 to provide a three-thousand-word outline for a Philo Vance mystery to feature the popular comedians George Burns and Gracie Allen. Eventually, Burns was eliminated from the project, but Gracie Allen is featured in the movie and in the novel, *The Gracie Allen Murder Case* (1938), which Van

Dine expanded from his outline and which Scribners published, counting on the Allen name to boost the dwindling sales of Philo Vance books.

The plot depends upon several coincidences, as when Vance, strolling through the woods in Riverdale, meets Gracie at the exact spot in which a murder weapon has been thrown. Equally coincidental is the connection between Gracie and an escaped criminal who has vowed to kill Markham. Vance is smitten—though not romantically—with Gracie and allows her to help him solve the murder of a man identified as her brother. Van Dine does a good job of capturing Gracie's voice, but the character named George Burns does not have the comedian's unmistakable speech. The Burns character was deleted from the movie. Most reviewers agreed that this book was not up to the standards of prior Vance novels, but some found it enjoyable because of the idea of Gracie Allen assisting Philo Vance in detection, though she calls him "Fido."

Van Dine's expenses were already exceeding his income when his wife's serious illnesses, requiring surgery, added to his problems. He began to sell some of the objects and books he had acquired and continued to be receptive to moneymaking projects. *The Winter Murder Case* was another outline "ordered" from Van Dine by a movie studio. An old friend from California, Julian Johnson, head of the story department at 20th Century-Fox, proposed that Van Dine tailor a mystery for one of his studio's stars. Since he had ice-skater Sonja Henie in mind, the story was to include at least one skating sequence. Van Dine agreed and wrote a mystery about murder at a midwinter house party in the Berkshire Mountains. Vance uses a skating exhibition by the daughter of the estate caretaker to distract the party while he solves the case.

Van Dine suffered what appeared to be a mild heart attack in February 1939; he was hospitalized but soon returned home. On 11 April 1939, he suffered another heart attack and died. 20th Century-Fox gave up the idea of making a movie from what Vance had written, but Scribners published this last Vance book, though it was incomplete by Van Dine's usual standards. He normally wrote his mysteries in three stages: a ten-thousand-word outline, a twenty- to thirty-thousand-word expanded version, and a final version of about sixty thousand words. Van Dine died after the second stage of this process, so *The Winter Murder Case* lacked the final elaboration of character, dialogue, atmosphere, and footnotes.

Contemporary reviewers did not miss what had been omitted. In *The New York Times* (15 October 1939), Anderson called it "As good a story as Van Dine ever wrote." He recognized "where it might have been embroidered with learned dissertations upon emeralds, figure skating, and other topics . . . but these . . . would have added nothing to the tale as a detective story." Perkins wrote an introduction to the posthumous publication of this book, praising the author's "integrity." This characterization is at considerable odds with Van Dine as Wright, who emerges from interviews with family and acquaintances in Loughery's biography as an unfaithful husband, a neglectful father, and a man of dubious honesty.

S. S. Van Dine's influence on other American detective-story writers was profound, if not long lasting. The early Ellery Queen novels, beginning in 1929, also presented a somewhat priggish hero of formidable reasoning ability. Anthony Abbot's Thatcher Colt, beginning in 1930, was another detective of great intelligence and, like Van Dine, had a secretary who narrates the stories and bears the same name as the author. Though Rex Stout's narrator, Archie Goodwin, is far from being as faceless as Van Dine's, Stout's Nero Wolfe is as eccentric as Vance, with the same sort of multifaceted intellect.

The fame of Philo Vance proved short-lived, though his name continued to be marketable. When he appeared in media adaptations after Van Dine's death, major changes were made in his image. In the movie *Calling Philo Vance* (1940), a remake of *The Dragon Murder Case,* Vance was made a Secret Service agent. In three low-budget movies made in 1947 he became a private detective. He was also a private detective in a radio series that aired during the 1940s.

In *Murder for Pleasure,* Haycraft says Van Dine had rejuvenated and reestablished detective fiction in America and that his name and that of his sleuth would endure. Both are still known, especially among scholars, but for more than thirty years, scholars have wondered at the reasons for Van Dine's success. In *A Catalogue of Crime* (1971), Jacques Barzun and Wendell Hertig Taylor found hard to believe that Van Dine's books were once the leading sellers of detective fiction and had so great an appeal to intellectual readers. Similarly, in 1982, in an article in *The Armchair Detective* on collecting Van Dine's works, Otto Penzler found the Vance books so hopelessly dated that he could not imagine that they had ever enjoyed great popularity. Writing in *1001 Midnights,* Nevins recognized Van Dine's faults and admitted that present-day readers have trouble reading his works, but he still found them of crucial historical importance and called Philo Vance "the first important character in the history of novel-length American detective fiction."

Bibliography:

Walter B. Crawford, "The Writings of Willard Huntington Wright," *Bulletin of Bibliography* (May–August 1963): 11–16.

Biography:

John Loughery, *Alias S. S. Van Dine: The Man Who Created Philo Vance* (New York: Scribner, 1992).

References:

Bruce R. Beaman, "S. S. Van Dine: A Biographical Sketch," *Armchair Detective,* 8 (February 1975): 133–135;

Ernest Boyd, "Willard Huntington Wright," *Saturday Review of Literature,* 19 (22 April 1939): 8;

Edward Connor, "The Nine Philo Vances," *Films in Review,* 9 (March 1958): 133–137, 154;

Fred Dueren, "Philo Vance," *Armchair Detective,* 9 (November 1975): 23–24;

E. R. Hagemann, "Philo Vance's Sunday Nights at the Old Stuyvesant Club," *Clues: A Journal of Detection,* 1 (Fall/Winter 1980): 35–41;

John Loughery, "The Rise and Fall of Philo Vance," *Armchair Detective,* 20 (Winter 1987): 64–71;

R. A. W. Lowndes, "Dear Me, Mr. Van Dine," *Armchair Detective,* 7 (November 1973): 30–31;

Otto Penzler, "Collecting Mystery Fiction: S. S. Van Dine," *Armchair Detective,* 15 (Fall 1982): 350–356;

Penzler, "Philo Vance," in *The Private Lives of Private Eyes* (New York: Grosset & Dunlap, 1977), pp. 185–193;

Theodor Reik, "The Canary Murder Case," in his *The Unknown Murderer* (New York: International Universities Press, 1945), pp. 238–243;

Roger Rosenblatt, "The Back of the Book: S. S. Van Dine," *New Republic,* 26 (July 1975): 32–34;

David Smith, "S. S. Van Dine at 20th Century-Fox," *Views and Reviews,* 2 (Fall 1970): 48–58;

Karl Thiede, "S. S. Van Filmography," *Views and Reviews,* 2 (Fall 1970): 43–46;

Jon Tuska, *"The Casino Murder Case,"* *Views and Reviews,* 2 (Fall 1970): 36–43;

Tuska, *Philo Vance: The Life and Times of S. S. Van Dine* (Bowling Green, Ohio: Bowling Green University Popular Press, 1971);

Tuska, "The Philo Vance Murder Case," *Views and Reviews,* 1 (Winter 1970): 54–62; 1 (Spring 1970): 38–46; 2 (Summer 1970): 45–54.

Papers:

The Willard Huntington Wright Scrapbooks are at the Princeton University Library. The Willard Huntington Wright correspondence is at the University of Virginia Library.

Judith Van Gieson

(24 January 1941 –   )

Carol McGinnis Kay
University of South Carolina

BOOKS: *North of the Border* (New York: Walker, 1988;
    London: Virago, 1990);
Raptor (New York: Harper & Row, 1990);
The Other Side of Death (New York: HarperCollins,
    1991);
The Wolf Path (New York: HarperCollins, 1992);
The Lies That Bind (New York: HarperCollins, 1993);
Mercury Retrograde (Huntington Beach, Cal.: James
    Cahill, 1994);
Parrot Blues (New York: HarperCollins, 1995);
Hotshots (New York: HarperCollins, 1996);
Ditch Rider (New York: HarperCollins, 1998);
The Stolen Blue (New York: New American Library,
    2000);
Vanishing Point (New York: New American Library,
    2001);
Confidence Woman (New York: New American Library,
    2002);
Land of Burning Heat (New York: New American
    Library, 2003);
The Shadow of Venus (New York: New American
    Library, 2004).

Judith Van Gieson is a refiner and polisher rather
than a radical reshaper of the genre of detective fiction.
Her first series, the eight Neil Hamel novels, are spare,
lean evocations of what Raymond Chandler calls the
world of the hard-boiled loner detective who "can walk
mean streets without becoming mean himself." Her second series, the five Claire Reynier novels, may at first
glance appear "cozy" because the central detective is a
fiftyish, book-loving archivist at the Center for Southwest Research at the University of New Mexico
Library who has many friends and a cat. But, while
Claire Reynier shoots no one on any mean street, the
novels featuring her are decidedly unlike the puzzle-
mysteries exemplified by Agatha Christie's Miss Marple novels. Nothing about the Reynier series is cute or
cuddly, and the wit is dry and sardonic. With their
unblinking look at the varieties of human corruption,
the Claire Reynier novels might more appropriately be

*Judith Van Gieson (photograph © by Robert R. White;
from* Ditch Rider, *1998; Richland County
Public Library)*

called hard-boiled novels for grown-ups. They secure
Van Gieson's place as an important contemporary
writer of the genre.

Since both series are set in Albuquerque and are
known for what *Kirkus Reviews* calls in a 1998 review of
North of the Border their "absolutely magical descriptions" of the Southwestern landscape, readers are often
surprised to learn that Judith Van Gieson is originally
from New York City and lived most of her young
adulthood on the East Coast. She was born on 24 January 1941 to Claire and John Van Gieson, who already
had a son, John. Something of the family structure is
echoed in Van Gieson's first series: Neil Hamel's family

is also composed of father, mother, son, and daughter. Much like Hamel's father, Joe, who worked for the telephone company for thirty years, John Van Gieson worked at Bell Labs for close to thirty years. He, like Joe, encouraged his daughter to be athletic. John Van Gieson was an accomplished athlete, not the stay-at-home armchair adventurer who is Hamel's father. Van Gieson's father died when she was twenty-seven years old, a loss that may be reflected in Hamel's losses of nurturing men from her life: Hamel loses her father at an even earlier age (twenty). In *Hotshots* (1996), she tells her lover about her father teaching her about risk taking, and she concludes, "After he died I completed his life." In a 14 March 1998 personal interview in Albuquerque, Van Gieson revealed that Hamel's hallucination during a life-threatening firestorm in *Hotshots*—seeing herself skiing a perfect run down the side of a mountain with her father waiting for her at the bottom—is actually one of her own childhood memories.

Van Gieson's mother was a nurse, and, unlike Hamel's mother, she did not abandon her family when her daughter was eight years old. On the contrary, Van Gieson had a close relationship with both parents and her brother, who is sixteen months older. Her mother remarried at the age of sixty and enjoyed twenty-five years in a second marriage before her death in 1998. Van Gieson clearly had a good relationship with her stepfather, as evidenced by her dedicating one of her novels to him.

Almost as reticent as her protagonist Neil Hamel, Van Gieson says little about her childhood. She does recall that the family moved twice to towns in New Jersey, when she was five and eight. Not until college at Northwestern University, when a course in creative writing struck a receptive chord, did Van Gieson begin to write short stories. She graduated from Northwestern in 1962 with a degree in English and went to work for G. P. Putnam's Sons in New York, an experience that she says temporarily squelched her budding enthusiasm for writing, because she found the sheer volume of books being printed intimidating.

In 1964, through mutual friends, Van Gieson met John Woodruff, a realtor who shared her interests in skiing and writing. They married and the next day moved to Waitsfield, Vermont, where they started a real-estate business. Woodruff had a son from a previous marriage, but they had no children together. During the next seven years Van Gieson wrote little, but the knowledge she gained about the inner workings of law offices and realtors' offices is clearly reflected in her first series: Neil Hamel is an attorney specializing in real estate and divorce. Experience with divorce law came when Van Gieson and Woodruff were divorced in 1971.

With the end of her marriage, Van Gieson decided to see if she could become the writer she had earlier wanted to be. She soon sold everything and moved to the writers' colony at San Miguel de Allende in Mexico. Thanks to the low cost of living there, Van Gieson lived comfortably in San Miguel and studied writing under Cameron Gray, who was an encouraging mentor. As she immersed herself in the process of writing, Van Gieson found herself increasingly attracted to two seemingly disparate effects, one highly conscious and one unconscious: she was fascinated by developing a sense of writing for an audience, and at the same time she discovered that she enjoyed losing herself in her writing. In the 1998 personal interview in Albuquerque, Van Gieson stated that she found that she worked best by starting with an idea for a plot and then creating the characters, who she hoped would "take off on their own." "Getting the voice right" for Van Gieson is the hardest part of writing. She learned from Gray to "trust the unconscious to create characters" while applying her conscious mind to honing the plotline.

After Gray died in 1979, Van Gieson and several other writers at San Miguel moved to Santa Fe, New Mexico. Throughout the early 1980s, Van Gieson worked a series of temporary, part-time jobs—for example, as a bookkeeper and secretary, at attorneys' offices in Santa Fe and later in Boston, where she also had contacts. In every spare moment, she wrote. She wrote some poetry, but mostly short stories. When she finally sold a story, "El Alicante," to the *Capilano Review* for $20 and five copies, she recalls thinking, "For this amount of work I could write a novel and actually get paid real money" (1998 Albuquerque interview). Drawing on her knowledge of Vermont, she set about writing her first novel, a nondetective work that was not picked up by a publisher. Some of her early poems and stories were collected in *Mercury Retrograde* (1994) after Van Gieson had published five detective novels.

In the early 1980s, an Albuquerque attorney friend introduced Van Gieson to the novels of Chandler and Dashiell Hammett; reading their works marked a turning point in her writing career. Previously an omnivorous reader, not especially a reader of detective fiction, she was attracted to the brilliance of the style of these two authors. She responded most strongly to Chandler's use of figurative language, calling him the "master of the metaphor" (in a 20 August 1996 personal interview in Charleston, S.C.). His work provided a model she wanted to emulate. In 1984, when she was living and working in Santa Fe, she began writing the first Neil Hamel book. She had moved to Boston by the time this work, *North of the Border,* was published in 1988, but she continued to visit New Mexico, specifically Santa Fe and Albuquerque, in order to conduct research for her writing. Reviews of *North of the Border* in both regional and national venues were positive–for example, *Kirkus Reviews* gave it a starred review (15 May 1988), praising the novel for its "well-thought out plot," "magical descriptions," and strong characterization, calling Neil Hamel "a find." The positive response to that first novel convinced Van Gieson that she could make a living with a series set in Albuquerque, and she chose to make that city her full-time residence. She has lived in Albuquerque since 1992. She currently lives in an adobe house similar to the ones owned by Neil Hamel in *Ditch Rider,* where she tries to write on a daily basis.

Among the hard-boiled women detectives who appeared in the 1980s, Neil Hamel is one of the most clearly descended from Philip Marlowe–that is, in every way except her profession and her gender. While she is an attorney whose detecting arises from doing her own investigative work for her cases, and she is decidedly female, she is also a loner and a tough fighter with a smart mouth. She has "a wry, intelligent voice," according to the *Orlando Sentinel.* A *Boston Globe* review calls her "tough-minded . . . funny, sexy, and very bright." Her world is marked by random violence and corruption in systems nominally established for the benefit of social order. She smokes and drinks too much, especially in the first novel, and describes herself in *Ditch Rider* (1998) as having "two moods. Either I'm pissed off or I'm not." Beneath her smart-alecky exterior, however, beats the heart of a female knight errant who is driven to seek justice in her own way. As *The New York Times Book Review* describes her, "Neil is a real maverick . . . and just the person to clean up . . . dirty secrets" in her town.

Van Gieson's knowledge of the life of an attorney was one of the reasons she chose that profession for her detective. She was also "impressed by the large number of women entering the legal profession in the eighties, powerful women with an idealistic core." One reason she decided not to make her detective a traditional private investigator (PI) was that she knew little about the actual lives of PIs.

The more philosophical basis for choosing to make Neil Hamel an attorney was Van Gieson's sense that "The lawyer is the symbol for our times the way the private eye was for the forties," as she states in her 1996 Charleston personal interview. According to Van Gieson, the tough private eyes of the 1930s and 1940s may have been cynical, hard-drinking, quick to swing a fist or shoot a gun, and equally quick to bed a woman or crack a joke, but they kept the corruption of America during and after the Great Depression in some sort of check. "The moral ambiguity of having one corruption eliminated by another, perhaps lesser, corruption was

Dust jacket for Van Gieson's first novel, published in 1988, which introduces lawyer-sleuth Neil Hamel (Richland County Public Library)

readily understood by the readers of hard-boiled detective novels in the thirties and forties." Today, according to Van Gieson, such moral ambiguities are most often played out in America through the legal system.

Moral and ethical choices for people and for systems are dealt with in an objective and often subtle fashion in the Neil Hamel series. According to *The Bloomsbury Review,* "characters and issues are nicely marbled" in the novels. Van Gieson's "strength is her ability to swirl inventiveness and research into timely plots with timeless themes." Van Gieson is not a preacher; she is an illuminator. *Kirkus Reviews,* in a 15 January 1992 review of *The Wolf Path,* lauds her "nonhectoring, clear prose." While unfolding the investigations of Neil Hamel, she explores many contemporary issues, particularly medical, legal, and environmental ones. In the initial novel of the series, *North of the Border,* she deals with problems associated with international child adoption and with burying nuclear waste. *Raptor* (1990) explores the fascination people have for endangered birds and the various ways, legal and illegal, in which that fascination is manifested. *The Other Side of Death* (1991) questions the effectiveness of zoning regulations in maintaining the character of historical districts. *The Wolf Path* (1992) shows the risks to humans and animals alike that accompany the seemingly laudable practice of reintroducing wolves to their natural Western habitat. In *The Lies That Bind* (1993), Van Gieson explores several issues. She questions both the ethics of overprescribing Halcion for the elderly and the morality of a defendant claiming diminished responsibility for a vehicular manslaughter as a consequence of the drug. She also reveals the corrupt workings of real estate developers as they are involved with savings-and-loan-association frauds similar to those that were making headlines in the early 1990s. In *Parrot Blues* (1995) Van Gieson returns to problems surrounding endangered birds as Hamel's case involves the smuggling of rare parrots. *Hotshots* offers a look at the risks—and ethics—of fighting forest fires. The environmental issues of the needs of the farmer versus the suburban homeowner for water and both of them versus the arid ecosystem of the Southwest are exemplified in the changing landscape of the North Valley of Albuquerque in *Ditch Rider,* the latest, and perhaps the last, Neil Hamel novel.

If *Ditch Rider* proves to be the last appearance by Neil Hamel, readers of the detective genre will likely feel a sense of loss. Reviewers have praised her as "a classic" *(Firsts),* "a great addition to the ranks of contemporary women sleuths" and "top-notch" character *(Booklist),* and "a solid addition to the sleuth pantheon" *(Boston Globe).* In a January 1990 review of *The Other Side of Death, Kirkus Reviews* calls her "A standout . . . Neil may actually be more interesting than Kinsey [Milhone] and as staunch as V. I. [Warshawski]—but with a better love life." The reviewer in *First for Women* asserts that "Judith Van Gieson, more than any other writer so far, seems to me capable of joining the ranks of [Sue] Grafton and [Sara] Paretsky. Her character, Neil Hamel, is intelligent, funny, tough, sexy, independent, and committed to causes."

Indeed, Neil Hamel has a strong sense of fair play. She likes solving puzzles, and she is relentless in moving toward a resolution. When March Augusta in *Raptor* is accused of murder, and Hamel is convinced he is incapable of deliberately killing another person, she offers her legal services, thinking "If I couldn't prove he didn't do it, I might have to find out who did." The sentiment is typical of the way in which Hamel keeps straying from her legal office into murder investigations.

Hamel's relentless determination to find answers leads her into risky, even foolhardy actions. Although Van Gieson says she is "not much interested in violence," she concludes each novel in the series with the de rigueur scene in which brute force concludes the search for the killer, with Hamel taking serious personal risks. For example, at the end of *Raptor,* she gets

into a violent fistfight, in which she nearly beats the male killer to death. At the end of *Ditch Rider,* she goes out alone at night to try to prevent a gang killing. While the novels are repeatedly praised for their sense of pacing and complicated plots that turn on Hamel's skills in logic and rational analysis, the detective also admits to liking the rush of adrenaline generated by such physical scrapes. Since she always handles herself well in these situations, readers must assume she is in good physical condition in spite of smoking, drinking to excess, and poor eating habits. (Readers must "assume," because Van Gieson says little about Hamel's looks.)

Part of the appeal of contemporary detective fiction lies in the immediacy of its impact on the readers, who recognize the fictional world as quite similar to the one they wake up to and read about in morning newspapers. Van Gieson's novels offer the reader a chance to consider many sides of contemporary social issues, typically without being coerced into any particular position except a broad concern for the health of the natural world—which includes human beings. The writer does not show a knee-jerk devotion to the spotted owl above all other living creatures. For example, in *Hotshots,* Hamel initially assumes that fighting all forest fires is an obvious obligation of the United States Forest Service, but as she learns more about the nature of forests and fires, she begins to question that assumption. She learns that fire suppression has actually interrupted forest regeneration, as well as created a fuel buildup that makes fires bigger, hotter, and more deadly. Yet, if the policy of fire suppression were to be altered to one of containment only, what about the homes and businesses that would be at risk? Further, is there no responsibility to be assumed by the person who knowingly builds in an isolated wooded area? The questions, Hamel learns, are myriad, and clear answers are elusive. Neither she nor Van Gieson offers a solution, but the reader finishes the novel with a definite awareness that this issue needs addressing.

Hotshots provides a good example of Hamel's unrelenting drive for justice. Unlike most practicing attorneys, she will work without pay if she thinks an injustice is occurring, and she will not stop until resolution is reached. When Eric Barker, the father of the deceased firefighter in *Hotshots,* suggests that they have all searched enough for answers about his daughter's death, he concludes, "Sometimes bad things just happen, Neil. Sometimes conditions are so severe there's nothing anyone can do." Understanding that this resignation satisfies him, Hamel does not argue, because, she thinks to herself, these "were the words that got him through the day, but if I believed them I'd have to take down my license to practice law."

The Hamel novels are also characterized by a strong sense of detachment, not from issues, but from people. "The writing is crisp and wry," says the blurb from the *Boston Globe* review of *The Lies That Bind*. Like Philip Marlowe, Hamel tells her own stories and is a keen observer of others. Like Marlowe, she lives and works alone. In the early novels, she has a bumbling, incompetent law partner, Brinkley Harrison, who has left the firm by the time *Hotshots* opens. The only other person in her legal office is Anna, a secretary who spends most of her time adjusting her nail polish or her bouffant hair and learning new lawyer jokes. Neither person is ever involved in her investigations. Hamel is divorced, in her thirties, and has no friends (a few are mentioned only in the early novels). She considers her "lawyer clothes" a costume for work and wears them only when she has to. She eschews wearing a watch. In every novel she drives long distances in the New Mexico desert, savoring the privacy and the solitude. "There's a lot of nothing out there," she observes on one of her drives in *Parrot Blues*, "more than I've ever seen. Some people find emptiness terrifying. I find it exhilarating." Until *Hotshots*, Hamel lives in an apartment complex named La Vista, a name that underscores her fondness for distance, space, and observation. Even her legal specialties—divorce and real estate—are the branches of law of that deal with psychological and physical spaces between people.

Hamel's intense need for personal space is underscored by Van Gieson's device of never naming the detective's lover, a young man in his twenties, some ten years younger than she. He is known only as "the Kid," a nickname given to him by one of his older brothers, not by Hamel. He is an auto mechanic by day and an accordion player at a tavern in the barrio by night; they met when her car broke down prior to the first novel. The reader learns a bit more about him in every novel, but not his name. His own story is a tale of aloneness and displacement: he was born in Argentina; his family fled to Mexico during political upheavals; then he fled alone to the United States as a teenager.

Hamel's fondness for physical space and distance is underscored by Van Gieson's frequent use of such distancing literary devices as flashbacks, journals, and diaries. For example, Hamel gets to know her recently deceased Aunt Joan only through reading her journal, which is the frame for the entire sequence of action in *Raptor*. Hamel even cuts back on her consumption of tequila and beer when she reads how much her aunt was concerned about Hamel's drinking. Through this indirect communication of a diary, her deceased aunt has far more impact on Hamel than she ever did while she was alive. Hamel takes her first case, in *North of the Border,* because she is asked to by a former lover, and in

Dust jacket for Van Gieson's 1996 novel, in which Neil Hamel investigates the death of a female firefighter during a forest fire (Richland County Public Library)

The Lies That Bind, she takes on a client only because the problem involves a childhood friend whom she has not seen for years. While the past is always a frame for action in detective fiction because it is the locus for a murder that must be investigated, the past in the Hamel series is typically the distant past, and it becomes more than a triggering device for the plot. Hamel's efforts to know or touch another person are always carried out indirectly, at an emotional distance. The novels always include a filter, such as the past, or a barrier, such as space, to intimacy with another person. Hamel is the epitome of the loner detective.

Hamel's quest for justice does not prevent her from tangling with her own ethical demons. In *Ditch Rider,* Hamel faces a curious dilemma: her client, a young neighbor, insists on confessing to a shooting that the detective is convinced she is lying about, presumably to protect the real shooter. As an attorney, Hamel is obligated to represent her client's wishes, but in this instance, she is not convinced that the client's wishes will lead to justice for anyone. She is in the morally ambiguous position of wanting to prove her own client a liar in order to prove her innocent. She does unearth the real shooter. Then, to the reader's surprise at the conclusion, the account of the events she gives to the police includes a significant omission: she fails to mention an accomplice to the murder. She makes the questionable decision to protect a young girl in the hope that she will come forward and confess. That the girl eventually volunteers a confession does not completely erase the ethically tainted nature of Hamel's tactics in this novel—the latest, and perhaps the last, novel in the series.

In the late 1990s Van Gieson decided to begin a different series of mystery novels. Her frustration with the corporate upheavals of HarperCollins, during which the publication of *Hotshots* was delayed a year and all the earlier Hamel novels were allowed to go out of print, was a major reason for her decision to create a new character and to look for a new publisher. Another reason may be that Hamel was so clearly created as a contemporary female version of an earlier male prototype; she is modeled on fiction, not life. Van Gieson says there is little of herself in Neil Hamel.

More of Van Gieson is found in the next series, five novels to date, featuring Claire Reynier, an archivist for the Center for Southwest Research at the University of New Mexico. The protagonist—her first name honoring Van Gieson's mother and her last name honoring one of Van Gieson's Dutch ancestors who came to America in the seventeenth century—is distinctly modeled on real life, not a fictional icon. Reynier is consistently praised in reviews for her intelligence and resolution and, importantly, unlike Neil Hamel, she is never compared to other fictional detectives. Both the author and her protagonist love books, the Southwest, their quiet homes, and solitude. Reynier is in her early fifties, has a pet cat named Nemesis, and enjoys Mozart. While her adventures are not awash in blood and violence, the new series is decidedly hard-boiled for its cool, dispassionate laying bare of human vagaries. Reynier is a keen analyst of the ways in which human beings entrap themselves in lies, corruption, and murder. The result is a richer, more complex series than the previous one. As Tony Hillerman said for the cover of the first Reynier novel, "Van Gieson's back—and better than ever."

Unlike Hamel, Reynier does not tell her own story. Van Gieson switches to third-person narration for this series, a change that might lead a reader to be more distanced from the central figure, but the reverse is true. Reynier is more real than her predecessor, or as the *Midwest Book Review* describes her, she is "multilayered and complex." (Only *Publishers Weekly* [2001]

finds Reynier lacking "emotional depth," in *Vanishing Point* [2001].) She lives a life filled with her job, her interests—art, literature, history, rare books, and music—and a score of friends, coworkers, and acquaintances, as well as two grown children, who are to date only voices on the phone. Van Gieson told J. C. Martin in an interview, "She is just a cool, middle-aged woman with a career." Delete the word "just" with its implied diminution, and this characterization explains the foundation for the success of the series: Reynier is a fully realized person, with strengths and weaknesses, quiet but brave, and she is active in an intellectual career that focuses on understanding the present in the context of the past—a perfect position from which to investigate murder.

In the first novel of the series, *The Stolen Blue* (2000), Reynier slips easily into such an investigation. When she responds to an invitation from an older mentor, Burke Lovell, to come to his ranch to collect some of his rare books for the Center for Southwest Research, she is dismayed when he dies suddenly during her first night there. Reynier quickly suspects that his death may have been a murder, not the suicide claimed by an alleged daughter who recently joined the household. Since Reynier is his executor and the newly discovered "daughter" is the primary heir, Reynier is thrown into exploring Burke Lovell's history and that of the new daughter in order to settle the estate and to protect her own professional reputation after some of his rare books are stolen from her truck.

In the second book, *Vanishing Point,* Reynier's job as archivist also leads her straight into a murder investigation, one inspired by an actual missing-person case in the mid 1930s. She is responsible for maintaining all material relating to an environmental activist in the 1960s, Jonathan Vail, who wrote one novel that achieved cult status. Vail disappeared in a canyon in Utah in 1966, but no one has ever been able to confirm his death. The novel opens with a young graduate student bringing Reynier a leather briefcase he has just discovered in a cave in the same canyon. They both think it belonged to Vail, and they are elated because the briefcase contains a journal apparently kept by Vail during his final hike in the canyon. Shortly afterward, Reynier finds the body of the graduate student in the canyon, and intertwining past and present murders must be resolved.

The opening line of *Confidence Woman* (2002)— "The fear of anyone who lives alone is to die alone and not be missed or discovered until the body begins to smell"—provides a clear indication of the tone of the gritty mystery about to unfold. The need to investigate murder in this novel does not come from Reynier's career but is instead highly personal. In the opening pages, she is horrified to discover that Evelyn Martin, a classmate from the University of Arizona who dropped in months ago for an unexplained visit, has just died in Santa Fe, apparently murdered. Further complications quickly ensue as a policeman's questions to Reynier make her realize that, during her visit, Evelyn must have stolen some of her credit cards, one of her rare books, and, in fact, her identity. Reynier's career training is again valuable in the investigation, during which she uses many of her skills as an archivist to research Evelyn Martin's story, the stories of their classmates, and ultimately to name the killer.

Land of Burning Heat (2003) opens with a visit to Reynier in her capacity as archivist, and the novel explores a subject little written about: crypto Jews in the Southwest. Isabel Santos has found a wooden cross with a paper hidden inside under the brick floor of her old adobe home in Bernalillo, and she brings it to the Center for Southwest Research for an explanation of its meaning. The paper excites Reynier, because it appears to be the final words of a Jewish mystic who was martyred during the Inquisition in Mexico City four hundred years earlier. She wants to know if they are in fact the final words of Joaquin Rodriguez, and if so, how they could have arrived in New Mexico to be secreted away for centuries. She barely gets started on her research into the Inquisition and possible connections between the Rodriguez and the Santos families, before Isabel is found murdered and the paper missing. Reynier pursues her research into the Inquisition and, convinced that the police are mistaken in thinking the murder is a burglary gone bad, she simultaneously pursues the identity of Isabel's killer, who does prove to be linked to the missing paper. Along the way, Reynier learns firsthand about two exotic and secretive worlds–that of crypto Jews, the descendants of those who in the fifteenth century were forced to convert to Christianity in order to save their lives, and who continue to practice their "old ways" secretly; and that of contemporary academics, many of whom believe they have a personal hold on truth and will use any weapon at their disposal to keep others out of their area of expertise. Reynier is respectful of the former and infuriated by the latter. "Just like a scholar," she thinks about one of the experts she consults, "to deny the existence of something that might contradict his scholarship."

The fifth Reynier novel, *The Shadow of Venus* (2004), is triggered by things both professional and personal. The body of a homeless woman is found in the Zimmerman Library, along with evidence of drug use and an illustration of the Spiral Rocks in Colorado cut from a rare book, *Ancient Sites*. Reynier's immediate involvement is to track down the vandalized book and check others for similar abuse, but she is also interested in finding the murderer, or the one who pushed the

Dust jacket for Van Gieson's 1998 novel, in which the lawyer tries to prove her client innocent of murder despite the young woman's confession (Richland County Public Library)

young woman into suicide, because the police seem to think that a homeless woman, known as Ansia, may be responsible, but Reynier has reasons to doubt this theory. As she pursues both threads of interest, Reynier develops a more intense, highly personal reason for finding the killer: the dead girl, known locally as Maia, came from an abusive home in Taos. This background reminds Reynier of something she has tried to forget about her own youth: the father of one of her childhood friends sexually fondled her when she was a child, and she never told anyone because he was also her father's friend. She has felt guilty for years on behalf of anyone else he may have abused. Now, she will do whatever she must to avenge Maia's death as a way of expiating her own guilt. The hidden worlds explored in this novel are that of the victims of child molestation and that of the homeless. Hovering teasingly behind all the human tragedies is the psychological power of astronomy and myth. "The shadow of

VANISHING POINT

A Claire Reynier Mystery

JUDITH VAN GIESON

Dust jacket for Van Gieson's 2001 mystery novel, the second to feature University of New Mexico Library archivist and sleuth Claire Reynier (Richland County Public Library)

that, what is more, he is not the author of the novel for which he achieved cult status. Nobody and nothing can be trusted to be what they seem in Reynier's world. Basic facts keep sliding into something else. Perhaps the most blatant example is found in *Confidence Woman* with Evelyn's theft of identity of former classmates, in part for financial gain, but also in part to satisfy a personal hunger for a whole self. Throughout this novel, Reynier comes to question her own sense of who she is, and the novel ends with Reynier toying with the idea of contacting a former lover from years ago, when she was effectively another person. Interestingly, in *Land of Burning Heat,* the Santos men are not aware of their Jewish background until the women, who serve as the family's historians, choose to tell them. In *The Shadow of Venus,* Reynier has chosen to close the door to a part of her own history and identity until Maia's death forces her to open it.

While one of the basic premises of most detective novels is that the killer does not at first appear to be the killer, thus making the detective and the reader scrutinize everyone for the reality behind the mask, Van Gieson takes this unreliability one step farther to suggest that for every character two contrary perspectives may be true simultaneously. Much of life cannot be seen in an either-or format; it must be seen as both-and. Reynier may shy away from developing a romantic relationship with a book-dealer friend, but, as she considers trying to find a former lover, she wonders if the sexy black nightgown sent to her by Evelyn as a macabre joke might turn out to be something she will actually wear one night. Just when the reader dismisses her pretentious boss, Harrison Hough, as a harmless petty bureaucrat, he turns out to have plagiarized his dissertation, the ultimate violation of ethics in the world of books and academe. *Confidence Woman* stands on its own as Reynier's investigation of a woman who kept shifting her own identity and stealing others' identities, but the novel is simultaneously Van Gieson's version of Herman Melville's *The Confidence-Man* (1857), and the reader is frequently reminded of this second lens through which to view the story. In *The Shadow of Venus,* Edward Girard may have installed an impressive work of art at the Spiral Rocks, an interpretation of nature that dazzles Reynier when she sees the Maximum Moon framed by the rocks, but he turns out to be a neglectful human being who ignored signs that his daughter needed help. The great artist and the deficient father—neither identity erases the other. Both exist simultaneously.

A significant reason for the superior literary quality of the Claire Reynier series lies in the way in which Van Gieson's much-praised descriptions of the New Mexico landscape become an organic part of her over-

Venus" looms large in this novel, literally and figuratively. The name chosen by the young woman reflects one way of escape: in Greek mythology, Maia was one of the seven daughters of Atlas and Pleione, who escaped the pursuing Orion by fleeing into the sky and becoming the constellation of stars known as the Pleiades.

At the core of the five Reynier novels is the mutability of human life, or as *The Bloomsbury Review* says, "the evanescence of things." Identity of others and even of self is a slippery business. All five novels of the series—*The Stolen Blue, Vanishing Point, Confidence Woman, Land of Burning Heat,* and *The Shadow of Venus*—ultimately turn on shifting identities. In *The Stolen Blue,* Reynier unearths a different story from the one she thought she knew about her old friend, his ranch, and his relationship with his alleged daughter. As Reynier observes in *Vanishing Point,* "history is revisionist." Certainly, *Vanishing Point* demonstrates the validity of that observation as Reynier discovers that Jonathan Vail is still alive and

all vision of the shifting nature of life. In *Vanishing Point,* the journal found in Slickrock Canyon includes a cryptic description of the canyon walls: "Canyon slipping and sliding like the walls of La Sagrada Familia." Reynier explains the image to the young man who found the journal: "It's an unfinished church in Barcelona designed by the architect Antoni Gaudi. The walls give the effect of sliding off the frame." While Hamel's descriptions of empty vistas may help to define her character as a loner and are praised by *The New York Times* as displaying "a poet's flair for imagery," many descriptions in that earlier series seem inserted into the narrative, particularly when compared to descriptions and figurative language in the Reynier series, in which they are an organic part of the narrative. For example, the reader of *Vanishing Point* is told that adobe "always" gives Reynier "the impression that it was rising out of the earth at the same time that it was sinking back in" just as she is exploring the possibility that someone presumed dead is alive and someone presumed an author is not. What may be most striking about so much of the imagery is a new attention to movement: the landscape shimmers, drifts, ripples, and moves, offering one shape from this spot, another identity from another perspective. The accuracy of the landscape and the accuracy of "truth" are equally hard to decipher in Reynier's world.

Reynier's ability to find the truth is primarily a result of her analytical skills, her determination, and her dispassionate willingness to face even unpleasant facts, but she is helped in more subtle ways by little details, such as practicing tai chi, "which had taught her how to keep an opponent off balance by embracing the opposite" *(Vanishing Point).* A blurb from *Albuquerque Arts* calls her "a resourceful, self-sufficient heroine with a scalpel-sharp mind and resilient poise." The combination of Reynier's mature and credible crime solving, organically underscored by the beauty and dangers of the natural world captured in writing that Gaye Brown de Alvarez in *Independent* (19 June 2002) calls "crisp and smart . . . there isn't an extraneous word in all her text." Clever plots emerging from her meticulous research into myriad subjects result in an outstanding detective series that, says Barbara Bibel in *Booklist,* "deserves a larger audience" (1 and 15 January 2002).

Judith Van Gieson is widely known and admired as a Southwestern writer. She is actively involved in the literary scene in the Southwest, especially with such groups as Sisters in Crime and Left Coast Crime, and in 2002 she won a Bravos Award for Excellence in Literary Arts from the Arts Alliance in New Mexico. In 2004 the Zia Book Award for best work of fiction by a New Mexico woman went to Van Gieson for *The Shadow of Venus.* Her novels have not yet, however, reached best-seller status nationwide despite the fact that her reviews in *Publishers Weekly, Booklist, Kirkus Reviews, Entertainment Weekly,* and a host of newspapers, such as *The New York Times, Boston Globe,* and *Denver Post,* are consistently strong, and her novels have been nominated for national awards. *The Lies That Bind* was nominated for a Shamus Award by the Private Eye Writers of America in 1994, and currently *The Shadow of Venus* is a nominee for a Barry Award from *Deadly Pleasures,* the magazine. Perhaps the long period when the early novels were allowed to lapse from print had a significant impact. Or perhaps the high praise in so many reviews for her descriptions of the Southwest makes a prospective buyer think "regional author," a serious misunderstanding of this writer of cool, classy detective novels.

Interview:

J. C. Martin, "Good Writing Not a Mystery," *Arizona Daily Star,* 11 March 2001, p. E13.

References:

Raymond Chandler, "The Simple Art of Murder," *Atlantic Monthly* (December 1944): 53–59;

Claire F. Fox, "Left Sensationalists at the Transnational Crime Scene: Recent Detective Fiction from the U.S.-Mexico Border Region," in *World Bank Literature,* edited by Amitava Kumar (Minneapolis: University of Minnesota Press, 2003), pp. 184–200;

Carol McGinnis Kay, "'I'm Not a Girl, I'm a Lawyer': Neil Hamel, Attorney at Law," *Clues: A Journal of Detection,* 22, no. 2 (Fall–Winter 2001): 5–22;

Jean Swanson and Dean James, *By a Woman's Hand: A Guide to Mystery Fiction by Women* (New York: Berkley, 1994);

Swanson and James, *Killer Books: A Reader's Guide to Exploring the Popular World of Mystery and Suspense* (New York: Berkley, 1998).

Checklist of Further Readings

Babener, Liahna K. "California Babylon," *Clues,* 1 (Fall 1980): 77–89.

Baker, Robert A., and Michael T. Nietzel. *Private Eyes: One Hundred and One Knights. A Survey of American Detective Fiction, 1922–1984.* Bowling Green, Ohio: Bowling Green State University Popular Press, 1985.

Bargainnier, Earl F., ed. *Comic Crime.* Bowling Green, Ohio: Bowling Green State University Popular Press, 1987.

Barzun, Jacques, and Wendell Hertig Taylor. *A Catalogue of Crime,* revised and enlarged edition. New York: Harper & Row, 1989.

Benstock, Bernard, ed. *Art in Crime Writing: Essays on Detective Fiction.* New York: St. Martin's Press, 1983.

Bloom, Harold, ed. *Classic Crime and Suspense Writers.* New York: Chelsea House, 1994.

Cawelti, John G. *Adventure, Mystery, and Romance: Formula Stories as Art and Popular Culture.* Chicago & London: University of Chicago Press, 1976.

Collins, Michael. "Expanding the *Roman Noir:* Ross Macdonald's Legacy to Mystery/Detective Authors," *South Dakota Review,* 24 (Spring 1986): 121–130.

Crowther, Bruce. *Film Noir: Reflections in a Dark Mirror.* New York: Ungar, 1989.

Docherty, Brian, ed. *American Crime Fiction: Studies in the Genre.* New York: St. Martin's Press, 1988.

Emck, Katy. "Feminist Detectives and the Challenges of Hardboiledness," *Canadian Review of Comparative Literature,* 21, no. 3 (1994): 383–398.

Geherin, David. *The American Private Eye: The Image in Fiction.* New York: Ungar, 1985.

Geherin. *Sons of Sam Spade: The Private-Eye Novel in the Seventies: Robert B. Parker, Roger L. Simon, Andrew Bergman.* New York: Ungar, 1982.

Goulart, Ron. *The Dime Detectives.* New York: Mysterious Press, 1988.

Gray, Piers. "On Linearity," *Critical Quarterly,* 38, no. 3 (1996): 122–133.

Gruber, Frank. *The Pulp Jungle.* Los Angeles: Sherbourne, 1967.

Guetti, James. "Aggressive Reading: Detective Fiction and Realistic Narrative," *Raritan,* 2 (Summer 1982): 128–138.

Gurko, Leo. *Heroes, Highbrows and the Popular Mind.* Indianapolis: Bobbs-Merrill, 1953.

Hagemann, E. R., ed. *A Comprehensive Index to* Black Mask, *1920–1951.* Bowling Green, Ohio: Bowling Green State University Popular Press, 1982.

Hamilton, Cynthia S. *Western and Hard-Boiled Detective Fiction in America: From High Noon to Midnight.* Iowa City: University of Iowa Press, 1987.

Henderson, Leslie, ed. *Twentieth Century Crime and Mystery Writers,* third edition. Chicago: St. James, 1991.

Hoppenstand, Gary, ed. *The Dime Novel Detective.* Bowling Green, Ohio: Bowling Green State University Popular Press, 1982.

Hubin, Allen J. *Crime Fiction, 1749–1980: A Comprehensive Bibliography.* New York: Garland, 1984.

Hubin. *1981–1985 Supplement to Crime Fiction, 1749–1980.* New York: Garland, 1988.

Irons, Glenwood. *Feminism in Women's Detective Fiction.* Toronto & Buffalo: University of Toronto Press, 1995.

Kittredge, William, and Steven M. Krauser. *The Great American Detective: 15 Stories Starring America's Most Celebrated Private Eyes.* New York: New American Library, 1978.

Klein, Kathleen Gregory. *The Woman Detective: Gender and Genre,* second edition. Urbana: University of Illinois Press, 1995.

Klein, ed. *Great Women Mystery Writers: Classic to Contemporary.* Westport, Conn.: Greenwood Press, 1994.

Klein, ed. *Women Times Three: Writers, Detectives, Readers.* Bowling Green, Ohio: Bowling Green State University Popular Press, 1995.

Klein, Marcus. *Easterns, Westerns, and Private Eyes: American Matters, 1870–1900.* Madison: University of Wisconsin Press, 1994.

Landrum, Larry N., Pat Browne, and Ray B. Browne, eds. *Dimensions of Detective Fiction.* Bowling Green, Ohio: Bowling Green State University Popular Press, 1976.

Madden, David, ed. *Tough Guy Writers of the Thirties.* Carbondale: Southern Illinois University Press, 1968.

Magill, Frank N., ed. *Critical Survey of Mystery and Detective Fiction: Authors.* Pasadena, Cal.: Salem Press, 1988.

Margolies, Edward. *Which Way Did He Go? The Private Eye in Dashiell Hammett, Raymond Chandler, Chester Himes and Ross Macdonald.* New York: Holmes & Meier, 1982.

Most, Glenn W., and William W. Stowe, eds. *The Poetics of Murder: Detective Fiction and Literary Theory.* New York: Harcourt Brace Jovanovich, 1983.

Munt, Sally R. *Murder by the Book? Feminism and the Crime Novel.* London & New York: Routledge, 1994.

Niebuhr, Gary Warren. *A Reader's Guide to the Private Eye Novel.* New York: G. K. Hall, 1993.

Nolan, William F. *The Black Mask Boys: Masters in the Hard-Boiled School of Detective Fiction.* New York: Morrow, 1985.

Nye, Russell B. *The Unembarrassed Muse: The Popular Arts in America.* New York: Dial, 1970.

Nyman, Jopi. *Hard-Boiled Fiction and Dark Romanticism.* New York: Peter Lang, 1998.

Panek, Leroy Lad. *Probable Cause: Crime Fiction in America.* Bowling Green, Ohio: Bowling Green State University Popular Press, 1990.

Porter, Dennis. *The Pursuit of Crime: Art and Ideology in Detective Fiction*. New Haven: Yale University Press, 1981.

Reddy, Maureen T. *Sisters in Crime: Feminism and the Crime Novel*. New York: Continuum, 1988.

Reilly, John M., ed. *Twentieth-Century Crime and Mystery Writers*. New York: St. Martin's Press, 1980.

Ruehlmann, William. *Saint with a Gun: The Unlawful American Private Eye*. New York: New York University Press, 1974.

Ruhm, Herbert, ed. *The Hard-Boiled Detective: Stories from* Black Mask *Magazine, 1920–1951*. New York: Vintage, 1977.

Shaw, Joseph T., ed. *The Hard-Boiled Omnibus: Early Stories from* Black Mask. New York: Simon & Schuster, 1949.

Silver, Alain, and Elizabeth Ward, eds. *Film Noir: An Encyclopedic Reference to the American Style,* third edition, revised and enlarged. Woodstock, N.Y.: Overlook Press, 1992.

Skinner, Robert E. *The Hard-Boiled Explicator: A Guide to the Study of Dashiell Hammett, Raymond Chandler and Ross Macdonald*. London: Scarecrow Press, 1985.

Skinner. *The New Hard-Boiled Dicks: Heroes for a New Urban Mythology,* second edition, revised and expanded. San Bernardino, Cal.: Brownstone Books, 1995.

Stephens, Michael L. *Film Noir: A Comprehensive, Illustrated Reference to Movies, Terms and Persons*. Jefferson, N.C.: McFarland, 1995.

Symons, Julian. *Mortal Consequences: A History: From the Detective Story to the Crime Novel*. New York: Harper & Row, 1972.

Van Dover, J. Kenneth. *Murder in the Millions: Erle Stanley Gardner, Mickey Spillane, Ian Fleming*. New York: Ungar, 1984.

Walker, Ronald G., and June M. Frazer, eds. *The Cunning Craft: Original Essays on Detective Fiction and Contemporary Literary Theory*. Macomb: Western Illinois University Press, 1990.

Walton, Priscilla L., and Manina Jones. *Detective Agency: Women Rewriting the Hard-Boiled Tradition*. Berkeley: University of California Press, 1999.

Wilt, David E. *Hardboiled in Hollywood*. Bowling Green, Ohio: Bowling Green State University Popular Press, 1991.

Winks, Robin W., and Maureen Corrigan, eds. *Mystery and Suspense Writers: The Literature of Crime, Detection, and Espionage,* 2 volumes. New York: Scribner, 1998.

Contributors

Wendi Arant . . . . *Texas A&M University*

John L. Cobbs . . . . *Montgomery County Community College*

Tim Cummings . . . . *Harrisonburg, Virginia*

Tim Dayton . . . . *Kansas State University*

Peter Dempsey . . . . *University of Sunderland, U.K.*

Marcia B. Dinneen . . . . *Bridgewater State College*

Charles L. Etheridge Jr. . . . . *McMurry University*

Anita G. Gorman . . . . *Slippery Rock University of Pennsylvania*

Douglas G. Greene . . . . *Old Dominion University*

Peter Gunn . . . . *University of Texas at Austin*

Donna Waller Harper . . . . *Middle Tennessee State University*

Carol McGinnis Kay . . . . *University of South Carolina*

Peter Kenney . . . . *Birmingham, Alabama*

Martin Kich . . . . *Wright State University–Lake Campus*

Marvin S. Lachman . . . . *Santa Fe, New Mexico*

Ward B. Lewis . . . . *University of Georgia*

Katherine M. Restaino . . . . *Fairleigh Dickinson University*

Bobbie Robinson . . . . *Abraham Baldwin College*

Karl L. Stenger . . . . *University of South Carolina Aiken*

Matt Theado . . . . *Gardner-Webb University*

Cumulative Index

Dictionary of Literary Biography, Volumes 1-306
Dictionary of Literary Biography Yearbook, 1980-2002
Dictionary of Literary Biography Documentary Series, Volumes 1-19
Concise Dictionary of American Literary Biography, Volumes 1-7
Concise Dictionary of British Literary Biography, Volumes 1-8
Concise Dictionary of World Literary Biography, Volumes 1-4

Cumulative Index

DLB before number: *Dictionary of Literary Biography,* Volumes 1-306
Y before number: *Dictionary of Literary Biography Yearbook,* 1980-2002
DS before number: *Dictionary of Literary Biography Documentary Series,* Volumes 1-19
CDALB before number: *Concise Dictionary of American Literary Biography,* Volumes 1-7
CDBLB before number: *Concise Dictionary of British Literary Biography,* Volumes 1-8
CDWLB before number: *Concise Dictionary of World Literary Biography,* Volumes 1-4

B

I

J

K

P

Cumulative Index

W

ISBN: 0-7876-6843-5

90000